Preface

In 1980 the International Bureau of Education published an *International directory of educational research institutions.* The first edition contained 550 entries covering national institutions identified in 117 countries. Some regional institutions were also included. With use, the first edition of the *Directory* proved to be inadequate: either by reason of the absence of some highly qualified institutions, or because of the fragmentary - and so perforce inadequate - nature of the information given or again because a certain number of institutions should not have been included as their programmes had little or nothing to do with research.

The second edition of the *Directory* therefore attempts not only to fill in the gaps, but also to adopt an entirely new approach in identifying and selecting institutions and giving users the necessary and relevant information to enable them to find institutions concerned with any given thematic field. The introduction by Geneviève Lefort, to whose patience, able and devoted work it is fitting to pay tribute here, gives full details on the method adopted, the stages of the development of the work and the final outcome. We would add, however, that the inclusion of information on research subjects for each institution makes it possible for research specialists and educators at all levels using the new edition of the *Directory* to see how interests shared on a worldwide and/or regional scale are organized under certain major themes which are in fact simply the expression of the problems and difficulties met by several countries throughout the world, independently of any political, economic and cultural differences there may be between them. This fact is likely to highlight not only the sharing of questions and difficulties among educational leaders in most countries, but also the necessity for international co-operation seen as an essential means of solving the problems posed by education throughout the world.

While renewing our cordial thanks to Mrs. Geneviève Lefort for her invaluable collaboration, we should point out that the designations employed and the presentation of the material throughout the publication do not imply the expression of any opinion whatsoever on the part of Unesco concerning the legal status of any country, territory, city or area or of its authorities, or concerning the delimitations of its frontiers or boundaries.

Préface

En 1980, le Bureau international d'éducation a publié un *Répertoire international des institutions de recherche en éducation.* Cette première édition comportait 550 entrées portant sur des institutions identifiées dans 117 pays. Certaines institutions régionales ont été aussi retenues. A l'usage, cette première édition du *Répertoire* s'est révélée insuffisante : soit par l'absence d'un certain nombre d'institutions hautement qualifiées, soit par l'aspect fragmentaire — et donc, nécessairement insuffisant — des renseignements fournis, soit, enfin, parce qu'un certain nombre d'institutions n'auraient jamais dû y figurer du fait que leurs programmes d'activités ne touchaient que peu ou prou à la recherche.

Aussi la deuxième édition du *Répertoire* tente-t-elle non seulement de combler ces lacunes mais encore d'adopter une méthodologie entièrement nouvelle pour ce qui est d'identifier et de sélectionner les institutions et de fournir aux utilisateurs les informations nécessaires et pertinentes qui leur permettent, à propos de n'importe quel champ thématique, de retrouver les institutions concernées. L'introduction rédigée par Geneviève Lefort, à qui nous tenons à rendre hommage pour la patience, la compétence et le dévouement avec lesquels elle a mené ce travail jusqu'à son terme, fournit tous les détails sur la méthode adoptée, les étapes franchies dans l'élaboration de l'ouvrage et les résultats obtenus. Nous ajouterons cependant que le fait de comporter des renseignements sur les thèmes de recherche de chaque institution, permettra aux chercheurs, comme aux responsables de l'éducation à tous les niveaux, de saisir à l'aide de cette nouvelle édition du *Répertoire* la façon dont la communauté d'intérêt, à l'échelle mondiale et/ou régionale, s'organise autour de certains thèmes majeurs qui ne sont en fait que l'expression des problèmes et des difficultés que rencontrent plusieurs pays, à travers le monde, et ce en dépit des différences politiques, économiques et culturelles qui existent entre eux. Une telle constatation est de nature à mettre en évidence non seulement la communauté d'interrogations et de difficultés qui existe entre les responsables de l'éducation dans la plupart des pays, mais aussi la nécessité d'une coopération internationale conçue comme moyen primordial de résoudre les problèmes que pose le développement de l'éducation à travers le monde.

Tout en renouvelant à Madame Geneviève Lefort nos plus vifs remerciements pour sa précieuse collaboration, nous tenons à signaler que les appellations employées dans cette publication et la présentation des données qui y figurent n'impliquent de la part de l'Unesco aucune prise de position quant au statut juridique des pays, territoires, villes ou zones, ou de leurs autorités, ni quant au tracé de leurs frontières ou limites.

IBEdata

Directory of educational research institutions

Second edition

Prepared by the International Bureau of Education

Répertoire des institutions de recherche en éducation

Deuxième édition

Préparé par le Bureau international d'éducation

Repertorio de instituciones de investigación educational

Segunda edición

Preparado por la Oficina Internacional de Educación

unesco

Titles in the IBEdata series include:

- Terminology of special education/Terminologie de l'éducation spéciale/Terminología de educación especial/Terminologija defektologii
- Terminology of scientific and technological education (Arabic, English, French, Russian, Spanish, in preparation)
- Terminology of technical and vocational education (Arabic, English, French, Russian and Spanish)
- Terminology of adult education/Terminología de educación de adultos/Terminologie de l'éducation des adultes (in preparation)
- Directory of educational documentation and information services/Répertoire des services de documentation et information sur l'éducation/Repertorio de servicios de documentación e información educacionales
- Directory of adult education documentation and information services/Répertoire des services de documentation et information relatives à l'éducation des adultes/Repertorio de servicios de documentación e información sobre educación de adultos
- Unesco:IBE education thesaurus (also in Russian/English edition)
- Thesaurus de l'éducation Unesco:BIE
- Tesauro de la educación Unesco:OIE
- Directory of educational research institutions/Répertoire des institutions de recherche en éducation/Repertorio de instituciones de investigación educacional
- International directory of higher education research institutions/Répertoire international des institutions de recherche sur l'enseignement supérieur/Repertorio internacional de instituciones de investigación sobre la enseñanza superior
- Glossary of educational technology terms/Glossaire des termes de technologie éducative (Also in English/Spanish and English/Russian editions)
- Directory of special education/Répertoire de l'éducation spéciale/Repertorio de educación especial

Published in 1986 by the
United Nations Educational,
Scientific and Cultural Organization,
7 Place de Fontenoy, 75700 Paris (France)

Publié en 1986 par
l'Organisation des Nations Unies pour
l'éducation, la science et la culture,
7, place de Fontenoy, 75700 Paris (France)

Publicado en 1986 por la
Organización de las Naciones Unidas
para la Educación, la Ciencia y la Cultura,
7, place de Fontenoy, 75700 París (Francia)

ISBN 92-3-002405-8

Printed in Switzerland by Presses Centrales, Lausanne

Prefacio

En 1980, la Oficina Internacional de Educación publicó un *Repertorio internacional de instituciones de investigación educacional.* Esa primera edición comprendía 550 entradas correspondientes a otras tantas instituciones identificadas en 117 países e incluía también a algunas instituciones regionales. El uso del primer *Repertorio* no tardó en poner de manifiesto sus insuficiencias, entre ellas la ausencia de cierto número de instituciones altamente calificadas, el carácter fragmentario, y por lo tanto necesariamente incompleto, de las informaciones contenidas en el mismo y el hecho de que algunas instituciones no deberían haber figurado porque sus programas de actividades tenían poco que ver con la investigación.

Esta segunda edición del *Repertorio* no sólo trata de llenar dichas lagunas, sino también de adoptar una metodología totalmente nueva para la identificación y selección de las instituciones y para proporcionar a los usuarios las informaciones necesarias y pertinentes que les permitan encontrar las instituciones correspondientes, cualquiera sea el área temática de que se trate. En la introducción, Geneviève Lefort, a quien queremos expresar nuestro reconocimiento por la paciencia, la idoneidad y la dedicación con que llevó a cabo este trabajo, proporciona todos los detalles sobre el método adoptado, las etapas cumplidas en la elaboración de la obra y los resultados obtenidos. Podemos agregar, sin embargo, que el hecho de que esta nueva edición del *Repertorio* incluya informaciones sobre los temas de investigación de cada institución, permitirá a los investigadores y a los encargados de la educación de todos los niveles, captar cómo la comunidad educacional se organiza, a escala mundial y/o regional, en torno a ciertos temas fundamentales, que no son otra cosa que los problemas y dificultades que deben afrontar numerosos países en todo el mundo, no obstante las diferencias políticas, económicas y culturales que existen entre ellos. Esta comprobación no sólo sirve para poner en evidencia la identidad de interrogantes y de dificultades que se plantean a los encargados de la educación de la mayoría de los países, sino también la necesidad de una cooperación internacional concebida como medio primordial para resolver los problemas del desarrollo de la educación en el mundo.

Al mismo tiempo que reiteramos nuestro más sincero agradecimiento a la señora Geneviève Lefort por su invalorable colaboración, queremos precisar que las denominaciones empleadas y la presentación de las informaciones en esta publicación, no implican por parte de la Unesco juicio alguno en cuanto a la situación jurídica de los países, territorios, ciudades o zonas o sobre sus autoridades, ni en lo que se refiere a sus fronteras o límites.

Contents

Introduction *p. vii*

Bibliography *p. xviii*

National institutions *p. 1*

Regional institutions *p. 321*

International institutions *p. 326*

Keywords index *p. 328*

Main subject index *p. 417*

Table des matières

Introduction *p. x*

Bibliographie *p. xviii*

Institutions nationales *p. 1*

Institutions régionales *p. 321*

Institutions internationales *p. 326*

Index des mots clés *p. 357*

Index des matières principales *p. 419*

Indice

Introducción *p. xiv*

Bibliografía *p. xviii*

Instituciones nacionales *p. 1*

Instituciones regionales *p. 321*

Instituciones internacionales *p. 326*

Indice de palabras claves *p. 387*

Indice de materias principales *p. 421*

Introduction

With this second edition of the *Directory of educational research institutions*, Unesco has updated the information contained in the first edition, published in 1980. An attempt has been made, by prospecting afresh, to overcome the shortcomings which use had brought to light in the first edition.

The dissemination of research findings has been a major objective of national and international authorities over the last decade. Publication of the *Directory* is a contribution to this effort at communication. It is designed to enable research specialists, decision makers and teacher trainers to make direct contact with the institutions they locate, and so to have access to documents which do not come into the commercial circuit (reports, theses, etc.), or which have not yet been published. In the field of social sciences, there is often actually a gap of several years between the first research report and its subsequent publication in specialist journals.

The *Directory* also offers a general survey of educational research. For example, it shows that the computer is often used in research projects, or that Latin American countries are very well represented. But the heterogeneous character of the information gathered makes it unwise to draw any conclusion of a comparative nature.

An account of the methodology used to update the *Directory* will make clear its limits.

Search for new institutions

A glance at the entries in the first edition suffices to show that the institutions listed cover a wide range of disciplines (educational theory, teaching methods, psychology, sociology, economics, etc.) and also of audiences (from pre-school age children to adult workers) and types of research (from empirical research to development of materials).

To the extent that it represents an actual reality, this wide range of approaches and objectives has been respected in the prospection carried out to identify new institutions. However, to avoid duplicating the *Directory of higher education research institutions* published by Unesco in 1981 [14] and currently being updated, institutions oriented exclusively towards research in higher education listed in that volume have not been included. (Numbers in brackets refer to the bibliography.)

Reference was made to several types of sources for this identification. First, all the information addressed to the IBE following the first edition was examined: forms which arrived too late for inclusion; requests from institutions which had not been solicited; readers' criticisms and suggestions.

Next came a systematic review of directories concerned with educational research. These fall into three categories:

1. *National* directories of educational research institutions [see entries 2 to 5 in the bibliography] or of scientific research institutions devoting a chapter to education [entries 6 to 10].
2. *International* directories of educational research institutions, referring either to a region [entries 11 to 14], or to a particular field of education [entries 15 to 17].
3. *Regional* directories, indicating periodically, for a particular geographical area, either educational research projects or reports published. Institutions mentioned frequently were identified [entries 18 to 21].

General documents on trends and methods in educational research, and the proceedings of international meetings dealing with the subject [entries 22 to 26] were also consulted in order to include institutions mentioned.

Finally, reference was made to various directories [entries 27 to 34] to complete or check information.

In addition, National Commissions for Unesco, solicited in each Member State, forwarded the form directly to the IBE with several more addresses. Thirty-eight new institutions have been identified in this way.

Selection

Out of 1,300 forms sent, 868 were returned to the IBE duly completed. This figure does not include replies indicating that the institutions no longer existed or had moved without giving a forwarding address. Of these, 155 were eliminated either because the institution did not belong to the specific field of the directory: some universities, for example, responded for the institution as a whole whereas the form was addressed strictly to the faculty of education (note that the term 'education' does not appear in the title of the form); or because the replies did not meet the selection criteria which had been established.

In order to eliminate institutions considered too marginal because of their small dimension, their activity, or the field concerned, three criteria were applied.

1. less than two full-time research workers (or equivalent);
2. less than 10% of the activities devoted to research, and among the research activities less than 10% concerning education;
3. complete absence of information on objectives, publications and projects.

However, these conditions were applied with some flexibility in some cases: for example, when the institution publishes a journal listed in an international directory; or when it is frequently mentioned in educational research literature, or again when it is the only one in a country.

Furthermore, some ten institutions listed in the first edition of the directory but which did not reply, yet which we considered important, appear in this new edition together with a minimum of information necessary for their identification.

Limits

Despite the precautions taken, the *Directory* is bound to have its shortcomings. Insufficient search for new institutions, due to a lack of information sources on certain countries. This is the case with China, where only one institution appeared in the 1980 edition. Having received no reply from this institution nor from the Chinese Commission for Unesco, we have retained for this new edition the basic reference (title and address). For other countries or regions the only sources available are out of date (1976 for Africa, 1972 for Eastern Europe, for example).

Shortcomings due to the fact that 40% of the institutions did not reply, and that many forms were incompletely filled in; in this last case, the selection criteria could not always be applied, hence the presence of institutions of limited interest, which, when in doubt, we decided to retain.

Should there then be some doubt about the usefulness of a directory at worldwide level? Of course, a field such as this can be covered neither exhaustively, since for some countries no information is available; nor with rigorous precision, because elements which would make it possible to check or to complete data which are sometimes ambiguous and often incomplete are also lacking. Furthermore, the extent of the undertaking does not make it easy to update frequently, although the mobility of the institutions makes this necessary.

Subject to these reservations, the international dimension of the directory is nonetheless entirely justified by the possibilities it offers for exchanges, particularly in countries where it is quite impossible to locate institutions otherwise. Moreover, the interest that the institutions contacted showed by responding to Unesco in a proportion of 61% shows that a real need exists.

And if this tool is not perfect, it is at least perfectible, particularly in the light of readers' criticisms and suggestions. A form is included at the end of the volume which may be returned to us for the next edition.

Access to the information: how to use this directory

Our first concern has been to improve the content of the directory; but in order to make it easier to use, we have also made some alterations in its presentation, while still retaining the general lay-out of the previous edition.

Entries concerning institutions, now numbered sequentially, are grouped by country, in the English alphabetical order as it appears in the *Unesco thesaurus*. Each institution is also classified alphabetically according to its official name and, if that is lacking, by its translation, within each country.

An index of descriptors, those of the *Unesco:IBE education thesaurus*, cross-references institutions by subjects represented mainly in publications and current research, but does not enable institutions specializing in a field of education to be located. For this reason it has been considered useful to include in this new edition a second index by main subjects grouping into seventeen major fields the institutions whose title indicates the specification. The first index makes it possible to find the answer to such questions as: in which institutions is current research mainly focused on methods of teaching physics?; whereas the second one provides an answer to such questions as: which institutions are permanently devoted to science teaching?

Introduction

Avec cette seconde édition du *Répertoire des institutions de recherche en éducation*, l'Unesco a procédé à la mise à jour des informations consignées dans la première édition, parue en 1980. On a essayé, par un nouveau travail de prospection, de remédier aux lacunes apparues à l'usage du premier document.

La diffusion des résultats de la recherche concernant l'éducation a constitué depuis la dernière décennie un des objectifs primordiaux des instances nationales et internationales. La publication du répertoire participe à cet effort de communication. Il devrait permettre à des chercheurs, décideurs, formateurs d'enseignants de s'adresser directement aux institutions repérées, et d'avoir ainsi accès à des documents qui échappent aux circuits commerciaux (rapports, thèses, etc.), ou qui n'ont pas encore été publiés. Dans le domaine des sciences sociales, il s'écoule, en effet, souvent plusieurs années entre la première rédaction d'un travail de recherche et sa publication dans les revues spécialisées.

Le répertoire apporte par ailleurs un panorama général de la recherche en éducation. Il permet par exemple de constater que l'utilisation de l'ordinateur revient souvent dans les projets de recherche, ou que les pays d'Amérique latine sont très largement représentés. Mais l'hétérogénéité des informations recueillies rendrait imprudente toute conclusion de nature comparée.

L'exposé de la démarche méthodologique suivie pour sa mise à jour mettra en évidence les limites du répertoire.

Recherches de nouvelles institutions

On peut constater, en parcourant les notices de la première édition, que les institutions recensées présentent une grande diversité tant dans les disciplines impliquées (pédagogie, didactique, psychologie, sociologie, économie, etc.) que dans les publics étudiés (des jeunes enfants non encore scolarisés aux travailleurs adultes) et dans le matériel.

Dans la mesure où elle représente un état de fait, cette variété dans les approches et dans les objectifs a été respectée dans le travail de prospection réalisé pour identifier de nouvelles institutions. Toutefois, pour éviter la redondance avec le *Répertoire des institutions de recherche sur l'enseignement supérieur* publié par l'Unesco en 1981 [14], on n'a pas retenu, parmi les institutions orientées exclusivement vers la recherche dans l'enseignement supérieur, celles qui figurent dans ce document. (Les chiffres entre parenthèses renvoient à la bibliographie.)

Plusieurs types de sources ont été sollicitées pour cette identification. On a d'abord recueilli toutes les informations adressées au BIE à la suite de la première édition : formulaires reçus après échéance, demandes d'organismes non sollicités, critiques et suggestions de lecteurs.

On a ensuite entrepris un dépouillement systématique des répertoires concernant la recherche en éducation. Ces répertoires appartiennent à trois catégories :

1. Répertoires *nationaux* d'institutions de recherche en éducation [voir de 2 à 5] ou d'institutions de recherches scientifiques consacrant un chapitre à l'éducation [voir de 6 à 10].
2. Répertoires d'institutions de recherche en éducation de caractère *international*, soit concernant une région [voir de 11 à 14], soit spécialisés dans un domaine de l'éducation [voir de 15 à 17].
3. Répertoires à caractère *régional*, diffusant périodiquement, pour une aire géographique donnée, soit les projets de recherche en éducation, soit les rapports publiés. On y a repéré les institutions fréquemment mentionnées [voir de 18 à 21].

Ont été consultés par ailleurs, pour y relever les institutions citées, des documents généraux sur les tendances ou les méthodes de la recherche en éducation, et des comptes rendus de réunions internationales en rapport avec le sujet [voir de 22 à 26].

Enfin, pour des compléments d'information ou pour des vérifications, on a eu recours à divers répertoires [voir de 27 à 34].

D'un autre côté, les Commissions nationales pour l'Unesco, sollicitées dans chaque Etat membre, ont fait parvenir directement le formulaire à quelques autres adresses. Trente-huit nouvelles institutions ont ainsi été identifiées.

Sélection

Sur 1300 formulaires envoyés, 868 sont parvenus au BIE après avoir été remplis. Ce chiffre ne comporte pas les réponses indiquant que l'institution n'existait plus ou qu'elle avait déménagé sans laisser d'adresse. Parmi ceux-ci, 155 ont été éliminés soit parce que l'organisme n'appartenait pas au champ spécifique du répertoire : des universités, par exemple, ont répondu pour l'ensemble de l'institution alors que le formulaire était adressé strictement à la faculté d'éducation (il faut dire que le terme «éducation» ne figure pas dans l'intitulé du formulaire.); soit parce que les réponses ne satisfaisaient pas aux conditions de sélection retenues.

Pour éliminer les institutions estimées trop marginales en raison de leur taille réduite, de leur activité, ou du domaine concerné, trois critères ont été définis :

1. moins de deux chercheurs à temps complet (ou équivalent) ;
2. moins de 10 % des activités consacrées à la recherche, et parmi les activités de recherche moins de 10 % concernant l'éducation ;
3. l'absence complète d'information sur les objectifs, les publications, les projets.

Ces conditions ont cependant été assouplies dans quelques cas : par exemple lorsque l'institution est éditrice d'une revue recensée dans un répertoire international; ou losqu'elle est fréquemment citée dans la littérature de la recherche en éducation, ou encore lorsqu'elle est seule à représenter un pays.

D'autre part, une dizaine d'institutions qui figuraient dans la première édition du répertoire et n'ont pas répondu, mais que nous estimons importantes, apparaissent dans cette nouvelle édition accompagnées du minimum d'information nécessaire à leur identification.

Limites

Malgré les précautions prises, il ne faut pas se dissimuler les insuffisances du répertoire. Insuffisances dans la recherche de nouvelles institutions, dues à l'absence de sources d'information concernant certains pays. Ainsi en est-il pour la Chine. Une seule institution figurait dans l'édition de 1980. N'ayant reçu de réponse ni de cet organisme ni de la Commission chinoise pour l'Unesco, nous avons conservé pour cette nouvelle édition les références minimum (intitulé et adresse). Pour d'autres pays ou régions, les seules sources disponibles sont trop anciennes (1976 pour l'Afrique, 1972 pour l'Europe de l'Est, par exemple) pour être entièrement valables.

Insuffisances dues au fait que 40 % des institutions n'ont pas répondu, et que bien des formulaires ont été incomplètement remplis; dans ce dernier cas, les critères de sélection n'ont pas toujours pu être appliqués, d'où la présence d'institutions d'intérêt limité, que dans le doute, nous avons pris le parti de conserver.

Faut-il alors mettre en doute l'utilité d'un répertoire réalisé à l'échelle mondiale ? On ne peut en effet couvrir un tel domaine ni exhaustivement, puisque pour certains pays les sources d'information sont absentes; ni avec une exactitude rigoureuse : les éléments de contrôle manquant, qui permettraient de vérifier ou de compléter des données parfois ambiguës et souvent lacunaires. D'autre part, l'étendue de l'entreprise ne facilite pas les fréquentes mises à jour pourtant rendues nécessaires par la mobilité des institutions.

Ces réserves étant faites, il reste que la dimension internationale du répertoire est tout à fait justifiée par les possibilités d'échange qu'il apporte, en particulier aux pays totalement dépourvus de moyens de repérage. D'ailleurs, l'intérêt qu'ont manifesté les institutions pressenties en répondant à l'Unesco dans une proportion de 61 % montre qu'il existe bien là un besoin.

Et si cet instrument de travail n'est pas parfait, il est du moins perfectible en particulier à partir des critiques et suggestions qui seront faites par ses lecteurs. Ceux-ci trouveront à la fin du document un formulaire qui peut nous être adressé en vue de la prochaine mise à jour.

Accès à l'information : comment utiliser ce répertoire

Ainsi notre premier souci a-t-il été d'améliorer le contenu du répertoire; mais nous avons aussi, dans le but de rendre la consultation plus aisée, apporté quelques modifications à sa présentation, tout en gardant l'organisation générale de l'édition précédente.

Les notices des institutions, numérotées maintenant séquentiellement, sont regroupées par pays, ceux-ci apparaissant dans l'ordre alphabétique de leur dénomination anglaise, telle qu'elle figure au thésaurus de l'Unesco. Chaque institution est également classée alphabétiquement sous son nom officiel et, si celui-ci est absent, selon sa traduction pour chaque pays.

Un index des descripteurs, ceux du *Thesaurus de l'éducation Unesco:BIE*, renvoie aux institutions d'après les sujets représentés principalement dans les publications et les recherches en cours, mais ne permet pas de repérer les organismes spécialisés dans un domaine de l'éducation. C'est pourquoi il nous a semblé utile de réaliser pour cette nouvelle édition un second index par matière principale qui regroupe suivant 17 grands domaines les institutions dont l'intitulé précise la spécification. Le premier index permet, par exemple, de répondre à la question : quelles sont les institutions dont la didactique de la physique est actuellement un des sujets principaux de recherche ?; alors que le second fournit une réponse à la question : quelles sont les institutions dont la vocation permanente est l'enseignement des sciences ?

Introducción

Con esta segunda edición del *Repertorio de instituciones de investigación educacional*, la Unesco ha puesto al día las informaciones contenidas en la primera edición, publicada en 1980. Con un nuevo trabajo de prospección, se ha procurado poner remedio a las lagunas que se manifestaron con la utilización del primer documento.

En el último decenio, uno de los objetivos primordiales de los organismos nacionales e internacionales ha sido la difusión de los resultados de la investigación educacional. La publicación del *Repertorio* forma parte de este esfuerzo de divulgación, que debería permitir a los investigadores, a las autoridades y a los formadores de docentes, dirigirse a las instituciones que figuran en el mismo y tener así acceso a documentos que no entran en los circuitos comerciales (informes, tesis, etc.) o que aún no han sido publicados. En efecto, en la esfera de las ciencias, a menudo pasan varios años entre la primera redacción de un trabajo de investigación y su publicación en las revistas especializadas.

Por otra parte, el *Repertorio* proporciona un panorama general de la investigación educacional. Permite, por ejemplo, comprobar que es frecuente el uso de la computadora en los proyectos de investigación o que los países de América Latina están ampliamente representados. Pero la heterogeneidad de las informaciones recogidas haría imprudente toda conclusión de carácter comparativo.

Los límites del *Repertorio* se pondrán en evidencia a través de la exposición del método empleado para su puesta al día.

Identificación de nuevas instituciones

Se puede comprobar, recorriendo las reseñas de la primera edición, que las instituciones enumeradas ofrecen una gran diversidad, tanto en lo que se refiere a las disciplinas que abarcan (pedagogía, didáctica, psicología, sociología, economía, etc.) como a los grupos que estudian (desde niños pequeños en edad preescolar hasta trabajadores adultos) y a los tipos de investigación que realizan (de la investigación experimental al desarrollo de material).

En la medida que constituye un dato de la realidad, esta diversidad de enfoques y de objetivos ha sido respetada en la prospección realizada para identificar nuevas instituciones. Sin embargo, para evitar repeticiones, no se incluyeron las instituciones orientadas exclusivamente a la investigación sobre la enseñanza superior que ya figuran en el repertorio de ese tipo de instituciones, publicado por la Unesco en 1981 [14]. (Los números entre paréntesis remiten a la bibliografía.)

Para esta identificación se ha recurrido a una gran variedad de fuentes. En primer lugar, se han recogido todas las informaciones recibidas en la OIE después de la publicación de la primera edición: formularios recibidos cuando ya estaba vencido el plazo, pedidos de organismos cuyos datos no se había solicitado, críticas y sugerencias de lectores, etc.

Se emprendió después un examen detenido y sistemático de los repertorios referidos a la investigación educacional. Esos repertorios son de tres categorías:

1. Repertorios *nacionales* de instituciones de investigación educacional [de 2 a 5] o de instituciones de investigación científica que consagran una parte de sus actividades a la educación [de 6 a 10].
2. Repertorios de instituciones de investigación educacional de carácter *internacional*, referidos a una región [de 11 a 14] o especializados en una esfera de la educación [de 15 a 17].
3. Repertorios de carácter *regional* que difunden periódicamente, para una zona geográfica determinada, proyectos de investigación educacional o informes ya publicados. Se han identificado las instituciones mencionadas más frecuentemente en estos repertorios [de 18 a 21].

Por otra parte, han sido consultados documentos generales sobre las tendencias o los métodos de la investigación educacional y actas de reuniones internacionales relacionadas con el tema, a fin de extraer los nombres de las instituciones citadas [de 22 a 26].

Finalmente, para completar la información o para hacer verificaciones, se han consultado diversos repertorios [de 27 a 34]. Además, las Comisiones Nacionales de Cooperación con la Unesco, requeridas en cada Estado Miembro, han hecho llegar directamente los formularios a algunas otras direcciones. Así han sido identificadas 38 nuevas instituciones.

Selección

Sobre 1300 formularios enviados, 868 retornaron a la OIE completados por sus destinatarios. Sin contar las respuestas indicando que la institución había cesado sus actividades o que se había mudado, desconociéndose su nuevo domicilio. Fueron eliminados 155 de ellos, a causa de que el organismo no formaba parte del campo específico del *Repertorio* (por ejemplo hubo universidades que respondieron por el conjunto de la institución, cuando el formulario había sido dirigido concretamente a la facultad de educación) (Es preciso aclarar que la palabra «educación» no figura en el título del formulario.) o en razón de que las respuestas no satisfacían las condiciones de selección establecidas.

Se definieron tres criterios para eliminar las instituciones consideradas muy marginales por su pequeña dimensión, por su actividad o por los temas abarcados por las mismas:

1. menos de dos investigadores con plena dedicación (o equivalente);
2. menos del 10 por ciento referidas a la educación;
3. ausencia completa de información concerniente a los objetivos, a las publicaciones y a los proyectos.

Estas condiciones fueron sin embargo flexibilizadas en algunos casos, por ejemplo cuando la institución edita una revista que figura en un repertorio internacional o cuando se la cita frecuentemente en las obras sobre investigación educacional o también en el caso que sea la única identificada en un país dado.

Por otra parte, una decena de instituciones que figuraban en la primera edición del repertorio y que no devolvieron el formulario, pero que hemos considerado importantes, aparecen en esta nueva edición con el mínimo de información necesaria para su identificación.

Límites

A pesar de todos los recaudos adoptados, el repertorio no está exento de insuficiencias en la búsqueda de nuevas instituciones, a causa de la falta de fuentes de información concerniente a algunos países. Es el caso de la República Popular China. En la edición de 1980 figuraba una sola institución. No habiendo recibido respuesta ni de ese organismo ni de la Comisión china de cooperación con la Unesco, hemos conservado para esta nueva edición las referencias mínimas (nombre y dirección). Para otros países o regiones las únicas fuentes disponibles son demasiado anticuadas (1976 para Africa y 1972 para Europa oriental, por ejemplo) como para considerarlas completamente válidas.

También hay insuficiencias a causa de que el 40 por ciento de las instituciones no respondieron y que muchos formularios fueron devueltos con los datos incompletos. En este último caso los criterios de selección no siempre pudieron ser aplicados, lo que explica la presencia de instituciones de escaso interés, pero que, en la duda, hemos decidido conservar.

¿Hay que poner entonces en duda la utilidad de un repertorio realizado a escala mundial? Es verdad que no se puede abarcar un campo tan vasto, ni exhaustivamente, porque para algunos países no existen fuentes de información, ni con una exactitud rigurosa, pues faltan los elementos de control que permitirían verificar o completar los datos a veces ambiguos y con frecuencia fragmentarios. Además, la magnitud de la empresa no facilita puestas al día frecuentes, que son sin embargo necesarias dada la movilidad de las instituciones.

Hechas estas reservas, no es menos cierto que la dimensión internacional del *Repertorio* se justifica plenamente por las posibilidades de intercambio que procura, en particular a los países completamente desprovistos de medios para localizar a las instituciones de investigación educacional. Además el interés manifestado por las instituciones requeridas, que respondieron a la Unesco en una proporción del 61 por ciento, es la prueba de que existe una necesidad en ese aspecto.

Si este instrumento de trabajo no es perfecto, es por lo menos perfectible, en particular a partir de las críticas y sugerencias que harán sus lectores. Estos encontrarán al final del documento un formulario que nos pueden enviar con vistas a la próxima puesta al día.

Acceso a la información: cómo utilizar este repertorio

Nuestro primera preocupación ha sido mejorar el contenido del *Repertorio*, pero también hemos hecho algunas modificaciones en su presentación para facilitar la consulta, aunque conservando la organización general de la edición precedente.

Las reseñas sobre las instituciones, numeradas ahora de manera secuencial, están agrupadas por países, que aparecen en el orden alfabético de su denominación en inglés, tal como figuran en el *Tesauro de la Unesco.* Cada institución está también clasificada alfabéticamente por su nombre oficial y, a falta de éste, por su traducción para cada país.

Un índice de descriptores, los del *Tesauro de la educación Unesco:OIE,* remite a las instituciones según los temas más representados en las publicaciones y en las investigaciones en curso, pero no permite localizar los organismos especializados en una esfera de la educación. Por esa razón nos ha parecido útil confeccionar para esta nueva edición un segundo índice por tema principal que reagrupa en 17 áreas las instituciones cuyo nombre identifica su naturaleza específica. El primer índice permite, por ejemplo, responder a la pregunta : ¿ Cuáles son las instituciones en las que la didáctica de la física es actualmente uno de los principales temas de investigación ? ; el segundo permite, por ejemplo, responder a la pregunta : ¿ Cuáles son las instituciones que se dedican de manera permanente a la enseñanza de las ciencias ?

Bibliography/Bibliographie/Bibliografía

1. **Garvey, W.D.; Lin, N.; Nelson, C.E.** A comparison of scientific communication behaviour of social and physical scientists. *International social science journal* (Paris, Unesco), vol. XXIII, no. 2, 1971, p. 256-272. [Also published in French]
2. **Bourgeois, M.E.; Lambert, O.** *Répertoire des organismes français de recherche en sciences de l'éducation : inventaire 1980.* Paris, Centre de documentation sciences humaines, Centre national de la recherche scientifique; Centre de documentation recherche, Institut national de recherche pédagogique, 1981. 148 p.
   ——.——. *mise à jour 1982.* Paris, CDSH, CNRS; Centre de documentation recherche, INRP, 1982. 231.
3. **Lehming, R., ed.** *Directory of research organizations in education: research, development, dissemination, evaluation and policy studies.* San Francisco, CA, Far West Laboratory for Educational Research and Development, 1982. 417 p. [ERIC microfiche ED 218 271]
4. **Thomas, R.C.; Ruffner, J.C., eds.** *Research centers directory.* 7th ed. Detroit, MI, Gale Research, 1982.
5. **British Library. Lending Division. RBUPC Office.** *Research in British universities, polytechnics and colleges. Vol. 3: Social sciences.* Wetherby, United Kingdom, 1982. 500 p.
6. **Istituto nazionale dell'informazione, Italy.** *Doc Italia: annuario degli enti di studio, ricerca, cultura e informazione, 1982.* Roma, 1982.
7. **Stifterverband für die Deutsche Wissenschaft.** *Vademecum deutscher Lehr- und Forschungstätten (VDLF).* Essen, Federal Republic of Germany, 1978.
8. **Kruzas, A.T.; Gill, Kay, eds.** *Government research centres directory.* 2nd ed. Detroit, MI, Gale Research, 1982. 434 p.
9. **Unesco. Regional Office for Education in Latin America and the Caribbean.** *Repertorio de instituciones de investigación educacional en América Latina y el Caribe.* Santiago de Chile, 1980. 53 p.
10. **African Bureau of Educational Sciences.** *Directory of African institutions of research in education/Répertoire des institutions africaines de recherche en éducation.* 2nd ed. Kisangani, Zaïre, Service de bibliothèque et de documentation, Bureau africain des sciences de l'éducation, 1976. 227 p.
11. **Birzéa, C., comp.** *Educational research in five European socialist countries: a survey, 1972/Recherche pédagogique dans cinq pays socialistes européens: une enquête, 1972.* Hamburg, Unesco Institute for Education, 1973. 198 p.
12. **Asian Programme of Educational Innovation for Development.** *Directory of national centres associated with APEID, 1983-1984.* Bangkok, Unesco Regional Office for Education in Asia and the Pacific, 1983. 277 p.
13. **Unesco. Division of Educational Policy and Planning.** *Directory of governmental bodies and institutions dealing with educational planning and administration.* Preliminary version. Paris, 1980. 337 p. (Reports and studies on educational policy and planning, S.86) (ED.80/WS/121) [Unesco microfiche 81s0088]

14. **European Centre for Higher Education.** *International directory of higher education research institutions/Répertoire international des institutions de recherche sur l'enseignement supérieur/Repertorio internacional de instituciones de investigación sobre enseñanza superior/Meždunarodnyj spravočnik učreždenij, veduščih issledovanija v oblasti vysšego obrazovanija.* Paris, Unesco, 1981. 139 p. (Ibedata)

15. **Unesco. Division of Science, Technical and Vocational Education.** *World directory of selected research and teacher training institutions in the field of technical and vocational education.* Rev. ed. Paris, 1983. 87 p. (ED/MD/72)

16. *EUDISED R&D Bulletin* (Windsor, United Kingdom, NFER-Nelson Pub. Co. for Documentation Centre for Education in Europe, Council of Europe, Strasbourg), no. 1, 1976- . 4/yr.

17. **Québec (Province). Ministère de l'éducation. Service de la recherche.** *Répertoire des projets de recherche en éducation.* Vol. 1, juillet 1979 à juin 1980. Québec, Canada, Secteur de la planification, Ministère de l'éducation, 1980. 550 p.

18. *Resources in education* (Washington, DC, Superintendent of Documents, U.S. Govt. Print. Off. for the Educational Resources Information Center, Washington, DC), v. 10, 1975- . 12/yr.

19. *EDUQ: bibliographie analytique sur l'éducation au Québec* (Montréal, Canada, Centrale des bibliothèques pour la Direction de la recherche, Ministère de l'éducation, Québec), n° 1, 1981-. 2/yr.

20. **All-European Conference for Directors of National Research Institutions in Education, 1st, Hamburg, 1976.** *Educational research in Europe,* collected and edited by M.D. Carelli and P. Sachsenmeier. Amsterdam, Swets & Zeitlinger, 1977. 142 p. [Also published in French]
All-European Conference for Directors of Educational Research Institutions, 2nd, Madrid, 1979. *A new look at the relationship between school education and work,* edited by M.D. Carelli. Lisse, Netherlands, Swets & Zeitlinger; Hamburg, Unesco Institute for Education, 1980. 164 p. (International studies in education, 37)
European Colloquy for Directors of National Research Institutions in Education, 3rd, Hamburg, 1978. *Equality of opportunity reconsidered: values in education for tomorrow,* collected and edited by M.D. Carelli and J.G. Morris. Lisse, Netherlands, Swets & Zeitlinger, 1979. 232 p. (International studies in education, 36)
Educational Research Colloquy, 4th, Hamburg, 1981. *Changing role of guidance for educational and vocational development at different stages of the life cycle: report.* Strasboug, Council for Cultural Co-operation, Council of Europe, 1981. 14, iv p. (DECS/Rech (81) 45) [Also published in French]

21. **Association internationale de pédagogie expérimentale de langue française.** Colloque, 27e, Lausanne, 1983. Enseignement de la langue maternelle et recherche pédagogique. *Les sciences de l'éducation: pour l'ère nouvelle* (Caen, France, Laboratoire de psychopédagogie, Université de Caen), n° 1/2, janvier-juin 1984, 197 p.; n° 3, juillet-septembre 1984, 168 p.

22. **Organization for Economic Co-operation and Development.** *Research & development in education: a survey.* Paris, 1974. 57 p. [Also published in French]

23. **Council of Europe. Documentation Centre for Education in Europe.** *Educational research policies in European countries: 1978-1979 survey.* Strasbourg, 1979. 97 p. [Also published in French]

24. **Landsheere, G. De.** *Empirical research in education.* Paris, Unesco, 1982. 113 p., bibl. (IBE. Educational sciences) [Also published in French and Spanish]

25. *The World of learning, 1983-84.* 34th ed. London, Europa Publications, 1983.

26. **International Association of Universities.** *World list of universities/Liste mondiale des universités, 1977-1978.* London, Macmillan, 1978. xxiv, 653 p.

27. **Hegener, Karen, ed.** *Peterson's annual guides to graduate and undergraduate study, 1979. Book 2: Humanities and social sciences.* 13th ed. Princeton, NJ, Peterson's Guides. 1978.

28. *Ulrich's international periodicals directory.* 22nd ed., 1983. New York, Bowker, 1983. 2 v. (1,969 p.)
29. *Irregular serials and annuals: an international directory.* 7th ed., 1982. New York, Bowker, 1981. 1,542 p.
30. **Foundation for Educational Research, Netherlands. Information Department.** *Directory of educational research information sources, 1983/Répertoire des sources d'information en matière de recherche pédagogique, 1983.* 2nd rev. ed. The Hague, 1983. 167 p.
31. **American Council on Education.** *American universities and colleges.* 12th ed. New York; Berlin, Walter de Gruyter, 1983. 2,156 p.
32. *Encyclopedia of associations, 1983.* 17th ed. Detroit, MI, Gale Research, 1982. 2 v. (1791 p.)
33. **Centre suisse de coordination pour la recherche en matière d'éducation.** *Institutions suisses de recherche et de développement éducationnels/Schweizerische Institutionen der Bildungsforschung und Entwicklung.* Aarau, Switzerland, 1983. 239 p.
34. **Australia. Department of Education and Youth Affairs.** *Australian education directory, 1983.* Canberra, Australian Govt. Pub. Service, 1983. 148 p.

National institutions
Institutions nationales
Instituciones nacionales

ALBANIA

Instituti i Studimeve Pedagogjike **0001**

Translation: Institut d'études pédagogiques
Address: Rue Naim Frasheri, TIRANA
Year of creation: 1970
Parent Organization: Ministère de l'éducation et de la culture
Present Head: M. Sotir Temo
Size of staff. Total: 45 — Full time: 29 — Part time: 16
Researchers: 35 — Full time: 19 — Part time: 16
Research activities: more than 50%
Educational research: from 25% to 50%
Type of research: Recherches de base et appliquées.
Functional objectives of research: Etudier les solutions justes et scientifiques pour le développement ultérieur du système de l'éducation, du contenu de l'école, des formes et méthodes de l'enseignement et de l'éducation, les expériences progressistes, les préparations des monographies nécessaires pour obtenir les titres scientifiques.
Periodical publications: Revue pédagogique. La mathématique et la physique à l'école. La chimie et la biologie à l'école. Les sciences sociales à l'école. La langue et la littérature albanaise à l'école. YLLKAT, revue illustrée littéraire pour enfants. Les écoles de 8 ans (cycle inférieur). Les langues étrangères à l'école.
Monographs: Dictionnaire pédagogique. Le contrôle du travail de l'enseignement et éducatif à l'école. La lutte pour une école socialiste et athée. Elever le niveau qualitatif de l'école (recueil d'études). L'éducation des élèves avec les traditions patriotiques et révolutionnaires. L'instituteur dans l'époque du Parti (le Parti du travail d'Albanie). Liste complète sur demande.
Studies and surveys in preparation: Elever le niveau et la qualité du travail à l'école afin de donner aux jeunes des connaissances du niveau contemporain. Renforcer les liens de l'école avec la vie et la production. Problèmes de l'éducation sociale et familiale de la jeune génération. Le développement de l'éducation en République populaire socialiste d'Albanie. Liste complète sur demande.

ALGERIA

al-Ma'had at-tarbawī al-waṭanī

0002

Translation: Institut pédagogique national
Address: 11 rue Ali Haddad, ALGER
Year of creation: 1963
Parent Organization: Ministère de l'éducation et de l'enseignement fondamental
Present Head: M. Mahi Rachid
Size of staff. Total: 890 — Full time: 870 — Part time: 20
Researchers: 140 — Full time: 120 — Part time: 20
Research activities: from 10% to 25%
Educational research: more than 50%
Type of research: Recherches appliquées.
Functional objectives of research: Réalisation de méthodes et moyens didactiques.
Monographs: Manuels scolaires destinés à l'enseignement fondamental. Documents didactiques pour les enseignants. Supports audio-visuels (diapositives, cassettes, films, cartes, etc.).

al-Marqaz al-waṭanī li-ăt-tawtīq wa-ăl-baḥt al-'ilmī

0003

Translation: Centre national de documentation et de recherche pédagogique (CNDRP)
Address: Cité Universitaire de garçons, Ben-Aknoun, ALGER
Year of creation: 1981
Parent Organization: ONRS
Present Head: M. M. Bensmaine
Size of staff. Total: 32 — Full time: 14
Researchers: 22 — Full time: 4 — Part time: 18
Research activities: 50%
Educational research: 50%
Type of research: Recherche appliquée en priorité.
Functional objectives of research: Etudes d'orientation; fournir des prestations.
Periodical publications: Préparation d'une revue semestrielle pour 1984.
Studies and surveys in preparation: Proposition d'enrichissement des sciences physiques. Etude de l'insertion professionnelle des diplômés des sciences humaines: promotion 1975/82 de l'Université d'Oran. Analyse et évaluation du système universitaire. Analyse comparée des coûts et rendements d'institutions post-secondaires. Place et rôle des techniques éducatives audiovisuelles dans l'enseignement supérieur et la recherche. Didactique de l'anglais.

ANGOLA

Centro de Investigação Pedagógica

0004

Translation: Centre de recherches pédagogiques
Address: Ministère de l'éducation, B.P. 1281, LUANDA
Year of creation: 1977
Parent Organization: Ministère de l'éducation

Present Head: Pedro Domingos Peterson
Size of staff. Total: 85 — Full time: 84 — Part time: 1
Researchers: 48 — Full time: 48
Research activities: from 25% to 50%
Educational research: more than 50%
Type of research: Recherche appliquée basée sur l'enseignement général.
Functional objectives of research: Donner satisfaction aux besoins présents et assurer l'anticipation des futurs: contribuer à trouver des solutions pour l'amélioration de la qualité de l'enseignement.
Studies and surveys in preparation: Causes des échecs scolaires (étude collective). Education sexuelle. Formation des maîtres.

ARGENTINA

Centro de Investigación Educativa

0005

Address: Nuestra Señora del Buen Viaje 161, MORÓN (1708)
Year of creation: 1968
Parent Organization: Ministerio de Educación y Cultura de la Provincia de Buenos Aires
Size of staff. Total: 10 — Full time: 10
Researchers: 6 — Full time: 6
Research activities: 50%
Educational research: more than 50%
Type of research: Aplicada.
Functional objectives of research: Obtener datos actualizados de índole pedagógica, a través de la aplicación de técnicas de investigación, para el mejoramiento mediato e inmediato del sistema educativo.
Periodical publications: Boletines de apoyo pedagógico. C.I.E. Asesora — informa (publicación semestral).
Monographs: Enfoque didáctico sobre temas de interés vinculados con los programas vigentes en la escuela primaria. Monografías realizadas por los docentes que asisten a los seminarios de perfeccionamiento. Las mismas permanecen en la institución para eventuales consultas.
Studies and surveys in preparation: Se realizan informes de investigación a cargo de grupos de seminaristas sobre temas que competen a la realidad educativa. Asimismo, un grupo de asesoras se halla abocado a la confección de una monografía sobre la enseñanza de las ciencias en la escuela primaria.

Centro Interdisciplinario en Investigaciones en Psicología Matemática y Experimental (CIIPME)

0006

Address: Cangallo 2158, BUENOS AIRES
Year of creation: 1971
Parent Organization: Consejo Nacional de Investigaciones Científicas y Técnicas; Universidad de Buenos Aires
Present Head: Dr. Horacio José Ambrosio Rimoldi
Size of staff. Total: 25

Researchers: 23
Type of research: Investigación básica.
Monographs: El papel de la educación matemática en una sociedad de cambio. La unidad funcional de enseñanza. Análisis de algunos factores relacionados con inteligencia en escuela primaria. El proceso educativo en la formación profesional. Lista completa a disposición.
Studies and surveys in preparation: Educación y ciencias sociales en el mundo moderno. Análisis de estructuras lógico matemáticas en niños de escuela primaria. Habilidad matemática y desarrollo intelectual. Lista completa a disposición.

Dirección General de Programación Educativa

0007

Address: Paraguay No. 1657, 2o. piso, BUENOS AIRES, (1062)
Year of creation: 1973
Parent Organization: Subsecretaría de Educación
Present Head: Contador Felipe G. De Carli
Size of staff. Total: 40
Researchers: 9
Educational research: more than 50%
Type of research: Investigación básica.
Functional objectives of research: Prestación de servicios a la administración educacional.
Periodical publications: Situación de la investigación educativa (publicación bianual).
Monographs: Aguerrondo, I. Estado de los estudios sobre deserción escolar en el sistema educativo argentino. 1981.
Studies and surveys in preparation: La regionalización educativa en la República Argentina. La orientación en las instituciones educativas del país. Innovaciones educacionales en Argentina. Estudio sobre experiencias de mejoramiento del sistema educativo argentino.

Facultad de Ciencias de la Educación, Universidad Nacional de Entre Rios

0008

Address: Rivadavia no. 106, 3100 PARANA, Entre Ríos
Year of creation: 1919
Parent Organization: Ministerio de Educación
Present Head: Carlos Antonio Uzin, Profesor en Pedagogía, Docente Universitario
Size of staff. Total: 57 — Part time: 17
Researchers: 23 — Part time: 6
Research activities: from 25% to 50%
Educational research: from 25% to 50%
Type of research: Básico.
Functional objectives of research: Formación de investigadores; mejoramiento del sistema educativo.
Monographs: Bases axiológicas de la educación personalizada. La escuela normal de Paraná. La educación jesuítica en las reducciones de guaraníes. Bases antropológicas de la educación personalizada. Causas que producen deserción escolar a nivel primario.
Studies and surveys in preparation: Los valores en Lavelle. La filosofía en Castellani. Causas que producen deserción escolar a nivel medio.

Instituto de Investigaciones Educativas, Buenos Aires

0009

Address: Cangallo 1605, 3er. piso, Of. 10, 1037 BUENOS AIRES
Year of creation: 1974
Parent Organization: Fundación para el Avance de la Educación
Present Head: Luis Jorge Zanotti
Size of staff. Total: 7 — Full time: 3 — Part time: 4
Researchers: 2 — Full time: 2
Research activities: from 10% to 25%
Educational research: more than 50%
Type of research: Básica y aplicada.
Functional objectives of research: Prestación de servicios a la administración educacional.
Periodical publications: Revista del IIE.
Monographs: Oñativa, O. Fundamentos psicológicos de los métodos de alfabetización. 1984.
Studies and surveys in preparation: Computadoras y educación. Perfil del docente musical en nuestro país.

Instituto de Investigaciones Educativas, La Plata

0010

Address: Calle 45 No. 582, Planta alta, Código postal 1900, LA PLATA
Year of creation: 1981
Parent Organization: Universidad Nacional de La Plata, Facultad de Humanidades y Ciencias de la Educación, Departamento de Ciencias de la Educación
Present Head: Carolita Sierra de Rogati, Jefe del Departamento de Ciencias de la Educación
Size of staff. Total: 9 — Full time: 8 — Part time: 1
Researchers: 6 — Full time: 6
Research activities: more than 50%
Educational research: more than 50%
Type of research: Básica, aplicada, investigación y desarrollo.
Functional objectives of research: Obtención de grados; prestación de servicios a la administración educacional.
Periodical publications: En preparación.
Monographs: En preparación.
Studies and surveys in preparation: Fundamentos psicológicos y pedagógicos de la necesidad de iniciar al niño en la lectoescritura durante la etapa del jardín de infantes como facilitador del proceso de enseñanza-aprendizaje de la lectoescritura en la escuela primaria. Incidencia del lenguaje escrito, sobre el rendimiento escolar de los alumnos de primer año de las Escuelas de Enseñanza Técnica y Profesional, dependientes del C.O.N.E.T. en la asignatura historia. Estrategias de desarrollo de un programa de educación a distancia para la formación y/o perfeccionamiento docente. Modelo de programa de capacitación continua para docentes en ejercio de escuela media. Lista complete a disposición.

Instituto de Investigaciones, Facultad de Psicopedagogía — Universidad del Salvador

0011

Address: Corrientes 4471, BUENOS AIRES (1195)
Year of creation: 1975
Parent Organization: Universidad del Salvador, Buenos Aires
Present Head: Prof. Aurora Constanza Mazás de Pérez
Size of staff. Total: 9 — Full time: 2 — Part time: 7
Researchers: 6 — Part time: 6
Research activities: 50%
Educational research: 50%
Type of research: Investigación aplicada, básica y operativa.
Functional objectives of research: Promover la investigación a partir de las cátedras.
Periodical publications: Revista de psicopedagogía (actualmente interrumpida).
Monographs: La orientación en la escuela primaria. Vínculo y aprendizaje.
Studies and surveys in preparation: El primer año de vida. El perfil del docente en nivel superior. Dificultades más frecuentes en el aprendizaje de la lecto-escritura. Dificultades más frecuentes en el aprendizaje del cálculo.

Instituto Rosario de Investigaciones en Ciencias de la Educación (IRICE)

0012

Address: 9 de Julio no. 80, 2000 ROSARIO, Pcia. Santa Fe
Year of creation: 1977
Parent Organization: Consejo Nacional de Investigaciones Científicas y Técnicas; Universidad Nacional de Rosario
Present Head: Prof. Ricardo Pedro Bruera
Size of staff. Total: 46
Researchers: 40
Type of research: Investigación básica y aplicada.
Functional objectives of research: Desarrollar las investigaciones en el campo teórico y en el experimental de las ciencias de la educación; promover la transferencia de los conocimientos pedagógicos elaborados al sistema educativo nacional; instrumentar un programa de desarrollo de recursos humanos en lo referente a formación y perfeccionamiento docente.
Periodical publications: Boletín trimestral.
Monographs: Teoría de la enseñanza, curriculum, materiales didácticos, información escolar y política educativa. Lista a disposición.
Studies and surveys in preparation: Fundamentación epistemológica del curriculum. Innovaciones curriculares en la enseñanza media. Curso de postgrado en ciencias de la educación. Bases políticas para la fundamentación de un proyecto de Ley de Educación. Modelo de análisis para el planeamiento de institutos terciarios no universitarios. Lista completa a disposición.

Proyecto Multinacional de Investigación Educativa

0013

Address: Paseo Colón 533, 4to. piso, Código postal 1063, BUENOS AIRES
Parent Organization: Ministerio de Educación de la Nación con aportes de la O.E.A.
Present Head: Sra. María Dolores Olano de Araujo
Size of staff. Total: 20 — Full time: 8 — Part time: 12
Researchers: 6 — Full time: 2 — Part time: 4
Research activities: more than 50%

Educational research: more than 50%
Type of research: Investigaciones aplicadas; investigación y desarrollo de programas (en coordinación con organismos específicos).
Functional objectives of research: Objetivo general: obtener información que sirva para tomar decisiones que permitan mejorar la calidad de la educación.
Monographs: Educación Universitaria a Distancia. 1983. Evaluación de la relación escuela y comunidad. 1983. Pautas para la planificación, desarrollo y evaluación de las actividades de perfeccionamiento docente. 1983. Dinámica de grupo y educación — fundamentación. 1983. Dinámica de grupo y educación — curso a distancia. 1983. Articulación de la educación preescolar con la escuela primaria. 1983. La escuela trabaja con la comunidad — fundamentación. 1983. La escuela trabaja con la comunidad — curso a distancia. 1983. Docencia y democracia. 1983. Demanda de carreras agrotécnicas. 1983. Fundamentación de un aprendizaje sobre estudio autodirigido — módulo I. 1983. Encuadre didáctico del estudio autodirigido — módulo II. 1983.
Studies and surveys in preparation: La supervisión y el curriculum. Interacción escuela y comunidad (La escuela trabaja con la comunidad). Capacitación de la mujer en áreas de escasa densidad de población. El perfeccionamiento docente en la República Argentina.

AUSTRALIA

Australian Council for Educational Research

0014

Address: Radford House, 9 Frederick Street, HAWTHORN, Vic. 3122
Year of creation: 1930
Present Head: Dr J.P. Keeves
Size of staff. Total: 74 — Full time: 58 — Part time: 16
Researchers: 33 — Full time: 25 — Part time: 8
Research activities: more than 50%
Educational research: more than 50%
Type of research: Basic, applied, research and development.
Functional objectives of research: Conduct research and undertake development in matters affecting education. Publish and disseminate the results of research. Develop tests and materials. Collect and document information concerning Australian education.
Periodical publications: Australian education index. Australian journal of education. ACER Newsletter. Bulletin for psychologists. Research information for teachers. Annual report. Bibliography on education theses in Australia.
Monographs: Ross, K.N. Social area indicators of educational need: a study of the use of census descriptions of school neighbourhood in guiding decisions concerning the allocation of resources to educationally disadvantaged schools in Australia. Fordham, A.M. The context of teaching and learning: report on the first phase of the IEA classroom environment study. Mills, J. Bilingual education and Australian schools. Smith, R.S. Australian independent schools, yesterday, today and tomorrow. Wilson, M. Adventures in uncertainty. Complete list on request.
Studies and surveys in preparation: Patterns of school organization. Devolution of curriculum development. Youth in transition. Second IEA science study. Complete

list on request.

Centre for Continuing Education

0015

Address: GPO Box 4, CANBERRA, ACT 2601
Year of creation: 1970
Parent Organization: Australian National University
Present Head: Dr. Chris Duke, Director
Size of staff. Total: 26 — Full time: 22 — Part time: 4
Researchers: 6 — Full time: 6
Research activities: less than 10%
Educational research: more than 50%
Type of research: Action, basic, participatory.
Functional objectives of research: Increasing knowledge in the areas of adult education; recurrent education and participatory strategies for learning and development.
Periodical publications: Canberra papers in continuing education (occasional).
Monographs: Adult education and development: some important issues. DVV–ASPBAE partnership: evaluative review 1977–1980. Haines, N. Education and leisure. Reflections on work, ethics and learning to be free. Model for planning and conducting a training activity. In Proceedings of the AAAE Conference on Training Adult and Community Educators. C. Cookson and B. Peace (eds.). Canberra, AAAE, 1981.
Studies and surveys in preparation: Adult education and poverty (comparative international study). Recurrent education in Australia. Recurrent education and the professions (revision for publication). Nonformal adult education provision in Australian universities and colleges. Complete list on request.

Commonwealth Schools Commission

0016

Address: P.O. Box 34, WODEN, ACT 2606
Year of creation: 1973
Parent Organization: The Commission is a statutory body created by the Federal Australian Parliament
Present Head: Dr. Peter Tannock
Size of staff. Total: 165 — Full time: 146 — Part time: 19
Researchers: 10 — Full time: 10
Research activities: less than 10%
Educational research: less than 10%
Type of research: Applied research.
Functional objectives of research: Formulating policy advice to the Commonwealth Government; information bases for Commonwealth funding programs for schools.
Periodical publications: Annual cycle of publications related to the Commonwealth government's budget cycle: Recommendations. Report (in response to Government Guidelines). Program guidelines. Statistical bulletin.
Monographs: The Commission has published more than 150 titles, many of them no longer in print. A list is available on request.
Studies and surveys in preparation: Computers in education. Survey on aboriginal education in Australia. School resources study. 15–16 year-old study. Participation and equity. Options for funding Government and non-government schools. Aboriginal education. Integrated school census. Education for girls. Complete list on

request.

Curriculum Development Centre

0017

Address: P.O. Box 52, DICKSON, ACT 2602
Year of creation: 1973
Parent Organization: Commonwealth Schools Commission (will become 'parent organization' in the near future)
Present Head: Mr. David Francis
Size of staff. Total: 26 — Full time: 23 — Part time: 3
Researchers: 8 — Full time: 8
Research activities: from 25% to 50%
Educational research: from 25% to 50%
Type of research: Applied research and development.
Functional objectives of research: Develop policies on national curriculum priorities; promote and assist in the devising and development of school curricula and educational materials; undertake and assist in R&D; make available school curricula and materials; collect, assess and disseminate information.
Periodical publications: Curriculum digest. Pacific Circle Consortium newsletter. Asia in the classroom. Study of society.
Monographs: English and the aboriginal child (text/audiotape). The English spoken by Aboriginal entrants to Traeger Park School. Curriculum evaluation: case studies; how it can be done; selected readings. School based curriculum development Series (set of 9). Complete list on request.
Studies and surveys in preparation: Environmental Education Project evaluation report. Friends and critics: a perspective on the theory of practice of co-operative curriculum development. Personalising instruction in mathematics. Teacher tactics for problem solving. All teachers teach language: strategies for teachers of ESL students in the mainstream classroom. Complete list on request.

Directorate of Research and Planning, South Australian Department of Education

0018

Address: G.P.O. Box 1152, ADELAIDE, S.A. 5001
Year of creation: 1969
Parent Organization: South Australian Education Department
Present Head: John Cusack
Size of staff. Total: 33 — Full time: 29 — Part time: 4
Researchers: 11 — Full time: 11
Research activities: from 25% to 50%
Educational research: from 25% to 50%
Type of research: Applied; research and development.
Functional objectives of research: Service to schools; service to educational administration.
Monographs: Affective Education Project. Talking about schools: parents and evaluation. Support project for school controlled evaluation. Portraits from an institution: a study of secondary schooling. Schools within schools: sub-schooling in Australian secondary schools. Developing the classroom group (Reports 1-5). Case studies in school evaluation.
Studies and surveys in preparation: Teenage mothers. Review of school libraries. English as a foreign language. Development of ability in written English. Development of

public examinations. Revision of school year. Sub-school structure. Transition from school.

Directorate of Studies

0019

Address: New South Wales Department of Education, Box 33, G.P.O., SYDNEY 2001
Year of creation: 1971
Parent Organization: NSW Department of Education
Present Head: Dr. Fenton G. Sharpe
Size of staff. Total: 77 — Full time: 77
Researchers: 59 — Full time: 59
Research activities: from 10% to 25%
Type of research: Applied research.
Functional objectives of research: Preparation for curriculum development: work towards the development of education as a unified process (K–12).
Periodical publications: Primary journal. Secondary journal. Insight. Contemporary issues. School magazine.
Studies and surveys in preparation: Curricula — Writing K–12. Drama K–12. Mass media. Music K–12. Health K–12. Visual arts K–12.

Evaluation and Assessment Unit

0020

Address: P.M.B. 25, WINNELLIE, N.T. 5789
Year of creation: 1977
Parent Organization: Professional Services Branch, NT Department of Education
Present Head: Dr. Jack Smith
Size of staff. Total: 6 — Full time: 6
Researchers: 5 — Full time: 5
Research activities: less than 10%
Type of research: Curriculum development; assessment of student performance.
Functional objectives of research: Servicing educational administration.
Studies and surveys in preparation: Accreditation of bilingual schools. Assessment of student performance. Evaluation of core curriculum.

Management Information Services

0021

Address: 50 Hunter Street, Box 33 G.P.O., SYDNEY, N.S.W. 2001
Parent Organization: New South Wales Department of Education
Present Head: Mr. B. Henry
Size of staff. Total: 67 — Full time: 67
Researchers: 9 — Full time: 9
Research activities: from 10% to 25%
Educational research: more than 50%
Type of research: Applied.
Functional objectives of research: Servicing educational administration.
Periodical publications: Occasional Departmental reports.
Monographs: Contribution of articles to Departmental publications, e.g. 'Insight'.
Studies and surveys in preparation: Survey of student background and class placement. Development of student data base. Programme evaluation. Development of enrolment projections data base at individual school level. Sex differences in subject choice and

academic performance. Documentary research in current educational issues. Study of school retention rates.

Planning Directorate, Education Department of Western Australia

0022

Address: 151 Royal Street, EAST PERTH, W.A. 6000
Year of creation: 1973
Parent Organization: Education Department of Western Australia
Present Head: Mr. J. Quinn
Size of staff. Total: 52 — Full time: 26 — Part time: 26
Researchers: 26 — Part time: 26
Research activities: from 10% to 25%
Educational research: less than 10%
Type of research: Research and development.
Functional objectives of research: Servicing the educational administration.
Periodical publications: Education Department pocket yearbook (biannual). Education statistics bulletin (biannual).
Monographs: Design brief for Senior High Schools: flexible area secondary schools for the 80's. 1975. Primary schools design brief. 1976. Care and maintenance of buildings and equipment in schools. 1976.
Studies and surveys in preparation: An anthropometric study of children of secondary school age in relation to design of school furniture (carried out in collaboration with the Department of Human Movement and the Department of Anatomy at the University of Western Australia).

Research and Curriculum Services

0023

Address: P.O. Box 33, North Quay, BRISBANE, Q. 4000
Parent Organization: Queensland Department of Education
Present Head: J.E. Fitzgerald
Size of staff. Total: 30 — Full time: 30
Researchers: 22 — Full time: 22
Research activities: more than 50%
Educational research: more than 50%
Type of research: Applied.
Functional objectives of research: Servicing schools and the administration.
Periodical publications: Research bulletin.
Monographs: Evaluation series. Research project (summaries of current projects). Interim reports.
Studies and surveys in preparation: Primary physical education evaluation. Foreign languages in secondary schools. Primary health education evaluation. Evaluation of special programme schools scheme. Evaluation of music in Queensland primary schools. Complete list on request.

Research and Statistics Branch, Commonwealth Department of Education and Youth Affairs

0024

Address: MLC Tower, P.O. Box 826, WODEN, ACT 2606
Present Head: Mr. B.E. Morey, Acting Assistant Secretary, Research and Statistics Branch

Size of staff. Total: 14 — Full time: 14
Researchers: 8 — Part time: 8
Research activities: from 25% to 50%
Educational research: from 25% to 50%
Type of research: Applied, research and development.
Functional objectives of research: Servicing educational administration and policy.
Monographs: Hubbert. G. An evaluation of the education program for unemployed youth. Young, C. Education and employment of Turkish and Lebanese youth. Elsworth, G. An evaluation of the adult secondary education assistance scheme. Drs. Rado, Foster and Bradley. Language needs of newly arrived youth in Australia. Complete list on request.
Studies and surveys in preparation: Case studies of innovative and traditional career counselling and guidance programs. ASAT sex bias study. Complete list on request.

Research Branch

0025

Address: 31 Flinders Street, GPO Box 2352, ADELAIDE, S.A. 5000
Year of creation: 1972
Parent Organization: Department of Technical and Further Education
Present Head: Mr. L.P. Fricker, Director-General
Size of staff. Total: 16 — Full time: 15 — Part time: 1
Researchers: 14 — Full time: 14
Research activities: more than 50%
Educational research: more than 50%
Type of research: Basic and applied research.
Functional objectives of research: Development, implementation of statistics systems as research tools; to assist in the effective provision of technical and further education of adults, by means of curriculum evaluation, planning and social research.
Periodical publications: Research bulletin.
Monographs: Broderick, J.S. An investigation into the curriculum development process in TAFE in Australia, 1982. Brown, P.J. The City College: an educational needs analysis, 1982. Parkinson, K.J., et al. Motivations for enrolments in external studies. 1982. Raffery, J.; Brown, A.; Kuhl, D.H. A survey of the educational and training needs of the pastoral industry of South Australia. 1981. Some perspectives on the participation of females in transition education. Port Augusta College of Technical and Further Education: an educational needs analysis. Complete list on request.
Studies and surveys in preparation: Fitting and machining skill survey. Evaluation of women's introductory trades courses. Evaluation of staff development programme for transition education personnel. Evaluation of transition education programmes. Complete list on request.

Research Branch, Tasmanian Department of Education

0026

Address: G.P.O. Box 169B, HOBART, Tasmania 7001
Year of creation: 1960
Parent Organization: Tasmanian Department of Education
Present Head: Mr. L.D. Blazely
Size of staff. Total: 18 — Full time: 12 — Part time: 6
Researchers: 15 — Full time: 11 — Part time: 4
Research activities: more than 50%

Educational research: more than 50%
Type of research: Applied.
Functional objectives of research: Support policy development; support curriculum development.
Periodical publications: Research studies (series). Statistical information (series).
Studies and surveys in preparation: Mobility of teachers. Parent participation in education. Integration of special education students. Education and minor physical impairments (3 studies). Transition from grade 10 (2 studies). Day and block release for apprentices. Evaluation of training of resource teacher.

AUSTRIA

Institut für berufsbezogene Erwachsenenbildung

0027

Translation: Institute for Vocationally-Oriented Adult Education
Address: Johannes Kelper Universität, Grillparzerstrasse 50, 4020 LINZ
Year of creation: 1980
Present Head: Mag. Dr. Walter Blumberger
Size of staff. Total: 10 — Full time: 2 — Part time: 8
Researchers: 9 — Full time: 1 — Part time: 8
Research activities: more than 50%
Educational research: more than 50%
Type of research: Adult education; vocational/professional training; workers' education; new technologies and professional training; technologies and trade unions; vocational rehabilitation.
Functional objectives of research: Preparation of courses; servicing the educational administration and trade-unions.
Periodical publications: Schriftenreihe des Institutes für Berufsbezogene Erwachsenenbildung.
Monographs: Projektberichte des Institutes für Berufsbezogene Erwachsenenbildung.
Studies and surveys in preparation: CAD in vocational training of handicapped. New technologies in vocational training of electricians. Vocational training of unskilled workers. Job-career of handicapped.

Institut für Erwachsenenbildung im Ring Öesterreichischer Bildungswerke

0028

Translation: Institute for Adult Education
Address: Imbergstr. 24, 5020 SALZBURG
Year of creation: 1962
Parent Organization: Ring Öesterreichischer Bildungswerke
Present Head: Dr. Hannelore Blaschek
Size of staff. Total: 3 — Full time: 3
Researchers: 2 — Full time: 2
Research activities: from 10% to 25%
Educational research: more than 50%
Type of research: Applied research.
Functional objectives of research: Preparing training of adult educators; contribution to philosophy of adult education.

Periodical publications: Bibliographische Mitteilungen zur Öesterreichischen Erwachsenenbildung I–IX.
Monographs: Gemeinwesenearbeit und Erwachsenenbildung (Introduction and redaction). 1983.
Studies and surveys in preparation: Begleituntersuchung zu Bildungswochen. Studie über den Bildungswerkleiter.

Institut für Erziehungswissenschaften der Universität Graz

0029

Translation: Institute of Educational Science
Address: Hans-Sachs-Gasse 3, 8010 GRAZ
Year of creation: 1969
Parent Organization: Universität Graz
Present Head: Univ. Prof. Dr. Hans Wurzwallner
Size of staff. Total: 18
Researchers: 15
Type of research: Basic and applied research.
Functional objectives of research: Partial fulfilment of degree requirements; teacher education; special education.
Studies and surveys in preparation: Methods of school-centred in-service training. Evaluation of a teacher education programme. Psychosomatic disorders.

Institut für Erziehungswissenschaften der Universität Innsbruck

0030

Translation: Institute of Education
Address: Innrain 52, 6020 INNSBRUCK
Year of creation: 1669
Parent Organization: University of Innsbruck
Present Head: Prof. Dr. Helmwart Hierdeis
Size of staff. Total: 11 — Full time: 11
Researchers: 11 — Full time: 11
Research activities: from 10% to 25%
Type of research: Research and development.
Functional objectives of research: Degree requirements.
Periodical publications: Arbeiten aus dem Institut für Erziehungswissenschaften. Impulse für Erwachsenenbildung und Hochschuldidaktik.
Monographs: Hierdin, H. Basiswissen Pädagogik. Bd. I. Erziehungstheorie. 1981. Hierdin, H. Erziehungsinstitutionen. 1983. Weiss, R. Grundfragen der pädagogischen Psychologie. 1982. Weiss, R. Grundfragen der Unterricht. 1982.
Studies and surveys in preparation: Untersuchungen zu den Bereichen Alltagstheorien, Kindheit auf dem Lande, Schulleben, Selbstevaluation von Lehrern, Lehrerverhalten.

Institut für Erziehungswissenschaften der Universität Salzburg

0031

Translation: Institute for Educational Sciences, University of Salzburg
Address: Franziskanergasse 1, 5020 SALZBURG
Year of creation: 1964
Parent Organization: Bundesministerium für Wissenschaft und Forschung
Size of staff. Total: 12
Researchers: 9

Research activities: from 25% to 50%
Educational research: from 25% to 50%
Type of research: Basic and applied research.
Functional objectives of research: Fulfilment of degree requirements; preparation of courses; individual researches/projects.
Periodical publications: Spectrum paedagogicum.
Monographs: Thonhauser, J. Determinanten unterschiedlicher Bildungswünsche. 1977.
Studies and surveys in preparation: Historische Entwicklungen und gegenwärtige Aspekte des Berufsbildenden Unterrichts. Die Stellung der Berufsschule im dualen Ausbildungssystem. Geschichtsdidaktik. Medienprofile. Interaktionen im Kindergarten.

Institut für Erziehungswissenschaften der Universität Wien

0032

Translation: Institute for Pedagogics
Address: Garnisongasse 3/8, 1090 WIEN
Parent Organization: University of Vienna; Bundesministerium für Wissenschaft und Forschung
Present Head: Univ. Prof. Dr. Richard Olechowski
Size of staff. Total: 21 — Full time: 20 — Part time: 1
Researchers: 21 — Full time: 20 — Part time: 1
Research activities: from 25% to 50%
Educational research: from 25% to 50%
Type of research: Basic and applied research.
Functional objectives of research: Partial fulfilment of degree requirements.
Periodical publications: Vierteljahresschrift für wissenschaftliche Pädagogik. Religion, Wissenschaft, Kultur.
Monographs: Datler, W. Was leistet die Psychoanalyse für die Pädagogik? 1983. Olechowski, R. Schule ohne Angst? 1983. Olechowski, R.; Weinzierl E. Neue Mittelstufe. 1981. Oswald, F. Familie und Gesellschaft. 1982. Schirlbauer, A. Didaktik und Unterricht. 1981. Schwendenwein, W. Erfolg und Versagen in technischen Schulen. 1982.
Studies and surveys in preparation: Menschenerweckende Erwachsenenbildung. Authentische Wissenschaft. Die Geschichte der Gesamtschulidee im deutschen Sprachraum. Religionsunterricht in der offenen Gesellschaft.

Institut für Pädagogik und Psychologie der Universität Linz

0033

Translation: Institute of Education and Psychology, University of Linz
Address: Altenbergerstrasse 69, 4045 LINZ
Year of creation: 1978
Parent Organization: University of Linz
Present Head: Prof. Dr. Hermann Brandstätter
Size of staff. Total: 19 — Full time: 16 — Part time: 3
Researchers: 11 — Full time: 11
Research activities: from 25% to 50%
Educational research: from 10% to 25%
Type of research: Basic and applied research.
Functional objectives of research: Career development, vocational and educational counselling, integration of disabled children, school climate, evaluation of teacher training and of courses for unemployed youth.

Monographs: Seifert, K.H. Die Bedeutung der Beschäftigungsaussichten im Rahmen des Berufswahlprozesses. 1982. Seifert, K.H.; Stangl, W. Einstellungen zu Körperbehinderten und ihrer beruflich-sozialen Integration. 1981. Sageder, J. Die Optimumhypothese: neue Aspekte der Angewandten Sozial-psychologie. 1982.
Studies and surveys in preparation: Evaluation of courses for unemployed youth. Career development of senior high school students.

Öesterreichisches Institut Bildung und Wirtschaft, Institut für Bildungsforschung der Wirtschaft

0034

Translation: Austrian Institute for Education and Economy, Institute for Educational Research and Economy
Address: Judenplatz 3-4, 1010 WIEN
Year of creation: 1975
Parent Organization: Federal Chamber of Commerce
Present Head: Kom.-Rat C.H. Schönbichler
Size of staff. Total: 9 — Full time: 7 — Part time: 2
Researchers: 7 — Full time: 5 — Part time: 2
Research activities: more than 50%
Educational research: more than 50%
Type of research: Fundamental and applied research.
Functional objectives of research: Job analysis; vocational information; vocational training; vocational training for adults; basic materials for examinations in the field of vocational training.
Periodical publications: Mitteilungen (12/yr). Abstracts Forschungsberichte (4/yr).
Monographs: Betriebliche Bildungsarbeit. Motive der Lehrlingseinstellung. Auswirkungen der Mikroelektronik. Jugend und Politik. Berufsentscheidung. Betriebserkundungen und Schnupperlehren. Studienfinanzierung. Jugendarbeit in Betrieben. Analyse der AHS-Schulbücher.
Studies and surveys in preparation: Lehrberufe mit geringen Lehrlingszahlen. Beschäftigungsprobleme der 19-25 jährigen. Das IBW Ausbildungsberaterseminar. Berufswahlentscheidung. Motive zum Selbständigwerden. Lehrabschlussprüfung 84.

Oesterreichisches Institut für Berufsbildungsforschung

0035

Translation: Austrian Institute of Vocational Training Research
Address: Kolingasse 15, 1090 WIEN
Year of creation: 1970
Parent Organization: Independent association
Present Head: Mag. Dr. Ilan Knapp
Size of staff. Total: 16 — Full time: 14 — Part time: 2
Researchers: 4 — Full time: 4
Research activities: more than 50%
Educational research: more than 50%
Type of research: Research and development.
Functional objectives of research: Servicing the educational administration.
Periodical publications: ÖIBF-Info. Lehrlingsprognose, Facharbeterprognose. Tätigkeitsberichte (Prognostics of needs of apprentices and skilled workers. Reports of activities).
Monographs: Berufslaufbahn von Handelsakademikern und Handelsakademikerinnen.

Lehrlingsentwicklung in den 80er Jahren. Berufsspezifische Ausbildungspläne für Blinde und stark sehbehinderte Menschen verschiedener Länder. Lebensweise von Arbeitslosen mit besonderer Berücksichtigung der Mediennutzung. Neue Technologien und Lehrlingsausbildung.

Studies and surveys in preparation: Bildungsmassnahmen für Jugendliche ohne Berufsbildung. Soziale Einstellung und Berufssituation des jungen Facharbeiters. Umweltschutzprogramme und deren Auswirkungen auf zukünftige Berufsinhalte und Berufsformen.

Pädagogische Akademie der Diözese Graz-Seckau

0036

Translation: School (College) of Education
Address: Georgigasse 85-89, 8026 GRAZ
Year of creation: 1968
Parent Organization: Bischöfliches Ordinariat der Diözese Graz-Seckau
Present Head: Dr. Gerhard Berger
Size of staff. Total: 120 — Full time: 45 — Part time: 75
Research activities: less than 10%
Educational research: more than 50%
Type of research: Applied.
Functional objectives of research: Servicing the educational administration.
Studies and surveys in preparation: Projects for playgrounds for children. Parents-teachers-children cooperation.

Pädagogisches Institut der Stadt Wien

0037

Translation: Vienna Metropolitan Institute of Education
Address: Burggasse 14-16, 1070 WIEN
Year of creation: 1868
Parent Organization: Magistrat der Stadt Wien
Present Head: Dr. Karl Sretenovic
Size of staff. Total: 17 — Full time: 13 — Part time: 4
Researchers: 6 — Full time: 4 — Part time: 2
Research activities: from 10% to 25%
Type of research: Applied; research and development.
Functional objectives of research: Preparation of courses; school focussed in-service; reduction of school anguish and similar phenomena.
Periodical publications: Mitteilungen des Pädagogischen Instituts der Stadt Wien (published monthly, contains essays, reports and announcements).
Studies and surveys in preparation: Problems connecting integration of socially, physically and otherwise handicapped children.

Pädagogisches Institut des Bundes für Oberösterreich

0038

Translation: Federal Institute for Teachers Inservice Training
Address: Rainerstrasse 11, 4020 LINZ
Year of creation: 1962
Parent Organization: Bundesministerium für Unterricht und Kunst
Present Head: Dr. Johann Sturm
Size of staff. Total: 11 — Full time: 8 — Part time: 3

Researchers: 1 — Full time: 1
Research activities: from 10% to 25%
Educational research: more than 50%
Type of research: Empiric research.
Functional objectives of research: Evaluation of the efficiency of teaching.
Periodical publications: Unterrichtspraktische Veröffentlichungen (publications on teaching practice).
Studies and surveys in preparation: Empirical research on special classes for handicapped children. Empirical research on school classes visiting museums.

Pädagogisches Institut des Bundes in Steiermark, mit Abteilungen für Lehrer an allgemeinbildenden Pflichtschulen, allgemeinbildenden höheren Schulen, Berufsschulen und berufsbildenden Schulen

0039

Translation: College for the Inservice Training of Teachers: Departments for schools for the 6–15 age group, schools for the 10–18 age group (grammar schools), for vocational schools
Address: Theodor Körner-Strasse 38, 8010 GRAZ
Year of creation: 1947
Parent Organization: Landesschulrat für Steiermark, Bundesministerium für Unterricht und Kunst
Present Head: Hofrat Direktor Professor Karl Haas
Size of staff. Total: 2000 — Full time: 13 — Part time: 1987
Researchers: 20 — Part time: 20
Educational research: less than 10%
Type of research: Training of teachers; qualification of teachers.
Functional objectives of research: In-service training of teachers, micro-teaching.
Monographs: Aspekte der Lehrerfortbildung in Österreich: Beispiel Steiermark. Wien, OBV.

Universität für Bildungswissenschaften Klagenfurt

0040

Translation: University of Klagenfurt
Address: Universitätsstrasse 65/67, 9020 KLAGENFURT
Year of creation: 1970
Parent Organization: Bundesministerium für Wissenschaft und Forschung
Present Head: Prof.Dr. Hans-Joachim Bodenhöfer, Rector
Size of staff. Total: 215 — Full time: 190 — Part time: 25
Researchers: 190 — Full time: 190
Research activities: from 25% to 50%
Educational research: from 10% to 25%
Type of research: Basic, applied as well as research and development.
Periodical publications: Klagenfurter Universitätsreden. Klagenfurter Beiträge zur wissenschaftlichen Forschung.
Monographs: Zehn Jahre Universität für Bildungswissenschaften Klagenfurt: 1. Geschichte und Dokumentation; 2. Forschungsperspektiven; 3. Forschungsperspektiven 1983 (in preparation).
Studies and surveys in preparation: Regular reports about current research projects.

Zentrum für Schulversuche und Schulentwicklung, Abteilung II

0041

Translation: Centre for School Experiments and School Development, Division II
Address: Hans Sachs–Gasse 14, 8010 GRAZ
Year of creation: 1968
Parent Organization: Bundesministerium für Unterricht und Kunst
Present Head: Dr. Gottfried Petri
Size of staff. Total: 10 — Full time: 10
Researchers: 4 — Full time: 4
Research activities: more than 50%
Educational research: more than 50%
Type of research: Evaluation of school experiments; methodology of educational development; curriculum research.
Functional objectives of research: Supporting educational development by fundamental, methodological and evaluative information.
Periodical publications: Arbeitsberichte des Zentrums für Schulversuche und Schulentwicklung, Reihe II.
Studies and surveys in preparation: Methodology of curricular development in the field of social sciences.

BAHRAIN

Murāqabat at–tawtīq wa–ăl–ma'lumāt wa–ăl–buḫūt at–tarbawiyya

0042

Translation: Superintendence of Educational Documentation, Information and Educational Research
Address: P.O.Box 43, MANAMA
Year of creation: 1975
Parent Organization: Directorate of Plans and Programming, Ministry of Education
Present Head: Miss Anisa Ali Al–Maskati, Superintendent
Size of staff. Total: 10
Researchers: 2
Research activities: less than 10%
Educational research: more than 50%
Type of research: Descriptive and comparative research.
Functional objectives of research: Servicing the educational administrators, teachers and students of colleges in Bahrain.
Periodical publications: Education systems in the world (monthly series in Arabic). Educational indicative abstracts (quarterly bulletin in Arabic). Educational informative abstracts (quarterly bulletin in Arabic). Bulletin of educational selections (quarterly bulletin in Arabic). Educational information bulletin: newsletter & acquisition list (quarterly bulletin in Arabic with acquisition list in English).
Monographs: Miḫriz, Z.M. at–Ta'līm al–asāsī: dirāsa muqārana fī ba'ḍ ad–duwal al–ağnabiyya (Basic education: comparative study in some foreign countries). 1980. Miḫriz, Z.M. at–Ta'līm al–asāsī: amtila min taṭbīgāt mabādi' wa usus at–ta'līm al–asāsī fī ba'ḍ ad–duwal al–'rabiyya ḫatā 'am 1979 (Basic education: examples from practice of principles and bases of basic education in some Arab States till 1979). as–Ṣāliḫ, F.S. Taḫdīt at–ta'līm fī ăl–baḫrayn fī ăl–fatra min 1978–80 (Educational

innovation and reform in Bahrain from 1978–80). 1981.
Studies and surveys in preparation: Development of girls education in Bahrain.

BANGLADESH

Institute of Education and Research

0043

Address: University of Dhaka, DHAKA-2
Year of creation: 1959
Parent Organization: University of Dhaka
Present Head: Dr. Mazharul Haque
Size of staff. Total: 62 — Full time: 60 — Part time: 2
Researchers: 32 — Full time: 32
Research activities: from 10% to 25%
Educational research: more than 50%
Type of research: Applied research.
Functional objectives of research: Meet degree requirements; assist Government in the field of education.
Periodical publications: Teachers' world (3/yr).
Monographs: A survey on the teaching of agriculture in the primary schools. An evaluation of the experimental adult education programmes in the eight thanas of Bangladesh. Feasibility study for introducing universal primary education in Bangladesh. A study on relevance of work education in Bangladesh.
Studies and surveys in preparation: Development of objective tests in Bengali. English and mathematics for secondary school certificate (SSC) examination.

BELGIUM

Centre de recherche et d'innovation en sociopédagogie familiale et scolaire (CERIS)

0044

Address: Université de l'Etat, Faculté des sciences psychopédagogiques, 18, place du Parc, 7000 MONS
Year of creation: 1982
Parent Organization: Université de l'Etat, Mons
Present Head: Jean-Pierre Pourtois, docteur en Sciences psychopédagogiques, professeur à l'Université de l'Etat à Mons
Size of staff. Total: 11 — Full time: 6 — Part time: 5
Researchers: 7 — Full time: 3 — Part time: 4
Research activities: more than 50%
Educational research: more than 50%
Type of research: Recherche fondamentale; recherche et action.
Functional objectives of research: Formation des parents, des enseignants, des futures enseignants, des éducateurs et des adolescents à l'éducation familiale.
Monographs: Comment les mères enseignent. 1979. Eduquer les parents.
Studies and surveys in preparation: Influence de la famille sur le développement et l'adaptation scolaire des enfants. Le changement des acteurs dans une recherche–

action. La perception des signifiants scolaires en milieu parental. Les comportements éducatifs et la syntaxe. Liste complète sur demande.

Département des sciences et de la technologie de l'éducation (DESTE)

0045

Address: 21, place du Parc, 7000 MONS
Year of creation: 1971
Parent Organization: Université de l'Etat à Mons
Present Head: Professeur L. D'Hainaut
Size of staff. Total: 14 — Full time: 9 — Part time: 5
Researchers: 10 — Full time: 7 — Part time: 3
Research activities: more than 50%
Educational research: more than 50%
Type of research: Fondamentale et appliquée.
Functional objectives of research: Contribution à l'amélioration des connaissances et des capacités d'action en éducation; prestations pour l'administration de l'éducation.
Monographs: Catalogue des publications de DESTE disponible sur demande.
Studies and surveys in preparation: Méthologie de la construction de questions d'évaluation formative. Méthode complexe de questionnement interactif à l'aide de micro-ordinateurs. Opérationalisation des objectifs de l'enseignement d'une seconde langue dans une perspective communicative. Etude sur la métacognition en situation scolaire. Evaluation des documents pédagogiques et des didacticiels. La difficulté réelle et la difficulté apparente dans la résolution de problèmes. Taxonomie d'objectifs à composante principale psychomotrice, en relation avec la pédagogie du travail. Liste complète sur demande.

Didactiek en psychopedagogiek

0046

Translation: Educational and Instructional Psychology
Address: Vesaliusstraat 2, 3000 LEUVEN
Year of creation: 1967
Parent Organization: Katholieke Universiteit te Leuven, Faculteit der psychologie en pedagogische wetenschappen
Present Head: Prof. Dr. G. Tistaeert
Size of staff. Total: 32 — Full time: 30 — Part time: 2
Researchers: 20 — Full time: 18 — Part time: 2
Research activities: 50%
Educational research: 50%
Type of research: Recherche et développement; appliquée à l'instruction.
Functional objectives of research: Recherches pratiquables dans l'instruction, soit primaire, secondaire ou tertiaire.
Periodical publications: Collaboration à plusieurs périodiques scientifiques surtout des périodiques américains.
Monographs: Une série de rapports.
Studies and surveys in preparation: Les comportements verbaux des enseignants. Stress des élèves dans les situations d'examen. Le feedback dans la formation des futurs enseignants. Le comportement de solutions des enfants de 5 à 7 ans pour les problèmes arithmétiques. Les directeurs de l'école primaire comme innovateurs.

Institut de psychologie et des sciences de l'éducation, Université de Liège

0047

Address: Service de méthodologie générale, Université de Liège, Sart Tilman, 4000 LIEGE
Parent Organization: Université de Liège
Present Head: A. Roosen, professeur ordinaire, docteur en Sciences pédagogiques
Size of staff. Total: 12 — Full time: 8 — Part time: 4
Researchers: 10 — Full time: 6 — Part time: 4
Research activities: more than 50%
Educational research: more than 50%
Type of research: Recherches appliquées; recherches-actions.
Functional objectives of research: Préparation de cours; mise au point de documents méthodologiques à l'intention de l'enseignement secondaire.
Periodical publications: Education. Tribune libre d'informations et de discussions pédagogiques.
Monographs: Dossiers pédagogiques interdisciplinaires: L'Homme et l'Etat; La santé; L'énergie; La paix. Dossier pédagogique: L'échec scolaire.
Studies and surveys in preparation: L'interdisciplinarité: fondements théoriques et applications pratiques. La rentabilité sociale et économique de l'enseignement.

Laboratoire de pédagogie expérimentale

0048

Translation: Laboratory for Experimental Educational Research
Address: Université de Liège, Institut de psychologie et des sciences de l'éducation, Sart Tilman, 4000 LIEGE I
Year of creation: 1963
Parent Organization: Université de l'Etat à Liège
Present Head: Prof. G. de Landsheere
Size of staff. Total: 60 — Full time: 50 — Part time: 10
Researchers: 45 — Full time: 40 — Part time: 5
Research activities: more than 50%
Educational research: more than 50%
Type of research: Recherche fondamentale et appliquée, recherche et développement.
Functional objectives of research: Recherches de 'graduat', de 'postgraduat', doctorat; recherches d'initiative des laboratoires; recherches commanditées.
Periodical publications: Nouvelles (bulletin d'information du Laboratoire). Rapport d'activité (triennal).
Monographs: De Landsheere, V. et G. Définir les objectifs de l'éducation. 1982. De Landsheere, G. Introduction à la recherche en éducation. 1982. De Landsheere, G. La recherche expérimentale en éducation. 1982. Crahay, M. Agir avec les objets pour construire la connaissance, Bruxelles, Ministère de l'éducation nationale, 1984. Henry, G.; Massoz, D. Connaissances et attitudes socio-politiques d'élèves de l'enseignement secondaire. 1980. Liste complète sur demande.
Studies and surveys in preparation: Histoire de la pédagogie expérimentale. Pourquoi Logo dans un contexte éducatif? Les questions à choix multiples. L'enseignement assisté par ordinateur. Les indices de certitude. Attitudes, valeurs et pratiques linguistiques. Les échecs scolaires: mirage de l'évaluation. Liste complète sur demande.

Laboratorium voor experimentele, differentiële en genetische psychology, en Centrum voor ontwikkelingspsychologie

0049

Translation: Département de psychologie expérimentale, différentielle et génétique, et Centre de psychologie du développement
Address: H. Dunantlaan 2, 9000 GENT
Year of creation: 1891
Parent Organization: Université de l'Etat, Gent
Present Head: Prof. Dr. W. De Coster, chef de projet au Ministère de la coopération au développement
Size of staff. Total: 39 — Full time: 34 — Part time: 5
Researchers: 23 — Full time: 20 — Part time: 3
Research activities: 50%
Educational research: more than 50%
Type of research: Fondamentale et appliquée.
Functional objectives of research: Connaissance fondamentale plus guidance psychologique et stimulation pédagogique.
Periodical publications: Mededelingen en werkdocumenten van het Laboratorium voor experimentele, differentiële en genetische psychologie en Centrum voor ontwikkelingspsychologie.
Monographs: De ontwikkeling van sociaal-onaangepaste jongens en meisjes tot jonge volwassenen. Handboek voor ontwikkelingspsychologie. I. Grondslagen en theorieën.
Studies and surveys in preparation: Diagnosis and fostering of development in young children; optimization of the development, especially of socially disadvantaged children and youth. Psychological intervention in problem children and adolescents. The effects of TV-programmes on children and youth. Studies on the development of cognitive processes, aiming at the fostering and optimization of cognitive development. Instructional psychology and studies about the self-concept. Experimental and developmental research on the psychosocial aspects of the human interface in the use of computers. Values and attitudes in adolescents and their parents. Modification and resistance to modification of motivation and attitudes in social interactions. Complete list on request.

Onderzoekscentrum Vrouw en opvoeding

0050

Translation: Research Centre Woman and Education
Address: Vesaliusstraat 2, 3000 LEUVEN
Year of creation: 1979
Parent Organization: Katholieke Universiteit Leuven
Present Head: Dr. Agnes De Munter
Size of staff. Total: 15 — Full time: 15
Researchers: 11 — Full time: 11
Research activities: more than 50%
Educational research: more than 50%
Type of research: Fondamentale, appliquée.
Functional objectives of research: The research team's main concern is the way in which people nowadays go in for education.
Monographs: De Munter, A. Moeden en opvoeding. Vandemenlebroecke, L. Wordt gezinsopvoeding anden?

Seminarie en Laboratorium voor didactiek 0051

Translation: Séminaire et Laboratoire de didactique
Address: H. Dunantlaan 2, 9000 GENT
Year of creation: 1964
Parent Organization: Université de l'Etat, Gent
Present Head: Prof. Dr. A. De Block
Size of staff. Total: 15 — Full time: 15
Researchers: 10 — Full time: 10
Research activities: 50%
Educational research: more than 50%
Type of research: Recherche fondamentale et appliquée.
Functional objectives of research: Elaborer la théorie didactique; fournir des instruments (processus d'apprentissage et évaluation) aux écoles (secondaires).
Monographs: Creativiteit en didactiek. 1980. In-service vorming van leerkrachten. 1981. Algemene didactiek. 1982.
Studies and surveys in preparation: L'ordinateur dans l'école. Construction de tests de rendement (item banking) pour la biologie. Rendement de l'enseignement des mathématiques. Créativité à l'école. Construction de cours individualisés pour les mathématiques. Evaluation de l'enseignement primaire rénové.

Seminarie en laboratorium voor experimentele, psychologische en sociale pedagogiek 0052

Translation: Séminaire et Laboratoire de pédagogie expérimentale, psychologique et sociale
Address: Henri Dunantlaan 1, 9000 GENT
Year of creation: 1948
Parent Organization: Université de l'Etat à Gent
Present Head: Prof. Dr. M.-L. van Herreweghe (Mrs), docteur en sciences de l'éducation, secrétaire générale ad vitam de l'Association mondiale des sciences de l'éducation
Size of staff. Total: 20 — Full time: 20
Researchers: 14 — Full time: 14
Research activities: more than 50%
Educational research: more than 50%
Type of research: Recherches de base et appliquées.
Functional objectives of research: Promouvoir les sciences de l'éducation dans différents domaines au niveau de l'école primaire: — par rapport à l'enseignement des mathématiques, de la langue maternelle, de la langue étrangère, — par rapport à la formation de la personnalité, l'importance de la famille pour l'éducation cognitive, sociale, morale; l'étude des problèmes psycho-pédagogiques; les problèmes de relation dans la formation des maîtres.
Periodical publications: Scientia paedagogica experimentalis/Revue internationale de pédagogie expérimentale.
Monographs: Gelber, L. Psychologie du chant autonome. Schuyten-Plancke, G.; Vossen, I.; Yde-Zenner, K.; De Craene, B. Wiskunde op de basisschool 3. Meetkundeactiviteiten. De tweede stap. 1982. Liste complète sur demande.
Studies and surveys in preparation: Influence of disturbance in relation between formal and informal education as regards personality variables. Tonal melodic behaviour of six-year olds. L'arithmétique à l'école. L'ordinateur à l'école. Education physique et

sports à l'école.

Service de didactique expérimentale (ULB)

0053

Address: 50, avenue F.D. Roosevelt, 1050 BRUSSELS, CP 186
Year of creation: 1968
Parent Organization: Université libre de Bruxelles
Present Head: Prof.Dr. Louis Vandevelde
Size of staff. Total: 19 — Full time: 7 — Part time: 12
Researchers: 16 — Full time: 4 — Part time: 12
Research activities: 50%
Educational research: more than 50%
Type of research: Recherches fondamentales; recherches commanditées.
Functional objectives of research: Evaluation; formation de formateurs; dispositifs expérimentaux en pédagogie.
Periodical publications: Revue belge de psychologie et de pédagogie (4/an).
Monographs: Cahiers et documents. Travaux de recherche réalisés par le Service de didactique expérimentale.
Studies and surveys in preparation: Formation par micro-enseignement (formation des maîtres). Enquête et entraînement à la consultation de références. Les questions et consignes à réponses fermes à réponses multiples.

BENIN

Institut national pour la formation et la recherche en éducation (I.N.F.R.E.)

0054

Address: Boîte postale 200, PORTO-NOVO
Year of creation: 1975
Parent Organization: Ministère des enseignements moyens général, technique et professionnel (MEMGTP)
Present Head: Mede Moussa Yaya
Size of staff. Total: 108
Researchers: 20
Research activities: from 10% to 25%
Educational research: more than 50%
Type of research: Recherches appliquées, recherche et développement.
Functional objectives of research: Fournir des prestations à l'administration de l'éducation.
Periodical publications: L'éducation béninoise (revue pédagogique).
Monographs: Document Education et développement. Document Education relative à l'environnement. Document sur l'opération pilote Comé. Fiches pédagogiques par discipline. Guide de coopérative scolaire.
Studies and surveys in preparation: Education relative à l'environnement. Démarginalisation de l'école. Interaction travail productif et travail intellectuel. Introduction des langues nationales à l'école. Relation entre système formel et non formel de l'éducation.

BOLIVIA

Centro Boliviano de Investigación y Acción Educativas (CEBIAE)

0055

Address: Casilla 1479, Hermanos Manchego No. 2518, LA PAZ
Year of creation: 1976
Parent Organization: Institución autónoma
Present Head: Ramón Alaix Busquets
Size of staff. Total: 21 — Full time: 21
Researchers: 15 — Full time: 15
Educational research: more than 50%
Type of research: Investigación básica y aplicada.
Functional objectives of research: Colaborar para que la educación sea un factor de cambio.
Periodical publications: Resúmenes analíticos educativos. Estudios educativos. Cuadernos educativos.

Dirección Nacional de Investigación Educativa

0056

Address: Av. Arce No. 2529, LA PAZ
Year of creation: 1963
Parent Organization: Dirección General de Planificación Educativa, Ministerio de Educacíon y Cultura
Present Head: Prof. Oscar Barriga Barahona
Size of staff. Total: 5
Researchers: 5
Research activities: 50%
Educational research: more than 50%
Type of research: Básica.
Functional objectives of research: Prestación de servicios a la educación, al servicio central y al magisterio a nivel nacional.
Periodical publications: Sólo informes de trabajos realizados.
Studies and surveys in preparation: Se ha establecido una serie de actividades de investigación educativa, requeridas por el Plan Nacional de Acción de Bolivia e el Proyecto de Educación en América Latina y el Caribe, en las áreas de expansión de la educación primaria, en educación del analfabetismo, y mejoramiento de la calidad de la educación.

BRAZIL

Centro de Educação

0057

Translation: Centre of Education
Address: Centro de Educação, UFSM, 97100 SANTA MARIA, RS
Year of creation: 1969
Parent Organization: Universidade Federal de Santa Maria
Present Head: Prof. Paulo Danton Benites
Size of staff. Total: 70 — Full time: 64

Researchers: 26 — Full time: 25 — Part time: 1
Research activities: less than 10%
Educational research: more than 50%
Type of research: Applied research.
Functional objectives of research: Improve instruction at primary, secondary and tertiary levels; satisfy requirements of M.A. degree.
Periodical publications: Educação (4 yr).
Monographs: Grau de satisfação dos egressos de habilitação em audio-comunicação do curso de pedagogia, em relação à formação profissional e ao mercado de trabalho. 1983. Avaliação das atividades curriculares do departamento de matemática da UF SM. 1983. Implicações da formação pedagógica do currículo do Centro da Educação Física e Deportos da Universidade de Santa-Maria, 1972-1979. 1984. Complete list on request.
Studies and surveys in preparation: Validation of a method for teaching children to read. Teacher's performance. Supervision of instruction. Student's perceptions of teachers' teaching style.

Centro de Educação da Universidade Federal de Pernambuco

0058

Translation: Centre d'éducation de l'Université fédérale de Pernambuco
Address: Cidade Universitária, Av. Prof. Moraes Rego, 1235, Engenho do Meio, RECIFE, PE
Year of creation: 1950
Parent Organization: Ministère de l'éducation et de la culture — MEC
Present Head: Alayde Gouveia Machado
Size of staff. Total: 120 — Full time: 68 — Part time: 52
Researchers: 22 — Full time: 22
Research activities: from 10% to 25%
Educational research: more than 50%
Type of research: Appliquée.
Functional objectives of research: Satisfaire aux conditions d'obtention d'un grade et fournir des prestations.
Periodical publications: Tópicos educacionais. Informativo.
Monographs: Aspectos metodológicos de comunicação de massa na educação de adultos. Evolução histórica do colégio pernambucano. Estudo sobre o liceu de artes e ofícios. Absorção dos diplomados em pedagogia no mercado do trabalho local. A qualidade do ensino de lo grau no Recife. Avaliação o melhoria dos cursos de licenciatura da Universidade Federal de Pernambuco. Educação primária em Pernambuco, na primeira República. Liste complète sur demande.
Studies and surveys in preparation: Aspecto de personalidade e desempenho acadêmico. Avaliação dos cursos de licenciatura. Educação de adultos e leitura para recém-alfabetizados. Um exemplo de anti-pedagogia — livro-texto de psicologia educacional no Brasil. A qualidade 1o. grau no Recife. Professorado leigo do 1o. e 2o. graus — situação em 1978. Liste complète sur demande.

Departamento de Pesquisas Educacionais da Fundação Carlos Chagas

0059

Translation: Département de recherches pédagogiques de la Fondation Carlos Chagas
Address: Av. Prof. Francisco Morato, 1565, Jardim Guedala, Caixa Postal 11478, 05513 SÃO PAULO

Year of creation: 1964
Parent Organization: Fundação Carlos Chagas
Present Head: Bernadete A. Gatti
Size of staff. Total: 28
Researchers: 14 — Full time: 2 — Part time: 12
Research activities: more than 50%
Educational research: more than 50%
Type of research: Recherches appliquées et fondamentales.
Functional objectives of research: Effectuer des recherches pédagogiques; préparer les cours; offrir des services à l'administration de l'éducation.
Periodical publications: Cadernos de pesquisa. Educação e seleção.
Studies and surveys in preparation: A escola básica de 8 anos em São Paulo. Currículos, métodos e programas: uma avaliação crítica. Representações dos professores a respeito da escola, do aluno pobre e de sua prática docente: um confronto entre a realidade e sua apreensão subjetiva. O ensino obrigatório e as crianças fora da escola: reavaliação do problema pela população de dois bairros da cidade de São Paulo. Liste complète sur demande.

Divisão de Avaliação, Métodos e Pesquisa

0060

Translation: Research, Methods and Evaluation Division
Address: Rua da Alfândega, 214/5o. andar, Centro-CEP 20070, RIO DE JANEIRO
Year of creation: 1973
Parent Organization: Fundação Movimento Brasileiro de Alfabetização (MOBRAL)
Present Head: Regina de Figueiredo Avelar-Linguist
Size of staff. Total: 30 — Full time: 26 — Part time: 4
Researchers: 27 — Full time: 23 — Part time: 4
Research activities: 50%
Educational research: more than 50%
Type of research: Applied and basic.
Functional objectives of research: To support — through the systematical practice of evaluation, the development of research and the study of new methods — the fixation of general directives of MOBRAL's educational projects and programmes.
Periodical publications: None.
Monographs: Lovisolo, H.R. O Programa de Alfabetização Funcional do MOBRAL e a redução da probreza. 1981. Wiggers de Almeida, T.; Leon Leblond, J.R. Análise comparativa do desempenho de adultos e crianças em classes do Programa de Alfabetização Funcional. 1981/1982. Complete list on request.
Studies and surveys in preparation: A articulação entre a educação escolar e extra-escolar: o caso MOBRAL. A literatura infantil na educação pré-escolar. O Programa Pré-Escolar e seu impacto na comunidade. Em busca do diálogo: a criança, a família e a pré-escola nas camadas populares. Complete list on request.

Faculdade de Educação da Universidade de Brasília

0061

Translation: Faculty of Education
Address: Caixa postal 15-3021, 70.910 BRASILIA D.F.
Year of creation: 1961
Parent Organization: Universidade de Brasília
Present Head: Professora Iria Gehlen Closs, PhD.

Size of staff. Total: 36 — Full time: 29 — Part time: 7
Researchers: 16 — Full time: 11 — Part time: 5
Research activities: from 25% to 50%
Educational research: more than 50%
Type of research: Appliquée et fondamentale.
Functional objectives of research: Satisfaire aux exigences académiques; fournir des informations pour la prise de décisions et développer des connaissances théoriques.
Periodical publications: Aucune.
Monographs: Velloso, J., et al. Can educational policy equalize income distribution in Latin America? In collab. with M. Carnoy. 1979. Vasconcellos, J.V. Igreja, mundo e educação: ensaios. 1980. Sander, B. Administração da educação no Brasil: evolução do conhecimento. 1982. Câmara da Silva, J. Academicismo versus pragmatismo. 1980. Liste complète sur demande.
Studies and surveys in preparation: Criatividade para deficientes visuais. Proposta para definição do papel profissional do orientador educacional: modelo teórico. Aplicações das posições teóricas de Jerome Bruner e David Ausubel a aspectos de ensino. Etapas para elaboração de plano curricular, a nível de escola: aplicação e análise. Brasília. A importância da brincadeira na pré-escola. Liste complète sur demande.

Faculdade de Educação da Universidade do Estado do Rio de Janeiro

0062

Translation: Faculté d'éducation
Address: Rua São Francisco Xavier, 542, 12o. andar, CEP 20.550, MARACANÃ
Parent Organization: Universidade do Estado do Rio de Janeiro
Present Head: Maria Violeta Coutinho Villas Boas
Size of staff. Total: 91 — Full time: 21 — Part time: 70
Researchers: 22 — Full time: 7 — Part time: 15
Research activities: from 10% to 25%
Educational research: from 10% to 25%
Type of research: Recherche appliquée; recherche et développement.
Functional objectives of research: Rechercher les aspects institutionnels et le processus de l'enseignement/apprentissage.
Periodical publications: Delfos.
Monographs: Definição das atribuições do supervisor educacional em atuação nos três níveis do sistema de ensino e dos pré-requisitos mínimos para o exercício de supervisor.
Studies and surveys in preparation: Tendências filosóficas de alunos e professores da Universidade do Estado do Rio de Janeiro. Interdisciplinaridade, polivalência e especialização: um estudo dos cursos de graduação superior no Brasil. Educação em saúde: proposta de ação integrada na Universidade do Estado do Rio de Janeiro. Proposta de capacitação de rondonistas da operação nacional/regional para o desenvolvimento de trabalho participativo em comunidades de Baixa Renda.

Faculdade de Educação da Universidade Federal de Juiz de Fora

0063

Translation: Faculty of Education
Address: Cidade Universitaria, CEP 36100, JUIZ DE FORA — MG
Year of creation: 1968
Parent Organization: Universidade Federal de Juiz de Fora

Present Head: José Geraldo Teixeira, Director, Mestre em Educação
Size of staff. Total: 36 — Full time: 31 — Part time: 5
Researchers: 16 — Full time: 14 — Part time: 2
Research activities: from 10% to 25%
Educational research: from 10% to 25%
Type of research: Appliquée.
Functional objectives of research: Préparation de cours; fournir des prestations à l'administration de l'éducation.
Monographs: Sarento, Liva Chaves. Educação e poder na sociedade brasileira. Monteiro, Maria Bellini A. Uma experiência de individualização no curso de química da UFJF.
Studies and surveys in preparation: Projets sur les thèmes suivants: Innovations dans les cursus universitaires et dans l'orientation des étudiants. Suivi psychopédagogique de déficients visuels. Education préscolaire.

Faculdade de Educação da Universidade Federal do Rio Grande do Sul

0064

Translation: Federal University of Rio Grande do Sul, Faculty of Education
Address: Av. Paulo Gama, s/no., Prédio da FACED, 9o. andar
Year of creation: 1970
Parent Organization: Ministério de Educação e Cultura, Universidade Federal do Rio Grande do Sul
Present Head: Juracy C. Marques
Size of staff. Total: 163 — Full time: 133 — Part time: 30
Researchers: 40 — Full time: 40
Research activities: from 25% to 50%
Educational research: from 25% to 50%
Type of research: Fundamental and practical research.
Functional objectives of research: For graduate degree; as a centre of research; special services for the system.
Periodical publications: Educação e realidade (4/yr). Bulletins of the Biblioteca Setorial de Educação (revisões bibliográficas). Sumários correntes em educação.
Monographs: The work of the researchers is published in national and international journals.
Studies and surveys in preparation: Avanço progressivo nas escolas de 1o. grau em Santa Catarina: balanço e perspectivas. Crenças e realidades acerca da escola. Educação rural: fator de migração ou de fixação? Estudio comparativo dos sistemas educacionais dos paises da Bacia do Prata. A espectativa do professor como fator determinante do rendimento escolar do aluno. Produção e adaptação de materiais instrucionais para escola de 1o. grau.

Fundação CENAFOR, Centro Nacional de Aperfeiçoamento de Pessoal para a Formação Profissional

0065

Translation: Fondation CENAFOR, Centre national de perfectionnement du personnel pour la formation professionnelle
Address: Rua Rodolfo Miranda 636, Bom Retiro, CEP 01121, SÃO PAULO
Year of creation: 1969
Parent Organization: Fondation liée au Ministère de l'éducation et de la culture — MEC

Present Head: Dr. Paulo Nathanael Pereira de Souza
Size of staff. Total: 179 — Full time: 179
Researchers: 20 — Full time: 16 — Part time: 4
Research activities: from 10% to 25%
Educational research: more than 50%
Type of research: Recherche appliquée; recherche et développement.
Functional objectives of research: Offrir des éléments de base à la politique de développement des resources humaines du CENAFOR.
Periodical publications: Aucune.
Monographs: CENAFOR. Serviço de Pesquisa. Trabalho participativo em educação: experiencias e reflexões. 1983. CENAFOR. Serviço de Pesquisa. Educação e trabalho: experiências junto a camadas populares. 1983. CENAFOR. Divisão de Tecnologia Educacional. Programa de Materiais Instrucionais. Literatura e criatividade da Criança de 1o. grau, por I. Palange e S. Guimarães. 1983. Liste complète sur demande.
Studies and surveys in preparation: Política educacional, educação básica, profissionalização e camadas populares: uma experiência no Estado do Acre. Definir participativamente critérios para estabelecer alternativas de capacitação de recursos humanos para o 2o. grau com as Secretarias de Educação e Cultura dos Estados de Alagoas e Paraíba. Trabalho participativo em educação: experiências e reflexões.

Instituto Nacional de Estudos e Pesquisas Educacionais

0066

Translation: Institut national d'études et de recherches éducationnelles
Address: Esplanada dos Ministérios, Bloco 'L' Anexo 1, 1o. andar, BRASILIA, CEP 70047
Year of creation: 1937
Parent Organization: Ministério da Educação e Cultura
Present Head: Lena Castello Branco Ferreira Costa, Professeur de l'Universidade Federal de Goiás-Brasil
Size of staff. Total: 135 — Full time: 135
Researchers: 3 — Full time: 3
Research activities: 50%
Educational research: more than 50%
Type of research: Fondamentale et appliquée.
Functional objectives of research: Répondre à des questions posées par la problematique de l'éducation en approfondissant sa connaissance; coopérer dans la planification, l'administration et la politique éducationnelles.
Periodical publications: Revista brasileira de estudos pedagógicos. Bibliografia brasileira de educação. Em aberto. Informativo.
Monographs: Educação no meio rural (anais do Seminário — IJUI, RS.) 1983. Encontro sobre estudos e pesquisas no ensino de 1o. grau, Região Centro-Oeste. 1980. Encontro sobre estudos e pesquisas no ensino de 1o. grau, Região Norte. 1980. Encontro técnico sobre a pesquisa educacional na área do ensino de 1o. grau. 1980. Kerlinger, F.N. Metodologia da pesquisa em ciências sociais. 1980. Caiafa, M.U., et al. Profissionalização do ensino na lei 5692/71. 1982.
Studies and surveys in preparation: O trabalho infantil e a questão do menor. Estudos sobre relação entre a solicitação do meio e o desenvolvimento intelectual. Origens e aplicações de recursos financeiros no ensino superior brasileiro 1960–1980. Os pioneiros da educação brasileira — atualidade de Lorenço Filho. Liste complète sur

demande.

Núcleo de Ciências em Educação

0067

Translation: Groupe d'étude de sciences en éducation
Address: Campus Universitário, Jardim Rosa Elze, 49.000 ARACAJU/SERGIPE
Year of creation: 1982
Parent Organization: Universidade Federal de Sergipe
Present Head: Pró-Reitora de Pós-Graduação e Pesquisa da UFS
Size of staff. Total: 12 — Full time: 12
Researchers: 10 — Full time: 10
Research activities: from 25% to 50%
Educational research: from 10% to 25%
Type of research: Fondamentale et appliquée.
Functional objectives of research: Connaissance de la situation de l'éducation dans l'Etat de Sergipe; satisfaire partiellement aux conditions d'obtention du grade de spécialiste.
Monographs: Aspectos do desenvolvimento do grafismo no pré-escolar. Aprendizagem de conceitos.
Studies and surveys in preparation: Projet d'intégration université enseignement du 1er degré.

Sector de Educação

0068

Translation: Faculté d'éducation
Address: Rua General Carneiro 460, 80.000 CURITIBA, Paraná
Year of creation: 1970
Parent Organization: Université fédérale du Paraná
Present Head: José Alberto Pedra, Doutor em Psicologia Social
Size of staff. Total: 100 — Full time: 70 — Part time: 30
Researchers: 30 — Full time: 30
Research activities: from 10% to 25%
Educational research: more than 50%
Type of research: Fondamentale et appliquée.
Functional objectives of research: Satisfaire partiellement aux conditions d'obtention d'un grade; préparation de cours; fournir des prestations à l'administration de l'éducation.
Periodical publications: Educar.
Monographs: Paula, V. Borges de. Modelo teórico tridimensional da atuação do supervisor pedagógico a nível de 2o. grau. Ribeiro, E. Eschholz. Competências docentes para o curso de habilitação específica, para magistério 2o. grau no Paraná. Gomide, N.M. Proposta de treinamento de pais para atuarem em estimulação de crianças entre quatro e sete anos de idade com deficiência auditiva severa ou externa. Procotte, A. Proposta curricular para a sensibilização de alunos de curso de magistério, a nível de 2o. grau, em relação a crianças excepcionais.
Studies and surveys in preparation: Interferência de um programa de atividades de expressão plástica no desenvolvimento integral de pré-escolares de 04 a 06 anos. Validação de competências docentes para o curso de habilitação específica para magistério — 2o. grau — Instituto de Educação do Paraná. Educação artística. Um projeto de viabilizacão aos professores atuantes em escolas afastadas dos grandes

centros. Feedback: metodologia da auto-regularização aplicada nos processos educacionais de ensino-aprendizagem, a nível de 4o. grau. Papel da interação social de pares na evolução da inteligência da criança e na aprendizagem de conteúdos trabalhados pela escola (matemática e linguagem).

BULGARIA

Institut supérieur de culture physique 'G. Dimitrov'

0069

Address: 1 rue Tina Kirkova, 1000 SOFIA
Year of creation: 1942
Parent Organization: Ministère de l'éducation nationale
Present Head: Prof. N. Hadjiev
Size of staff. Total: 536 — Full time: 536 — Part time: 7-8
Researchers: 48 — Full time: 48
Research activities: from 25% to 50%
Educational research: from 10% to 25%
Type of research: Fondamentale, appliquée.
Functional objectives of research: Satisfaire aux conditions d'obtention d'un grade, fournir des données aux différentes institutions intéressées.
Periodical publications: Trudove na VIF (Travaux de l'Institut supérieur de culture physique).
Studies and surveys in preparation: Investigation longitudinale du développement physique et de la capacité physique des élèves des écoles sportives et de leurs performances pendant la période de leur préparation et pendant la pratique du sport de compétition. Le développement et la capacité physique de la population de la R.P. de Bulgarie pour la période 1981-1985. Formation idéologique et éducation des sportifs d'élite. Problèmes psychologiques de l'éducation physique et du sport. Liste complète sur demande.

Institute for Foreign Students "G.A. Nasser"

0070

Address: 27, "Asen Velchev", 1111 SOFIA
Year of creation: 1963
Parent Organization: Ministry of Education
Present Head: Professor Victor Donov
Size of staff. Total: 439 — Full time: 389 — Part time: 150
Researchers: 11 — Full time: 11
Research activities: from 25% to 50%
Educational research: from 10% to 25%
Type of research: Applied (80 %), fundamental (10 %), research and development (10 %).
Functional objectives of research: Meeting the needs of acquiring a degree; obligations towards the educational administration.
Periodical publications: Yearbook of the Institute for Foreign Students "G.A. Nasser"
Monographs: Lexical minimum of English for Bulgarian learners. 1983. Bulgarian transcription of English names. 1982. The Bulgarian language, Bulgaria and the Bulgarians. 1982. The Bulgarian norms of word associations.

Studies and surveys in preparation: Contrastive linguistics. Psycholinguistics. Problems of measurement in psychology and education. Linguistic — didactic fundamentals of foreign students' education in Bulgaria during the preliminary stage. A study of the efficiency in foreign language teaching of adults.

Naučno-izsledovatelski institut po obšto obrazovanie "Todor Samodumov"

0071

Translation: Todor Samodumov Research Institute of General Education
Address: 125 Lenin Bulvar, Bl. V, 1113 SOFIA
Year of creation: 1950
Parent Organization: Ministry of Public Education
Present Head: Prof. Lyubomir Stoev Gheorgiev, PhD. in Pedagogical Sciences
Size of staff. Total: 110 — Full time: 110
Researchers: 70 — Full time: 70
Research activities: more than 50%
Educational research: more than 50%
Type of research: Fundamental and applied research.
Functional objectives of research: Scientific service of the development of education.
Periodical publications: Izvestija (2/yr).
Monographs: Gheorgi Dimitrov on education. 1982. One thousand and three hundred years of Bulgaria and Bulgarian education. 1983. Problems of education and instruction in the protection of the environment. Reports presented at the International Scientific Symposium on Education and Environment's Protection. 1981. Radov, V. Graphic visualness in mathematics education at the primary grades of ESPU. 1982. The effective use of training appliances and teacher's training. 1983. Complete list on request.
Studies and surveys in preparation: System of qualitative indicators and criteria of the IV–VIIth Grade students' training and development. Methodological and methodical foundations of forming oecological consciousness in students. Effect of scientific and technological progress on the technology of educative work (educational television, micro-processors, computer systems). Education of visually handicapped children in public schools. Optimizing information and educative work in individual classes with deaf students. Complete list on request.

Naučno-izsledovatelski institut po profesionalno obrazovanie

0072

Translation: Institut de recherches sur l'enseignement professionnel
Address: 125 Lenin bulvar, Bl. V, 1413 SOFIA
Year of creation: 1978
Parent Organization: Ministère de l'éducation nationale
Present Head: Pavlina A. Miševa
Size of staff. Total: 79 — Full time: 79
Researchers: 57 — Full time: 57
Educational research: more than 50%
Type of research: Fondamentale (25%); appliquée (65%); recherche et développement (10%).
Monographs: Miševa, P. Săvremenni metodi i organizacia na učebno–văzpitatelnija procese v sredno politehničeskite utčilišta, naušto rakovodstvo. 1982. Makedonska, M. Obrazovanie i profesionalno maistorstvo. 1982.
Studies and surveys in preparation: Teoretiko–metodologišteski osnovi na novata sistema

za profesionalna podgotovka. Planirane u prognozirane na razvitieto na profesionalnoto obrazovanie. Teoritičeski osnovi i sadarganie na trudovo-politenničeskoto o obučenie. Postigane na visok profesionalizam v mladečka vazrast.

Naučno-izsledovatelski institut po ruski ezik i literatura

0073

Translation: Institut de recherche sur la langue et la littérature russes
Address: 125 Bulvar Lenin, Bl. V, 1113 SOFIA
Year of creation: 1978
Parent Organization: Ministère de l'éducation nationale
Present Head: Prof. Maria Léonidova
Size of staff. Total: 22 — Full time: 20 — Part time: 2
Researchers: 18 — Full time: 16 — Part time: 2
Research activities: more than 50%
Educational research: more than 50%
Type of research: Fondamentales et appliquées.
Periodical publications: Bălgarskaja rusistika (en collaboration avec la Société des russistes en Bulgarie).
Monographs: 5.
Studies and surveys in preparation: Problèmes spécifiques de l'enseignement en langue russe en 3e. col. Problèmes de la communication dans l'enseignement du russe. Caractère du contenu scolaire en 9e et 1Oe. Organisation du lexique dans les manuels de langue russe (5–8 classes). Principes de la création des films scolaires de TV. Problèmes de la combinaison du lexique en russe et en bulgare (aspect lexicographique). Liste complète sur demande.

Naučno-izsledovatelski institut po visše obrazovanie

0074

Translation: Institut de recherche sur l'enseignement supérieur
Address: 125 Bulvar Lenin, Bl. V, SOFIA 1113
Year of creation: 1978
Parent Organization: Ministère de l'éducation nationale
Present Head: Prof. agr. Tseko Tsekov
Size of staff. Total: 24
Researchers: 20
Research activities: more than 50%
Educational research: more than 50%
Type of research: Recherche appliquée et développement, information et coordination.
Functional objectives of research: Fournir des prestations à l'administration de l'éducation.
Periodical publications: Bulletin d'information scientifique.
Monographs: Kvalifikacionni harakteristuki na specialištite s visše obrazovanie. Utčebni planove i programi za VUZ-teoria i metodika na izrabotvane. Metodika za normativi za prodaljitelnost, periodičnost i posledovatelnost pri povičavane kvalifikatsiata na specialištite.
Studies and surveys in preparation: Etude sur les facteurs d'intensification de l'éducation dans les établissements d'enseignement supérieur. Conception sur l'automatisation de l'éducation dans les établissements d'enseignement supérieur. Critères et indices des caractéristiques de la formation dans les établissements d'enseignement supérieur comme centres complexes d'éducation et de recherche. Critères d'effectivité de la

qualification post-universitaire des cadres. Liste complète sur demande.

Problemna grupa po obrazovanieto pri BAN i MNP

0075

Translation: Research Group on Education, Bulgarian Academy of Sciences and Ministry of Education
Address: 5 Boulevard Vitosha, P.O. Box 405, 1000 SOFIA
Year of creation: 1979
Parent Organization: Bulgarian Academy of Sciences
Present Head: Prof. Dr. Blagovest Sendov
Size of staff. Total: 155 — Full time: 31 — Part time: 124
Researchers: 120 — Full time: 6 — Part time: 114
Research activities: more than 50%
Educational research: more than 50%
Type of research: Research and development.
Functional objectives of research: Experimental project on primary and secondary education.
Periodical publications: None issued.
Monographs: None issued.
Studies and surveys in preparation: About twenty textbooks for the first five years (age 6–10) plus about twenty auxiliary leaflets.

Visš pedagogičeski institut, Blagoevgrad

0076

Translation: Higher Pedagogical Institute
Address: 16 Maritza Str., 2700 BLAGOEVGRAD
Year of creation: 1976
Parent Organization: Ministry of Public Education
Present Head: Associate Prof. Petar Nikolov Petzev
Size of staff. Total: 272
Researchers: 149
Research activities: from 25% to 50%
Educational research: from 10% to 25%
Type of research: Fundamental and applied.
Functional objectives of research: Amelioration of the educational process.
Periodical publications: None published.
Monographs: 28 monographs: list on request.
Studies and surveys in preparation: Formation and development of the adolescent's personality. Study on the abilities of pupils of primary and pre-school age. Psycho-pedagogical problems of the pupils' abilities.

Visš pedagogičeski institut, Shumen

0077

Translation: Institut pédagogique supérieur
Address: 9700 SHUMEN
Year of creation: 1971
Parent Organization: Ministère de l'éducation nationale
Present Head: Professeur Todor Bojadžiev, Recteur de l'Institut pédagogique supérieur et professeur à l'Université de Sofia
Size of staff. Total: 310 — Full time: 265 — Part time: 45

Researchers: 196 — Full time: 151 — Part time: 45
Research activities: 50%
Educational research: from 10% to 25%
Type of research: Fondamentales, appliquées.
Functional objectives of research: Obtention d'un grade; préparation de cours.
Periodical publications: Annuaire de l'Institut pédagogique supérieur. Bulletin bibliographique.
Monographs: Jovéva, Rumjana. Filosovsko-istoričeskite romani na Emilijan Stanev: obrazi i kompozicija. 1981. Dimkova, Guínka. Ot edno gărlo dva glasa. Narodni pesni ot selo Gostilica, Gabrovsko. 1982. Bojadžiev, Todor, et al. Gramatika na săvremennija bălgarski knižoven ezik: 3 vol. V.1–1982.
Studies and surveys in preparation: Ekologo–fiziologičeskie mehanizmi podderžanija populjacionnogo gomeostaza nekotorih melkih grizunov v norme i pod vozdejstviem pesticidov. B A N. Specialni polymeri.

BURKINA FASO

Institut de la réforme et de l'action pédagogique

0078

Address: B.P. 7043, OUAGADOUGOU
Year of creation: 1966
Parent Organization: Ministère de l'éducation nationale, des arts et de la culture
Present Head: M. Zoungrana, Ali Pascal
Size of staff. Total: 147 — Full time: 147 — Part time: 107
Researchers: 26 — Full time: 13 — Part time: 13
Research activities: from 10% to 25%
Educational research: more than 50%
Type of research: Recherche appliquée.
Functional objectives of research: Assurer le passage du système d'éducation ancien au système d'éducation nouveau : améliorer le système existant, préparer et mettre en oeuvre la réforme de l'éducation.
Periodical publications: Action–réflexion et culture (ARC).
Monographs: Dossiers de langage (français) pour le 1er degré. Documents de français pour l'enseignement du 2e degré. Dossiers de langage en langues nationales. Fiches de mathématiques pour l'enseignement du 1er degré (langues nationales) et du 2e degré (français). Productions audiovisuelles: émissions et films vidéo.
Studies and surveys in preparation: Formation et perfectionnement du personnel enseignant; système de la réforme avec langues nationales; production à l'école; l'échec scolaire — extension de la radio scolaire.

BURMA

Myanma Nainggan Pyinnya Ye Thu Tay Thana A Phwe

0079

Translation: The Burma Educational Research Bureau
Address: Institute of Education Compound, University P.O., Prome Road, RANGOON
Year of creation: 1965
Parent Organization: Ministry of Education
Present Head: Dr. Ye Aung
Size of staff. Total: 110 — Full time: 81 — Part time: 29
Researchers: 40 — Full time: 22 — Part time: 18
Research activities: more than 50%
Educational research: more than 50%
Type of research: Basic and applied research.
Functional objectives of research: Servicing the educational administration.
Periodical publications: Pyinnya lawka (The world of education) (4/yr).
Studies and surveys in preparation: An evaluation of the new basic education curriculum.

BURUNDI

Bureau d'études de l'enseignement technique (BEET)

0080

Address: B.P. 1990, BUJUMBURA
Year of creation: 1978
Parent Organization: Ministère de l'éducation nationale
Present Head: Jean Kabahizi, directeur
Size of staff. Total: 22 — Full time: 22
Researchers: 17 — Full time: 17
Research activities: more than 50%
Educational research: less than 10%
Type of research: Recherche scientifique, adaptée à l'enseignement technique et recherche appliquée.
Functional objectives of research: Adapter l'enseignement technique aux réalités nationales; préparer des cours, programmes.
Periodical publications: Cours-programmes. Vade-mécum de l'enseignement technique. Les grilles horaires et programmes.
Studies and surveys in preparation: Suivi socio-économique des lauréats de l'enseignement technique. Différents cours enseignés dans nos établissements d'enseignement technique.

Bureau d'études des programmes de l'enseignement secondaire (BEPES)

0081

Address: B.P. 2990, BUJUMBURA
Year of creation: 1976
Parent Organization: Ministère de l'éducation nationale, Direction générale de l'enseignement secondaire
Present Head: Aimable Nibishaka

Size of staff. Total: 56 — Full time: 53 — Part time: 3
Researchers: 50 — Full time: 47 — Part time: 3
Research activities: more than 50%
Educational research: more than 50%
Type of research: Recherches appliquées.
Functional objectives of research: Production de curricula; livres du maître, livres de l'élève; fourniture de matériel didactique.
Periodical publications: Echanges pédagogiques. Information.
Monographs: Livres du maître et livres de l'élève produits suivant les différents niveaux du secondaire.
Studies and surveys in preparation: Trés variées.

Faculté de psychologie et des sciences de l'éducation

0082

Address: B.P. 1550, BUJUMBURA
Year of creation: 1977
Parent Organization: Université du Burundi
Present Head: Mgr Michel Karikunzira, docteur en sciences de l'éducation
Size of staff. Total: 15 — Full time: 13 — Part time: 2
Researchers: 13 — Part time: 13
Research activities: from 25% to 50%
Educational research: more than 50%
Type of research: Fondamentale et appliquée.
Functional objectives of research: Satisfaire aux conditions d'obtention d'un grade; préparation de cours; fournir des prestations à l'administration.
Periodical publications: Revue de l'Université.
Monographs: Le professeur de l'enseignement secondaire et supérieur.
Studies and surveys in preparation: Constitution de la bibliographie nationale dans le domaine de la psychologie et de la pédagogie. Les facteurs d'échec à l'Université du Burundi. Les facteurs motivationnels dans le choix d'une carrière professionnelle au Burundi.

CAMEROON UR

Centre national d'éducation (CNE)

0083

Address: B.P. 1721, YAOUNDE
Year of creation: 1973
Parent Organization: Ministère de l'éducation nationale
Present Head: M. Etienne Bebbe-Njoh
Size of staff. Total: 67
Researchers: 24 — Full time: 24
Research activities: more than 50%
Educational research: more than 50%
Type of research: Recherches et développement.
Functional objectives of research: Eclairer les décisions des responsables de la politique éducative du Cameroun.
Monographs: La réforme éducative au Cameroun: orientations générales, implications et

contraintes. Education, emploi, salaire au Cameroun (en collaboration avec l'IIPE). Etude préliminaire sur l'éducation non formelle au Cameroun (en collaboration avec 'Creative Associates').

Studies and surveys in preparation: Mise au point d'une taxonomie d'objectifs pédagogiques utilisable par les enseignants camerounais. Etudes de cas sur l'éducation traditionnelle. Etude expérimentale des conditions d'éveil et de développement de l'esprit scientifique et technologique en milieu scolaire africain.

Institut de pédagogie appliquée à vocation rurale (IPAR)

0084

Address: Boîte postale 4135, YAOUNDE
Year of creation: 1969
Parent Organization: Ministère de l'éducation nationale
Present Head: M. Joseph Mballa
Size of staff. Total: 68 — Full time: 68
Researchers: 23 — Full time: 23
Research activities: more than 50%
Educational research: more than 50%
Type of research: Appliquée.
Functional objectives of research: Réforme de l'enseignement primaire.
Periodical publications: Recherche pédagogique et formation permanente.
Monographs: Réforme de l'enseignement au Cameroun: perspectives et difficultés. Estimation des coûts des manuels et supports didactiques de la réforme. Programme de formation dans les écoles normales: objectifs et finalités. L'enseignement par objectifs: quelques fiches de préparation. La technologie éducative dans un institut de recherche et de formation.
Studies and surveys in preparation: Evaluation de l'apprentissage de la lecture par les méthodes synthétiques et à point de départ global. Evaluation des nouveaux programmes de l'école primaire: approche comparative; français, mathématiques; activités d'éveil. Evaluation des manuels de lecture en usage dans les écoles (niveau I).

Institute for the Reform of Primary Education

0085

Address: P.O. Box 8, BUEA, South West Province
Year of creation: 1974
Parent Organization: Ministry of National Education
Present Head: Mr. Kajih John Tansam
Size of staff. Total: 65
Researchers: 22
Research activities: more than 50%
Educational research: more than 50%
Type of research: Applied research.
Functional objectives of research: To contribute to the reform of primary school education; adapt primary school education to meet the socio-economic needs of the country.
Monographs: Report on an International Seminar on Appropriate Technologies in Education held in Nairobi, Kenya from 21st to 26th March 1983. Report of the Seventh Intensive Workshop organised by the African Curriculum Organisation (ACO) on Book Production Techniques held at the Institute of Education University

of Ibadan, Nigeria from 6th to 19 March 1983, presented by Ashu, C. and Endeley, J. Boma, A.N. The ideologies, strategies and implications of the reform of primary education in Cameroon. 1980. Complete list on request.
Studies and surveys in preparation: Syllabuses for all areas of the curriculum. Primary level teachers' guides to conform to new proposed syllabuses. Teaching and class materials implemented on trial basis for classes 5, 6, and at Mile 17 classroom.

CANADA

Atlantic Institute of Education

0086

Translation: Institut d'éducation de l'Atlantique
Address: 5244 South Street, HALIFAX, N.S., B3J 1A4
Year of creation: 1970
Parent Organization: Autonomous institution
Present Head: Dr. William B. Hamilton
Size of staff. Total: 27
Researchers: 12
Type of research: Applied research.
Functional objectives of research: Partial fulfilment of degree requirements; teacher education; curriculum development and evaluation; survey work; testing and measurement.
Periodical publications: ACT (Atlantic Canada teacher).
Monographs: A guide to public education in Nova Scotia. Learning outside. Public attitudes toward post secondary education in the Maritime Provinces. Teachers at the centre. Educational research series. Professional development series. Complete list on request.
Studies and surveys in preparation: Five monographs for teachers on socio-economic conditions in Canada. Basic designs in Canadian career education. Assessment of approaches to continuing teacher education. Influences on teacher implementation of educational innovations. Use of television and the teaching of second languages. Complete list on request.

Brock College of Education

0087

Address: College of Education, Brock University, ST. CATHARINES, Ont., L2S 3A1
Year of creation: 1971
Parent Organization: Brock University
Present Head: Peter J. Atherton
Size of staff. Total: 58 — Full time: 28 — Part time: 30
Researchers: 14 — Part time: 14
Research activities: from 25% to 50%
Educational research: from 25% to 50%
Type of research: Applied research and development.
Functional objectives of research: Supervision of graduate thesis; support of PRAISE Centre (Personnel Review and Evaluation Centre); support of Reading Clinic; individual faculty research.
Monographs: Trouble shooting manual for managers of the change process.

Performance appraisal instruments for teachers, principals, superintendents.

Studies and surveys in preparation: Performance appraisal instrument design and processing, PRAISE Centre. Project 'THRIVE': pupil characteristics and teacher problem-solving strategies. Diagnosis and research into reading difficulties at all age levels including development of micro-computerized reading tests within the framework of a level of processing theory.

Centre d'animation, de développement et de recherche en éducation (CADRE) **0088**

Address: 1940 est, Henri-Bourassa, MONTREAL, Qué. H2B 1S2
Year of creation: 1968
Parent Organization: Corporation privée
Present Head: Mathieu Girard, directeur général
Size of staff. Total: 23 — Full time: 21 — Part time: 2
Researchers: 9 — Full time: 9
Research activities: more than 50%
Educational research: more than 50%
Type of research: Recherche appliquée; recherche et développement.
Functional objectives of research: Analyse et évaluation des établisssements d'enseignement.
Periodical publications: Prospectives (revue trimestrielle d'éducation).
Monographs: Liste complète sur demande.
Studies and surveys in preparation: Dossier-souche sur la formation fondamentale. Un instrument d'évaluation de la formation fondamentale. Autonomie, évaluation et financement de l'enseignement privé.

Centre for Teaching and Learning Services, McGill University **0089**

Address: 815 Sherbrooke Street West, MONTREAL, Que., H3A 2K6
Year of creation: 1969
Parent Organization: Office of University Teaching and Learning, McGill University
Present Head: Dr. Janet G. Donald, Director
Size of staff. Total: 10 — Full time: 4 — Part time: 6
Researchers: 6 — Part time: 6
Research activities: 50%
Educational research: more than 50%
Type of research: Basic, applied, research and development.
Functional objectives of research: Knowledge, training, degree requirements, servicing of educational administration.
Periodical publications: Not applicable.
Monographs: Cartwright, G.F. The impact of symbionic technology on education. 1982. Cranton, P.A. Evaluating complex student learning. 1982. Cranton, P.A. McGill evaluation system: user's guide and resource file bibliography. 1982. Donald, J.G. Objective tests: a guide to assist faculty. 1983. Logsdon, D.; Shore, B.M. Student needs and services: undergraduate and mature student perceptions. 1982. Complete list on request.
Studies and surveys in preparation: The improvement of instruction in natural settings. La représentation et les stratégies de la connaissance: une étude comparative. Socialization and the intellectual abilities of gifted children. Expanding the parameters of interactive computer applications in education.

Conseil supérieur de l'éducation 0090

Translation: Superior Council of Education
Address: 2050 ouest, boul. St-Cyrille, 4e étage, STE FOY, Qué. G1V 2K8
Year of creation: 1964
Parent Organization: Gouvernement du Québec
Present Head: Claude Benjamin, président
Size of staff. Total: 34 — Full time: 33 — Part time: 1
Researchers: 4 — Full time: 4
Research activities: more than 50%
Educational research: more than 50%
Type of research: Recherches appliquées.
Functional objectives of research: Conseiller le ministre de l'Education et contribuer aux orientations de l'éducation.
Periodical publications: Rapport annuel sur l'état et les besoins de l'éducation.
Monographs: L'égalité des chances en éducation. 1979. Le projet éducatif de l'école. 1980. Après l'école secondaire, étudier ou travailler: choisit-on vraiment? 1982.
Studies and surveys in preparation: Recherche sur les attentes des jeunes, leurs attitudes et leur environnement socio-culturel en vue d'une meilleure adaptation du système éducatif.

Département des sciences de l'éducation, Université de Québec à Hull 0091

Address: 283, boulevard Alexandre-Taché, C.P. 1250, succursale 'B', HULL, Qué.
Year of creation: 1970
Parent Organization: Réseau de l'Université du Québec
Present Head: Raoul Côté, directeur du département des sciences de l'éducation; Jean R. Messier, recteur de l'Université du Québec à Hull
Size of staff. Total: 33 — Full time: 16 — Part time: 17
Researchers: 6 — Full time: 6
Research activities: from 10% to 25%
Educational research: more than 50%
Type of research: Recherche-action, appliquée.
Functional objectives of research: Services éducationnels.
Studies and surveys in preparation: Application pédagogique de l'ordinateur. Apprentissage. Formation initiale et perfectionnement des maîtres.

Educational Research Institute of British Columbia 0092

Address: 701-601 West Broadway, VANCOUVER, B.C., V5Z 4C2
Year of creation: 1967
Parent Organization: Independent, non-profit institute
Present Head: Mrs. Audrey Sojonky, Executive Director
Size of staff. Total: 16 — Full time: 14 — Part time: 2
Researchers: 4 — Full time: 4
Research activities: more than 50%
Educational research: more than 50%
Type of research: Applied research and research and development.
Functional objectives of research: To provide research services on contractual basis for education and social service agencies with educational programmes.

Periodical publications: EDGE (newsletter) (4/yr). Reports list (updated annually). Annual report.

Monographs: Hambleton, R.K., ed. Applications of item response theory. Ruggles, R., ed. Learning at a distance and the new technology.

Studies and surveys in preparation: Test development projects. English placement test project. Community school evaluation. Adaptive testing project. Career education needs assessments.

Faculté d'éducation, Université d'Ottawa

0093

Address: 651 Cumberland, OTTAWA, Ont., K1N 6N5
Year of creation: 1967
Parent Organization: Université d'Ottawa
Present Head: Dr. Yves Poirier
Size of staff. Total: 300 — Full time: 80 — Part time: 220
Researchers: 40 — Part time: 40
Research activities: from 25% to 50%
Educational research: from 25% to 50%
Type of research: Fondamentales, appliquées et développement.
Functional objectives of research: Etudes doctorales; contrats gouvernementaux et des Conseils scolaires.
Periodical publications: Participation à la Revue des sciences de l'éducation.
Monographs: Plusieurs monographies dans les domaines de l'enfance en difficulté, du développement international, de l'éducation des adultes, de l'administration éducationnelle.
Studies and surveys in preparation: Plusieurs études et enquêtes dans les domaines de l'administration éducationnelle, du développement international, de l'enfance en difficulté.

Faculté des sciences de l'éducation, Université Laval

0094

Address: STE-FOY, Qué., G1K 7P4
Year of creation: 1852
Parent Organization: Université Laval
Present Head: Eddy Slater
Size of staff. Total: 235 — Full time: 235
Researchers: 105
Research activities: from 10% to 25%
Educational research: from 25% to 50%
Type of research: Appliquées; recherche et développement.
Functional objectives of research: Satisfaire partiellement aux conditions d'obtention d'un grade.
Periodical publications: Revue des sciences de l'éducation. Revue canadienne de l'éducation. Profil. Apprentissage et socialisation. L'orientation professionnelle. P.P.M.F. Laval.
Monographs: Mesure et évaluation en éducation.
Studies and surveys in preparation: L'inégalité des chances en éducation au Québec. Analyse des politiques d'admission et taux d'accès à l'université au Québec. Identification de certaines variables influençant le type d'enseignement, et recherche de leur relation avec les attitudes du professeur. Compréhension des histoires,

développement cognitif et compréhension de marques temporelles dans le langage. Réseau de communication pédagogique et technologie. Application d'un modèle d'éducation des attitudes propres à l'éducation morale auprès d'étudiants du secondaire III.

Faculty of Education, McGill University

0095

Address: 3700 McTavish, MONTREAL, P.Q. H3A 1Y2
Size of staff. Total: 127 — Full time: 117 — Part time: 10
Researchers: 160 — Full time: 120 — Part time: 40
Research activities: from 10% to 25%
Educational research: from 25% to 50%
Type of research: Largely applied and some basic; also research and development.
Functional objectives of research: Partial fulfilment of degree, personal research interest of staff.
Periodical publications: McGill Journal of Education.

Faculty of Education, Queen's University

0096

Address: KINGSTON, Ont., K7L 3N6
Year of creation: 1971
Present Head: Dean T.R. Williams
Size of staff. Total: 64 — Full time: 64
Researchers: 32 — Full time: 32
Research activities: from 10% to 25%
Educational research: more than 50%
Studies and surveys in preparation: Development of self instructional learning modules in language arts. Documenting a primary classroom, and ethnographic study. Monitoring, self-monitoring and education. Is there too much community in community education? The mathematics curriculum and the base of mathematical knowledge and skills in Canada in the era of high technology. Prisoners as learners: a description and analysis.

Faculty of Education, University of Alberta

0097

Address: EDMONTON, Alta., T6G 2G5
Year of creation: 1945
Parent Organization: University of Alberta
Present Head: Dr. R.S. Patterson
Size of staff. Total: 204 — Full time: 166 — Part time: 38
Researchers: 155 — Full time: 155
Research activities: from 10% to 25%
Educational research: more than 50%
Type of research: Research projects include all types: basic, applied, and research and development.
Functional objectives of research: Advance knowledge base in field of education; contribute to improvements in educational practices.
Periodical publications: The Alberta journal of educational research. Canadian journal of native education. Elements. The Canadian administrator. The Association of Canadian Educators of the Hearing Impaired journal. Mental retardation and

learning disabilities bulletin.
Monographs: Monographs have been published on topics in all major areas: administration, curriculum and instruction, educational foundations, educational psychology, and teacher education.
Studies and surveys in preparation: Research is in progress in all areas of education including curriculum studies; history, sociology and philosophy of education; educational administration and governance; couselling; learning theory; and special education.

Faculty of Education, University of Calgary

0098

Address: 2500 University Drive N.W., CALGARY, Alta., T2N 1N4
Year of creation: 1966
Parent Organization: Board of Governors, University of Calgary
Present Head: Dr. N.E. Wagner, President; Dr. R.F. Lawson, Dean
Size of staff. Total: 162 — Full time: 147 — Part time: 15
Researchers: 103 — Full time: 103
Research activities: from 10% to 25%
Educational research: more than 50%
Type of research: Basic, applied and developmental.
Functional objectives of research: Increased basic knowledge, e.g., technology in education, special education, curriculum development, applied classroom research.
Monographs: Braun, C. Integrating the language arts in the primary school (3 modules).
Studies and surveys in preparation: Assessing cognitive levels in classrooms. Critical studies in education and how they impact upon the image and role of the classroom teacher. Belief systems of teachers and the implementation of prescribed curricula. Telidon — Teleconference Distance Education Project. Complete list on request.

Faculty of Education, University of Victoria

0099

Address: P.O. Box 1700, VICTORIA, B.C., V8W 2Y2
Year of creation: 1963
Parent Organization: University of Victoria
Present Head: Dr. John J. Jackson
Size of staff. Total: 130 — Full time: 80 — Part time: 50
Researchers: 80 — Full time: 70 — Part time: 10
Research activities: from 25% to 50%
Educational research: more than 50%
Type of research: Basic and applied.
Functional objectives of research: Advancing knowledge and improving practice.
Monographs: Physical education series.
Studies and surveys in preparation: All researchers have studies in progress.

International Council for Adult Education

0100

Address: 29 Prince Arthur Avenue, TORONTO, Ont., M5R IB2
Year of creation: 1973
Present Head: Dr. Budd Hall, Secretary General; Dr. Chris Duke, Associate Secretary-General

Size of staff. Total: 20 — Full time: 9 — Part time: 11
Researchers: 8 — Full time: 2 — Part time: 6
Research activities: from 25% to 50%
Educational research: from 25% to 50%
Type of research: Adult education and human and social development in a global context, particularly the consideration of critical social issues relating to and arising from this (basic and applied research).
Functional objectives of research: Advancing the theory, practice, and methodology of adult education in collaboration with affiliated groups throughout the world.
Periodical publications: Convergence (4/yr). ICAE Newsletter (4/yr).
Monographs: Occasional publications and reports in the following areas: primary health care; literacy; peace education; participatory research; the political economy of adult education; radio learning group campaigns; womens' studies. Complete list on request.
Studies and surveys in preparation: The political economy of adult education. Womens' studies. Workers' education. Micro-technology. Leadership training. Library services. An international directory of regional and national associations affiliated with the ICAE.

International Development Research Centre

0101

Translation: Centre de recherche pour le développement international/Centro Internacional de Investigaciones para el Desarrollo
Address: Box 8500, OTTAWA, Ont., K1G 3H9
Year of creation: 1970
Parent Organization: Government of Canada
Present Head: Ivan Head
Size of staff. Total: 350 — Full time: 350
Researchers: 100 — Full time: 100
Research activities: more than 50%
Educational research: less than 10%
Type of research: Applied research and development activities.
Functional objectives of research: Identifying and examining development problems.
Periodical publications: Reports (Le CRDI explore, El CIID informa (12/yr)). Searching (Quête d'avenirs, Busqueda (1/yr)). Annual report (Rapport annuel).
Monographs: Teaching yourself in primary school: report of a Seminar on Self-Instructional Programs held in Quebec, Canada, 12–15 May 1981. Avalos, B.; Haddad, W. A review of teacher effectiveness research in Africa, India, Latin America, Middle East, Malaysia, Philippines, and Thailand: synthesis of results. 1981. Schiefelbein, E.; Farrell, J.P. Eight years of their lives: through schooling to the labour market in Chile. 1982. Schiefelbein, E. Educational financing in developing countries: research findings and contemporary issues. 1983. Universal primary education in Tanzania: a continuation of the educational revolution. 1983. Complete list on request.
Studies and surveys in preparation: Not applicable.

Ontario Institute for Studies in Education

0102

Address: 252 Bloor Street West, TORONTO, Ont., M5S 1V6
Year of creation: 1965
Present Head: Dr. Bernard J. Shapiro
Size of staff. Total: 478
Researchers: 154
Research activities: from 25% to 50%
Type of research: Basic research and development.
Functional objectives of research: To study matters and problems relating to or affecting education, and disseminate results; to assist in the implementation of the findings of educational studies; to establish and conduct courses leading to certificates and graduate degrees in education.
Periodical publications: Curriculum inquiry. Interchange on education. Orbit: ideas about teaching and learning. Ethics in education. Fun with mathematics.
Monographs: List on request from OISE Press.
Studies and surveys in preparation: Implementation of assessment instrument pool. Collection and development of heritage language materials. Studies of second language learning. Implementation of and development of materials for the Canadian Educational Computer. Canadian women's history: materials and methodology.

CENTRAL AFRICAN REPUBLIC

Institut national d'éducation et de formation (I.N.E.F.)

0103

Address: B.P. 921 et 772, BANGUI
Year of creation: 1974
Parent Organization: Ministère de l'éducation nationale
Present Head: Pierre Sammy, inspecteur de l'enseignement
Size of staff. Total: 115 — Full time: 115
Researchers: 60 — Full time: 60
Research activities: more than 50%
Educational research: more than 50%
Type of research: Recherches appliquées en éducation.
Functional objectives of research: Adaptation du contenu des programmes aux besoins nationaux; adéquation des techniques, des méthodes et des moyens didactiques; formation continue des enseignants.
Periodical publications: Revue pédagogique INEF. Bulletin de liaison concernant les EPC (Ecole de promotion collective). BIEN: journal du Ministère de l'éducation nationale.
Monographs: Divers manuels didactiques.
Studies and surveys in preparation: Education et développement. La réforme éducative centrafricaine. Programme de mathématiques, 1er degré. Enseignement du français 2e degré. Programme des sciences physiques et technologiques.

CHAD

Institut national des sciences de l'éducation (INSE)

0104

Address: Boîte postale No 473, N'DJAMENA
Year of creation: 1968
Parent Organization: Ministère de l'enseignement supérieur, de la recherche et des bourses
Present Head: Oumar Ben Moussa, licencié en sciences de l'éducation
Size of staff. Total: 70
Researchers: 12
Research activities: 50%
Educational research: 50%
Type of research: Recherches appliquées.
Functional objectives of research: Formation des enseignants (primaire); réforme de l'enseignement; élaboration du matériel didactique.
Periodical publications: Revue pédagogique tchadienne.

CHILE

Centro de Estudio, Investigación y Experimentación, Instituto de Educación, Universidad Católica de Valparaiso

0105

Address: Av. El Bosque 1290, Casilla 4059, VALPARAISO
Year of creation: 1969
Parent Organization: Facultad de Filosofía y Educación. Universidad Católica de Valparaiso
Present Head: Alvaro M. Valenzuela
Size of staff. Total: 14 — Full time: 9 — Part time: 5
Researchers: 14 — Full time: 9 — Part time: 5
Research activities: from 25% to 50%
Educational research: from 25% to 50%
Type of research: Investigación básica y aplicada.
Functional objectives of research: Apoyo a labores docentes; mejoría del sistema educacional; avance de las ciencias de la educación; perfeccionamiento de maestros y de la escuela.
Periodical publications: Perspectiva educacional.
Monographs: Valenzuela, A.; Onetto, L. Clima organizacional. Ahumada, P., otros. Modelos y metodologías para la evaluación de la eficiencia docente. Nuñez, O.M. La educación científico humanística en la década de los años 30. Gonzales, E. El pensamiento universitario de Don Juan Gomez Millas. Villagran, G.J. El pensamiento educacional de Francisco Antonio Encina.
Studies and surveys in preparation: Diseño de una metodología para la micro-enseñanza. La familia como entidad educativa. Tendencias e influencias en la educación media chilena. Programa integral acelerado (PIA) para trabajo grupal de niños con trastornos de aprendizaje.

Centro de Investigación y Desarrollo de la Educación (CIDE)

0106

Address: Erasmo Escala 1825, SANTIAGO
Year of creation: 1965
Present Head: Patricio Cariola, S.J. M.Ed. (Harvard)
Size of staff. Total: 61 — Full time: 61
Researchers: 40 — Full time: 40
Research activities: more than 50%
Educational research: more than 50%
Type of research: Investigación aplicada; investigación y desarrollo.
Functional objectives of research: Realizar estudios en relación con la educación y procurar que éstos sean conocidos y difundidos y que contribuyan al mejoramiento de la educación.
Periodical publications: Resúmenes analíticos en educación (2/año). Cuadernos de educación (12/año). Boletín REDUC.
Monographs: Mifsud, T. Los seis estadios del juicio moral: con aplicación pedagógica. 1983. Infante, I. La Red de Documentación en Educación para A.L. (REDUC). 1983. Richards, H. La evaluación de la acción cultural: estudio evaluativo del P.P.H. 1983. Ochoa, J. La sociedad vista desde los textos escolares. 1983. Lista completa a disposición.
Studies and surveys in preparation: Programas destinados a servir las necesidades básicas de campesinos y pobladores. Investigaciones acerca de la relación educación y familia, empleo y valores sociales.

Centro de Perfeccionamiento, Experimentación e Investigaciones Pedagógicas (CPEIP)

0107

Address: Casilla 16162, Correo 9, SANTIAGO
Year of creation: 1967
Parent Organization: Ministerio de Educación Pública
Present Head: Jorge Jimenez Espinoza, Profesor de Estado en química, Master en ciencias con mención en química, Doctor en administración de la educación superior
Size of staff. Total: 224 — Full time: 224
Researchers: 16 — Full time: 8 — Part time: 8
Research activities: from 10% to 25%
Educational research: more than 50%
Type of research: Investigación básica y aplicada.
Functional objectives of research: Mejoramiento cualitativo del sistema; prestación de servicios en la administración y gestión educativa.
Periodical publications: Revista de educación. Revista de tecnología educativa. English teaching newsletter. Revista chilena de educación química. Boletín informativo 'Perfeccionamiento'. Informativo (educación física). Alemán en Chile — Deutsch in Chile. Boletín bibliográfico.
Monographs: Factores de la repetitión en la educación básica chilena. 1981. Efectos del kindergarten en la repetición observada en la educación básica fiscal. 1981. Conocimiento que tienen los docentes sobre velocidad de lectura. 1982. Factores asociados al rendimiento en castellano y matematica en el primer ciclo de la enseñanza básica rural. 1982. Modelo tentativo para realizar estudios del efecto del curriculum en el rendimiento del alumno. 1983. Lista completa a disposición.
Studies and surveys in preparation: La educación parvularia y su quehacer educativo con padres en situación de extrema pobreza urbana: Programa 'Conozca a su hijo'.

Tendencia de rendimiento, repetición y deserción escolar. Formación, destino y demanda de profesores. Diagnóstico de la situación del alcoholismo y de la drogadicción en niños y jóvenes de la educación general básica y media de la región de Coquimbo.

Departamento de Educación, Facultad de Humanidades y Educación

0108

Address: Casilla 721, TALCA, Region del Maule
Year of creation: 1981
Parent Organization: Universidad de Talca
Present Head: Sr. Enrique López Bourasseau, Decano
Size of staff. Total: 17 — Full time: 17
Researchers: 4 — Full time: 4
Research activities: from 10% to 25%
Educational research: more than 50%
Type of research: Aplicadas.
Functional objectives of research: Prestación de servicios a la administración educacional.
Periodical publications: Cuadernos de educación (boletín anual de la Universidad de Talca). Documento de trabajo (boletín trimestral de la División de Planificación y Estudio de la Universidad de Talca).
Studies and surveys in preparation: Evaluación de la realidad de la docencia — 1, en la Universidad de Talca. Evaluación externa de la docencia. Seguimiento de la carrera de educación general básica de la Universidad de Talca. Seguimiento de profesionales del programa de enfermería de la Universidad de Chile-Talca y Universidad de Talca. Estudio descriptivo de los principales trastornos de conducta de los párvulos del jardín de infantes de la Universidad de Talca. Descripción de las actitudes facilitantes del aprendizaje a través de las interacciones verbales en aula. Lista completa a disposición.

Dirección General Académica

0109

Address: Avenida Libertador Bernardo O'Higgins 1058, SANTIAGO
Year of creation: 1974
Parent Organization: Rectoría Universidad de Chile
Present Head: Prof. Marino Pizarro Pizarro, Profesor de Castellano
Size of staff. Total: 46 — Full time: 39 — Part time: 7
Researchers: 17 — Full time: 10 — Part time: 7
Research activities: from 10% to 25%
Type of research: Investigación aplicada.
Functional objectives of research: Prestación de servicios a la administración educacional.
Periodical publications: Anales de la Universidad de Chile. Proyectos de investigación (1/año). Publicaciones originadas en proyectos de investigación apoyados con el fondo central de investigación (1/año). Cuadernos de la Universidad de Chile.
Studies and surveys in preparation: Proyecto internacional sobre evaluación de la redacción en lengua materna.

División Estudios, Servicio de Selección y Registro de Estudiantes

0110

Address: José Pedro Alessandri 685, SANTIAGO
Year of creation: 1975
Parent Organization: Universidad de Chile
Present Head: Luz Eliana Díaz Becerra
Size of staff. Total: 21 — Full time: 21
Researchers: 10 — Full time: 10
Research activities: more than 50%
Educational research: more than 50%
Type of research: Investigación aplicada.
Functional objectives of research: Apoyo a la toma de decisiones en materia de educación superior, principalmente en selección y admisión de alumnos.
Periodical publications: Resultados estadísticos de las pruebas del examen de admisión a la educación superior en Chile (boletín informativo (1/año)). Matrícula de los alumnos de pregrado de la Universidad de Chile (boletín estradístico (1/año)). Análisis cualitativos de los resultados de las pruebas de conocimientos.
Monographs: Rodríguez, C.; Donoso, G.; Zunino, E. Deserción y cambio de carrera en la Universidad de Chile. 1982. Avila, E., y otros. Medición de la redacción. 1982. Rodríguez, C.; Zunino, E. Demanda por las carreras de la Universidad de Chile en 1983. 1983. Bocchieri, A.; Rojas, R. Características de los candidatos rezagados y su incidencia en los resultados de la prueba de aptitud académica, 1982. 1983. Donoso, G.; Zunino, E Análisis cualitativo de los resultados de la prueba de aptitud académica matemática, admisión 1982. 1983. Lista completa a disposición.
Studies and surveys in preparation: Medición de la ortografía. Estudio sobre el rendimiento de los estudiantes en las distintas habilidades involucradas en la comprensión de lectura. Diferencias de rendimiento entre las secciones que conforman la parte verbal de la prueba de aptitud académica. El léxico activo de los estudiantes de 4o. año de enseñanza media. Lista completa a disposición.

Facultad de Educación, Humanidades y Arte

0111

Address: Casilla 82-C, CONCEPCION
Year of creation: 1920
Parent Organization: Universidad de Concepción
Present Head: Astrid Raby, Master of Arts, Profesor de literatura angloamericana
Size of staff. Total: 181 — Full time: 176 — Part time: 5
Researchers: 89 — Full time: 89
Research activities: from 10% to 25%
Educational research: from 10% to 25%
Type of research: Aplicada y básica.
Functional objectives of research: Contribuir al avance del conocimiento; preparar cursos; obtener grado; prestar servicios a la administración educacional regional, a la administración universitaria, y a otras faculdades.
Periodical publications: RLA (Revista de lingüística aplicada). Acta literaria.
Monographs: Evaluación del nivel de conocimientos alcanzados en francés por los estudiantes de 4o. año de enseñanza media de Concepción. Medición del grado de lecturabilidad del material de lectura en la enseñanza media. Evaluación de vocabulario pasivo y disponibilidad léxica en niños y adolescentes del Gran Concepción. Uso de modelos televisivos. Feed-back en el entrenamiento de

profesores en una situación de micro-enseñanza.
Studies and surveys in preparation: 10 investigaciones en curso tratando de enseñanza de las lenguas, computador como ayuda en el proceso docente, factores afectivos en el rendimiento escolar, etc.

Facultad de Educación, Pontificia Universidad Católica de Chile

0112

Address: Presidente J. Baltle y Ordoñez 3.300, SANTIAGO
Year of creation: 1943
Parent Organization: Pontificia Universidad Católica de Chile
Present Head: Sra. Josefina Aragoneses A., Decana de la Facultad
Size of staff. Total: 213 — Full time: 69 — Part time: 134
Researchers: 52 — Part time: 52
Research activities: from 10% to 25%
Educational research: more than 50%
Type of research: Básica, aplicada, investigación y desarrollo.
Functional objectives of research: Aumentar el conocimiento en las áreas disciplinarias relacionadas con educación; aplicar el conocimiento a la solución de problemas detectados en el proceso E — A y en general, en el sistema de educación; generar un ambiente científico de excelencia académica que retroalimente las labores de docencia en la Facultad.
Periodical publications: Anales de la Facultad de Educación.
Studies and surveys in preparation: Geometria, naturaleza y arte: un nuevo enfoque para la enseñanza de la geometria en la educación básica. Los estudiantes: sus valores, imagenes y aspiraciones sociales. Estudio longitudinal. Alumnos de la escuela de educación de la U.C.: caracterización según variables relevantes desde el punto de vista vocacional. La presencia del catolicismo en la vida intelectual chilena en la primera mitad del Siglo XX: filosofia y educación. La República de Platon: un pensamiento sobre la educación. Lista completa a disposición.

Facultad de Educación, Universidad del Norte

0113

Address: Av. Angamos 0610, Casilla 1280, ANTOFAGASTA
Year of creation: 1956
Parent Organization: Institución aútonoma
Present Head: Sr. Tito Pizarro Castro
Size of staff. Total: 56 — Full time: 55 — Part time: 1
Researchers: 19 — Full time: 19
Research activities: from 10% to 25%
Educational research: from 10% to 25%
Type of research: Investigación básica y aplicada.
Functional objectives of research: Apoyo a la docencia; prestación de servicios a la administración educacional; aporte de nuevos antecedentes científico-técnico-pedagógicos.
Periodical publications: Boletín de educación (Publicación semestral de circulación internacional). Ponencias jornadas de psicología educacional. Revista educación física — DEFUN (1/año).
Monographs: Gallardo, O.J. Motricidad: estructuraciones específicas. 1983. Santander Wannhoff, W. Programa de salud cardiorespiratorio para alumnos universitarios. 1983. Moreno Villanfana, A. Estudio comparativo de planes curriculares para la

formación de licenciados en educación física de las universidades del Valle (Colombia) y del Norte (Chile). 1983. Pizzaro Castro, T. Adolescencia y creatividad. 1982. Lista completa a disposición.

Studies and surveys in preparation: Investigaciones multidisciplinarias en la Costa Centro-Sur Andina. Estudiantes con problemas de rendimiento de nivel universitario. Estudio de la actitud de los padres y apoderados frente al proceso educativo en las comunas de Antofagasta. Estudio de desarrollo sicomotor en alumnos de primer año de enseñanza general básica. Estudio de motivaciones y causales de deserción de los usuarios en un programa de educación a distancia. Lista completa a disposición.

Programa Interdisciplinario de Investigaciones en Educación (PIIE)

0114

Address: Brown Sur, No 247, Nuñoa, SANTIAGO
Year of creation: 1971
Parent Organization: Academia de Humanismo Cristiano
Present Head: Professor Iván Núñez
Size of staff. Total: 30 — Full time: 30
Researchers: 13 — Full time: 13
Research activities: more than 50%
Educational research: more than 50%
Type of research: Investigación básica sobre el sistema educacional y sobre la cultura escolar e investigación-acción en educación no-formal y comunitaria.
Functional objectives of research: Contribuir al avance del conocimiento; promover procesos de organización y educación popular.
Monographs: Hevia, R.; Vera, R.; Latorre, C. Estudio descriptivo-analítico: las maestrías en educación en América Latina. 1981. Latorre, C. Análisis de un sistema de capacitación a trabajadores del sector informal. 1981. Magendzo, A. Una contribución al desarrollo de innovaciones curriculares en el ámbito de la educación no-formal. 1981. Latorre, C. Educación y capacitación en sectores de pobreza: el caso de la población San Antonio de Lo Barnechea. 1981. Lista completa a disposición.
Studies and surveys in preparation: Políticas históricas comparadas de gasto público en educación. Efectos distributivos del gasto en educación (1977-1978). La educación y los ingresos en una economía en crisis. Chile: 1977-1982. Actores y procesos del sistema educativo: el sector docente. Análisis del proceso de descentralización educacional en Chile durante el régimen militar (1973-1983). El fracaso escolar en la escuela básica chilena (2a. etapa).

CHINA

Zhong Yang Jiao Yu Ke Xue Yan Jiu Suo

0115

Translation: Central Institute of Educational Research
Address: 35 Damucanhutong Xidan, BEIJING
Year of creation: 1960
Parent Organization: Ministry of Education
Type of research: Basic and applied research.
Functional objectives of research: Undertake research centring on the theory, history

and current issues of education in China in order to develop the socialist cause of education; lay emphasis on scientific investigation and experiments, proceeding from actual conditions and combining theory with practice; coordinate educational research programmes, establish bases for educational research and entrust them with certain major research.
Periodical publications: Educational research (6/yr). Foreign education (6/yr).

COLOMBIA

Centro de Investigación y Educación Popular

0116

Address: Carrera 5, No. 33A-08, BOGOTA 2
Year of creation: 1972
Parent Organization: Organización privada independiente
Present Head: Manuel Uribe
Size of staff. Total: 55 — Full time: 55
Researchers: 30 — Full time: 30
Research activities: 50%
Educational research: from 10% to 25%
Type of research: Investigación y desarrollo; economía; sociopolítica; pedagogía no escolarizada.
Functional objectives of research: Organización popular.
Periodical publications: Qué paso (4/año). Análisis coyuntural sociopolítico.
Monographs: Colección Controversia. Colección Teoría y sociedad.
Studies and surveys in preparation: El plan de desarrollo de Colombia 1983-1986. Historia del movimiento campesino. Un model de escuela sindical.

Centro de Investigaciones de la Universidad del Norte (CIUN)

0117

Address: Kilómetro 5 Puerto Colombia, Apartado aéreo 1569, BARRANQUILLA
Year of creation: 1975
Parent Organization: Universidad del Norte
Present Head: Pedro Falco González M.S.
Size of staff. Total: 42 — Full time: 32 — Part time: 10
Researchers: 40 — Full time: 30 — Part time: 10
Research activities: more than 50%
Educational research: from 10% to 25%
Type of research: Aplicada.
Functional objectives of research: Cumplimiento parcial de registros para obtener grados.
Periodical publications: Huellas: revista de la Universidad del Norte. Anuario Uninorte.
Studies and surveys in preparation: Atención integral pre-escolar Costa Atlántica. Partes de crianza predominantes en los diferentes sectores socio-económicos de la ciudad de Barranquilla, Colombia. Elaboración, aplicación y evaluación de programas de prevención primaria del abuso de medicamentos dirigidos a grupos de pre-escolar, adolescentes y adultos. Estudio evaluativo de los métodos para la enseñanza de la lectura en las escuelas y colegios de enseñanza básica pre-escolar y elemental en Barranquilla, Colombia.

Centro de Investigaciones de la Universidad Pedagógica Nacional (CIUP) **0118**

Address: Avenida 46, No. 15–99, Apdo. aéreo 5304, BOGOTA
Year of creation: 1976
Parent Organization: Universidad Pedagógica Nacional que a su vez depende del Ministerio de Educación Nacional
Present Head: Guillermo Torres Zambrano
Size of staff. Total: 26 — Full time: 22 — Part time: 4
Researchers: 14 — Full time: 14
Research activities: more than 50%
Educational research: more than 50%
Type of research: Investigación básica y aplicada.
Periodical publications: Revista colombiana de educación (2/año).
Monographs: Las relaciones sociales de la práctica pedagógica de las escuelas normales (Informe final). Los estudios generales en el Nuevo reino de Granada 1600–1767. Escuela, maestro y métodos en la sociedad colonial. Curso audiovisual para padres de comunidades marginadas sobre el desarrollo integral del niño de 0 a 3 años de edad. 4392 diapositivas, 68 cassettes, manual general y 3 guías. La escuela primaria en Colombia: una perspectiva etnográfica (Informe final).
Studies and surveys in preparation: Curso de educación para padres de comunidades marginadas sobre el desarrollo integral del niño de 0 a 3 años de edad. Mecanismos de aprendizaje social. La efectividad del maestro: sus inicios en las escuelas normales. El maestro y la calidad de la educación. Catedráticos y colegiales en la sociedad colonial. Historia de la práctica pedagógica durante la Colonia — II Fase. La escuela primaria y la vida comunitaria y extracomunitaria. Programa de investigación: maestros currículo y organización escolar.

Centro de Investigaciones Educativas (CIED) **0119**

Address: Universidad de Antioquia, Apartado aéreo 1226, MEDELLIN, Antioquia
Year of creation: 1970
Parent Organization: Universidad de Antioquia
Present Head: Enrique E. Batista J., Ph.D.
Size of staff. Total: 6 — Full time: 1 — Part time: 5
Researchers: 5 — Full time: 5
Research activities: more than 50%
Educational research: more than 50%
Type of research: Aplicada, evaluativa, básica.
Functional objectives of research: La investigación educativa del CIED comprometida tanto con el descubrimiento de lo nuevo que caracteriza por ejemplo la etapa actual de la educación colombiana, como con el pronóstico o creación de condiciones para favorecer, recomendar o incluso experimentar innovaciones que eleven significativamente su calidad y cobertura en el futuro próximo del país.
Periodical publications: No se tienen publicaciones períodicas.
Monographs: Batista, E.; Vallejo, L.A.; Villa, G. Refinamiento psicométrico de un instrumento de evaluación de docentes. Carillo, D.; Correa, S. Educación a distancia y la profesionalización docente en Antioquia. Batista, E. Evaluación de algunos aspectos del programa de educación a distancia. Batista, E.; Bechara, R.; Duque, N. Aspectos sociales, culturales y educativos de los estudiantes de educación a distancia. Lista completa a disposición.

Studies and surveys in preparation: Estudio evaluativo de la educación de adultos de Comfama. Identificación, documentación y caracterización de innovaciones educativas: estudio de seis casos de innovaciones en Antioquia. Lista completa a disposición.

Facultad de Educación, Universidad del Valle

0120

Address: Ciudad Universitaria del Valle, Meléndez, CALI, Valle
Year of creation: 1945
Parent Organization: Universidad del Valle, Ministerio de Educación Nacional
Present Head: Gustavo Ignacio de Roux
Size of staff. Total: 70 — Full time: 58 — Part time: 12
Researchers: 15 — Part time: 15
Research activities: less than 10%
Educational research: more than 50%
Type of research: Aplicada.
Functional objectives of research: Aplicación en desarrollo curricular; innovaciones metodológicas; asesoría a instituciones y comunidades.
Periodical publications: Reflexiones pedagógicas (revista). Cuadernos de psicología (revista). Educación popular (boletín). Educación física, deportes y recreación (serie).
Monographs: Una enseñanza centrada en el alumno. La administración y planificación del núcleo de desarrollo educativo. Desde uno versus uno hasta once versus once. Características curriculares de programas de educación primaria en Colombia: análisis descriptivo y comparativo.
Studies and surveys in preparation: Perfil pedagógico de la región IDOC. Conceptualización de la docencia en ingeniería. Mejoramiento de la enseñanza de las ciencias. Análisis estructural del juego en grupo. Los procedimientos de partición, las hipótesis y la autoregulación.

Facultad de Educación, Universidad Pedagógica y Tecnológica de Colombia

0121

Address: Carretera Central del Norte, TUNJA, Boyacá
Parent Organization: ICFES
Present Head: Rosendo Castro Jiménez, D.
Size of staff. Total: 250 — Full time: 250 — Part time: 30
Researchers: 50 — Full time: 50
Research activities: from 25% to 50%
Educational research: from 25% to 50%
Type of research: Aplicada a la educación; desarrollo.
Functional objectives of research: Tesis y trabajos personales de profesores.
Periodical publications: Pensamiento y acción (12/año).
Monographs: Arbeláez Arbeláez, B. Corrientes pedagógica contemporaneas. 1982. Arbeláez Arbeláez, B. Juventud universitaria e ideológica. 1980. Aplicación de principios de modificación de conducta a un problema de aprendizaje. Ardila Espinel, N. La educación en tres paises socialistas.

Fundación para la Aplicación y Enseñanza de las Ciencias (FUNDAEC)

0122

Address: Apartado aéreo 6555, CALI
Year of creation: 1974
Present Head: Gustavo Correa
Size of staff. Total: 42 — Full time: 9 — Part time: 33
Researchers: 14 — Full time: 9 — Part time: 5
Research activities: more than 50%
Educational research: more than 50%
Type of research: Aplicada.
Functional objectives of research: Curriculo para educación rural; tecnología agropecuaria; busqueda de nuevas estrategias para desarollo rural.
Periodical publications: Textos educativos.
Monographs: FUNDAEC, una descripción.
Studies and surveys in preparation: A new alternative for rural development.

Instituto SER de Investigación

0123

Address: Carrera 15a., No. 45-65, Apartado aéreo 1978, BOGOTA
Year of creation: 1973
Parent Organization: Institución autónoma, privada, sin ánimo de lucro
Present Head: Dr. Jorge Aceredo
Size of staff. Total: 36 — Full time: 20 — Part time: 16
Researchers: 25 — Full time: 15 — Part time: 10
Research activities: more than 50%
Educational research: more than 50%
Type of research: Investigación básica y aplicada.
Functional objectives of research: Ayudar en la definición de políticas del Estado en educación, salud, justicia, seguridad social, desarrollo comunitario; asesor en planeación.
Periodical publications: Series. (Boletín publicado 3 veces al año).
Monographs: Características del Bachiller colombiano. 1981. Planteles de educación media. 1982. El joven universitario: características logro en los examenes de Estado. 1983. Lista completa a disposicíon.
Studies and surveys in preparation: Evaluación del bachillerato colombiano. Los examenes de Estado y el ingreso a la universidad. Desarrollo cognitivo y rendimiento en ciencias.

Programa de Investigación y Tecnología Educativa

0124

Address: Carrera 10a., No.65-48, BOGOTA
Year of creation: 1975
Parent Organization: Pontificia Universidad Javeriana
Present Head: Benjamín Alvarez Heredia
Size of staff. Total: 20 — Full time: 6 — Part time: 14
Researchers: 10 — Full time: 5 — Part time: 5
Research activities: 50%
Educational research: 50%
Type of research: Desarrollo, básica, aplicada.
Functional objectives of research: Desarrollo educativo; crítica, social y educativa;

docencia.
Monographs: Alvarez, E. de; Campo, R. Proceso de transferencia de tecnología de computadores al país y la formación de recursos humanos. Rodríguez, E., y otros. Rentabilidad y crecimiento de la educación superior en Colombia.
Studies and surveys in preparation: Modernización en el medio universitario. Creatividad y estilos de docente universitario. La educación católica. La mujer en la universidad. El libro de texto. El niño trabajador rural. Algunas características sico-sociales de los estudiantes de la Universidad Javeriana que ingresaron en julio de 1983. Nivelas de desarrollo moral y valores en niños provenientes de ambientes de pobreza en Bogotá. Factores asociados con la repitencia en secundaria. Educación a distancia.

CONGO

Institut de recherche et d'action pédagogique (INRAP)

0125

Address: Boîte postale 2128, BRAZZAVILLE
Year of creation: 1955
Parent Organization: Ministère de l'éducation nationale
Type of research: Recherches appliquées.

COSTA RICA

Centro de Investigación y Perfeccionamiento para la Educación Técnica (CIPET)

0126

Address: Costado Norte, Parque Central, ALAJUELA
Year of creation: 1976
Parent Organization: Ministerio de Educación Pública
Present Head: Dr. Rafael Angel Arguedas Marín
Size of staff. Total: 45 — Full time: 45
Researchers: 5 — Full time: 5
Research activities: 50%
Educational research: 50%
Type of research: Relacionados con la educación técnica y profesional.
Functional objectives of research: Investigar y difundir estudios sobre sectores técnicos y profesionales.
Periodical publications: Semestral sobre investigaciones.
Studies and surveys in preparation: Estudios de mercado en las zonas rurales y marginadas urbanas.

Instituto de Investigaciones para el Mejoramiento de la Educación Costarricense (IMMEC)

0127

Address: Facultad de Educación, Universidade de Costa Rica, Ciudad Universitaria Rodrigo Facio, SAN JOSE
Year of creation: 1980

Parent Organization: Universidad de Costa Rica
Present Head: Juan M. Esquivel
Size of staff. Total: 19 — Full time: 11 — Part time: 8
Researchers: 17 — Full time: 6 — Part time: 11
Research activities: more than 50%
Educational research: more than 50%
Type of research: Aplicada, investigación y desarrollo.
Functional objectives of research: Estimular y apoyar experiencias destinadas a introducir y probar innovaciones educativas; apoyo a trabajos finales de graduación; planificar, coordinar y realizar la investigación interdisciplinaria en ciencias de la educación en la Universidad de Costa Rica.
Periodical publications: Los investigadores contribuyen a la revista de la Universidad de Costa Rica, Educación, publicada por la Facultad de Educación.
Monographs: Diagnóstico evaluativo de la enseñanza de la matemática en la educación general básica y educación diversificada. Diagnóstico de las necesidades de investigación en la enseñanza de español, inglés, francés, matemática, estudios sociales y educación física, señaladas por los docentes que trabajan en las instituciones oficiales del país. Mendez, Z.; Chaves, C.; Escalante, A.C. Desarrollo del pensamiento formal en estudiantes de enseñanza secundaria del area metropolitana de San José. Lista completa a disposición.
Studies and surveys in preparation: Relación entre uso de algunos modelos de explicación en la historia de la física y la utilización de esos modelos por parte de sujetos no especializados. Adquisición de conceptos básicos de física, necesarios para la comprensión de la climatología en estudiantes de enseñanza general básica del area metropolitana.

Instituto de Investigaciones Psicológicas

0128

Address: Ciudad Universitaria Rodrigo Facio, SAN JOSE
Year of creation: 1969
Parent Organization: Facultad de Ciencias Sociales, Universidad de Costa Rica
Present Head: Rosa Isabel Blanco de Acuña, Lic. en ciencias y letras
Size of staff. Total: 22 — Full time: 8 — Part time: 14
Researchers: 16 — Full time: 2 — Part time: 14
Research activities: more than 50%
Educational research: from 25% to 50%
Type of research: Enfasis en la investigación aplicada.
Functional objectives of research: Estudios en psicología social, de la salud, educativa y metodología de la investigación; prestación de servicios a la administración educacional.
Periodical publications: Informes de investigación.
Monographs: Lista a disposición.
Studies and surveys in preparation: Manual de orientación a padres de familia en técnicas de comunicación. Ansiedad, percepción del ambiente y rendimiento académico en la Universidad de Costa Rica. Inventario de intereses vocacionales. Análisis factorial de la prueba de aptitud académica. Experimentación de una metodología para mejorar la capacidad de razonamiento lógico. Algunas características psicosociales del niño sordo y su familia. Algunas características psicosociales de la juventud costarricense.

CUBA

Departamento de Estudios para el Perfeccionamiento de la Educación Superior

0129

Address: Calle 23 No. 453 entre H e I, Vedado, Zona postal 4, CIUDAD HABANA
Year of creation: 1982
Parent Organization: Universidad de la Habana
Present Head: C.Dr. Elvira Martin Sabina
Size of staff. Total: 79 — Full time: 36 — Part time: 43
Researchers: 66 — Full time: 25 — Part time: 41
Research activities: more than 50%
Educational research: more than 50%
Type of research: Aplicadas.
Functional objectives of research: Perfeccionamiento del subsistema de educación superior; complimiento parcial de requisitos para obtener grados; preparación de cursos; prestación de servicios a la administración educacional.
Periodical publications: Ninguna.
Monographs: Estudio diagnóstico del desarrollo de la educación superior, período 1959–1980. Metodología para la planificación anual de la cantidad de profesores en los centros de educación superior. Organización y planificación de las inversiones en fondos básicos en la educación superior. Propuesta de nuevo sistema de financiamiento para la actividad científico-investigativa de carácter aplicado.
Studies and surveys in preparation: La demografía y su vinculación con el desarrollo de la educación superior. Perfeccionamiento de la estructura organizativa para la educación superior. La calidad del especialista graduado de la educación superior.

Instituto Central de Ciencias Pedagógicas

0130

Address: Obispo 160, Habana Vieja, CIUDAD HABANA
Year of creation: 1976
Parent Organization: Ministerio de Educación
Present Head: Dr. Max Figueroa Araújo
Size of staff. Total: 122 — Full time: 122
Researchers: 62 — Full time: 48 — Part time: 14
Research activities: more than 50%
Educational research: more than 50%
Type of research: Investigación básica y fundamentalmente aplicada y de desarrollo.
Functional objectives of research: Atender a la unidad de enfoque científico-pedagógica en los documentos sobre contenido de la enseñanza y la educación en las actividades teórico prácticas: planes, programas, textos de estudio y medios de enseñanza, organización escolar en todos los tipos y niveles de educación. Estas tareas las asume el Instituto Central de Ciencias Pedagógicas como trabajos científicos de desarrollo. Promoción y control de los temas de investigación del Plan Unico de Investigaciones Pedagógicas y de Psicología Pedagógica del MINED. El plan de traducciones y de importación de libros y revistas.
Periodical publications: Revista referativa (3/año). La educación por el mundo (12/año). Sistemas educativos (4/año). Ciencias pedagógicas (2/año). Experiencias pedagógicas de avanzada (11/año). Bibliografía temática (4/año).

Monographs: Ministerio de Educación. Plan de perfeccionamiento y desarrollo del sistema nacional de educación de Cuba. Estudio de cambios e innovaciones en la educación técnica y formación profesional en América Latina y el Caribe. Política de educación, empleo y trabajo productivo en Cuba. La experiencia cubana en materia de asociación de estudio y trabajo. Relación entre la formación de especialistas de nivel medio y superior y el desarrollo de la industria azucarera cubana.

Studies and surveys in preparation: Del Plan único de investigaciones pedagógicas y de psicología pedagógica del Ministerio de Educación — años 1981-1985 — hay 70 temas en curso. De ellos 43 son dirigidos por personal del Instituto, y son orientados y controlados por el Instituto, 21 de distintas instancias del Ministerio, y 6 de otros organismos.

CYPRUS

Paidagōgiko institouto

0131

Translation: Pedagogical Institute
Address: P.O. Box 5365, NICOSIA
Year of creation: 1972
Parent Organization: Ministry of Education
Present Head: Mr. Michalakis Maratheftis
Size of staff. Total: 31 — Full time: 19 — Part time: 12
Researchers: 11 — Full time: 7 — Part time: 4
Research activities: from 25% to 50%
Educational research: more than 50%
Type of research: Survey, experimental, case studies, Monte Carlo.
Functional objectives of research: To provide information for educational administration and for educational improvement.
Monographs: Personality and educational achievement in the public schools of Cyprus. Physical fitness of Cypriot adolescents on the basis of Kraus and Weber test. Clarity of instruction in science teaching. An evaluation of the Technician Education Council as programme at Brighton Technical College. Investigating the learning capabilities of maladjusted children. In-service training of teachers in Cyprus. The socialization of adolescents in Cyprus.
Studies and surveys in preparation: Punishment inflicted by Cypriot parents on their children. Complete list on request.

CZECHOSLOVAKIA

Evropské informační středisko pro další vzdělávání učitelů Univerzity Karlovy

0132

Translation: European Information Centre of Charles University for Further Education of Teachers
Address: Kaprova 14, 110 00 PRAHA 1
Year of creation: 1973

Parent Organization: Charles University
Present Head: Doc. JUDr. Svatopluk Petráček, CSc.
Size of staff. Total: 10 — Full time: 10
Researchers: 6 — Full time: 6
Research activities: from 10% to 25%
Educational research: from 10% to 25%
Type of research: Research and development.
Functional objectives of research: Servicing the educational administration; research and in-service teacher training.
Periodical publications: Newsletter EIC-FET (Czech, English, Russian 2/yr). Further education of teachers: annotated bibliography (Czech, English, Russian 2/yr).
Monographs: In-service teacher education. Educational documentation and information, no. 218/219. 1981. Information system for administration of higher education. 1981. Systems of educational information in some socialist countries. 1981. Scientific and technical education in Czechoslovakia. 1982.
Studies and surveys in preparation: Personality of teachers. Unity of the initial and in-service training of teachers (based on the experience from the Bulgarian People's Republic, the Czechoslovak Socialist Republic, the German Democratic Republic, the Rumanian Socialist Republic and the Union of Soviet Socialist Republics). Training of teachers for environmental education. Complete list on request.

Oddelenie biodromálnej a poradenskej psychológie. Psychologický ústav Univerzity Komenského

0133

Translation: Department of Biodromal Psychology and Counselling. Psychological Institute of Comenius University
Address: ul. 29. augusta 5, 811 08 BRATISLAVA
Year of creation: 1957
Parent Organization: Rectorate of Comenius University
Present Head: Prof. PhDr. Jozef Koščo, CSc
Size of staff. Total: 15 — Full time: 15
Researchers: 11 — Full time: 11
Research activities: more than 50%
Educational research: from 10% to 25%
Type of research: Basic and applied research.
Functional objectives of research: In theory development of biodromal psychology; in applied field conceptions and methods of work in biodromal counselling/life-span from the aspect of life-long education; education of scientific workers for higher degrees; theoretical and practical preparation of university students of counselling psychology.
Periodical publications: Psychologica. Miscellany of Comenius University.
Monographs: Teoreticko-metodologické základy procesu psychologického poradenstva. 1981. Identifikácia nadaných pre vedecké dráhy (so zameraním na prírodné vedy). 1982. Biodromálny model životnej cesty afunkcia niektorých aspektov dimenzie budúcnosti pri jej rozvíjaní. 1982. Profesionálny vývin v adulciu. 1983. Problémy vývinu a životnej cesty človeka v epigenetickej teórii Erika H. Eriksona (monografická stúdia). 1982.
Studies and surveys in preparation: In the framework of the Department's collective research work, the following problems are elaborated: theory and methodology of biodromal psychology; models of life-span development; problems of personal

maturity; self-concept; problems of talented and gifted persons with special regard to educational, vocational and marital development. Problems are solved in the team cooperation on the theoretical and empiric-research level. Results will be: a) monography — Biodromal psychology in the theory and practice of services for man; b) university textbook — Principles of counselling psychology; c) university scriptum — Pre-marital, marital and parental counselling.

Pedagogická Fakulta Univerzity Karlovy

0134

Translation: Pedagogical Faculty of Charles University
Address: M.D. Rettigové 4, 116 39 PRAHA 1
Year of creation: 1964
Parent Organization: Univerzita Karlova
Present Head: Prof. Dr. Miroslav Kořínek, Dr. Sc.
Size of staff. Total: 422.4 — Full time: 395.28 — Part time: 27.12
Researchers: 25.9 — Full time: 24.15 — Part time: 1.75
Research activities: from 25% to 50%
Educational research: more than 50%
Functional objectives of research: Educational and vocational guidance and counselling.
Periodical publications: Výchova k péči o životní prostředí. Didaktika ruštiny a ostatních cizích jazyků. General didactics. Pedagogical psychology. Preschool education. Educational and vocational guidance and counselling. Complete list on request.
Monographs: Jaroš, J. Výchova k vědeckému světovému názoru na základní škole. Klímová, M. Volba dalšího studia a přípravy pro povolání žáky 8. a 9. ročníků ZDŠ. Martincová, O. Problematika neologismů v současné spisovné češtině. Schneiderová, H. Vliv estetické výchovy na utváření postojů a životního stylu dospívající mládeže. Bezručková, V. Výchova řeči mentálně retardovaných žáků. Kořínek, M. Zdokonalování přípravy a dalšího vzdělávání učitelů prvního stupně ZŠ.
Studies and surveys in preparation: Výchova k míru. Výchova k péči o životní prostředí ve vysokoškolské přípravé učitelů. Dějiny socialistického školství. Společenské postavení a funkce učitele v socialistické společnosti. Podstata audiovizuální globálně strukturální metody při výuce cizích jazyků. Lingvodidaktická problematika výuky dospělých cizím jazykům. Současná francouzská didaktická literatura.

Ústav rozvoja vysokých škôl SSR

0135

Translation: Institute for the Development of Higher Education of the Slovak Socialist Republic
Address: Konventná 1, 812 41 BRATISLAVA
Year of creation: 1979
Parent Organization: Ministry of Education of the Slovak Socialist Republic
Present Head: Prof. Ing. Andrej Piškanin, CSc.
Size of staff. Total: 96 — Full time: 86 — Part time: 10
Researchers: 64 — Full time: 56 — Part time: 8
Research activities: more than 50%
Educational research: more than 50%
Type of research: Applied.
Functional objectives of research: Educational and economic problems of the development of higher education.

Periodical publications: Information bulletin.
Monographs: The analysis of the development of womens' education in the Slovak Socialist Republic and its portion in the total number of the qualified workers. 1981. Application of mathematical models in the economics of education, especially in educational prognosis. 1981. Hapala, D., et al. Equipment of the universities of the Slovak Socialist Republic with the apparatus for school teaching. 1982. Complete list on request.
Studies and surveys in preparation: The analysis of the development of the number of students and teachers at universities. The university classroom and its complex equipment. Questions of the improvement of communist education at universities during the stage of building the developed socialist society. Methodology for evaluating the teaching load of the teachers at universities. Complete list on request.

Ústřední ústav pro vzdělávání pedagogických pracovníků

0136

Translation: Central Institute for the Training of Educational Workers
Address: Celetná 20, Staré Město, 110 00 PRAHA 1
Year of creation: 1974
Parent Organization: Ministry of Education ČSR
Present Head: Doc. PhDr. Karel Tmej, CSc.
Size of staff. Total: 80 — Full time: 70 — Part time: 10
Researchers: 51 — Full time: 51
Research activities: from 10% to 25%
Educational research: more than 50%
Type of research: Applied research.
Functional objectives of research: Continuing education of teachers.
Periodical publications: Bulletin Učitelské vzdělání (2/an).
Monographs: Kymlička, M. Sociálně ekonomické problémy vzdělání. 1981. Somr, M. Cesta k socialistické výchově, škole a pedagogice. 1980. Somr, M. Od reformního úsilí ke škole reálného socialismu. 1982. Tmej, K. Úloha vlastního poznání ve výchově žáků k socialistickému vlastenectví a internacionalismu. 1980. Tmej, K., a kolekt. Uvádění začínajících učitelek mateřských škol do praxe. 1982.

Ústredný ústav pre vzdelávanie učitelov v Bratislave

0137

Translation: Central Institute for Teacher Education in Bratislava
Address: Budyšínska 3, BRATISLAVA
Year of creation: 1975
Parent Organization: Ministry of Education
Present Head: PhDr. Anton Auxt
Size of staff. Total: 41 — Full time: 40 — Part time: 1
Researchers: 30 — Full time: 29 — Part time: 1
Research activities: more than 50%
Educational research: more than 50%
Type of research: Basic and applied.
Functional objectives of research: Preparation of courses.
Periodical publications: Učitelské vzdělání.
Monographs: Aktuálne otázky pedagogickej diagnostiky. 1983. Aktuálne otázky riadenia škôl. 1983. O systémovom prístupe ku komunistickej výchove. Pedagogické a psychologické otázky uvádzania začínajúcich učitelov. Základy knižnej techniky v

školskej knižnici.

Výskumný ústav pedagogický

0138

Translation: Research Institute of Education
Address: Štúrova 5, 886 35 BRATISLAVA
Year of creation: 1947
Parent Organization: Ministry of Education of the Slovak Socialist Republic
Present Head: Doc. Dr. Juraj Koutun, CSc.
Size of staff. Total: 146 — Full time: 136 — Part time: 10
Researchers: 100 — Full time: 93 — Part time: 7
Research activities: more than 50%
Educational research: more than 50%
Type of research: Applied research.
Functional objectives of research: Preparation of school documents; construction of new content of teaching in individual subjects (pre-school, primary school, gymnasium).
Periodical publications: Jednotná škola.
Monographs: Binder, R. Úvod do pedagogiky tvorivosti. Milec, A. Pracovná výchova mimo vyučovania v sovietskej škole. Fedorová, V. Socialistické vlastenectvo a internacionalizmus vo výchovnom systéme PO SZM.
Studies and surveys in preparation: Výchovné vyučovanie v základnej škole. Poslanie a funkcia Programu komunistickej výchovy žiakov gymnázií. Technické myslenie a jeho rozvoj u žiakov. Vzťah medzi utváraním vedomostí a rozvíjaním rozumových schopností žiakov. Complete list on request.

Výzkumný ústav inženýrského studia při ČVUT

0139

Translation: Research Institute for Engineering Education at ČVUT
Address: Na Florenci 25, 115 18 PRAHA 1
Year of creation: 1961
Parent Organization: Czech Technical University (ČVUT)
Present Head: Jiří Měřička
Size of staff. Total: 59 — Full time: 55 — Part time: 4
Researchers: 33 — Full time: 30 — Part time: 3
Research activities: more than 50%
Educational research: more than 50%
Type of research: Applied research.
Functional objectives of research: Improvement of methods of education of engineers; development and application of audiovisual educational means and computers.
Periodical publications: Bulletin VÚIS (annual survey of activities of the Institute). Acta polytechnica VI. (General topics).
Monographs: Casové zatízení studentu 4. rocníku CVUT. 1980. Slavícek, P. Psychologie pro techniky. 1981. Holý, K. Sledování a vyhodnocení experimentu v řízení samostatné práce studentů. 1982. Beneš, J., Mazák, E. K metodice stanovení výukových cílů. 1981. Byčkovský P. Základy měření výsledků výuky. Tvorba didaktického testu. 1982.
Studies and surveys in preparation: Research reports on self-studies, control of study, development of audiovisual educational means and use of computers.

Výzkumný ústav odborného školství

0140

Translation: Research Institute of Vocational and Technical Education
Address: Karlovo nám. 17, Nové Město, 120 00 PRAHA 2
Year of creation: 1950
Parent Organization: Ministry of Education
Present Head: Ing. Václav Rohlíček
Size of staff. Total: 131 — Full time: 112 — Part time: 19
Researchers: 79 — Full time: 74 — Part time: 5
Research activities: more than 50%
Educational research: more than 50%
Type of research: Research and development.
Functional objectives of research: Curriculum development; development of documentation services; educational innovations; educational projects; educational statistics.
Periodical publications: Technické aktuality a metodické rozhledy pro SPŠ. Hospodářské aktuality a metodické rozhledy pro ekonomické studijní obory. Bulletin Výzkumného ústavu odborného školství pro učnovská zařízení.
Monographs: Kolektiv. Příprava středních odborných pracovníků na středních průmyslových školách po r. 1984. Průcha, J. Didaktická prognostika. Bacík, J., a kol. Systémové pojetí řízení práce škol. Complete list on request.
Studies and surveys in preparation: Obsahová přestavba odborného školství 1981–1983. Dynamika obsahu odborného vzdělání na středních školách a jeho vztahu ke vzdělání všeobecnému. Proces diferenciace a integrace obsahu. Specifika žáků jednotlivých druhů středních škol. Empirický výzkum znaků charakterizujích žáky. Complete list on request.

DENMARK

Danmarks laererhøjskole

0141

Translation: The Royal Danish School of Educational Studies
Address: Emdrupvej 101, 2400 KØBENHAVN NV
Year of creation: 1856
Parent Organization: Ministry of Education
Present Head: Mr. Henning Andersen
Size of staff. Total: 508 — Full time: 357 — Part time: 151
Researchers: 148 — Full time: 148
Research activities: from 25% to 50%
Educational research: more than 50%
Type of research: Basic research, educational R&D.
Functional objectives of research: Training of teachers (Grade 1–10); educational R&D.
Periodical publications: Annual syllabus and report.

Danmarks paedagogiske institut

0142

Translation: Danish Institute for Educational Research
Address: 28 Hermodsgade, 2200 KØBENHAVN N
Year of creation: 1955
Present Head: Jesper Florander, Director
Size of staff. Total: 49 — Full time: 45 — Part time: 4
Researchers: 17 — Full time: 15 — Part time: 2
Research activities: more than 50%
Educational research: more than 50%
Type of research: Basic; applied; research and development.
Functional objectives of research: Scientific research of importance to educational activities; developmental projects requiring scientific support; advisory service, planning, collection and analysis of educational material.
Periodical publications: NYT. Danmarks paedagogiske institut. Beretning 1982-83.
Monographs: Curriculum change and teacher qualification: an attempt to print out some consequences for the teacher qualifications of a change in the Danish social curriculum. Undervisningsmønstre — en kritisk analyse af Flanders' observationsteknik. Complete list on request.
Studies and surveys in preparation: Styring og samarbejde mellem laerer og elever. Paedagogisk miljø, dets tilblivelse og virkninger. Complete list on request.

Institut for paedagogik

0143

Translation: Institute of Education
Address: Store Kannikestraede 18, 1169 KØBENHAVN K
Year of creation: 1970
Parent Organization: University of Copenhagen
Present Head: Per Fibaek Laursen
Size of staff. Total: 15 — Full time: 12 — Part time: 3
Researchers: 9 — Full time: 9
Research activities: from 25% to 50%
Educational research: from 25% to 50%
Type of research: Basic.
Periodical publications: None.
Monographs: Complete list on request.
Studies and surveys in preparation: History of Danish school. The educational sociology of Bourdieu. The study of medicine. Instruction in the gymnasium. Education and new technology. Kindergarten activities. History of didactics. Education in developing countries.

DOMINICAN REPUBLIC

Centro de Investigaciones

0144

Address: Km. 5 1/2 Autopista Duarte, SANTO-DOMINGO
Parent Organization: Rectoría de la Universidad
Present Head: Ing. Ezequiel García Tatis

Size of staff. Total: 3
Researchers: 2
Research activities: more than 50%
Educational research: 50%
Type of research: Básica, aplicada, investigación y desarrollo.
Functional objectives of research: Preparación de cursos.
Periodical publications: Ninguna.
Studies and surveys in preparation: Evaluación del Plan Mejoramiento Docente de la Universidad Nacional Pedro Henríquez Ureña (estudio descriptivo). Análisis de los instrumentos de evaluación docente de la Universidad Nacional Pedro Henríquez Ureña (estudio experimental). Validación de materiales diseñados para la enseñanza de la matemática. Efectividad de la enseñanza modular (programada 1984–1985).

Centro de Investigaciones (UCMM)

0145

Address: Km. 1 1/2 Autopista Duarte, SANTIAGO DE LOS CABALLEROS
Year of creation: 1974
Parent Organization: Vicerrectoría Académica, Universidad Católica Madre y Maestra
Present Head: Profesor Ing. Nelson Gil Gil
Size of staff. Total: 22 — Full time: 17 — Part time: 5
Researchers: 11 — Full time: 6 — Part time: 5
Research activities: more than 50%
Educational research: from 10% to 25%
Type of research: Básica y aplicada (técnica, social y de otros tipos).
Functional objectives of research: Promover el fortalecimiento de la investigación institucional; incentivar y promover investigaciones de interés para el país.
Periodical publications: Aún no existen; se publican los proyectos una vez que han sido terminados.
Studies and surveys in preparation: La enseñanza y el aprendizaje de la matemática en la República Dominicana (segunda etapa). Proyecto co-auspiciado por el International Development and Research Centre, de Canadá.

ECUADOR

Sección de Investigación y Evaluación Curricular

0146

Address: San Gregorio y Juan Murillo, Edificio de la Dinamed, 4to. piso, QUITO
Year of creation: 1983
Parent Organization: Dirección Nacional de Mejoramiento de la Educación, Ministerio de Educación y Cultura
Present Head: Lcdo. Armando Raza Quelal
Size of staff. Total: 8
Researchers: 8
Research activities: more than 50%
Educational research: more than 50%
Type of research: Investigación y desarrollo.
Functional objectives of research: Investigación y evaluación curricular.
Periodical publications: Ninguna por ser institución de reciente creación.

Monographs: Ninguna.
Studies and surveys in preparation: Investigación evaluativa de planes y programas de la educación pre-primaria, primaria y media en el ciclo básico.

EGYPT

Kulliyyat at-tarbiya, Ǧāmi'at al-Mīniyā

0147

Translation: Faculty of Education
Address: Minia University, EL-MINIA
Year of creation: 1957
Parent Organization: Ministry of Higher Education
Present Head: Prof. Dr Mohamed A. Elnaghy
Size of staff. Total: 50 — Full time: 21
Researchers: 29
Research activities: less than 10%
Educational research: more than 50%
Type of research: Applied and research and development.
Functional objectives of research: Partial fulfilment of degrees requirements; preparation of courses; servicing the local educational environment.
Periodical publications: Bulletin of educational research.
Monographs: Effect of science process training on science understanding of science teachers. Content analysis of science textbooks of the intermediate stage (science process skills). The use of interaction analysis systems in the foreign language classroom. Attitude of the prospective teachers towards science, scientists and scientific career. The range of practising problem solving method by the science teachers in the second stage of basic education. Complete list on request.

Kulliyyat at-tarbiya, Ǧāmi'at 'Ayn Šams

0148

Translation: Faculty of Education
Address: Ain-Shams University, Roxy, CAIRO
Year of creation: 1929
Parent Organization: Ain-Shams University and Ministry of Education
Present Head: Prof. Dr. Abd El Salam Abd El Gafar
Size of staff. Total: 120 — Full time: 60
Researchers: 60 — Part time: 60
Research activities: from 10% to 25%
Type of research: Applied and basic research.
Functional objectives of research: Partial fulfilment of degree requirements; development of all aspects of education in Egypt.
Periodical publications: The Faculty yearbook.
Monographs: Lectures and studies of training sessions on educational research. Lectures of faculty teacher training sessions.
Studies and surveys in preparation: Studies in basic education. Research in alienation. Evaluation of the programme of upraising primary school teachers in Egypt.

Kulliyyat at-tarbiya, Ǧāmi'at Mansūra

0149

Translation: Faculty of Education
Address: Mansoura University, Ahmed Maher Street, Zip Cod. 35516, MANSOURA
Year of creation: 1969
Parent Organization: Mansoura University
Present Head: Prof. Dr. Sayed Khaer Allah
Size of staff. Total: 150 — Full time: 91 — Part time: 59
Researchers: 71 — Full time: 53 — Part time: 18
Type of research: Applied, basic and experimental research.
Functional objectives of research: Partial fulfilment of degree requirements; contribute to educational development.
Periodical publications: A half-year educational review (First issue: October 1978). Annual statistical bulletin (First issue: 1981). Annual dissertation bulletin (First issue: May 1983). Educational news journal (First issue: January 1983).
Monographs: None published.
Studies and surveys in preparation: None published.

Kulliyyat at-tarbiya, Ǧāmi'at Tantā

0150

Translation: Faculty of Education, Tanta University
Address: Tanta University, Osman Mohamad Street, TANTA
Year of creation: 1969
Parent Organization: Tanta University
Present Head: Dr. Mahmoud El Sayed Soultan
Size of staff. Total: 276 — Full time: 176 — Part time: 100
Research activities: more than 50%
Educational research: more than 50%
Type of research: Basic, applied, research and development.
Functional objectives of research: Fulfilment of degree requirements; development of society; preparation of courses.
Periodical publications: Revue de la Faculté de l'éducation de Tanta (1/an).
Monographs: Grille d'évaluation des stagiaires de langue française. Grille d'évaluation des stagiaires des sciences. Grille d'évaluation des stagiaires de l'anglais.
Studies and surveys in preparation: Personality profile and business competencies needed for the education of the Egyptian business man: a field study. Preparation of a dictionary of preschool spoken language.

Kulliyyat at-tarbiya, Ǧāmi'at Zaqāzīq

0151

Translation: Faculty of Education
Address: University of Zagazig, Mustafa Kamel St, ZAGAZIG
Year of creation: 1972
Parent Organization: University of Zagazig
Present Head: Prof. Dr. M. Abdel-Latif
Size of staff. Total: 202 — Full time: 128 — Part time: 74
Researchers: 146 — Full time: 116 — Part time: 30
Research activities: more than 50%
Educational research: more than 50%
Type of research: Applied and basic research.

Functional objectives of research: Preparation of courses; fulfilment of degree requirements.
Periodical publications: Educational journal (under establishment).
Studies and surveys in preparation: A psychological study of some aspects related to verbal development in child tales on children from 4–8 years of age. The development of the concept of correlation from the age of 4 and upward in the agricultural and industrial environments.

Markaz taṭwīr tadrīs al-'ulūm

0152

Translation: Science Education Centre
Address: Ain-Shams University, Abbassia, CAIRO
Year of creation: 1974
Parent Organization: Ain Shams University
Present Head: Prof. Dr. Yousef Salah El-Din Kotb
Size of staff. Total: 65 — Full time: 35 — Part time: 30
Researchers: 41 — Full time: 11 — Part time: 30
Research activities: more than 50%
Educational research: more than 50%
Type of research: Research and development.
Functional objectives of research: Improving science education for Egypt.
Periodical publications: Annual reports. Journal of modern science (Arabic, 3/yr).
Monographs: Resource units for science and mathematics curricula. Proceedings of six conferences and seminars organized by the Centre since 1974.
Studies and surveys in preparation: Development of science curricula for student teachers in faculties of education in Egyptian universities. Development of science education for the compulsory stage of basic education. Construction of item bank of science questions for secondary schools. Finalizing the project on science and mathematics curricula for secondary schools.

ETHIOPIA

Curriculum Evaluation and Educational Research Division

0153

Address: P.O.Box 31160, ADDIS ABABA
Year of creation: 1982
Parent Organization: Curriculum Department, Ministry of Education
Present Head: Tekle Ayano
Size of staff. Total: 8
Researchers: 8
Research activities: more than 50%
Educational research: more than 50%
Type of research: Applied research.
Functional objectives of research: To improve the quality of education by carrying out various evaluation activities.
Monographs: Only the results of the study.
Studies and surveys in preparation: Evaluative research of the general educational system in Ethiopia.

Institute of Educational Research (IER)

0154

Address: Addis Ababa University, P.O. Box 1176, ADDIS ABABA
Year of creation: 1983
Parent Organization: Autonomous institution under Addis Ababa University
Present Head: Yusuf Omer Aldi (Ph.D.)
Size of staff. Total: 25 — Full time: 24 — Part time: 1
Researchers: 15
Research activities: more than 50%
Educational research: more than 50%
Type of research: Basic, applied, R&D.
Functional objectives of research: Resolving national educational problems; research material for publication; production of instructional material.
Periodical publications: Ethiopian journal of education. News bulletin.
Monographs: Guideline to educational research. Study habits of AAU students.
Studies and surveys in preparation: Identification and classification of handicapped persons in Ethiopia. Study of the nature of the current practice of training teachers in AAU and its effect on the education in senior secondary schools in Ethiopia.

FINLAND

Aikus- ja nuorisokasvatuksen laitos

0155

Translation: Department of Adult Education and Youth Work, University of Tampere
Address: PL 607, 33101 TAMPERE 10
Year of creation: 1946
Parent Organization: University of Tampere
Present Head: Prof. Matti Peltonen
Size of staff. Total: 8
Researchers: 6
Type of research: Basic and applied research.
Periodical publications: Research reports.
Monographs: List on request.

Helsingin yliopisto, Lahden tutkimus ja koulutuskeskus

0156

Translation: University of Helsinki, Research and Training Centre at Lahti
Address: Oikokatu 1, 15100 LAHTI 10
Year of creation: 1979
Parent Organization: University of Helsinki
Present Head: Mr. Heikki Lampi
Size of staff. Total: 100 — Full time: 100
Researchers: 11 — Full time: 10 — Part time: 1
Research activities: from 10% to 25%
Educational research: from 25% to 50%
Type of research: Applied (50%), research and development (50%).
Functional objectives of research: Development of new branches in economic life; increase of employment; development of education and preparation of courses;

increase of extramural interaction.
Periodical publications: Planned.
Monographs: Vehviläinen, M.R. Avoin korkeakoulu opiskelijoiden näkökulmasta. 1982. Kantola, S. Tutkimus eräiden Päijät-Hämeen piiripaikallishallintoviranomaisten ammatillisen täydennyskoulutuksen tarpeesta. 1982. Complete list on request.
Studies and surveys in preparation: Sarala, U. Training and education in developing an industrial organisation. Köppä, T.; Pääkkönen, J. Follow up stud. Nurmi, K.E. Methods of teaching and learning in open university distance education. Eerola, M. Follow up study of educational project of the personnel in Kouvola labour administration.

Kasvatustieteen laitos, Helsingin yliopisto

0157

Translation: Department of Education, University of Helsinki
Address: Fabianinkatu 28, 00100 HELSINKI 10
Year of creation: 1974
Parent Organization: University of Helsinki
Present Head: Prof. Pertti Kansanen
Size of staff. Total: 148 — Full time: 122 — Part time: 26
Researchers: 1 — Full time: 1
Research activities: 50%
Type of research: Basic, applied, research and development.
Functional objectives of research: Partial fulfilment of degree requirements and various research objects.
Periodical publications: Research bulletin, Department of Education, University of Helsinki (Tutkimuksia, Helsingin yliopisto, Kasvatustieteen laitos). Research bulletin, Institute of Teacher Education, University of Helsinki (Tutkimuksia, Helsingin yliopisto, Opettajankoulutuslaitos). Complete list on request.

Kasvatustieteen laitos, Jyväskylän yliopisto

0158

Translation: Department of Education, University of Jyväskylä
Address: Seminaarinkatu 15, 40100 JYVÄSKYLÄ 10
Year of creation: 1944
Parent Organization: University of Jyväskylä
Present Head: Prof. Dr. Paavo Päivänsalo
Size of staff. Total: 19
Researchers: 12
Type of research: Basic and applied research.
Monographs: Research reports.

Kasvatustieteen laitos, Tampereen yliopisto

0159

Translation: Department of Education
Address: PL 607, 33101 TAMPERE 10
Year of creation: 1974
Parent Organization: University of Tampere
Present Head: Prof. Jarkko Leino
Size of staff. Total: 11 — Full time: 11
Researchers: 7 — Full time: 7

Research activities: from 25% to 50%
Educational research: more than 50%
Type of research: Basic and applied research.
Functional objectives of research: Servicing educational administration, classroom teaching and educational planning and preparation of courses.
Monographs: Virtanen, A., ed. Korkeakouluopetuksen tehostaminen. Ojanen, S. Opettajien stressi. Raivola, R. Koulutuksen yhteiskunnalliset tehtävät eduskuntapuolueiden ohjelmien valossa. Pentti, V. Kadettien suoritusmotivaatio. Gutsa, J. Foundations of integrating education with working life in Zimbabwe. Mhene, A. The role of social studies in nation building in Zimbabwe. Complete list on request.
Studies and surveys in preparation: Computer-based education. Cognitive psychology in education. Sport activities of young children. In-service teacher education in comparative point of view. Vocational education.

Kasvatustieteiden laitos, Turun yliopisto

0160

Translation: Institute of Education, University of Turku
Address: PL 23, 20521 TURKU 52
Year of creation: 1957
Parent Organization: University of Turku
Present Head: Erkki Olkinuora
Size of staff. Total: 18 — Full time: 18
Researchers: 7 — Full time: 7
Research activities: from 10% to 25%
Educational research: more than 50%
Type of research: Basic and applied research.
Functional objectives of research: Learning difficulties, history of education, development of curricula.
Monographs: List on request.
Studies and surveys in preparation: The interactive formation of learning difficulties. The changes of the secondary school curriculum in Finland in 1890–1920. The changes of curriculum of Finnish compulsory education in 1916–1970.

Kasvatustieteiden tutkimuslaitos, Jyväskylän yliopisto

0161

Translation: Institute for Educational Research
Address: Seminaarinkatu 15, 40100 JYVÄSKYLÄ 10
Year of creation: 1968
Parent Organization: University of Jyväskylä
Present Head: Prof. Jouko Kari
Size of staff. Total: 80 — Full time: 69 — Part time: 11
Researchers: 55 — Full time: 49 — Part time: 6
Research activities: more than 50%
Educational research: more than 50%
Type of research: Basic and applied research.
Functional objectives of research: Basic research related to curriculum development; research related to teaching arrangements; research related to educational achievement; research on the educational system; research on home education and collaboration between home and school; research serving the research activity of the

Institute.

Periodical publications: The Finnish journal of education/Kasvatus (6/yr). Reports from the Institute for Educational Research (ca. 10/yr). The Institute for Educational Research bulletin (ca. 20–25/yr).

Monographs: Developing the comprehensive school on the basis of research results. Articles written by researchers on the comprehensive school and its developments. Dialects, bilingualism, and mother tongue teaching in the Swedish-speaking comprehensive school in Finland. On the development of the education of study counsellors for the upper secondary school based on the ratings of contact teachers in vocational guidance, studying to become study counsellors. School–home cooperation as a special theme in the time resource quota experiment. Teachers' experiences of cooperation between home and school in the time resource quota system on the upper level of the comprehensive school. Tutor-method. Introduction to the tutor-method and experience gained on its application in Finnish experimental schools following the time resource quota-system. Complete list on request.

Studies and surveys in preparation: International composition study. The educational profile of the class teacher. Research on the teaching of the mother tongue. Second international school achievement study in natural sciences. International study of school achievement in mathematics. Research project on the administrative effects of the time resource. Research on vocational structure and education. Complete list on request.

Käyttäytymistieteiden laitos, Joensuun yliopisto

0162

Translation: Department of Education, University of Joensuu
Address: PL 111, 80101 JOENSUU 10
Year of creation: 1969
Parent Organization: University of Joensuu
Present Head: Prof. Yrjö-Paavo Häyrynen
Type of research: Basic and applied research.
Monographs: List on request.

Liikunnan ja kansanterveyden edistämissäätiön tutkimuslaitos

0163

Translation: The Research Institution of Physical Culture and Health
Address: Rautpohjankatu 10, 40700 JVYÄSKYLÄ 70
Year of creation: 1970
Parent Organization: The Foundation for Promotion of Physical Culture and Health
Present Head: Dr. Pauli Vuolle
Size of staff. Total: 3 — Full time: 2 — Part time: 1
Researchers: 14 — Full time: 6 — Part time: 8
Research activities: more than 50%
Educational research: from 25% to 50%
Type of research: Firstly, applied and research and development; secondly, basic research.
Functional objectives of research: To produce, acquire and pass on information connected with the health and welfare of man.
Periodical publications: Yearbook.
Monographs: In 1983, 36 monographs in the series Reports of physical culture and

health.

Studies and surveys in preparation: Research into physical education and training. Research into the adult population's sports behaviour. Physical exercise and physical sciences from the body cultural point of view. The follow-up study of the sport law. Research on the effects of physical rehabilitation. The origin of modern sport. Women and sport. The health and physical activity of employees of the machine industry in Finland.

Opettajankoulutuslaitos, Jyväskylän yliopisto

0164

Translation: Teacher Training Department
Address: Seminaarinkatu 15, 40100 JYVÄSKYLÄ
Year of creation: 1972
Parent Organization: University of Jyväskylä
Present Head: Dr. Paavo Malinen, Ass. Professor
Size of staff. Total: 113 — Full time: 93 — Part time: 20
Researchers: 7 — Full time: 7
Research activities: from 10% to 25%
Educational research: from 10% to 25%
Type of research: Basic and applied research connected with teacher education and school instruction.
Functional objectives of research: Instruction in elementary and secondary education; teacher training programmes.
Periodical publications: Research reports, Teacher Training Department, University of Jyväskylä.
Studies and surveys in preparation: Teacher training programme for elementary school teachers. Curriculum for elementary education. Curriculum theory.

Pedagogiska institutionen vid Pedagogiska fakulteten

0165

Translation: Institute of Education, Faculty of Education
Address: Kyrkoesplanaden 12–14, 65100 VASA 10
Year of creation: 1974
Parent Organization: Åbo Akademi
Present Head: Håkan Andersson
Size of staff. Total: 6 — Part time: 1
Research activities: from 25% to 50%
Educational research: from 25% to 50%
Type of research: Basic, applied.
Functional objectives of research: Educational objectives; servicing teacher training; curriculum research.
Periodical publications: Reports from the Faculty of Education (Dokumentation från Pedagogiska fakulteten).
Studies and surveys in preparation: Bedömning av undervisningsförmågan inom lärarutbildningen. I kulturens och samhällets tjänst: Studier i finländsk skol- och läroplansutveckling 1860–1980. Tobalk-projektet. Complete list on request.

Psykologian laitos, Jyväskylän yliopisto 0166

Translation: Department of Psychology
Address: University of Jyväskylä, Seminaarinkatu 15, 40100 JYVÄSKYLÄ 10
Year of creation: 1936
Parent Organization: University of Jyväskylä
Present Head: Lea Pulkkinen, PhD, Professor
Size of staff. Total: 49 — Full time: 46 — Part time: 3
Researchers: 39 — Full time: 18 — Part time: 21
Research activities: from 25% to 50%
Educational research: from 10% to 25%
Type of research: Basic.
Periodical publications: Reports from the Department of Psychology. Jvyäskylä studies in education, psychology and social research.
Monographs: Makkonen, T., et al. Operaatio Perhe: isä ja synnytys. 1981. Pulkkinen, L. Nuorten tupakointi ja alkoholinkäyttö pitkittäistutkimuksen valossa. (Youthful smoking and drinking: a longitudinal study). 1982. Stranden, P. Nuori lapsiperhe: tutkimus nuorten perheiden elämäntilanteesta ja toimintaedellytyksistä. 1982.
Studies and surveys in preparation: Developing day care for small children: at present, mental load and stress of children in day care system. Health education in day care. Social development in a longitudinal perspective; from childhood to adulthood. Family education in the comprehensive school system. Peace education in day care, family and school.

FRANCE

Agence nationale pour le développement de l'éducation permanente (ADEP) 0167

Address: Le Central 430, La Courtine Mont d'Est, 93160 NOISY LE GRAND
Year of creation: 1973
Parent Organization: Ministère de l'éducation nationale
Present Head: Jean-François Cuby
Size of staff. Total: 60 — Full time: 57 — Part time: 3
Researchers: 35 — Full time: 35
Research activities: from 25% to 50%
Educational research: from 25% to 50%
Type of research: Recherche appliquée au développement de systèmes de formation.
Functional objectives of research: Prestations à la demande des administrations (ministères de l'éducation nationale, de la formation professionnelle, du plan, de l'emploi, ...) et de clients privés.
Periodical publications: Courrier de l'A.D.E.P. L'oeil sur la formation et son environnement socio-économique.
Monographs: La planification régionale de la formation professionnelle. La formation des formateurs pour la formation en alternance. La formation professionnelle au service de l'exportation. Les comités locaux pour l'emploi. Liste complète sur demande.
Studies and surveys in preparation: La régionalisation de la formation professionnelle. Le dispositif de formation des jeunes de 16 à 25 ans. Les nouvelles qualifications

liées aux changements technologiques.

Centre de didactique des langues

0168

Address: Université de Grenoble III, BP 25 X, 38040 GRENOBLE CEDEX
Year of creation: 1975
Parent Organization: Université de Grenoble III
Present Head: Louise Dabene, docteur en lettres et sciences humaines, professeur
Size of staff. Total: 8 — Part time: 8
Researchers: 7 — Part time: 7
Research activities: 50%
Educational research: more than 50%
Type of research: Recherches fondamentales et appliquées.
Functional objectives of research: Recherches linguistiques et sociolinguistiques en rapport avec l'enseignement des langues étrangères.
Monographs: La grammaire en langue maternelle et en langue étrangère. 1979. Les jeunes issus de l'immigration algérienne et espagnole à Grenoble: quelques aspects sociolinguistiques. Sociolinguistique en milieu urbain en France. Langues et migrations.
Studies and surveys in preparation: Enquête sur les problèmes sociolinguistiques des migrants de la 2e génération. Etude sur l'enseignement de la grammaire en langue maternelle (LM) et langue étrangère (LE). Analyse des phénomènes de communication dans la classe de langue étrangère.

Centre de recherche appliquée en informatique pédagogique (C.R.A.I.P.)

0169

Address: Grille d'Honneur, Parc de Saint-Cloud, 92211 SAINT-CLOUD
Year of creation: 1983
Parent Organization: Ecole normale supérieure de Saint-Cloud
Present Head: Monsieur André Poly
Size of staff. Total: 14 — Full time: 6 — Part time: 4 à 10
Researchers: 6 — Full time: 3 — Part time: 3
Research activities: from 25% to 50%
Educational research: more than 50%
Type of research: Recherches appliquées en informatique pédagogique.
Functional objectives of research: Développement d'outils pédagogiques et didactiques.

Centre de recherche en psychologie de l'éducation (C.R.P.E.)

0170

Address: Université d'Aix-Marseille I, UER de psychologie, Avenue de l'Arc de Mayran, 13621 AIX EN PROVENCE
Year of creation: 1977
Parent Organization: Université d'Aix-Marseille I et C.N.R.S.
Present Head: Michel Gilly
Researchers: 8 — Full time: 7 — Part time: 1
Research activities: more than 50%
Educational research: more than 50%
Type of research: Surtout fondamentale, mais en partie tournée vers les applications.
Functional objectives of research: Développement de la recherche fondamentale à caractère universitaire; préparation de thèses et formation à la recherche; recherches

contractuelles: pour le C.N.R.S. en tant que 'laboratoire associé'; pour le Ministère de l'éducation nationale, pour la région.
Monographs: Bonniol, J.J. Déterminants et mécanismes des comportements d'évaluation d'épreuves scolaires. 1980. Gilly, M. Maître-élève: rôles institutionnels et représentations. 1980. Massonnat, J. Rapports entre conditions de travail, activité cognitive et attitudes des étudiants appartenant à deux filières scientifiques. 1981. Gilly, M. Psychosociologie de l'éducation. In: Psychologie sociale. 1984. Menez, M. Procédure de pilotage de la classe et fonctionnement cognitif des élèves: deux outils d'analyse des situations scolaires. In: La pensée naturelle: structures, procédures, logique du sujet. 1983. Liste complète sur demande.
Studies and surveys in preparation: Interactions sociales, socio-éducatives et acquisitions cognitives individuelles. Education, formation et identification. Représentations réciproques maître-élève. Evaluation formative acquisitions et socialisation des élèves.

Centre de recherche et d'étude pour la diffusion du français (CREDIF)

0171

Address: 11, Avenue Pozzo di Borgo, 92211 SAINT-CLOUD
Year of creation: 1956
Parent Organization: Ecole normale supérieure de Saint-Cloud
Present Head: Professeur Jacques Cortes
Size of staff. Total: 65
Researchers: 40
Research activities: 50%
Educational research: from 25% to 50%
Type of research: Recherches fondamentales et appliquées.
Functional objectives of research: Etudes pour les ministères; méthodes de langues (didactique des langues); thèses de doctorat.
Periodical publications: Bulletin bibliographique (7/an). Revue Reflet (5/an).
Monographs: Collection Langues et apprentissage des langues (LAL). Collection Essais.
Studies and surveys in preparation: Evaluation des expériences pilotes de scolarisation des enfants des travailleurs migrants. Action pilote éducative en vue de l'insertion sociale et professionnelle des jeunes d'origine étrangère. La variété des pratiques langagières dans le français des années 80.

Centre de recherche interdisciplinaire — Vaucresson

0172

Address: 54, rue de Garches, 92420 VAUCRESSON
Year of creation: 1951
Parent Organization: Ministère de la justice, Ministère de l'industrie et de la recherche
Present Head: Jacques Commaille, maître de recherche
Size of staff. Total: 77 — Full time: 65 — Part time: 12
Researchers: 27 — Full time: 26 — Part time: 1
Research activities: more than 50%
Educational research: from 25% to 50%
Type of research: Recherche appliquée et fondamentale.
Functional objectives of research: Amélioration de la politique de la justice dans le domaine de l'enfance, de la jeunesse et de la famille.
Periodical publications: Les Annales de Vaucresson. Le Droit de l'enfance et de la famille. Marginalités.
Monographs: Commaille, J. Familles sans justice? Le droit et la justice face aux

transformations de la famille. 1982. Koeppel, B. De la pénitence à la sexologie: Essai sur le discours tenu aux jeunes filles. 1982. Délits des jeunes et jugement social: recherche comparative internationale. 1983. Malewska-Peyre, H., éd. Crise d'identité et problèmes de déviance chez les jeunes immigrés: comparaison des adolescents français et immigrés. Sous presse. Liste complète sur demande.
Studies and surveys in preparation: Sociologie des régulations sociales dans le domaine de la famille à partir de l'analyse des fonctions de la justice et du droit. Fonctionnement des tribunaux pour enfants et incidences sur le devenir des mineurs délinquants. L'évolution des relations parents-enfants dans la période 1945-1982. Recherche comparative franco-polonaise sur la formation et l'intériorisation des normes en institution de rééducation. L'approche familiale systémique appliquée au champ de la rééducation (ses applications dans le cadre de la formation continue et de l'expérimentation éducative et clinique).

Centre de recherches et d'applications pédagogiques en langues (CRAPEL)

0173

Address: B.P. 33.97, 54015 NANCY CEDEX
Year of creation: 1969
Parent Organization: Université de Nancy II
Present Head: Professeur Henri Holec
Size of staff. Total: 17 — Full time: 4 — Part time: 13
Researchers: 13 — Part time: 13
Research activities: 50%
Educational research: more than 50%
Type of research: Recherche fondamentale, appliquée; recherche-action.
Functional objectives of research: Amélioration de l'enseignement/apprentissage des langues étrangères.
Periodical publications: Mélanges pédagogiques (1/an).
Monographs: Autonomie et apprentissage des langues. 1981.
Studies and surveys in preparation: L'interaction d'aide. Utilisation du milieu. Apprentissage assisté par ordinateur.

Centre d'étude des politiques d'éducation (C.E.P.E.)

0174

Address: Université de Paris VIII, Département des sciences de l'éducation, C 420, 2, rue de la Liberté, 93526 SAINT DENIS CEDEX 02
Year of creation: 1973
Parent Organization: Université de Paris VIII
Present Head: Michel Debeauvais
Size of staff. Total: 7 — Full time: 1 — Part time: 6
Researchers: 5 — Full time: 1 — Part time: 4
Research activities: more than 50%
Educational research: more than 50%
Type of research: Recherche appliquée: éducation comparée; politiques d'éducation; politiques d'innovation; Tiers Monde; planification de l'éducation; évaluation.
Functional objectives of research: Recherches interdisciplinaires sur les interrelations entre les systèmes éducatifs, la société et l'emploi dans les pays du Tiers Monde; recherche-action sur l'innovation.
Periodical publications: Cahiers du C.E.P.E. (à paraître à partir de 1984).
Monographs: L'Université ouverte: les dossiers de Vincennes. 1976.

Studies and surveys in preparation: Inventaire des travaux français (recherches et publications) sur l'éducation dans le Tiers-Monde. Sous-programme: Analyse du rôle des universités françaises dans l'étude des problèmes d'éducation dans le Tiers-Monde et dans la formation des chercheurs sur ces questions. Méthodes d'évaluation institutionnelle et d'auto-évaluation assistée, appliquées aux innovations dans l'enseignement supérieur et la formation des adultes.

Centre d'études et de recherches sur les qualifications (CEREQ)

0175

Address: 9, rue Sextius Michel, 75732 PARIS Cedex 15
Year of creation: 1970
Parent Organization: Ministères de l'éducation nationale et de l'emploi
Present Head: M. Paul-Pierre Valli
Size of staff. Total: 130 — Full time: 130
Researchers: 60 — Full time: 60
Research activities: more than 50%
Educational research: from 10% to 25%
Type of research: Appliquée; recherche et développement.
Functional objectives of research: Analyse des relations entre la formation et l'emploi et les transformations du travail.
Periodical publications: Formation-emploi (4/an). Collection des études (5 à 10 numéros par an).
Monographs: Enseignement et organisation du travail du XIXe siècle à nos jours. 1979. Les conditions d'emploi des anciens élèves des classes de BEP. 1979. Recherches sur les compétences professionnelles à développer dans les enseignements: analyse du travail dans les systèmes énergétique-thermiques. 1980. La formation par la recherche et l'emploi: les docteurs de 3e cycle. 1979. Liste complète sur demande.
Studies and surveys in preparation: L'appel aux jeunes issus de l'enseignement secondaire (niveaux VI — V bis et V). Contribution du système de formation supérieure au renouvellement des emplois. Stratégie de qualification des jeunes sans bagage scolaire. Itinéraires professionnels et emplois occupés à l'issue des LEP. Les débuts de carrières professionnelles à la fin des études supérieures. Liste complète sur demande.

Centre international d'études pédagogiques de Sèvres (CIEP)

0176

Address: 1, avenue Léon-Journault, 92310 SEVRES
Year of creation: 1945
Parent Organization: Institut national de recherche pédagogique à Paris
Present Head: Madame Jeannine Feneuille
Size of staff. Total: 64 — Full time: 61 — Part time: 3
Researchers: 26 — Full time: 26
Research activities: less than 10%
Educational research: more than 50%
Type of research: Didactique du français langue étrangère; recherche appliquée et de développement.
Functional objectives of research: Améliorer la formation en français-langue étrangère.
Periodical publications: Amis de Sèvres (4/an). Dossiers (4 au minimum par an). Informations-SODEC (10/an). Echos (4/an).
Studies and surveys in preparation: Logiciels d'enseignement du français-langue

étrangère.

Centre technique national d'études et de recherches sur les handicaps et les inadaptations (C.T.N.E.R.H.I.)

0177

Address: 27, quai de la Tournelle, 75005 PARIS
Year of creation: 1975
Present Head: Monsieur Robert Moreau
Size of staff. Total: 38 — Full time: 21 — Part time: 17
Researchers: 12 — Full time: 5 — Part time: 7
Research activities: from 10% to 25%
Educational research: from 10% to 25%
Functional objectives of research: Internat, internement sous l'Ancien Régime; l'intégration des enfants et des adultes handicapés; l'école et l'accueil des enfants en difficulté; action éducative auprès des mineurs signalés par la justice; intégration en crèche et en maternelle.
Periodical publications: Flash informations législatives (1/an). Handicap et inadaptation: les cahiers du C.T.N.E.R.H.I. (4/an).
Studies and surveys in preparation: Etude pour des pédagogies adaptées aux personnes en risque de désinsertion.

Centre universitaire de recherche, d'information et de documentation sur l'éducation permanente (CUIDEP)

0178

Address: Université des sciences sociales, 2, place de l'Etoile, 38000 GRENOBLE
Year of creation: 1975
Parent Organization: Université des sciences sociales de Grenoble
Present Head: Noël Terrot
Size of staff. Total: 8 — Full time: 6 — Part time: 2
Researchers: 5 — Full time: 3 — Part time: 2
Research activities: more than 50%
Educational research: more than 50%
Type of research: Fondamentale et appliquée sur la formation des adultes.
Functional objectives of research: Information et conseil aux responsables de formation publics et privés (administrations, associations et entreprises).
Periodical publications: Flash formation continue (2/an) — national. Flash Rhône-Alpes (1/mois) — régional.

CREPCO (Psychologie génétique et de l'enfant)

0179

Address: CREPCO Psychologie, Université de Provence, 29, ave. R. Schuman, 13621 AIX EN PROVENCE
Parent Organization: C.N.R.S. et Université de Provence
Present Head: CREPCO: J.-P. Codol; Equipe 1: F. Orsini-Bouichou
Size of staff. Total: 10
Researchers: 2
Research activities: 50%
Educational research: less than 10%
Type of research: Adaptation des exercices "scolaires" au niveau de fonctionnement de l'enfant.

Studies and surveys in preparation: Projet de film: modes de présentation d'exercices à l'école maternelle. 1984–85. L'enfant et l'ordinateur (utilisation LOGO).

Equipe de recherche sur la première enfance

0180

Address: Université de Tours, 3, rue des Tanneurs, 37041 TOURS CEDEX
Year of creation: 1978
Parent Organization: Université de Tours, Département de psychologie
Present Head: Mme G. Boulanger-Balleyguier
Size of staff. Total: 4 — Full time: 2 — Part time: 2
Research activities: from 25% to 50%
Educational research: from 25% to 50%
Type of research: Recherche et développement.
Functional objectives of research: Préparation de cours et recueil de données scientifiques en vue de publication.
Monographs: Boulanger Balleyguier, G. Le caractère de l'enfant en fonction de son mode de garde pendant les premières années. 1982.
Studies and surveys in preparation: Enquête sur 'le consolateur': étude longitudinale. Etude sur le cycle tensionnel et son contrôle.

Greco "Didactique et acquisition des connaissances scientifiques"

0181

Address: 54, Boulevard Raspail, 75270 PARIS CEDEX 06
Year of creation: 1984
Parent Organization: C.N.R.S.
Present Head: Gérard Vergnaud, directeur de recherche au CNRS; Guy Brousseau et Michel Hulin, co-directeurs
Size of staff. Total: 80 — Full time: 6 — Part time: 74
Researchers: 80 — Full time: 6 — Part time: 74
Research activities: from 25% to 50%
Educational research: more than 50%
Type of research: Didactique et psychologie des mathématiques de la physique et de l'informatique; recherche fondamentale et appliquée.
Functional objectives of research: Améliorer l'enseignement, les programmes, et les méthodes d'enseignement.
Periodical publications: Recherches en didactiques des mathématiques (3/an).
Studies and surveys in preparation: Thèmes généraux des recherches: interactions entre mathématiques et physique dans la conceptualisation et la modélisation du réel par les élèves et les étudiants. L'espace comme objet d'étude en mathématiques, en physique et comme support des représentations symboliques. Signification et fonctionnement des concepts informatiques chez l'élève, en interaction avec la formation des connaissances mathématiques et physiques. Problèmes théoriques et méthodologiques de la didactique des mathématiques et de la physique.

Groupe de recherche sur l'éducation et l'emploi (GREE)

0182

Address: Université de Nancy II, 23, boulevard Albert 1er, 54000 NANCY
Year of creation: 1970
Parent Organization: Université de Nancy II
Present Head: Annie Vinokur

Size of staff. Total: 12 — Full time: 12
Researchers: 12 — Full time: 12
Research activities: more than 50%
Educational research: 50%
Type of research: Fondamentale et appliquée; théorique et empirique.
Monographs: Mehaut, P. Patronats, syndicats et formation: les Fonds d'assurance — formation. 1982. Mehaut, P.; Vinokur, A. Régulation de branche et gestion des rapports emploi — formation. In: Formation et emploi, Colloque de Toulouse. 1982. Lhotel, H.; Humbert, C. La destructuration du Pays-Haut: ses rapports à l'emploi et la formation et les perspectives démographiques. 1982. Mehaut, P., et al. Mission d'observation-évaluation du Plan 16–18 ans: méthodologie et premiers résultats. 1983. Mehaut, P., et al. Mission d'observation-évaluation du Plan 16–18 ans: analyse de la phase accueil. 1983. Gehin, J.P.; Mehaut, P. Evolution d'un appareil régional de formation continue: approche financière et méthodologique. 1981. Liste complète sur demande.
Studies and surveys in preparation: Insertion sociale et professionnelle des jeunes. Evaluation de la politique française de formation continue. Les flux d'étudiants dans l'université.

Groupe de recherches de sociologie de l'éducation

0183

Address: UER des sciences du comportement et de l'éducation, rue Lavoisier, 76130 MONT-SAINT-AIGNAN
Year of creation: 1975
Parent Organization: Université de Rouen
Present Head: Professeur Jacques Testanière, directeur du Département de sciences de l'éducation
Size of staff. Total: 10 — Full time: 4 — Part time: 6
Researchers: 10 — Full time: 4 — Part time: 6
Research activities: 50%
Educational research: more than 50%
Type of research: Recherche fondamentale.
Functional objectives of research: Obtention de doctorats; enseignement; publications.
Periodical publications: Publications dans les revues françaises.
Studies and surveys in preparation: Les classes populaires et l'école.

Institut de recherche sur l'économie de l'éducation (IREDU)

0184

Address: Faculté des sciences Mirande, B.P. 138, 21004 DIJON Cedex
Year of creation: 1971
Parent Organization: C.N.R.S.
Present Head: Prof. Jean-Claude Eicher
Size of staff. Total: 20 — Full time: 16 — Part time: 4
Researchers: 15 — Full time: 13 — Part time: 2
Research activities: more than 50%
Educational research: more than 50%
Type of research: Fondamentale et appliquée en économie de l'éducation.
Periodical publications: Cahiers de l'IREDU.
Monographs: Mingat, A.; Rasera, J.B. Enquête longitudinale, 3: après la première année d'études: réorientation, réussite, scolarité. 1981. Mingat, A.; Rapiau, M.T.

L'insertion professionnelle des apprentis en Bourgogne. 1982. Mingat, A.; Perrot, J. Les déterminants de l'orientation en classe de troisième. 1983. Giffard, A., Lacaille, C.; Paul, J.J. Analyse d'un système régional de formation professionnelle continue: le cas de la Bourgogne. 1983. Mingat, A. Evaluation analytique d'une action Z.E.P. au cours préparatoire. 1983. Liste complète sur demande.
Studies and surveys in preparation: Rapport scientifique 1983.

Institut de recherche sur l'enseignement des mathématiques

0185

Address: Domaine Universitaire, 45046 ORLEANS CEDEX
Year of creation: 1973
Parent Organization: Ministère de l'éducation nationale
Present Head: Rémy Charpentier
Researchers: 5
Research activities: from 25% to 50%
Educational research: from 25% to 50%
Type of research: Recherches sur les processus de construction des connaissances en situation scolaire; recherches en didactique des mathématiques.
Periodical publications: Soutien à la revue Recherches en didactique des mathématiques (4/an).
Monographs: PERPE SP (Perception par les élèves des relations professeurs-élèves), guide d'utilisation des questionnaires, guide d'analyse des résultats. Recherche et utilisation d'objectifs pédagogiques (sciences physiques: polymères et matières plastiques). Etude des locutions 'de plus que' 'de moins que' dans des choix opératoires. Acquisition des 'structures multiplicatives' dans le 1er cycle du second degré. Liste complète sur demande.
Studies and surveys in preparation: Rapport CIEAEM, Orléans, 1982. Rapport recherche A.D.I.; informatique et didactique des mathématiques.

Institut de recherche sur l'enseignement des mathématiques de Rouen (IREM)

0186

Address: Boîte postale 27, 76130 MONT-SAINT-AIGNAN
Year of creation: 1972
Parent Organization: Ministère de l'éducation nationale
Present Head: Alain Cardon
Size of staff. Total: 40 — Full time: 2 — Part time: 38
Researchers: 71 — Part time: 71
Research activities: from 25% to 50%
Type of research: Recherche fondamentale et recherches appliquées.
Functional objectives of research: Recherche fondamentale en matière d'enseignement des mathématiques et les recherches appliquées qui en découlent.
Monographs: Le raisonnement dans les situations-problèmes. 1981. Actes du colloque de Pacy-sur-Eure. Histoire et enseignement des mathématiques. 1982. Notion d'astronomie. En liaison avec les programmes de terminale A. 1983. La notion de fractions au C.M. Rapport sur une recherche action au cycle élémentaire. 1984.
Studies and surveys in preparation: Etude des objectifs, contenus et méthodes de l'enseignement des mathématiques pour les 10-16 ans dans différents pays. Pédagogie de l'enseignement des probabilités et statistiques. Experiences interdisciplinaires en analyse des données. Réalisation de didacticiels. Pédagogie de l'enseignement de l'informatique. Liste complète sur demande.

Institut national de recherche pédagogique (INRP)

0187

Address: 29, rue d'Ulm, 75230 PARIS Cedex 05
Year of creation: 1976
Parent Organization: Ministère de l'éducation nationale
Present Head: Francine Best
Researchers: 130
Research activities: 50%
Educational research: more than 50%
Type of research: Recherches fondamentales et appliquées.
Functional objectives of research: Amélioration des conditions de réussite scolaire; lutte contre les situations d'échec; amélioration de l'insertion professionnelle des jeunes par la rénovation et le développement des filières technologiques.
Periodical publications: Revue française de pédagogie (4/an). Histoire de l'éducation (4/an). Repères (3/an). Perspectives documentaires en sciences de l'éducation (3/an). Etapes de la recherche (2/an).
Monographs: Collections: Rapports de recherche. Cresas. Rencontres pédagogiques. Liste complète sur demande.
Studies and surveys in preparation: Parmi les grands thèmes de recherche: Articulation école-collège. Caractères de la fréquentation des collèges sous l'Ancien Régime. L'autonomie et l'unité d'un établissement dans sa région, facteurs d'harmonie dans les actions éducatives. Approches du fonctionnement des collèges dans la recherche "Etude du fonctionnement de l'établissement scolaire" Les objets matériels fabriqués comme support du développement cognitif et socio-affectif dans l'enseignement. Liste complète sur demande.

Institut national de recherches et d'applications pédagogiques (INRAP)

0188

Address: 2, rue des Champs Prévois, 21100 DIJON
Year of creation: 1966
Parent Organization: Ministère de l'agriculture
Present Head: Michel Méaille, ingénieur en chef d'agronomie
Size of staff. Total: 50 — Full time: 47 — Part time: 3
Researchers: 20 — Full time: 18 — Part time: 2
Research activities: 50%
Educational research: more than 50%
Type of research: Recherche appliquée.
Functional objectives of research: Etudes visant à l'adaptation permanente de l'enseignement agricole aux nécessités de la pédagogie et aux besoins du secteur agricole.
Periodical publications: Bulletin INRAP (4/an). INRAP Documentation trimestrielle.
Monographs: Thesaurus de l'enseignement agricole. 1983. L'évaluation (recueil de textes). 1982. Contribution à la formation des chefs d'exploitation agricole. 1981. Les qualifications professionnelles de l'agriculture. 1980.
Studies and surveys in preparation: La pédagogie de l'alternance. Elaboration et transmission des savoirs professionnels agricoles. Les unités de valeur en BTS.A. Les unités de contrôle capitalisables en CAP.A. Méthode d'études des systèmes dc production agricole. Education relative à l'environnement.

Institut national d'éducation populaire (I.N.E.P.) **0189**

Address: Val Flory, 78160 MARLY-LE-ROY
Year of creation: 1946
Parent Organization: Ministère de la jeunesse, des sports et des loisirs
Present Head: Henri Hutin
Size of staff. Total: 110 — Full time: 108 — Part time: 2
Researchers: 10 — Full time: 8 — Part time: 2
Research activities: from 25% to 50%
Educational research: from 10% to 25%
Type of research: Recherche fondamentale et recherches appliquées (études de conjoncture).
Functional objectives of research: Etablir une 'mémoire nationale' dans le domaine de l'éducation populaire, de l'éducation extrascolaire, des pratiques culturelles populaires.
Periodical publications: Les cahiers de l'animation (5/an).
Monographs: Les 'Documents de l'INEP'.
Studies and surveys in preparation: Etude de la socialisation des jeunes par utilisation du temps libre et du temps de non travail. L'éducation populaire et la télévision. Histoire de l'éducation populaire.

Institut national d'étude du travail et d'orientation professionnelle **0190**

Address: 41, rue Gay-Lussac, 75005 PARIS
Year of creation: 1928
Parent Organization: Conservatoire national des arts et métiers
Present Head: M. Reuchlin
Size of staff. Total: 52 — Full time: 50 — Part time: 2
Researchers: 12 — Full time: 11 — Part time: 1
Research activities: from 25% to 50%
Educational research: from 10% to 25%
Type of research: Psychologie différentielle; orientation; éducation.
Functional objectives of research: Recherche fondamentale; applications en éducation et en orientation.
Periodical publications: L'orientation scolaire et professionnelle.
Monographs: Bariaud, F. La genèse de l'humour chez l'enfant. 1983. Mullet, E. Les paramètres du jugement. 1982.
Studies and surveys in preparation: Aspects cognitifs de la maîtrise de la langue chez les élèves des collèges. Etude des rapports entre structures et fonctionnement dans les conduites cognitives. Etude différentielle inter et intra-sexes des opérations spatiales: liaison avec les opérations logico-mathématiques, les intérêts et l'éducation. Les processus cognitifs dans les tests d'intelligence. Les relations forme-contenu dans le raisonnement technique. Les processus intellectuels lors d'un apprentissage technologique. Liste complète sur demande.

Institut national du sport et de l'éducation physique (INSEP) **0191**

Address: 11, avenue du Tremblay, 75012 PARIS
Year of creation: 1975
Parent Organization: Ministère de la jeunesse, des sports et des loisirs
Present Head: Claude Bouquin, docteur en droit

Size of staff. Total: 427 — Full time: 406 — Part time: 22
Researchers: 50 — Full time: 35 — Part time: 15
Research activities: from 10% to 25%
Educational research: from 10% to 25%
Type of research: Appliquée, recherche et développement.
Functional objectives of research: Consignes d'enseignement: stratégies pédagogiques.
Periodical publications: Dossier documentaire (6/an). Motricité humaine (2/an).
Monographs: Bos, J.C. Les objectifs de l'éducation physique à l'école élémentaire. Fleurance, P. Apprentissage et procédures pédagogiques. Kusmierczyk, G. Adaptabilité et éducation physique (approche expérimentale avec des pré-adolescents de 12–13 ans). Margot, A. De l'école maternelle à l'école élémentaire: rupture ou continuité? Le cas de l'éducation physique. Liste complète sur demande.
Studies and surveys in preparation: Les stratégies pédagogiques et l'apprentissage moteur. Dynamique de l'action motrice dans les jeux sportifs. Emplois et formations du secteur sportif: marchés du travail et stratégies de formation. Les modèles sportifs diffusés par les média et reçus par les enfants. Liste complète sur demande.

Institut supérieur de pédagogie

0192

Address: 3, rue de l'Abbaye, 75006 PARIS
Year of creation: 1963
Parent Organization: Institut catholique de Paris
Present Head: Jean Furri
Size of staff. Total: 50 — Full time: 10 — Part time: 40
Researchers: 11 — Full time: 6 — Part time: 5
Research activities: from 25% to 50%
Educational research: more than 50%
Type of research: Recherche et développement.
Functional objectives of research: Améliorer la qualité des formations; aider à l'innovation dans les écoles.
Periodical publications: Les cahiers de l'I.S.P.
Studies and surveys in preparation: Les conditions à satisfaire pour que le recours à l'E.A.O.A. (système E.S.O.P.E.) se traduise par un gain pédagogique.

Laboratoire de pédagogie expérimentale de l'Université Lyon II

0193

Address: 16 quai Claude Bernard, 69007 LYON
Year of creation: 1956
Parent Organization: Université Lyon II
Present Head: Professeur Guy Avanzini
Type of research: Recherches fondamentales et appliquées.
Functional objectives of research: Améliorer la pratique éducative, surtout par des apports de didactique expérimentale.
Periodical publications: In: Bulletin de la Société Alfred Binet et Théodore Simon.

Laboratoire de psychologie et de sociologie de l'éducation, Centre de recherche et de formation en éducation, (CREFED)

0194

Address: Ecole normale supérieure de Saint-Cloud, Parc de Saint-Cloud, Grille d'Honneur, 92211 ST-CLOUD Cédex

Year of creation: 1968
Parent Organization: Ecole normale supérieure de Saint-Cloud
Present Head: Yves Guyot
Size of staff. Total: 6
Researchers: 5
Research activities: 50%
Educational research: 50%
Type of research: Recherches fondamentales et appliquées.
Functional objectives of research: Compréhension et maîtrise des relations enseignants–enseignés et des situations éducatives.
Periodical publications: N'en publie pas.
Monographs: Obstacles à la communication dans l'enseignement supérieur. Réussite et échec scolaire. Insertion professionnelle des jeunes. Objectifs et curricula d'enseignement et théorie de l'éducation. Langage et communications sociales chez l'enfant. Psychosociologie de la recherche. Les communications non verbales en situation inter-spécifique. Liste complète sur demande.
Studies and surveys in preparation: Acquisition des règles d'usage social du langage. Développements récent de la sociologie de l'éducation en Grande Bretagne. Adaptation aux populations africaines d'épreuve de développement mental et de tests de facteur 'G'. Communications non verbales et paraverbales en situation d'autorité.

Laboratoire de psychopédagogie de l'Université de Caen

0195

Address: Palais de l'Université, 14032 CAEN CEDEX
Year of creation: 1958
Parent Organization: Université de Caen
Present Head: Gaston Mialaret
Size of staff. Total: 29 — Full time: 9 — Part time: 20
Researchers: 20 — Part time: 20
Research activities: more than 50%
Educational research: more than 50%
Type of research: Recherche fondamentale et appliquée.
Functional objectives of research: Facteurs de la réussite scolaire; formation des enseignants; technologie de l'éducation.
Periodical publications: Les sciences de l'éducation — Pour l'ère nouvelle.
Monographs: H. Wallon.

Laboratoire de recherches sur l'acquisition et la pathologie du langage chez l'enfant — ERA 357

0196

Address: Université René Descartes, UER de linguistique, 12 rue Cujas, 75005 PARIS
Year of creation: 1972
Parent Organization: C.N.R.S.
Present Head: Fréderic François
Size of staff. Total: 8 — Full time: 4 — Part time: 4
Researchers: 3 — Full time: 3
Research activities: more than 50%
Educational research: from 25% to 50%
Type of research: Fondamentale.
Monographs: François, F. Ebauche d'une dialogique.

Studies and surveys in preparation: Communication non verbale. Le dialogue chez l'enfant. Le récit chez l'enfant. La conscience linguistique chez l'enfant.

Laboratoire des techniques et méthodes modernes d'éducation. ex Centre audio-visuel

0197

Address: Grille d'Honneur, Parc de Saint-Cloud, 92211 SAINT-CLOUD
Year of creation: 1947
Parent Organization: Ecole normale supérieure de Saint-Cloud
Present Head: Robert Lefranc
Size of staff. Total: 28
Researchers: 8
Research activities: more than 50%
Educational research: more than 50%
Type of research: Fondamentale et appliquée.
Functional objectives of research: Information pour l'innovation des organismes éducatifs français, étrangers et internationaux.
Periodical publications: Aucune.
Monographs: Rapports de recherche publiés par le laboratoire (liste sur demande). Livres et articles dans revues.
Studies and surveys in preparation: Historique des enseignements à distance. La méthodologie multi-media dans les enseignements supérieurs à distance. Les modalités d'étude et d'apprentissage des étudiants du télé-enseignement universitaire. Analyse de contenu des composantes audio-visuelles des systèmes d'enseignement supérieur à distance. Production expérimentale de cassettes sonores destinées au télé-enseignement universitaire. Les applications des nouvelles technologies de communication aux enseignements supérieurs à distance.

Laboratoire interuniversitaire de recherche sur l'enseignement des sciences physiques et de la technologie (L.I.R.E.S.P.T.)

0198

Address: Université Paris 7, Tour 23, 2, place Lussieu, 75251 PARIS CEDEX 05
Year of creation: 1971
Parent Organization: Université Paris 7
Present Head: Professeur Goery Delacote
Size of staff. Total: 19 — Full time: 14
Researchers: 17 — Full time: 12 — Part time: 5
Research activities: more than 50%
Educational research: more than 50%
Type of research: Recherches fondamentales et appliquées.
Functional objectives of research: Le laboratoire est chargé de quelques recherches demandées et financées par le Ministère de l'éducation nationale.
Periodical publications: European journal of science education (4/an).
Monographs: Articles et contributions diverses: liste sur demande.
Studies and surveys in preparation: Recherches sur les curriculums: formation des maîtres et expérimentation du module électronique; objectifs de l'initiation aux sciences et techniques; etc. Recherches sur les représentations et l'apprentissage: les concepts de chaleur et température; l'état gazeux et le concept de pression; etc. Recherches sur la résolution de problèmes. Innovation: contrôle au 2e cycle et épreuves du baccalauréat; micro-ordinateurs; etc.

Recherches coopératives en didactique de la chimie (ReCoDiC)

0199

Address: Chimie XIII, Faculté des sciences, 40, avenue du Recteur Pineau, F 86022 POITIERS CEDEX
Year of creation: 1976
Parent Organization: Réseau interuniversitaire (et international) — Subvention DESUP — Minstère de l'éducation nationale
Present Head: Maurice Gomel
Size of staff. Total: 800 — Part time: 800
Researchers: 200 — Part time: 200
Research activities: less than 10%
Educational research: more than 50%
Type of research: Appliquée et recherche et développement.
Functional objectives of research: Améliorer l'enseignement universitaire de la chimie.
Periodical publications: Bulletin général ReCoDiC informations. Bulletins de liaisons des Groupes ReCoDiC.
Monographs: Gomel, M. La didactique de la chimie: mythes et réalités 25 ans après. 1983. Liste complète sur demande.
Studies and surveys in preparation: Chimie universitaire et information du grand public. Chimie et enseignement médical. Didactique de la chimie théorique. Didactique de la thermodynamique. Docimologie–enseignement par objectif. Enseignement assisté par multimédia. Enseignement assisté par ordinateur. Liste complète sur demande.

Séminaire Gournay

0200

Address: Faculté des sciences économiques, 7, place Hoche, 35000 RENNES
Parent Organization: Laboratoire d'économie de l'éducation de l'Université de Rennes
Present Head: Philippe Cazenave
Size of staff. Total: 4 — Full time: 3 — Part time: 1
Researchers: 3 — Part time: 3
Research activities: 50%
Educational research: more than 50%
Type of research: Appliquée.
Functional objectives of research: Analyse économique de l'enseignement supérieur en France.
Periodical publications: Cahiers du CREFAUR.
Monographs: Ressources et dépenses des étudiants en 1978–79. Répartition des subventions de fonctionnement liées à l'activité pédagogique dans les universités françaises en 1979–80 (hors IUT et secteur santée).
Studies and surveys in preparation: Zones d'attraction des villes universitaires françaises.

Service d'études et de recherches appliquées (SERA), Association nationale pour la formation professionnelle des adultes (AFPA)

0201

Address: 13, place de Villiers, 93108 MONTREUIL CEDEX
Year of creation: 1966
Parent Organization: Ministère de la formation professionnelle
Present Head: M. Guy Metais
Researchers: 14 — Full time: 12 — Part time: 2
Research activities: less than 10%

Ontario

Library Reference Request

Requestor's Name

From

☐ Ministry

☐ Ont. Gov't:

☐ Other:

Nature of Request

Directory of educational research institutions

UNESCO

Time Taken

Request

☐ Answered in full ☐ Referred to:

Initials	Date

19 -0490 (2/82) Formerly 09-2370

Educational research: more than 50%
Type of research: Appliquée.
Periodical publications: Objectif formation (revue de l'AFPA). Bulletin bibliographique (SERA-Documentation).
Studies and surveys in preparation: Etudes concernant la formation professionnelle, formation individualisée, formation modulaire, évaluation de la formation, enseignement assisté par ordinateur.

UER de didactique des disciplines (mathématiques, physique, biologie, histoire et géographie, français, anglais)

0202

Address: Couloir 45-46, 1er étage, Université Paris VII, 2, Place Jussieu, PARIS 5e
Year of creation: 1969
Parent Organization: Université de Paris VII
Present Head: André Gauthier, Professeur de linguistique et didactique des langues
Size of staff. Total: 15 — Full time: 4 — Part time: 11
Researchers: 12 — Full time: 2 — Part time: 10
Research activities: more than 50%
Educational research: more than 50%
Type of research: Théorie de la pratique (enseignement); recherche et développement; enseignement assisté par ordinateur.
Functional objectives of research: Amélioration de l'enseignement dans les diverses disciplines — DEA et thèses de 3e cycle.
Monographs: Publications dans diverses revues spécialisées. Thèses de didactique.
Studies and surveys in preparation: Echecs scolaires en mathématiques.

Unité d'enseignement et de recherche de sciences de l'éducation

0203

Address: 28 rue Serpente, 75006 PARIS
Year of creation: 1967
Parent Organization: Université René Descartes (Paris V)
Present Head: Madame Viviane Isambert-Jamati, Professeur à l'U.E.R. de sciences de l'éducation
Size of staff. Total: 49 — Full time: 38 — Part time: 11
Researchers: 44 — Full time: 16 — Part time: 28
Research activities: 50%
Educational research: more than 50%
Type of research: Appliquée, recherche et développement.
Functional objectives of research: Satisfaire partiellement aux conditions d'obtention d'un grade; préparation de cours; fournir des prestations à l'administration de l'éducation et de la recherche.
Periodical publications: Thèses de sciences de l'éducation (Recueil de titres soutenus en sciences de l'éducation dans les universités françaises). (Parution annuelle ronéotypée).
Monographs: Langouet, G. Technologie de l'éducation et démocratisation de l'enseignement: méthodes pédagogiques et classes sociales. 1982. Mylonas, T. La reproduction des classes sociales à travers les mécanismes scolaires en Grèce. 1982. Tanguy, L.; Kieffer, A. Ecole et production dans les deux Allemagnes. 1983. Chobaux, J.; Segré, M. L'enseignement du français à l'école élémentaire: quelle réforme? 1981. Le Than Khoi. L'éducation comparée. 1981. Liste complète sur

demande.

Studies and surveys in preparation: Recherches dans les domaines suivants : psychologie de l'apprentissage, psychosociologie de l'éducation, sociologie et histoire de l'éducation, économie de l'éducation, pédagogie des adultes, éducation populaire et diffusion des connaissances scientifiques.

GERMAN DR

Institut für Didaktik

0204

Translation: Research Institute of Didactics
Address: Otto-Grotewohl-Str. 11, 1080 BERLIN
Year of creation: 1970
Parent Organization: Academy of Pedagogical Sciences of the GDR
Research activities: more than 50%
Educational research: more than 50%
Type of research: Basic and applied research.
Functional objectives of research: Theoretical and practical problems of didactics and teaching methods in general education; servicing the educational administration; preparation of courses.
Periodical publications: None issued.
Monographs: Drews, U.; Fuhrmann, E. Fragen und Antworten zur Gestaltung einer guten Unterrichtsstunde. 1980, 2. Auflage 1981. Weck, H. Bewertung und Zensierung. In: Ratschläge für Lehrer. 1981. Faust, H., et al. Probleme der Könnensentwicklung im Unterricht. In: Beiträge zur Pägagogik. Band 28, 1982. Becher, J.; Scheibner, E. Wie arbeite ich im Unterricht mit Problemstellungen? In: Ratschläge für Lehrer. 1983. Drews, U. Zum dialektischen Charakter des Unterrichtsprozesses in der allgemeinbildenden Schule. In: Beiträge zur Pädagogik. 1983.
Studies and surveys in preparation: Problems of the pupil's activity. Problems of teacher's activity in the educational process.

Institut für Leitung und Organisation des Volksbildungswesens

0205

Translation: Research Institute for Management and Organization of the Education System
Address: Friedrich-Ebert-Str. 4/7, 1500 POTSDAM
Parent Organization: Academy of Pedagogical Sciences of the GDR
Present Head: Prof. Dr. Günter Wilms
Research activities: from 10% to 25%
Educational research: from 10% to 25%
Type of research: Basic and applied research.
Functional objectives of research: Management and organization of education systems; servicing the educational administration.
Periodical publications: Beiheft für Leiter im Volksbildungswesen (in connection with the journal Pädagogik (4/yr)).
Monographs: Grundlagen und Grundfragen der staatlichen Leitung der Volksbildung (engl. und portug.) 1980. Qualifizierung von Schulräten und leitenden Kadern der Volksbildung am Institut für Leitung und Organisation des Volksbildungswesens

Potsdam. 1981. Zur Theorie und Praxis der Leitung der Volksbildung. 1982. Die Lebenskraft des Marxismus-Leninismus und seine grundlegende Bedeutung für die Leitung gesellschaftlicher Prozesse in den Schulen. 1983.

Institut für mathematischen und naturwissenschaftlichen Unterricht

0206

Translation: Research Institute of Mathematics and Scientific Education
Address: Otto-Grotewohl-Str. 11, 1080 BERLIN
Year of creation: 1970
Parent Organization: Academy of Pedagogical Sciences of the GDR
Research activities: more than 50%
Educational research: more than 50%
Type of research: Basic and applied research.
Functional objectives of research: Improvement of content and methods in mathematics and scientific education; theoretical problems in this field; servicing the educational administration; preparation of courses.
Periodical publications: Mathematik in der Schule (12/yr). Physik in der Schule (12/yr). Chemie in der Schule (12/yr). Biologie in der Schule (12/yr).
Monographs: Some articles; list on request.
Studies and surveys in preparation: Teacher's aid for mathematics and science education.

Institut für Oekonomie und Planung des Volksbildungswesens

0207

Translation: Research Institute for Economics and Planning of the Education System
Address: Schulstr. 29, 1100 BERLIN
Year of creation: 1970
Parent Organization: Academy of Pedagogical Sciences of the GDR
Type of research: Basic and applied research.
Functional objectives of research: Educational economics and planning; contents, methodology and methods of education.
Periodical publications: None issued.
Monographs: List on request.

Institut für Pädagogische Psychologie

0208

Translation: Research Institute of Pedagogical Psychology
Address: Böcklinstr. 1-5, 1035 BERLIN
Year of creation: 1970
Parent Organization: Academy of Pedagogical Sciences of the GDR
Research activities: more than 50%
Educational research: more than 50%
Type of research: Basic and applied research.
Functional objectives of research: Theoretical and methodological problems of pedagogical psychology; servicing the educational administration.
Monographs: Kossakowski, A. Erziehung älterer Schüler — psychologisch betrachtet. 1983. Kossakowski, A.; Obuchowski, K. Progress in psychology of personality. 1983. Lompscher, J. Psychische Besonderheiten leistungsschwacher Schüler und Bedingungen ihrer Veränderung. 1978. Ausbildung der Lerntätigkeit bei Schülern. 1982. Lompscher, J. Persönlichkeitsentwicklung in der Lerntätigkeit. 1984. Witzlack, G.

Verhaltensbewertung und Schülerbeurteilung. 1982. Complete list on request.

Institut für polytechnische Bildung

0209

Translation: Research Institute of Polytechnical Education
Address: Otto-Grotewohl-Str. 11, 1080 BERLIN
Year of creation: 1970
Parent Organization: Academy of Pedagogical Sciences of the GDR
Research activities: more than 50%
Type of research: Basic and applied research.
Functional objectives of research: Improvement of content and methods in polytechnical education; theoretical problems in this field; servicing the educational administration; preparation of courses.
Periodical publications: Polytechnische Bildung und Erziehung (12/yr).
Monographs: Wettstädt, G. Combining instruction with productive work at general schools in the GDR. 1983. Some articles: list on request.
Studies and surveys in preparation: Teacher's aid for polytechnical education (forms 7 to 10).

Institut für Unterrichtsmittel

0210

Translation: Research Institute of School Equipment and Technical Aids in Education
Address: Krausenstr. 8, 1080 BERLIN
Year of creation: 1970
Parent Organization: Academy of Pedagogical Sciences of the GDR
Research activities: from 25% to 50%
Educational research: more than 50%
Type of research: Basic and applied research; research and development.
Functional objectives of research: Elaboration of rules for school equipment, materials and technical aids for the educational process; servicing the educational administration.
Periodical publications: None published.
Monographs: List on request.

Pädagogische Hochschule

0211

Translation: Pedagogical University
Address: Kröllwitzerstrasse 44, 402 HALLE/Saale
Year of creation: 1953
Type of research: Applied and basic research.
Functional objectives of research: Training of "Diplomlehrer", R&D in pedagogics and methodology.
Monographs: Correlation between pedagogical and scientific training of teachers. The role of methodology in teacher training. The importance of polytechnical education for the comprehensive education of children.

Zentralinstitut für Berufsbildung der DDR **0212**

Translation: Central Institute of Vocational Education of the GDR
Address: Reinholdt-Huhn-Str. 5, Postfach 1292, 1086 BERLIN
Year of creation: 1950
Parent Organization: State Secretariat of Vocational Education
Present Head: Prof. Dr. Rudolph
Size of staff. Total: 150
Researchers: 100
Research activities: more than 50%
Educational research: more than 50%
Type of research: Basic and applied research.
Functional objectives of research: All aspects of vocational education.
Periodical publications: Forschung der sozialistischen Berufsbildung. Beiträge zur Berufsbildung.
Monographs: List on request.

GERMANY FR

Arbeitsbereich Erwachsenenbildung, Institut für Erziehungswissenschaft II, Universität Tübingen **0213**

Translation: Division of Adult Education and Continuing Education, Institute of Educational Studies, University of Tübingen
Address: Holzmarkt 7, 74 TUEBINGEN
Year of creation: 1979
Parent Organization: University of Tübingen
Present Head: Prof. Dr. Günther Dohmen
Size of staff. Total: 8 — Full time: 4 — Part time: 4
Researchers: 4 — Full time: 4
Research activities: from 25% to 50%
Type of research: Basic research.
Periodical publications: Prof. Dr. G. Dohmen is co-editor of "Unterrichtswissenschaft", München.
Monographs: Dohmen, G. Several long articles in omnibus-volumes and periodicals. Vogel, N. Professionalisierung in der dänischen Erwachsenenbildung. 1981. Vogel, N., (Mithrsg.) Lernort Heimvolkshochschule.
Studies and surveys in preparation: Research on educational needs of people without jobs, psychological and educational conditions and prerequisites. Comparative study on Scandinavian adult education and the folk high school. Adult education in Germany 1919-1933. Evaluatory research survey on "Zeitungskolleg" (open learning by newspapers).

Arbeitsgruppe Empirische mathematikdidaktische Forschung **0214**

Translation: Centre of Empirical Research in Mathematical Education
Address: Universität Osnabrück, Fachbereich Mathematik, Albrechtstr. 28, 4500 OSNABRUECK

Year of creation: 1974
Parent Organization: Universität Osnabrück, Fachbereich Mathematik
Present Head: Prof. Dr. E. Cohors-Fresenborg
Size of staff. Total: 12 — Full time: 8 — Part time: 4
Researchers: 9 — Full time: 8 — Part time: 1
Research activities: 50%
Educational research: from 25% to 50%
Type of research: Basic, applied, research and development.
Functional objectives of research: Basic research: mathematical abilities; cognitive styles in mathematical thinking; computers in mathematics education; curriculum development.
Periodical publications: Osnabrücker Schriften zur Mathematik: Reihe, D. Mathematikdidaktische Manuskripte: Reihe, U. Materialien zum Mathematikunterricht (some booklets are available in English translation).
Monographs: Sommer, N; Viet, U. Leistungsdifferenzierung im Mathematikunterricht der Sekundarstufe I. 1981. Sommer, N. Fehleranalyse als empirische Forschungsmethode der Mathematikdidaktik: Dissertation. 1982. Schmidt, V. Der Begriffsbildungsprozess im Mathematikunterricht. 1983.
Studies and surveys in preparation: Underachievement in mathematics. Algorithmic thinking in mathematics curriculum. Cognitive styles of algorithmic thinking at secondary level. Intercultural studies in learning mathematics.

Arbeitsgruppe Internationale Forschung in der Lehrerbildung

0215

Translation: Centre for International Research in Teacher Education
Address: c/o Universität Osnabrück, Postfach 4469, 4500 OSNABRÜECK
Year of creation: 1983
Parent Organization: Universität Osnabrück
Present Head: Professor Dr. K. Hartong
Size of staff. Total: 5 — Full time: 5
Researchers: 4 — Full time: 4
Research activities: 50%
Educational research: more than 50%
Type of research: Applied, R&D (in the field of teacher education); basic (in the field of maths education).
Functional objectives of research: Research cooperation with educational institutions of Third World countries in the field of special didactics (maths) and innovation in teacher education/further education.
Periodical publications: None.
Monographs: Schepers, R. Beratung in der entwicklungspolitischen Zusammenarbeit. 1978. Teacher education and training as objects of international educational research: the case of Indonesia, Yogyakarta. 1984 (also in German). Escuela y formación docente en communidades indigenas del Chaco Central (Paraguay). 1982 (also in German). Bericht über die Gastprofessoren an der East China Normal University. 1983.
Studies and surveys in preparation: Comparative/intercultural studies on mathematical thinking of children. Comparative education and maths education in cooperation with the East China Normal University, Shanghai. Educational research and teaching methods in teacher education in cooperation with teacher institutions in Indonesia and Paraguay.

Arbeitsgruppe 'Wissenschafts- und Hochschulforschung', Fachbereich Erziehungswissenschaften, Universität Frankfurt

0216

Translation: Research Group 'Research on Science and Higher Education'
Address: Senckenberganlage 15, Universität Frankfurt, 6000 FRANKFURT M.
Year of creation: 1982
Parent Organization: Universität Frankfurt
Present Head: Professor Dr. Egon Becker
Size of staff. Total: 8 — Full time: 4 — Part time: 4
Researchers: 7 — Full time: 4 — Part time: 3
Research activities: more than 50%
Educational research: from 10% to 25%
Type of research: Basic, applied.
Functional objectives of research: Historical and systematic research in the field of history, philosophy and theory of science and of higher education.
Periodical publications: Hochschuldidaktische Forschungsberichte (co-editor).
Monographs: Becker, E. Curriculare Sackgassen: eine Analyse theoretischer Probleme der Curriculumforschung und curricularer Planungsstrategien. 1980. Becker, E.; Klüver, J. Hochschulkrise und Studienberatung. In: Rieck, W., Hrsg. Studienberatung. 1981. Becker, E. Hrsg. Reflexionsprobleme der Hochschulforschung. Beiträge zur Theorie- und Methodendiskussion. 1983. Complete list on request.
Studies and surveys in preparation: Social history of social science. Constitutional theory of natural science. Ecological education.

Arnold-Bergstrasser-Institut für kulturwissenschaftliche Forschung (e.V.)

0217

Translation: Arnold-Bergstrasser-Institut for Socio-political Research
Address: Windausstrasse 16, 7800 FREIBURG
Year of creation: 1960
Present Head: Prof. Dr. Dieter Oberndörfer; Prof. Dr. Theodor Hanf; Dr. Herbert Weiland
Size of staff. Total: 35 — Full time: 26 — Part time: 9
Researchers: 15 — Full time: 11 — Part time: 4
Research activities: more than 50%
Educational research: from 25% to 50%
Type of research: Basic (30%), applied(70%).
Periodical publications: Aktuelle Informationspapiere (AIP).
Monographs: Goetze, D.; Weiland, H., Hrsg. Soziokulturelle Implikationen technologischer Wandlungsprozesse. 1983. Dias, P.V. Erziehung, Identitätsbildung und Reproduktion in Zaire. 1979. Schmitt, K. Politische Erziehung in der DDR. 1979. Hundsdörfer, V. Die politische Aufgabe des Bildungswesens in Tanzania: Entwicklungen von der Arusha-Deklaration 1967 zur Musoma-Deklaration 1975. 1977. Complete list on request.
Studies and surveys in preparation: Significance of cultural and religious factors as determinants of attitudes to development (with special regard to education). Informal youth training. Cultural dimension in development policies.

Deutsches Institut für Fernstudien an der Universität Tübingen

0218

Translation: German Institute for Distance Studies at the Unversity of Tübingen
Address: Wöhrdestr. 8, 7400 TUEBINGEN
Year of creation: 1967
Parent Organization: Universität Tübingen
Present Head: Prof. Dr. Karlheinz Rebel
Size of staff. Total: 127 — Full time: 122 — Part time: 11
Researchers: 85 — Full time: 83 — Part time: 4
Research activities: more than 50%
Educational research: more than 50%
Type of research: Research and development.
Functional objectives of research: Preparation of courses; basic research of teaching-learning problems; evaluation.
Monographs: Mandl, H.; Stein, N.L; Trabasso, T., eds. Learning and comprehension of text. 1984. Schnotz, W. On the influence of text organization on learning outcomes. In: Rickheit, G.; Bock, M., eds. Psycholinguistics studies in language processing. 1983. Schnotz, W. Zur Diagnose von Verstehensleistungen. In: Kornmann, R.; Meister, H.; Schlee J., Hrsg. Förderungsdiagnostik in der Pädagogik. 1983. Fischer, P.M.; Mandl, H. Metakognitive Regulation von Textverarbeitungsprozessen: Aspekte und Probleme des Zusammenhangs von metakognitiven Selbstaussagen und konkretem Leitstungsverhalten. 1981. Complete list on request.
Studies and surveys in preparation: Learning with texts. Learning aids for the independent study of adults. Evaluation. Learning by dialogue with computers.

Deutsches Institut für internationale pädagogische Forschung

0219

Translation: German Institute for International Educational Research
Address: Schloss Str. 29, 6000 FRANKFURT/Main 90
Year of creation: 1950
Parent Organization: The Institute is an independent body
Present Head: Prof. Dr. Hermann Avenarius
Size of staff. Total: 72 — Full time: 72
Researchers: 41 — Full time: 41
Research activities: more than 50%
Educational research: more than 50%
Type of research: Basic and applied research.
Functional objectives of research: Develop interdisciplinarity in educational research; establish international contacts on education; improve the quality and content of curricula on the basis of research results.
Periodical publications: Zeitschrift für Erziehungswissenschaft und Sozialforschung.
Monographs: List on request.
Studies and surveys in preparation: Comparative studies on education and society in different fields of research (amongst others, sociology, economics, administration) and various regions (Eastern Europe, Africa, South-East Asia).

Deutsches Jugendinstitut

0220

Translation: German Youth Institute
Address: Saarstr. 7, 8000 MUNCHEN 40
Year of creation: 1961
Parent Organization: Bundesministerium für Jugend, Familie, Gesundheit (Federal Ministry for Youth, Family, Health)
Present Head: Dr. Böhnisch
Size of staff. Total: 140 — Full time: 130 — Part time: 10
Researchers: 70
Research activities: more than 50%
Educational research: from 10% to 25%
Type of research: Basic research; research and development.
Monographs: Research reports. List on request.
Studies and surveys in preparation: Numerous research projects in the areas of preprimary education, youth policy and young adult socialization.

Didaktisches Zentrum

0221

Translation: Centre for Didactics
Address: Johann Wolfgang Goethe-Universität, Senckenberganlage 15, 6000 FRANKFURT AM MAIN 1
Year of creation: 1971
Parent Organization: Johann Wolfgang Goethe-Universität
Present Head: Prof. Dr. H.D. Schlosser
Size of staff. Total: 26 — Full time: 23 — Part time: 3
Researchers: 15 — Full time: 15
Research activities: 50%
Educational research: 50%
Type of research: Applied, research and development.
Functional objectives of research: Improving service and development in several specific fields on account of research (school affairs, German as a foreign language, media, distance study and continuing education affairs).
Periodical publications: DZ — Schriftenreihe. Impulse.
Studies and surveys in preparation: Dealing with school affairs. German as a foreign language. Educational media. Distance study and continuing education affairs. List on request.

Diplomstudiengang Erziehungswissenschaft

0222

Translation: Postgraduated Studies in Educational Science
Address: Universität Bremen-FB-12, Bibliothekstrasse, 28 BREMEN
Year of creation: 1971
Parent Organization: Universität Bremen
Present Head: Professor Dr. Leo Roth
Size of staff. Total: 8 — Full time: 8
Researchers: 8 — Full time: 8
Research activities: from 25% to 50%
Educational research: from 25% to 50%
Type of research: Research and development.

Functional objectives of research: Research on school and instruction; political counselling based on empirical research; comparative educational research.
Periodical publications: none.
Monographs: See the annoted bibliography of "Forschungsberichte der Universität Bremen, Band 1-4 (Research documentation, Vol. I-IV).
Studies and surveys in preparation: Will be documented in Forschungsberich der Universität Bremen, Band 5 (Research documentation, Vol. V).

Erziehungswissenschaftliche Hochschule Rheinland-Pfalz

0223

Translation: University of Educational Sciences (Pedagogics) of Rhineland-Palatinate
Address: Grosse Bleiche 60-62, PB 1864, 6500 MAINZ
Year of creation: 1969
Present Head: Prof. Dr. phil. Franz Fippinger, President of University
Size of staff. Total: 362 — Full time: 343 — Part time: 19
Researchers: 238 — Full time: 238
Research activities: 50%
Educational research: more than 50%
Type of research: Research and development.
Functional objectives of research: Servicing the educational administration.
Periodical publications: Pressemitteilungen der Erziehungswissenschaftlichen Hochschule Rheinland-Pfalz. Personal- und Vorlesungsverzeichnis der Erziehungswissenschaftlichen Hochschule Rheinland-Pfalz. Jahresbericht des Präsidenten der Erziehungswissenschaftlichen Hochschule Rheinland-Pfalz.
Monographs: Complete list in: Jahresbericht des Präsidenten der EWH Rheinland-Pfalz für das Jahr 1982.
Studies and surveys in preparation: MUD — Mathematik-Unterrichts-Dokumentation. Theoretisch/empirische Ermittlung und Konzeption von Nutzungsmöglichkeiten der 'Neuen Medien' zur Förderung der sozio-kulturellen Kommunikationskompetenz und Integration. For complete list see above.

Erziehungswissenschaftliches Institut der Universität Düsseldorf

0224

Translation: Institute for Pedagogics
Address: Universität Düsseldorf, Universitätsstr. 1, 4000 DÜESSELDORF
Year of creation: 1969
Parent Organization: Universität Düsseldorf
Present Head: Prof. Dr. Christine Schwarzer
Size of staff. Total: 35 — Full time: 32 — Part time: 3
Researchers: 21 — Full time: 21
Research activities: from 25% to 50%
Type of research: Basic, research and development.
Functional objectives of research: Philosophy of education; didactics; theory of school; educational diagnostics; educational counselling; inservice training; applied educational research; history of education.
Monographs: Luth, C. Gesamthochschulpolitik in der Bundesrepublik Deutschland. 1983. Steuber, H. Grundlagen der Methodologie der Didaktik. 1981. Steuber, H. Methodologie der Didaktik: ein Versuch. 1982. Schwarzer, C. Pädagogische Diagnostik. 1982. Schwarzer, C. Gestörte Lernprozesse. 1982. Koblitz, J. Leistungserwartungen von Lehrern und die Lehrer-Schüler-Interaktion: eine

empirische Untersuchung aus der Sicht sozial-kognitiver Lerntheorie. 1981. Posse, N. Selbststeuerung: Theoretische Analysen, Diagnose und pädagogisch-therapeutische Förderungskonzepte. Diss. Univ. Düsseldorf. 1982.

Studies and surveys in preparation: Cross-cultural diagnostics in anxiety. Critical life events and coping. Educational strategies for diabetic patients. Computerized adaptive testing. Diagnosing text comprehension based on psycho-linguistic theories. Zur Relation von Arbeit und Bildung.

Fach Erziehungswissenschaft im Fachbereich 2 der Universität-Gesamthochschule — Paderborn

0225

Translation: Faculty 2 of the University of Paderborn (Education)
Address: Warburger Str. 100, Postfach 1621, 479 PADERBORN
Year of creation: 1972
Parent Organization: University of Paderborn
Present Head: Prof. Dr. Gerhard Tulodziecki
Size of staff. Total: 22 — Full time: 19 — Part time: 3
Researchers: 17 — Full time: 17
Research activities: from 25% to 50%
Educational research: more than 50%
Type of research: Basic research, applied research, research and development.
Functional objectives of research: Improving educational practice.
Periodical publications: Publications in different educational journals.
Monographs: A list of publications is being prepared and may be requested later.

Fachbereich 22, Erziehungs- und Unterrichtswissenschaften

0226

Translation: Faculty for Educational and Instructional Sciences
Address: Franklinstrasse 28/29, 1000 BERLIN 10
Year of creation: 1980
Parent Organization: Technische Universität Berlin
Present Head: Professor Dr.-Ing. Carl-Hellmut Wagemann
Size of staff. Total: 110 — Full time: 110
Researchers: 90 — Full time: 90
Research activities: 50%
Educational research: more than 50%
Type of research: Basic and applied.
Functional objectives of research: Diverse, e.g.: fulfilment of degree requirements (doctoral dissertation, 'Habilitation'); evaluation of pedagogical experiments ('Modellversuche'); extension of scientific knowledge; preparation of courses.
Monographs: Bamme, A.; Holling, E. Die Alltagswirklichkeit des Berufsschullehrers. 1982. Boye, H. Die Kinder des Elfenbeinturms. 1982. Kaufmann-Sauerland, L.; Collingro, P. Berufliche Bildung ausländischer Jugendlicher. Tub-Dokumentation Weiterbildung, Heft 8. 1982. Northemann, W.U.A. Neue didaktische Modelle, Band 1, 2 und 3 (Bd.1: Frauen; Bd.2: Verbrauchererziehung; Bd.3: Frieden). 1981–1982. Preuss-Lausitz, U. Projekt Planung und Realisierung integrativer Grundschulen im Bezirk Schoeneberg zur Vermeidung der Ueberweisung in Sonderschulen. 1980–1982. Schonig, B.; du Bois-Reymond, M. Lehrerlebensgeschichten. Lehrerinnen und Lehrer aus Berlin und Leiden (Holland) erzählen. 1982. Weber, N.H. Frieden: Theoretische Ansätze und didaktische Vorschläge zur Friedenserziehung in Grundschule und

Sekundarstufe I. Neue didaktische Modelle, Bd.3. 1982.
Studies and surveys in preparation: At the moment, it is not possible to give a list of titles in preparation.

Fachhochschule für Sozialarbeit und Sozialpädagogik Berlin

0227

Address: Karl-Schrader-Str. 6, 1000 BERLIN 30
Year of creation: 1971
Parent Organization: Senator für Wissenschaft und Forschung, Berlin
Present Head: Prof. Dr. Hans Jochen Brauns
Size of staff. Total: 64 — Full time: 60 — Part time: 4
Researchers: 49 — Full time: 49
Research activities: from 25% to 50%
Educational research: from 25% to 50%
Type of research: Applied, research and development; field survey (panel); qualitative; longitudinal; process (action) research.
Functional objectives of research: All fields of social work practice.
Monographs: Danzig, H.; Kesting, H.; Werder, L. von. Entwicklung eines Curriculums für den Bereich der Fort- und Weiterbildung von Sozialarbeitern und Sozialpädagogen. 1982. Karberg, W. Untersuchung zur Effizienz von sozialpädagogischer Methodik in der Gemeinwesenarbeit an einem Beispiel der ländlichen Entwicklungshilfe eines Landkreises der Elfenbeinküste. 1979. Koch, G. Entwicklung einer Didaktik des Spiels als einer sozio-kulturellen Aktionsform ausgehend von der Theorie und Praxis Brechtscher Lehrstücke. 1982. Schneider, J., mit Projektgruppe. Forschungs- und Entwicklungsvorhaben 'Schule als Berufsfeld für Sozialpädagogen'. 1982. Brauns, H.-J.; Müller, W.C. (TU). Symposium zum Berufsfeld von an Fachhochschulen und Hochschulen ausgebildeten Sozialarbeitern und Sozialpädagogen. 1980. Complete list on request.
Studies and surveys in preparation: Sozialpädagogische Betreuung in ausserbetrieblicher Berufsausbildung. Grundzüge der Entwicklung demokratisch-emanzipatorischer Erziehung im Nachkriegsdeutschland, erforscht und dargestellt am Beispiel der sozialistischen Jugend Deutschlands — die Falken-Landesverband Berlin, nach 1945. Analyse der gesellschaftspolitischen Funktion von Jugendwerkheim, Werkstadt für Behinderte und Konzeptionen praktischer Alternativen. Die Stadt als Schule. Complete list on request.

Fachrichtung Allgemeine Erziehungswissenschaft

0228

Translation: Department of General Education
Address: St. Johanner Stadtwald, 6600 SAARBRUCKEN
Year of creation: 1948
Parent Organization: University of Saarland
Present Head: Professor Dr. L. Koetter
Size of staff. Total: 24 — Full time: 21
Researchers: 6 — Full time: 6
Research activities: 50%
Educational research: 50%
Type of research: Basic and applied.
Functional objectives of research: Conditions for teaching and education; cognition, anxiety, motivation, aggression, social perception and variables of environment.

Periodical publications: Arbeitsberichte aus der Fachrichtung allgemeine Erziehungswissenschaft der Universität des Saarlandes (up to 1983: 15 issues).
Monographs: Jacobs, B. Angst in der Prüfung. 1981. Kornadt, H.J. Aggressionsmotiv und Aggressionshemmung (2 vols.). 1982. Seel, N.M. Lernaufgaben und Lernprozesse. 1981.
Studies and surveys in preparation: Conditions of forming cognitive structures by means of instruction. Cross-cultural studies (Japan, Indonesia, West Germany, Switzerland) on education and aggression. Social and educational integration of handicapped children. Using knowledge in understanding and solving applied problems. Interventions to decrease test anxiety in school settings.

Fachrichtung Erziehungswissenschaft

0229

Translation: Département des sciences de l'éducation
Address: Wilhelm Röpkestr. 6/B, 3550 MARBURG AN DER LAHN
Year of creation: 1973
Parent Organization: Universität Marburg
Size of staff. Total: 29 — Full time: 22 — Part time: 7
Researchers: 19 — Full time: 17 — Part time: 2
Research activities: from 25% to 50%
Educational research: from 25% to 50%
Monographs: Ausländerpolitik in einem ländlichen Zentrum — dargestellt am Beispiel Stadtallendorf. Massnahmen zur Berufsvorbereitung und sozialen Eingliederung junger Ausländer (MBSE) in einem ländlichen Raum.
Studies and surveys in preparation: Schulnahe Curriculumentwicklung und Handlungsforschung. Forschungsbericht des Marburger Grundschulprojekts. Die Pädagogik Theodor Litts: eine kritische Vergegenwärtigung. Genesis der Subjektivität. Zur Bedeutung der kritischen Psychologie für die materialistische Pädagogik. Kritik und Neuorientierung des Musikunterrichts. Liste complète sur demande.

Forschungsstelle Arbeit-Wirtschaft-Technik

0230

Translation: Institute for Vocational Training
Address: Kirchplatz 2, 7987 WEINGARTEN
Year of creation: 1980
Parent Organization: Pädagogische Hochschule, Weingarten
Present Head: Prof. Dr. Rolf Prim (geschäftsführend); Prof. Dr. Eva Schmidt; Prof. Heinz-J. Stührmann
Size of staff. Total: 3 — Full time: 2 — Part time: 1
Researchers: 2 — Full time: 2
Research activities: more than 50%
Educational research: more than 50%
Type of research: Entwicklungsforschung auf empirisch-hermenentischer Grundlage.
Periodical publications: "AWT-Info"
Monographs: Complete list on request.
Studies and surveys in preparation: Probleme über fachlichen Unterricht in der Arbeitslehre. Das Betriebspraktikum im Studiengang Arbeit-Wirtschaft-Technik für das Lehramt an Hauptschulen. Die allgemeinbildende Funktion der Arbeitlehre in der Hauptschule.

Forschungsstelle für pädagogische Psychologie und Entwicklungspsychologie

0231

Translation: Research Centre for Educational Psychology and Developmental Psychology
Address: Philosophische Fakultät I der Universität Augsburg, Alter Postweg 120, 8900 AUGSBURG
Year of creation: 1967
Parent Organization: Universität Augsburg
Present Head: Prof. Dr. Dieter Ulich
Size of staff. Total: 15 — Full time: 13
Researchers: 10 — Full time: 10
Research activities: more than 50%
Educational research: 50%
Type of research: Research and development.
Functional objectives of research: Empirical basic research.
Monographs: Oerter, R.; Montada, L., et al. Entwicklungspsychologie. 1982. Ulich, D. Das Gefühl. 1982.

Forschungsstelle für politisch-gesellschaftliche Erziehung

0232

Translation: Institution for Social Education
Address: Kirchplatz 2, 7987 WEINGARTEN
Year of creation: 1973
Parent Organization: Pädagogische Hochschule Weingarten
Present Head: Prof. Dr. Willy Rehm
Size of staff. Total: 2.5 — Full time: 2 — Part time: 0.5
Researchers: 2 — Full time: 2
Research activities: 50%
Educational research: from 25% to 50%
Type of research: Research and development.
Functional objectives of research: Preparation of courses.
Monographs: Social Support im Erziehungswesen. Die neuen Medien. Herkömmliche Strategien zur Bewältigung Gesundheitsgefährdender Belastungen im Raum der Schule. Aktivierung von Selbsthilfepotentialen im lebensweltlichen Kontext von Schülern.
Studies and surveys in preparation: Social support and well-being in educational systems. The influence of new mass communication media. Computers and education.

Hessisches Institut für Bildungsplanung und Schulentwicklung (HIBS)

0233

Translation: Hesse Institute of Educational Planning and School Development (HIBS)
Address: Bodenstedtstrasse 7, 6200 WIESBADEN
Year of creation: 1975
Parent Organization: Der Hessische Kultusminister
Present Head: Bernd Frommelt
Size of staff. Total: 67 — Full time: 45 — Part time: 22
Research activities: less than 10%
Educational research: less than 10%
Type of research: Research and development, applied.

Functional objectives of research: Servicing the educational administration and curriculum development.
Monographs: Didaktische Differenzierung im Englischunterricht, Klasse 7/8. Die Kleingruppe als Ort sozialen Lernens. Lernen in hessischen Gesamtschulen. Schulrechnerberatung: Erfahrungen und Tendenzen. Technische Kommunikation: eine Herausforderung an den Einsatz des Computers im Unterricht. Computer an hessischen Schulen: Ergebnisse der landesweiten Erhebung. 1982. Complete list on request.
Studies and surveys in preparation: Cooperation of teachers. Criteria for quality of schools. Learning in projects.

Hochschuldidaktisches Zentrum der Universität Augsburg

0234

Translation: Institute for Higher Education at the University of Augsburg
Address: Eichleitnerstr. 30, 8900 AUGSBURG
Year of creation: 1972
Parent Organization: University of Augsburg
Present Head: Prof. Dr. Konrad Schröder; Dr. Johann Nowark, Manager
Size of staff. Total: 7 — Full time: 6 — Part time: 1
Researchers: 5 — Full time: 4 — Part time: 1
Research activities: 50%
Educational research: more than 50%
Type of research: Basic as well as applied.
Functional objectives of research: Curriculum evaluation, preparation of courses, servicing faculties.
Periodical publications: Jahresbericht des Hochschuldidaktischen Zentrums (Annual report).
Monographs: Braun, M. Berufseingangsphase der ersten Absolventen des Augsburger Modells "Einphasige Juristenausbildung". 1981. Wissner, B. Weiterbildungsprobleme von Lehrern: eine Befragung über das Kontaktstudium an der Universität Augsburg. 1982.
Studies and surveys in preparation: Familie, Schicht und Schule. Empirische Untersuchung zur Fremdsprachenmotivation. How to improve note-taking. The language of lecturing.

Institut für Berufs-, Wirtschafts- und Sozialpädagogik der Universität zu Köln

0235

Translation: Institute of Vocational, Economic and Social Pedagogics, University of Cologne
Address: Haedenkampstrasse 2, 5000 KÖELN 41
Year of creation: 1941
Parent Organization: Universität zu Köln
Present Head: Professor Dr. Wolfgang Stratenwerth (geschäftsführend); Professor Dr. Martin Twardy
Size of staff. Total: 18 — Full time: 12 — Part time: 6
Researchers: 10 — Full time: 10
Research activities: more than 50%
Educational research: more than 50%
Type of research: Basic and applied.
Functional objectives of research: Grundlage der Lehre; Anwendung in der Praxis der

Berufs-, Wirtschafts- und Sozialerziehung.
Periodical publications: Jahresberichte des Instituts für Berufs-, Wirtschafts- und Sozialpädagogik der Universität zu Köln.
Monographs: Manstetten, R. Kommunikation und Interaktion im Unterricht: eine fachdidaktische Analyse. 1983. Twardy, M. Kompendium Fachdidaktik Wirtschaftswissenschaften. 1983. Henning, G.; Schannewitzky, G. Leitfaden zum Hospitieren und Unterrichten: mit einer systematisierten Auswahlbibliographie von Lothar Förmer. 1983. Complete list on request.
Studies and surveys in preparation: Pädagogische Konzeption zur beruflichen Erstausbildung von ausländischen Jugendlichen. Didaktische Logik. Methodische und methodologische Grundlegung einer vergleichenden Wirtschaftspädagogik am Beispiel der Handwerkspädagogik unter besonderer Berücksichtigung deutscher und französischer Ausbildungskonzeptionen. Kooperation zwischen Schule und Betrieb. Complete list on request.

Institut für Bildungsinhalte- und Lehrmittelforschung

0236

Translation: Institute for Research on Contents of Education and Educational Aids
Address: Flandernstrasse 103, 7300 ESSLINGEN
Year of creation: 1966
Parent Organization: Berufspädagogische Hochschule Esslingen
Present Head: Prof. Dr. F. Wagner
Size of staff. Total: 5 — Full time: 5
Researchers: 2 — Full time: 2
Research activities: more than 50%
Educational research: more than 50%
Type of research: Applied research.
Functional objectives of research: Research on educational aids for vocational schools.
Periodical publications: Beiträge zur Didaktik und Unterrichtstechnologie. Mitteilungen.
Studies and surveys in preparation: Rationelle Energieverwendung als Lerninhalt beruflicher Schulen. (Beiträge zur Didaktik und Unterrichtstechnologie. Nr. 11). CNC-gesteuerte Werkzeugmaschinen.

Institut für Didaktik der Physik im Fachbereich Physik, Universität Frankfurt

0237

Translation: Institute for Physics Education, Physics Department, University of Frankfurt
Address: Gräfstr. 39, 6000 FRANKFURT
Year of creation: 1970
Parent Organization: University of Frankfurt
Present Head: Prof. Dr. K. Weltner
Size of staff. Total: 12 — Full time: 12
Researchers: 6 — Full time: 6
Research activities: 50%
Educational research: 50%
Type of research: Basic research and development.
Monographs: Jung, W. Aufsätze zur Didaktik der Physik und Wissenschaftstheorie. (Reihe Beiträge zur Methodik und Didaktik der Physik). 1979. Jung. W. Mechanik für die Sekundarstufe 1. (Reihe Beiträge zur Methodik und Didaktik der Physik). 1980. Duit, R.; Jung, W.; Pfundt, H. Alltagsvorstellungen und naturwissenschaftlicher

Unterricht. 1981. Complete list on request.

Studies and surveys in preparation: Investigations of motivations of adolescents especially interested in science, and of the kind of scientific activities preferred by them. Experiments in optics teaching. The project aims at modernizing the traditional inventory of school experiments in optics. Studies in problem solving in elementary physics. Studies in representation of knowledge (electricity). Development of techniques to support autonomous learning of students with science text books, e.g. programmed study guides, computer based study aids. Complete list on request.

Institut für Didaktik des Schulsports, Abt. II, der Deutschen Sporthochschule Köln

0238

Translation: Institute of Didactics in School Physical Education, Department II
Address: Deutsche Sporthochschule Köln, Postfach 45 03 27, Carl Diem-Weg, 5000 KOELN 41
Year of creation: 1975
Parent Organization: Deutsche Sporthochschule Köln
Present Head: Prof. Dr. G. Hecker
Size of staff. Total: 6 — Full time: 3 — Part time: 3
Researchers: 3 — Full time: 3
Research activities: from 25% to 50%
Educational research: from 25% to 50%
Type of research: Field research.
Functional objectives of research: Development motivation; (public) schools; teacher training/evaluation.
Monographs: Erdmann, R. Motive und Einstellungen im Sport. Kleine, W., et al. Lehrerfortbildung. Bd. II. Wessling-Lünnemann, G. Lehrertraining für Leistungsmotivationsförderung im Sportunterricht.
Studies and surveys in preparation: DFG-Projekt 'Motivförderung im Sport'. Motiventwicklung und motorische Fertigkeiten. Lehrerfortbildung; Motive und Einstellungen; Wissenschaftstheorie.

Institut für die Pädagogik der Naturwissenschaften (IPN)

0239

Translation: Institute for Science Education
Address: Olshausenstrasse 40, 2300 KIEL 1
Year of creation: 1966
Parent Organization: Schleswig-Holstein Ministry of Education
Present Head: Prof. Karl Frey
Size of staff. Total: 91 — Full time: 72 — Part time: 19
Researchers: 42 — Full time: 41 — Part time: 1
Research activities: more than 50%
Educational research: more than 50%
Type of research: Basic and applied research.
Functional objectives of research: Improvement of science education by research and development of teaching materials.
Periodical publications: Active part in the publication of the European journal of science education. Studies in educational evaluation.
Monographs: List of publications 1979 to 1981 can be obtained free of charge from Institute upon request. All publications are written in German.
Studies and surveys in preparation: List on request.

Institut für Erziehungswissenschaft der RWTH Aachen, Lehrstuhl II

0240

Translation: Department of Education at the Technical University of Aachen
Address: Eilfschornsteinstrasse 7, 5100 AACHEN
Parent Organization: University of Aachen
Present Head: Prof. Dr. Karl Josef Klauer
Size of staff. Total: 10 — Full time: 10
Researchers: 7 — Full time: 7
Research activities: more than 50%
Educational research: more than 50%
Type of research: Mainly applied, some basic.
Functional objectives of research: Preparation of courses, partial fulfilment of degree requirements, continuation of previous research.
Periodical publications: Aus dem Institut für Erziehungswissenschaft der RWTH Aachen.
Studies and surveys in preparation: Various aspects of criterion-referenced measurement.

Institut für Erziehungswissenschaft I der Universität Oldenburg

0241

Translation: Institute of Education I, University of Oldenburg
Address: Universität Oldenburg, Postfach 2503, Ammerländer Heerstr. 67-99, 2900 OLDENBURG
Year of creation: 1983
Parent Organization: Fachbereich 1 Pädagogik der Universität Oldenburg
Present Head: Prof. Dr. F.W. Busch (Forschungsbeauftragter); Prof. Dr. J. Wolff, Dean of Department
Size of staff. Total: 69 — Full time: 9 — Part time: 60
Researchers: 30 — Full time: 5 — Part time: 25
Research activities: 50%
Educational research: more than 50%
Type of research: Case studies; applied research; research and development.
Monographs: Busch; Winter. Lehren und Lernen in der Lehrerausbildung. 1981. Lange. Problemlösender Unterricht und selbständiges Arbeiten von Schülern. 1982. Maydell, V. Bildungsforschung und Gesellschaftspolitik. 1982. Heller; Semmerling. Das ProWo-Buch: Leben, Lernen, Arbeiten in Projekten und Projektwochen. 1983. Busch, A. Die vergleichende Pädagogik in der DDR: eine disziplingeschichtliche Untersuchung. 1983.
Studies and surveys in preparation: Untersuchungen zum Problem der semantischen Validität. Jugendarbeit und Sozialhilfe. Weiterbildung in einer ländlichen Region. Arbeitsschwerpunkt Erwachsenenbildung.

Institut für Grundschulforschung

0242

Translation: Institute of Research in Primary Education
Address: Regensburger Strasse 160, 8500 NÜRNBERG 90
Year of creation: 1974
Parent Organization: Universität Erlangen-Nürnberg
Present Head: Prof. Dr. Wolfgang Einsiedler
Size of staff. Total: 8 — Full time: 7 — Part time: 1
Researchers: 6 — Full time: 6

Research activities: from 25% to 50%
Educational research: more than 50%
Type of research: Applied research.
Functional objectives of research: Prescriptions for practical teaching in primary schools.
Monographs: Berichte und Arbeiten aus dem Institut für Grundschulforschung.
Studies and surveys in preparation: Writing research. Play research.

Institut für Migrationsforschung, Ausländerpädagogik und Zweitsprachendidaktik

0243

Translation: Institute of Migration Research, Multicultural Education, Didactics of Second Language Teaching
Address: Universität-Gesamthochschule Essen, Universitätsstr. 11, 4300 ESSEN 1
Year of creation: 1981
Parent Organization: Universität-Gesamthochschule Essen
Present Head: Prof. Dr. Ursula Boos-Nünning
Size of staff. Total: 32 — Full time: 21 — Part time: 11
Researchers: 32 — Full time: 21 — Part time: 11
Research activities: 50%
Educational research: from 25% to 50%
Type of research: Migration research; basic multicultural education, didactics of second language teaching; applied research and development.
Functional objectives of research: Initial and in-service teacher training, preparation of courses for German as a second language, servicing educational politics and administration.
Periodical publications: Berichte und Materialien der Forschungsgruppe ALFA.
Monographs: Boos-Nünning, U., et al. Aufnahmeunterricht, Muttersprachlicher Unterricht, Interkultureller Unterricht: Ergebnisse einer vergleichenden Untersuchung zum Unterricht für ausländische Kinder in Belgien, England, Frankreich und den Niederlanden. 1983. Boos-Nünning, U. Schulmodelle für ethnische Minderheiten: drei Bundesländer im Vergleich. 1981. Nieke, W.; Budde, H.; Henscheid, R. Benachteiligung ausländischer Jugendlicher: die Marginalisierung der zweiten Generation. 1983. Meyer-Ingwersen, J.; Neumann, R. Türkisch für Lehrer, I. 1982. Complete list on request.
Studies and surveys in preparation: Vergleichende Evaluation von Modellversuchen zum Aufnahmeunterricht, zum Muttersprachlichen Unterricht und zur Curriculumentwicklung für den Unterricht von Migrantenkindern in Mitgliedsländern der Europäischen Gemeinschaften. Entwicklung von Studienelementen für die Ausbildung von Lehrern, die ausländischen Schüler in regelklassen Unterrichten. Entwicklung Problemorientierter Sprachkurse für Lehrer auf der Basis von türkisch und griechisch als Herkunftssprache. Complete list on request.

Institut für Pädagogik der Ruhr-Universität Bochum

0244

Translation: Institute of Education
Address: Universitätsstrasse 150, Postfach 10 21 48, 4630 BOCHUM 1
Year of creation: 1964
Parent Organization: Ruhr-Universität Bochum
Present Head: Prof. Dr. Jakob Muth
Size of staff. Total: 62 — Full time: 54 — Part time: 8
Researchers: 42 — Full time: 41 — Part time: 1

Research activities: 50%
Educational research: more than 50%
Type of research: Basic and applied research and development.
Periodical publications: Bildung und Erziehung (6/yr). Internationales Jahrbuch der Erwachsenenbildung.
Monographs: List on request.
Studies and surveys in preparation: List on request.

Institut für Psychologie, Abt. Medienforschung, Freie Universität Berlin

0245

Translation: Institute of Psychology, Department of Media Research, Free University Berlin
Address: Malteserstr. 74–100, 1000 BERLIN WEST 46
Year of creation: 1980
Parent Organization: Institute of Psychology, Free University of Berlin
Present Head: Prof. Dr. Ludwig J. Issing
Size of staff. Total: 9 — Full time: 5 — Part time: 4
Researchers: 3 — Full time: 3
Research activities: from 25% to 50%
Educational research: more than 50%
Type of research: Basic, applied, research and development.
Functional objectives of research: Preparation of courses; servicing the educational administration.
Monographs: Issing, L.; Hannemann, J., Hrsg. Lernen mit Bildern. 1983. Issing, L. Die Entwicklung der neuen Medien und ihre Bedeutung für den Bildungsbereich. 1983.
Studies and surveys in preparation: Bildverarbeitung und Bildgestaltung.

Lehrstuhl für Didaktik der Mathematik

0246

Translation: Department of Mathematics Education
Address: Am Hubland, 8700 WÜRZBURG
Year of creation: 1970
Parent Organization: Universität Würzburg
Present Head: Prof. Dr. H.-J. Vollrath
Size of staff. Total: 8 — Full time: 6 — Part time: 2
Researchers: 7 — Full time: 5 — Part time: 2
Research activities: from 10% to 25%
Educational research: more than 50%
Type of research: Research and development.
Functional objectives of research: Knowledge about teaching and learning in mathematics, fulfilment of degree requirements, development of instructional materials.
Studies and surveys in preparation: Concept teaching in mathematics. Problem solving in geometry. Language in mathematics. Error analysis in mathematics. Mathematics on the primary level.

Lehrstuhl für Didaktik des Englischen, Universität Augsburg

0247

Translation: Chair for the Didactics of E.L.T., University of Augsburg
Address: Alter Postweg 120, 8900 AUGSBURG
Year of creation: 1973
Parent Organization: Universität Augsburg
Present Head: Prof. Dr. Konrad Schröder
Size of staff. Total: 5 — Full time: 4 — Part time: 1
Researchers: 3 — Full time: 3
Research activities: more than 50%
Educational research: more than 50%
Type of research: Empirical and applied research.
Functional objectives of research: Servicing the educational admininstration; servicing decision-making in the sphere of language politics.
Periodical publications: Augsburger I&I — Schriften.
Monographs: Ostberg, H.K. Gesprächsverhalten in der Fremdsprache (Englisch) und fremdsprachlicher Unterricht. 1982. Walter, A.V. Zur Geschichte des Englischunterrichts an höheren Schulen. Die Entwicklung bis 1900 vornehmlich in Preussen. 1982. Schröder, K.; Macht, K. Wieviele Sprachen für Europa? Fremdsprachenunterricht, Fremdsprachenlernen und europäische Sprachenvielfalt im Urteil von Studierenden des Grundstudiums in Deutschland, Belgien und Finnland. 1983. Zapp, F.; Schröder, K. Deutsche Lehrpläne 1900 bis 1970: ein Lesebuch. 1983. Finkenstaedt, T.; Weller, F.R. Der Schülerwettbewerb Fremdsprachen im Stifterverband für die Deutsche Wissenschaft: Referate eines Symposiums in Wildsteig. 1983. Els, T. van; Oud-de Glas, M. Research into foreign language needs. 1984. Complete list on request.

Max-Planck Institut für Bildungsforschung

0248

Translation: Max-Planck Institute for Educational Research
Address: Lentzeallee 94, 1000 BERLIN 33
Year of creation: 1963
Parent Organization: Max-Planck Gesellschaft zur Förderung der Wissenschaften
Present Head: Prof. Dr. Paul B. Baltes
Size of staff. Total: 158
Researchers: 78
Research activities: more than 50%
Educational research: more than 50%
Type of research: Applied and basic research.
Functional objectives of research: Educational research.
Monographs: Veröffentlichung des Max-Planck-Instituts für Bildungsforschung. Materialien aus der Bildungsforschung.

Osteuropa Institut, Abteilung für Bildungswesen in Osteuropa, Freie Universität Berlin

0249

Translation: Section of Education in Eastern Europe, Eastern European Institute, Free University, Berlin
Address: Garystr. 55, 1000 BERLIN 33
Year of creation: 1956
Parent Organization: Freie Universität Berlin

Present Head: Prof. Dr. Siegfried Baske
Size of staff. Total: 4 — Full time: 3 — Part time: 1
Researchers: 2 — Full time: 2
Research activities: 50%
Educational research: 50%
Periodical publications: Informationsdienst zum Bildungswesen in Osteuropa.

Pädagogische Hochschule Flensburg

0250

Translation: College of Higher Education Flensburg
Address: Mürwiker Str. 77, 2390 FLENSBURG
Year of creation: 1946
Present Head: Professor Dr. Willfried Janssen
Size of staff. Total: 200 — Full time: 110 — Part time: 90
Researchers: 40 — Full time: 40
Research activities: from 10% to 25%
Educational research: more than 50%
Type of research: Basic and applied.
Functional objectives of research: Varied.
Monographs: Annual reports on faculty research. Complete list on request.
Studies and surveys in preparation: Complete list on request.

Pädagogische Hochschule Karlsruhe

0251

Translation: College of Education, Karlsruhe
Address: Bismarckstrasse 10, Postfach 4960, 7500 KARLSRUHE 1
Year of creation: 1768
Parent Organization: Ministerium für Wissenschaft und Kunst, Baden-Württemberg
Size of staff. Total: 152 — Full time: 108 — Part time: 44
Researchers: 100 — Full time: 100
Type of research: Basic, applied, research and development.
Functional objectives of research: Developments in academic subjects; curriculum development; methodology of teaching; educational concepts, etc.
Periodical publications: Karlsruher pädagogische Beiträge.
Monographs: Günzler, C., Hrsg. Bildung und Erziehung im Denken Goethes. 1981. Günzler, C., Hrsg. Ethik und Lebenswirklichkeit: theologische und philosophische Beiträge zur ethischen Dimension von Gegenwartsproblemen. Festschrift für Heinz-Horst Schrey zum 70. Geburtstag. 1982. Nayhauss, H.-Chr. v., Hrsg. Das Taschenbuch im Unterricht: Analysen, Modelle, Praxisberichte. 1982. Behr, W. Jugendkrise und Jugendprotest. 1982.
Studies and surveys in preparation: Bilanz der gegenwärtigen Jugendforschung in der Bundesrepublik Deutschland. Probleme der Rezeption von Literatur bei Grund-, Haupt- und Realschülern. Erziehung zur Ehrfurcht vor dem Leben. Präventive Erziehung zum Abbau von Gewalt und Vandalismus.

Pädagogische Hochschule Kiel

0252

Translation: College of Higher Education
Address: Olshausenstrasse 75, 2300 KIEL
Year of creation: 1926

Parent Organization: Ministry of Education and Cultural Affairs in Schleswig-Holstein
Present Head: Prof. Dr. rer. nat. Helmut Dahncke
Size of staff. Total: 178 — Full time: 161 — Part time: 17
Researchers: 73 — Full time: 73
Research activities: 50%
Educational research: from 25% to 50%
Type of research: Applied, partly basic.
Functional objectives of research: Concerning teacher's training.
Periodical publications: Annual report of the President. Research report (published biennually).
Monographs: Biller, K. Unterrichtsstörungen. 1981. Bornhöft, G. Einige Probleme der Kinder beim Übergang in die Orientierungsstufe. In: Schröter, G. Schulkinderprobleme. 1981. Niermann, J. Methoden der Unterrichtsdifferenzierung. 1981. Complete list on request.
Studies and surveys in preparation: Erforschung und Entwicklung eines Modells zur Gestaltung des Theorie–Praxis–Verhältnisses in der Lehrerausbildung an der Pädagogischen Hochschule Kiel. Akustische Medien im Elementar- und Primarbereich — Kinderschallplatte. Sozialisationsrelevante Inhalte auf Schallplatten und Tonkassetten für Kinder und Jugendliche. Medien im Unterricht mit ausländischen Kindern. Video-feedback und Schulerverhalten im Unterricht. Sprache im Unterricht. Complete list on request.

Pädagogische Hochschule Ludwigsburg

0253

Address: Reuteallee 46, 7140 LUDWIGSBURG
Year of creation: 1962
Parent Organization: Ministry of Science and Art, Baden–Württemberg
Present Head: Prof. Karl-Dieter Klose, Rektor
Size of staff. Total: 210 — Full time: 200 — Part time: 10
Researchers: 90 — Full time: 90
Research activities: 50%
Educational research: more than 50%
Type of research: Basic, applied.
Functional objectives of research: Research in all fields of education.
Periodical publications: Ludwigsburger Hochschulschriften.
Studies and surveys in preparation: Several projects are described in the Forschungsberichten der Pädagogischen Hochschule Ludwigsburg. Special demands will be answered on request. Complete list on request.

Pädagogische Hochschule Reutlingen

0254

Translation: College of Education/Teachers' Training College
Address: Postfach 680, 7410 REUTLINGEN
Year of creation: 1962
Parent Organization: Ministerium für Wissenschaft und Kunst des Landes Baden-Württemberg
Present Head: Professor Dr. Hermann Wenzel
Size of staff. Total: 319 — Full time: 178 — Part time: 141
Researchers: 102 — Full time: 8 — Part time: 94
Research activities: from 10% to 25%

Educational research: more than 50%
Type of research: Basic, applied, development.
Functional objectives of research: Preparation of courses; improvement of teaching practice.
Periodical publications: PH-Information (containing, among institutional news, information on current research projects).
Studies and surveys in preparation: Cultural technique in special education. Social and emotional learning in primary and secondary school. Compensatory training for children of foreign origin. Special training for potentially handicapped children. Children of unemployed parents. Differences in motivation between girls and boys.

Pädagogisches Zentrum Berlin

0255

Translation: Educational Centre, Berlin
Address: Uhlandstrasse 97, 1000 BERLIN 31 (Wilmersdorf)
Year of creation: 1965
Parent Organization: Ministry of Education, Youth and Sports
Present Head: Dr. Erwin Voigt
Size of staff. Total: 135
Researchers: 40
Research activities: from 10% to 25%
Educational research: from 10% to 25%
Type of research: Research and development.
Functional objectives of research: Screening of R&D for use in educational practice; empirical R&D to evaluate educational practice primarily in Berlin schools; counselling of Berlin teachers.
Monographs: List on request.

Schulbauinstitut der Länder

0256

Translation: Institut for School Facilities of the Laender
Address: Schillstrasse 9–10, D–1000 BERLIN 30
Year of creation: 1962
Parent Organization: Conference of Standing Ministers of Culture in Germany
Present Head: Leitender Baudirektor Christoph Köhler
Size of staff. Total: 23 — Full time: 21 — Part time: 2
Researchers: 7 — Full time: 7
Research activities: more than 50%
Educational research: less than 10%
Type of research: Research and development, e.g. building and running costs for schools, modernization, equipment of special room-types for vocational education, sports for handicapped students, energy conservation.
Functional objectives of research: Means for planning and construction of school building as recommendations for the governments of the Laender (States) and the local authorities.
Periodical publications: List on request.
Monographs: Planungs- und Kostendaten von Schulen: Zusammenfassung Teil 5 und 7. 1983. Weiterverwendung bestehender Schulen: Planungs- und Bewertungsverfahren. 1981. Baunutzungskosten im Schulbau: Betriebskosten. 1982. Fachraumtypen: Fachraumausstattung für berufliche Schulen für Elektrotechnik. 1981. Complete list

on request.
Studies and surveys in preparation: Dokumentation berufliche Schulbauten. Sportbauten für Behinderte. Energieeinsparung im Schulbau. Kunst an Schulen. Complete list on request.

Seminar für allgemeine Pädagogik an der Technischen Universität Braunschweig

0257

Translation: Institute for Education, University of Braunschweig
Address: Seminar für allgemeine Pädagogik TU/FB 9, Postfach 3329, 3300 BRAUNSCHWEIG
Year of creation: 1978
Parent Organization: Universität Braunschweig
Present Head: Prof. Dr. Hein Retter (geschäftsführender Leiter)
Size of staff. Total: 9 — Full time: 7 — Part time: 2
Researchers: 7 — Full time: 7
Research activities: 50%
Educational research: more than 50%
Type of research: Basic, applied.
Functional objectives of research: Geisteswissenschaftliche Pädagogik, empirische Pädagogik (insbes. Vorschulpädagogik, Spiel und Spielzeug).
Periodical publications: Complete list on request.
Monographs: Hein Retter, Spielzeug: Handbuch zur Geschichte und Pädagogik der Spielmittel. Weinheim, Beltz, 1979. Complete liste on request.
Studies and surveys in preparation: Die Orientierungsstufe in Niedersachsen. Complete list on request.

Stiftung Rehabilitation Heidelberg

0258

Translation: Rehabilitation Foundation of Heidelberg
Address: Bonhoefferstrasse, 6900 HEIDELBERG 1
Year of creation: 1960
Present Head: Friedrich Löffler
Size of staff. Total: 3000 — Full time: 2900 — Part time: 100
Researchers: 8 — Full time: 7 — Part time: 1
Research activities: less than 10%
Educational research: from 25% to 50%
Type of research: Applied research on vocational rehabilitation.
Functional objectives of research: Vocational reintegration of handicapped persons.

Universität Hamburg. Fachbereich Erziehungswissenschaft. Fachausschuss Sonderpädagogik. Institut für Behindertenpädagogik

0259

Translation: University of Hamburg. Department of Education. Institute of Special Education
Address: Sedanstrasse 19, 2000 HAMBURG 13
Year of creation: 1945
Parent Organization: University of Hamburg
Present Head: Prof. Hartwig Claussen, Kommerz. Geschf., Direktor
Size of staff. Total: 22 — Full time: 22
Researchers: 20 — Full time: 20

Research activities: 50%
Educational research: more than 50%
Type of research: Research on special education; applied; research and development.
Functional objectives of research: All problems of special education.
Periodical publications: None issued.
Monographs: Diverse, by the staff members.

Zentrales Institut für Fernstudienforschung

0260

Translation: Central Institute for Research into Distance Education
Address: Postfach 940, 5800 HAGEN
Year of creation: 1975
Parent Organization: Fernuniversität — Gesamthochschule — Hagen
Present Head: Professor Börje Holmberg
Size of staff. Total: 18 — Full time: 10 — Part time: 8
Researchers: 15 — Full time: 9 — Part time: 6
Research activities: more than 50%
Educational research: more than 50%
Type of research: Basic and applied research into the conditions, methods and media of distance education.
Functional objectives of research: Servicing the distance-teaching institutions in the world and particularly the Fernuniversität.
Periodical publications: Ziff Papiere. Ziff Hinweise.
Monographs: Graff, K. Die jüdische Tradition und das Konzept des autonomen Lernens (Studien und Dokumentationen zur vergleichenden Bildungsforschung, Bd. 14). 1980. Holmberg, B. Status and trends of distance education. 1981. Sewart, D.; Keegan, D.; Holmberg, B., eds. Distance education: international readings. 1983.
Studies and surveys in preparation: Ongoing research projects of particular interest are: Comparative distance education. Evolutionist and constructivist approaches to learning. Financial input (into media) and educational output. Decision models for the identification of an optimal media combination.

Zentrum für empirische pädagogische Forschung

0261

Translation: Centre of Empirical Pedagogical Research
Address: Industriestr. 15, 6740 LANDAU
Year of creation: 1969
Parent Organization: Erziehungswissenschaftliche Hochschule Rheinland-Pfalz
Present Head: Prof. Dr. Karlheinz Ingenkamp
Size of staff. Total: 19 — Full time: 9 — Part time: 10
Researchers: 16 — Full time: 8 — Part time: 8
Research activities: more than 50%
Educational research: more than 50%
Type of research: Basic research and development.
Functional objectives of research: Advancing knowledge; servicing the educational administration.
Periodical publications: Jahresbericht des Zentrums für empirische pädagogische Forschung.
Monographs: Arbinger, R.; Seitz, H.; Todt, E. La investigación de la motivación en la escuela. In: Todt, E. La motivación. 1982. Brandt, W.; Geyer, A.; Ingenkamp, K.;

Rüchner, M.; Wolf, B. Materialien zur institutionellen Lernumwelt: Beobachtung und Interview im Kindergarten. 1982. Complete list on request.
Studies and surveys in preparation: Kognitive Verarbeitungsprozesse in leistungsbezogenen schulischen Situationen. Sozialklima von Schulklassen. Wirkungen der Klassenfrequenzen auf Schülermerkmale. Probleme von Kindern in der Grundschule. Complete list on request.

Zentrum für neue Lernverfahren, Institut für Erziehungswissenschaft II

0262

Translation: Center for New Learning Methods, Institute of Education II
Address: Münzgasse 11, 7400 TUEBINGEN
Year of creation: 1965
Parent Organization: Universität Tübingen
Present Head: Prof. Dr. Walther Zifreund
Size of staff. Total: 10 — Full time: 4 — Part time: 6
Researchers: 5 — Full time: 4 — Part time: 1
Research activities: 50%
Educational research: more than 50%
Type of research: Basic and applied research.
Functional objectives of research: Effective teacher training. Meaningful use of personal computers in schools and universities. Improvisation training in teacher education.
Periodical publications: Unterrichtswissenschaft (4/yr).
Monographs: Book series 'Neue Lernverfahren' and other volumes published by various publishers in all research and development areas of the Institute mentioned below.
Studies and surveys in preparation: Microteaching. Microcounselling. Interaction analysis. Computer assisted simulation. Development and research of interactional games.

GHANA

Centre for Development Studies

0263

Address: P.O. Box 01, University Post Office, CAPE COAST
Year of creation: 1967
Parent Organization: University of Cape Coast
Present Head: J.K.A. Boakye
Size of staff. Total: 61 — Full time: 56
Researchers: 17 — Full time: 12 — Part time: 5
Research activities: more than 50%
Educational research: from 10% to 25%
Type of research: Development issues such as: education and development; technology and development; agriculture and rural development; women in development.
Functional objectives of research: To provide information based on empirical work for use by policy makers and educational institutions.
Periodical publications: Research report series.
Monographs: French, S.; Boyd, T.A. An enquiry concerning employment opportunities for secondary school leavers in Ghana. 1971. Boaky, J.K.A. The continuation school system and the unemployment problem among middle school leavers in Ghana.

1975. Wagenbuur, T.M. Asuansi school leavers: a study of the impact of agricultural training.

Curriculum Research and Development Division, Ghana Education Service

0264

Address: P.O. Box 2739, ACCRA
Year of creation: 1967
Parent Organization: Ghana Education Service
Present Head: Robert A. Ntumi
Size of staff. Total: 67 — Full time: 60 — Part time: 7
Researchers: 7 — Part time: 7
Research activities: from 25% to 50%
Educational research: more than 50%
Type of research: Mainly survey research.
Functional objectives of research: Improve quality of instruction, curriculum and assessment.
Monographs: Attitude of primary school children in Ghana. Family life education. Drug abuse among students.
Studies and surveys in preparation: Second science study. Evaluation of Science Programme for Africa. Continuation schools and junior secondary schools.

Faculty of Education

0265

Address: University of Cape Coast, CAPE COAST
Year of creation: 1962
Parent Organization: University of Cape Coast
Present Head: Professor S.K. Odamtten
Size of staff. Total: 33 — Full time: 45 — Part time: 33
Type of research: Basic and applied research.
Functional objectives of research: To increase knowledge and to improve teaching and learning.
Periodical publications: Oguaa educator.
Monographs: Pecku, N.K. Psychoeducational consultation: a personal model. Collinson, G.O. The development of science education in elementary schools. Tufuor, J.K. Aspects of outdoor education programme which appear to contribute to the enhancement of positive attitudes towards conservation of natural resources; a case study. Saah, M. Concepts in educational psychology with implications for effective teaching/learning. Ocansey, P.K. The role of the Faculty of Education, University of Cape Coast in the use of in-service education and training in the training of primary school teachers in Ghana. Complete list on request.

GREECE

Kentro Ekpaideutikōn Meletōn kaì Epimorfōsēs

0266

Translation: Centre for Educational Research and Teacher In-Service Training
Address: 396 Messoghion Street, Aghia Paraskevi, ATHENS
Year of creation: 1976

Parent Organization: Ministry of National Education and Religion
Present Head: Prof. Pavlos Sakellaridis
Type of research: Applied research.
Functional objectives of research: Provision of guidance and programming in primary, secondary-general, technical and vocational and higher education; research and study of areas related to education; consulting services; elaboration and analytical school programmes; training of teaching personnel employed in the national education system.

Kentro Meletōn kaì Automorfōsēs

0267

Translation: Centre d'études et d'autoformation
Address: Dioskouron 11, Plaka 10555, ATHENS
Year of creation: 1983
Parent Organization: Centre pour les études méditerranéennes
Present Head: Georges Papandreou
Size of staff. Total: 10 — Full time: 6 — Part time: 4
Researchers: 8 — Full time: 6 — Part time: 2
Research activities: 50%
Educational research: more than 50%
Type of research: Participative.
Functional objectives of research: Fournir des prestations; organiser des séminaires en recherche participative.
Periodical publications: Automorfōsē (3/an).
Monographs: Education populaire: le cas de la Grèce. 1983. Plusieurs textes dans notre revue concernent l'acte pédagogique et l'analyse du processus d'apprentissage.
Studies and surveys in preparation: Projet pilote sur un groupe de jeunes chômeurs. Analyse des propositions faites par le Gouvernement de Pasok concernant l'éducation populaire.

Paidagōgiko Ergastērio Filosofikēs Sholēs

0268

Translation: Laboratoire pédagogique de la Faculté des lettres
Address: Université de Jannina, 45332 JANNINA
Year of creation: 1977
Parent Organization: Faculté des lettres, Université de Jannina
Present Head: M. Christos Frangos
Size of staff. Total: 14 — Full time: 14
Researchers: 14 — Full time: 14
Research activities: from 10% to 25%
Educational research: from 10% to 25%
Type of research: Fondamentale et appliquée.
Functional objectives of research: Préparation de thèses; fournir des éléments de réflexion aux instances et personnes concernées par l'éducation: administration, enseignants, usagers.
Studies and surveys in preparation: Le personnel enseignant dans les universités grecques: origine socio-économique, attitudes. Les causes de la déperdition scolaire durant les trois dernières années de l'enseignement obligatoire. La discrimination sociale dans la pratique pédagogique à l'école primaire. Idéologie scolaire et décoration de l'école. Echec scolaire et attitudes des enseignants dans l'enseignement

secondaire. Reintégration scolaire des enfants des migrants de retour au pays d'origine. Liste complète sur demande.

GUATEMALA

Instituto de Investigaciones y Mejoramiento Educativo (IIME)

0269

Address: Ciudad Universitaria, Zona 12, GUATEMALA
Year of creation: 1962
Parent Organization: Universidad de San Carlos de Guatemala
Present Head: Lic. Josefina Antillón Milla
Size of staff. Total: 28 — Full time: 6 — Part time: 22
Researchers: 10 — Full time: 4 — Part time: 6
Research activities: from 25% to 50%
Educational research: from 10% to 25%
Type of research: Investigación básica y aplicada.
Functional objectives of research: Sobre temas específicos ubicados en el sistema educativo nacional o en el área social.
Periodical publications: Boletín documental. Boletín informativo.
Studies and surveys in preparation: Nivel académico de la Universidad de San Carlos de Guatemala. Determinación de la estructura aptitudinal del estudiante de física a nivel superior. Diagnóstico operativo de la Universidad de San Carlos. Acceso a la Universidad de San Carlos. Evaluación de catedráticos a nivel superior. Permanencia de los estudiantes de la USAC. Diagnóstico descriptivo de la creatividad en estudiantes de primer años de ingenieria de la USAC.

Unidad Sectorial de Investigación y Planificación Educativa (USIPE)

0270

Address: 6a. Avenida 3-11, Zona 4, GUATEMALA
Year of creation: 1977
Parent Organization: Ministerio de Educación
Present Head: Lic. Miguel Angel Barrios Escobar, Director
Size of staff. Total: 122 — Full time: 122
Research activities: 50%
Educational research: from 25% to 50%
Type of research: Básica, aplicada; investigación desarrollo.
Functional objectives of research: Objectivos funcionales de la investigación.
Periodical publications: Boletín estadísticas educacionales: cifras preliminares. Boletín bibliográfico (3/año à partir de 1984).
Studies and surveys in preparation: División de infraestructura física: criterios normativos para el diseño de edificios escolares. Estudio de microplanificación educativa (proyecto EDUPRIMUR). Manual preliminar sobre mantenimiento de edificios escolares. Recolección de la información estadística final ciclo escolar. 1983.

GUYANA

Faculty of Education, University of Guyana

0271

Address: P.O. Box 10 1110, GEORGETOWN
Year of creation: 1967
Parent Organization: University of Guyana
Present Head: Dr. Irma I. King
Size of staff. Total: 47
Researchers: 4 — Full time: 3 — Part time: 1
Research activities: from 10% to 25%
Type of research: Applied research.
Functional objectives of research: Curriculum development. Servicing the educational system. Partial fulfilment of degree requirements.
Periodical publications: Teacher forum.
Monographs: Oluikpe, G. Elementary statistics for educational research. Oluikpe, G. How to respond to essay questions.
Studies and surveys in preparation: Writing test items as a means of achieving instructional objectives. The relative merits of the analytical and the global methods of marking essay questions. Community attitudes towards the community high schools. Separate sciences curricula for secondary schools. Student achievement in integrated science at the Caribbean Examinations Council (CXC) examinations. Complete list on request.

Planning and Research Unit

0272

Address: 26 Brickdam, P.O. Box 1014, GEORGETOWN
Year of creation: 1976
Parent Organization: Ministry of Education, Social Development and Culture
Present Head: Dr. Una M. Paul
Size of staff. Total: 13 — Full time: 3
Researchers: 3 — Full time: yes
Research activities: from 25% to 50%
Type of research: Research and development.
Functional objectives of research: Servicing the educational administration.
Monographs: An analysis of education wastage at the primary level, 1980–1981. An analysis of overaged pupils (age group 12–17) enrolled at the primary level, 1980–1981. A performance appraisal of the education system of Guyana. 1982. Evaluation of the nursery training programme. 1981. A follow-up study of 1979 community high school graduates. 1982. A digest of educational statistics, 1980–1981.
Studies and surveys in preparation: The effectiveness of the change of school hours in region 4. The degree and pattern of overcrowding in primary schools in region 4. Agricultural resources in school programmes. An evaluation of the broadcast to schools. Development of a monitoring mechanism for efficient book distribution in schools. An analysis of demand for trained teachers in the school system. An analysis of teacher employment costs and other charges of the school system.

HOLY SEE

Facoltá di scienze dell'educazione

0273

Translation: Faculté de sciences de l'éducation
Address: Piazza dell'Ateneo Salesiano, 1, 00139 ROMA
Year of creation: 1956
Parent Organization: Université pontificale salesienne
Present Head: P. Guglielmo Malizia, professeur d'organisation et législation scolaire
Size of staff. Total: 50 — Full time: 29 — Part time: 21
Researchers: 24 — Full time: 20 — Part time: 4
Research activities: 50%
Educational research: more than 50%
Type of research: Fondamentale et appliquée.
Functional objectives of research: Préparation de cours; fournir des prestations à l'administration de l'éducation.
Periodical publications: Orientamenti pedagogici. Tuttogiovani notizie.
Monographs: Alberich, E. Catechesi e prassi ecclesiale. 1982. Franta, H. Individualità e formazione integrale. 1982. Milanesi, G.C., ed. Educare con lo sport. 1983. Pellerey, M. Per un insegnamento della matematica dal volto umano. 1983. Liste complète sur demande.
Studies and surveys in preparation: La sperimentazione delle fasce di professionalità. La formazione dei formatori. La formazione scientifica di fronte all'innovazione tecnologica. Verifica di un modello pedagogico di 'Scuola per genitori'. L'ambiente familiare e la dinamica dell'orientamento scolastico-professionale. Liste complète sur demande.

HONDURAS

Unidad de Investigación Educativa

0274

Address: Ministerio de Educación Pública, 1a. Calle, 2-4 Avenida, Comayaguela, TEGUCIGALPA D.C.
Year of creation: 1978
Parent Organization: Dirección General de Planeamiento y Reforma Educativa, Ministerio de Educación Pública
Present Head: Prof. Ivis Orlando Boquín Madrid, Estudiante Universitario-Administración Pública
Size of staff. Total: 9 — Full time: 1 — Part time: 8
Researchers: 8 — Full time: 1 — Part time: 7
Research activities: more than 50%
Educational research: more than 50%
Type of research: Investigación básica y aplicada.
Functional objectives of research: Prestación de servicios a la administración educacional.
Periodical publications: No publica periódicas.
Studies and surveys in preparation: Proyecto multinacional de investigación evaluativa de logros de los sistemas educativos. Realizar una investigación acerca de las

características de los niños hondureños de 4 a 6 años de edad. Realizar un estudio acerca de la vinculación de la escuela primaria al trabajo productivo. Realizar una investigación sobre la vinculación del plan de estudio del ciclo común de cultura general al trabajo productivo.

HUNGARY

Felnøttnevelési és Közmüvelødési Tanszék, Kossuth Lajos Tudományegyetem **0275**

Translation: Department of Adult and Public Education, Lajos Kossuth University
Address: Egyetem tér 1., Pf. 25, 4010 DEBRECEN 1O
Year of creation: 1971
Parent Organization: Ministry of Education
Present Head: Prof. Mátyás Durkó dr.
Size of staff. Total: 17 — Full time: 12 — Part time: 5
Researchers: 6 — Full time: 2 — Part time: 4
Research activities: from 25% to 50%
Educational research: more than 50%
Type of research: Basic (70%) and applied (30%).
Functional objectives of research: Partial fulfilment of degree requirements, preparation of courses.
Periodical publications: Felnőttnevelés, Müvelődés. Acta andragogiae et culturae.
Monographs: Educational — acquisitional process in adult education. 1982. Essays on contemporary cultural studies. 1983.
Studies and surveys in preparation: Psychological and pedagogical pecularities of adulthood. Specific problems of learning and knowledge acquisition in adulthood. Capability for self-education in adulthood taken as a function of different ages and educational levels. Aspects of didactics in distance education. Self education habits of adults. Motivated education and personality of adults of different ages and with different educational levels. Interdependence of public education, cultural degree attained at school and public culture-administration. Structure, mechanism and management of public education administration. The effectiveness of adult educational, cultural acquisitional processes and its evaluation.

Ho Si Minh Tanárképző Főiskola **0276**

Translation: Ho Chi Minh Teacher's Training College
Address: Szabadság tér 2, Pf. 43,3301, EGER
Year of creation: 1948
Parent Organization: Ministry of Education
Present Head: Dr. László Szücs, General Director of the College
Size of staff. Total: 572 — Full time: 532 — Part time: 40
Researchers: 108 — Full time: 2
Research activities: from 10% to 25%
Educational research: from 10% to 25%
Type of research: Basic research.
Functional objectives of research: Mainly for teaching/educational purposes and for obtaining scientific degrees; and, in a lesser number, research under contract.

Periodical publications: Ho Si Minh Tanárképző Főiskola tudományos közleményei és füzetei (Scientific publications and of the Ho Si Minh Teacher Training College). Ho Si Minh Tanárképző Főiskola évkönyve (Annual of the Ho Si Minh Teacher Training College). Szervezeti életünk (Our life).
Monographs: Complete list on request.
Studies and surveys in preparation: A mozgalmi képzés rendszertani, tartalmi és módszertani problémái. A televizió szerepe és lehetőségei a szülők nevelésében. Complete list on request.

Neveléstudományi Tanszék, Kossuth Lajos Tudományegyetem

0277

Translation: Department of Education, Lajos Kossuth University of Arts and Sciences
Address: Pf.17, 4010 DEBRECEN
Year of creation: 1912
Parent Organization: Müvelődési Minisztérium
Present Head: Dr. Petrikás Árpád, egyetemi tanár
Size of staff. Total: 26 — Full time: 13 — Part time: 13
Researchers: 12 — Full time: 1 — Part time: 11
Research activities: from 10% to 25%
Educational research: from 10% to 25%
Type of research: Basic and applied research.
Functional objectives of research: Educational history; community research; educational problems of personality.
Periodical publications: Acta paedagogica Debrecina.
Monographs: Research reports. Forum.
Studies and surveys in preparation: 3 studies in preparation.

Oktatáskutató Intézet

0278

Translation: Institute for Educational Research
Address: Victor Hugo u.18-22, 1395 Pf. 427, BUDAPEST XIII
Year of creation: 1981
Parent Organization: Ministry of Education
Present Head: Károly Soós, director p.i.
Size of staff. Total: 70
Researchers: 40
Type of research: Basic and applied research to cover the entire vertical structure of the established system of education (kindergarten, primary, secondary, higher education); research team pertinent to policy research and planning; school research team; higher educational research team; research team pertinent to socialization in schools.
Functional objectives of research: To establish educational policy decisions of strategic nature in a scientific manner, and to expedite the prudent realisation of decisions aimed at the development of education.
Monographs: Mühelytanulmányok (Workshop studies series). Kutatások az oktatási rendszer témaköréből (Researches from the subject fields of the education system). Volumes of essays and studies and monographs are published by the Institute with the co-operation of commercial publishing houses.

Oktatástechnikai Központ, Kossuth Lajos Tudományegyetem

0279

Translation: Educational Technology Centre, Lajos Kossuth University
Address: Egyetem tér 1., 4010 DEBRECEN
Year of creation: 1979
Parent Organization: Lajos Kossuth University of Arts and Sciences
Present Head: Dr. László.Magyari
Size of staff. Total: 14 — Full time: 13 — Part time: 1
Researchers: 6 — Full time: 6
Research activities: from 25% to 50%
Educational research: from 25% to 50%
Type of research: Applied research.
Functional objectives of research: Work out methods for improving the effectiveness of secondary and higher education; plan and build educational machines to help in teaching.
Monographs: Magyari, L. A KLTE Oktatástechnikai Központja az egyetemi oktatástechnológia szolgálatában. Agócs, L. A fakultativ oktatástechnológiai képzés tapasztalatai a KLTE-n. Complete list on request.
Studies and surveys in preparation: A szaktárgyra orientált egyetemi oktatástechnológiai ismeretanyag modulszerü kimunkálása. Szovremennaja vüszsaja skola. Complete list on request.

Országos Oktatástechnikai Központ (OOK)

0280

Translation: National Centre for Educational Technology
Address: POB 260, 1519 BUDAPEST
Year of creation: 1973
Parent Organization: Ministry for Culture and Education
Present Head: Mr. Genzwein Ferenc
Size of staff. Total: 154 — Full time: 140 — Part time: 14
Researchers: 9 — Part time: 9
Research activities: less than 10%
Educational research: more than 50%
Type of research: Development, applied research.
Functional objectives of research: To examine: the use of AV media, produced by the Centre; the role of educational technology in schools; educational technology in teacher training and further training; preparation for decisions in the field of educational technology.
Periodical publications: Audio-vizuális közlemények (AV Proceedings). Pedagógiai technológia (Educational technology). Uj média (New media).
Monographs: OOK: towards educational technology in Hungary. Oktatástechnológia a neveléstudomány rendszerében (Educational technology in the system of pedagogical sciences). Oktatás és technológia (Education and technology).
Studies and surveys in preparation: Az oktatás, mint a tanulás szabályozása (Education as control for learning). Pedagógusok előadóképességének fejlesztése video-technika segitségével (Developing lecturing skills of pedagogues with the help of videotechnics).

Országos Pedagógiai Intézet

0281

Translation: National Institute for Education
Address: 1071 Gorkij fasor 17-21, PF. 33, 1406 BUDAPEST
Year of creation: 1962
Parent Organization: Ministry of Cultural Affairs
Present Head: Prof. Miklós, Szabolcsi, Academicin, President of FILLM
Size of staff. Total: 450 — Full time: 450
Researchers: 29 — Full time: 29
Research activities: from 10% to 25%
Educational research: from 10% to 25%
Type of research: Applied and basic research and development.
Functional objectives of research: Continuing development of education.
Periodical publications: Educational theory and school research. Child and youth protection.
Monographs: Gál, E.; Lászlóné Majzik. Modern educational methods in the school. 1982. Mohás, L., ed. The profession of parents. 1982. Vizy, J., ed. Handbook on education to environmental protection. 1982. Mihály, O. Tasks of the Hungarian National Institute of Education in the field of innovation. 1982. Complete list on request.

Pedagogógia Tanszék, Eötvös Loránd Tudományegyetem

0282

Translation: Département de l'éducation, Université des sciences, Loránd Eotvos
Address: Pesti Barnabas u.1, BUDAPEST 1052
Year of creation: 1814
Parent Organization: Recteur de l'Université
Present Head: Joseph Szarka
Size of staff. Total: 20 — Full time: 20
Researchers: 7 — Full time: 2 — Part time: 5
Research activities: from 25% to 50%
Educational research: more than 50%
Type of research: Fondamentale et appliquée.
Functional objectives of research: Préparation de cours.
Periodical publications: Magyar pedagógia (Pédagogie hongroise).
Monographs: Nagy, S. Az oktatáselmélet alapkérdései. Bábosik, I. Személyiségformálás közvetett hatásokkal. Mészáros, I. Az iskolaügy története.
Studies and surveys in preparation: Préparation des instituteurs.

INDIA

Bharatiya Shikshan Sanstha (Marathi)

0283

Translation: Indian Institute of Education
Address: 128/2 Kothrud, Karve Road, PUNE-411029
Year of creation: 1948
Parent Organization: Indian Institute of Education
Present Head: Professor M.P. Rege

Size of staff. Total: 7 — Full time: 7
Research activities: more than 50%
Educational research: more than 50%
Type of research: Basic and action research related to education and rural development, non-formal education, educational planning and administration.
Functional objectives of research: Full-fledged research; research for partial fulfilment of M.Phil and Ph.D. degrees; to evolve alternatives to the formal education system; to discover and evolve linkages between education and development; to experiment and innovate in all aspects of the educational process with a view to benefiting the disadvantaged sections of society.
Periodical publications: Shikshan ani samaj (Marathi, 4/yr). Bulletin (English, 4/yr). I.I.E. News (English, 4/yr). Samvadini (Marathi, 6/yr). State Resource Centre newsletter (English, 4/yr).
Monographs: Naik, Chitra. India: extending primary education through non-formal approaches (English, French, Spanish, Arabic). Gogate, S.B. Problems of education in Marathwada (Marathi, English).
Studies and surveys in preparation: Studies in regional problems of education. Educational reform in India (1921-80): a basic study for perspective planning up to the year 2000. Universalization of primary education: an action research project. Science and technology for rural women: an action-research project. Education and literacy among scheduled castes. Education and rural development.

Central Institute of Educational Technology

0284

Address: NCERT, NEW DELHI-110 016
Year of creation: 1973
Parent Organization: National Council of Educational Research and Training
Present Head: Prof. M.M. Chaudhri
Size of staff. Total: 200 — Full time: 190 — Part time: 10
Researchers: 30 — Full time: 25 — Part time: 5
Research activities: from 10% to 25%
Educational research: from 10% to 25%
Type of research: Formative and developmental; summative; planning and research.
Functional objectives of research: To improve the quality of instructional packages; to assess effectiveness and achievement; to evaluate the programmes.
Periodical publications: Newsletter (to be published soon).
Monographs: A report on quick feed-back obtained from the user teachers on ETV programmes in Andhra Pradesh and Orissa, India. A report on ETV utilisation with special reference to TV maintenance in Sambalpur, India. Report on ETV utilisation in Orissa (for the period ending December, 1983). A report on ETV utilisation in Orissa (1983-84). A study of the impact of the ETV programmes on the children of classes IV-V in Sambalpur district, India. Complete list on request.
Studies and surveys in preparation: Audience profiles of INSAT-I studies in respect of primary school children and teachers for ETV support. Assessment of the needs of primary school children and teachers for ETV support. Formative evaluation and field testing of educational TV programmes. Impact of educational TV on primary school children and teachers. Complete list on request.

National Council of Educational Research and Training

0285

Address: Sri Aurobindo Marg, NEW DELHI-110016
Year of creation: 1961
Parent Organization: Ministry of Education and Culture, Government of India, New Delhi
Present Head: Dr. P.L. Malhotra, Director
Size of staff. Total: 3035 — Full time: 3035
Researchers: 965 — Full time: 965
Research activities: from 25% to 50%
Educational research: from 25% to 50%
Type of research: Basic, applied and developmental research.
Functional objectives of research: Preparation of courses, servicing the educational administration; undertake help and coordinate research in all branches of education; organize preservice and inservice training in the field of education (advanced level); organise extension programmes and clearing house activities.
Periodical publications: The primary teacher (English, 4/yr). Primary shikshak (Hindi, 4/yr). School science (English, 4/yr). Journal of Indian education (English, 6/yr). Indian education review (English, 4/yr). Bhartiya adhunik shiksha (Hindi, 4/yr).
Monographs: The effect of environmental process variables on school achievement: the report of Bangalore Centre. The effect of environmental process variables on school achievement: the report of Varanasi centre. Fourth All-India Educational Survey. Core teaching skills: microteaching approach. Research on examination in India (reprint). Play-way activities in primary schools. Readings in language and language teaching book I: reading comprehension. Complete list on request.
Studies and surveys in preparation: Primary education curriculum renewal and developmental activities in community education and participation. Comprehensive access to developing socially useful productive work activities and vocational education courses at higher secondary levels. Educational technology, development of criteria for evaluating syllabus in environmental studies, social sciences and humanities, and sciences. 5th All-India educational survey. Value oriented education. Education for international understanding, peace and human rights. Integrated education of the disabled. Computer education. Preparation and publication of textbooks, etc.

National Institute of Educational Planning and Administration

0286

Address: 17-B, Sri Aurobindo Marg, NEW DELHI-110016
Year of creation: 1962
Parent Organization: Ministry of Education and Culture, Government of India
Present Head: Professor Moonis Raza
Size of staff. Total: 202 — Full time: 202
Researchers: 53 — Full time: 53
Research activities: from 25% to 50%
Educational research: more than 50%
Type of research: Applied research.
Functional objectives of research: Improvement of educational planning and administration; preparation and enrichment of training courses; seminars and workshops.
Periodical publications: EPA Bulletin (4/yr).

Monographs: Revitalising school complexes in India. 1983. Education and the new international order. 1983. Women's education: the regional dimension. 1983. In-depth study of Ashraw schools. 1982. Exposure of scheduled castes and tribes to ITIs. 1982. Administration of elementary education in relation to universalisation of elementary education in Assan, Bihar, Madhya Pradesh, Andhra Pradesh, Jammu & Kashmir, Orissa, Rajasthan, U.P. and West Bengal (9 reports). Demographic and educational statistics in India. 1981.

Studies and surveys in preparation: 24 projects dealing with disparities in educational development. Educational economics. School organization. Complete list on request.

Proudh Shiksha Nideshalaya

0287

Translation: Directorate of Adult Education
Address: Block No. 10, Jamnagar Hutments, Shahjahan Road, NEW DELHI-110011
Year of creation: 1956
Parent Organization: Ministry of Education and Culture
Present Head: Mr. S.K. Tuteja
Size of staff. Total: 110 — Full time: 110
Researchers: 38 — Full time: 38
Research activities: from 10% to 25%
Educational research: more than 50%
Type of research: Applied research; action-oriented research having relevance to improvement of on-going adult education programme.
Functional objectives of research: To emanate useful and high quality research; to coordinate research activites; to disseminate research findings in a manner that would be comprehensible and practical for the improvement of the on-going programmes of adult education.
Periodical publications: DAE's Newsletter, bibliographies and summary reports of research studies for dissemination to the adult educators.
Monographs: Adult education for women: developing a research base through four case studies. First study. Educative component to a holistic health-care for rural communities in West Bengal.
Studies and surveys in preparation: Adult education for women: developing a research base through four case studies. Second study. Education and training in industries, 1983-84: an exploratory study in the public sector. Evolving a methodology for numeracy, learning and teaching for adults in rural areas. Effect of socio-psychological variates on participation and use of message by literates under adult education programme.

Regional College of Education, Ajmer

0288

Address: Pushkar Road, Rajasthan, AJMER-305004
Year of creation: 1963
Parent Organization: National Council of Educational Research and Training, New Delhi
Present Head: Prof. S.N. Dutta, Principal
Size of staff. Total: 63 — Full time: 63
Researchers: 30 — Full time: 1 — Part time: 29
Research activities: from 10% to 25%
Educational research: from 10% to 25%

Type of research: Basic and applied research.
Functional objectives of research: Partial fulfilment of degree requirements; serving the educational administration.
Periodical publications: The educational trends: a research journal.
Studies and surveys in preparation: The determination and development of thought in science during adolescence: an ERIC project.

Regional College of Education, Bhopal

0289

Address: Shyamla Hills, BHOPAL–462013, Madhya Pradesh
Year of creation: 1964
Parent Organization: National Council of Education, Research and Training, New Delhi
Present Head: Dr. J.S. Rajput
Size of staff. Total: 71
Type of research: Basic and applied research.
Functional objectives of research: Creation of modalities of integrated teacher training programme; undertake pilot studies and research projects on curricula, teaching methods, teacher education, elementary and secondary education.
Periodical publications: College news–letter. College hand–book.
Monographs: Vocationalizing secondary education: report of an occupational survey. Teacher education in the Western Region: report based on a regional study. Environmental studies: report of a research project. Non–formal education centres: report of a developmental project. Hoshangabad Science Education Project: report (in Hindi).
Studies and surveys in preparation: Institutional research projects on environmental studies, the learning environment and nonformal education. Research for degree programmes on science education, teacher education, guidance, elementary education.

Regional College of Education, Mysore

0290

Address: Manasagangotri Campus, MYSORE–570006
Year of creation: 1963
Parent Organization: National Council of Educational Research and Training, New Delhi
Present Head: Dr. A.K. Sharma
Size of staff. Total: 299 — Full time: 293 — Part time: 6
Researchers: 2 — Full time: 2
Research activities: from 10% to 25%
Educational research: more than 50%
Type of research: Applied research.
Functional objectives of research: To improve the quality of education in secondary schools in the Southern region of India.
Monographs: Occasional publications. List on request.
Studies and surveys in preparation: Acceptance, awareness and impact of RCE (Mysore) programmes. An experimental model for a cooperative remedial centre in an institutional campus (RCE Mysore). A comparison of psycho–social development of primary aged (1 to 4 years old) children with and without the background of preprimary education. Complete list on request.

Regional College of Education, Orissa 0291

Address: Bhubaneswar, 751007 ORISSA
Year of creation: 1963
Parent Organization: National Council of Educational Research and Training, New Delhi
Present Head: Dr. G.B. Kanungo
Size of staff. Total: 56 — Full time: 56
Researchers: 56
Research activities: less than 10%
Educational research: less than 10%
Type of research: Applied, research and development.
Functional objectives of research: Partial fulfilment of degree requirements; preparation of materials; advanced research.
Periodical publications: Current issues in education (1/yr).
Monographs: Mathemagenic activities of prose learning. Universalization of elementary education. Adult education: plan and action strategies.
Studies and surveys in preparation: Development of attribution of responsibility in children. A technique for establishing scale values, reliability and validity index of attitude scales. Teacher perception of training curriculum. Teacher perception of exceptional children. Adjunct questioning and prose learning. Complete list on request.

INDONESIA

Badan Penelitian dan Pengembangan Pendidikan dan Kebudayaan 0292

Translation: Office of Educational and Cultural Research and Development
Address: Jalan Jenderal Sudirman, Senayan, P.O. Box 297 Kby., JAKARTA
Year of creation: 1974
Parent Organization: Ministry of Education and Culture
Present Head: Prof. Dr. Harsja W. Bachtiar
Size of staff. Total: 368
Researchers: 146
Type of research: Applied research.
Functional objectives of research: Developing policy recommendations.
Periodical publications: School statistics. Education in Indonesia.
Studies and surveys in preparation: Policy studies.

Pusat Penelitian Unika Atma Jaya 0293

Translation: Atma Jaya Research Centre
Address: Jalan Jenderal Sudirman 49A, P.O. Box 2639/Jkt, JAKARTA
Year of creation: 1972
Parent Organization: Atma Jaya Foundation
Present Head: Prof. Dr. Anton M. Moeliono
Size of staff. Total: 36 — Full time: 36
Researchers: 25 — Full time: 25

Research activities: more than 50%
Educational research: 50%
Type of research: Basic and applied research.
Functional objectives of research: Servicing the research and training needs of educational institutes in Indonesia.
Periodical publications: Atma Jaya Research Centre newsletter (6/yr). Atma Jaya Research Centre Library bulletin (12/yr). Annual report. Educational research report series.
Monographs: Kurnia, N. Inventory of opinions on affective instructional objectives in the Atma Jaya Medical School. 1981. Noegroho, E.D. Principles of instructional design: a summary from the book by R.M. Gagné and L.J. Briggs. 1981. Noegroho, E.D. Affective student characteristics relevant to the instructional process. 1982. Tusin, M.R. Cognitive student characteristics relevant to the instructional process. 1982. Wouw, H.M.W.J.; Kurnia, N. Analysing instructional objectives: some remarks... 1982.
Studies and surveys in preparation: Indonesian overseas contract workers in the Middle East. Youth problems in the urban centres of West Java. External productivity of four private universities on Java. Tracer study among the alumni of the Dutch International Education Programme. Development of a research strategy for urban health problems.

IRAN (ISLAMIC REPUBLIC)

Sazemane Pazhuhesh va Barname Rizee Amovzeshee

0294

Translation: Organization of Research and Educational Planning
Address: Martyr Mousavi Building, Iranshahr, Shomali Ave, Postal code 14367, TEHRAN
Year of creation: 1975
Parent Organization: Ministry of Education
Present Head: Dr. G.A. Haddad Adel
Size of staff. Total: 250 — Full time: 200 — Part time: 50
Researchers: 15 — Full time: 10 — Part time: 5
Research activities: from 10% to 25%
Educational research: more than 50%
Type of research: Applied.
Functional objectives of research: To help solve educational problems.
Periodical publications: Several types of educational journals published for primary and secondary school students as well as for teachers.
Studies and surveys in preparation: Evaluation of school text books. Evaluation of an experimental educational project in schools called the TAM Project.

IRAQ

Markaz al-buḥūt at-tarbawiyya wa-ăn-nafsiyya **0295**

Translation: Center for Educational and Psychological Research (CEPR)
Address: University of Baghdad, Adhamiyyah, P.O. Box 4095, BAGHDAD
Year of creation: 1967
Parent Organization: Ministry of Higher Education and Scientific Research, Baghdad University
Present Head: Dr. Ibrahim Kadhem Ibrahim (PhD.)
Size of staff. Total: 42 — Full time: 42
Researchers: 3024 — Full time: 24
Research activities: more than 50%
Educational research: more than 50%
Type of research: Basic and applied research.
Functional objectives of research: Increase the effectiveness of education for economic and social development.
Periodical publications: Annual report of the Educational and Psychological Research Center.
Monographs: To what extent do universities' students rely on the teaching staffs' lectures and how much do they use books and references available in their colleges' libraries. Difficulties which hinder vocational education students from benefiting from practical training in Iraq. Evaluation of reading skills for understanding of the sixth primary pupils. Complete list on request.
Studies and surveys in preparation: Students' behavioural problems of some colleges of Baghdad University as seen by those in charge. To what extent is there interest in psychological and educational subjects in the College of Education and departments of teacher training of Baghdad University. Complete list on request.

IRELAND

Department of Education, University College **0296**

Address: CORK
Year of creation: 1911
Parent Organization: National University of Ireland
Present Head: Professor D.G. Mulcany
Size of staff. Total: 9 — Full time: 9
Researchers: 9 — Full time: 9
Research activities: from 10% to 25%
Educational research: from 10% to 25%
Type of research: Various.
Functional objectives of research: General advancement of knowledge in the field.
Studies and surveys in preparation: The real world of secondary education. Through a glass darkly: aspects of education in Northern Ireland. Educational policy in the Republic of Ireland.

Institiúid Teangeolaíochta Éireann

0297

Translation: Linguistics Institute of Ireland
Address: 31 Plás Mhic Liam, BAILE ATHA CLIATH, 2, Eire
Year of creation: 1972
Parent Organization: Department of Education
Present Head: Dr. Cathair Ó Dochartaigh
Size of staff. Total: 15 — Full time: 15
Researchers: 10 — Full time: 10
Research activities: more than 50%
Educational research: more than 50%
Type of research: Applied research in the field of linguistics with special reference to Irish and learning and teaching of modern European languages.
Functional objectives of research: Servicing needs of educational administrators and teaching profession; preparation of courses.
Periodical publications: Teangeolas (2/yr). Annual report.
Monographs: Language syllabus planning for the development of communicative skills. Language policy and socioeconomic development in Ireland. I.T.E. experimental test in spoken French: report. Some problems in the design of a functional syllabus. All-Irish primary schools in the Dublin area. Complete list on request.
Studies and surveys in preparation: Survey of language attitudes in an Irish-speaking area in Kerry. Survey on spoken Irish of teachers and pupils of 11 and 17 years, respectively. Oral Irish tests in primary schools. Irish language attitudes research. Development of materials for teaching French and German in post-primary schools in connection with ITE Modern Languages Project.

ISRAEL

Beit Hasefer Le Chinuch

0298

Translation: School of Education
Address: University of Haifa, Mt. Carmel, HAIFA 31 999
Parent Organization: University of Haifa
Present Head: Prof. Pearla Nesher
Research activities: from 25% to 50%
Educational research: from 25% to 50%
Type of research: Research and development.
Functional objectives of research: Partial fulfilment of degree; servicing educational needs.
Periodical publications: Studies in education. Reading and children's literature. Studies in administration.
Monographs: Ben-Peretz, M. Curriculum analysis as a tool in evaluation. In: Levy, A., ed. Evaluation. In press. Feitelson, D. Fads and facts in reading instruction. In press. Schwarcz, J. Ways of the illustrator-visual communication in children's literature. In press. Complete list on request.

Machon Henrietta Szold — Hamachon Haartzi Lemechkar Bemada'ei Hahitnahagut **0299**

Translation: Henrietta Szold Institute — The National Institute for Research in the Behavioral Sciences
Address: 9 Colombia Street, Kiryat-Menachem, JERUSALEM 96583
Year of creation: 1941
Present Head: Dr. Y. Friedman
Size of staff. Total: 54
Researchers: 10
Research activities: 50%
Educational research: more than 50%
Type of research: Applied research.
Periodical publications: Megamot. Current research in the social sciences.
Monographs: Youth Aliya — the education of the culturally disadvantaged. 1983. Administrative styles in Israeli elementary schools. 1982. Immigrant students in pre-academic courses in institutes of higher learning in Israel. 1982. Problems raised by mothers in parent-education groups. 1982. Violence in schools: patterns of coping by the educational system. 1981.
Studies and surveys in preparation: The testing and assessment of Israel's academically gifted and talented youngsters. A nation-wide survey of kindergarten reading readiness programmes. Minimal competency testing project of Israeli 3rd graders in reading comprehension and arithmetic. Instructional staff burn-out.

Hamerkaz Haisraeli Lehorat Hamadaim, Hauniversita Haivrit Yerushaliem **0300**

Translation: Israel Science Teaching Center, Hebrew University Jerusalem
Address: Givat Ram, JERUSALEM
Year of creation: 1967
Parent Organization: Hebrew University and the Ministry of Education and Culture
Present Head: Professor Alexandra Poljakoff-Mayber
Size of staff. Total: 40 — Full time: 8 — Part time: 32
Researchers: 10 — Full time: 2 — Part time: 8
Research activities: from 25% to 50%
Educational research: from 25% to 50%
Type of research: Basic, applied, research and development, evaluation.
Functional objectives of research: Development of research instruments and tests; design and analysis of matriculation examinations; partial fulfilment of degree requirements; providing data for decision markers (e.g. administrators, curriculum developers, teachers, ministry officials).
Periodical publications: Alow lemoray habiologia (Biology teacher bulletin). Mabat (A science journal for grades 7-10). Alow lemoray hachimia (Chemistry teacher bulletin).
Monographs: Preservice and inservice education of science teachers. 1984. Report on the structure and activities of the Science Teaching Department at the Hebrew University.
Studies and surveys in preparation: Second IEA International Science Study: cognitive preferences of 12th grade students. Computers in science and math education. Teaching and learning in the high school laboratory. Assessment of two innovative biology courses at the University. Comparison of biology achievement of Jewish and Arab students. Curriculum development through master's and Ph.D. dissertations.

Science Teaching Department

0301

Address: Weizmann Institute, REHOVOT 76100
Year of creation: 1969
Parent Organization: Weizmann Institute
Present Head: Prof. M. Bruckheimer
Size of staff. Total: 49 — Full time: 11 — Part time: 38
Researchers: 15 — Full time: 11 — Part time: 4
Research activities: from 25% to 50%
Type of research: Applied to curriculum development and implementation.
Periodical publications: Shevavim (for maths teachers) (in Hebrew). Tehuda (for physics teachers) (in Hebrew). Hakesher hachimi (for chemistry teachers) (in Hebrew).
Studies and surveys in preparation: Cognitive processes of mathematics learning as evidenced by analysis of students' mistakes. The role of the history of mathematics in the curriculum. Students' understanding of the function concept. A model relating teachers' perception to students' difficulties. Study of learning difficulties in grade 9, and development of remedial teaching methods. Evaluation of these methods in schools. Research of problem solving processes in high school physics and development of strategies for improving student performance. Study of concept learning and misconceptions in high school physics. Evaluation of teachers and teaching methods. Identification of learning difficulties in the context of high school chemistry with regard to concept formation, scientific thinking and Piagetian developmental stages. Complete list on request.

ITALY

Biblioteca di documentazione pedagogica

0302

Translation: Bibliothèque de documentation pédagogique
Address: Via M. Buonarroti 10, 50122 FIRENZE
Year of creation: 1980
Parent Organization: Ministère de l'éducation nationale
Present Head: Prof. Renato Bortoli
Size of staff. Total: 30 — Full time: 30
Researchers: 25 — Full time: 25
Research activities: 50%
Educational research: 50%
Type of research: Recherches appliquées.
Functional objectives of research: Réunir la documentation pédagogique; diffuser des orientations pour l'expérimentation et la recherche.
Periodical publications: Segnalibro. Annuario delle letture dall'infanzia all'adolescenza. Schedario. Letteratura giovanile, gioco e animazione tempo libero.
Monographs: Le biblioteche scolastiche. Attindei corsi residendiaziali di aggiornamento per docenti (...). 1983. La documentazione pedagogica: un presente e un futuro. 1983. Le pubblicazione dell'Unesco. Atti del Convegno europeo dei Club Unesco. 1984. Leggere: movimenti letterari e letteratura giovanile. 1984.
Studies and surveys in preparation: Progetti di documentazione del sistema scolastico italiano quali l'aggiornamento degli insegnanti, la sperimentazione scolastica e

l'inserimento dei portatori di handicap. Progetti di tipo bibliografico relativi alla letteratura nell'ambito delle scienze dell'educazione, con creazione del thesaurus pedagogico e di basi-dati bibliografiche su tematiche attinenti la ricerca educativa, l'educazione degli adulti, storia dell'educazione, letteratura giovanile e scienza dell' educazione.

Centro de ricerca delle tecnologie dell'istruzione (CRTI)

0303

Translation: Research Centre of Educational Technology
Address: Largo Gemelli 1, 20123 MILANO
Year of creation: 1969
Parent Organization: Università cattolica del Sacro Cuore — Milano
Present Head: Prof. Mario Groppo
Size of staff. Total: 14 — Full time: 3 — Part time: 11
Researchers: 11 — Full time: 1 — Part time: 10
Research activities: 50%
Educational research: more than 50%
Type of research: Basic and applied.
Functional objectives of research: Basic qualifications for primary schools, educational technology, models for teacher training.
Monographs: Groppo, M.; Liverta Sempio, O. La scheda di valutazione. 1981. Groppo, M. (a cura di). La psicologia dell'educazione. Vol. I: Aspetti psicopedagogici. 1983.
Studies and surveys in preparation: La psicologia dell'educazione. Vol. II: Interventi rieducativi, in corso di stampa. Il tempo educativo nella scuola dell'obbligo.

Centro di orientamento professionale, servizio istruzione e assistenza scholastica

0304

Translation: Guidance and Counselling Bureau, Teaching and School Assistance Service
Address: Via Petrarca 32, TRENTO
Year of creation: 1958
Parent Organization: Self-governing Province of Trient
Present Head: Dott. Mauro Marcantoni, laurea in sociologia
Size of staff. Total: 18 — Full time: 9
Researchers: 9
Research activities: from 25% to 50%
Educational research: from 25% to 50%
Type of research: Applied.
Functional objectives of research: Preparation of courses; servicing the educational administration; working information.
Periodical publications: Spazio orientamento. L'Impegno di una scelta. Scelte universitarie e para-universitarie.
Monographs: L'impegno di una scelta: orientamento al laboro per aree professionali e percorsi formativi. 1983. Scelte universitarie e para universitarie. 1983. Materiali di lavoro — progetto scuola-laboro. 1983. Complete list on request.
Studies and surveys in preparation: Attivazione della III fase della sperimentazione con finalità orientative presso la Scuola elementare "V. Veneto" di Trento nell'anno scolastico 1983-84. Sperimentazione didattica con finalità orientative presso la Scuola elementare Madonna Bianca di Trento nell'anno scolastico 1983-84. Sperimentazione nell'a.s. '82/83 presso l'Istituto magistrale "A. Rosmini" di Trento, riguardante una ipotesi progettuale quadriennale di una classe sul tema: "Il libro e i settori connessi

alla sua produzione, distribuzione, conservazione, classificazione, restauro" Complete list on request.

Centro europeo dell'educazione (CEDE)

0305

Translation: European Centre of Education/ Centre européen de l'éducation
Address: Villa Faconieri, 00044 FRASCATI, Roma
Year of creation: 1974
Parent Organization: Ministero della pubblica istruzione
Present Head: Aldo Visalberghi, Professor of education at the University of Rome
Size of staff. Total: 46 — Full time: 46
Researchers: 24 — Full time: 24
Research activities: from 25% to 50%
Educational research: more than 50%
Type of research: Applied and R&D.
Functional objectives of research: Research on educative problems and structures both within the country and (chiefly) between countries.
Periodical publications: Ricerca educativa (4/yr).
Monographs: I quaderni di Villa Falconieri, n.1: Innovazione educativa e riforma dell'insegnamento primario. 1983. I quaderni di Villa Falconieri, n.2: L'educazione plurilingue in Italia. 1983.
Studies and surveys in preparation: Second IEA Science Study. IEA Study of Written Composition. Information sciences and technologies in general education. In-service training of teachers at distance in Italy: a survey. The teaching of literature both Italian and foreign. Mastery learning. Introduction of information technologies in the CEDE Research Organization.

Centro nazionale italiano tecnologie educative (CNITE)

0306

Translation: Centre national italien de technologie éducative (CNITE)
Address: Via Marche 84, 00187 ROMA
Year of creation: 1969
Parent Organization: Organisme semi-officiel
Present Head: Dottore Giorgio Panizzi
Size of staff. Total: 7 — Full time: 4 — Part time: 3
Researchers: 14 — Full time: 4 — Part time: 10
Research activities: from 25% to 50%
Educational research: from 25% to 50%
Type of research: Recherche et développement.
Functional objectives of research: Fournir des prestations à l'administration de l'éducation; préparation de cours.
Periodical publications: Quaderni CNITE.
Monographs: La valutazione nella scuola media dell'obbligo. Informazione e documentazione nel settore sociale ed educativo. Thesaurus multilingue Eudised: traduzione italiana per il Consiglio d'Europa. La necessità di formazione del personale operante nelle Unità sanitarie locali della Regione Campania. Corso multimediale di statistica sociale. Corso modulare sui temi delle scienze dell'educazione.
Studies and surveys in preparation: La gaming simulation nei processi formativi. Progetto di applicazione dell'informatica alla didattica della letteratura. Progetto per

la costituzione di un laboratorio didattico-informatico per motu-video audiolesi. Progetto di fattibilità per la costituzione di una base dati sulle tecnologie educative. Progetto di informazione e formazione di quadri delle piccole e medie imprese del Lazio.

Dipartimento di scienze dell'educazione

0307

Translation: Département des sciences de l'éducation
Address: Palazzo Ateneo, Piazza Umberto 1, 70121 BARI
Year of creation: 1983
Parent Organization: Università degli studi di Bari
Present Head: Professora Luisa Santelli Beccegato, Ordinario di pedagogia
Size of staff. Total: 29 — Full time: 29
Researchers: 29 — Full time: 29
Research activities: from 25% to 50%
Educational research: more than 50%
Type of research: Fondamentale et appliquée.
Functional objectives of research: Formation des formateurs; fournir des prestations à l'administration de l'éducation.
Periodical publications: "Quaderni" del dipartimento di scienze dell'educazione.
Studies and surveys in preparation: Nuovi curricula per la formazione degli insegnanti della scuola di base. Educazione e formazione ricorrente.

Fondazione Rui

0308

Translation: Rui Foundation
Address: Via Crescenzio 16, 00193 ROMA
Year of creation: 1959
Present Head: Prof. Ing. Luigi Fortina
Size of staff. Total: 15 — Full time: 10 — Part time: 5
Researchers: 8 — Full time: 5 — Part time: 3
Research activities: from 10% to 25%
Educational research: more than 50%
Type of research: R & D.
Functional objectives of research: Research requested by the Ministry of Education.
Periodical publications: Documenti di lavoro.
Monographs: Camiciotti, G. L'orientamento personale degli alumni. 1981. Castillo, G. L'adolescenza e i suoi problemi. 1981. Dallo studio al lavoro: esperienze europee nell'ambito scolastico e universitario: atti del XXIV Convegno. 1982. Scelta e riuscita negli studi e transizione alla vita attiva nell'insegnamento superiore: atti del Colloquio europeo, Castelgandolfo 1982. Fondazione Rui. L'orientamento e il "counselling" nelle Università della Comunità Europea. 1982.
Studies and surveys in preparation: L'orientamento nella scuola media dell'obbligo. L'orientamento e la riforma della scuola secondaria superiore. La formazione nel settore dei beni culturali.

Instituto regionale di ricerca, sperimentazione e aggiornamento educativi (IRRSAE) **0309**

Translation: Regional Institute for Educational Research, Experimentation and In-service Training for Sicily
Address: Via Resuttana Colli 360, 90146 PALERMO
Year of creation: 1979
Parent Organization: Ministero della pubblica istruzione
Present Head: Professor Vincenzo Rapisarda, Director of Catania Neuropsychiatric Clinic (University)
Size of staff. Total: 16 — Full time: 16
Research activities: less than 10%
Educational research: more than 50%
Type of research: Applied, R&D.
Functional objectives of research: Knowledge of school system, behaviour of teachers.
Periodical publications: Funzione docente (Teaching function) (4/yr).
Studies and surveys in preparation: Beginning training and in-service training of teachers.

Istituto di pedagogia **0310**

Translation: Institute of Education
Address: Via Tigor 22, 34124 TRIESTE TS
Year of creation: 1954
Parent Organization: Università di Trieste
Present Head: Enzo Petrini, Professore ordinario di pedagogia
Size of staff. Total: 14 — Full time: 14
Researchers: 4 — Full time: 4
Research activities: more than 50%
Educational research: more than 50%
Type of research: Basic and applied research.
Functional objectives of research: Training and in-service training of teaching staff.
Monographs: Educare l'infanzia. 1983. Maestri domani. 1981. Profilo di storia della pedagogia. 1981. Nuove prospettive della professionalità docente. 1982. Socrate e dopo. 1983. Dalla parte di Collodi. 1982.
Studies and surveys in preparation: University training of the teaching staff in the primary school. Some problems of the history of education.

Istituto di pedagogia della facoltà di magistero della Università di Palermo **0311**

Translation: Institut de pédagogie de la Faculté des maîtres de l'Université de Palermo
Address: Piazza Ignazio Florio 24, 90139 PALERMO
Year of creation: 1980
Parent Organization: Università degli studi di Palermo
Present Head: Mario Manno
Size of staff. Total: 10 — Full time: 10
Researchers: 5 — Full time: 5
Type of research: Fondamentale, appliquée.
Periodical publications: Annali della Facoltà di magistero.
Monographs: Funzione pubblica della pedagogia. Nuove ricerche sul personalismo. Introduzione critica all'educazione etico-politica. Scelte educative. Sicilia giornali.

Pinocchio: storia di un burattino che diventa uomo. Ipotesi pedagogica del problematicismo. Educazione stetica. Valutazione scolastica. Studio e lavoro al termine della scuola dell'obbligo. Aspetti pedagogici dell'orientamento universitario.
Studies and surveys in preparation: Teorie pedagogiche e prassi educativa in Sicilia. Educazione politica da Kant alla scuola di Francoforte. Educazione permanente. Educazione al lavoro. Uso didattico del quotidiano. La formazione degli insegnanti della scuola dell'obbligo.

Istituto di pedagogia, Facoltà di lettere e filosofia, Università degli studi di Milano **0312**

Translation: Institut de pédagogie, Faculté de lettres et philosophie, Université des études de Milan
Address: Via Festa del Perdono, n. 3, 20122 MILANO
Parent Organization: Università degli studi di Milano
Present Head: Prof. Riccardo Massa
Size of staff. Total: 11 — Full time: 9 — Part time: 2
Researchers: 5 — Full time: 4 — Part time: 1
Research activities: 50%
Educational research: more than 50%
Type of research: Fondamentale et appliquée, recherche et développement.
Functional objectives of research: Préparation de cours; fournir des prestations à l'administration de l'éducation.
Monographs: Rezzara, A. Il bambino davanti all'imagine: studi di pedagogia infantile. 1983.
Studies and surveys in preparation: Il microprocessori in educazione. La struttura epistemologica della ricerca educativa. L'educazione politica dei giovani.

Istituto di scienze pedagogiche e psicologiche **0313**

Translation: Institut de sciences pédagogiques et psychologiques
Address: Piazza Universita 2, 95125 CATANIA
Year of creation: 1984
Parent Organization: Facoltà di lettere e filosofia, Università degli studi, Catania
Present Head: Prof. Gino Corallo
Size of staff. Total: 16 — Full time: 15 — Part time: 1
Researchers: 14 — Full time: 13 — Part time: 1
Research activities: from 25% to 50%
Educational research: more than 50%
Type of research: Fondamentale et appliquée.
Functional objectives of research: Préparation de cours, fournir des prestations à l'administration de l'éducation.
Monographs: Corallo, G. I giovani e l'educazione morale. In: Problemi educativi della condizione giovanile. 1983. Patané, L.R. Spirito scientifico e insegnamento della scienza in Gaston Bachelard. 1981. Vittone, F. Educazione e ordinamento giuridico. 1981. Moscato, M.T. Educazione familiare e insuccesso scolastico. In: La famiglia e la scuola. 1983. Henry Bouchet e l'individualizzazione dell'insegnamento. In: Studi di storia dell'educazione. 1982. Liste complète sur demande.
Studies and surveys in preparation: Ricerche sulla storia della scuola e dell'educazione in Italia fra 800 e 900. Ricerca sul campo su alcuni contenuti proposti dai libri di testo. Ricerca sul senso dello spazio e del tempo nel bambino a livello di scuola

elementare. Ricerca sul campo sul fenomeno dell'insuccesso scolastico. Ricerca sperimentale sulle modalità d'apprendimento dell'adulto in piccolo gruppo, con la metodologia del caso.

Istituto per le tecnologie didattiche

0314

Translation: Institute for Instructional Technology
Address: Via all'Opera Pia 11, 16145 GENOVA
Year of creation: 1970
Parent Organization: Consiglio nazionale delle ricerche
Present Head: Prof. Ing. Giorgio Olimpo
Size of staff. Total: 9 — Full time: 9
Researchers: 6 — Full time: 6
Research activities: more than 50%
Educational research: more than 50%
Type of research: Applied research.
Functional objectives of research: To develop methodologies, models and prototypes of instructional systems.
Studies and surveys in preparation: Instructional application of videodisc. Development of the material for a course of computer literacy.

Istituto regionale di ricerca, sperimentazione e aggiornamento educativi della Basilicata

0315

Translation: Regional Institute for Educational Research, Experimentation and In-service Training
Address: Via IV Novembre 14, 85100 POTENZA
Year of creation: 1979
Parent Organization: Ministero della pubblica istruzione
Present Head: Prof. Leddomade Beatrice, Docente psicologia, Università di Bari
Size of staff. Total: 15 — Full time: 2 — Part time: 13
Research activities: more than 50%
Educational research: from 25% to 50%
Type of research: Recherche et développement.
Functional objectives of research: Préparation de cours; fournir des propositions.
Periodical publications: Bolletino "Scuola e territorio"
Studies and surveys in preparation: Il bambino di 5 anni e la sua scuola. Ricerca-formazione sul tempo pieno in Basilicata. Il bilinguismo in Basilicata.

Istituto regionale di ricerca, sperimentazione e aggiornamento educativi (I.R.R.S.A.E.)

0316

Translation: Institut régional pour la recherche et l'expérimentation éducatives et la formation en cours d'emploi
Address: Via Melo 231, 70121 BARI
Year of creation: 1979
Parent Organization: Ministero della pubblica istruzione
Present Head: Prof. Luisa Santelli Beccegato, titulaire de pédagogie à l'Université de Bari
Size of staff. Total: 24 — Full time: 10 — Part time: 14
Researchers: 6 — Full time: 4 — Part time: 2
Research activities: from 10% to 25%

Educational research: from 25% to 50%
Type of research: Appliquée.
Functional objectives of research: Fournir un soutien et une orientation au Ministère de l'instruction publique.
Periodical publications: Bollettino di ricerca, sperimentazione e aggiornamento (4/an). Quaderni dell'IRRSAE di Puglia (trois cahiers déjà parus).
Monographs: Uno spazio per il rinnovamento educativo. 1981. Aggiornamento e ricerca. 1982. La ricerca educativa. 1984.
Studies and surveys in preparation: Sur l'enseignement des langues étrangères, de la géographie; rapports entre l'école et la recherche.

Istituto regionale di ricerca, sperimentazione e aggiornamento educativi per l'Emilia/Romagna (IRRSAE)

0317

Translation: Regional Institute for Educational Research, Experimentation and In-service Training — Emilia/Romagna
Address: Via Testoni 5, 40123 BOLOGNA
Year of creation: 1974
Parent Organization: Ministero della pubblica istruzione
Present Head: Prof. Lucio Guasti
Size of staff. Total: 52 — Full time: 22
Researchers: 30 (teachers seconded to IRRSAE)
Research activities: from 10% to 25%
Educational research: from 10% to 25%
Type of research: Educational research and development.
Functional objectives of research: School improvement.
Periodical publications: Innovazione educativa.
Monographs: Quaderni.
Studies and surveys in preparation: Insegnamento storia letteratura 1o anno scuole sec. superiori. Passaggio giovani dagli studi alla vita attiva (Progetto CEE). Potenzialità intellettive dei ragazzi diversi strati sociali. Insegnamento educazione tecnica. Scuole medie Emilia/Romagna.

Istituto S.E.F.O.R. (Istituto siciliano per la formazione, l'orientamento e la ricerca educativa)

0318

Translation: S.E.F.O.R. Institute (Sicilian Institute for Training, Counselling and Educational Research)
Address: Viale Regina Margherita 10, 95100 CATANIA
Year of creation: 1984
Parent Organization: Independent, self-financing association
Present Head: Prof.ssa Maria Teresa Moscato
Size of staff. Total: 9 — Part time: 9
Researchers: 9 — Part time: 9
Research activities: more than 50%
Educational research: more than 50%
Type of research: Applied.
Functional objectives of research: Servicing the educational administration and school personnel.
Monographs: The Institute being too recent, a list of publications of present research

staff, covering the last 3 years, is available on request.
Studies and surveys in preparation: Ricerca permanente sui metodi e le tecniche della formazione in servizio degli insegnanti; ricerca sulle difficoltà scolastiche dei figli degli emigrati italiani e degli immigrati stranieri in Italia.

Movimento di collaborazione civica

0319

Translation: Mouvement de collaboration civique
Address: Via Filippo Corridoni n.6, 00195 ROMA
Year of creation: 1945
Present Head: Dott. Prof. Ebe Flamini
Size of staff. Total: 18 — Full time: 3 — Part time: 15
Researchers: 10 — Full time: 1 — Part time: 9
Research activities: from 25% to 50%
Educational research: from 25% to 50%
Type of research: Appliquée; recherche et développement.
Functional objectives of research: Sur l'éducation permanente, satisfaire partiellement aux conditions d'obtention d'un grade; préparation de cours; fournir des prestations à l'administration de l'éducation soit nationale soit locale.
Monographs: Processi formativi ed intervento educativo in Calabria. Libro e lettura nella scuola. Strutture culturali e sociali nelle 20 circoscrizioni di Roma. Indagine sulle biblioteche-centri culturali della città di Roma. La figura dell'assistente di biblioteca nelle scuole e nei comuni della Provincia di Roma.
Studies and surveys in preparation: Ricerca per proposte di sviluppo di attività economiche nella zona di Pomezia. Progetto di formazione di base (mise à niveau) per disoccupato, (i due progetti sono approvati dal Fondo sociale europeo). Progetto per una programmazione educativa e culturale nella prospettiva dell'educazione permanente, nella Provincia di Roma. Progetto di intervento educativo in Calabria.

Organizzazione per la preparazione professionale degli insegnanti (O.P.P.I.)

0320

Translation: Organisation pour la préparation professionnelle des enseignants
Address: Via Orseolo n.1, 20144 MILANO
Year of creation: 1965
Present Head: Piero Cattaneo — Preside Scuola media
Size of staff. Total: 46 — Full time: 6
Researchers: 40 — Part time: 40
Research activities: 50%
Educational research: 50%
Type of research: Recherche et développement.
Functional objectives of research: Préparation et évaluation de cours de formation en cours de service; fournir des prestations à l'administration de l'éducation.
Periodical publications: Oppidocumenti. Oppinformazioni.
Monographs: L'educazione ecologica: un contributo sul campo alla soluzione dei problemi dell'ambiente. Riforma scuola secondaria superiore e determinazione dei contenuti formativi dell'area comune. Scuola e salute dei minori. La condizione e la formazione degli insegnanti in alcuni paesi della CEE (en collaboration avec ATEE).
Studies and surveys in preparation: Sistema di informazione sulle professioni. Prevenzione dalle tossicodipendenze nella scuola secondaria superiore. Scienze sociali e curricoli nella scuola secondaria superiore.

Pontificia facoltà di scienze dell'educazione "Auxilium"

0321

Translation: Faculté pontificale des sciences de l'éducation "Auxilium"
Address: Via Cremolino, 141, 00166 ROMA
Year of creation: 1954
Present Head: Colombo Antonia
Size of staff. Total: 43 — Full time: 27 — Part time: 16
Researchers: 9 — Part time: 9
Research activities: from 25% to 50%
Educational research: from 25% to 50%
Type of research: Fondamentale, appliquée.
Functional objectives of research: Satisfaire partiellement aux conditions d'obtention d'un grade; préparation de cours; fournir des prestations à l'administration de l'éducation.
Periodical publications: Rivista di scienze dell'educazione.
Monographs: Chang, Hiang Chu Ausilia. La pedagogia comparata come disciplina pedagogica. 1982. Lanfranchi, R. Genesi degli scritti pedagogici di Antonio Rosmini. 1983. Marchi, M. Menottic. Il cristianesimo come profezia in Mario Pomilio. 1984 (sous presse).
Studies and surveys in preparation: Giovani e riconciliazione: ricerca sociologica su un campione di giovani (18–19 anni). Ricerca sulla cultura di base nei corsi di formazione professionale in relazione al biennio della scuola secondaria superiore.

Unione cattolica italiana insegnanti medi

0322

Translation: Union catholique italienne des enseignants de l'enseignement secondaire
Address: Via Crescensio 25, 00193 ROMA
Year of creation: 1944
Present Head: Prof. Cesarina Checcacci, professore di scuola media, membro del C.N.P.I.
Size of staff. Total: 20 — Full time: 12 — Part time: 8
Researchers: 6 — Part time: 6
Research activities: from 25% to 50%
Educational research: more than 50%
Type of research: Recherche et développement.
Functional objectives of research: L'actualisation de la profession enseignante.
Periodical publications: La Scuola e l'uomo.
Monographs: La scuola media degli anni 80. Proposte per la scuola. Istituti tecnici industriali. L'integrazione scolastica degli andicappati. I problemi della scuola italiana. Gli esami di licenza media. Giovani, culture contemporanea e scuola. La famiglia e la scuola.
Studies and surveys in preparation: Proposte per gli indirizzi matematico, naturalistico, meccanico, elettronico, elettrotecnico, giuridico, amministrativo e economico, aziendale della nuova scuola secondaria superiore. L'UCIIM sulla riforma della scuola secondaria superiore. Il problema del secolo: l'informatica e la scuola.

IVORY COAST

Centre d'enseignement et de recherches audio-visuels (CERAV) 0323

Address: B.P. V34, ABIDJAN
Year of creation: 1969
Parent Organization: Université nationale
Present Head: Roger Alangba
Size of staff. Total: 20 — Full time: 19 — Part time: 1
Researchers: 7 — Full time: 4 — Part time: 3
Research activities: 50%
Educational research: from 10% to 25%
Type of research: Appliquée, recherche et développement.
Functional objectives of research: Adaptation du contenu et des méthodes d'éducation (accent mis sur l'audiovisuel).
Periodical publications: Communication audio-visuelle (1/an).
Monographs: L'enfant ivoirien et la technologie. 1981. Transfert des technologies de communication pour le développement: leçons de l'éducation télévisuelle de Côte d'Ivoire (paru en anglais).
Studies and surveys in preparation: Les médias et l'acquisition des connaissances: élèves du primaires/adultes. Modèles culturels véhiculés par les manuels de français de l'enseignement primaire.

Centre national de formation permanente des personnels de l'éducation (CNFP) 0324

Address: B.P. 1189, BOUAKE 01
Year of creation: 1976
Parent Organization: Direction de la pédagogie
Present Head: M. Maurice Kouyate
Size of staff. Total: 36 — Full time: 36
Research activities: less than 10%
Educational research: from 10% to 25%
Type of research: Recherches appliquées à l'enseignement fondamental (méthodes, programme, formation permanente).
Functional objectives of research: Elaborer, harmoniser et développer les contenus et méthodes d'enseignement pour l'école primaire; élaborer, harmoniser, développer les contenus et méthodes pour la formation initiale et continue des enseignants et des personnels d'encadrement.
Periodical publications: L'Ecole permanente (1/semaine).
Studies and surveys in preparation: Projet d'enseignement par correspondance à l'intention des instituteurs du primaire pour la préparation des examens et concours professionnels.

JAMAICA

Faculty of Education, University of the West Indies

0325

Address: Mona, KINGSTON 7
Year of creation: 1953
Parent Organization: University of the West Indies
Present Head: Professor Dennis R. Craig, Dean
Size of staff. Total: 71 — Full time: 71
Researchers: 41 — Full time: 41
Research activities: 50%
Educational research: 50%
Type of research: Basic, applied, developmental.
Functional objectives of research: Fulfilment of degree requirements; servicing of national educational institutions; advancing knowledge in all disciplines serving education.
Periodical publications: Caribbean journal of education. Occasional papers of the Society for Caribbean Linguistics.
Monographs: Monograph series of the Caribbean journal of education.
Studies and surveys in preparation: Cognitive development and learning disabilities. Evaluation of student performance. Evaluation of the tutorial system in the experimental project for primary schools.

Jamaican Movement for the Advancement of Literacy

0326

Address: 47B South Camp Road, P.O. Box 40, KINGSTON 4
Year of creation: 1972
Parent Organization: Ministry of Education
Present Head: Miss Leila T. Thomas
Size of staff. Total: 642 — Full time: 400 — Part time: 242
Researchers: 6 — Full time: 6
Research activities: less than 10%
Educational research: more than 50%
Type of research: Surveys for educational development.
Functional objectives of research: Servicing educational requirements.
Periodical publications: New readers' page — daily gleaner (2/mth). Let's read (4/yr). Lamplight (4/yr). Light magazine (12/yr).
Monographs: Occasional.
Studies and surveys in preparation: Jamal communications skills, literacy survey, 1981.

JAPAN

Hikaku Kyoiku Bunka Kenkyushisetsu

0327

Translation: Research Institute of Comparative Education and Culture
Address: 6-19-1 Hakozaki, Higashi-ku, FUKUOKA CITY, 812
Year of creation: 1955
Parent Organization: Faculty of Education, Kyushu University

Present Head: Prof. Kazuhiko Hironaka
Size of staff. Total: 20 — Full time: 6 — Part time: 14
Researchers: 19 — Full time: 5 — Part time: 14
Research activities: less than 10%
Educational research: less than 10%
Type of research: Basic research.
Functional objectives of research: Carry out comprehensive comparative research in education and culture in Asia.
Periodical publications: Research bulletin.
Studies and surveys in preparation: Comparative research on the development of educational policies and their socio-cultural bases in Asian countries during the post-war period.

Hokkaido Kyoiku Daigaku

0328

Translation: Hokkaido University of Education
Address: Nishi 13-chome, Minami 24-jo, Chuo-ku, SAPPORO, Hokkaido 064
Year of creation: 1949
Parent Organization: Ministry of Education, Science and Culture
Present Head: Hisashi Ishii
Size of staff. Total: 984 — Full time: 915 — Part time: 69
Researchers: 414 — Full time: 414
Research activities: 50%
Educational research: more than 50%
Type of research: Basic and applied.
Functional objectives of research: Training of teachers.
Periodical publications: Hokkaido Kyoiku Daigaku kiyo (Journal of Hokkaido University of Education). C.A.I. Kenkyu hokoku (Bulletin of C.A.I. research). Kushiro ronshu. Kyoiku kogaku Center kenkyu hokoku. Hekichi kyoiku kenkyu (Bulletin of Rural Education Institute). Seibutsu kyozai. Taisetsuzan Sizen Kyoiku Kenkyu Sisetu kenkyu hokoku (Reports of the Taisetsuzan Institute of Science). Nenpo iwamizawa.
Studies and surveys in preparation: Basic studies and development of teaching materials in elementary education through a visual-informational analysis system. Development of curriculum for environmental education. Usage of computer in education — C.M.I, C.A.I. and programme for educational information.

National Institute for Educational Research (NIER)

0329

Address: 6-5-22 Shimomeguro, Meguro-ku, TOKYO 153
Year of creation: 1949
Parent Organization: Ministry of Education, Science and Culture
Present Head: Mr. Isao Suzuki
Size of staff. Total: 99 — Full time: 99 — Part time: Some
Researchers: 71 — Full time: 71 — Part time: some
Research activities: more than 50%
Educational research: more than 50%
Type of research: Basic and applied research.
Functional objectives of research: Mostly serving the researchers in education and partially serving the administration.

Periodical publications: Research bulletins (Japanese and English).
Monographs: Research bulletin No. 21: Development of criteria and procedures for the evaluation of school curricula. Low-cost aids for elementary science teaching in Asia and the Pacific. Research and educational reform: problems and issues. Scanning the new horizons: essays on the preparation of educational research personnel in Asia and the Pacific. Vocational and technical teacher preparation. Complete list on request.
Studies and surveys in preparation: Comprehensive study on the role of educational research in the reform of the educational system, content and methods. Comprehensive and comparative study on international exchange and assistance in education. A comprehensive study of juvenile delinquency. List on request.

Osaka-fu Kagaku Kyoiku Center

0330

Translation: Osaka Prefectural Science Education Institute
Address: 13-23, 4-chome, Karita, Sumiyoshi-ku, OSAKA 558
Year of creation: 1962
Parent Organization: Osaka Prefectural Board of Education
Present Head: Shigeru Shimanaka
Size of staff. Total: 91 — Full time: 83 — Part time: 8
Researchers: 32 — Full time: 32
Research activities: 50%
Educational research: more than 50%
Type of research: Research and development.
Functional objectives of research: Obtaining data for the improvement of the educational administration, improvement of teaching methods in each subject for use in in-service training, development of teaching materials, and finding effective ways and means to cope with problems arising in school education today.
Periodical publications: Kenkyu hokoku shuroku (Compilation of research reports). Osaka no chigakukyoiku (Earth science education in Osaka). Butsuri to kyoiku (Physics and education). Seibutsu to kyozai (Biology and its teaching materials). Kagaku to kyoiku (Chemistry and education). Kyoikukeikaku Kenkyushitsu kenkyukiyo (Bulletin of Educational Planning Section).
Monographs: Sugakka shindan chiryo yo kyozai. Speech and Sketch — Ryakuga o katsuyoshita eigo no shido.
Studies and surveys in preparation: Studies on the influence of new curricula on individual school programmes. Development of a teaching system emphasizing individualized learning in the classroom. Studies on methods and techniques for teaching handicapped children. A survey of pre-school children's language abilities and development of the curriculum for their language education. Complete list on request.

Research Institute for Higher Education

0331

Address: Higashisenda-machi, HIROSHIMA CITY 730
Year of creation: 1972
Parent Organization: Hiroshima University
Present Head: Inaga Keiji
Size of staff. Total: 56 — Full time: 11 — Part time: 45
Researchers: 52 — Full time: 7 — Part time: 45

Research activities: more than 50%
Educational research: more than 50%
Type of research: Basic research.
Functional objectives of research: Improve the performance of universities in Japan.
Periodical publications: Research in higher education (Daigaku ronshu). Notes on higher education. Record of the annual staff meeting.

Tokyo Metropolitan Institute for Educational Research and In-Service Training **0332**

Address: 1-14, Meguro 1-chome, Meguro-ku, TOKYO 153
Year of creation: 1954
Parent Organization: Tokyo Metropolitan Board of Education
Present Head: Yakichiro Kitazawa
Size of staff. Total: 129 — Full time: 128 — Part time: 1
Researchers: 88 — Full time: 88
Research activities: 50%
Type of research: Basic and applied research.
Functional objectives of research: Diffuse result of educational reearch findings to all involved in education in Tokyo Metropolis.
Periodical publications: Bulletins.
Monographs: Handled by individual project. List on request.
Studies and surveys in preparation: List on request.

JORDAN

Markaz al-baḥt wa-ăt-taṭwīr at-tarbawī **0333**

Translation: Educational Research and Development Center
Address: Ed. R&D Center, Yarmouk University, IRBID
Year of creation: 1981
Parent Organization: Yarmouk University
Present Head: Dr. Farid K. Abu Zeineh
Size of staff. Total: 15 — Full time: 10 — Part time: 5
Researchers: 5 — Full time: 2 — Part time: 3
Research activities: 50%
Educational research: more than 50%
Type of research: Basic, applied, research and development.
Functional objectives of research: Partial fulfilment of degree requirements, preparation of courses, servicing the educational administration.
Periodical publications: Theses abstracts. Bulletin (to be published soon).
Monographs: Translation of two studies on concepts. Sampling and data gathering in education and social studies. Others in preparation.
Studies and surveys in preparation: Evaluation of teaching effectiveness. Evaluation of the different programmes and plans at the University. Promoting teaching practices.

KENYA

Bureau of Educational Research

0334

Address: P.O. Box 43844, NAIROBI
Year of creation: 1973
Parent Organization: Kenyatta University College
Present Head: Professor G.S. Eshiwani
Size of staff. Total: 19 — Full time: 17 — Part time: 2
Researchers: 9 — Full time: 7 — Part time: 2
Research activities: more than 50%
Educational research: more than 50%
Type of research: Research and development.
Functional objectives of research: The major objectives of the BER are : to initiate and conduct long-term and fundamental research in the field of education; to assist public and private agencies through application of methods and results of educational research to on-going social problems; to undertake feasibility and evaluation studies of projects; to document and disseminate research materials; to provide a venue for objective discussion and analysis of major issues in the educational field through seminars, workshops and symposia; to develop a cadre of trained educational researchers through staff development programmes, undergraduate and graduate programmes, and through workshops.
Periodical publications: The Kenya educational review.
Monographs: Karugu, A.M. Primary school teachers in Kenya: a study of teachers' views on promotion. 1982. Kathuri, N.J. Factors that influence the performance of pupils in C.P.E. 1982. Digolo, O.O. A study of the suggested needs of 8th and 9th year of primary education in Kenya. 1982. Ogula, A.P. Evaluating the status of the teaching of social studies in primary schools in Busia District. 1982. Complete list on request.
Studies and surveys in preparation: Equity of educational system. Relevance of educational system. Efficiency of educational system. Management and administration of the educational system.

Research and Evaluation Section, Kenya Institute of Education

0335

Address: P.O. Box 30231, NAIROBI
Year of creation: 1967
Parent Organization: Ministry of Education, Science and Technology
Present Head: A.O. Waka
Researchers: 8 — Full time: 2 — Part time: 6
Research activities: more than 50%
Educational research: less than 10%
Type of research: Basic, applied, curriculum evaluation.
Functional objectives of research: Preparation of curriculum materials, measurement of programme outcomes.
Periodical publications: Kenya Institute of Education journal (in preparation).
Monographs: Drug education in Kenya. Identification of learning needs in rural areas. Evaluation of the Kenya Science Teachers College. The profile of the Kenyan child. Training youths for employment.
Studies and surveys in preparation: Evaluation of the primary education project. Pre-

school education in Kenya.

KOREA R

Busan City Education Research Institute

0336

Address: 88-1 Bumil-dong, Dong-ku, BUSAN CITY
Year of creation: 1963
Parent Organization: Busan City Board of Education
Present Head: Mr. Kim Gab Seok
Size of staff. Total: 30 — Full time: 30
Researchers: 13 — Full time: 13
Research activities: more than 50%
Educational research: more than 50%
Type of research: Applied and basic research.
Functional objectives of research: Conduct surveys and research relating to education; guide research schools; produce and lend teaching-learning media; service educational administration.
Periodical publications: Busan education. Report on research school. Report on teachers' educational study.
Monographs: Materials of teaching-learning on sexual morality. Materials for Korean national spirit. Materials of moral discourse for students. Materials on club activities for pupils.
Studies and surveys in preparation: History of Busan education. A study of classroom support.

Chung Buk Provincial Educational Research Institute

0337

Address: 44-12 San, Sannam-dong, CHEONGJU CITY, Chung Buk
Year of creation: 1969
Parent Organization: Chung Buk Provincial Board of Education
Present Head: Mr. Im Chang Soon
Size of staff. Total: 24 — Full time: 24
Researchers: 12 — Full time: 12
Research activities: more than 50%
Educational research: more than 50%
Type of research: Applied and basic research.
Functional objectives of research: Study and investigation of educational theory and practice; manufacture and distribution of audiovisual material for teaching; guidance of research schools and investigators.
Periodical publications: Education of Chung Buk Province.
Monographs: The standard of music practical test for primary school. The standard of training practical test for senior school. The standard of action development test. The criticism of educational material against communism. The thesis of study about teaching way of teachers.

Institute for Adult Education, Keimyung University

0338

Address: 2139 Daemyung-dong, TAEGU 634
Year of creation: 1973
Parent Organization: Keimyung University
Present Head: Lee Hee-Doe
Size of staff. Total: 40 — Full time: 10 — Part time: 30
Researchers: 12 — Full time: 4 — Part time: 8
Research activities: from 10% to 25%
Educational research: more than 50%
Type of research: Applied.
Functional objectives of research: Servicing adult and continuing education.
Periodical publications: Adult education quarterly. Lifelong education (newsletter).
Monographs: The philosophy of adult education. Adults and adult learning. Adult education for women's self-realization. Philosophy of adult religious education.
Studies and surveys in preparation: Teaching materials and methods for adults.

Kangweon Provincial Educational Research Institute

0339

Address: 32 Yarksa-dong, CHUNCHEON 200, Kangweon-do
Year of creation: 1969
Parent Organization: Provincial Board of Education under the Ministry of Education
Present Head: Mr. Kang Yoon Taek
Size of staff. Total: 19 — Full time: 19
Researchers: 12 — Full time: 12
Research activities: from 10% to 25%
Educational research: from 25% to 50%
Type of research: Applied research.
Functional objectives of research: Inquiry studies into educational theory and fact; selection and implementation of teaching materials; teacher's service training; counselling; implementation of audio-visual materials and the guidance for their practical use.
Periodical publications: Research report of the Institute. Annual report of the Institute. Journal of guidance and counselling. Teachers' actual study report. The Journal of Kangweon education.
Studies and surveys in preparation: Improved teaching plan for preventing accumulation of study loss in making out teaching materials at schools (both primary and secondary schools).

Korean Educational Development Institute (KEDI)

0340

Address: 20-1 Umyeon-dong, Gangnam-gu, SEOUL 135
Year of creation: 1972
Parent Organization: Independent autonomous centre, funded by Government
Present Head: Dr. Young Shik Kim
Size of staff. Total: 464
Researchers: 138
Research activities: 50%
Educational research: 50%
Type of research: Educational development; curriculum research; basic and applied

research in education; educational technology; educational broadcasting; international education.

Functional objectives of research: Undertake comprehensive and systematic studies on educational goals, contents and methodology. Provide an effective mechanism for solving educational problems by developing innovative educational programmes for schools in Korea.

Periodical publications: The journal of Korean education. Educational development. Research abstract. Current content of foreign journals.

Studies and surveys in preparation: A long-term plan of national development. A study on evaluation of elementary school curriculum. An applied study of the instruction model with TV programme.

Korean Institute for Research in the Behavioral Sciences (KIRBS) **0341**

Address: 163 Ankook-dong, IPO Box 3528, Chongno-ku, SEOUL
Year of creation: 1968
Parent Organization: Independent, autonomous, non-profit organization
Present Head: Dr. Lee Sung Jin
Size of staff. Total: 45 — Full time: 45
Researchers: 35 — Full time: 35
Research activities: more than 50%
Educational research: 50%
Type of research: Basic and applied.
Functional objectives of research: Research and training of personnel in behavioural sciences.
Periodical publications: Research bulletin. Research notes.
Monographs: Human problems in the future society (Korean). Development of morality of Korean children and its implications for education (Korean). Behaviour modification: principles and applications (4 vols. Korean).
Studies and surveys in preparation: Early childhood education. Use of psychological tests in industry. Development of system. Complete list on request.

Kyeonggi Provincial Education Research Institute **0342**

Address: 495 Joewon-dong, SUWEON CITY, Kyeonggi Province, Postal Zone 170
Year of creation: 1962
Parent Organization: Kyeonggi Provincial Board of Education
Present Head: Mr. Lee Tae Hun
Size of staff. Total: 12 — Full time: 12
Researchers: 12 — Full time: 12
Research activities: from 10% to 25%
Educational research: from 10% to 25%
Type of research: Applied research.
Functional objectives of research: Survey and research relating to education; educational action research (workshop); guidance to research schools; producing and lending AV materials; inservice training.
Periodical publications: Kyeonggi supervision (4/yr).
Monographs: Manual on the Korean classical music instruments. Educational manual for teachers. Extra learning strategies for slow learners. A study of Japanese education status for the purpose of the improvements of Korean elementary schools.

Theory and practice of one classroom school education. Value learning manual on social studies in secondary school. Foundation of english teaching and learning. English evaluation manual.

Studies and surveys in preparation: Evaluation item sampling of moral education in elementary school level. A study on teacher's basic attitude. Community curriculum in secondary school level.

National Institute for Educational Research and Training

0343

Address: 25-1 Samchong-dong, Jongno-ku, SEOUL
Year of creation: 1974
Parent Organization: Ministry of Education
Present Head: Choi Yeol Gon
Size of staff. Total: 146 — Full time: 146
Researchers: 55 — Full time: 55
Research activities: from 25% to 50%
Educational research: from 25% to 50%
Type of research: Research and development.
Functional objectives of research: Servicing the educational administration.
Periodical publications: Education in Korea (English, 1/yr). Statistical yearbook of education (English, 1/yr). Educational administration (Korean, 12/yr).
Monographs: National Institute for Educational Research and Training. A guide book for evaluation study in 2nd IEA science education (Korean). Ha In Ho, et al. Evaluation of student achievement degree in science education (Korean). Yoon Eung Sup, et al. Comparative study on the entrance examination in foreign countries (Korean). Kim Ho Kyun; Jo Dae Kyung, et al. Basic study to improve student life-records (1) (Korean). Choi Ji Hoon; Lee Myung Woo. Study on development of O.M.R. card to be used in scholastic achievement examination (Korean). Complete list on request.
Studies and surveys in preparation: Evaluation of student achievement in science education (IEA-SISS). Studies on the improvement of college entrance examination test items. Studies on training programmes.

Research Institute for Human Development

0344

Address: College of Education, Ewha Women's University, 11-1 Daihyun-dong, Sehdaimoon-ku. SEOUL
Year of creation: 1970
Parent Organization: College of Education, Ewha Women's University
Size of staff. Total: 6 — Full time: 1 — Part time: 5
Researchers: 5 — Full time: 1 — Part time: 4
Research activities: more than 50%
Educational research: more than 50%
Type of research: Research and development.
Functional objectives of research: Basic research; servicing the educational administration.
Periodical publications: Human development bulletin (1/yr).
Monographs: Human development, vol. 9. 1981. Human development, vol. 10. 1982. Human development, vol. 11. 1983.
Studies and surveys in preparation: Analytic study of children's language.

Research Institute of Education, Korea University (Riekou)

0345

Address: 1, 5-ka Anam-dong, Sungbug-ku, SEOUL
Year of creation: 1972
Parent Organization: Korea University
Present Head: Dr. Yu In Jong
Size of staff. Total: 12 — Full time: 1 — Part time: 11
Researchers: 4 — Full time: 4
Research activities: more than 50%
Educational research: more than 50%
Type of research: Applied research.
Functional objectives of research: Study of theory and practices on educational problems at large; contribution to the innovation and development of education of Korea.
Monographs: An explorative study on the evaluative criteria for development of affective characteristics and extra-curricular activities. 1981. A study of the latent functions of educational environments. 1981. Socio-psychological characteristics of college environments. 1982.
Studies and surveys in preparation: A study on Korean education under the Japanese rule — with special reference to segregation of educational policy.

Seoul Special City Educational Research Institute

0346

Address: 2-77, 2-ka, Sinmoon-ro, Chongno-ku, SEOUL
Year of creation: 1958
Parent Organization: Seoul Special City Board of Education
Present Head: Mr. Zin Ki Zeong
Size of staff. Total: 64 — Full time: 60 — Part time: 4
Researchers: 25 — Full time: 25
Research activities: from 25% to 50%
Educational research: from 25% to 50%
Type of research: Applied and basic research and development.
Functional objectives of research: To conduct surveys and research on educational theory and practice; to provide inservice training of teachers; to produce and distribute audiovisual materials; to operate the demonstration schools and research schools (Grades 1-11).
Periodical publications: Research bulletin. Guidance and counselling journal. Report for research teachers. Journal of Seoul education.
Monographs: Eighties' subjects (tasks) of Seoul education. Modern society and teacher. Teaching profession and duty of a teacher. Sex moral education. Statistical yearbooks of Seoul education.
Studies and surveys in preparation: Way of evaluation for experiment and practice in science (for high school). Way of evaluation for music, fine art and physical exercice (for primary school). Reports of research schools and demonstration schools. Series of collective reports of various researches. Material for admonitory speech. Guidelines for self-control. Pollution (film). Attitude for studying science (slides). '83 Guidance and counselling (Series 9).

KUWAIT

College of Education, Kuwait University

0347

Address: P.O.Box 1328, Keifan, KUWAIT
Year of creation: 1980
Parent Organization: Kuwait University
Present Head: Dr. Abdul Rahman Ahmad Al-Ahmad
Size of staff. Total: 59 — Full time: 59
Researchers: 4 — Full time: 4
Research activities: from 25% to 50%
Educational research: from 10% to 25%
Type of research: Theoritical and experimental and field studies.
Functional objectives of research: To solve school problems; to help educational planners in their decisions.
Periodical publications: Educational Journal (4/yr).
Studies and surveys in preparation: There is many studies in process in our four departments.

Curricula Research Centre

0348

Address: No. 7, Street No. 75, QADESSIA
Year of creation: 1974
Parent Organization: The Ministry of Education
Present Head: Dr. Abd El-Aziz El-Ghanem
Size of staff. Total: 76 — Full time: 76
Researchers: 49 — Full time: 49
Research activities: more than 50%
Educational research: more than 50%
Type of research: Educational.
Functional objectives of research: Defining educational objectives and study plans for each educational stage; defining objectives for each factor of the curriculum, and evaluating them; making studies and researches necessary for planning curricula; designing and executing the experiments necessary for developing the content of curricula and teaching methods.
Periodical publications: Yearly plan of educational research: yearbook of main activities of the centre.
Studies and surveys in preparation: Most studies and surveys in preparation concern curricula. About 33% deal with evaluating various subject matters in credit system. The rest deal with various educational matters such as teacher training, visual aids, handicapped, dropouts, educational skills, educational experiences in preschool stage.

LEBANON

Division of Education and Extension Programs

0349

Address: D.E.E.P. — A.U.B., P.O. Box 11-0-236, BEIRUT
Year of creation: 1976
Parent Organization: American University of Beirut
Present Head: Professor George I. Za'rour
Size of staff. Total: 43 — Full time: 43
Researchers: 24 — Full time: 22 — Part time: 2
Research activities: from 10% to 25%
Educational research: from 10% to 25%
Type of research: Applied and basic research.
Functional objectives of research: Faculty academic interests and partial fulfilment of degree requirements.
Periodical publications: None, but our faculty publish in internationally refered journals.
Monographs: The planning of future careers by Lebanese students. The predictive influence of the principal on school effectiveness in Lebanon. Construct validity of a set of mathematical superitems. Ittiğāhāt fī ăt-tarbiya al-'arabīyya (Trends in Arab education). Tadrīs al-luğa al-'arabiyya fī ăl-marḫala al-ibtidā'iyya fī ba'ḍ ad-duwal al-'arabiyya (The teaching of Arabic in elementary schools in Arab countries). Complete list on request.
Studies and surveys in preparation: Educational reform and development in Sudan, 1970–1980. Counselling in the Middle East. Development of anxiety scales. Development and norming of personnel preference schedule and norming of vocational interest battery. Moral and civic development and education. Complete list on request.

LIBERIA

Division of Research and Publication, Ministry of Education

0350

Address: P.O. Box 9012, Broad Street, MONROVIA
Year of creation: 1970
Parent Organization: Ministry of Education
Present Head: J.C. Gbanyon Natt
Size of staff. Total: 9 — Full time: 9
Researchers: 3 — Full time: 3
Research activities: more than 50%
Educational research: more than 50%
Type of research: Basic scientific data gathering, mainly in the social research fashion.
Functional objectives of research: Providing data of important significance in all programme planning in the Education Ministry; providing information concerning the efficient functioning of the Education Ministry.
Periodical publications: The Diary. The Education review. Newsletter. A Journal.
Monographs: Tracer studies of the 1982 national examination results.
Studies and surveys in preparation: Teacher education and benefits. A recommended

strategy for dealing with Liberia's education problem. Access to education. Philosophy of Liberia education. Student personnel services and the Liberian school system. Women in development: a geographic impact of Liberian women in domestic market development.

LUXEMBOURG

Institut supérieur d'études et de recherches pédagogiques

0351

Address: Route de Diekirch, Boite postale 2, 7201 WALFERDANGE
Year of creation: 1983
Present Head: Dr. Gaston Schaber
Size of staff. Total: 31 — Full time: 10 — Part time: 21
Researchers: 12 — Full time: 3 — Part time: 9
Research activities: from 10% to 25%
Educational research: from 25% to 50%
Type of research: Recherche appliquée.
Functional objectives of research: Prestation à l'administration de l'éducation et éducation des enseignants (primaire, préscolaire, spécial).
Monographs: Storoni, A. Der Borden, unsere Lebensgrundlage. 1980. Dieschbourg, R. Les fractions à l'école primaire. 1981. Dieschbourg, R. Le langage des flèches et la résolution de problèmes arithmétiques. 1981. Dickes, P.; Kneip, N.; Wirtgen, G. Recherche sur l'enseignement complémentaire (Résumé). 1982.

Service d'innovation et de recherche pédagogiques (SIRP) du Ministère de l'éducation nationale

0352

Address: 6, boulevard Royal, LUXEMBOURG
Year of creation: 1979
Present Head: Lex Kaiser
Size of staff. Total: 47 — Full time: 2 — Part time: 45
Researchers: 46 — Part time: 46
Research activities: from 10% to 25%
Educational research: from 10% to 25%
Type of research: Elaboration de curricula; évaluation d'innovations pédagogiques; développement du système éducatif.
Functional objectives of research: Adaptation du système éducatif au développement économique, social et culturel.
Periodical publications: Courrier de l'innovation et de la recherche pédagogiques.
Studies and surveys in preparation: Evaluation du premier cycle harmonisé pour les élèves de 12 à 15 ans. Education et migration au Luxembourg.

MALAYSIA

Bahagian Perancangan dan Penyelidikan Pelajaran

0353

Translation: Educational Planning and Research Division
Address: 21-23 Floor, Bank Pertanian Building, Leboh Pasar Besar, KUALA LUMPUR 01-23
Year of creation: 1963
Parent Organization: Ministry of Education
Present Head: Mr. Omar bin Mohd. Hashim
Size of staff. Total: 111 — Full time: 111
Researchers: 51 — Full time: 51
Research activities: 50%
Educational research: more than 50%
Type of research: Applied research and research and development.
Functional objectives of research: To ensure that national educational planning and development effectively and efficiently meet national education policies and objectives; servicing the educational administration.
Periodical publications: Education in Malaysia (1/yr). Education statistics Malaysia (1/yr). Nadi pendidikan (3/yr).
Monographs: Research studies conducted do not generally culminate in reports for publication but serve as an empirical basis for decision making in the formulation of policies and implementation strategies in educational programme administration/management.
Studies and surveys in preparation: Equality and equity in education opportunities. Participation and achievement by levels according to national needs. Financing in the education sector. Identification of major problems and innovative intervention measures. School mapping.

Universiti Sains Malaysia

0354

Translation: University of Science, Malaysia
Address: MINDEN, Penang
Year of creation: 1969
Parent Organization: Ministry of Education
Present Head: The Honourable Datuk Musa Bin Mohamad, Vice-Chancellor
Size of staff. Total: 2367 — Full time: 2349 — Part time: 219
Researchers: 18 — Full time: 18
Research activities: 50%
Educational research: more than 50%
Type of research: Basic and applied research.
Functional objectives of research: Assist in improving teaching methods and curriculum development; contribute to national development by encouraging scientific research.
Periodical publications: Bulletin penyelidikan (Research bulletin) — mainly in Bahasa Malaysia. Laporan tahunan (Annual report) — all in Bahasa Malaysia. Jernal pendidik-pendidikan (Educators and education journal) — mainly in Bahasa Malaysia. Kajian Malaysia (Journal of Malaysian studies) — mainly in Bahasa Malaysia.
Monographs: List on request.
Studies and surveys in preparation: INSPIRE Project (Integrated System of Programme

Instruction for Rural Environment). Project on vector control. KANITA Project (Project on women and children).

MALI

Direction nationale de l'Institut pédagogique national et de l'enseignement normal **0355**

Address: B.P. 1583, BAMAKO
Year of creation: 1962
Parent Organization: Ministère de l'éducation nationale
Present Head: Ousmane Sidi Touré, professeur d'enseignement secondaire
Size of staff. Total: 170
Researchers: 12
Research activities: from 25% to 50%
Educational research: more than 50%
Type of research: Recherche appliquée.
Functional objectives of research: Confection de documents scolaires; suivi des expérimentations pédagogiques; amélioration de la qualité de l'enseignement.
Periodical publications: Contact.

MALTA

Fakulta ta' l-Edukazzjoni **0356**

Translation: Faculty of Education
Address: University of Malta, Msida, MALTA
Year of creation: 1979
Parent Organization: University of Malta
Present Head: Prof. Charles J. Farrugia
Size of staff. Total: 55 — Full time: 40 — Part time: 15
Type of research: Basic and applied research.
Functional objectives of research: General pedagogical research and pedagogical research in specific subject areas; partial fulfilment of degree requirements; preparation of courses; servicing the educational administration.
Periodical publications: Journal 'Education'.
Monographs: Trends in teacher education. Teacher education: the need for greater coherence between theory and practice.
Studies and surveys in preparation: Status of teachers in Malta.

MAURITIUS

Mauritius Institute of Education

0357

Address: REDUIT
Year of creation: 1973
Parent Organization: A council constituted of various representatives of Ministries, Government, University and teachers, M. and M.I.E. staff
Present Head: Professor Ramesh Ramdoyal
Size of staff. Total: 291 — Full time: 286 — Part time: 5
Researchers: 86
Research activities: from 10% to 25%
Educational research: from 10% to 25%
Type of research: Action research.
Functional objectives of research: Improvement of education at pre-primary, primary and secondary levels.
Periodical publications: Annual reports. M.I.E. Journal.
Studies and surveys in preparation: Underachievement: remedial education. Profile of the Mauritian child. Curriculum innovation: implementation. Evaluation (curriculum, examinations, tests, etc.). Teacher education: classroom interaction. Education and development. Language in education resources for education.

MEXICO

Centro de Estudios Educativos, A.C.

0358

Address: Av. Revolución 1291, Deleg. Alvaro Obregón, C.P. 01040, COL TLACOPAC-SAN ANGEL
Year of creation: 1963
Parent Organization: Institución autónoma
Present Head: Lic. Luis M. Narro Rodríguez
Size of staff. Total: 80 — Full time: 40 — Part time: 40
Researchers: 30 — Full time: 30
Research activities: from 10% to 25%
Educational research: more than 50%
Type of research: Aplicada; investigación y desarrollo.
Functional objectives of research: Contribuir a la planificación educativa del país.
Periodical publications: Revista latinoamericana de estudios educativos (4/año).
Studies and surveys in preparation: Modelo alternativo de educación secundaria en zonas rurales. Proyecto alternativo de educación preescolar en zonas marginadas. Presente y futuro de la educación secundaria.

Centro de Investigaciones y Servicios Educativos

0359

Address: Edificio Técnico de la Universidade Abierta, Circuito Exterior, Ciudad Universitaria, Apartado postal 20-089, 04510 MEXICO, D.F.
Year of creation: 1977
Parent Organization: Universidad Nacional Autónoma de México

Present Head: Dr. Enrique Suárez-Iñiguez
Size of staff. Total: 128 — Full time: 127 — Part time: 1
Researchers: 43 — Full time: 43
Research activities: 50%
Educational research: more than 50%
Type of research: Investigación aplicada y propositiva.
Functional objectives of research: Prestación de servicios a la administración educativa.
Periodical publications: Perfiles educativos (4/año). Criterios (12/año). Boletín bibliográfico (12/año). Síntesis informativa (52/año; circulación interna).
Monographs: Enseñanza programada. Evaluación del aprovechamiento escolar. Sistematización de la enseñanza. Técnicas para el aprendizaje grupal (grupos numerosos). Diseño de planes de estudio.
Studies and surveys in preparation: Evaluación del rendimiento escolar. Perfiles universitarios. Los profesionistas y el mercado de trabajo: un acercamiento al fenómeno de la producción y la utilización de la cualificación universitaria del trabajo.

Centro Interdisciplinario de Investigación y Docencia en Educación Técnica (CIIDET) **0360**

Address: Av. Tecnológico y Mariano Escobedo, Apartado postal 752, Codigo postal 7600, QUERETARO
Year of creation: 1976
Parent Organization: Dirección General de Institutos Tecnológicos
Present Head: Dr. José Antonio Lopez y Maldonado
Size of staff. Total: 80 — Full time: 55
Researchers: 25 — Full time: 25
Research activities: more than 50%
Educational research: more than 50%
Type of research: Investigaciones orientadas a las necesidades concretas de los tecnológicos, a través de la maestria en ciencias de la educación, al desarrollo del propio CIIDET, solicitadas o desarrolladas mediante convenios con la SEP y organizaciones educativas.
Functional objectives of research: Organizar y desarrollar programas de investigación en áreas o disciplinas de la educación técnica de tipo medio superior y de tipo superior.
Periodical publications: Revista de educación e investigación del Sistema Nacional de Institutos Tecnológicos (2/año). Informe de actividades del CIIDET. Boletines (12/año).
Monographs: Adaptación de un instrumento para el diagnóstico del estilo de liderazgo y su eficacia. Evaluación de la eficiencia de un programa de maestria en ciencias de la educación. Factores codeterminantes en el éxito escolar. Estudio comparativo de las capacidades físicas de estudiantes de nivel escolar. Estudio piloto de las variables relacionadas con la actitud de los maestros de los institutos tecnológicos hacia el uso de medios audiovisuales en el aula. Lista completa a disposición.
Studies and surveys in preparation: Adaptación de la técnica de LIKERT para su utilización en instituciones de educación superior. Diseño de un modelo orgánico que responda mejor a las necesidades de los institutos tecnológicos. Estudio de las espectativas y aspiraciones de los estudiantes de los sistemas de educación de adultos en México. Educación y trabajo productivo: una alternativa para carreras tecnológicas en los institutos tecnológicos. Lista completa a disposición.

Dirección General de Planeación

0361

Address: Añil No. 571, 9o. piso, Col. Granjas México, C.P. 08400 MEXICO
Year of creation: 1970
Parent Organization: Secretaría de Educación Pública
Present Head: Mtro. Arturo Velázquez Jiménez
Size of staff. Total: 315 — Full time: 310 — Part time: 5
Researchers: 99 — Full time: 99
Research activities: from 25% to 50%
Educational research: from 25% to 50%
Type of research: Investigación aplicada en campo educativo.
Functional objectives of research: Fomentar la investigación y planeación educativa; apoyar la descentralización de los servicios educativos y mejorar la calidad de la educación.
Periodical publications: Boletín de planeación e investigación educativas (Intercambio).
Monographs: Microplaneación regional educativa de las entidades federativas. Monografías estatales.
Studies and surveys in preparation: 7 Diagnósticos regionales de la investigación educativa. Uso intensivo de los medios de comunicación en la educación. Uso de las computadoras en programas educativos.

Fomento Cultural y Educativo, A.C.

0362

Address: Miguel Laurent 340, Colonia del Valle, 03100 MEXICO, D.F.
Year of creation: 1972
Present Head: Sr. Enrique Gutiérrez Martín del Campo
Size of staff. Total: 38 — Full time: 38
Researchers: 33 — Full time: 33
Research activities: 50%
Educational research: more than 50%
Type of research: Investigación en la acción.
Functional objectives of research: Encontrar métodos educativos que puedan quedar en manos del pueblo.
Studies and surveys in preparation: Investigación de apoyo a la educación del adulto campesino a partir de la comunicación radiofónica rural.

Fundación Javier Barros Sierra, A.C.

0363

Address: Carretera Al Ajusco S/N, Col. Pedregal de Santa Teresa, Del. Contreras, 01790 MEXICO, D.F.
Year of creation: 1975
Present Head: Ing. Antonio Alonso Concheiro
Size of staff. Total: 13 — Full time: 12 — Part time: 1
Researchers: 4 — Full time: 4
Research activities: more than 50%
Educational research: from 25% to 50%
Type of research: Investigación básica e investigación y desarrollo.
Functional objectives of research: Investigación prospectiva y prestación de servicios a la investigación educacional.
Monographs: McGinn, N. La asignación de recursos económicos para la administración

pública en México.
Studies and surveys in preparation: EDFOREM (Modelo econométrico para el estudio de la vinculación entre educación, formación y empleo).

Instituto Ajijic sobre Educación Internacional (IASEI) 0364

Address: Av. Patria, 1201, Apdo. postal 1-440, 44100 GUADALAJARA, Jalisco
Year of creation: 1978
Parent Organization: Universidad autónoma de Guadalajara (UAG)
Present Head: Dr. Oscar Soria Nicastro, Director de Investigaciones
Size of staff. Total: 17 — Full time: 5 — Part time: 12
Researchers: 15 — Full time: 3 — Part time: 12
Research activities: more than 50%
Educational research: more than 50%
Type of research: Exploratoria, iluminativa, prospectiva; problem-solving.
Functional objectives of research: Estudio problemas urgentes para quienes toman decisiones sobre el nivel terciario de la educación.
Periodical publications: Docencia-postsecundaria (4/año). Series de documentos.
Monographs: Diseño de proyectos de investigación educativa. La educación superior en América Latina a través de quince tendencias. Universidad y desarrollo rural. Educación superior particular en ALyC: pasado presente y futuro.
Studies and surveys in preparation: Líneas de investigación. Educación superior en América Latina: calidad. Educación superior en América Latina: eficiencia externa. Educación superior particular en América Latina y el Caribe. Fundaciones privadas norteamericanas en América Latina.

Instituto de Investigaciones en Psicología y Pedagogía 0365

Address: San Fernando no. 42, Z.P. 36000 GUANAJUATO, GTO
Year of creation: 1973
Parent Organization: Universidad de Guanajuato
Present Head: Mtra. María del Carmen Carrasco Hernández
Size of staff. Total: 14 — Full time: 11 — Part time: 3
Researchers: 10 — Full time: 7 — Part time: 3
Research activities: more than 50%
Educational research: more than 50%
Type of research: Básica y aplicada.
Functional objectives of research: Calidad y cobertura de la educación; análisis de la problemática social en relación con la educación; factores que propician el desarrollo adecuado del proceso educativo y proposición de estrategias innovadores de tecnología educativa; tesis de postgrado en investigación educativa.
Periodical publications: Publicaciones del Instituto de Investigaciones en Psicología y Pedagogía (2/año).
Monographs: No se publica.
Studies and surveys in preparation: Estudio diferencial de actitudes, aspiraciones y expectativas hacia la educación formal de tres subgrupos sociales en el estado de Guanajuato (obreros, campesinos y burócratas). Estudio comparativo del incremento de razonamiento abstracto y aptitudes específicas del estudiante al ingresar y egresar de la Universidad. Modelo para apreciar la calidad del desempeño del docente.

NEPAL

Pathyakram Phthyapustak Tatha Nirikshan Bikhs Kendra

0366

Translation: Curriculum Textbook and Supervision Development Centre
Address: Harihar Bhawan, Pulchowk, LALITPUR
Year of creation: 1971
Parent Organization: Ministry of Education and Culture
Present Head: Dr. Kedar Nath Shrestha
Size of staff. Total: 107 — Full time: 107
Researchers: 31 — Full time: 31
Research activities: 50%
Educational research: 50%
Type of research: Survey, applied research; basic research and evaluation studies.
Functional objectives of research: To enrich the curriculum and improve the teaching-learning situation.
Periodical publications: Education (2/yr). Supervision bulletin (4/yr).
Monographs: Administrative guides. Supervision guides. Teachers' guide for all textbooks.
Studies and surveys in preparation: A study of the effectiveness of the present supervisory system. Knowledge and attitude: survey of parents on population evaluation.

Shikshya Shastra Adhayan Ṣamsthan

0367

Translation: Institute of Education
Address: Dean's Office, Sanothimi, BHAKTAPUR
Year of creation: 1956
Parent Organization: Tribhuvan University
Present Head: Dr. Berendra Kumar Mallik
Size of staff. Total: 406 — Full time: 406
Researchers: 45 — Part time: 45
Type of research: Applied research.
Functional objectives of research: Preparation of courses; servicing the educational administration; improving instruction.
Periodical publications: Education quarterly.
Monographs: Tracer study of students graduating with the School Learning Certificate in education: study of the job performance of IOE trained secondary school teacher. Socio-personal characteristics of students enrolled in the prevocational teacher education programme. Preliminary survey of science teaching in selected schools of Kathmandu Valley. Distance learning. Higher education in Nepal. Teacher education in Nepal. Educational experiment in Nepal. Education in Nepal. Complete list on request.

NETHERLANDS

Afdeling onderzoek en ontwikkeling van onderwijs, Rijksuniversiteit Utrecht

0368

Translation: Department of Research and Development in Higher Education, State University of Utrecht
Address: Maliebaan 5, 3581 CA UTRECHT
Year of creation: 1968
Parent Organization: State University of Utrecht
Present Head: Drs. P.J.C. Veltman
Size of staff. Total: 17 — Full time: 11 — Part time: 6
Researchers: 11 — Full time: 10 — Part time: 1
Research activities: from 10% to 25%
Educational research: more than 50%
Type of research: Applied research and development.
Functional objectives of research: Course development; educational administration and policy-making; doctoral dissertations; marketing research.
Periodical publications: Onderwijsmemo.
Monographs: Eijl, P.J. van. Modulaire onderwijsvormen in het hoger onderwijs. 1983. Holleman, J.W. Contouren van het universitaire studiepuntenstelsel. 1983. Holleman, J.W. Project- en lijnorganisatie in de universitaire bestuursstructuur. 1983. Holleman, J.W. Doelen van de wet Tweefasenstructuur. 1983. Muyden, J.N. Blokonderwijs in het kort. 1983. Complete list on request.
Studies and surveys in preparation: Sense and non-sense about the relationship between group size and educational achievement in higher education. Skimming the milk and whipping the cream: articulation between school and university. Controlling study duration. Influence of academic environments on study habits.

Bureau onderzoek van onderwijs

0369

Translation: Educational Research Center
Address: Boerhaavelaan 2, 2334 EN LEIDEN
Year of creation: 1968
Parent Organization: University of Leyden
Present Head: Prof. dr. H.F.M. Crombag
Size of staff. Total: 12 — Full time: 9 — Part time: 3
Researchers: 7 — Full time: 6 — Part time: 1
Research activities: more than 50%
Educational research: more than 50%
Type of research: Research and development.
Functional objectives of research: Servicing faculty.
Monographs: Distance learning: on the design of an Open University. 1983. Crombag, H.F.M. Een manier van overleven: psychologische grondslagen van moraal en recht. 1983. Gruijter, D.N.M. de. Tentamineren en beslissen: tentamens met goed of fout gecodeerde itemantwoorden: Een cijfermatige analyse. 1982. Heuvel, J.H. van den. Wetgeving belicht. 1982. Complete list on request.
Studies and surveys in preparation: Onderwijstechnologie. Onderzoek naar tekstbegrip. Het interpreteren van afbeeldingen door chemiestudenten. Doelmatigheid van het onderwijs. Complete list on request.

Centraal instituut voor toetsontwikkeling

0370

Translation: National Institute for Educational Measurement
Address: Oeverstraat 65, Postbus 1034, 6801 MG ARNHEM
Year of creation: 1968
Parent Organization: Ministry of Education
Present Head: Dr. F.P. Carpaij
Size of staff. Total: 242 — Full time: 142 — Part time: 100
Researchers: 120 — Full time: 77 — Part time: 43
Research activities: from 25% to 50%
Educational research: more than 50%
Type of research: Applied, research and development.
Functional objectives of research: Servicing the educational administration and educational product development.
Periodical publications: Algemene publicaties (general publications). Specialistische bulletins (research bulletins).
Studies and surveys in preparation: Problem solving. Indices for inter-observer-agreement. Latent trait-models. Measurement of affective goals. Teachers' thought processes during their interactive teaching. Scaling of judges on implicit dimensions.

Centrum voor de Studie van het Onderwijs in Ontwikkelingslanden (CESO)

0371

Translation: Centre for the Study of Education in Developing Countries (CESO)
Address: P.O. Box 90734, 2509 LS THE HAGUE
Year of creation: 1963
Parent Organization: Netherlands Universities Foundation for International Cooperation (NUFFIC)
Present Head: Prof. drs. J.H. Kraak
Size of staff. Total: 18 — Full time: 11 — Part time: 7
Researchers: 10 — Full time: 9 — Part time: 1
Research activities: from 25% to 50%
Educational research: more than 50%
Type of research: Basic, applied and evaluative research.
Functional objectives of research: Servicing institutions of development cooperation; giving advice in policy matters.
Monographs: Kasey, M. Youth education in Iraq and Egypt. 1984. Kidd, Ross. The Popular performing arts, non-formal education and social change in the Third World: a bibliography and review essay. 1981. Heerdink, R. Anthropology of education/indigenous education. 1981. Hoppers, W. Education in a rural society, primary pupils and school leavers in Mwinilunga, Zambia. 1980. Omari, I.M., et al. Universal primary education in Tanzania. 1983. Kater, Adri, ed. Anthropoligists approaching education: papers presented at the Symposium Anthropology of Education, held at the occasion of the 1981 Intercongress of the International Union of Anthropological and Ethnological Sciences, April 1981. 1982.
Studies and surveys in preparation: DELSILIFE, Phase II: The implementation of an educational method (developed in phase I) aimed at improving the situation of the rural poor in four countries of Southeast Asia. Drama as a means of rural development in Zambia (a case-study).

Groep onderwijsresearch

0372

Translation: Educational Research Group
Address: Eindhoven University of Technology, P.O. Box 513, 5600 MB EINDHOVEN
Year of creation: 1963
Parent Organization: Eindhoven University of Technology
Present Head: Prof. dr. D.W. Vaags
Size of staff. Total: 15 — Full time: 11 — Part time: 4
Researchers: 6 — Full time: 6
Research activities: more than 50%
Educational research: more than 50%
Type of research: Research and development.
Functional objectives of research: Development and evaluation of new educational systems.
Periodical publications: List on request.
Monographs: List on request.
Studies and surveys in preparation: Evaluation-research. Problem solving in a technological domain. Measurement of insight. Learning of prototypical concepts. Non-technical aspects of engineering education.

Hoofdinspectie speciale diensten

0373

Translation: Main Inspectorate Special Services
Address: Postbus 255, 1850 AG HEILOO
Year of creation: 1981
Parent Organization: Ministry of Education and Science
Present Head: Drs. N.J. Heijkoop
Size of staff. Total: 8 — Full time: 4 — Part time: 4
Researchers: 3 — Full time: 3
Research activities: from 25% to 50%
Educational research: from 25% to 50%
Type of research: Action research.
Functional objectives of research: Inform the Ministry of Education about actual problems in school.
Periodical publications: Only irregular publications.
Monographs: Comment on plans for new educational policy: first stage secondary education; second stage secondary education. Advising the Ministry of Education about results in experimental comprehensive schools.
Studies and surveys in preparation: Classwork with mixed abbility groups. Problems with fusion of schools.

Instituut voor toegepaste sociologie

0374

Translation: Institute for Applied Sociology
Address: Graafseweg 274, 6532 ZV NIJMEGEN
Year of creation: 1964
Parent Organization: Katholieke universiteit Nijmegen
Present Head: Dr. F. Carpay
Size of staff. Total: 113 — Full time: 101.6
Researchers: 68 — Full time: 63.5

Research activities: more than 50%
Educational research: 50%
Type of research: Applied; some basic and some research and development.
Monographs: Smets, P. Experimenteren: in wiens belang? 1980. Claessen, J.F.M.; Burgt, J.H.F., van der. Van hoger beroepsonderwijs naar wetenschappelijk onderwijs. 1981. Jungbluth, P. Docenten over onderwijs aan meisjes. 1982. Galen, A., van; Bulte, J. Veranderen is gewoon. 1982. Pelkmans, A.H.W.M. Scholen met een samenwerkingskarakter van dichtbij gezien. 1981. Complete list on request.
Studies and surveys in preparation: Mavo-projekt. Het schoolonderzoek onder de loupe. Samenwerkingsscholen in ontwikkeling. Kwalitatieve behoeftencriteria ten behoeve van de planning voortgezet onderwijs. Follow-up onderzoek middenschool. Complete list on request.

Katholiek pedagogisck centrum

0375

Translation: Catholic Pedagogic Centre
Address: P.O.Box 482, 5201 AL DEN BOSCH
Year of creation: 1949
Parent Organization: Private foundation
Present Head: Drs. G.A.J. Janssen
Size of staff. Total: 128 — Full time: 100 — Part time: 28
Researchers: 8 — Full time: 8
Research activities: from 10% to 25%
Educational research: from 10% to 25%
Type of research: Applied.
Functional objectives of research: Evaluation research; developmental work; policy analysis.
Monographs: Kwantes, N.; Stekelenburg, A. The MAVO-project: International School Improvement Project. 1982. Kwantes, N.; Karstanje, P. Dilemma of evaluation in large-scale innovations in education: International School Improvement Project. 1983. Kwantes, N. The role of the internal (change-agent) coordinator in school improvement processes. 1983. Berg, R.M., van der. The functioning of school principals in relation to large-scale change efforts in the Netherlands. 1983.
Studies and surveys in preparation: Grootschaligheid in de onderwijsvernieuwing. Publication in English: Large-scale innovations in education. 1984.

Leids interdisciplinair centrum voor onderwijsresearch (LICOR), Rijksuniversiteit te Leiden

0376

Translation: Leiden Interdisciplinary Centre for Educational Research (LICOR), State University of Leiden
Address: Stationsplein 10, 2312 AK LEIDEN
Year of creation: 1968
Parent Organization: State University of Leiden
Present Head: Drs. D. de Jong
Size of staff. Total: 40 — Full time: 2 — Part time: 38
Researchers: 30 — Full time: 1 — Part time: 29
Research activities: more than 50%
Educational research: more than 50%
Type of research: Basic and applied research.
Functional objectives of research: Theory; development; educational services;

innovation; course prototypes; partial fulfilment of degree requirements.
Periodical publications: Plans and proposals (in Dutch).
Monographs: Research reports on topics mentioned below (in Dutch).
Studies and surveys in preparation: Pre- and in-service education of teachers. Differentiation of staff and organization. Values clarification. Computer managed instruction. Individualized education. Education for minority groups. Vocational education.

Onderafdeling toegepaste onderwijskunde

0377

Translation: Department of Education
Address: Postbus 217, 7500 AE ENSCHEDE
Year of creation: 1980
Parent Organization: Twente University of Technology
Present Head: Prof. dr. Tj. Plomp
Size of staff. Total: 40 — Full time: 38.7 — Part time: 1.3
Researchers: 9 — Full time: 8 — Part time: 0.8
Research activities: from 25% to 50%
Type of research: Research and development.
Functional objectives of research: Various.
Periodical publications: Twente educational report.
Studies and surveys in preparation: Instruction. Information technology. Curriculum. Item banking.

Onderwijs research centrum, katholieke hogeschool Tilburg

0378

Translation: Educational Research Centre, Tilburg University
Address: P.O.Box 90153, 5000 LE TILBURG
Year of creation: 1969
Parent Organization: Tilburg University
Present Head: E. van Hees
Size of staff. Total: 10 — Full time: 8 — Part time: 2
Researchers: 7 — Full time: 5 — Part time: 2
Research activities: more than 50%
Educational research: more than 50%
Type of research: Research and development.
Functional objectives of research: Staff development; curriculum development.
Periodical publications: None published.
Monographs: Dorp, C. van; Kok, E. Onderwijsextensivering via rendementsverbetering. Paper for the National Consortium on Research into Higher Education. 1983. Hees, E.J.W.M. van. Some design considerations on EDUSERVICE, a computer assisted evaluation system. Paper prepared for CAL '81 (Leeds). 1981. Wijffels, H.J.C. On testing student learning at intellectual level higher than factual recall. Paper presented at the Fifth International Symposium on Educational Testing, Stirling, Scotland. 1982. Complete list on request.
Studies and surveys in preparation: Handbook on educational testing for teachers (development of questions and tests — test marking — test analyses — itembanking — on line/tailored testing). Handbook on computers in schools (CAT-CMI — informatics and computer education — administrative applications). Individuele studiesystemen (personalized systems of instruction in higher education). Testing of

higher cognitive levels. Complete list on request.

Onderwijskunding centrum CDO/AVC, Technische hogeschool Twente

0379

Translation: Centre for Educational Research and Development, Twente University of Technology
Address: P.B. 217, 7500 AE ENSCHEDE
Year of creation: 1965
Parent Organization: Twente University of Technology
Present Head: Drs. J.M. Donders
Size of staff. Total: 33 — Full time: 23 — Part time: 10
Researchers: 17 — Full time: 14 — Part time: 3
Research activities: from 10% to 25%
Educational research: more than 50%
Type of research: Research and development.
Functional objectives of research: Servicing teachers, students, and educational administration.
Periodical publications: OC — Bulletins (3–4/yr). OC — Reports (irregular).
Monographs: Schriftelijk studiemateriaal. Studiemethoden. Oriëntatie op leren en onderwijs. Het leren oplossen van natuurwetenschappelijk problemen. Het leren oplossen van mechanika–problemen. Mentorencursus gespreksvoering. Hoorkollege geven.
Studies and surveys in preparation: Computer assisted learning (Pascal, algebra, etc.). Giving feedback to students in training problem solving. Problem solving in governmental administration. Course construction in learning to make computer programmes.

Orthopedagogische instituut van de Universiteit van Amsterdam

0380

Translation: Orthopedagogical Institute of the University of Amsterdam
Address: Ÿsbaanpad 9, 1076 CV AMSTERDAM
Year of creation: 1965
Parent Organization: University of Amsterdam
Present Head: Prof. dr. A.T.G. van Gennep
Size of staff. Total: 44 — Full time: 10 — Part time: 34
Researchers: 22 — Full time: 6 — Part time: 12
Research activities: from 25% to 50%
Educational research: from 10% to 25%
Type of research: Research and development.
Functional objectives of research: Treatment of developmental disabilities.
Monographs: Wolf, J.C. van der; Drapers, J.C. Kwalitatief onderzoek in het kader van het samenwerkingsproject buo–bao Amersfoort. 1981. Leemans, P.A.M. Zelfstandigheid, hoe zo? Een onderzoek naar zelfstandigheidsbevordering bij meervoudig gehandicapte mensen. 1982. Gennep, A. van, red. Inleiding tot de orthopedagogiek. 1983. Complete list on request.
Studies and surveys in preparation: Early detection of development disabilities. Residential treatment of emotional disturbances. School drop–outs.

Research instituut voor het onderwijs in het Noorden (RION)

0381

Translation: Research Institute for Education in the North of the Netherlands
Address: Nieuwe Stationsweg 5-9, 9751 SZ HAREN (Gr.)
Year of creation: 1973
Parent Organization: State University of Groningen; Foundation of Educational Research (SVO)
Present Head: Prof. dr. Bert P.M. Creemers
Size of staff. Total: 55
Researchers: 25
Type of research: Applied research.
Functional objectives of research: Advance, on non-profit basis, educational research for teaching practice, educational science and policy.
Periodical publications: RION Bulletins. Annual reports.
Monographs: Ontwikkeling von een observatieinstrument. 1979. Theorie en oefeningen. 1979. Toetsen bij de leesmethoden: zo/veilig leren lezen en letterstad. 1980. Eindrapportage DVO-projekt PO 417 I: evaluatie van het programme 'Leren participerend leren'. 1980. Signaleren, diagnostiseren en remediëren als functie van de school. 1980. Complete list on request.
Studies and surveys in preparation: Primary education. Secondary education. Link-up between regular education and special education. Curriculum research. Participation education. Regional administration.

Stichting centrum voor onderwijsonderzoek van de Universiteit van Amsterdam

0382

Translation: Foundation for Educational Research of the University of Amsterdam
Address: Singel, 138, AMSTERDAM
Year of creation: 1981
Parent Organization: University of Amsterdam
Present Head: Drs. W.G. Zijlstra
Size of staff. Total: 60 — Full time: 20 — Part time: 40
Researchers: 47 — Full time: 5 — Part time: 42
Research activities: more than 50%
Educational research: more than 50%
Type of research: Applied, research and development.
Functional objectives of research: Servicing the educational administration.
Periodical publications: SCO Cahiers.
Monographs: Godefrooij, P. Hoe spelen leerlingen op basisscholen in Rotterdam met woorden? 1983. Oostwoud Wijdenes, J.; Otto, F.; Kamp, M. van der; Oijen, L. van. Leren musiceren. Een onderzoek naar het instrumentale en vocale muziekvakonderwijs. 1983. Erp, M. van; Visch Eybergen, A. de. Op basis van de kleuterschool: een onderzoek naar de verworvenheden van het kleuteronderwijs in de nieuwe basisschool. 1983. Glopper, K. de. Opstelkenmerken en opstelbeoordelingen: onderzoek naar de validiteit van globale opstelbeoordeling. 1983. Complete list on request.

Stichting interuniversitair instituut voor sociaal-wetenschappelijk onderzoek **0383**

Translation: Netherlands Universities' Joint Social Research Centre
Address: Oude Zijds Achterburgwal 128, P.O.Box 19079, 1000 GB AMSTERDAM
Year of creation: 1960
Present Head: Dr. J.G.M. Sterk
Size of staff. Total: 35 — Full time: 19 — Part time: 16
Researchers: 17 — Full time: 13 — Part time: 4
Research activities: from 25% to 50%
Educational research: from 10% to 25%
Type of research: Basic.
Functional objectives of research: Stimulation and cooperation among educational researchers.
Periodical publications: Berichten over onderzoek. SISWO-studiebijeenkomsten onderwijssociologie. Nieuwsbrief projectonderwijs.
Monographs: Guldenmund, A. Literatuuroverzicht projectonderwijs. 1980. Hoff, J.J. van; Dronkers, J. Onderwijs en arbeidsmarkt. 1980. Verschoor, F. Jeugdcultuur en onderwijs: een literatuuroverzicht. 1981. Kleijer, H., red. Onderwijs, kwalificatie en arbeidsmarkt. 1981. Complete list on request.
Studies and surveys in preparation: Changing educational opportunities overtime. Relation between educational and occupation attainment.

Stichting voor de leerplanontwikkeling (SLO) **0384**

Translation: Institute for Curriculum Development
Address: Postbox 2041, 7500 CA ENSCHEDE
Year of creation: 1975
Parent Organization: Private institution; budget voted by Department of Education
Present Head: Drs. B. Wildeboer
Size of staff. Total: 200
Type of research: Applied research.
Functional objectives of research: Devise/have devised models for common-core curricula, school curricula and teaching-learning packages for educational organizations outside university sector. Advise and coordinate tasks in the field of curriculum development.

Stichting voor onderzoek van het onderwijs (SVO) **0385**

Translation: Foundation for Educational Research in the Netherlands
Address: Pletterijkade 50, 2515 SH DEN HAAG
Year of creation: 1966
Present Head: Mr. Chris W. van Seventer
Size of staff. Total: 41
Researchers: 12
Type of research: The Foundation itself does not conduct research, but promotes and coordinates educational research. In practice, coordinating this at the national level comprises in the main: coordinating the demand for research articulated in various quarters (co-)organizing research structures, improving the climate and framework within which the individual researcher operates, systematically evaluating quality of research, allocating research funds and promoting dissemination of research findings.

Periodical publications: SVO Annual report (presents a detailed account of research policy, development and financial matters; list of subsidized projects for the year; description of number of projects added). Didaktief (information bulletin, 12/yr). Literatuurdocumentatie onderwijs (abstract journal, 10/yr). Literature documentation on education (English version of the abstract journal, 4/yr). Directory of educational research information sources (English overview of most important bibliographical publications and databases in educational research and associated social sciences). SVO Projectlist: concise survey of complete and ongoing educational research (English, first published for year 80–81).

Monographs: SVO Series (book series publishing research reports, popularized versions of research projects, dissertations, documents on research policy, conference reports, etc.). SVO Memo series (periodical series of policy and advisory reports on subjects of concern to SVO but which deserve wider publication). SVO Brochures (occasional publications on topics of current public interest, with condensed and popularized information from research reports, etc.).

Studies and surveys in preparation: SVO Sheets (short descriptions, in looseleaf format, of new research projects). A selection from the SVO Series in English.

Subfaculteit voor pedagogische en andragogische wetenschappen

0386

Translation: Institute for Pedagogy and Andragology (Adult education and social work and community organisation)

Address: Rijksuniversiteit Utrecht, Instituut voor pedagogische en andragogische wetenschappen, Heidelberglaan 1 Postbus 80.140, 3508 TC UTRECHT

Year of creation: 1963

Parent Organization: Institute of Social Science

Present Head: Prof. dr. L.M. Stevens (Dean)

Researchers: 112 — Full time: 75 — Part time: 37

Research activities: from 25% to 50%

Educational research: from 10% to 25%

Type of research: Basic and applied.

Functional objectives of research: Education and educational institutions in relation to the development of children.

Periodical publications: Wetenschappelijk jaarverslag Rijksuniversiteit Utrecht.

Monographs: Andree, T.G.I.M. Gelovig word je niet vanzelf, godsdienstige opvoeding van rk–jongeren tussen 12 en 20 jaar. 1983. Linden, J.L. van der; Kanselaar, G. Sociaal kognitieve complexiteit: een onderzoek naar individuele verschillen in complexiteit van de organisatie van sociale kennis bij kinderen in samenhang met het verwerken van informatie en sociaal interageren. 1983. Tilleman, H.H. Leerkrachten als ontwerpers: een studie naar de mogelijkheden tot het instrumenteren van leerkrachten uit het basisonderwijs t.b.v. het ontwerpen van onderwijsleersituaties binnen het leerstofdomein verbale informatie. 1983. Dirksen, W. Vakoverschrijdend bewegingsonderwijs: een ontwikkelingspsychologisch georiënteerde studie ter verheldering en verbreding van de vakoverschrijdende doelen van het bewegingsonderwijs aan 5- tot 8 jarige kinderen. 1983. Goudena, P.P. Private speech: an analysis of its social and self regulatory functions. 1983. Zwarts, M.A. Criteriumtoetsen bij de aansluiting van primair en secundair onderwijs. 1983. Complete list on request.

Studies and surveys in preparation: Problematisch leren. Problemen in de ontwikkeling van jonge kinderen. Innovatie van onderwijs en curriculum. Ontwerpen van sociale systemen. Onderwijs en leren. Complete list on request.

Vakgroep interdisciplinaire onderwijskunde, Rijksuniversiteit te Groningen **0387**

Translation: Department of Interdisciplinary Education and Educational Research, State University of Groningen
Address: Westerhaven 16, 9718 AW GRONINGEN
Year of creation: 1964
Parent Organization: State University of Groningen
Present Head: Prof. dr. K.B. Koster
Size of staff. Total: 61 — Full time: 18 — Part time: 43
Researchers: 28 — Part time: 28
Research activities: from 25% to 50%
Educational research: more than 50%
Type of research: Basic, applied, research and development.
Periodical publications: Info. Informatiebladen van het Instituut voor onderwijskunde der RU/Groningen, 1-, 1969 —
Monographs: Corte, E. de; Peters, J.J. Beknopte didaxologie: 5e dr. Groningen. 1981. Creemers, B.P.M. Pedagogiek in de jaren tachtig in Nederland. In: Visies op onderzoek in enkele sociale wetenschappen. 1982. Gelder, L. van. Ervaring en opdracht: enkele notities over een persoonlijke visie op de onderwijskunde. 1981. Koetsier, J.M.B. Education and the social commitment: report of a workshop for teachers in Tiruvanmiyur, India, 11-13 August 1982. 1982. Complete list on request.
Studies and surveys in preparation: Research project on didactic behaviour. Research project on educational policy and innovations in the content of education. Research project on teaching-learning processes and stagnations in these processes. The position of interdisciplinary educational research within the framework of international, national and local scientific research. Complete list on request.

Vereniging werkverband van plaatselijke en regionale onderwijsbegeleidingsdiensten **0388**

Translation: Organisation of Local and Regional Educational Guidance Services
Address: Noordeinde 94a, 2514 GM 's-GRAVENHAGE
Year of creation: 1969
Present Head: Drs. H.G. van Noordenburg
Size of staff. Total: 9 — Full time: 7 — Part time: 2
Researchers: 4 — Full time: 3 — Part time: 1
Research activities: from 25% to 50%
Educational research: from 25% to 50%
Type of research: Applied, policy-directed.
Functional objectives of research: Preparation of courses for inservice training of teachers and of the personnel of guidance services; documentation; servicing the educational administration.
Periodical publications: W.P.R. Overzicht.
Monographs: W.P.R.O.-commentaar op het discussiestuk 'Voorontwerp van wet op de onderwijsverzorging'. W.P.R.O.-enquêtes 1980. 1982. Jaarverslag 1981. 1982. Onderzoeksnota 1. Scholingsnota 1. Beleidsnota '80-'83.
Studies and surveys in preparation: Onderwijsbegeleiding 1984-1994. W.P.R.O.-beleidsplan 1984-1987.

VOU (Vakgroep onderwijskunde der Rijksuniversiteit Utrecht)

0389

Translation: VOU (Section for Educational Research of the State University of Utrecht)
Address: Heidelberglaan 1, 3584 CS UTRECHT
Year of creation: 1963
Parent Organization: State University of Utrecht
Present Head: Prof. dr. N.A.J. Lagerweij
Size of staff. Total: 37 — Full time: 26 — Part time: 11
Researchers: 37 — Full time: 7 — Part time: 30
Research activities: from 25% to 50%
Educational research: more than 50%
Type of research: Basic and applied research.
Functional objectives of research: Curriculum development and implementation; public policy and educational policy (within the research-programme Innovation of education and curriculum).
Periodical publications: Journal of the VOU (Dutch title: VOU-blad).
Monographs: List on request.
Studies and surveys in preparation: Structuring school-based educational planning. Developing and functioning of curricula. Developing and functioning of educational beliefs. Public policy and educational innovation. Educational counseling and educational innovation. Dissemination and implementation of innovations (within the programme Innovation of education and curriculum). The use of computers as a plentiful resource in instruction. Descriptive and prescriptive studies of cognitive processes. Contribution of social learning processes and communication among pupils to cognitive development. Contribution of qualitative methods to the diagnosis of learning problems (within the programme Teaching and learning).

NEW ZEALAND

Curriculum Development Unit, Directorate, Department of Education

0390

Address: Private Bag, WELLINGTON
Year of creation: 1963
Parent Organization: Department of Education
Present Head: Mr. Jack Cox
Size of staff. Total: 40 — Full time: 40
Researchers: 37
Research activities: from 10% to 25%

New Zealand Council for Educational Research (NZCER)

0391

Address: P.O. Box 3237, WELLINGTON
Year of creation: 1934
Parent Organization: Independent
Present Head: Mr. John E. Watson
Size of staff. Total: 31 — Full time: 26 — Part time: 5
Researchers: 14 — Full time: 12 — Part time: 2
Research activities: from 25% to 50%

Educational research: from 25% to 50%
Type of research: Basic and applied research.
Functional objectives of research: Foster the study of and R&D in educational and other like matters; give assessment on these matters; supply information and assistance to persons and organizations concerned with education.
Periodical publications: NZ Journal of educational studies. NZCER Newsletter. NZCER Annual report. SET: research information for teachers. NZCER Mail order newsletter.
Monographs: Benton, R. The flight of the amokura: oceanic languages and formal education in the Pacific. 1981. Hall, C. Grandma's attic or Aladdin's cave: museum education service for children. 1981. McDonald, G. Working and learning: a participatory project on parent helping in the New Zealand playcentre. 1982. Routledge, M.; Hall, C. Young people and alcohol: a national survey. 1981. Sutton-Smith, B. A history of children's play: the New Zealand playground 1840–1950. 1982. McNaughton, S., et al. Parents as remedial reading tutors: issues for home and school. 1981. Buckton, R. Sing a song of six-year-olds. 1983.
Studies and surveys in preparation: Adult education. Early childhood education. Test development. Maori schooling.

Research and Statistics Division, Department of Education

0392

Address: Private Bag, WELLINGTON
Year of creation: 1977
Parent Organization: Department of Education
Present Head: L.J. Ingham
Size of staff. Total: 19 — Full time: 19
Researchers: 15 — Full time: 15
Research activities: more than 50%
Educational research: more than 50%
Type of research: Applied research.
Functional objectives of research: To provide information for education planning, policy-making and practice.
Periodical publications: Research and Statistics Division bulletin (2/yr).
Monographs: Absence from school. Teacher career and promotion study. An evaluation of nursing courses in technical institutes. Complete list upon request.
Studies and surveys in preparation: Demographic, survey and evaluative research. Major projects include: an evaluation of physiotherapy training. A survey of social studies subjects. A study of teachers' perceptions of children with special needs. Second IEA Mathematics Study. IEA Written Expression Study.

NICARAGUA

Departamento de Investigaciones y Documentación

0393

Address: Complejo Cívico "Camilo Ortega Saavedra", MANAGUA
Year of creation: 1974
Parent Organization: División General de Planificación, Ministerio de Educación
Present Head: Juan Bautista Arríen

Size of staff. Total: 11 — Full time: 10 — Part time: 1
Researchers: 5 — Full time: 5
Research activities: more than 50%
Educational research: more than 50%
Type of research: Investigación aplicada.
Functional objectives of research: Orientación en la toma de decisiones en la planificación de la educación nacional.
Periodical publications: Resúmenes analíticos en educación (Nicaragua). Bibliografía educativa (Nicaragua, a iniciarse).
Monographs: Demanda de carreras técnicas cortas y capacitación para el trabajo en el sector agroindustrial. Evaluación de proceso para determinar el grado de dominio en los idiomas extranjeros. Consulta para obtener insumos que ayuden a definir los fines y objetivos de la educación nicaragüense. Estudio sobre la "Calidad de la educación" Necesidades de información y comunicación a través de los CEP y TEPCE en el proceso de implementación y evaluación de la transformación educativa en Nicaragua.
Studies and surveys in preparation: Investigación- evaluativa en el programa de primer grado.

NIGER

Institut national de documentation, de recherche et d'animation pédagogiques (INDRAP) **0394**

Address: B.P. 10184, NIAMEY
Year of creation: 1974
Parent Organization: Etablissement public de l'Etat jouissant de l'autonomie financière et de la personnalité civile
Present Head: Monsieur Abache Chaibou, directeur général
Size of staff. Total: 88
Researchers: 30 — Full time: 30
Research activities: from 25% to 50%
Educational research: more than 50%
Type of research: Recherche linguistique et pédagogique.
Functional objectives of research: Production de documentation pédagogique; formation des formateurs; études de planification de l'éducation.
Periodical publications: Informations pédagogiques (6/an).
Monographs: Série 'Etudes et documents': 175 titres parus.
Studies and surveys in preparation: Manuels d'enseignement en langues nigériennes (Hausa, Zarma, Fulfulde, Tamajaq, Kanuri). Perspectives de développement du système scolaire nigérien. Projet de réforme de l'enseignement.

NIGERIA

Advanced Teachers College (Ahmadu Bello University)

0395

Address: P.M.B. 3045, KANO
Year of creation: 1967
Parent Organization: Ahmadu Bello University, Zaria
Present Head: Dr. M.I. Ayeni
— Full time: 69 — Part time: 26
Researchers: 69 — Full time: 69
Research activities: from 10% to 25%
Educational research: more than 50%
Type of research: Basic.
Functional objectives of research: Partial fulfilment of degree requirements; servicing educational administrators.
Periodical publications: The Educator. Geomophone.
Studies and surveys in preparation: Learning orientations of participants in the Nigeria Certificate in Education by correspondence programme. A survey of personnel problems in science teaching at post-primary level in Kano State. The functions of art and ifa in promoting informal education in Oyo State with particular reference to Ibarapa division. School participation by girls (and women) in Kano State. Attitudes of female students participating in sports — a study of some post secondary institutions in northern States of Nigeria. Complete list on request.

Comparative Education Study and Adaptation Centre (CESAC)

0396

Address: University of Lagos, P.O. Box 116, Akoka, LAGOS
Year of creation: 1968
Parent Organization: University of Lagos, Lagos
Present Head: Dr. U.M.O. Ivowi
Size of staff. Total: 44 — Full time: 44
Researchers: 11 — Full time: 11
Research activities: from 10% to 25%
Educational research: more than 50%
Type of research: Research and development.
Functional objectives of research: Servicing curriculum development.
Periodical publications: Journal of research in curriculum. Newsletter.
Monographs: Textbooks. Occasional papers.
Studies and surveys in preparation: A survey of resources for teaching/learning agriculture in some urban secondary schools of Lagos. Research on teacher effectiveness: the Nigerian experience. Research on Public attitudes towards public education. A survey of teacher perception of the new agriculture curriculum for the JSS. Use of aids in concept formation in physics. Content analysis representation as a method of evaluating curricular and instructional materials. Students misconception about energy, conservation principles and fields.

Department of Adult Education and Extra-Mural Studies

0397

Address: University of Nigeria, NSUKKA
Year of creation: 1980
Parent Organization: University of Nigeria
Present Head: Dr. E.O. Okeem
Size of staff. Total: 40 — Full time: 40 — Part time: 35
Researchers: 12 — Full time: 12
Research activities: from 25% to 50%
Educational research: from 25% to 50%
Type of research: Applied research and development.
Functional objectives of research: Academic servicing of courses; national development.
Monographs: Adult education in the 80s: problems and solutions.
Studies and surveys in preparation: An appraisal of adult education programmes and their implementation in Nigeria, 1976–1982.

Department of Adult Education, University of Ibadan, Ibadan

0398

Address: University of Ibadan, IBADAN
Year of creation: 1949
Parent Organization: The University of Ibadan
Present Head: Professor J.T. Okedara
Size of staff. Total: 59 — Full time: 51 — Part time: 8
Researchers: 13 — Full time: 12 — Part time: 1
Research activities: from 25% to 50%
Educational research: more than 50%
Type of research: Basic, applied, research and development.
Functional objectives of research: Partial fulfilment of higher degree requirements; servicing the educational administration.
Periodical publications: Departmental newsletter.
Monographs: Report of Annual Conference on Functional Literacy. Report of Annual Conference on Industrial Relations. Directory of adult education.
Studies and surveys in preparation: Urban Experimental Literacy Project — Department. Rural Experimental Literacy Project. Literacy Documentation Project. Extra-mural Documentation Project.

National Teachers' Institute

0399

Address: College Road, P.M.B. 2191, KADUNA
Year of creation: 1976
Parent Organization: Federal Ministry of Education, Lagos
Present Head: Alhaji Hafiz Wali
Size of staff. Total: 755
Researchers: 60 — Full time: 20 — Part time: 40
Research activities: from 25% to 50%
Educational research: more than 50%
Type of research: Action research, research and development.
Functional objectives of research: Preparation of courses, servicing of teacher education and professional development of teachers.
Monographs: Reports of seminars, workshops, course books.

Studies and surveys in preparation: An investigation on the use of audiovisual aids by teachers in Nigerian primary schools. An investigation into the types of inservice education programmes offered to teachers in Nigeria.

Nigerian Educational Research Council (NERC)

0400

Address: 3 Jibowu Street, Yaba, P.O. Box 8058, LAGOS
Year of creation: 1965
Parent Organization: Federal government educational parastatal set up by law
Present Head: Mr. J.M. Akintola, Executive Secretary
Size of staff. Total: 330 — Full time: 330 — Part time: 500
Researchers: 69 — Full time: 69 — Part time: 2
Research activities: more than 50%
Educational research: more than 50%
Type of research: Applied research and special studies; research commissioned to universities; research activities in the sectors of curricular development and design for primary, secondary and teacher education levels.
Functional objectives of research: Encourage, promote and co-ordinate educational research programmes in Nigeria; identify and establish priorities of educational problems; undertake and support R&D; maintain relationships with other institutions.
Periodical publications: Education and development. NERC News. IPR Bulletin.
Monographs: Paper prepared by Nigerian Educational Research Council in support of Nigerian participation in the Pan-Commonwealth Specialists Conference on 'Science, Mathematics, Technical and Vocational Education'. 1983. Directory of special education personnel and facilities in Nigeria. Approved national curriculum for junior secondary schools — Hausa language, Igbo language, Yoruba language. 1982. Complete list on request.
Studies and surveys in preparation: Universal primary education. Adult and continuing education. Special project on science and mathematics.

NORWAY

Bergen Laererhøgskole

0401

Translation: Bergen College of Education
Address: Landåssvingen 15, 5030 LANDÅS
Year of creation: 1953
Parent Organization: Ministry of Culture and Research
Present Head: Ivar Drevland
Size of staff. Total: 86 (teaching staff)
Research activities: from 10% to 25%
Type of research: Research and development.
Functional objectives of research: Partial fulfilment of degree requirements; servicing the school system (pre-school; elementary/junior/high).
Periodical publications: Report from Bergen College of Education (3/4 yr).

Forsøksrådet for skoleverket

0402

Translation: National Council for Innovation in Education
Address: Erich Mogensønsvei 38, Linderud, OSLO 5
Year of creation: 1954
Parent Organization: Ministry of Education
Present Head: Per Østerud
Size of staff. Total: 35
Researchers: 15
Type of research: Research and development.
Functional objectives of research: Research into educational conditions; follow-up work on new development; promotion of educational research and development.
Periodical publications: Forsøksnytt (News on current research).
Monographs: Informasjon om forsøksarbeid (series). Complete list on request.
Studies and surveys in preparation: Teacher training projects. School in relation to the local community. Coordination and cooperation of education for 4–9 year olds. Projects concerning handicapped children. Vocational orientation and practical-experience careers guidance. Upper secondary education in sparsely populated areas. Connection between school and working life. Organizational development in school.

Institute of Educational Psychology, University of Bergen

0403

Address: Sydnesplass 12, 5000 BERGEN
Year of creation: 1971
Parent Organization: University of Bergen, School of Psychology
Present Head: Professor Hans-Jørgen Gjessing
Size of staff. Total: 7 — Full time: 6 — Part time: 1
Researchers: 5 — Full time: 5
Research activities: more than 50%
Educational research: 50%
Type of research: Applied.
Functional objectives of research: Learning process; learning disabilities; remedial teaching; self concept; blind and partially sighted; emotional problems in the classroom; school organization and system theory.
Studies and surveys in preparation: Several studies within the mentioned topics.

Oppland distriktshøgskole

0404

Translation: Oppland College
Address: P.O. Box 1004, Skurva, 2601 LILLEHAMMER
Year of creation: 1972
Parent Organization: Ministry of Culture and Science
Present Head: Olav R. Spilling
Size of staff. Total: 68 — Full time: 55 — Part time: 13
Researchers: 41 — Full time: 34 — Part time: 7
Research activities: from 25% to 50%
Educational research: from 25% to 50%
Type of research: Basic, applied and development.
Functional objectives of research: Research (in itself) and research servicing the educational administration.

Monographs: Monsen, L. LMB-studiet: rapport fra en observatør. Monsen, L. Form og innhold i den spesial-pedagogiske utdanninga. Ålvik, T.; Monsen, L. Larerutdanning i samfunnsfag.
Studies and surveys in preparation: List on request.

Pedagogisk forskningsinstitutt

0405

Translation: Institute for Educational Research
Address: University of Oslo, Box 1092, Blindern, OSLO 3
Year of creation: 1938
Parent Organization: University of Oslo
Present Head: Ass. Prof. Oddbjørn Evenshaug
Size of staff. Total: 55 — Full time: 44 — Part time: 11
Researchers: 44 — Full time: 2 — Part time: 42
Research activities: from 25% to 50%
Educational research: from 25% to 50%
Type of research: Basic research (mostly).
Functional objectives of research: Fulfilment of degree requirements for the approximately 200 higher level students, no 'external' functional objectives for the staff.
Periodical publications: Rapporter fra Pedagogisk forskningsinstitutt (Reports from Institute for Educational Research. Only in Norwegian).
Monographs: (in progress).
Studies and surveys in preparation: Laererrollen i den videregående skole. Ungdom som elever i den videregående skole. Laerebøkene og skolens innhold. Peace begins in the minds of women.

Pedagogisk institutt, Den allmennvitenskapelige høgskolen, Universitetet i Trondheim

0406

Translation: Education Department, The University of Trondheim
Address: 7055 DRAGVOLL
Year of creation: 1922
Parent Organization: University of Trondheim
Present Head: Oskar Solberg
Size of staff. Total: 17
Researchers: 14
Research activities: 50%
Educational research: 50%
Type of research: Educational research, comprising historical, psychological and sociological topics.
Functional objectives of research: A variety of objectives, related to both special and general education.
Periodical publications: None issued.
Monographs: None issued.
Studies and surveys in preparation: List on request.

Statens spesiallaererhøgskole

0407

Translation: The Norwegian Postgraduate College of Special Education
Address: Granaasen 4, N-1347 HOSLE
Year of creation: 1961
Parent Organization: Kultur- og vitenskapsdepartementet
Present Head: Mr. Edvard Befring, Dr. Philos.
Size of staff. Total: 62 — Full time: 40 — Part time: 22
Researchers: 39 — Full time: 32 — Part time: 7
Research activities: from 25% to 50%
Educational research: from 25% to 50%
Type of research: Special education and rehabilitation.
Functional objectives of research: Prevention of learning problems etc., and development of education practice for all groups of handicapped children, youth and adults.
Periodical publications: Spesialpedagogiske forskningsbidrag (Summaries of compiled research projects). Informasjon (Information journal covering the current activities of the institution).
Monographs: Dissertations and books.
Studies and surveys in preparation: 24 projects dealing with handicapped students and special education. Complete list on request.

Stavanger laerarhøgskole

0408

Translation: Stavanger College of Education
Address: P.O. Box 2521, 4000 ULLANDHAUG
Year of creation: 1954
Present Head: Sigmund Sunnanå
Size of staff. Total: 77 — Full time: 48 — Part time: 29
Researchers: 3 — Full time: 2 — Part time: 1
Research activities: less than 10%
Type of research: All types, but mostly research and development.
Functional objectives of research: Partly fulfilment of degree requirements, partly servicing the educational administration.
Periodical publications: Skriftserie for Stavanger laerarhøgskole.
Monographs: List on request.
Studies and surveys in preparation: Project on the connections between childhood experiences and religious faith. Project on echoic memory and auditive perception. Project on stress among teachers.

PAKISTAN

Board of Intermediate Education, Karachi

0409

Address: Bakhtiari Youth Centre, North Nazimabad, KARACHI-33
Year of creation: 1962
Parent Organization: Ministry of Education
Present Head: Prof. Mohammad Ali Khan, Chairman
Size of staff. Total: 181

Researchers: 8
Research activities: more than 50%
Educational research: more than 50%
Type of research: Applied research.
Functional objectives of research: Curriculum evaluation; evaluation of teaching facilities; classroom testing; examination reforms.
Studies and surveys in preparation: Collection of statistics to study the academic achievement of students in the annual examinations held by this Board.

Board of Secondary Education **0410**

Address: 2/V/C, Nazimabad, KARACHI–45
Year of creation: 1950
Parent Organization: Government of Sind
Present Head: Mr. Mir Muhammad Siyal
Size of staff. Total: 157
Researchers: 2
Research activities: less than 10%
Educational research: less than 10%
Type of research: Historical survey, statistical survey, descriptive.
Functional objectives of research: To obtain quantitative information regarding different aspects of secondary education, sometimes used for decision making.
Periodical publications: None published.
Monographs: Survey of general science curriculum at secondary level in Pakistan since 1947. 1974. Survey of classroom testing practices at secondary level in Karachi schools. Evaluation of proposed geography curriculum at H.S.C. level. 1982.
Studies and surveys in preparation: Study of the psychological needs of secondary school children in Karachi. Selection procedure for President's talent farming scheme.

Committee for Coordination of Research Activities in Education in Sind **0411**

Address: St–22, Block–6, Gulshan–e–Iqbal, University Road, KARACHI
Year of creation: 1982
Parent Organization: Department of Education, Government of Sind
Present Head: Prof. Razi–ur–Rahman, Additional Secretary, Education Department
Size of staff. Total: 30 — Full time: 28 — Part time: 2
Researchers: 5 — Full time: 3 — Part time: 2
Research activities: from 10% to 25%
Educational research: more than 50%
Type of research: Fundamental and applied.
Functional objectives of research: To undertake research activities relevant to local and regional needs; to assist the Government in planning educational programmes on the basis of studies and research; to publish a journal to disseminate research activities.
Periodical publications: Sind educational journal (4/yr).
Monographs: Classroom testing practices. Survey of agro–technical studies. Causes of students' unrest.
Studies and surveys in preparation: Causes of falling of standard of education. Predictive validity of high school results. Causes of drop–outs in primary education.

Institute of Education and Research **0412**

Address: University of the Punjab, New Campus, LAHORE 20
Year of creation: 1960
Parent Organization: Board of Governors, Institute of Education and Research, University of the Punjab
Present Head: Professor. Dr. Munir-ud-Din Chughtai
Size of staff. Total: 40 — Full time: 40
Researchers: 7
Research activities: from 25% to 50%
Educational research: more than 50%
Type of research: Basic, applied as well as research and development.
Functional objectives of research: Partial fulfilment of degree requirements, preparation of courses, and servicing the educational administration and planning, etc.
Periodical publications: Bulletin of education and research (1/yr, English). Taleem-o-tahqeeq (1/yr, English and Urdu).
Monographs: Tests and guidance materials. Basic Urdu vocabulary study for students of grade 1 to 8 in West Pakistan. Preference and interests of ten-year old children in Punjab. Semi-standardization of mental ability test for children aged 5, 6 and 7. Family factors and school opportunities. Supply system of educated manpower in West Pakistan. A statistical profile of education in West Pakistan. A study on teachers in West Pakistan. Complete list on request.
Studies and surveys in preparation: Functional literacy and adult education pilot research and training. Experimental study on internal evaluation in primary and secondary schools in Punjab. Experimental study on the feasibility of open school strategies in Punjab. Curriculum development in: primary education; industrial arts education; secondary education; business education. Research and evaluation components of the primary education project. Complete list on request.

National Institute of Psychology **0413**

Address: K-14, F-8 Markaz, ISLAMABAD
Year of creation: 1976
Parent Organization: Quaid-e-Azam University, Islamabad
Present Head: Z.A. Ansari
Size of staff. Total: 54 — Full time: 54
Researchers: 18 — Full time: 18
Research activities: more than 50%
Educational research: more than 50%
Type of research: Both basic and applied.
Functional objectives of research: Providing tools for school teachers and developing understanding of the educational process.
Monographs: Hassan, I.N. The sociocultural variables of dropout syndrome in rural primary schools Pakistan. Kazim, A. Financial, organizational and technical innovation in education: evaluation report on five target villages in federal capital area, Islamabad. Pervez, S.; Bokhari, T. Study of personality dynamics of children. Ansari, Z.A. Scales for measuring attitude of women towards male and female education. Complete list on request.
Studies and surveys in preparation: Content analysis of text-books and story books. Studies in learning and teaching of science and mathematics. Guidance and

counselling in Pakistani schools. Development and adaptation of psychological tests. Study of drop-out in schools.

PAPUA NEW GUINEA

Educational Research Unit

0414

Address: University of Papua New Guinea, Box 320, WAIGANI
Year of creation: 1970
Parent Organization: University of Papua New Guinea
Present Head: Dr. Sheldon G. Weeks
Size of staff. Total: 13 — Full time: 13
Researchers: 6 — Full time: 6
Research activities: more than 50%
Educational research: more than 50%
Type of research: Basic and applied.
Functional objectives of research: Evaluation of innovative projects.
Periodical publications: ERU Reports.
Monographs: List on request.
Studies and surveys in preparation: Evaluation of secondary schools community extension project. West sepik non-formal education study. Comprehensive education of disavantaged children. Standards in community schools: New Ireland study. National literacy policy development. An evaluation of secondary teacher training. Complete list on request.

PERU

Centro de Investigación y Promoción Educativa (CIPE)

0415

Address: Camilo Carrillo 225, Of. 703, Jesus Maria, Apartado 11570, LIMA
Year of creation: 1978
Present Head: Luz Landazuri de Maurtua, Presidente Ejecutivo Educadora
Size of staff. Total: 5 — Full time: 2 — Part time: 3
Researchers: 4 — Full time: 1 — Part time: 3
Research activities: more than 50%
Educational research: more than 50%
Type of research: Investigación aplicada e investigación y desarrollo.
Functional objectives of research: Planificación curricular, administración escolar, planificación del desarrollo educativo.
Periodical publications: Folleto de divulgación del CIPE (Las publicaciones son realizadas por las instituciones que financian los estudios e investigaciones).
Monographs: El crecimiento de la población y las necesidades de la educación peruana. Seminario de la Asociación Multidisciplinaria de Investigación y Docencia en Población, Tarma, Perú. La participación de los padres de familia en la atención educativa de sus hijos: un estudio de caso de los programas no escolarizados de educación inicial. Estudio elaborado para la OREALC-UNESCO. Descentralización y

desconcentración administrativa en la educación peruana: antecedentes y perspectivas. Estudio elaborado para el CINTERPLAN-OEA. Lista completa a disposición.
Studies and surveys in preparation: Proyecto experimental de educación forestal en comunidades rurales de la sierra peruana. Formación y capacitación de personal para empresas: estudio de caso en el Peru.

Instituto Nacional de Investigación y Desarrollo de la Educación (INIDE) **0416**

Address: Dirección de Investigaciones Educacionales, Van de Velde 160, Urb. San Borja, Apdo. 1156, LIMA 100
Year of creation: 1972
Parent Organization: Ministerio de Educación
Present Head: Dr. Antonio Arenas, Director General; Prof. Rodolfo Sanchez, Direction de Investigaciones
Size of staff. Total: 296 — Full time: 296
Researchers: 24 — Full time: 24
Research activities: from 10% to 25%
Type of research: Investigaciones básicas y aplicadas en las siguientes áreas: tecnología educativa, psicopedagógicas, socioeconómicas, de economía de la educación y programas aplicados de carácter integral.
Functional objectives of research: Contribuir al desarrollo de la educación y el sistema educativo; ejecutar investigaciones orientadas al conocimiento de las características bio-psio-sociales de los educandos; ejecutar estudios sobre los factores contextuales socio-económicos que afectan el fenómeno educativo; generar tecnologías adecuadas, preparar programas pedagógicos y materiales educativos adecuados a la realidad nacional.
Periodical publications: Ediciones Retablo de papel. Ediciones previas. Informes de investigación. INIDE Informa. Cuadernos de información educacional RIDECAB (Revista de información educacional). RAE (Resúmenes analíticos en educación).
Monographs: Educación, Migración y Empleo. Educación superior tecnologica. Situación profesional e intereses de capacitación de los docentes en servicio. Exploración del desarrollo socio-emocional e intelectual en el niño en un programa de autoeducación. Autoeducación y aprendizaje creativo en el desarrollo del niño.
Studies and surveys in preparation: Estudio psicosocial del niño en edad escolar. Investigaciones en educación bilingue-puno. Convenio Peru-RFA. Hacia una alternativa en educación de adultos en el marco del desarrollo rural: problemas y posibilidades. Perspectivas educacionales y laborales de los jóvenes de las aŕeas urbanas del Perú.

Programa Académico de Administración de la Educación, Universidad de Lima **0417**

Address: Prolongación Av. Javier Prado Este s/n, Monterrico, Apartado 852, LIMA
Year of creation: 1960
Present Head: Dr. Luis Salazar Larrain
Size of staff. Total: 15 — Full time: 5 — Part time: 10
Researchers: 4 — Part time: 2
Research activities: from 10% to 25%
Educational research: more than 50%
Type of research: Aplicada.
Functional objectives of research: Obtención del grado de Magister e Especialista.

Monographs: Caballero Romero, A.E. Criterios de los governantes sobre el gasto destinado a educación a través de la historia presupuestal educativa peruana. 1982. Bullon Campos, H.F. Educación del sistema educativo en el ámbito rural con fines de desarrollo endógeno local micro regional: el caso del distrito de Huaylas. 1982. Castañeda Pilo Pais, M. La tutilidez de la escuela superior profesional (ESEP) de Sullana. 1983. Chumpitaz Cuadros, M.G. Posibilidades de aplicación de un sistema de evaluación para docentes de educación secundaria en centros educativos estatales. Iliovich Penfold, A.B. El trabajo infantil en Lima.
Studies and surveys in preparation: El proceso de institucionalización de las ESEP del 1o. ciclo en el período 1975-1980.

PHILIPPINES

Research and Development Office, College of Education, University of the Philippines
0418

Address: Diliman, QUEZON CITY
Year of creation: 1975
Parent Organization: University of the Philippines
Present Head: Dr. Josefina R. Cortes, Ph.D.
Size of staff. Total: 7 — Full time: 2 — Part time: 5
Research activities: 50%
Educational research: 50%
Type of research: Basic and applied research.
Functional objectives of research: Identify priority areas in educational research to set up a comprehensive R&D programme for the college; provide preservice, continuing education and training programmes in educational research; retrieve, publish, disseminate and utilize worthwhile and relevant researches and studies in education.
Periodical publications: R & D Bulletin. Education quarterly.
Monographs: Numerous articles issued in R & D Bulletin and in Education quarterly.
Studies and surveys in preparation: Attitudinal and motivational variables affecting the learning of Philipino to implement the bilingual policy in education. Evaluation and improvement of secondary education. Follow-up of the graduates of the U.P. College of Education, 1971-1980. Complete list on request.

Science Education Center
0419

Address: Vidal Tan Hall, University of Philippines, Diliman, QUEZON CITY
Year of creation: 1964
Parent Organization: University of the Philippines
Present Head: Dr. Dolores F. Hernandez, Director
Size of staff. Total: 105 — Full time: 104 — Part time: 1
Researchers: 43 — Full time: 42 — Part time: 1
Research activities: from 25% to 50%
Educational research: from 25% to 50%
Type of research: Basic and applied research in science education.
Functional objectives of research: Undertake studies related to teaching/learning of science/mathematics in Philippine situations, develop curriculum materials for students at pre-university level, conduct evaluative studies; to improve science and

math education curricular materials at pre-university levels; to provide information/data for decision makers at various levels.
Periodical publications: SEC Newsletter.
Monographs: Textbooks, resource materials, R & D publications, monographs & occasional papers on current topics of interest. Complete list upon request.
Studies and surveys in preparation: IEA International Study of Science Education (Philippine national survey is being conducted by this Centre). Science Educational Development Plan (several studies on national level have been commissioned), a project of the Ministry of Education, Culture and Sports and the National Science and Technology Authority. Science and technology in Philippine society. Study of misconceptions of science principles among students. Summative evaluation of curriculum materials already planned.

POLAND

Instytut Badań Pedagogicznych

0420

Translation: Institute of Educational Research
Address: ul. Górczewska 8, 01-180 WARSZAWA
Year of creation: 1950
Parent Organization: Ministry of Education
Present Head: Prof. dr hab. Maksymilian Maciaszek
Size of staff. Total: 134 — Full time: 127 — Part time: 7
Researchers: 80 — Full time: 76 — Part time: 4
Research activities: more than 50%
Educational research: from 25% to 50%
Type of research: Basic and applied research.
Functional objectives of research: General theory of education; new methods of teaching; improvements in organization and financial systems of education.
Periodical publications: Edukacja (4/yr). Studia — badania — innowacje (Study — research — innovation. Previous title: Badania oświatowe).
Monographs: The development of education in Polish People's Republic 1979-1980. 1981. Pańtak G.; Winiarski M. Szkoła środowiskowa na wsi (Community school in the country). 1982. Programowana gramatyka języka polskiego. Dla szkół dla pracujących (Programmed grammar of Polish language. For adults). 1981. Raport z badań przeprowadzonych w latach 1976-1980 (Report from researches conducted in the period 1976-1980). 1981. Szkolnictwo podstawowe (Elementary education). 1981. Korczak, J. Życie i dzieło (Life and work). 1982.
Studies and surveys in preparation: The concept of the educational system of A.S. Neill: Summerhill. The little dictionary of protective pedagogics. Psychosocial problems of school class. Retrospective evaluation of school work by retiring teachers. Conditions and possibility of generalizing secondary education.

Instytut Kształcenia Nauczycieli im. Władysława Spasowskiego

0421

Translation: Institut de formation et de perfectionnement des enseignants
Address: ul. Mokotowska 16/20, 00-561 WARSZAWA
Year of creation: 1972

Parent Organization: Ministère de l'instruction et de l'éducation
Present Head: Doc. dr Edmund Staszyński
Size of staff. Total: 162 — Full time: 146 — Part time: 16
Researchers: 100 — Full time: 84 — Part time: 16
Research activities: more than 50%
Educational research: more than 50%
Type of research: Recherches appliquées; recherche en développement propre; fondamentale.
Functional objectives of research: Préparation de la conception du système de la formation et du perfectionnement des enseignants; préparation des guides didactiques des matières de classe de base; des outils de contrôle de l'efficacité du travail scolaire des élèves et des enseignants; participation à la modernisation du système d'éducation; programme de perfectionnement pour les cadres de l'administration scolaire; préparation du pronostic des besoins de cadres d'enseignants jusqu'à la fin du XX siècle.
Periodical publications: Zeszyty naukowe filologia Polska. Zeszyty naukowe historia. Zeszyty naukowe matematyka. Kształcenia ustawiczne: materiały pomocnicze dla nauczycieli. Bibliografia analityczna Polskiego piśmiennictwa z zakresu teorii i praktyki wychowania. Bibliografia analityczna Polskiego piśmiennictwa z zakresu ogólnej teorii nauczania. Bibliografia analityczna Polskiego piśmiennictwa pedeutologicznego.
Monographs: Sykut, M. Osiągnięcia dydaktyczne a wydolność fizyczna nauczycieli wychowania fizycznego. 1983. Nowacki, J. Nauczycielski Uniwersytet Radiowo-Telewizyjny. 1982. Liste complète sur demande.
Studies and surveys in preparation: Conception générale et fondements méthodologiques du système de formation des enseignants. Analyse comparative des systèmes de formation des enseignants dans différents pays du monde. Ethique de la profession d'enseignant. Efficacité scolaire des élèves et des enseignants. Efficacité de l'activité de l'Université de la radio et de la télévision dans la formation des enseignants. Conditions sociales du perfectionnement professionnel des enseignants. Modernisation du système administratif de l'éducation. Didactique de l'éducation musicale. Didactique de l'enseignement de la physique, de la biologie, de la géographie.

Instytut Kształcenia Zawodowego

0422

Translation: Institute of Vocational Education and Training
Address: Mokotowska 16/20, 00-561 WARSZAWA
Year of creation: 1972
Parent Organization: Ministry of Education
Present Head: Prof. Tadeusz Nowacki
Size of staff. Total: 118 — Full time: 103 — Part time: 15
Researchers: 82 — Full time: 70 — Part time: 12
Research activities: more than 50%
Educational research: more than 50%
Type of research: Fundamental and applied research.
Functional objectives of research: Preparation of teaching/learning materials, curriculum development; research in teaching/learning methods and techniques; educational planning; educational development; occupational qualifications; career development; lifelong education.
Periodical publications: Pedagogika pracy (Pedagogics of work, 1/yr). Szkoła-zawód-

praca (School-occupation-work, 1/yr). Bibliografia pedagogiki pracy (Bibliography of pedagogics of work).
Monographs: Kształcenie zawodowe. Elementy diagnozy. 1983.
Studies and surveys in preparation: Modernization of vocational/technical education and training. Research in adult education. Curriculum development.

Instytut Nauk Pedagogicznych i Społecznych

0423

Translation: Institute for Pedagogical and Social Sciences
Address: Uniwersytet Śląski Filia w Cieszynie, ul. Bielska 62, 43-400 CIESZYN
Year of creation: 1984
Parent Organization: Uniwersytet Śląski w Katowicach
Present Head: Doc. dr hab. Kazimierz Ślęczka
Size of staff. Total: 47 — Full time: 44 — Part time: 3
Researchers: 44 — Full time: 41 — Part time: 2
Research activities: from 25% to 50%
Educational research: 50%
Type of research: Basic and applied research.
Functional objectives of research: Fulfilment of degree requirements.

Instytut Oświaty Rolniczej

0424

Translation: Institute of Agricultural Education
Address: Akademia Rolniczo-Techniczna, bl. 23, 10-725 OLSZTYN-KORTOWO
Year of creation: 1973
Parent Organization: Akademia Rolniczo-Techniczna, Olsztyn
Present Head: Zdzisław Czyż, Senior Lecturer
Size of staff. Total: 21 — Full time: 21
Researchers: 16 — Full time: 16
Research activities: 50%
Educational research: more than 50%
Type of research: Applied research.
Periodical publications: Zeszyty naukowe Akademii Rolniczo-Technicznej w Olsztynie. Seria Ekonomika.
Monographs: Czyż, Z. Evolution of education of dairy workers in Poland and some other countries with a particular respect to vocational education (In Polish, summary in English). 1983. Najmowicz, W. Cultural interests and aspirations of State farm workers in the Olsztyn province (In Polish, summary in English). 1982. Malewska, E.; Trawiński, W. Educational training of agricultural secondary school teachers at Academy of K.A. Timiriazev in Moscow and at Agricultural and Technical Academy in Olsztyn (In Polish, summary in English). 1982. Kuziel, F.; Kobus, K. Organizational and methodical aspects of functioning of qualifying courses for individual farmers (In Polish, summary in English). 1982. Ziajka, H.; Chmielewska, M.C.; Nowak, H. Professional qualification and the role of country-household instructresses in extension of everyday cultural practices (In Polish, summary in English). 1982.
Studies and surveys in preparation: Education and professional effectiveness of graduates of agricultural and food technology schools. Education and professional effectiveness of alumni of agricultural academies. Post graduate studies. Training for the agricultural services.

Instytut Pedagogiki i Psychologii

0425

Translation: Institut de pédagogie et psychologie
Address: 3 Fosa Staromiejska, 87-100 TORUŃ
Year of creation: 1976
Parent Organization: Université de Mikołaj Kopernik
Present Head: Prof. dr hab. Georges Danielewicz
Size of staff. Total: 52 — Full time: 49 — Part time: 3
Researchers: 46 — Full time: 43 — Part time: 3
Research activities: more than 50%
Educational research: from 25% to 50%
Type of research: Recherche fondamentale.
Functional objectives of research: Préparation des dissertations pour les titres scientifiques; préparation des autres ouvrages scientifiques; organisation du processus d'enseignement; organisation des sessions et conférences scientifiques.
Periodical publications: Acta Universitatis Nicolai Copernici — pedagogika.
Monographs: Les aspects psychologiques et pédagogiques des études. 1981. Kosakowski, C. L'adaptation sociale de l'enfant. 1981. Lróblewska, T. L'université allemande de Poznan (1941–1945) comme modèle d'école supérieure hitlérienne. 1983. Zachowicz, H. Les actuels problèmes d'éducation des enfants au seuil de l'école primaire. 1983.
Studies and surveys in preparation: Les relations entre les pédagogies française et polonaise au XIX et XX siècles. Précis d'histoire d'éducation universelle et polonaise. Histoire des écoles, de l'instruction publique et de la culture en Pologne (1918–1945). Liste complète sur demande.

Instytut Pedagogiki i Psychologii, Wyższa Szkoła Pedagogiczna w Rzeszowie

0426

Translation: Department of Pedagogy and Psychology, Pedagogical College in Rzeszów
Address: ul. Turkienicza 24, 35-959 RZESZÓW
Year of creation: 1966
Parent Organization: Ministerstwo Nauki, Szkolnictwa Wyższego i Techniki
Present Head: Andrzej Meissner, Ph.D.
Size of staff. Total: 48 — Full time: 46 — Part time: 2
Researchers: 5 — Full time: 2 — Part time: 3
Research activities: from 25% to 50%
Educational research: more than 50%
Type of research: Basic and applied research.
Functional objectives of research: Partial fulfilment of degree requirements and group research.
Periodical publications: Pedagogical sciences (1/yr).
Monographs: Meissner, A. Restoration of school system in Rzeszów county in 1944–49. 1982. Pilecka, B. Personal correlates of suicidal behaviour in youth. 1981. Horbowski, A. Functions of socio-cultural associations in Rzeszów county. 1982. Berling, Z.; Sowa, J. Determinants of effectiveness of revalidation process in mentally retarded children. 1982. Zeleźny, E. System of education of rural youth in 1973–1980. 1983.
Studies and surveys in preparation: Family psychotherapy: selected problems of theory and practice. Restoration of cultural life in Rzeszów county in 1944–1950. Vocational aspirations of primary school pupils. Social binds of pupils with the school.

Instytut Pedagogiki, Uniwersytet Jagielloński 0427

Translation: Institute of Pedagogy, Jagiellonian University
Address: ul. Manifestu Lipcowego 13, 31-110 KRAKÓW
Year of creation: 1924
Parent Organization: Jagiellonian University
Present Head: Doc. dr hab. Stanisław Palka
Size of staff. Total: 68 — Full time: 63 — Part time: 5
Researchers: 58 — Full time: 54 — Part time: 4
Research activities: from 25% to 50%
Educational research: from 25% to 50%
Type of research: Basic and applied research.
Functional objectives of research: Theory of pedagogy and theory of particular disciplines; giving scientific and methodological information for school practice.
Periodical publications: Zeszyty naukowe Uniwersytetu Jagiellońskiego. Prace pedagogiczne.
Monographs: Urban, B. Social maladjustment among children without family. 1982. Grochulska-Stec, J. Reeducation of aggressive children. 1982. Adamski, F. Sociology of marriage and a family. 1984. Palka, S. Research work as a method of education in school practice. 1984.
Studies and surveys in preparation: Modernization of the education process at all levels of education. How to increase the effectiveness of the education process. Culture and science in education. Problem of pedagogical methodology and pedagogical research work.

Instytut Polityki Naukowej, Postępu Technicznego i Szkolnictwa Wyższego 0428

Translation: Institute of Science Policy, Technological Progress and Higher Education
Address: ul. Nowy Świat 69, 00-046 WARSZAWA
Year of creation: 1973
Parent Organization: Ministerstwo Nauki, Szkolnictwa Wyższego i Techniki
Present Head: Prof. dr hab. Jan Kluczyński
Size of staff. Total: 125 — Full time: 111 — Part time: 14
Researchers: 71 — Full time: 61 — Part time: 10
Research activities: more than 50%
Educational research: more than 50%
Type of research: Basic and applied.
Functional objectives of research: To establish the size, structure and model of education based on the projected needs for qualified workers in developing the nation's economy and culture; to determine the size, structure and distribution of resources in higher education; to modernize the system of organization and management of higher education; to develop methods for determining the tasks and content of education and character formation through higher education.
Periodical publications: Dydaktyka szkoły wyższej. Sovremennaja vysšaja škola.
Monographs: List on request.
Studies and surveys in preparation: Planning and forecasting of the development of higher education. Organization of higher education. Modernization of educational and instructional process in higher education. Studies of students and academic staff. Studies of graduates. Comparative higher education.

Instytut Programów Szkolnych Ministerstwa Oświaty i Wychowania

0429

Translation: Institut des programmes scolaires du Ministère de l'éducation
Address: ul. I Armii Wojska Polskiego 25, 00–918 WARSZAWA
Year of creation: 1972
Parent Organization: Ministère de l'éducation
Present Head: Dr. Stanisław Frycie, Professeur adjoint
Size of staff. Total: 139 — Full time: 115 — Part time: 14
Researchers: 65 — Full time: 58 — Part time: 7
Research activities: more than 50%
Educational research: more than 50%
Type of research: Etudes théoriques et recherches expérimentales concernant les programmes et les manuels scolaires de tous les types d'écoles primaires et secondaires.
Functional objectives of research: Elaboration des bases théoriques de la construction et de l'évaluation des programmes scolaires; perfectionnement et modernisation des programmes et des manuels scolaires.
Periodical publications: N'en publie pas.
Monographs: Série: Bibliothèque de l'Institut des programmes scolaires.
Studies and surveys in preparation: Modernisation des programmes et des manuels scolaires pour tous les types d'écoles secondaires. Recherches expérimentales concernant lesdits programmes et manuels.

Katedra Pedagogiki Rolniczej

0430

Translation: Chaire de pédagogie agronomique
Address: Nowoursynowska 166, 02–675 WARSZAWA
Year of creation: 1958
Parent Organization: L'Université d'agronomie de Varsovie
Present Head: Prof. dr hab. Tadeusz Wieczorek
Size of staff. Total: 14 — Full time: 14
Researchers: 13 — Full time: 13
Research activities: 50%
Educational research: 50%
Type of research: Fondamentale et appliquée.
Functional objectives of research: Satisfaire partiellement aux conditions d'obtention d'un grade: fournir des prestations à l'administration de l'éducation.
Monographs: Wieczorek, T. Kształcenie i dokształcanie nauczycieli szkół rolniczych. 1981. Wieczorek, T., i inni. Dzieje szkolnictwa i oświaty na wsi polskiej do 1919. 1982. Wieczorek, T. Historia szkolnictwa rolniczego w Polsce.
Studies and surveys in preparation: Aptitude professionnelle des élèves dans les écoles agricoles. Fonctions de l'enseignement agricole primaire et secondaire.

Wrocławska Szkoła Przyszłości

0431

Translation: L'Ecole de l'avenir de Wroclaw
Address: Instytut Pedagogiki, Uniwersytet Wrocławski, ul. Dawida 1, 50527 WROCŁAW
Year of creation: 1973
Parent Organization: Université de Wroclaw

Present Head: Prof. Richard Lukaszewicz
Size of staff. Total: 15 — Full time: 9 — Part time: 6
Researchers: 10
Research activities: more than 50%
Educational research: from 25% to 50%
Type of research: Fondamentale et appliquée.
Functional objectives of research: Expérimenter à l'école un de ses modèles possibles; étudier la personnalité de l'écolier; les changements fondamentaux dans les principes d'organisation.
Periodical publications: L'Ecole de l'avenir de Wroclaw.
Monographs: L'Ecole de l'avenir de Wroclaw: Le développement de l'école — le développement de l'homme. 1981.
Studies and surveys in preparation: Les confrontations dans la réalisation. 1984. Rapport officiel au Ministère de la science.

Wydział Pedagogiczny, Wyższa Szkoła Pedagogiczna w Bydgoszczy

0432

Translation: Educational Department, Higher School of Education in Bydgoszcz
Address: ul. Chodkiewicza 30, 85-064 BYDGOSZCZ
Year of creation: 1978
Parent Organization: Ministry of Science, Higher Education and Technology
Present Head: Doc. dr hab. Zygmunt Wiatrowski
Size of staff. Total: 151 — Full time: 145 — Part time: 6
Researchers: 136 — Full time: 130 — Part time: 6
Research activities: 50%
Educational research: 50%
Type of research: Basic and applied.
Functional objectives of research: Partial fulfilment of degree requirements; servicing the educational administration.
Periodical publications: Studia pedagogiczne (2/yr). Studia psychologiczne (1/yr). Studia z wychowania muzycznego (1/yr).
Monographs: Wiatrowski, Z. Pedagogika pracy w zarysie. 1984. Trempała, E. Działalność pedagogiczna wychowawców nieprofesjonalnych w środowisku. 1984. Jakóbowski, J. Młody nauczyciel w kolektywie pedagogicznym. 1984. Rulka, J. Historia w szkole podstawowej: przewodnik metodyczny do klasy czwartej. 1983. Niemierko, B. Obiektywizacja stopni szkolnych. 1984. Complete list on request.
Studies and surveys in preparation: Rozwijanie zainteresowán zawodem nauczycielskim. Ekonomiczno finansowe instrumenty zarządzania kultura w województwie bydgoskim. Edukacja wczesnoszkolna procesem stymulującym rozwój zdolności specjalnych. Complete list on request.

Wydział Pedagogiki i Psychologii

0433

Translation: Faculty of Pedagogy and Psychology
Address: ul. Tyszki 53, 40-126 KATOWICE
Year of creation: 1976
Parent Organization: University of Silesia
Present Head: Prof. dr hab. Wanda Bobrowska-Nowak
Size of staff. Total: 137 — Full time: 137
Researchers: 137 — Full time: 135 — Part time: 2

Research activities: more than 50%
Educational research: from 10% to 25%
Type of research: Basic and applied.
Periodical publications: Prace pedagogiczne — wydawnictwo Uniwersytetu Śląskiego Katowice.
Monographs: Żechowska, B. Efektywność pracy nauczyciela. 1982. Maszczyk, D. Młodzież a szkoła równoległa. 1983. Ekiert-Grabowska, D. Dzieci nieakceptowane w klasie szkolnej. 1983. Bobrowska-Nowak, W. Historia wychowania przedszkolnego. 1983.

Wydział Pedagogiki i Psychologii, Uniwersytet Warszawski Filia w Białymstoku

0434

Translation: Department of Pedagogy and Psychology, Branch of Warsaw University in Bialystok
Address: Swierkowa St. 20, 15-328 BIAŁYSTOK
Year of creation: 1968
Parent Organization: Warsaw University
Present Head: Michał Balicki, Senior Lecturer
Size of staff. Total: 87 — Full time: 77 — Part time: 10
Researchers: 5 — Full time: 4 — Part time: 1
Research activities: from 10% to 25%
Educational research: more than 50%
Type of research: Implemented.
Functional objectives of research: Attainment of degrees, courses, guidance in education.
Periodical publications: Zeszyty naukowe FUW. Problemy oświatowe na wsi. Białostockie Towarzystwo Muzyczne. Badania oświatow twórczość. Problemy szkolnictwa nauk medycznych. Przegląd psychologiczny. Świata dorosłych. Harcerstwo. Oświata i wychowanie. Wydawnictwo Uniwersytetu Śląskiego. Polish art studies. Jednotna skola — Słowackie wydawnictwo pedagogiczne.
Monographs: Miejsce i funkcje wychowawcze środków masowego oddziaływania w czasie wolnym dzieci. Nowa sztuka teatralna. Poznanie struktury pojęć. Społeczne ogniska muzyczne.
Studies and surveys in preparation: Introduction to the theory of organizational effectiveness in education. Martyrology of the Polish teachers in the region of Białystok during the Nazi occupation 1939, 1941-1944.

Wyższa Szkoła Pedagogiczna

0435

Translation: Ecole supérieure de pédagogie
Address: Aleja Wojska Polskiego 69, 65-069 ZIELONA GÓRA
Year of creation: 1971
Parent Organization: Ministerstwo Nauki, Szkolnictwa Wyższego i Techniki
Present Head: Szczegóła Hieronim, professeur
Size of staff. Total: 613 — Full time: 475 — Part time: 138
Researchers: 357 — Full time: 252 — Part time: 105
Research activities: from 25% to 50%
Educational research: 50%
Type of research: Fondamentale, appliquée, recherche et développement.
Functional objectives of research: Obtention d'un grade; préparation de cours; prestations à l'administration de l'éducation.

Periodical publications: Etudes et documents. Didactique de la littérature. Méthodologie de l'enseignement des mathématiques (à paraître).
Monographs: Problèmes de civilisation dans l'enseignement des langues étrangères. Relations et dépendances entre les phases du processus de l'étude scolaire de la littérature. Les fonctions pédagogiques dans la formation des professeurs. Adaptation des étudiants aux conditions des études. Liste complète sur demande.
Studies and surveys in preparation: Education de l'enfant dans l'enseignement préscolaire et dans les classes primaires. Didactique de la littérature et des langues étrangères au niveau supérieur. Education politique des jeunes.

Zakład Pedagogiki, Wydział Pedagogiczny, Wyższa Szkoła Pedagogiczna

0436

Translation: Section de pédagogie, Faculté de pédagogie, Ecole supérieure pédagogique
Address: ul. Ogińskiego 16/17, 71-431 SZCZECIN
Year of creation: 1968
Parent Organization: Ministère de l'éducation
Present Head: Dr Zdzisław Zacha
Size of staff. Total: 12
Type of research: Recherches de base et appliquées.
Functional objectives of research: Pédologie, socialisation, histoire de l'éducation; l'école communautaire et l'école du milieu; sociologie de la culture et de l'éducation.
Periodical publications: Zeszyty naukowe WSP w Szczecinie.
Monographs: Zacha, Z. Orientation du choix professionnel des jeunes des écoles primaires. 1977. Błażejewski, Z. Relations entre les fugues (de la maison) et l'environnement domestique. 1979. Bielawiec, A. Dix ans de fonctionnement de l'école rurale à Pyrzyce. 1979. Zacha, Z., et al. Monographie socio-culturelle de la commune de Moryń. 1979.

PORTUGAL

Alternativas para o Ensino Da Ciência

0437

Translation: Alternatives for Science Education
Address: Departamento de Quīmica, Faculdade de Ciências de Lisboa, Universidade de Lisboa, R. da Escola Politécnica, 1294 LISBOA CODEX
Year of creation: 1983
Parent Organization: Universidade de Lisboa, Faculdade de Ciências
Present Head: Prof. Maria Elisabeth da Silva Fonseca Elias
Size of staff. Total: 8 — Part time: 8
Researchers: 8 — Part time: 8
Research activities: from 25% to 50%
Educational research: from 25% to 50%
Functional objectives of research: Implementation at secondary level.
Periodical publications: None issued.
Monographs: In preparation.
Studies and surveys in preparation: Learning difficulties. Materials development. Energy in curriculum.

Departamento de Ciências da Educação

0438

Translation: Département des sciences de l'éducation
Address: Universidade de Aveiro, 3800 AVEIRO
Year of creation: 1975
Parent Organization: Universidade de Aveiro
Present Head: Prof. Doutor Jorge de Carvalho Arroteia, Presidente do Conselho Directivo
Size of staff. Total: 28 — Full time: 28
Researchers: 22 — Full time: 22
Research activities: more than 50%
Educational research: from 25% to 50%
Type of research: Fondamentale et appliquée.
Functional objectives of research: Préparation des cours.
Periodical publications: Revista da Universidade de Aveiro. Série Ciências da Educação.
Monographs: Oliveira, A.J. Morgado Alves de. Etude d'un schème de résolution: l'exemple de l'organisation du produit de deux ensembles. Tavares, M.I. Lobo de Alarcão e Silva. Psychopedagogy and foreign language teacher education. David, M.M. Martins Soares. The nature of secondary school. Pupils spatial ability in mathematics: some instructional alternatives. Lopes, M. Carvalho. Enonciation, analyse de discours et évaluation à l'école: un essai sur le portugais.
Studies and surveys in preparation: A educação como factor de desinvolvimento psychológico. Psicologia do desinvolvimento e da aprendizagem. Analise psicológica e lingística do acto di leitura e a sua aplicação pedagógica. Aquisição fonética e fonológica de língua materna. Estudio casuístico. A população escolar de origem portuguesa no G.D. do Luxemburgo. Suas relações com o meio social e o contexto emigratório. Liste complète sur demande.

Gabinete de Estudos e Planeamento (GEP)

0439

Translation: Planning and Research Bureau
Address: Av. Miguel Bombarda No. 20, 1700 LISBÕA
Year of creation: 1965
Parent Organization: Ministry of Education
Size of staff. Total: 111 — Full time: 111
Researchers: 25 — Full time: 25
Research activities: 50%
Educational research: more than 50%
Type of research: Applied research; research and development.
Periodical publications: Complete list on request.
Monographs: Sousa, R.P. Acção piloto de formação profissional de jovens nas empresas. 1983. Costa, I.R., et al. Despesas de educação no contexto de uma politica de desenvolvimento. 1983. São Pedro, E., coord. Introdução ao diagnóstico da situação/previsões de discentes. 1983. Costa, I.R., coord. Matrizes: despesas por niveis de ensino — 1980. 1983. Cortesão, L., et al. Avaliação pedagógica II: perspectivas de sucesso. 1983. Complete list on request.
Studies and surveys in preparation: Womens' education and employment. Regional disparities and democratization. Basic education. European integration: impact on the Portuguese educational system. Simulation exercise in educational planning. Complete

list on request.

Unidade de Educação de Adultos da Universidade do Minho 0440

Translation: Department of Adult Education
Address: R. Abade Da Loureira, 4719 BRAGA CODEX
Year of creation: 1979
Parent Organization: University of Minho (State University)
Present Head: Prof. Dr. Licínio Chaínho Pereira
Size of staff. Total: 12 — Full time: 4 — Part time: 8
Researchers: 4 — Full time: 3 — Part time: 1
Research activities: from 25% to 50%
Educational research: from 10% to 25%
Type of research: Participatory research.
Functional objectives of research: Diagnosis and inventory of the regional needs in adult education; cultural and social development of under-privileged communities.
Monographs: Colecção de publicações em educação de adultos.
Studies and surveys in preparation: Survey on the needs expressed by local authorities (Braga District). Research and development methods (rural communities of Viana do Castelo).

QATAR

Idārat al-buḥūt al-fanniyya 0441

Translation: Department of Technical Research
Address: Ministry of Education, P.O.Box 80, DOHA
Year of creation: 1966
Parent Organization: Ministry of Education, Technical Affairs
Present Head: Dr. Ahmed Rajab Abdul Majid
Size of staff. Total: 40 — Full time: 40
Researchers: 22 — Full time: 22
Research activities: from 25% to 50%
Educational research: more than 50%
Type of research: Applied and basic research.
Periodical publications: Annual report covering all activities of the Ministry. Periodical statistical report (4/yr). Annual report of educational evaluation.
Monographs: Annual report from 1975 to 1980. Research on efficiency of education in Qatari schools for boys and girls. Education Strategy in Qatar Committee. Education policy.

Markaz al-buḥūt at-tarbawiyya 0442

Translation: Educational Research Centre
Address: University of Qatar, P.O. Box 2713, DOHA
Year of creation: 1979
Parent Organization: University of Qatar
Present Head: Dr. Mohamed Monir Morsi

Size of staff. Total: 27 — Full time: 5 — Part time: 22
Researchers: 25 — Full time: 3 — Part time: 22
Research activities: more than 50%
Educational research: more than 50%
Type of research: Applied and basic research.
Functional objectives of research: To serve the development of theory and practice of education in general and in Qatar in particular.
Monographs: Problems of university textbooks in universities of Arab Gulf States. Organizational climate of Qatari schools. Education and development of human resources in Qatar. The role of the Arab universities in labour education. Complete list on request.
Studies and surveys in preparation: Teacher education in the Gulf States. Headteachers' role in Qatari schools. Reading difficulties: their diagnosis and remedy in the primary schools in Qatar. Complete list on request.

ROMANIA

Catedra de pedagogie psihologie şi metodică

0443

Translation: Chaire de pédagogie–psychologie et méthodologie de l'enseignement
Address: 1, rue Kogălniceanu, Cod. 3400, CLUJ–NAPOCA
Year of creation: 1919
Parent Organization: Université de Cluj–Napoca
Present Head: Prof. dr. Andrei Dancsuly
Size of staff. Total: 40 — Full time: 40
Research activities: from 25% to 50%
Educational research: more than 50%
Type of research: Fondamentale (25%) et appliquée (75%).
Functional objectives of research: Contributer au développement de la théorie pédagogique et fournir des prestations à l'administration de l'éducation.
Periodical publications: Studia Universitatis 'Babeş–Bolyai', série de philosophie, pédagogie, psychologie.
Monographs: Rosca, Al. Creativitatea generală şi specifică. 1981. La sinteze de psihologie contemporană, vol. III: Psihologia educaţiei si dezvoltării. 1983. Ionescu, M. Lecţia între proiect şi realizare. 1982. Preda, V. Profilaxia delicvenţei şi reintegrarea socială. 1981. Liste complète sur demande.
Studies and surveys in preparation: Stratégies de valorisation efficace des moyens d'enseignement et d'utilisation des méthodes actives selon les exigences de la révolution technique et scientifique. Prémisses méthodologiques dans la formation de la pensée scientifique chez les étudiants, condition pour l'accroissement de leur rendement scolaire. Formation chez les élèves des notions et des valeurs à travers l'enseignement des sciences sociales, dans un contexte interdisciplinaire. Conditions d'intégration du style pédagogique créatif dans la pratique scolaire.

Catedra de pedagogie, Universitatea "Al.I. Cuza", Iaşi

0444

Translation: Chaire de pédagogie, Université "Al. I. Cuza", Iassy
Address: Rue 23 Août no. 11, Cod. 6600, IAŞI
Year of creation: 1980
Parent Organization: Faculté d'histoire et de philosophie de l'Université "Al. I. Cuza"
Present Head: Prof. Dr. Grigoraş Ioan, titulaire d'une chaire universitaire
Size of staff. Total: 21
Research activities: from 25% to 50%
Educational research: from 25% to 50%
Type of research: Fondamentale.
Periodical publications: Analele ştiinţifice ale Universităţii "Al. I. Cuza", seria ştiinţe sociale (Annales de l'Université, série Sciences sociales).
Studies and surveys in preparation: Recherches sur les contenus de l'éducation de demain. Recherches sur la psychologie de la personalité. Recherches d'histoire de la pédagogie roumaine.

Catedra de pedagogie–psihologie

0445

Translation: Chaire de pédagogie–psychologie, Department of Pedagogy and Psychology
Address: Bd. Gh. Gheorghiu-Dej. N.62–64, Sectorul 5, BUCUREŞTI 70608
Year of creation: 1878
Parent Organization: University of Bucharest
Present Head: Ioan Cerghit, Professor, DH.D.
Size of staff. Total: 36 — Full time: 36
Researchers: 30 — Full time: 30
Research activities: from 25% to 50%
Educational research: more than 50%
Type of research: Fundamental (25%); applied (75%).
Functional objectives of research: Working out variables solutions regarding problems of teaching and learning processes in the schools (structures, curricula, methods, etc.) at the request of the Ministry of Education.
Periodical publications: Analele Universităţii din Bucureşti.
Monographs: Cerghit, I. Metode de învaţămînt. 1980. Radu, I.T. Teorie şi practică în evaluarea eficienţei învăţămîntului. 1981. Radu, I.T. Perfecţionarea lecţiei în şcoala modernă. 1983. Stanciu, I. Scoala şi pedagogia în secolul. 1983. Complete list on request.
Studies and surveys in preparation: Comparative study concerning the dynamics of changes in the contemporary school. Research on teachers' personality. Integrating teaching with research and production (experimental study). A systematic model of personality: interpersonal level.

Catedra de pedagogie–psihologie, Facultatea de Invăţămînt Pedagogic, Universitatea din Galaţi

0446

Translation: Chaire de pédagogie–psychologie, Faculté d'enseignement pédagogique, Université de Galaţi
Address: Boulevard de la République nr. 47, GALAŢI, Cod. 6200
Year of creation: 1974
Parent Organization: Ministère de l'éducation et de l'enseignement

Present Head: Dr. Dumitru Vrabie, maître de conférences
Size of staff. Total: 60 — Part time: 20
Type of research: Fondamentale et appliquée.
Functional objectives of research: Fournir des prestations à l'administration de l'éducation.
Periodical publications: Bulletin de l'Université de Galaţi, série Sciences sociales (1/an).
Monographs: Vrabie, D. L'attitude de l'élève à l'égard de l'appréciation du professeur. 1975. Itu, M. Formes étatisées de l'éducation populaire en Roumanie. 1981. Potorac, E. L'élève entre attente et performance.
Studies and surveys in preparation: Intégration socio-professionnelle des diplômés ingénieurs. Psychologie des comportements et psychologie de l'évaluation scolaire.

Laboratorul de psiholingvistică al Universitătii din Bucureşti

0447

Translation: Laboratory of Psycholinguistics at the University of Bucharest
Address: Str. Pitar Mos 7-13, BUCUREŞTI
Year of creation: 1971
Parent Organization: University of Bucharest
Present Head: Prof. Dr. Tatiana Slama-Cazacu
Periodical publications: International journal of psycholinguistics (4/yr).

RWANDA

Bureau pédagogique de l'enseignement primaire et de l'enseignement rural et artisanal intégré (BPEPERAI)

0448

Address: B.P. 608, KIGALI
Year of creation: 1976
Parent Organization: Direction générale des études et recherches pédagogiques, Ministère de l'enseignement primaire et secondaire
Present Head: Froduald Bemeliki
Size of staff. Total: 77 — Part time: 77
Researchers: 47 — Part time: 47
Research activities: from 10% to 25%
Educational research: from 10% to 25%
Type of research: Appliquée: élaboration des programmes (pédagogie par objectifs) et des manuels; émissions scolaires; méthodologie spéciale.
Functional objectives of research: Meilleure adaptation de l'enseignement aux besoins économiques et au contexte socio-culturel.
Monographs: Profil de sortie du primaire. Programmes et manuels (par branche) destinés à l'enseignement primaire et à l'enseignement rural et artisanal intégré (de la 1ère à la 5e année et de la 1ère et 2e années).
Studies and surveys in preparation: Manuels de 6e année primaire. Programmes et manuels de 3e année de l'enseignement rural et artisanal intégré.

Bureau pédagogique de l'enseignement secondaire (BPES)

0449

Address: B.P. 816, KIGALI
Year of creation: 1972
Parent Organization: Direction générale des études et recherches pédagogiques, Ministère de l'enseignement primaire et secondaire
Present Head: Herman Trog
Size of staff. Total: 111 — Full time: 111
Researchers: 67 — Full time: 67
Research activities: from 10% to 25%
Educational research: from 10% to 25%
Type of research: Appliquée: élaboration de curricula (méthode des objectifs pédagogiques) et de manuels; évaluation des documents produits, des professeurs et des élèves; méthodologie spéciale des branches.
Functional objectives of research: Meilleure adaptation de l'enseignement aux besoins économiques et au contexte socio-culturel.
Monographs: Description des fonctions (par filière d'enseignement). Profils de sortie des élèves (par filière d'enseignement). Curricula et manuels pour les branches enseignées au secondaire.
Studies and surveys in preparation: Curricula et manuels pour les classes de 4e année secondaire.

SAUDI ARABIA

Markaz al-buḥūt at-tarbawiyya

0450

Translation: Educational Research Centre
Address: P.O. Box 2458, RIYADH
Year of creation: 1977
Parent Organization: College of Education, Riyadh University
Present Head: Dr. A. El-Mahdi Abdel-Halim, Director
Size of staff. Total: 7
Researchers: 4
Type of research: Applied, basic and conceptual research.
Functional objectives of research: Service to the Ministry of Education and Riyadh University.
Periodical publications: Participation in "Educational studies", the College of Education journal, and a newsletter to begin in 1979.
Monographs: Monograph series in preparation for publication April 1979. Occasional paper series underway. List on request.
Studies and surveys in preparation: Survey of Islamic educational thought. Investigations of Arabic language teaching. Complete list on request.

SENEGAL

Centre de linguistique appliquée de Dakar (CLAD)

0451

Address: Faculté des lettres, Université de Dakar
Year of creation: 1963
Parent Organization: Université de Dakar
Present Head: Monsieur Abdoulaye Balde
Size of staff. Total: 43
Researchers: 20
Research activities: more than 50%
Educational research: more than 50%
Type of research: Recherches appliquées.
Functional objectives of research: Fournir des prestations à l'administration de l'éducation.
Periodical publications: Réalités africaines et langue française.
Monographs: Cribier, J. La motivation à l'école primaire. Dreyfus, M. L'acquisition d'une langue maternelle. Gontier, D. Lexique fondamental et structure fondamentale: leur utilité et leur rôle dans ... linguistique. Niang, G. Enseignement en langue maternelle et valeur de civilisation: une réflexion sur la langue. Lexique Mandinka du Sénégal.
Studies and surveys in preparation: Recherches en linguistique appliquée. Recherches en phonétique. Recherches sur les langues nationales.

Centre de recherche, de documentation et d'équipement pédagogique (C.R.D.E.P.)

0452

Address: Ecole normale supérieure, Boulevard Habib Bourguiba, B.P. 5036, DAKAR-FANN
Year of creation: 1962
Parent Organization: Université de Dakar
Present Head: Bouna Gaye, professeur de mathématiques
Size of staff. Total: 29 — Full time: 10 — Part time: 19
Researchers: 19 — Full time: 10 — Part time: 9
Research activities: from 25% to 50%
Educational research: from 10% to 25%
Type of research: Appliquée.
Functional objectives of research: Amélioration de la méthodologie de la didactique des disciplines; amélioration des conditions d'obtention d'un grade; meilleure utilisation de l'audiovisuel.
Periodical publications: Liens ENS. DO.PE.DOC. (Dossiers pédagogiques documentaires).
Monographs: Liste complète sur demande.
Studies and surveys in preparation: Influences directes de l'éducation sénégalaise sur la formation de la main-d'oeuvre qualifiée et sur le développement économique et social du Sénégal. Etude des réactions des lycéens et des étudiants sénégalais devant leurs succès ou leurs échecs. Problématique de l'introduction de l'informatique dans le système scolaire sénégalais par le laboratoire "Informatique-Education"

Ecole normale régionale de Saint-Louis

0453

Address: Ndar-Toute, B.P. 381, SAINT-LOUIS
Year of creation: 1972
Parent Organization: Ministère de l'éducation nationale
Present Head: M. Kimingtang Tounkara
Size of staff. Total: 58 — Full time: 47 — Part time: 11
Researchers: 11 — Part time: 11
Research activities: from 25% to 50%
Educational research: from 25% to 50%
Type of research: Recherches appliquées.
Functional objectives of research: Préparation de cours.
Monographs: Documents ronéotypés à l'intention des élèves-maîtres et des instituteurs déjà en service.
Studies and surveys in preparation: Elaboration de matériel didactique. Expérimentation du travail de groupe au cours élémentaire. Analyse sociologique du monde enseignant sénégalais.

Institut national d'étude et d'action pour le dévéloppement de l'éducation (INEADE)

0454

Address: Rue 54 x 73 Gueule Tapee, DAKAR
Year of creation: 1981
Parent Organization: Ministère de l'éducation nationale
Present Head: Amadou Ndiaye Anne Tounkara
Size of staff. Total: 36 — Full time: 36
Researchers: 28 — Full time: 28
Research activities: more than 50%
Educational research: more than 50%
Type of research: Introduction des langues nationales dans l'enseignement; amélioration qualitative et quantitative du système éducatif; formation des maîtres; psychologie et sociologie.
Functional objectives of research: Fournir des prestations à l'administration de l'éducation.
Periodical publications: Animation pédagogique (revue de pédagogie pratique).
Monographs: Tounkara, A.N.A. L'évolution psycho-génétique de l'enfant dans ses rapports avec les programmes de l'enseignement élémentaire au Sénégal. 1983. Fall, S. L'étude du milieu à l'école élémentaire de l'organisation spatiale à la géographie. 1983. Sene, M.C. L'éducation préscolaire au Sénégal. 1983. L'orientation scolaire au Sénégal: objectifs, statut, perspectives. 1983. Gomis, D. Education traditionelle et programmes scolaires au Sénégal: l'école élémentaire en milieu diola (Casamance). 1983. Liste complète sur demande.

SIERRA LEONE

Centre for Research into the Education of Secondary Teachers (CREST)

0455

Address: Milton Margai Teachers College, Private Mail Bag, FREETOWN
Year of creation: 1980
Parent Organization: Milton Margai Teachers College
Present Head: Cream A.H. Wright
Size of staff. Total: 18 — Full time: 6 — Part time: 12
Researchers: 12 — Part time: 12
Research activities: from 25% to 50%
Educational research: more than 50%
Type of research: Action research, collaborative research (with teacher).
Functional objectives of research: Problem solving and quality improvement.
Monographs: Working papers series. Interim research papers. Seminar/workshop reports. Occasional research papers series.
Studies and surveys in preparation: A needs assessment study of French teachers in Sierra Leone. Factors influencing participation and performance in technical subjects at secondary school level. An investigation of implementation problems in the core course integrated science (CCIS) programme. Provision, use and organization of resources for integrated studies in secondary schools in Sierra Leone. Constraints in the management of secondary teachers education policies in Sierra Leone. Complete list on request.

Institute of Education, University of Sierra Leone

0456

Address: Private Mail Bag, Tower Hill, FREETOWN
Year of creation: 1968
Parent Organization: University of Sierra Leone
Present Head: Mr. T.J. Lemuel Forde
Size of staff. Total: 30 — Full time: 30
Researchers: 3 — Full time: 1 — Part time: 2
Type of research: Action and evaluative research.
Functional objectives of research: Servicing other Divisions of the Institute, the Ministry of Education and the University of Sierra Leone.
Monographs: First progress report on the study of the characteristics of the school-age population (5-19): a sample survey (1981). Pupils' mobility: primary to secondary education. 1983. Characteristics of the school-age population: the incidence of repetition among enrolled primary school children. 1983. Do children repeat classes? 1983. The attitudes of primary school age children in Sierra Leone (in print). A formative study on Bunumbu Project graduates and ex-pupils of Bunumbu Project pilot studies. 1980. Complete list on request.
Studies and surveys in preparation: Continuation of the characteristics of the school-age population (5-19): a sample survey. The general attitudes of secondary school students towards mathematics in Sierra Leone. A collaborative study between the Research Division and the Department of Mathematics, St. Andrew's Secondary School, Bo. Vocational and educational expectation of unplaced pupils of class seven (a research proposal seeking funding). Societal expectation of secondary education (a study to be undertaken prior to the development of a national teaching syllabus for secondary schools). Complete list on request.

Test Development and Research Division, Freetown

0457

Address: Tower Hill, P.O.Box 573, FREETOWN
Year of creation: 1971
Parent Organization: West African Examinations Council
Present Head: Mr. Alieu Swarray Deen
Size of staff. Total: 9 — Full time: 9
Researchers: 5 — Full time: 5
Research activities: from 25% to 50%
Educational research: more than 50%
Type of research: Basic and applied.
Functional objectives of research: Servicing the educational administration.
Periodical publications: Predicting success in trade centres in Sierra Leone (The West African journal of educational and vocational measurement).
Monographs: Deen, A.S. Investigating the performance of repeaters at the SC/GCE 0-level examination. Deen, A.S. Validity of teacher's estimates for fixing pupils actual grade: SC/GCE 0-level examination. Conton, C.P.L. Optimising item selection difficulty.
Studies and surveys in preparation: Investigating the performance of SC/GCE 0-level candidates in literature in English and Geography — Sierra Leone.

SINGAPORE

Institute of Education

0458

Address: 469, Bukit Timah Road, SINGAPORE 1025
Year of creation: 1973
Parent Organization: Ministry of Education
Present Head: Dr. Sim Wong Kooi, Director
Size of staff. Total: 178 — Full time: 165 — Part time: 13
Research activities: from 10% to 25%
Educational research: more than 50%
Type of research: Applied research.
Functional objectives of research: To serve the needs of the education system in Singapore.
Periodical publications: Singapore journal of education. Teaching and learning. Annual report. IE Newsletter. Prospectus. REACT (Research and evaluation abstracts for classroom teachers).
Monographs: Report on the moral education programmes — "Good citizen", and "Being and becoming". 1982. Student-teachers' backgrounds and motives for teaching: a 1968 and 1981 comparison. 1983. Student profiles and motives for teaching full-time students in the Institute of Education: a comparison between Dip. Ed. and Cert. Ed. students. 1982. Interdisciplinary approach in helping school pupils with learning problems. 1982. A standardized Chinese language test for primary one (research version). 1982. Complete list on request.
Studies and surveys in preparation: Evaluation of primary school curriculum materials, analysis of spoken English, development of curriculum materials for slow learners, development of computer assisted instructional software.

Research and Testing Division, Ministry of Education **0459**

Address: Kay Siang Road, SINGAPORE 1024
Year of creation: 1981
Parent Organization: Ministry of Education
Present Head: Dr. Soon Teck Wong
Size of staff. Total: 101 — Full time: 101
Researchers: 35
Research activities: 50%
Educational research: more than 50%
Type of research: Applied.
Functional objectives of research: Servicing the educational administration; policy formulation and evaluation.

SPAIN

Centro Nacional de Investigación y Documentación Educativa **0460**

Address: Ciudad Universitaria, MADRID 3
Year of creation: 1983
Parent Organization: Ministerio de Educación y Ciencia
Present Head: Juan Delval Merino
Size of staff. Total: 111 — Full time: 111
Researchers: 40 — Full time: 40
Research activities: 50%
Educational research: more than 50%
Type of research: Investigación básica, aplicada, I&D.
Functional objectives of research: Mejora calidad de los procesos educativos.
Periodical publications: Revista de educación. Temas de investigación educativa. Abstracts de investigaciones realizadas.
Monographs: Lista completa a disposición.
Studies and surveys in preparation: 100 investigaciones en curso.

Ikastola-Colegio Ekintza **0461**

Translation: Escuela-Colegio Ekintza
Address: Parque Nuevo Igueldo, s/n, SAN SEBASTIAN-DONOSTIA (Guipúzcoa)
Year of creation: 1978
Parent Organization: Titularidad Académica: Gobierno Vasco; gestión: Ikastaries S.A.
Present Head: Enrique Echeburúa Odriozola
Size of staff. Total: 75 — Full time: 58 — Part time: 17
Researchers: 8 — Full time: 7 — Part time: 1
Research activities: from 10% to 25%
Educational research: more than 50%
Type of research: Investigación aplicada.
Functional objectives of research: Experimentar un nuevo sistema de enseñanza del/en euskara para niños de ambiente familiar castellano; evaluación de resultados con el fin de difundir la experiencia a otros centros educativos de Euskadi.

Monographs: Glotodidáctica del euskara para alumnos castellano parlantes. 1980. Documentos de apoyo a la evaluación: preescolar, ciclo inicial y ciclo medio. 1982/83. Programaciones generales áreas: mat/sociales/nat/lengua/euskara. 1982. Informe sobre experiencia informática alumnos 12 años. 1983.
Studies and surveys in preparation: Reforma de enseñanzas medias. Características alumnos, profesor y método del proceso educativo de la Ikastola Ekintza. Material didáctico en euskara de apoyo al proceso lecto-escritor y del área de matemáticas.

Instituto de Ciencias de la Educación, Universidad Autónoma de Barcelona

0462

Address: Campus Universitario, Bellaterra, BARCELONA
Year of creation: 1970
Parent Organization: Universidad Autónoma de Barcelona
Present Head: Berta Gutierrez Reñon
Size of staff. Total: 40
Research activities: from 10% to 25%
Educational research: more than 50%
Functional objectives of research: Formación permanente del profesorado de todos los niveles académicos.
Periodical publications: Butlleti Informatiu. Revista de las ciencias.
Monographs: Primeras jornadas sobre 'Aprendizaje y enseñanza de las matemáticas', Barcelona, 1981. 1982. Encuentro sobre centros piloto y experimentales, Barcelona, 1982. 1982. Teaching language as communication.

Instituto de Ciencias de la Educación, Universidad Autónoma de Madrid

0463

Address: Cantoblanco, Carretera de Colmenar, MADRID — 34
Year of creation: 1970
Parent Organization: Ministerio de Educación y Ciencia
Present Head: Alfredo Poves Paredes, Profesor agregado, Dpto. de física teórica
Size of staff. Total: 23 — Full time: 21 — Part time: 2
Researchers: 6 — Full time: 6
Research activities: from 25% to 50%
Educational research: more than 50%
Type of research: Investigación básica y aplicada.
Functional objectives of research: Didáctica aplicada; relación entre el curriculum escolar y la capacidad cognitiva de los alumnos.
Periodical publications: Boletín del I.C.E. (4/año).
Monographs: Jordanas sobre la enseñanza de la ecología. Perspectivas actuales en sociología de la educación. Monografías del I.C.E., por ejemplo: Los juegos de simulación en E.G.B. y B.U.P.; La calculadora de bolsillo como instrumento pedagógico. Proyecto de enseñanza individualizada de ciencias experimentales.
Studies and surveys in preparation: La evaluación de la enseñanza universitaria en relación con los objetivos del profesor. La formación del espíritu científico en el niño. Las pruebas de selectividad en la Universidad Autónoma de Madrid. Lista completa a disposición.

Instituto de Ciencias de la Educación, Universidad de Barcelona

0464

Address: Sótano del Patio de Ciencias, Pza Universidad, BARCELONA-7
Year of creation: 1970
Parent Organization: Universidad de Barcelona
Present Head: Dr. Miguel Siguan Soler
Size of staff. Total: 35 — Full time: 29 — Part time: 6
Researchers: 7 — Full time: 3 — Part time: 4
Research activities: from 25% to 50%
Educational research: more than 50%
Type of research: Descriptiva; aplicada; experimental.
Functional objectives of research: Métodos y medios de enseñanza; mejora sistema educativo EGB y BUP; innovaciones educativas; formación y perfeccionamiento profesional.
Periodical publications: Informés investigación.
Monographs: Bohemer, M. Museo y escuela. Cuello, J. Didáctica de la genética. Vega, A., et al. Delincuencia y drogas. Bartolme, M., et al. Modelos de investigación educativa. L'entorn escolar: problematica psicológica, educativa i de disseny. Materiales del II Seminario de investigacionés psicopedagogicas. Lista a disposición.
Studies and surveys in preparation: Pedagógica cibernetica y ciencias sociales. Estudi comparatiu sobre la fonética segmental del catalá i de l'angles. El sabó com a eina en la didáctica de la física i la química. Lista a disposición.

Instituto de Ciencias de la Educación, Universidad de Bilbao

0465

Address: LEIOA (Vizcaya)
Year of creation: 1970
Parent Organization: Universidad del País Vasco — Euskal Herriko Unibertsitatea
Present Head: D. Iñaki Dendaluze, Adjunto Numerario de Universidad, Profesor de Pedagogía en la Facultad de Filosofía y Ciencias de la Educación
Size of staff. Total: 18 — Full time: 18
Researchers: 2 — Part time: 2
Research activities: from 25% to 50%
Educational research: more than 50%
Type of research: Investigación aplicada.
Functional objectives of research: Los objetivos han sido variados en función de las áreas temáticas investigadas.
Monographs: El problema del bilingüismo en el Estado Español. El lenguaje en la educación preescolar y ciclo preparatorio vasco-castellano. El preescolar en Euskadi; problemática, necesidades, bilingüismo e implicaciones psicopedagógicas. Lista completa a disposición.
Studies and surveys in preparation: Programación didáctica de geografía humana y económica, 2o. B.U.P. Seminario permanente de geografia e historia. Análisis de la estructura educativa en las escuelas de formación del profesorado del E.G.B. de la comunidad autónoma vasca.

Instituto de Ciencias de la Educación, Universidad de Córdoba

0466

Address: Carretera de Villaviciosa, Km. 5, Edificio La Aduana, Apartado de correos 496, CORDOBA
Year of creation: 1974
Parent Organization: Universidad de Córdoba
Present Head: Mr. José Porro Herrera
Size of staff. Total: 11 — Full time: 11
Researchers: 7 — Full time: 7
Research activities: from 25% to 50%
Educational research: more than 50%
Type of research: Investigación básica y aplicada.
Functional objectives of research: Prestación de servicios a la administración educativa y ayuda profesional al profesorado en ejercicio.
Monographs: Itinerarios geológicos de la Provincia de Córdoba como ejemplo de interés de las actividades de campo en la enseñanza de la geología. Curso de prácticas de física en BUP y COU. Determinación del grado de comprensión de las ciencias socio-naturales en los alumnos de la segunda etapa de E.G.B. Coordinación entre la E.G.B. y la F.P. en la búsqueda de modalidades profesionales para la Región Andaluza.
Studies and surveys in preparation: Determinación del grado de comprensión de las matemáticas en los alumnos de la segunda etapa de E.G.B. Coordinación entre la F.P. y el mundo del trabajo a la búsqueda de una programación y planificación de las diversas modalidades de la F.P. en Córdoba.

Instituto de Ciencias de la Educación, Universidad de Extremadura

0467

Address: Crta. de Portugal, s/n., BADAJOZ
Year of creation: 1974
Parent Organization: Universidad de Extremadura
Present Head: Antonio Sánchez Misiego, Doctor en ciencias químicas
Size of staff. Total: 20 — Full time: 17 — Part time: 3
Researchers: 3 — Full time: 3
Research activities: from 10% to 25%
Educational research: more than 50%
Type of research: Investigación básica y aplicada.
Functional objectives of research: Formación pedagógica y perfeccionamiento del profesorado; estructura educativa y planificación; evaluación y rendimiento; sociología de la educación.
Monographs: Palavecino, J.C.; García, R. Estudio experimental de la adquisición de conceptos en la segunda etapa de E.G.B.. 1982. Simón Galindo, M.; Cardalliaguet Quirant, M.; Mora Peña, A. Los medios didácticos para la enseñanza práctica de geografía e historia en bachillerato. 1983. Estudios metodológicos sobre la lengua griega. 1983. Lista completa a disposición.
Studies and surveys in preparation: Lenguaje y creatividad. Técnicas de motivación del lenguaje y la literatura en E.G.B. Aplicación y extensión de un programa y una metodología específica para la enseñanza del inglés en Extremadura. Aplicación de las teorías de Ausubel y Novak sobre adquisición de conceptos al aprendizaje de la física y la química en el B.U.P. y C.O.U. Lista completa a disposición.

Instituto de Ciencias de la Educación, Universidad de Granada

0468

Address: Campus Universitario de Fuentenueva, Edificio de 'El Mecenas', GRANADA
Year of creation: 1970
Parent Organization: Universidad de Granada
Present Head: Asunción Linares Rodriguez, Licenciada en ciencias, Catedrática de paleontología
Size of staff. Total: 12
Researchers: 6
Type of research: Investigación aplicada.
Functional objectives of research: Formación pedagógica y perfeccionamiento del profesorado; evaluación y rendimiento; curriculum; sociología de la educación.
Periodical publications: Relación alfabética de las publicaciones recibidas en la biblioteca (2/año).
Monographs: La música en el bachillerato. Sobre el origen de la vida del hombre: materiales para el desarrollo de un módulo interdisciplinar en bachillerato. El uso del franelograma en la formulación y nomenclatura química. La utilización de películas sonoras en la enseñanza del inglés. Iniciación al análisis transaccional en la educación. Orientación y tutorias. Didáctica sobre la pizarra. Sobre el problema de la evaluación: una técnica operativa analítica para bachillerato. Lista completa a disposición.
Studies and surveys in preparation: Orientaciones didácticas sobre todas las materias (ciencias y letras) de bachillerato. 3o. de bachillerato: un modelo de programación. Estudio mediante ordenador del dominio cognoscitivo inicial en matemáticas de 1o. de BUP. Lista completa a disposición.

Instituto de Ciencias de la Educación, Universidad de Málaga

0469

Address: Escuela de Ingeniería Técnica Industrial, Plaza del Ejido s/n, MALAGA
Year of creation: 1974
Parent Organization: Universidad de Málaga
Present Head: Profesor Dr. D. Eusebio Garcia Manrique
Size of staff. Total: 16 — Full time: 14 — Part time: 2
Researchers: 5 — Full time: 3 — Part time: 2
Research activities: from 25% to 50%
Educational research: more than 50%
Type of research: Investigación aplicada.
Functional objectives of research: Formación pedagógica y perfeccionamiento del profesorado; estructura educativa y planificación; innovación metodológica.
Monographs: Leer y escribir ¿Cuando? 1981. Teoría y práctica de la expresión dramática infantil. 1982. Folletos de autoevaluación: "Yo soy así", "Así voy yo", "Ya corro hacia el ciclo medio" Lista completa a disposición.
Studies and surveys in preparation: Mapa escolar de la Provincia de Málaga. Desarrollo intelectual del niño trisómico de 6 a 11 años: elaboración y aplicación de una nueva metodología para su educación. Estudio de la organización lingüística de los textos educativos y su influencia sobre el rendimiento escolar en la E.G.B. Lista completa a disposición.

Instituto de Ciencias de la Educación, Universidad de Salamanca

0470

Address: Paseo Canalejas, 169, 1o., SALAMANCA
Year of creation: 1969
Parent Organization: Universidad de Salamanca
Present Head: Agustín Escolano Benito
Size of staff. Total: 21 — Full time: 21
Researchers: 15 — Full time: 1 — Part time: 14
Research activities: from 10% to 25%
Educational research: more than 50%
Type of research: Investigación básica y aplicada.
Functional objectives of research: Prestación de servicios a la administración educativa y a los centros de enseñanza de los diversos niveles educativos.
Periodical publications: Studia paedagogica.
Monographs: Ortega Esteban, J. Platón: eros, política y educación. 1981. Pujante, A.L.; Hyde, J., comp. Metodología de la enseñanza de idiomas: aspectos y problemas. 1982. Prieto Adanez, G., et al. La universidad a través de sus alumnos. 1982. Lista completa a disposición.
Studies and surveys in preparation: Relaciones entre el subsistema educativo superior y el subsistema económico. Valoración de textos de EGB y obtención de normas para su elaboración. Fuerzas de resistencia a la innovación educativa en el BUP. Educación preescolar: problemática para su renovación.

Instituto de Ciencias de la Educación, Universidad de Santander

0471

Address: Avenida de Los Castros, s/n, SANTANDER
Year of creation: 1974
Parent Organization: Universidad de Santander, Ministerio de Educación y Ciencia
Present Head: D. José Angel García de Cortázar
Size of staff. Total: 15 — Full time: 14 — Part time: 1
Researchers: 7 — Full time: 7
Research activities: from 10% to 25%
Educational research: more than 50%
Type of research: Investigación aplicada (creación de material didáctico); educación ambiental; educación especial (niños deficientes); investigación prospectiva y básica.
Functional objectives of research: Desarrollar un plan de coordinación didáctica y renovación pedagógica en el distrito universitario de Santander; desarrollo de programas de educación especial; proyecto A.N.I.D.A. (Area natural de investigación didáctico-ambiental); formación y perfeccionamiento del profesorado.
Monographs: Coordinación didáctica y sistema educativo. Utilización didáctica del medio ambiente: el valle del río Miera. Utilización didáctica del medio ambiente: la bahía de Santander. El cine en el aula. Experiencias básicas en la enseñanza de las ciencias de la naturaleza (3 volúmenes). Pautas de programación en preescolar y ciclo inicial.
Studies and surveys in preparation: Utilización didáctica del medio ambiente: los valles de los ríos Saja y Besaya. Guía didáctica de la frauja costera Santander-Linares. Aplicación de métodos de simulación mecánica a la enseñanza de la mecánica de las rocas. Enseñanza de la informática en el bachillerato. Como individualizar el aprendizaje de las matemáticas en el contexto actual de la enseñanza: explicación de un método experimental. Proyecto de experiencia interdisciplinar del entorno escolar.

Instituto de Ciencias de la Educación, Universidad de Sevilla **0472**

Address: Av. Ramón y Cajal, s/n, Edificio de la Facultad de Económicas y Empresariales, SEVILLA 5
Year of creation: 1969
Parent Organization: Universidad de Sevilla
Present Head: D. Rafael Márquez Delgado
Size of staff. Total: 70 — Full time: 7 — Part time: 63
Researchers: 61 — Full time: 2 — Part time: 59
Research activities: from 10% to 25%
Educational research: more than 50%
Type of research: Investigación aplicada; investigación y desarrollo.
Functional objectives of research: Prestación de servicios a la administración educacional.
Monographs: Fernández Pozar, F., et al. Agrupamientos flexibles de alumnos y profesores: un nuevo concepto de organización de centros de E.G.B. 1980. Equipo de investigación del Colegio de Educación Especial 'Jesús del Gran Poder'. Coeducación de niñas deficientes físicas (motrices e hipoacúsicas) y límites intelectuales con niñas normales. Fase A: Estudio del nivel de tolerancia a la frustración y de las relaciones interpersonales. 1980. Estebán Arbués, A. El tutor y la orientación del alumno. 1983. Jimenez Nuñez, A. Análisis de la situación de la educación en Sevilla en relación con las variables sociales, culturales y económicas más significativas: importancia de los factores extra-escolares en el análisis y planificación de la educación. 1981. Gonzalez Alonso, J.M.; Perez Rios, J. Un programa de orientación vocacional para el ciclo superior de la E.G.B. 1982. Lista completa a disposición.
Studies and surveys in preparation: Determinación de prioridades en la actualización y perfeccionamiento del profesorado de enseñanzas medias, planificación de los cursos de perfeccionamiento. Factores y causas del fracaso académico de la Universidad. Diseño y experimentación de unidades programadas de recuperación para alumnos de 3o. de física y química de B.U.P. Estructuración de contenidos educativos y estilos cognitivos: incidencia en el aprendizaje universitario.

Instituto de Ciencias de la Educación, Universidad de Valencia **0473**

Address: C/ Nave, 2, VALENCIA 3
Year of creation: 1970
Parent Organization: Universidad Literaria de Valencia
Present Head: Vicente Montes Penades
Size of staff. Total: 18
Researchers: 10
Research activities: from 25% to 50%
Educational research: more than 50%
Type of research: Investigación aplicada.
Functional objectives of research: Educación especial; formación pedagógica y perfeccionamiento del profesorado; métodos y medios de enseñanza.
Periodical publications: Memorias anuales.
Monographs: Publicaciones sobre las distintas materias de enseñanza. Lista completa a disposición.

Studies and surveys in preparation: Didácticas especiales: sobre enseñanza de las ciencias (preconceptos, resolución problemas, trabajos prácticos); sobre enseñanza de las matemáticas; sobre otras materias (francés y griego). Informatización de la gestión administrativa. Agresividad en el contexto familiar y escolar. Comprensión de lectura y escritura. Curriculum para deficientes mentales.

Instituto de Ciencias de la Educación, Universidad de Zaragoza

0474

Address: Ciudad Universitaria, ZARAGOZA-9
Year of creation: 1970
Parent Organization: Universidad de Zaragoza
Present Head: Agustín Ubieto Arteta
Size of staff. Total: 23 — Full time: 23
Researchers: 7 — Full time: 7
Research activities: from 25% to 50%
Educational research: more than 50%
Type of research: Básica y aplicada.
Functional objectives of research: Prestación de servicios a la administración educacional; evaluación.
Periodical publications: Educación abierta. Anexos. Materiales para la clase. Informes. Investigación.
Monographs: Velasco Herrero, M. Maduración afectiva, motriz e intelectual a través movimiento. Método global (preescolar y ciclo inicial). Aguirre Gonzalez, J. Aprender en la biblioteca. Mallas Casas, S. Cómo programar y redactar guiones para audiovisuales didácticos. Sebastian Aguilar, C. Origen y desarrollo de la química: sus valores didácticos. Garces Campos, R. Tendencias a la escolarización en la ciudad de Zaragoza.
Studies and surveys in preparation: El éxito y el fracaso escolar en relación a los sistemas de modos de hablar y a las interacciones profesor-alumno. Formación de conceptos: estrategias y niveles de asimilación de la realidad circundante al finalizar el preescolar (5 años). Análisis del rendimiento de los alumnos de preescolar-ciclo inicial. La prensa en las escuelas rurales: estudio sobre su utilización para la mejora de la calidad de la enseñanza en EGB (análisis en Aragón). Lista completa a disposición.

Instituto de Ciencias de la Educación, Universidad Nacional de Educación a Distancia

0475

Address: Ciudad Universitaria, MADRID 3
Year of creation: 1972
Parent Organization: Universidad Nacional de Educación a Distancia
Present Head: Alejandro Tiana Ferrer
Size of staff. Total: 19 — Full time: 19
Researchers: 15 — Full time: 15
Research activities: 50%
Educational research: more than 50%
Type of research: Investigación básica y aplicada.
Functional objectives of research: Análisis y desarrollo de la educación a distancia.
Periodical publications: La UNED y sus alumnos (1/año). Boletín bibliográfico (2/ao).
Monographs: Los primeros licenciados de la UNED. Técnicas de estudio. Nuevas normas para la redacción de unidades didácticas.

Studies and surveys in preparation: Análisis de los programas renovados del ciclo superior en área de ciencias naturales. Desarrollo de hábitos lectores de estudio mediante textos socioliterarios seleccionados con criterios de lecturabilidad y propuesta de actividades fácilmente controlables válidos para el aprendizaje individualizado y a distancia. Hacia una homogeneización de programas y de baremos de evaluación de distintos profesores de una misma disciplina. Experimentación, ensayo, aplicación y análisis de resultados en el Colegio Universitario San Pablo de Madrid.

SRI LANKA

Adhyāpane Paripālane Abhyāse Āyatanaye

0476

Translation: Staff College for Educational Administration
Address: KALUTARA
Year of creation: 1976
Parent Organization: Ministry of Education
Present Head: Mr. L.D.P. Jayasinghe
Size of staff. Total: 5 — Full time: 5 — Part time: 4
Researchers: 5 — Full time: 5
Research activities: from 10% to 25%
Educational research: more than 50%
Type of research: Basic.
Functional objectives of research: Preparation of courses; servicing the educational administration.
Periodical publications: Kalamanākaranaya (Management: collection of articles on educational planning and management. 4/yr).
Monographs: 8 volumes of distance training materials for training of SLES V officers. Case study on training needs of educational administration and management for officers in the Sri Lanka education service. Identification of training needs of principals of 1A, 1B and 1C (collegiate) schools: a sample survey.
Studies and surveys in preparation: The effect of teacher absenteeism on school management. Preparation of a comprehensive inventory of grade 1A, 1B and 1C (collegiate) schools. Preparation of a glossary of technical terms in educational planning and management. The changing role of the teacher in the school system. Role perception of departmental principals of 10 selected 1A, 1B schools.

Agaeem Margopadesha Ha Paryeshana Ekakaya Adyapana Amathyansaya

0477

Translation: Evaluation, Guidance and Research Unit of the Ministry of Education
Address: P.O. Box 1509, Malay Street, COLOMBO 2
Year of creation: 1983
Parent Organization: Ministry of Education
Present Head: Dr. Mrs. T. Kariyawasam
Size of staff. Total: 27
Researchers: 26
Research activities: more than 50%
Educational research: more than 50%

Type of research: Research and development.
Functional objectives of research: Servicing the educational administration.
Monographs: Reports pertaining to the following research projects undertaken for UNICEF. Diagnostic survey of 6 project areas (Sri Lanka). Student competencies in mathematics and language in the 6 project areas (Sri Lanka). Evaluation design to evaluate competency in mathematics and language (Sri Lanka).
Studies and surveys in preparation: National assessment of educational progress. Identification of a minimum learning continuum. Remedial teaching techniques and material.

Faculty of Education, University of Colombo

0478

Address: P.O.Box 1490, COLOMBO 03
Year of creation: 1949
Parent Organization: The University of Colombo
Present Head: Prof. W.A. de Silva
Size of staff. Total: 33 — Full time: 33
Research activities: more than 50%
Educational research: more than 50%
Type of research: Applied, research and development.
Functional objectives of research: Partial fulfilment of degree requirements; preparation of courses; improvement of teaching and training; advancement of knowledge.
Periodical publications: The Journal of the National Education Society of Sri Lanka.
Studies and surveys in preparation: Students' learning orientations. The impact of adult education on the universalization of primary education.

Sri Lanka Adhyapana Paripalana Ayatanaya

0479

Translation: Sri Lanka Staff College for Educational Administration
Address: MAHARAGAMA
Year of creation: 1976
Parent Organization: Ministry of Education
Present Head: Mr. P. Kumarasiri
Size of staff. Total: 15 — Full time: 14
Researchers: 15 — Full time: 12
Research activities: from 10% to 25%
Educational research: from 10% to 25%
Type of research: Basic research, research and development.
Functional objectives of research: Preparation of courses; servicing the educational administration.
Monographs: Kalamanakarana prakasana (Sinhala) Vols. I and II. Identification of training needs of 1A B C principals: survey.
Studies and surveys in preparation: Field Projects: Training of educational administrators in Sri Lanka: problems and issues. A study of curricula and their impact on the roles of school principles. Intersectional comparative analysis of schools. Professional development of educational administration in the context of educational reform.

Vishayamala Sanwardhana Madyasthanaya **0480**

Translation: Curriculum Development Centre
Address: 255 Bauddhaloka Mawatha, COLOMBO 7
Year of creation: 1969
Parent Organization: Ministry of Education
Present Head: M.M. Premaratne
Size of staff. Total: 110 — Full time: 101 — Part time: 09
Researchers: 81 — Full time: 81
Research activities: from 25% to 50%
Educational research: from 25% to 50%
Type of research: Applied.
Functional objectives of research: Design and produce curriculum material for the primary, junior and senior secondary schools; initiate special projects in educational development work and educational innovations — field study centre, science education support centre and educational television.
Periodical publications: Bulletin. Newsletters.
Monographs: Syllabuses of instruction.
Studies and surveys in preparation: Study on the position of science education in Sri Lanka. Graphic communication: feasibility study.

SWEDEN

Institutionen för internationell pedagogik, Stockholms universitet **0481**

Translation: Institute of International Education, University of Stockholm
Address: 106 91 STOCKHOLM
Year of creation: 1971
Parent Organization: University of Stockholm
Present Head: Professor Ingemar Fägerlind
Size of staff. Total: 25 — Full time: 14 — Part time: 11
Researchers: 14 — Full time: 8 — Part time: 6
Research activities: more than 50%
Educational research: more than 50%
Type of research: Basic research.
Functional objectives of research: Studies of education in Third World countries.
Periodical publications: Institute of International Education report series. Studies in comparative and international education.
Monographs: Mauno Mbamba, A. Primary education for an independent Namibia: planning in a situation of uncertainty and instability. 1982. Duberg, R. Schooling, work experience and earnings: a study of determinants of earnings in a Third World corporate setting. 1982. Fägerlind, I.; Saha, L. Education and national development: a comparative perspective. 1983. Chinapah, V. Participation and performance in primary schooling: a study of equality of educational opportunity in Mauritius. 1983.
Studies and surveys in preparation: The Second IEA Science Study. The Malmö longitudinal study. Women and work: a comparative study. Educational research in Sweden 1944–1971. Instruments for educational reforms in Sweden 1950–1975.

Institutionen för lingvistik, Stockholms universitet

0482

Translation: Institute of Linguistics, University of Stockholm
Address: 106 91 STOCKHOLM
Year of creation: 1967
Parent Organization: University of Stockholm
Present Head: Professor Östen Dahl
Size of staff. Total: 40 — Full time: 20 — Part time: 20
Researchers: 30 — Full time: 15 — Part time: 15
Research activities: more than 50%
Educational research: from 10% to 25%
Type of research: Basic and applied within language learning and teaching, language disorders and therapy, language and ethnic minorities, sign language of the deaf.
Functional objectives of research: Degree requirements; research ordered by and paid for by external authorities, etc.; internal research in its own right.
Periodical publications: SSM Reports.
Monographs: Strömqvist, S. En orientering om NP, kasus och prepositioner i ryska. 1980. Viberg, A. Studier i kontrastiv lexikologi: perceptionsvert. 1983. Studium av ett invandrarsvenskt språkmaterial. 1983. Complete list on request.
Studies and surveys in preparation: An information brochure is in preparation presenting the Institute and describing ongoing research.

Institutionen för pedagogik vid Högskolan för lärarutbildning i Stockholm

0483

Translation: Department of Educational Research, Stockholm Institute of Education
Address: P.O. Box 34103, 100 26 STOCKHOLM
Year of creation: 1956
Parent Organization: University of Stockholm
Present Head: Prof. Bengt Erik Andersson
Size of staff. Total: 70 — Full time: 40 — Part time: 30
Researchers: 35 — Full time: 25 — Part time: 10
Research activities: 50%
Educational research: from 25% to 50%
Type of research: Basic and some applied.
Functional objectives of research: In coordination with the training of teachers at the Institute of Education.
Periodical publications: Studies in education and psychology. Reports on education and psychology.
Monographs: Adult education for social change. Research on the Swedish allocation policy. The development of school curricula as a context for work. Children's outdoor environment.

Institutionen för praktisk pedagogik, Göteborgs universitet

0484

Translation: Department of Educational Research, University of Göteborg
Address: P.O. Box 1010, 431 26 MÖLNDAL
Parent Organization: University of Göteborg
Present Head: Prof. Karl-Gustaf Stukát
Size of staff. Total: 102 — Full time: 43 — Part time: 59
Researchers: 44 — Full time: 12 — Part time: 32

Research activities: 50%
Educational research: 50%
Type of research: Basic, applied, research and development.
Functional objectives of research: Servicing the educational and childcare administration on different levels.
Periodical publications: The yellow series (which includes project reports and other research bulletins in Swedish). The brown series (of Research bulletins in English from projects and other research work). The red series (of essays including both interim reports from research projects and contributions to the 'Educational Debate', in Swedish).
Studies and surveys in preparation: Development and socialization. Special education. Subject oriented education. Teacher training research. Sports education research.

Pedagogiska institutionen, Göteborgs universitet

0485

Translation: Department of Education, University of Göteborg
Address: P.O. Box 1010, 431 26 MÖLNDAL
Parent Organization: University of Göteborg
Present Head: Jan-Eric Gustafsson
Size of staff. Total: 65 — Full time: 37 — Part time: 28
Researchers: 18 — Full time: 18
Research activities: from 25% to 50%
Educational research: more than 50%
Type of research: All types.
Functional objectives of research: Training and many different research and development objectives.
Periodical publications: Rapporter från Pedagogiska institutionen, Göteborgs universitet. Reports from the Department of Education, University of Göteborg. Göteborg studies in educational sciences.
Monographs: Lindström, B. Forms of representation, content and learning. 1980. Hasselgren, B. Ways of apprehending children at play: a study of pre-school student teachers' development. 1981. Balke-Aurell, G. Changes in ability as related to educational and occupational experience. 1982. Säljö, R. Learning and understanding: a study of differences in constructing meaning from a text. 1982. Complete list on request.
Studies and surveys in preparation: Phenomenographic studies of learning. Long-term effects of education. Studies in science teaching. Studies in vocational training. Individual differences in learning and abilities. Studies in sex role differentiation. Studies in curriculum. Studies in financial support to students.

Pedagogiska institutionen, Linköpings universitet

0486

Translation: Department of Education, Linköping University
Address: 581 83 LINKÖPING
Year of creation: 1970
Parent Organization: Linköping University
Present Head: Dr. Carl Holmberg
Size of staff. Total: 71
Researchers: 25
Research activities: 50%

Educational research: more than 50%
Type of research: Fundamental and applied research in education and other behavioural sciences concentrated in three areas: children, adult education, care and handicaps, and education in the classroom.
Functional objectives of research: Thesis work; staff research; commissioned research.
Periodical publications: s k arbetsrapporter ('Work-reports'). Eve Malmqvists särtrycksserie. Gula rapportserien LiU-PEK-R- Linköping studies in education: dissertations. Linköping studies in education: reports.
Monographs: Johansson, B. Arbetarkvinnor och barntillsyn i Norrköping: en studie av arbetarrörelsens inställning i barntillsynsfrågan speglad i Östergötlands Folkblad 1905-1912. 1983. Forslund, K. Lokalt utvecklingsarbete inom skolan: en försöksverksamhet med fortbildnings- och utvecklingsarbete baserad på lokala arbetslag. MOL-projektet. 1983. Ekholm, M.; Eklund, H.; Erasmie, T.; Eriksson, K.H.; Werdelin, I. Fem uppsatser om handledning och avhandlingsarbete. 1983. Ellström, E.; Ellström, P-E. Social interaktion mellan hörselskadade och hörande barn i integrerade förskolegrupper: en forskningsöversikt rörande integration av döva och hörselskadade barn i vanlig förskola. 1983. Complete list on request.
Studies and surveys in preparation: Language mixing in bilingual children. Facilitation of bilingual language acquisition in the context of the family. Project concerning concentrated study periods in the upper secondary school. Cooperative teaching in home economics, handicraft and technology. Complete list on request.

Pedagogiska institutionen, Lunds universitet

0487

Translation: Department of Education, University of Lund
Address: P.O. Box 7009, 220 07 LUND
Parent Organization: Lund University
Present Head: Prof. Göte Klingberg
Size of staff. Total: 24 — Full time: 13 — Part time: 11
Researchers: 5 — Full time: 5
Research activities: from 10% to 25%
Educational research: more than 50%
Type of research: All kinds of research in the field of education.
Functional objectives of research: Doctoral and post-doctoral research.
Periodical publications: Pedagogical reports. Pedagogical bulletin. Pedagogiska rapporter. Pedagogiska uppsatser. Studia psychologica et paedagogica. Series altera.
Monographs: Angerin, C. Prematura barn: utveckling och uppväxt till 26 månaders ålder. 1982. Löfgren, H.; Brenner, S.-O.; Tellenback, S. Arbetsmiljön i skolan: utveckling av en kausal modell för relationer mellan faktorer i arbetsmiljön för kommunalt anställda inom skolväsendet. 1982. Löfgren, H.; Ericsson, E. Undervisningsmodeller för barn med annat hemspråk än svenska: utvärdering av modersmålsklasser kontra sammansatta klasser. 1982. Nilsson, U. Pensionärer och studieverksamhet: en inledande diskussion. 1983. Complete list on request.

Pedagogiska institutionen, Stockholms universitet

0488

Translation: Institute of Education, University of Stockholm
Address: 106 91 STOCKHOLM
Year of creation: 1953
Parent Organization: University of Stockholm

Present Head: Prof. Dr. Åke W. Edfeldt
Size of staff. Total: 63 — Full time: 40 — Part time: 23
Researchers: 35 — Full time: 12 — Part time: 23
Research activities: from 25% to 50%
Educational research: from 25% to 50%
Type of research: Basic in educational psychology (language, reading, discourse comprehension, communication); applied (curriculum, adult education).
Functional objectives of research: Basic: general need for basic research; applied: objectives given by the State Board of Education.
Periodical publications: Research bulletins from the Institute of Education, University of Stockholm, Sweden.
Monographs: Stockholm studies in educational psychology.
Studies and surveys in preparation: Children's cultural communication. Reading: discourse comprehension. Violence in the family: violence towards children. Immigrant identity. Music therapy. An existential approach to the history of education.

Pedagogiska institutionen, Umeå universitet

0489

Translation: Department of Education, University of Umeå
Address: 901 87 UMEA
Year of creation: 1964
Parent Organization: Faculty of Social Science
Present Head: Professor Sigbrit Franke-Wikberg
Size of staff. Total: 90 — Full time: 70 — Part time: 20
Researchers: 43 — Full time: 23 — Part time: 20
Research activities: from 25% to 50%
Educational research: more than 50%
Type of research: Basic; applied; research and development.
Functional objectives of research: Basic research; servicing the educational administration.
Monographs: Educational reports: Holm, O. The effects of intent, reason and harm on attribution of aggression. Holm, O. Attribution of aggressiveness and judgment of behaviour as right or wrong. Egerbladh, T. Social decision schemes of the same dyads and tetrads on two different disjunctive tasks. Sjödin, S. Group norms, types of problems and group compositions on group and subsequent individual performances.
Studies and surveys in preparation: Evaluation research. Construction of tests and related research. Research related to sports activities. Research about minorities and multicultural contexts.

Pedagogiska institutionen, Uppsala universitet

0490

Translation: Department of Education, University of Uppsala
Address: Box 2109, 750 02 UPPSALA
Year of creation: 1977
Parent Organization: University of Uppsala
Present Head: Prof. Karl-Georg Ahlström; Prof. Urban Dahllöf; Prof. Erik Wallin
Size of staff. Total: 75
Researchers: 20

Type of research: Basic and applied research.
Functional objectives of research: Partial fulfilment of degree requirements; servicing the educational administration on a national level.
Periodical publications: Uppsala reports on education (English). Complete list on request.
Monographs: Söderström, M. Ledningsutveckling inom statsförvalningen. 1979. Hammarstedt, B.; Amcoff, S. Integration av hörselskadade elever i grundskolan. 1979. Svensson, H. En inventering av synskadade utvecklingsstörda elever i Stockholms län. 1979. Elander, I. Om de små högstadiernas roll i regionalpolitiken. 1979. Complete list on request.
Studies and surveys in preparation: Individualization and grouping of students. Treatment of drug addicts. Distance education and recurrent education. Education for peace. School and change.

Pedagogisk-psykologiska institutionen vid Lärarhögskolan i Malmö, Lunds Universitet **0491**

Translation: Department of Educational and Psychological Research, School of Education, University of Lund
Address: P.O. Box 23501, 200 45 MALMÖ
Year of creation: 1962
Parent Organization: University of Lund
Present Head: Prof. Åke Bjerstedt
Size of staff. Total: 63 — Full time: 25 — Part time: 38
Researchers: 22 — Full time: 7 — Part time: 15
Type of research: Applied; research and development.
Functional objectives of research: See research programmes.
Periodical publications: Utbildning och utveckling (Education and development). Didakometry and sociometry.
Monographs: Studia psychologica et paedagogica. Complete list on request.
Studies and surveys in preparation: Structural transformation in the economy of the need for education.

Psykologiska institutionen, Stockholms universitet **0492**

Translation: Department of Psychology, University of Stockholm
Address: 106 91 STOCKHOLM
Parent Organization: University of Stockholm
Present Head: Professor David Magnusson
Size of staff. Total: 150
Researchers: 85
Research activities: 50%
Educational research: from 10% to 25%
Type of research: Biological psychology; clinical psychology; information processes and decision making; environmental and organizational psychology; perception and psychophysic with application within ergonomic and environmental psychology; personality, social, and developmental psychology.
Functional objectives of research: Scientific.
Periodical publications: Reports from the Department of Psychology, University of Stockholm.
Monographs: Zuber, I.; Nystedt, L.; Smari, J. Social conditions in the family, self-

consciousness, and attribution style: an explorative study. 1983. Bergman, L.R. A developmental study of sex differences in some reactions to the school environment. 1983. Magnusson, D.; Allen, V.L., eds. Human development: an international perspective. 1983. Hagert, G.; Waern, Y. On implicit assumptions in reasoning. In: Myers, T. ed. Reasoning and discourse processes. (In press). Complete list on request.

Religionspedagogiska forskningsavdelningen

0493

Translation: Institute of Religious Education
Address: Slottsgränd 3, Box 1604, 751 46 UPPSALA
Year of creation: 1977
Parent Organization: University of Uppsala, Department of Theology
Present Head: Bergling, Kurt, Ph.D., D.D.
Size of staff. Total: 2 — Full time: 2
Researchers: 2 — Full time: 2
Research activities: more than 50%
Educational research: more than 50%
Type of research: Basic research.
Functional objectives of research: Basic research on the psychological foundations of religious education.
Periodical publications: Reports from the Institute of Religious Education, University of Uppsala.
Monographs: Bergling, K. Moral development: the validity of Kohlberg's theory. 1981. Bergling, K. Moralutveckling. (Moral development). 1982.
Studies and surveys in preparation: The psychology of religious conversion and developmental changes in religious and ideological orientation. The Sunday School movement in Sweden from its 100th anniversary in 1951 to 1979.

Skolöverstyrelsen

0494

Translation: National Swedish Board of Education
Address: 106 42 STOCKHOLM
Year of creation: 1905
Parent Organization: Ministry of Education
Present Head: Mr. Lennart Orehag
Size of staff. Total: 580 — Full time: 450 — Part time: 130
Researchers: 76
Educational research: more than 50%
Type of research: Basic and applied educational and social science research.
Functional objectives of research: Longitudinal studies on effects of reforms and developments and follow-up and evaluation of decentralization within the school system; specific projects on critical issues in primary, secondary (including vocational) and adult education.
Periodical publications: School research: newsletter. Svensk utbildningsforskning: projektkatalog (Swedish educational research: annual catalogue for R&D). Verksamhetsberättelse för anslaget pedagogiskt forsknings- och utvecklingsarbete (Annual report on the use of the R&D grant).
Monographs: Swedish research and debate about bilingualism: läsprocessen i ljuset av aktuell forskning (Current research on the reading process). Läs- och skrivsvårigheter

i ljuset av aktuell forskning (Current research on reading and writing difficulties). Elevers skolmiljö: en översikt av FoU i grundskolan (Working conditions for students in the compulsory school: an R&D review). Konsten att kunna vårda: om vårdpedagogik (The art of nursing: about teaching of nursing and care). Matematik i svensk skola (Mathematics in Swedish schools).
Studies and surveys in preparation: Reports on 54 research projects. Reports on 24 educational development projects.

SWITZERLAND

Abteilung Angewandte Psychologie, Psychologisches Institut der Universität

0495

Translation: Section de psychologie appliquée, Institut de Psychologie de l'Université
Address: Zürichbergstrasse 44, 8044 ZURICH
Parent Organization: Université/Département de l'instruction publique du canton de Zürich
Present Head: Prof. Dr. François C. Stoll
Size of staff. Total: 12 — Full time: 4 — Part time: 8
Researchers: 9 — Full time: 4 — Part time: 5
Research activities: from 10% to 25%
Educational research: from 10% to 25%
Functional objectives of research: Psychologie du développement scolaire et professionnel; psychologie de la lecture; psychométrie et sélection.
Monographs: Berichte der Abteilung. Schweizer Lehrlinge zwischen. Ausbildung und Produktion.
Studies and surveys in preparation: Influence de la formation professionnelle sur la personnalité.

Abteilung für Klinische Psychologie, Psychologisches Institut der Universität Freiburg

0496

Translation: Section Clinical Psychology, Institute of Psychology of the University
Address: 14, rue St-Michel, 1700 FREIBURG
Year of creation: 1981
Parent Organization: University of Fribourg
Present Head: Prof. Dr. Meinrad Perrez
Size of staff. Total: 6 — Full time: 5 — Part time: 1
Researchers: 5 — Full time: 5
Research activities: from 25% to 50%
Educational research: from 25% to 50%
Type of research: Basic and applied.
Functional objectives of research: Development and evaluation of interventional methods for the readjustment of disturbed children; parent-child-interaction-analysis.
Periodical publications: Forschungsberichte (bulletins de recherche).
Monographs: Lukesch, H.; Perrez, M.; Schneewind, K.A., Hrsg. Familiäre Sozialisation und Intervention. 1980. Perrez, M. Krise der Kleinfamilie, Hrsg. und Mitarbeit von L. Alberti u.a. 1979.
Studies and surveys in preparation: Analysis of the social contingencies in mother-baby-interaction (specially the crying-behaviour).

Abteilung für Unterrichts-Medien (AUM), Medizinische Fakultät der Universität Bern **0497**

Translation: Division of Instructional Media, Medical Faculty, University of Bern
Address: Inselspital, 38, 3010 BERNE
Year of creation: 1975
Parent Organization: Medical Faculty, University of Bern
Present Head: Dr. Jürg F. Steiger, M.D.
Size of staff. Total: 11 — Full time: 8 — Part time: 3
Researchers: 4 — Full time: 2 — Part time: 2
Research activities: from 10% to 25%
Educational research: from 10% to 25%
Type of research: Applied research (media communication).
Functional objectives of research: Feasibility and efficiency of self-instruction.
Periodical publications: Irregular internal bulletin (in German).
Monographs: Steiger, J. Availability and utilization of self-learning materials for continuing education of health professions in Switzerland: report written on request by the WHO Regional Office for Europe, Copenhagen, 1982. (In press).

Abteilung Pädagogische Psychologie der Universität Bern **0498**

Translation: Department of Educational Psychology of the University of Bern
Address: Waldheimstrasse 6, 3012 BERNE
Year of creation: 1971
Parent Organization: Department of Education of the canton of Bern
Present Head: Professor Dr. Hans Aebli, M.A.
Size of staff. Total: 9 — Full time: 3 — Part time: 6
Researchers: 7 — Full time: 1 — Part time: 6
Research activities: from 10% to 25%
Educational research: from 10% to 25%
Type of research: Metacognition on problem solving; type of problems: word problems in mathematics.
Functional objectives of research: Applications to mathematics teaching.
Monographs: Denken: das Ordnen des Tuns, 2 Bände. 1980/81. Zwölf Grundformen des Lehrens. 1983.
Studies and surveys in preparation: Metakognition bei Erziehern und Kindern: Förderung der Selbstbeobachtung und der Steuerung des Problemlöse- und Lernverhaltens bei Erziehern als Voraussetzung ihrer Befähigung zur Beobachtung und Anleitung des Problemlöse- und Lernverhaltens bei Kindern.

Abteilung Systematische und historische Pädagogik, Pädagogisches Seminar **0499**

Translation: Section pédagogie systématique et historique, Institut de pédagogie
Address: Gesellschaftsstrasse 6, 3012 BERNE
Parent Organization: Université de Berne
Present Head: Prof. Dr. T. Weisskopf
Size of staff. Total: 11 — Full time: 6 — Part time: 5
Researchers: 5 — Full time: 2,5 — Part time: 2,5
Research activities: from 25% to 50%
Educational research: more than 50%
Type of research: Appliquée et fondamentale.

Functional objectives of research: Satisfaire partiellement aux conditions d'obtention d'un grade; préparation de cours.
Monographs: Küffer, U. Die Darstellung der Fehlerziehung im Werke Jeremias Gotthelfs. 1982.
Studies and surveys in preparation: Pestalozzis Begriff der 'sehenden Liebe'. Die Disziplinierungsfunktion der Schule im 19. und zu Beginn des 20. Jahrhunderts, v.a. am Beispiel der Zürcher Volksschule. Arbeit, Beruf und Lebensalltag. Führung und Innovation: ein Grundmodell für die Führung von Volksschullehrern. Complete list on request.

Amt für Unterrichtsforschung und -planung des Kantons Bern

0500

Translation: Office de recherche pédagogique du canton de Berne
Address: Sulgeneckstrasse 70, 3005 BERNE
Year of creation: 1972
Parent Organization: Direction de l'instruction publique du canton de Berne
Present Head: Dr. phil. Hans Stricker
Size of staff. Total: 30 — Full time: 19 — Part time: 11
Researchers: 10 — Full time: 7 — Part time: 3
Research activities: 50%
Educational research: more than 50%
Type of research: Recherche d'action; recherche et développement.
Functional objectives of research: Prestations pour l'administration de l'éducation; prestations pour les enseignants.
Periodical publications: Tätigkeitsbericht (Rapport sur les activités).
Monographs: Hedinger, U.R.; Deppeler, R. Planung einer Weiterausbildungsphase für Primarlehrer. Allemann, A.; Meli, B. Gesundheitserziehung in der Schule. Guyer, Marianne. Elternmitarbeit am Schulversuch Manuel. 1981. Müller, P. Schulstrukturen in ländlichen Regionen des Kantons Bern. 1981. Ramseier, E.; Hohn-Freiburghaus, D. Befragung austretender Schüler über ihre Erfahrungen im Schulversuch Manuel. 1981. Complete list on request.
Studies and surveys in preparation: Evaluation der Lehrpläne für die Primar- und Sekundarschulen des Kantons Bern. Evaluation der Seminarreform. Studie über die Rekrutierung in die Ausbildung und den Beruf des Primarlehrers. Auswertung von Schulversuchen zu Schulstrukturen.

Centre de recherches psychopédagogiques

0501

Address: 15A, avenue Joli-Mont, Case postale 218, 1211 GENEVE 28
Year of creation: 1963
Parent Organization: Département de l'instruction publique, Cycle d'orientation de l'enseignement secondaire
Present Head: Gilbert Metraux
Size of staff. Total: 17 — Full time: 6 — Part time: 11
Researchers: 11 — Full time: 4 — Part time: 7
Research activities: 50%
Educational research: more than 50%
Type of research: 90% recherches et développement.
Functional objectives of research: Amélioration du système éducatif au sein de l'enseignement secondaire obligatoire.

Monographs: Bain, D. La démocratisation des études: problèmes et suggestions. 1980. Bain, D.; Hexel, D. Evaluation de l'expérience VORWARTS: travaux du CRPP (Budé et Sécheron 1976–1979). Imperiali, M.; Bain, D. Notes scolaires et pronostics d'orientation. Lehmann, W.; Favre, C. De l'épreuve commune à la banque d'items: analyse d'une épreuve commune de sciences naturelles. Méthodologie de la constitution d'une banque d'items pour les épreuves à référence normative. 1981.
Studies and surveys in preparation: Analyse des interviews de directeurs de collège sur les objectifs légaux de l'école. Analyse de stratégies d'orientation. Actualité de la démocratisation des études. Genèse des plans d'étude. Réactions à la nouvelle batterie et au questionnaire de pré-orientation. Fonctions des épreuves communes. Liste complète sur demande.

Centre vaudois de recherches pédagogiques

0502

Address: 56, rue Marterey, 1005 LAUSANNE
Year of creation: 1976
Parent Organization: Service de la formation et de la recherche pédagogiques, Département de l'instruction publique et des cultes du canton de Vaud
Present Head: Marise Paschoud, licenciée ès Lettres, ès sciences politiques, en psychologie
Size of staff. Total: 17 — Full time: 6 — Part time: 11
Researchers: 12 — Full time: 3 — Part time: 9
Research activities: more than 50%
Educational research: more than 50%
Type of research: Recherche appliquée.
Functional objectives of research: Fournir des prestations à l'administration de l'éducation.
Monographs: Observation de l'introduction d'une nouvelle méthodologie pour l'enseignement du français. Observation longitudinale de candidats à l'enseignement à l'Ecole normale. La réintégration: un problème d'orientation scolaire. Moyens d'enseignement du français en classes terminales à options. Observation de l'introduction expérimentale.
Studies and surveys in preparation: Observation de l'introduction du français 1 à 4 P. Etude longitudinale sur l'enfant de 12 à 14 ans. Etude sur la suppression des notes dans les premiers degrés de la scolarité. Etude sur la carrière scolaire de certains groupes d'élèves.

Fédération suisse pour l'éducation des adultes (FSEA)

0503

Address: Oerlikonerstr. 38, 8057 ZURICH Postfach
Year of creation: 1951
Present Head: Dr. H. Amberg
Size of staff. Total: 4
Researchers: 2
Type of research: Recherches appliquées.
Functional objectives of research: Aperçu des conditions et motifs de la participation à l'éducation des adultes; création de concepts pour différents types d'activités (par exemple : formation des collaborateurs de l'éducation des adultes).
Monographs: Vontobel, J. Ueber den Erfolg in der Erwachsenenbildung. Braunschweig, Westermann, 1972. Berufe in der Erwachsenenbildung. Zürich, SFAE, 1975.

Institut de psychologie appliquée, Université de Lausanne

0504

Address: Avenue Vinet 19, 1004 LAUSANNE
Year of creation: 1968
Parent Organization: Université de Lausanne
Present Head: Professeur Rémy Droz
Size of staff. Total: 34 — Full time: 9 — Part time: 25
Researchers: 29 — Full time: 1 — Part time: 28
Research activities: from 25% to 50%
Educational research: from 10% to 25%
Type of research: Choix professionnel des futurs bacheliers; passage de la vie scolaire à la vie professionnelle.
Studies and surveys in preparation: Les structures de l'individu et de son environnement déterminantes de l'adaptation professionnelle. L'image de l'infirmière et la réalité de la sélection. Le choix professionnel des futurs bacheliers.

Institut für Ausbildungs- und Examensforschung (IAE), Medizinische Fakultät der Universität Bern

0505

Translation: Research Institute for Teaching and Examinations, Medical Faculty, University of Bern
Address: Inselspital 14c, 3010 BERNE
Year of creation: 1971
Parent Organization: Medical Faculty, University of Bern
Present Head: H.G. Pauli, M.D., Professor of medecine
Size of staff. Total: 16 — Full time: 8 — Part time: 8
Researchers: 10 — Full time: 6 — Part time: 4
Research activities: from 25% to 50%
Educational research: from 10% to 25%
Type of research: Applied research and development.
Functional objectives of research: Relevance of medical education to medical practice; licencing procedures in the medical profession.
Monographs: Noack, H., ed. Medical education and primary health care. 1980. Noack, H. Prüfungsreform und Ausbildungsreform in der Medizin. Zeitschrift für Hochschuldidaktik 4, Sonderheft 2. 1980. Albisser, S., et al. Berufsfeldbezogene Fachdidaktik am Beispiel des Einführungskurses Gynäkologie/Geburtshilfe. Zeitschrift für Hochschuldidaktik 7, Sonderheft 8. 1983.
Studies and surveys in preparation: Der Patient in der ambulanten ärztlichen Versorgung. Probleme der Krankheitsbewältigung und Versorgungsbedürfnisse von Rheumakranken im Kanton Bern.

Institut für Leibeserziehung und Sport der Universität Bern

0506

Translation: Institut de l'éducation physique et du sport
Address: Bremgartenstr. 145, 3012 BERNE
Year of creation: 1968
Parent Organization: Universität Bern
Present Head: Prof. Dr. phil.K. Egger
Size of staff. Total: 16 — Full time: 10 — Part time: 6

Researchers: 6 — Part time: 6
Research activities: from 10% to 25%
Educational research: from 10% to 25%
Type of research: Appliquée.
Functional objectives of research: Divers.
Periodical publications: Diplomarbeiten. Beindle.

Institut romand de recherches et de documentation pédagogiques (IRDP)

0507

Address: Faubourg de l'Hôpital 43, 2000 NEUCHATEL
Year of creation: 1969
Parent Organization: Conférence intercantonale des chefs de Département de l'instruction publique de la Suisse romande et du Tessin
Present Head: M. Jacques-André Tschoumy, licencié en psychologie
Size of staff. Total: 27 — Full time: 13 — Part time: 14
Researchers: 6 — Full time: 3 — Part time: 3
Research activities: 50%
Educational research: more than 50%
Type of research: Recherches appliquées.
Functional objectives of research: Suivre le fonctionnement des mesures de coordination scolaire en Suisse romande.
Periodical publications: Rapports de recherche de l'IRDP.
Monographs: Huberman, M. L'analyse des données qualitatives: quelques techniques de réduction et de représentation. 1983. Huberman, M. "S'évaluer pour s'illusionner?" Promesses et écueils de l'évaluation 'adaptative/interactive' des innovations scolaires. Journée d'étude du 27 septembre 1983. 1983. Rebetez, G. Historique de l'évaluation de la radio-télévision éducative 1982-1983. 1983. Cardinet, J. Des instruments d'évaluation pour chaque fonction. 1983. Cardinet, J. Evaluer les conditions d'apprentissage des élèves plutôt que leurs résultats. 1983. Perret, J.-F. Mathématique et réalité. Regard sur le contenu des activités mathématiques à l'école primaire. 1983. Pochon, L.-O. Mathématique 6e année: pondération des objectifs. 1983.
Studies and surveys in preparation: Evaluation du nouvel enseignement du français et des ouvrages pour l'enseignement de l'allemand. Recherches didactiques en mathématique. Fonctions et formes de l'évaluation des élèves.

Laboratoire de didactique et d'épistémologie des sciences

0508

Address: Université de Genève, 24, rue du Général Dufour, 1211 GENEVE 4
Year of creation: 1980
Parent Organization: Université de Genève
Present Head: André Giordan, professeur ordinaire
Size of staff. Total: 28 — Full time: 3 — Part time: 25
Researchers: 28 — Full time: 3 — Part time: 25
Research activities: more than 50%
Educational research: more than 50%
Type of research: Recherche fondamentale et appliquée, recherche et développement.
Functional objectives of research: Formation des chercheurs, animateurs et vulgarisateurs scientifiques; analyse de système de formation en sciences (université scientifique, école d'ingénieurs, universités nationales).
Periodical publications: Activités du laboratoire. Actes des Journées internationales sur

l'éducation scientifique.

Monographs: Une pédagogie pour les sciences expérimentales. 1978. Quelle éducation scientifique pour quelle société? 1978. L'élève et/ou les connaissances scientifiques. 1983. Le guide du maître pour une éducation relative à l'environnement. (Sous presse).

Studies and surveys in preparation: Construction de quelques concepts en physique, chimie et en biologie. Analyse de livres et de matériel scientifiques (scolaires et non scolaires). Etude de muséologie. Informatique et éducation scientifique.

Pädagogische Abteilung der Erziehungsdirektion des Kantons Zürich

0509

Translation: Pedagogy Section of the Department of Education of the Canton of Zurich

Address: Haldenbachstr. 44, 8090 ZURICH

Year of creation: 1971

Parent Organization: Erziehungsdirektion des Kantons Zürich, Akademische Berufsberatung

Present Head: Herr Uri-Peter Trier, dipl. Psych.

Size of staff. Total: 40 — Full time: 13 — Part time: 27

Researchers: 19 — Full time: 7 — Part time: 12

Research activities: 50%

Educational research: 50%

Type of research: Evaluation of school experiments; developmental research; statistical research; situations' analysis.

Functional objectives of research: School innovations; development.

Periodical publications: Arbeits- und Forschungsberichte der pädagogischen Abteilung der Erziehungsdirektion des Kantons Zürich. Bildungsstatistische Berichte, Erziehungsdirektion des Kantons Zürich.

Monographs: None published.

Studies and surveys in preparation: Informatik und Schule.

Pädagogisches Institut der Universität Freiburg

0510

Translation: Institut de pédagogie de l'Université de Fribourg

Address: Petrus-Kanisius-Gasse 19, 1700 FRIBOURG

Parent Organization: Université de Fribourg

Present Head: Prof. Dr. Fritz Oser, prof. ord., président de la Société suisse de la recherche en éducation

Size of staff. Total: 37 — Full time: 17 — Part time: 20

Researchers: 3 — Full time: 2 — Part time: 1

Research activities: from 10% to 25%

Educational research: from 10% to 25%

Periodical publications: Berichte der Erziehungswissenschaft. Arbeitsmaterialien zur Didaktik.

Schweizerische Koordinationsstelle für Bildungsforschung

0511

Translation: Centre suisse de coordination pour la recherche en matière d'éducation

Address: Entfelderstrasse 61, 5000 AARAU

Year of creation: 1971

Parent Organization: Federal Department of the Interior (represented by Federal Office for Education and Science); Swiss Conference of Cantonal Directors of Public Education
Present Head: Armin Gretler
Size of staff. Total: 6 — Full time: 2 — Part time: 4
Researchers: 2 — Full time: 2
Research activities: from 10% to 25%
Educational research: from 10% to 25%
Type of research: Recherche de développement; recherche sur la recherche (méta-recherche).
Functional objectives of research: Etat de l'art et développement de la recherche pédagogique en Suisse.
Periodical publications: Enquête permanente sur la recherche et le développement éducationnels (6/an).
Monographs: Institutions suisses de recherche et de développement éducationnels: répertoire. 1983. Schweizerische Forschungs- und Entwicklungsprojekte im Bereich der obligatorischen Schulzeit. 1981. Trendbericht zur Berufsbildungsforschung: Aktuelle Themen der Forschung in einigen europäischen Ländern. 1980. Education et vie active des jeunes handicapés: quelques contributions de la recherche en Suisse et dans le cadre de l'OECD. 1981. Der Taschenrechner in der Schule: Probleme, Forschungsergebnisse und didaktische Ansätze. 1980. L'école et les enfants de travailleurs migrants en Suisse: projets suisses de recherche 1975–1979. 1980.
Studies and surveys in preparation: Plan de développement pour la recherche éducationnelle en Suisse. Rapport "Didactique intégrée de l'enseignement des langues maternelle et seconde"

Section des sciences de l'éducation (FPSE), Université de Genève

0512

Address: 24, rue Général Dufour, 1211 GENEVE 4
Year of creation: 1912
Parent Organization: Département de l'instruction publique de la République de Genève
Present Head: Pierre Dominicé
Size of staff. Total: 120
Researchers: 15
Type of research: Recherches fondamentales et appliquées.
Functional objectives of research: Contribuer à la connaissance du processus enseignement–apprentissage et des systèmes de formation.
Periodical publications: Cahiers de la Section des sciences de l'éducation.
Monographs: Recherche–action. La délinquance stigmatisée. Les sciences de l'éducation. Didactique de la langue maternelle. Liste complète sur demande.
Studies and surveys in preparation: Apprentissage et évaluation à travers des jeux pédagogiques. Analyse des processus d'enseignement. Inventaire du Fonds Adolphe Ferrière. Les conduites autonomes et dépendantes des élèves en situation d'éducation active. Comment enseigner l'arithmétique à la lumière de la théorie piagétienne? Education ouvrière et formation syndicale. L'insertion sociale et professionnelle des travailleurs migrants. Etudes sur les implications éducatives de la régionalisation. Les processus de formation, de connaissance et d'apprentissage des adultes.

Séminaire de pédagogie, Faculté des lettres

0513

Address: Clos-Brochet 30, 2000 NEUCHATEL
Year of creation: 1981
Parent Organization: Université de Neuchâtel
Present Head: Pierre Marc, prof. ord., vice-président de la Société suisse de recherche en éducation, rédacteur 'Education et recherche'
Size of staff. Total: 5 — Full time: 1 — Part time: 4
Researchers: 5 — Full time: 1 — Part time: 4
Research activities: from 25% to 50%
Educational research: more than 50%
Type of research: Socio-pédagogique (enquêtes); interprétations de nature psychanalytique le plus souvent.
Functional objectives of research: Théoriques; notion pédagogique d'attente; éclairages psychanalytiques.
Periodical publications: Vous avez dit Pédagogie... (créé en 1982). Echecs des uns, inéchecs des autres; de la re-connaissance dans le puzzle scolaire des attentes. Inégalités sociales et culturelles (Fribourg).
Monographs: Marc, P. Autour de la notion pédagogique d'attente. 1983. Marc, P. Contribution à une théorie pédagogique des comportements d'attente. 1980 (3 tomes).
Studies and surveys in preparation: Recherches plus théoriques sur la notion d'attente et plus largement d'attitude en psychosociologie éducative.

Service de la recherche pédagogique (SRP)

0514

Address: 11, rue Sillem, 1207 GENEVE
Year of creation: 1958
Parent Organization: Département de l'instruction publique, Genève
Present Head: Raymond Hutin
Size of staff. Total: 33 — Full time: 21 — Part time: 12
Researchers: 12 — Full time: 7 — Part time: 5
Research activities: 50%
Educational research: more than 50%
Type of research: Recherche et développement dans l'enseignement public.
Functional objectives of research: Améliorer la qualité de l'enseignement et la qualification des enseignants.
Periodical publications: Math-école.
Monographs: Bugniet, C. Evaluer la production écrite. Guignard, N. Les chemins de traverse de la mathématique. Bolsterli, M. Une forme d'évaluation en 1P-2P. Groupe math du SRP. Sur les pistes de la mathématique en division moyenne. Groupe math du SRP. Approcher la mathématique à cinq ans.
Studies and surveys in preparation: Apprentissage de la lecture. Didactique de la mathématique. Fonctionnement global de l'école primaire. Stratégies de différenciation et d'appui pédagogique. Evaluation.

Service de la recherche sociologique

0515

Address: 8, rue du 31 Décembre, 1207 GENEVE
Year of creation: 1965
Parent Organization: Département de l'instruction publique de la République et Canton

de Genève
Present Head: Walo Hutmacher
Size of staff. Total: 19 — Full time: 10 — Part time: 9
Researchers: 11 — Full time: 6 — Part time: 5
Research activities: more than 50%
Educational research: more than 50%
Type of research: Analyse statistique; monographies; enquêtes.
Functional objectives of research: Améliorer la connaissance du fonctionnement effectif de l'école, conçue comme lieu et carrefour de relations sociales.
Periodical publications: Annuaire statistique de l'éducation. Cahiers.
Monographs: Haramein, A.; Perrenoud, P. "Rapsodie", une recherche-action: du projet à l'acteur-collectif. 1981. Delay-Malherbe, N. Enfance protégée, familles encadrées: matériaux pour une histoire des services officiels de protection de l'enfance à Genève. 1982. Perrenoud, P. L'évaluation est-elle créatrice des inégalités de réussite scolaire? 1982. Favre, B. Du dire au faire: quelle formation pour quel changement: enquête auprès des maîtres genevois sur leur première année de formation à l'enseignement renouvelé du français. 1982. Magnin, C. La naissance de l'école dans la Genève médiévale: de l'enseignement cathédral à l'école communale (1179-1429). 1983. Liste complète sur demande.
Studies and surveys in preparation: Sortie de scolarité obligatoire. Entrée en apprentissage professionnel. Résiliations de contrats d'apprentissage. Succès et échecs scolaires à l'école primaire. Education familiale et école.

Ufficio studi e ricerche

0516

Translation: Bureau des études et des recherches
Address: Stabile Torretta, 6501 BELLINZONA, Ticino
Year of creation: 1968
Parent Organization: Dipartimento della pubblica educazione del Cantone Ticino
Present Head: Prof. Diego Erba, licenziato e diplomato in scienze dell'educazione
Size of staff. Total: 8 — Full time: 5 — Part time: 3
Researchers: 6 — Full time: 3 — Part time: 3
Research activities: more than 50%
Educational research: more than 50%
Type of research: Appliquée; recherche et développement; planification de l'enseignement.
Functional objectives of research: Fournir des prestations à l'administration de l'éducation.
Periodical publications: Bibliografia pedagogica.
Monographs: Struttura a livelli e struttura a sezioni: l'innovazione pedagogica nell'opinione dei docenti di scuola media. 1982. Controllo dell'apprendimento in matematica nelle classi pilota di I elementare, anno scolastico 1981/82. 1982. Attività di controllo dell'apprendimento della lingua italiana nelle classi pilota di I elementare. 1982. Controllo dell'apprendimento relativo allo studio dell'ambiente nelle classi pilota di I elementare. 1982. Prospettive occupazionali e finanziarie negli anni ottanta: ripercussioni dell'evoluzione demografica nei vari ordini di scuola. 1982.
Studies and surveys in preparation: Statistiche. Censimenti. Pianificazione scolastica. Liste complète sur demande.

Zentralschweizerischer Beratungsdienst für Schulfragen (ZBS)

0517

Translation: Service pédagogique pour la Suisse centrale
Address: Guggistrasse 7, 6005 LUCERNE
Year of creation: 1974
Parent Organization: Conférence des Directeurs de l'instruction publique de la Suisse centrale (les 7 cantons: Lucerne, Zoug, Uri, Schwyz, Obwalden, Nidwalden, Valais)
Present Head: Dr. Anton Strittmatter
Size of staff. Total: 10 — Full time: 5 — Part time: 5
Researchers: 4 — Full time: 4
Research activities: from 10% to 25%
Educational research: from 10% to 25%
Type of research: Appliquée; recherche et développement; évaluation de projets de réforme scolaire.
Functional objectives of research: Evaluation de projets de réforme scolaire; étude de problèmes scolaires dans tous les domaines de l'école obligatoire; fournir des prestations à l'administration de l'éducation.
Periodical publications: ZBS — Informationen (2-4/an). ZBS — Tätigkeitsbericht (1/an).
Monographs: Lehrplan Deutsch für die Primarschule: Erprobungsfassung 1982. 1982. Ergebnisse einer Befragung der Lehrerschaft zum Lehrplan: Laufbahnwahlorientierung. 1982. Argumentarium zu Schülerbeurteilung mit Noten und Worten. 1982. Bedenken gegen den prüfungsfreien Uebertritt. 1982. "Wie weiter?" Handweiser zur Entwicklung des Hilfsschulwesens in der Zentralschweiz. 1982. Tätigkeitsbericht 1981. 1982. Liste complète sur demande.
Studies and surveys in preparation: 11 projets de recherche portant sur les plans d'études et les structures d'école, l'évaluation des réformes. Liste complète sur demande.

SYRIAN AR

Department of Research

0518

Address: Ministry of Education, DAMASCUS
Year of creation: 1969
Parent Organization: Ministry of Education
Present Head: Mrs. Madiha Imam
Research activities: from 25% to 50%
Educational research: more than 50%
Type of research: Field and theoretical research.
Functional objectives of research: Serving the development of educational work.
Monographs: Some articles in al-Mu'allim al-'arabī magazine.
Studies and surveys in preparation: Preparing investigations to study educational work.

TANZANIA UR

Institute of Adult Education

0519

Address: P.O. Box 20679, DAR ES SALAAM
Parent Organization: Autonomous institution
Present Head: Mr. E.N. Ntirukigwa
Size of staff. Total: 590 — Full time: 479 — Part time: 111
Researchers: 6 — Full time: 6
Research activities: from 10% to 25%
Type of research: Applied research.
Functional objectives of research: Servicing the educational administration and preparation of courses.
Periodical publications: Journal of adult education. Studies in adult education. Adult education now.
Monographs: The Juhudi series (in Kiswahili).

Institute of Education

0520

Address: P.O. Box 35094, DAR-ES-SALAAM
Year of creation: 1975
Parent Organization: Ministry of National Education
Present Head: Mr. Raphael Kiyao
Size of staff. Total: 111
Researchers: 5
Research activities: from 25% to 50%
Educational research: more than 50%
Type of research: Applied (evaluation).
Functional objectives of research: Needs identification; formative and summative evaluation; quality control.
Periodical publications: Annotated bibliography of educational works. Handbook of the Institute of Education. Studies in curriculum development. Tanzania educational journal.
Studies and surveys in preparation: Evaluation of the teaching of advanced level mathematics in Tanzania. Evaluation of the post-primary craft centre programme. Evaluation of the teaching of English '0' Level in Tanzania.

THAILAND

Educational Planning Division

0521

Address: Office of the Permanent Secretary, Ministry of Education, BANGKOK 10300
Year of creation: 1963
Parent Organization: Office of the Permanent Secretary. Ministry of Education
Present Head: Mr. Muangchai Tajaroensuk
Size of staff. Total: 41 — Full time: 41
Researchers: 7 — Full time: 7
Research activities: from 10% to 25%

Educational research: more than 50%
Type of research: Applied R&D.
Functional objectives of research: Servicing the educational administration.
Periodical publications: None published.
Studies and surveys in preparation: Optimal secondary school size. Student's motive in education.

Gong Wijai Garnsuksa

0522

Translation: Educational Research Division
Address: Sukhothai Road, BANGKOK 10300
Year of creation: 1974
Parent Organization: Office of the National Education Commission
Present Head: Dr. Wichien Ketsingha
Size of staff. Total: 46 — Full time: 46
Researchers: 36 — Full time: 36
Research activities: more than 50%
Educational research: more than 50%
Type of research: Applied research, R&D.
Functional objectives of research: Servicing educational planning and policy formulation.
Periodical publications: Educational research newsletter.
Monographs: An evaluative study of primary school efficiency in Thailand. The assessment of grade 3 students' cognitive achievement in 1980. Vocational-technical education and the Thai labor market.
Studies and surveys in preparation: Research for the development of provincial educational planning. The efficiency of secondary education. Cost and contribution of higher education. An evaluative study of the pre-school programmes. Resource allocation for pre-school services.

Institute for the Promotion of Teaching Science and Technology (IPST)

0523

Address: 924 Sukhumvit Road, BANGKOK 10110
Year of creation: 1970
Parent Organization: Semi-autonomous Institute within the Ministry of Education
Present Head: Dr. Nida Sapianchai
Size of staff. Total: 293 — Full time: 187 — Part time: 106
Researchers: 25 — Full time: 18 — Part time: 7
Research activities: from 10% to 25%
Educational research: more than 50%
Type of research: Research and development.
Functional objectives of research: To evaluate the implementation of school science and mathematics curricula as well as to promote new trends in teaching and learning science and mathematics in schools.
Periodical publications: IPST Newsletter (4/yr).
Monographs: Research reports concerning science and mathematics curriculum development activities (available in Thai only).
Studies and surveys in preparation: The Second IEA Science Study. The development of courses in computer education for high school students. The development of instructional materials for school science talented students.

Kong-Wijai-tangkarnsueksa

0524

Translation: Educational Research and Planning Centre
Address: Rajdamnern nok Avenue, BANGKOK 10300
Year of creation: 1952
Parent Organization: Department of Curriculum and Instruction Development
Present Head: Dr. Sman Chatiyanonda
Size of staff. Total: 28 — Full time: 28
Researchers: 23 — Full time: 23
Research activities: more than 50%
Educational research: more than 50%
Type of research: Basic research and applied research.
Functional objectives of research: Servicing the educational administration.
Periodical publications: The Thai journal of educational research. Educational research information courier.
Studies and surveys in preparation: Primary school curriculum evaluation. Secondary school curriculum evaluation.

Soon Pattana Luksoot

0525

Translation: Curriculum Development Centre (CDC)
Address: Department of Curriculum and Instruction Development, Ministry of Education, Sukhumvit Rd., BANGKOK 10110
Year of creation: 1972
Parent Organization: Department of Curriculum and Instruction Development, Ministry of Education
Present Head: Mr. Swasdi Suwanna-agsorn, Director
Size of staff. Total: 95 — Full time: 95
Researchers: 10 — Full time: 10
Research activities: from 10% to 25%
Educational research: more than 50%
Type of research: Research and development.
Functional objectives of research: Development and implementation of curriculum and related materials.
Periodical publications: Curriculum development bulletin (6/yr).
Monographs: Instructional plans (grades 1–6). Curriculum guides (grades 7–12).
Studies and surveys in preparation: Follow-up and evaluation of curriculum implementation.

Soon Technology Thang Karn Suksa

0526

Translation: Centre for Educational Innovation and Technology
Address: Ministry of Education, Sri Ayudhaya Road, BANGKOK10400
Year of creation: 1972
Parent Organization: Department of Non-Formal Education, Ministry of Education
Present Head: Miss Napa Bhongbhibhat, Director
Size of staff. Total: 156 — Full time: 154 — Part time: 2
Researchers: 5 — Full time: 5
Research activities: from 10% to 25%
Educational research: from 10% to 25%

Type of research: Applied research.
Functional objectives of research: Assess the potential of radio as a medium for in-school direct teaching.
Periodical publications: Chankasem journal.
Monographs: Teacher's handbooks of school broadcast programmes: English, music, Thai language, maths, life experience, career building, arts, moral education, and physical education.
Studies and surveys in preparation: Direct teaching of mathematics and Thai language by radio.

Sthabunwijai Pluttikamsart

0527

Translation: Behavioural Science Research Institute
Address: Sukhumvit Soi 23, BANGKOK 10110
Year of creation: 1955
Parent Organization: Sri Nakharinwirot University
Present Head: Prof. Chancha Suvannathat
Size of staff. Total: 20 — Full time: 20
Researchers: 17 — Full time: 17
Research activities: more than 50%
Educational research: from 10% to 25%
Type of research: Basic and applied research.
Functional objectives of research: Serve the needs of Thai society. Improve the quality of learning strategies in educational institutions, and also improve the quality of child rearing practices in Thai homes and families.
Monographs: Thai people's awareness of socio-cultural changes. Family relations and mental health of Thai adolescents. Changing patterns of child rearing practices among low income families in Thailand.
Studies and surveys in preparation: Family size preference of Thai female migrants. Relationships between child rearing practices, physical development and school readiness in preschool children. Environmental and psychological correlates of child rearing practices for the promotion of desirable psychological characteristics in Thai children. Child rearing practices and some selected personality variables as predictors of elementary school student achievement. Inter-attitudes between parents and grandparents towards each other's child-rearing practices and their effects on some characteristics of child behaviour. Familial control of the mass media's influence and important psychological development of Thai youths. Moral qualities of Thai teachers in central plains.

TOGO

Institut national des sciences de l'éducation (INSE)

0528

Address: Université du Bénin, B.P. 1515, LOME
Year of creation: 1972
Parent Organization: Université du Bénin
Present Head: M. Messan Gnininvi, chef du département de physique, chef du Laboratoire sur l'énergie solaire, directeur de l'Office du baccalauréat

Size of staff. Total: 42 — Full time: 42
Researchers: 23 — Part time: 23
Research activities: from 25% to 50%
Educational research: more than 50%
Type of research: Recherches appliquées.
Functional objectives of research: Formation des formateurs; préparation de thèses.
Periodical publications: Etudes et documents de sciences humaines. Documents pédagogiques de sciences naturelles. Bulletin du Laboratoire de pédagogie. Bulletin pédagogique de sciences physiques.
Monographs: La formation des maîtres à l'Ecole normale d'instituteurs d'Atakpamé (Togo). La qualification professionnelle des enseignants togolais du 1er degré dans le cadre de la réforme. Analyse des particularités sémantiques d'élèves evephones.
Studies and surveys in preparation: La pédagogie à l'université. La formation des maîtres au Togo. Le système éducatif togolais. L'éducation précoloniale au Togo.

TRINIDAD AND TOBAGO

School of Education, University of the West Indies

0529

Address: ST. AUGUSTINE
Parent Organization: University of the West Indies
Present Head: Professor Dennis R. Craig, Dean
Size of staff. Total: 22 — Full time: 20 — Part time: 2
Researchers: 7 — Full time: 7
Research activities: from 25% to 50%
Educational research: from 25% to 50%
Type of research: Basic and applied research.
Functional objectives of research: Higher degrees and diplomas; preparation of courses; servicing the community.
Periodical publications: Social studies education. Caribbean journal of education.
Monographs: Occasional publications.
Studies and surveys in preparation: List on request.

TUNISIA

al-Ma'had al-qawmī li-'ulūm at-tarbiya

0530

Translation: Institut national des sciences de l'éducation
Address: 17, rue d'Iraq, TUNIS
Year of creation: 1969
Parent Organization: Ministère de l'éducation nationale

TURKEY

Eğitim Araştırmaları Merkezi

0531

Translation: Educational Research Center
Address: Ankara Üniversitesi Eğitim Bilimleri Fakültesi, Cebeci, ANKARA
Year of creation: 1976
Parent Organization: Faculty of Educational Sciences, Ankara University
Present Head: Prof. Dr. Hıfzı Doğan
Size of staff. Total: 16 — Full time: 6 — Part time: 10
Researchers: 4 — Full time: 1 — Part time: 3
Research activities: 50%
Educational research: more than 50%
Type of research: Basic, applied and developmental research.
Functional objectives of research: Support the Faculty's research activities and do own research to help solve educational problems of various kinds.
Monographs: Policies, planning and administration of vocational and technical education in Turkey. (In French). Determining of manpower needs in textile, food technology and commercial areas. (In Turkish). Vocational technical education project. Curriculum development curriculum materials. (In Turkish).
Studies and surveys in preparation: Vocational technical educational project (guidance, curriculum development, administration). Teacher education project for teachers of vocational technical education and research center, Dhaka, Bangladesh.

Eğitim Bilimleri Araştırma Merkezi

0532

Translation: Centre for Studies in Educational Sciences
Address: Istanbul Üniversitesi, Edebiyat Fakültesi, Eğitim Bilimleri Bölümü, Beyazıt, İSTANBUL
Year of creation: 1982
Parent Organization: Istanbul University
Present Head: Doç. Dr. Halûk Yavuzer
Size of staff. Total: 8 — Full time: 8
Researchers: 2 — Full time: 2
Research activities: from 10% to 25%
Educational research: from 10% to 25%
Type of research: All kinds of educational research from pre-school education to high school level.
Functional objectives of research: To solve educational problems.
Periodical publications: Pedagoji dergisi.
Studies and surveys in preparation: School readiness. Failure in schools. Reading abnormalities.

Eğitim Bilimleri Bölümü, Sosyal Bilimler Enstitüsü, Hacettepe Üniversitesi

0533

Translation: Department of Educational Sciences, Institute of Social Sciences, Hacettepe University
Address: Beytepe, ANKARA
Year of creation: 1980
Parent Organization: Hacettepe University

Present Head: Prof. Dr. Selâhattin Ertürk
Size of staff. Total: 30 — Full time: 30
Researchers: 15 — Full time: 15
Research activities: from 10% to 25%
Educational research: from 10% to 25%
Type of research: Fundamental and applied.
Functional objectives of research: To develop new practices and to improve the situation in Turkish education.
Studies and surveys in preparation: Some personal projects for theses.

Eğitim Bilimleri Fakültesi, Ankara Universitesi

0534

Translation: Faculté des sciences de l'éducation de l'Université d'Ankara
Address: Cebeci, ANKARA
Year of creation: 1965
Parent Organization: Université d'Ankara
Present Head: Prof. Dr. Ziya Bursalıoğlu, doyen de la Faculté
Size of staff. Total: 83 — Full time: 72 — Part time: 11
Researchers: 72 — Full time: 72
Research activities: from 25% to 50%
Educational research: more than 50%
Type of research: Fondamentale, appliquée, recherche et développement.
Functional objectives of research: Soutenir l'enseignement; contribuer au développement du secteur éducatif en Turquie.
Periodical publications: Revue de la Faculté des sciences de l'éducation.
Monographs: 127 publications (125 en turc et 2 en anglais).
Studies and surveys in preparation: 14.

Millî Eğitim Gençlik ve Spor Bakanlığı–Araştırma Geliştirme Planlama ve Koordinasyon Kurulu Başkanlığı

0535

Translation: Planning and Coordination Commission, Ministry of Education, Youth and Sport Research Development
Address: ANKARA
Year of creation: 1981
Parent Organization: Ministry of Education, Youth and Sport
Present Head: Dr. H. Nihat Bilgen
Size of staff. Total: 35
Researchers: 4
Type of research: Educational research.
Functional objectives of research: To serve and develop the educational system.
Monographs: Estimated report of decisions of 10th educational council. Research on European educational systems. Educational statistics. Education system of Japan.
Studies and surveys in preparation: Studies are planned in the subjects of educational planning, management and systems development.

Psikoloji Bölümü, Hacettepe Üniversitesi

0536

Translation: Department of Psychology, Hacettepe University
Address: Edebiyat Fakültesi, Beytepe, ANKARA
Year of creation: 1964
Parent Organization: Hacettepe University
Present Head: Prof. Dr. Hüsnü Arıcı
Size of staff. Total: 18 — Full time: 15 — Part time: 3
Researchers: 11 — Full time: 11
Research activities: from 10% to 25%
Educational research: from 25% to 50%
Type of research: Basic and applied.
Functional objectives of research: Partial fulfilment of degree requirements; finding solutions for theoretical and practical problems related to human behaviour; servicing the educational and administrative organizations.
Monographs: None published.
Studies and surveys in preparation: Developing tests for the university entrance examinations. A cross cultural analysis of drawing errors in young children. Selecting students for the secondary schools: a test-development project. Complete list on request.

Sosyal Bilimler Enstitüsü, Anadolu Universitesi

0537

Translation: Graduate Institute of Social Sciences, University of Anatolia
Address: Yunus Emre Kampüsü, ESKİŞEHİR
Year of creation: 1982
Parent Organization: University of Anatolia
Present Head: Prof. Dr. Şan Öz-Alp
Size of staff. Total: 7 — Full time: 7
Researchers: 5 — Full time: 5
Research activities: from 25% to 50%
Educational research: from 10% to 25%
Type of research: Fundamental and applied.
Functional objectives of research: Programme development for special education and distance education.
Periodical publications: None published.
Monographs: Graduate and post-graduate education (a case study on the Social Sciences Institute of the University of Anatolia).
Studies and surveys in preparation: Recent developments in educational and instructional technologies and their application in Turkish higher education.

UGANDA

National Curriculum Development Centre

0538

Address: P.O. Box 7002, KAMPALA
Year of creation: 1973
Parent Organization: Ministry of Education

Present Head: Mr. V.E. Bua
Size of staff. Total: 56 — Full time: 56 — Part time: 18
Researchers: 2 — Full time: 2
Research activities: from 25% to 50%
Educational research: from 25% to 50%
Type of research: Research and development.
Functional objectives of research: Preparation of courses and servicing the educational administration.
Periodical publications: Curriculum forum.
Monographs: Curriculum forum series, volumes 1, 2, 3.
Studies and surveys in preparation: The Namutamba Project: a case study. Objectives and implementation of the World Food Programme in post secondary institutions in Uganda: a survey.

UK

Cambridge Institute of Education

0539

Address: Shaftesbury Road, CAMBRIDGE CB2 2BX
Year of creation: 1951
Present Head: Mr. H.W. Bradley
Size of staff. Total: 24 — Full time: 24
Researchers: 3 — Full time: 3
Research activities: from 10% to 25%
Educational research: more than 50%
Type of research: Applied research.
Functional objectives of research: Action research with teachers; nationally commissioned projects.
Periodical publications: Cambridge journal of education. Bulletin of the classroom action research network.
Monographs: The education of feeling. Issues in school-centred in-service education. Case studies in school accountability. Curriculum provision in the small primary school.
Studies and surveys in preparation: An appraisal of the outcomes of the assessment of performance unit's mathematics testing. Development work and in-service training for an A-level syllabus in industrial studies. Classroom action research network.

Centre for Advanced Studies in Education

0540

Address: 7 Church Road, Edgbaston, BIRMINGHAM B15 3SH
Year of creation: 1977
Parent Organization: Birmingham Polytechnic
Present Head: Derek Cherrington
Size of staff. Total: 9 — Full time: 6 — Part time: 3
Researchers: 7 — Full time: 2 — Part time: 5
Research activities: more than 50%
Educational research: more than 50%
Type of research: Applied research and development.

Periodical publications: Educational studies. Collected original research in education. Behavioural psychology abstracts.
Studies and surveys in preparation: Early development of Down's syndrome: children 3 to 5 years old. Social education data base.

Centre for Applied Research in Education

0541

Address: School of Education, University of East Anglia, Keswick Hall, NORWICH NR4 6TL
Year of creation: 1970
Parent Organization: University of East Anglia
Present Head: Mr. Rob Walker
Size of staff. Total: 18 — Full time: 11 — Part time: 7
Researchers: 8 — Full time: 8
Research activities: more than 50%
Educational research: more than 50%
Type of research: Applied research in education, specializing in curriculum, research methodology, evaluation, examinations and assessment, innovations and change, in-service activities and research by school teachers, transition from school to work, computer-based innovations in education and training.
Functional objectives of research: To teach higher degrees in applied research in education. To achieve through systematic enquiry improvements in schools and other educational settings.
Periodical publications: Occasional publications.
Monographs: Bread and dreams: a case study of bilingual schooling in the USA. Observational work of LEA inspectors and advisors. School-based examining in England: a focus for school-based curriculum development and accountability. Mode III examining: a study of experience.
Studies and surveys in preparation: Sex-stereotyping and the early years of schooling. Partnership: an exploration of the student-tutor relationship in teaching practice. The Humanities Curriculum Project: an introduction.

Centre for Educational Research and Development

0542

Address: Cartmel College, University of Lancaster, LANCASTER LA1 4YL
Year of creation: 1974
Parent Organization: University of Lancaster, Department of Educational Research
Present Head: Prof. S.N. Bennett
Size of staff. Total: 2 — Full time: 2
Research activities: more than 50%
Educational research: more than 50%
Type of research: Collaborative research between the university and the local education authority service.
Functional objectives of research: To influence policy decisions related to schools.
Periodical publications: Link (3/yr).
Monographs: Option choice process in six 11–16 high schools. The school and its curriculum. Microcomputers in primary schools. The evaluation of an innovatory programme of 16–19. Provision by a local education authority, 1982-83. Computer timetabling in 11 Cumbria secondary schools.
Studies and surveys in preparation: LEA Teacher Fellowship topics 1983-84. Parent

participation in primary schools. Coping with disruptive pupils in schools. Integration of special needs pupils into normal schools. Sex stereotyping in lower infants and middle secondary schools.

Centre for Postgraduate Studies in Education, Leicester Polytechnic

0543

Address: Scraptoft Campus, Scraptoft, LEICESTER LE7 9SU
Parent Organization: Leicester Polytechnic
Present Head: Professor Brian Allison
Size of staff. Total: 18 — Full time: 13 — Part time: 5
Researchers: 10 — Full time: 1 — Part time: 9
Research activities: from 10% to 25%
Educational research: from 10% to 25%
Type of research: Basic, applied, research and development.
Functional objectives of research: Research degree requirements; course development; surveys; indexing.
Monographs: Allison. Guide to dissertation preparation. 3rd ed. Allison. British thesaurus of keywords in education. Allison. Index of British studies in art and design education. Moloney. Index to assessment techniques in aesthetics. Hassan. Reflections on Egyptian folk crafts and their implications for education.
Studies and surveys in preparation: Learning in art and design. Aesthetic criticism. Multi-cultural education. Student teacher classroom effectiveness. Complete list on request.

Centre for Research into the Education of Adults

0544

Address: B Block, Cherry Tree Buildings, University Park, NOTTINGHAM NG7 2RD
Year of creation: 1978
Parent Organization: University of Nottingham
Present Head: Professor J.E. Thomas
Size of staff. Total: 10 — Full time: 1 — Part time: 9
Researchers: 8 — Part time: 8
Research activities: more than 50%
Educational research: more than 50%
Type of research: Adult and continuing education.
Functional objectives of research: To improve the quality of practice.
Periodical publications: Newsletter.
Monographs: Policy and research in adult education: papers presented at the First Nottingham International Colloquium, July 1981. The training of part-time teachers of adults. 1982. Dalnes, J.; Elsey, B.; Gibbs, M. Changes in student participation in adult education. 1982. Stephens, M.D.; Roderick, G.W., eds. Essays on scientific and technical education in early industrial Britain. 1982. Complete list on request.
Studies and surveys in preparation: Nottinghamshire Oral History Project. 'Look after yourself' tutor training research project. International bibliography of adult education.

Centre for Science and Mathematics Education

0545

Address: Bridges Place, LONDON SW6 4HR
Year of creation: 1968
Parent Organization: Chelsea College, University of London

Present Head: Professor P.J. Black
Size of staff. Total: 62 — Full time: 22
Researchers: 40 — Full time: 40
Research activities: 50%
Educational research: more than 50%
Type of research: A mixture of basic research, applied research and curriculum development work.
Functional objectives of research: Understanding process of learning in science and mathematics; evaluation of school science performance for government policy; development of new curriculum materials; helping development of teachers through in-service training.
Periodical publications: Papers published in a variety of professional journals.
Monographs: Monographs and books published by a variety of publishers. Curriculum materials by Nuffield-Chelsea Curriculum Trust. Annual list of publications is available.
Studies and surveys in preparation: Assessment of school performance in science. Mathematical frameworks in children aged 8-13. Graded assessment in mathematics. Computers in the curriculum. School policy and attitudes to smoking. Physiological aspects of smoking education. Initiatives on in-service education in mathematics and science. Complete list on request.

Computer Based Learning Unit, The University of Leeds

0546

Address: LEEDS LS2 9JT
Year of creation: 1968
Parent Organization: University of Leeds
Present Head: J.R. Hartley
Size of staff. Total: 8 — Full time: 6 — Part time: 2
Researchers: 6 — Full time: 4 — Part time: 2
Research activities: more than 50%
Educational research: more than 50%
Type of research: Basic and applied learning systems.
Functional objectives of research: Research programme of the unit.
Monographs: Hartley, J.R. Computer assisted learning. In: Smith, H.T.; Green, T.R.G., eds. Human interaction with computers. 1980. Hartley, J.R. Computer assisted learning and the National Development Programme. In: Moore, J.L.; Thomas, F.H., eds. Computers in schools. 1980. Hartley, J.R. Learner initiatives in computer assisted learning. In: Howe, J.A.M.; Ross, P.M., eds. Microcomputers in secondary education. 1981. Sleeman, D.H.; Brown, J.S., eds. Intelligent tutoring systems. Academic Press, 1982. Complete list on request.
Studies and surveys in preparation: To study processes of learning cognition and problem-solving. To design and evaluate knowledgeable computer based learning materials.

Consultative Committee on the Curriculum (CCC)

0547

Address: Room 4/17, New St. Andrew's House, EDINBURGH EH1 3SY
Year of creation: 1965
Parent Organization: Secretary of State for Scotland, Scottish Office, Edinburgh
Present Head: Dr. J. Munn OBE MA

Size of staff. Total: 60 — Full time: 48 — Part time: 12
Researchers: 20 — Full time: 18 — Part time: 2
Research activities: from 25% to 50%
Educational research: more than 50%
Type of research: Applied research.
Functional objectives of research: Advise the Secretary of State for Scotland on development of the curriculum of primary and secondary schools.
Periodical publications: CCC News. Curriculum bulletins. Curriculum papers on specific subjects.
Monographs: List on request.
Studies and surveys in preparation: List on request.

Council for Educational Technology for the United Kingdom

0548

Address: 3 Devonshire Street, LONDON W1N 2BA
Present Head: Geoffrey Hubbard
Size of staff. Total: 34 — Full time: 28 — Part time: 6
Researchers: 19 — Full time: 9 — Part time: 10
Research activities: less than 10%
Educational research: more than 50%
Type of research: Development action research.
Functional objectives of research: Purpose of organization.
Periodical publications: British journal of educational technology. CET News. CAL News. OLS News.
Monographs: Duke, J. Interactive video: implications for education and training. Gilman, J.A. Information technology and the school library resource centre: the microcomputer as resourcerer's apprentice. Pope, D. Objectives model of curriculum planning and evaluation. Chandler, D. Exploring English with microcomputers. Complete list on request.
Studies and surveys in preparation: Projects dealing with: information technology, videotex, telesoftware, open learning systems, supported self study in secondary education, costing educational materials, etc.

Department of Education, Brunel University

0549

Address: Cooper's Hill, EGHAM, Surrey, TW20 0JZ
Year of creation: 1966
Parent Organization: Brunel University
Present Head: Mr. R. Schofield
Size of staff. Total: 17 — Full time: 14 — Part time: 3
Researchers: 5 — Full time: 3 — Part time: 2
Research activities: from 25% to 50%
Educational research: more than 50%
Type of research: Basic; applied; research and development.
Functional objectives of research: Sponsored research funded by grants from external bodies.
Monographs: Barr, G.V.; Rees, R.; Winter, C.F. An investigation of some common mathematical difficulties experienced by technicians students. Freeling, P.; Barry, S.M.K. In-service training and the study of the Nuffield courses of the Royal College of General Practitioners. Furneaux, W.D.; Curnyn, J.C.; Rees, R. An

experimental and statistical study of the structure and development of mathematical ability during the late primary and early secondary stages of education, together with an investigation of some of its cognitive and affective concomitants. Shinman, S. A chance for every child: access and response to pre-school provision. Complete list on request.

Studies and surveys in preparation: Medical and para-medical education. School pupils' attitude to science. The learning of mathematics.

Department of Education, Southampton University

0550

Address: SOUTHAMPTON S09 5NH
Parent Organization: Southampton University
Present Head: Professor P.J. Kelly
Size of staff. Total: 45 — Full time: 30 — Part time: 15
Researchers: 15 — Full time: 12 — Part time: 3
Research activities: from 25% to 50%
Educational research: from 25% to 50%
Type of research: Research and development.
Periodical publications: Department newsletter.
Monographs: Souper, P.C.; Kay, W.K. The School Assembly in Hampshire: report of a pilot study. 1982. Briggs, B.; Meredith, M. Electronic learning aids: enquiry one. 1981. Poulton, G.; Campbell, G. Families with young children. 1979. Opportunities for research and development work.
Studies and surveys in preparation: The role of teacher assessment in public examinations. Examining in a multicultural society. Possible methods of assessing pupils decision-making skills, developed in school health education programmes, with particular reference to 14/15 year-olds. "Bigtrak plus": exploiting programmable vehicle toys as aids in developing analytical problem-solving. The management of school experience for student teachers. Non-verbal communication and the teacher. Development of curricula and teaching methods for relating biological education to community development. Complete list on request.

Department of Education, University College of Swansea

0551

Address: Hendrefoilan, SWANSEA SA2 7NB
Parent Organization: University College of Swansea (University of Wales)
Present Head: Professor Maurice Chazan
Size of staff. Total: 17 — Full time: 16 — Part time: 1
Type of research: Varied, fundamental and applied.
Functional objectives of research: Partial or full fulfilment of degree requirements; individual staff projects.
Periodical publications: Faculty research newsletter.
Monographs: Chazan, M. Children with special needs: the early years. 1982. Chazan, M., et al. Helping young children with behaviour difficulties. 1984. Jones, G.E. Controls and conflicts in Welsh secondary education. 1982. Brissenden, T.H.F. Mathematics teaching: theory and practice. 1980. Carroll, H.C.M.; Kahn, J.H.; Nursten, J.P. Unwillingly to school. 1981. Complete list on request.
Studies and surveys in preparation: The prevalence and characteristics of children with specific learning difficulties. Project on assessment of A-level chemistry.

Department of Education, University of Aberdeen 0552

Address: Taylor Building, King's College, ABERDEEN AB9 2UB
Year of creation: 1984
Parent Organization: University of Aberdeen
Present Head: Dr. John Nisbet
Size of staff. Total: 11 — Full time: 10 — Part time: 1
Researchers: 8 — Full time: 6
Research activities: 50%
Educational research: 50%
Type of research: Mainly applied, also evaluation, and basic (psychology and sociology).
Functional objectives of research: Collaboration with schools and colleges in the region; higher degrees.
Monographs: No regular series but published as results become available.
Studies and surveys in preparation: Community education. Learning strategies 10–14. Pre-school children entering first school.

Department of Education, University of Cambridge 0553

Address: 17 Trumpington Street, CAMBRIDGE CB2 1PT
Year of creation: 1968
Parent Organization: University of Cambridge
Present Head: Professor P.H. Hirst
Size of staff. Total: 23 — Full time: 19 — Part time: 4
Researchers: 10 — Full time: 8 — Part time: 2
Research activities: from 25% to 50%
Educational research: more than 50%
Type of research: Basic research, research and development.
Functional objectives of research: Research for higher degrees, research projects funded by outside bodies, individual lecturer's research.
Studies and surveys in preparation: Developmental psycholingustics. Social psychology. Curriculum research and development. Islamic education. Studies in training of teachers. History of education. Political literacy in the classroom.

Department of Education, University of Keele 0554

Address: KEELE, Staffordshire, ST5 5BG
Year of creation: 1951
Parent Organization: University of Keele
Present Head: Professor S.J. Eggleston
Size of staff. Total: 96 — Full time: 38 — Part time: 58
Researchers: 62 — Full time: 14 — Part time: 48
Research activities: from 10% to 25%
Educational research: more than 50%
Type of research: Applied research and development in all aspects of education.
Functional objectives of research: Servicing all the needs of the education administration in schools, colleges, universities and the community.
Periodical publications: Studies in design and technology. Multicultural teaching. European journal of science education. Sociological review (edited within the

Department).
Monographs: Inservice teacher education in a multi-racial society. Keele Further Education Curriculum Adaptation Project. Archaeological educational resource materials. History teaching resource materials. Mathematics education handbooks. Range of other occasional publications in educational administration and curriculum issues.
Studies and surveys in preparation: The educational and vocational experiences of young people of minority ethnic groups. Minority arts and education. Certificate in health education Open Learning Project.

Department of Education, University of Stirling

0555

Address: STIRLING FK9 4LA
Year of creation: 1967
Parent Organization: University of Stirling
Present Head: Professor J. Duthie
Size of staff. Total: 30 — Full time: 22 — Part time: 8
Researchers: 13 — Full time: 6 — Part time: 7
Research activities: from 25% to 50%
Educational research: more than 50%
Type of research: Applied.
Functional objectives of research: Primarily study of teaching and curricula in secondary education with external funding.
Monographs: Criterion referenced assessment: an annotated bibliography. Introducing criterion-referenced assessment: teachers' views. Mastery learning in foreign language teaching: a case study. Skills and strategies of foreign language teaching. Accountability and professionalism. An independent evaluation of 'Tour de France'.
Studies and surveys in preparation: The feasibility of mastery learning. Multi-disciplinary courses. Assessment in modern languages education. Communicative use of foreign language in modern languages education. Media education. Literacy in secondary schools. Use of computers in modern languages education.

Department of Educational Studies

0556

Address: University of Surrey, GUILDFORD, Surrey, GU2 5XH
Year of creation: 1982
Parent Organization: University of Surrey
Present Head: Prof. David James
Size of staff. Total: 73 — Full time: 64 — Part time: 9
Researchers: 38 — Full time: 36 — Part time: 2
Research activities: 50%
Educational research: 50%
Type of research: Fundamental, applied and research and development.
Functional objectives of research: Improvement of educational provision in higher, further education and youth, continuing and adult education.
Monographs: Brownhill, R.J. Education and the nature of knowledge. 1983. Cryer, P.; Cryer, N. Basic programming on the BBC microcomputer. 1983. Helping young people to learn, part II: consultancy report for Manpower Services Commission. 1982. Evans, K.M. Innovation in continuing education and training in United Kingdom. 1983. Jarvis, P. Adult education in a small centre: a case study of

Lingfield. 1982. Complete list on request.
Studies and surveys in preparation: Personal construct psychology and education. Academic staff training. Computer assisted learning and information technology. Individualized systems of instruction. Teaching and learning in higher education. Comparative studies of innovation in post-compulsory education. Complete list on request.

Dundee College of Education

0557

Address: Gardyne Road, Broughty Ferry, DUNDEE DD5 1NY
Year of creation: 1906
Parent Organization: Dundee College of Education
Present Head: Dr. W.A. Illsley, Principal
Size of staff. Total: 95 — Full time: 95
Researchers: 10 — Full time: 8 — Part time: 2
Research activities: from 10% to 25%
Educational research: more than 50%
Type of research: Applied research, research and development.
Functional objectives of research: Development of techniques and material; advancing knowledge, servicing needs of educational system.
Periodical publications: Annual report.
Monographs: Development and evaluation of curriculum materials in S3 and S4 history. Microcomputers in primary education. Attitudes to reading. Problems confronting 'List D' pupils on return to day school. Writing across the curriculum.
Studies and surveys in preparation: Integrating the microcomputer into the language arts curriculum in the primary school. Perceptions and priorities in secondary teacher training. The role of the school and college in the training and assessment of primary school teachers. Assessment of music in S3 and S4. In-depth study of national in-service courses. Language Monitoring Project. New information technology and its impact on science curricula in secondary schools in the UK. Secondary Schools Computer Administration and Management Project.

Faculty of Education, King's College

0558

Address: The Strand, LONDON WC2 2LS
Year of creation: 1968
Parent Organization: University of London
Present Head: Professor David N. Aspin
Size of staff. Total: 20
Researchers: 6 (Plus postgraduate students)
Research activities: from 25% to 50%
Educational research: more than 50%
Type of research: Basic (research in education); applied (science education and urban education).
Functional objectives of research: Partial fulfilment of degree requirements (M.Phil. and Ph.D.); also separate research projects into particular aspects of education.

Faculty of Education, Kingston Polytechnic 0559

Address: Gipsy Hill Centre, Kenry House, Kingston Hill, KINGSTON UPON THAMES, Surrey, KT2 7LB
Year of creation: 1975
Parent Organization: Kingston Polytechnic
Present Head: Dr. R.J. Godfrey
Size of staff. Total: 48 — Full time: 45 — Part time: 3
Researchers: 7 — Full time: 7
Research activities: from 10% to 25%
Educational research: from 10% to 25%
Type of research: Applied research; research and development.
Functional objectives of research: To improve the education of pupils in schools and teachers in training (initial and in-service).
Monographs: Lomax, P.; Murphy, P. Teachers report. Montgomery, D., ed. Teaching reading through spelling diagnosis (Kingston Polytechnic — Learning Difficulties Project). Montgomery, D., ed. Study skills: learning and teaching strategies (Kingston Polytechnic — Learning Difficulties Project). Montgomery, D., ed. The way forward: the education and welfare of children in hospital (Kingston Polytechnic, Conference papers).
Studies and surveys in preparation: Children's learning difficulties. Course evaluation in higher education. Man, culture and the environment. The quality of reasoning attained by secondary school pupils in various subject disciplines. Teaching scientific thinking.

Faculty of Education, Ulster Polytechnic 0560

Address: Newtownabbey, CO. ANTRIM BT37 OQB
Year of creation: 1971
Present Head: Dr. A. Nicholls
Size of staff. Total: 55 — Full time: 40 — Part time: 15
Researchers: 4 — Full time: 4
Research activities: from 10% to 25%
Educational research: more than 50%
Type of research: Basic and applied.
Functional objectives of research: Curriculum development; educational management; partial fulfilment of degrees; preparation of courses.
Monographs: Collins, J. Television in N. Ireland secondary schools: paper delivered at E.S.A.I. Annual Conference, Carysfort, Dublin. 1984. Dwyer, E. Education and mental handicap in Ireland — cross border links: ATEE Annual Conference, Aalborg. 1983. Hutchinson, B. Consultancy project: promoting management, organisational staff and curriculum development in a college of further education. 1982. Saunders, E. The research, development and evaluation of students' teaching performance: proceedings of an International Symposium in School Physical Education, Jyväskylä. 1982. Complete list on request.
Studies and surveys in preparation: The role and provision of organized artistic and sporting activities in selected Japanese firms. The Northern Ireland dimension of the problem of adult literacy as it relates to the history of schooling, religion and the economics prospect. The curriculum in home economics. Language and thinking in deaf children. The effect of teaching action research in an MSc degree programme

on secondary school principal's attempt to initiate and sustain a curriculum review and development process. Complete list on request.

Faculty of Education, University College Cardiff

0561

Address: University College, P.O. Box 78, CARDIFF CF1 1XL
Year of creation: 1884
Parent Organization: University of Wales
Present Head: Professor A. Taylor
Size of staff. Total: 477 — Full time: 192 — Part time: 285
Researchers: 384 — Full time: 124 — Part time: 260
Research activities: from 25% to 50%
Educational research: more than 50%
Type of research: All types.
Functional objectives of research: Higher degree purposes by students; professional interests of staff researchers.
Periodical publications: Education for development (2/yr)(deals with matters of general educational concern in Wales and other parts of the world).
Studies and surveys in preparation: Educational psychology. Education for development. Educational administration.

Faculty of Education, University of Birmingham

0562

Address: P.O. Box 363, BIRMINGHAM B15 2TT
Year of creation: 1966
Parent Organization: University of Birmingham
Present Head: Professor M.G. Hughes
Size of staff. Total: 57 — Full time: 52 — Part time: 5
Researchers: 3 — Full time: 2 — Part time: 1
Research activities: from 10% to 25%
Educational research: more than 50%
Type of research: Research and development.
Functional objectives of research: Various aspects of education.
Periodical publications: Educational review.
Monographs: List on request.
Studies and surveys in preparation: GCE examinations: cross-moderation exercises. Education of visually handicapped. New technology and mathematics in employment. Plus individual research by staff.

Faculty of Educational Studies

0563

Address: Lady Spencer-Churchill College, Oxford Polytechnic, Wheatley, OXFORD OX9 1HX
Parent Organization: Oxford Polytechnic
Present Head: Mr. Cedric Cullingford
Size of staff. Total: 60 — Full time: 56 — Part time: 4
Researchers: 8 — Full time: 8
Research activities: from 10% to 25%
Educational research: from 10% to 25%
Type of research: Applied.

Functional objectives of research: Support of courses and staff development.
Periodical publications: Journal of applied educational studies.
Studies and surveys in preparation: Children and television. Classroom processes. Development education. Television research unit.

Further Education Staff College

0564

Address: Coombe Lodge, Blagdon, BRISTOL BS18 6RG
Year of creation: 1961
Present Head: Gordon Wheeler BSc (Econ.) FIIM FRSA
Size of staff. Total: 19 — Full time: 17 — Part time: 2
Researchers: 3 — Full time: 3
Research activities: from 25% to 50%
Educational research: from 25% to 50%
Type of research: Research and development, applied.
Functional objectives of research: To improve efficiency and effectiveness of further education service.
Periodical publications: Coombe Lodge reports.
Monographs: Measures to deal with youth unemployment in the Federal Republic of Germany. Vocational counselling and guidance in the FRG. Netherlands: 16–19 education. The Anglo-German report on curriculum development for vocational education. Vocational education and training in Sweden. Complete list on request.
Studies and surveys in preparation: FEMIS — Further Education Management Information System. YTS — evaluation of.

ILEA Research and Statistics Branch

0565

Address: Addington Street Annex, County Hall, LONDON SE1 7UY
Year of creation: 1963
Parent Organization: Inner London Education Authority
Present Head: Dr. Peter Mortimore
Size of staff. Total: 48 — Full time: 44 — Part time: 4
Researchers: 13 — Full time: 12 — Part time: 1
Research activities: from 25% to 50%
Educational research: more than 50%
Type of research: Basic and applied research.
Functional objectives of research: To meet the research needs of the elected members and the officers of the ILEA.
Periodical publications: Current reports. Current topics. Statistical information bulletins.
Monographs: The child at school: a new behaviour schedule. 1983. Suspensions and expulsions from school 1981/82. 1983. Women's careers in teaching: a survey of teachers views. 1983. Anti-sexist initiatives in ILEA schools. 1983. Comparison between the educational and economic activity of young people in inner London and nationally. 1983. Complete list on request.
Studies and surveys in preparation: A longitudinal study of ILEA junior schools. A series of studies in connection with the Authority's equal opportunities initiatives. A longitudinal study of the reformed West Indian pupils. A survey of pupils in special schools. A study of early school learners.

Institute of Education, University of Hull

0566

Address: 173 Cottingham Road, HULL
Year of creation: 1950
Parent Organization: University of Hull
Present Head: Professor V.A. McClelland
Size of staff. Total: 26 — Full time: 21 — Part time: 5
Researchers: 26
Research activities: from 25% to 50%
Educational research: more than 50%
Type of research: A wide range.
Functional objectives of research: A wide range: partial fulfilment of degree requirements; preparation of courses; chiefly advancing scholarship.
Periodical publications: Aspects of education. Research in science and technological education. English in education.
Monographs: Elliott, G.G. Self-evaluation and the teacher: an annotated bibliography and report on current practice. 1980. Elliott, G.G. The school curriculum in the 1980s. Richardson, G. Modern language teaching in the 1980s. Richardson, G. Teaching modern languages. Slean, M. Mini sport. Protherough, R. The development of readers. 1983.
Studies and surveys in preparation: Comparative and multicultural education with particular emphasis on special problems associated with educational development in small countries. Curriculum development in economics. Social and biological factors associated with intellectual, scholastic and emotional differences among school children. Early experience and later development. Curriculum development with particular emphasis on evaluation. The effects of continuity of educational experience. Complete list on request.

Institute of Education, University of London

0567

Address: 20 Bedford Way, LONDON WC1H 0AL
Year of creation: 1902
Parent Organization: University of London
Present Head: Professor Denis Lawton
Size of staff. Total: 528 — Full time: 395 — Part time: 133
Researchers: 59 — Full time: 44 — Part time: 15
Research activities: from 10% to 25%
Educational research: more than 50%
Type of research: Basic and applied research.
Functional objectives of research: Enlarge educational understanding and improve educational practice; carry out long and short-term projects and programmes commissioned or funded by government departments, research councils and foundations; offer research training to postgraduate students.
Periodical publications: Prospectus and calendar (1/yr).
Monographs: Studies in education (occasional papers). Inaugural and public lectures. Seminar papers.
Studies and surveys in preparation: The young child's representation of persons and the social world. Longitudinal study of child development. Assessment, screening and follow-up project. Community languages and education project. Training Third World educational administrators: methods and materials. Television in the

curriculum. Funding in education. Language information network. Linguistic minorities project. Complete list on request.

Institute of Educational Development

0568

Address: University of Surrey, GUILDFORD GU2 5XH
Year of creation: 1967
Parent Organization: University of Surrey
Present Head: Professor L.R.B. Elton
Size of staff. Total: 11 — Full time: 6 — Part time: 5
Researchers: 5 — Full time: 3 — Part time: 2
Research activities: 50%
Educational research: more than 50%
Type of research: Research and development.
Functional objectives of research: Improvement of teaching and learning; partial fulfilment of degree requirements.
Periodical publications: Studies in higher education. Higher education. European journal of science education. Aspects of educational technology. Physical education. British journal of educational technology.
Monographs: Training activities for teachers in higher education. Educational technology in science education and higher education.

Institute of Educational Technology, The Open University

0569

Address: Walton Hall, MILTON KEYNES MK7 6AA
Year of creation: 1970
Parent Organization: The Open University
Present Head: Professor David G. Hawkridge
Size of staff. Total: 100 — Full time: 95 — Part time: 5
Researchers: 60 — Full time: 60 — Part time: 3
Research activities: 50%
Educational research: more than 50%
Type of research: Research and development.
Functional objectives of research: Improve student learning in the university; extend and deepen knowledge base.
Periodical publications: Institute bibliography (1/yr, containing details of published and unpublished documents prepared by members of the Institute).
Monographs: Gibbs, G. Teaching students to learn. Hawkridge, D. New information technology in education. Hawkridge, D.; Robinson, J. Organizing educational broadcasting. Hawkridge, D., et al. Costs of new educational media, Vol 3. Henderson, E.; Perry, G. Change and development in schools. Kaye, T.; Harry, K. Using the media for adult basic education. Kaye, T., et al. Distance teaching for higher and adult education.
Studies and surveys in preparation: A wide range in the fields of: audiovisual media, continuing education, student assessment, textual communications.

International Centre for Multicultural Education

0570

Address: 9 Westbourne Road, Edgbaston, BIRMINGHAM B15 3TN
Year of creation: 1979
Parent Organization: Birmingham Polytechnic
Present Head: Derek Cherrington
Size of staff. Total: 5 — Full time: 5
Researchers: 1 — Part time: 1
Research activities: 50%
Educational research: 50%
Type of research: Applied research and development.
Functional objectives of research: Preparation of courses; partial fulfilment of degree requirements; international programme development; creation of data base.
Periodical publications: Multicultural education abstracts.
Studies and surveys in preparation: Review of West Indian literature in schools. Development of an international data base in multicultural studies.

National Foundation for Educational Research in England and Wales (NFER)

0571

Address: The Mere, Upton Park, SLOUGH, Berks., SL1 2DQ
Year of creation: 1946
Parent Organization: Private organization
Present Head: Dr. C. Burstall
Size of staff. Total: 125 — Full time: 106 — Part time: 19
Researchers: 53 — Full time: 47 — Part time: 6
Research activities: more than 50%
Educational research: more than 50%
Type of research: Applied research.
Functional objectives of research: Conduct applied research into problems of education at all levels within the State system; disseminate information and its findings.
Periodical publications: Book and test catalogues. Educational research (journal, 3/yr). Educational research news (newsletter).
Monographs: NFER Reports. Research in progress series.
Studies and surveys in preparation: Brochures and book lists on request from Library and Information Services.

National Institute for Careers Education and Counselling

0572

Address: Bateman Street, CAMBRIDGE CB2 1LZ
Year of creation: 1979
Parent Organization: Careers Research and Advisory Centre, Cambridge; Hatfield Polytechnic
Present Head: A.G. Watts, MA, MPhil
Size of staff. Total: 16 — Full time: 8 — Part time: 8
Researchers: 10 — Full time: 6 — Part time: 4
Research activities: from 25% to 50%
Educational research: more than 50%
Type of research: Career development; methods of careers guidance.
Functional objectives of research: To provide a sounder research base for the practice of careers guidance and related activities.

Periodical publications: British journal of guidance and counselling. NICEC Training and development bulletin. Supporting guidance.
Monographs: Complete list on request.
Studies and surveys in preparation: Guidance and the open tech. Curriculum-lead institutional development in further education. Education, unemployment and the future of work. Impact of new technology on female labour-force participation.

National Institute of Adult Continuing Education (England and Wales)

0573

Address: 19B De Montfort Street, LEICESTER LE1 7GE
Year of creation: 1949
Parent Organization: Independent body with official representation
Present Head: Arthur K. Stock
Size of staff. Total: 17 — Full time: 10 — Part time: 7
Researchers: 3 — Full time: 1 — Part time: 2
Research activities: from 10% to 25%
Type of research: Policy and applied research.
Functional objectives of research: To conduct applied research, usually connected with public policy, in area of adult continuing education.
Periodical publications: Studies in adult education (1/yr). Adult education (4/yr). Teaching adults (2/yr). Year book of adult continuing education (directory, 1/yr).
Monographs: Prison education in England and Wales. Preparation for retirement in England and Wales. Education and work (paid educational leave survey). Select bibliography of adult and continuing education in Great Britain. Research in adult education in the British Isles. Community colleges in England and Wales. Complete list on request.
Studies and surveys in preparation: Continuous update of 'Database I', a computer bank of research data in co-operation with Leicester University, resulting in various reports and print-outs, eg., 'Mature students', 'The elderly', etc. In collaboration with the Adult Literacy and Basic Skills Unit, creation of 'Database 2', on 'Resources for tutors in adult basic education', a computer printed bibliographical listing of resource material for specific enquiries.

Northern Ireland Council for Educational Research

0574

Address: NICER Research Unit, The Queen's University of Belfast, BELFAST BT9 5BS, Northern Ireland
Year of creation: 1963
Parent Organization: NICER (independent charitable foundation in receipt of grant-in-aid from the Department of Education for Northern Ireland)
Present Head: Dr. J.A. Wilson
Size of staff. Total: 15 — Full time: 14 — Part time: 1
Researchers: 10 — Full time: 10
Research activities: more than 50%
Educational research: more than 50%
Type of research: Applied and basic research.
Functional objectives of research: To encourage, organize and conduct educational research in Northern Ireland.
Periodical publications: NICER Bulletin (1/yr).
Monographs: List on request.

Studies and surveys in preparation: Participants' evaluation of the YTP curriculum. Curriculum evaluation in schools. Progress at 18: a follow-up of the 1975 cohort. Evaluation of management training for principal teachers. Area Board research and consultancy service. Preparation of a data archive. Follow-up of newly-trained teachers. APU in Northern Ireland.

Research Section, School Examinations Department, University of London

0575

Address: Stewart House, 32 Russell Square, LONDON WC1B 5DN
Year of creation: 1838
Parent Organization: University of London
Present Head: J.M. Kingdon BA, MEd, PhD, FSS
Size of staff. Total: 7 — Full time: 7
Researchers: 3 — Full time: 3
Research activities: more than 50%
Educational research: more than 50%
Type of research: Applied research into school examinations.
Functional objectives of research: Support for administrative and working parties developing new examinations.
Periodical publications: An annual report of the Section's work is contained in the Department's Research and development report.
Monographs: Wood, R.; Wilson, D.T. Determining a rank order when not all individuals are assessed on the same basis. In: Psychometrics for educational debates. 1980. Kingdon, J.M. Some statistical problems associated with the introduction of the new 16+ examination. 1982. Complete list on request.
Studies and surveys in preparation: Special staff interests include history of school examinations and geography of education.

Roehampton Institute

0576

Address: Roehampton Lane, LONDON SW15 5PJ
Year of creation: 1975
Present Head: K.W. Reohane
Size of staff. Total: 244 — Full time: 200
Research activities: less than 10%
Educational research: from 10% to 25%

School of Education, University College of North Wales

0577

Address: Lon Pobty, BANGOR, North Wales LL57 1DZ
Year of creation: 1884
Present Head: Professor I.W. Williams
Size of staff. Total: 31 — Full time: 23 — Part time: 8
Researchers: 8 — Full time: 8
Research activities: from 25% to 50%
Educational research: from 25% to 50%
Type of research: Action research, basic, applied, and R&D.
Functional objectives of research: Contributions to national policy; contributions to local classroom practice; higher degree work.
Periodical publications: None published.

Monographs: Complete list on request.
Studies and surveys in preparation: Bilingual education in Wales. Microcomputers and minority language contexts.

School of Education, University of Bristol

0578

Address: 35 Berkeley Square, BRISTOL BS8 1JA
Year of creation: 1969
Parent Organization: University of Bristol
Present Head: Professor Eric Hoyle, Dean
Size of staff. Total: 50 — Full time: 38 — Part time: 12
Researchers: 15 — Full time: 8 — Part time: 7
Research activities: from 25% to 50%
Educational research: more than 50%
Type of research: All types; basic and applied; research and development; evaluation.
Functional objectives of research: Degree requirements; government and other research grants bodies; various personal staff initiatives.
Monographs: Wells, G.G. Language, learning and education. 1982. McMahon, A.; Bolam, R. School-based induction: helping the beginning teacher. 1982. Bolam, R.; Baker, K. Staff development: Open University course. 1981. Kyle, J.G.; Allsop, L. Deaf people and the community. 1982. Complete list on request.
Studies and surveys in preparation: 10 projects dealing with communication, language, deafness, etc.

School of Education, University of Durham

0579

Address: Leazes Road, DURHAM DH1 1TA
Year of creation: 1979
Parent Organization: University of Durham
Present Head: Mr. P.R. May, J.P., B.A.
Size of staff. Total: 44 — Full time: 38 — Part time: 6
Researchers: 4 — Full time: 4
Research activities: from 25% to 50%
Educational research: more than 50%
Type of research: Basic, applied, research and development.
Functional objectives of research: Fulfilment of degree requirements (M.Ed, Ph.D.); individual staff research (usually in relation to staff interests); research commissioned by outside agencies.
Periodical publications: The Durham and Newcastle research review (a joint publication with Newcastle University School of Education).
Monographs: List on request.
Studies and surveys in preparation: Projects dealing with religious education, moral education, history teaching, teacher education, etc.

School of Education, University of East Anglia

0580

Address: University of East Anglia, NORWICH, Norfolk, NR4 7TJ
Year of creation: 1981
Parent Organization: University of East Anglia
Present Head: Professor H.T. Sockett

Size of staff. Total: 43 — Full time: 42 — Part time: 1
Researchers: 4
Research activities: from 25% to 50%
Educational research: more than 50%
Monographs: Bread and dreams: a case study of bilingual schooling in the USA. 1982. Torrance, H. Mode III examining: a study of experience. Final report of a Schools Council funded study: School-based examining and the professional development of teachers: a study of the worth and potential of the Mode III approach. 1982. Verma, G.K. The impact of innovation: a selection of evaluation papers about the Humanities Curriculum Project including an updated final account of the measurement programme. 1980. Brown, G.; Peelo, M. Aspirations and realizations: undergraduate attitudes to employment. 1982. Complete list on request.

School of Education, University of Exeter

0581

Address: Heavitree Road, EXETER EX1 2LU
Parent Organization: University of Exeter
Present Head: Professor E.C. Wragg, Director
Size of staff. Total: 91 — Full time: 84 — Part time: 7
Researchers: 6 — Full time: 6
Educational research: more than 50%
Type of research: Mainly applied, research and development.
Functional objectives of research: Various including higher degree work; funded projects and personal research.
Periodical publications: Perspectives in education.
Monographs: Research findings are published in national and international journals and in books.
Studies and surveys in preparation: There is presently an increased emphasis within the School on primary education, and research possibilities in this area will develop in the near future. Additionally, in the traditional disciplines of education: educational psychology and child development, sociology of education, philosophy of education, comparative education and curriculum studies. Finally, in some areas, special research projects are being followed: organisation of schools, classroom interaction, personal, social and moral education, health education, microcomputers in education, special educational needs, creative arts in education, education 16–19 and vocational guidance.

School of Education, University of Leeds

0582

Address: LEEDS LS2 9JT
Year of creation: 1976
Parent Organization: University of Leeds
Present Head: Mr. E.W. Jenkins
Size of staff. Total: 87 — Full time: 76 — Part time: 11
Researchers: 26 — Full time: 24 — Part time: 2
Type of research: All types.
Periodical publications: Journal of educational administration and history. Studies in science education. British journal of educational studies.
Monographs: Research in science and mathematics education 1968–82. Factors influencing the choice of advanced level mathematics by boys and girls. Teaching

microelectronics in schools. Concept development research in science and mathematics. Complete list on request.

Studies and surveys in preparation: Computer Based Learning Project. Children's Learning in Science Project. Assessment of performance unit (section of national investigation of performance in science at 11, 13–15). Participation of ethnic minority students in post-graduate teacher training.

School of Education, University of Leicester

0583

Address: 21 University Road, LEICESTER LE1 7RF
Year of creation: 1962
Parent Organization: University of Leicester
Present Head: Professor G. Bernbaum
Size of staff. Total: 37 — Full time: 35 — Part time: 2
Researchers: 7 — Full time: 7
Research activities: from 10% to 25%
Educational research: more than 50%
Type of research: Research and development.
Functional objectives of research: Personal and for funding bodies, e.g. SSRC, DES.
Monographs: Patrick, H.; Bernbaum, G.; Reid, K. The structure and process of initial teacher education within universities in England and Wales. Patrick, H.; Bernbaum, G.; Jackson, S. The national scholarships for priority teachers scheme. Sutton, C. Metaphorically speaking: the role of metaphor in teaching and learning science. Written work in science lessons: annotated extracts to illustrate a range of different kinds. Horsfield, J. Pupil controlled groups: small group discussion in biology. Complete list on request.

School of Education, University of Newcastle upon Tyne

0584

Address: St. Thomas' Street, NEWCASTLE UPON TYNE NE1 7RU
Year of creation: 1896
Parent Organization: University of Newcastle upon Tyne
Present Head: Professor A.D. Edwards
Size of staff. Total: 39 — Full time: 38 — Part time: 1
Researchers: 3 — Full time: 3
Research activities: from 10% to 25%
Educational research: more than 50%
Type of research: Basic and applied; research and development.
Functional objectives of research: Degree requirements sponsored; commissioned enquiries.
Periodical publications: Durham and Newcastle research review.
Monographs: Screening for early educational difficulties. 1983. Methods in social and educational caring. 1982. Skills in social and educational caring. 1983. Aims and priorities in upper secondary schools. 1983. Education in jeopardy. 1981. Doing better for fewer: education and falling rolls. 1983.
Studies and surveys in preparation: Music teaching and the development of young children. Training mathematics teachers in developing countries. The organization of post-compulsory schooling in England and Norway. The State and private education. Academic achievement and athletic achievement in multi-racial schools. Adolescents and solvent-abuse. Complete list on request.

Scottish Council for Educational Technology

0585

Address: 74 Victoria Crescent Road, Dowan Hill, GLASGOW G12 9JN
Year of creation: 1975
Parent Organization: Scottish Education Department
Present Head: Mr. R.B. Macluskie
Size of staff. Total: 203 — Full time: 186 — Part time: 17
Researchers: 12 — Full time: 10 — Part time: 2
Research activities: from 25% to 50%
Educational research: more than 50%
Type of research: Action research, development projects.
Functional objectives of research: Promote and encourage the understanding and application of educational technology in its widest sense throughout education and in commercial and industrial training. Promote and encourage the understanding of film and related media in their artistic and cultural aspects at all levels of the community.
Periodical publications: Educational technology news-sheet. News-sheet for industry and commerce. Journals listings.
Monographs: Henderson, J.; Humphries, F. Audio visual and microcomputer handbook: the SCET guide to educational and training equipment. Murray, J. Television studies in Scottish schools. Murray, J. Media education in Scotland: outline proposals for a curriculum. Hamilton, D.D.; Tucker, R.N. Resources centres in Scottish schools. Murray, J. The future of educational broadcasting: a discussion paper. Complete list on request.
Studies and surveys in preparation: Press studies in Scotland. Media studies development. Viewdata in special education. Electronic mail. Annotation of software information. Supported self study. Open learning systems. Educational broadcasting. Microelectronics in education. Resource organization and curriculum development. Details on request.

Scottish Council for Research in Education

0586

Address: 15 St. John Street, EDINBURGH EH8 8JR
Year of creation: 1928
Present Head: Dr. W. Bryan Dockrell
Size of staff. Total: 39 — Full time: 34 — Part time: 5
Researchers: 16 — Full time: 16
Research activities: more than 50%
Educational research: more than 50%
Type of research: Basic and applied research.
Functional objectives of research: To conduct educational research, to foster such activity within Scotland and to disseminate findings to all involved in education in Scotland.
Periodical publications: Research in education (free newsletter, 2/yr).
Monographs: Ryrie, A.C. On leaving school: a study of schooling, guidance and opportunity. Spencer, L. Soft skill competencies: their identification, measurement and development. Mangan, J.A.; Marker, W.B. Management and organization in a variety of open-plan schools. Cumming, C.E., et al. Making the change: a study of the process of the abolition of corporal punishment. Complete list on request.
Studies and surveys in preparation: Teaching strategies in the primary school. Second

International (IEA) Mathematics Survey. Community schools in Lothian region. After school: a study of young adults in Scotland. Evaluation of links between primary schools and non-formal education agencies. Complete list on request.

Scottish Curriculum Development Service: Glasgow Centre

0587

Address: Lymehurst House, Jordanhill College of Education, 76 Southbrae Drive, GLASGOW G13 1PP
Year of creation: 1971
Parent Organization: Consultative Committee on the curriculum (S.E.D.)
Present Head: Mr. T.K. Robinson, Director
Size of staff. Total: 18 — Full time: 11 — Part time: 7
Researchers: 5 — Full time: 5
Educational research: more than 50%
Type of research: Curriculum development (secondary education).
Functional objectives of research: Development of course guidelines and teaching materials.
Periodical publications: Social subjects (Newsletter of the Scottish Central Committee on Social Subjects). Newsletter of the Scottish Central Committee on Relegious Education. COSPEN News (Committee on Special Educational Needs). S.C.D.S. Annual joint centres newsletter.
Monographs: Curriculum guidelines for religious education. An inquiry into the teaching of modern studies in SI and SII. Integration in the social subjects in SII (third term). The SI/II social subjects curriculum. Primary/secondary liaison in environmental studies/social subjects. Series of 17 reports from the Education for the Industrial Society Project. Production of teaching materials.
Studies and surveys in preparation: Work in fields of money management. Consumer education. Special educational needs. Police and community courses. Environmental education.

Scottish Institute of Adult Education

0588

Address: 30 Rutland Square, EDINBURGH EH1 2BW
Year of creation: 1949
Parent Organization: Scottish Education Department
Present Head: Dr. Elisabeth Gerver
Size of staff. Total: 4 — Full time: 2 — Part time: 2
Research activities: from 10% to 25%
Educational research: from 10% to 25%
Type of research: Basic and applied.
Functional objectives of research: Servicing the educational administration.
Periodical publications: Scottish journal of adult education (2/yr). Scottish handbook of adult education.
Monographs: Gerver, E.; Wilson, V. Computers and adult learning: recent developments in new opportunities for women. Bryant, I. The educational needs of long-term unemployed adults. Cosgrove, D.; Nelson, P. Continuing education: recommendations in Strathclyde region. MacDonald, C. Mature students in higher and further education in Strathclyde region.
Studies and surveys in preparation: Computers in community education. Survey of counselling provision for adults in mid-career. History of network.

South Glamorgan Institute of Higher Education, Cardiff **0589**

Address: Western Avenue, CARDIFF CF5 2YB
Year of creation: 1976
Parent Organization: South Glamorgan County Council
Present Head: E.J. Brent
Size of staff. Total: 500 — Full time: 500
Research activities: from 10% to 25%
Educational research: from 10% to 25%
Type of research: Basic and applied.
Functional objectives of research: Fulfilment of degree requirements; servicing education.
Monographs: Scott, B. Historical enquiry and the younger pupil in 'New history: old problems'. Tattum, D.P. The general area of disruptive pupil behaviour. Complete list on request.
Studies and surveys in preparation: The universities and the development of public, further and higher (technological) education in England and Wales. A study of the developmental characteristics of the human figure schema in the drawings of children aged four to seven years. Personal autonomy and integrated curricula. Student attitudes to liberal studies. The development of 'consistency management' at school and classroom levels, with particular reference to the prevention of pupil indiscipline. Relationship between research and application in the field of educational technology. Student maturity as a factor in further education: implications for curriculum development and evaluation. Complete list on request.

UKRAINIAN SSR

Naučno-issledovatel'skij institut pedagogiki Ministerstva prosveščenija Ukrainskoj SSR **0590**

Translation: Research Institute of Pedagogics of the Ministry of Education of the Ukrainian SSR
Address: Ul. Lenina 10, KIEV 252030
Year of creation: 1926
Parent Organization: Ministry of Education of the Ukrainian SSR
Present Head: Prof. N.D. Jarmačenko
Size of staff. Total: 251
Researchers: 196
Type of research: Basic and applied research.
Functional objectives of research: Improvement of the content, forms and methods of teaching and education of children under school age and of school children; the problems of improvement in school management.
Periodical publications: None issued.
Monographs: List on request.
Studies and surveys in preparation: Content, forms and methods for education, upbringing and development of 6-year-old children. School and family work in building up students' maturity. Problems of labour education.

Naučno-issledovatel'skij institut psihologii Ministerstva prosveščenija Ukrainskoj SSR **0591**

Translation: Research Institute of Psychology of the Ministry of Education of the Ukrainian SSR
Address: Ul. S. Halturina 2, KIEV 252033
Year of creation: 1945
Parent Organization: Ministry of Education of the Ukrainian SSR
Present Head: Prof. L.N. Prokolienko
Size of staff. Total: 203
Researchers: 153
Research activities: more than 50%
Educational research: more than 50%
Type of research: Basic and applied research.
Functional objectives of research: Problems of general, child, adult and educational psychology.
Periodical publications: Psyhologij (Republican serial).
Monographs: Psyhologičeskij slovar'. 1982. Gitchan, I.S. Psyhologo-pedagogičeskaja kultura nastavnika. 1981.
Studies and surveys in preparation: Psychology of instruction and upbringing methodology of psychological research. Psychology of teachers' collective. Psychology of professional orientation and preparation for work.

UNITED ARAB EMIRATES

Kulliyyat at-tarbiya **0592**

Translation: Faculty of Education
Address: P.O. Box 15551, AL-AIN, Abu Dhabi
Year of creation: 1977
Parent Organization: United Arab Emirates University
Present Head: Dr. Sayed Mohamed Ghoneim
Size of staff. Total: 22 — Full time: 22
Researchers: all — Full time: all
Research activities: 50%
Educational research: from 25% to 50%
Type of research: Basic and applied research and development.
Functional objectives of research: Research into academic achievement; prepare courses; develop curricula; educational services and teacher training.
Periodical publications: United Arab Emirates University magazine.
Monographs: None published.
Studies and surveys in preparation: Attributional style in depression. Sex differences in attributional style. Draw a family test as a clinical tool. Public schools and technical and vocational education: problems and solutions.

Qism al-buḫūt wa-ăt-tawtīq wa-ăl-maktaba al-markaziyya

0593

Translation: Research and Documentation Department
Address: General Administration of Educational Planning, P.O. Box 3962, DUBAI
Year of creation: 1980
Parent Organization: Ministry of Education, General Administration of Educational Planning
Present Head: Abdul Hussain Al Haddad
Size of staff. Total: 2 — Full time: 2
Researchers: 1 — Full time: 1
Research activities: more than 50%
Educational research: more than 50%
Type of research: Basic and applied research.
Functional objectives of research: Research related to educational planning and field work in schools and analysing exam results.
Studies and surveys in preparation: Diagnostic testing and its effects on mathematics achievement. Survey of school buildings in U.A.E. Research priorities in education in U.A.E. Kindergarten and its effect on children's achievement in primary schools. Causes of lack of entry to technical schools in U.A.E.

URUGUAY

Departamento de Investigaciones Educacionales (DINED)

0594

Address: Av. Libertador Brigadier General Lavalleja 2025, MONTEVIDEO
Year of creation: 1975
Parent Organization: Consejo Nacional de Educación, Instituto Nacional de Docencia "General Artigas", Centro III
Present Head: Prof. Juan Antonio Vazquez Petrides
Size of staff. Total: 2 — Full time: 2
Researchers: 2 — Full time: 2
Type of research: Investigación básica y aplicada.
Functional objectives of research: Apoyo curricular y asistencia técnica a los cursos del Proyecto Multinacional de OEA y a los cursos para directores del Centro III.
Periodical publications: No publica.
Monographs: Memoria técnica 1982 PREDE de OEA. Memoria técnica 1981 PREDE de OEA. El método de asociación de McGinnis: material modular. Habilidades básicas: material modular. Detección de carencia de información y (o) aprendizaje en docentes que trabajan con niños con dificultades específicas de aprendizaje: investigación aplicada.
Studies and surveys in preparation: Proceso de validación de materiales modulares arriba mencionados. Estudio sobre las necesidades de actualización de adultos que no han realizado el ciclo básico: investigación básica. Material modular de educación a distancia para adultos que no realizaron ciclo básico.

USA

Appalachia Educational Laboratory, Inc.

0595

Address: P.O. Box 1348, CHARLESTON, WV 25325
Year of creation: 1966
Present Head: Dr. Terry L. Eidell
Size of staff. Total: 36 — Full time: 28 — Part time: 8
Researchers: 15 — Full time: 13 — Part time: 2
Research activities: 50%
Educational research: more than 50%
Type of research: Educational research and development.
Functional objectives of research: To improve education and educational opportunity for those who live in AEL's primarily non-urban region.
Periodical publications: The Link (6/yr).
Monographs: The decline of standardized test scores in the United States from 1965 to present. Effective schools are America's best bet: summary and proceedings of the 1983 AEL Regional Forum. Considering the research: what makes an effective school? School effectiveness: climate, goals and leadership. Community survey model for school districts: procedural guide. Improving school practice: summary and proceedings of the 1981 AEL Regional Forum. Forum of State procedures for validation of educational programs. (Papers available through ERIC).
Studies and surveys in preparation: AEL's current work is focused in the areas of basic skills, school/family relations and lifelong learning.

Bureau of Educational Evaluation, Inc.

0596

Address: 2 Rockaway Avenue, GARDEN CITY, NY 11530
Year of creation: 1974
Present Head: Dr. Esin Kaya-Carton
Size of staff. Total: 7 — Full time: 2 — Part time: 5
Researchers: 5 — Full time: 2 — Part time: 3
Research activities: more than 50%
Educational research: more than 50%
Type of research: Basic (less than 10%), applied (over 50%), R&D (from 10-25 %).
Functional objectives of research: Evaluation studies for improving education; basic research in cognitive processes, creativity, humour, research methodology; language development and semiotics.
Periodical publications: Annuar reports.
Monographs: Lieberman, L. Report on needs assessment of research and evaluation needs in Nassau County school districts. 1980. Kaya-Carton, E. Evaluation report on the bilingual/bicultural program of the Wyandanch school district. Annual reports: 1980, 1981, 1982, 1983. Kaya-Carton, E. Final report to the Ford Foundation on the preparation of a plan for the formative and summative evaluation of the instrumental enrichment program as implemented in the schools. 1982. Kaya-Carton, E. Diary of an independent evaluator: paper given at the Annual Conference of the Evaluation Network and Evaluation Research Society. 1983. Complete list on request.
Studies and surveys in preparation: Cross-cultural study of humour preferences and humour production of children, teenagers, adults. Correlation between humour preference category and creativity. Differences in humour production and preference

between monolingual and bilingual children. Evaluation of two different bilingual training programmes.

Bureau of Educational Research and Evaluation

0597

Address: College of Education, Mississippi State University, Box 5365, MISSISSIPPI STATE, MS 39762
Year of creation: 1963
Parent Organization: Mississippi State University
Present Head: James E. Wall
Size of staff. Total: 10 — Full time: 8 — Part time: 2
Researchers: 7 — Full time: 5 — Part time: 2
Research activities: more than 50%
Educational research: more than 50%
Type of research: Testing; measurement; curriculum design of evaluation, etc.; basic, applied, R&D.
Functional objectives of research: Curricular evaluation; servicing educational administration; test item bank development; test development; etc.
Periodical publications: BERE Annual report. Annual report of the program of research and evaluation for public schools.
Monographs: Individual project reports.
Studies and surveys in preparation: Testing. Curriculum evaluation. Administration data.

Center for Cross-Cultural Studies

0598

Address: 708A Gruening Building, University of Alaska, FAIRBANKS, AK 99701
Year of creation: 1971
Parent Organization: University of Alaska
Present Head: Gerald V. Mohatt
Size of staff. Total: 7 — Full time: 7 — Part time: 0.5
Researchers: 5 — Full time: 5 — Part time: 0.5
Research activities: from 25% to 50%
Educational research: more than 50%
Type of research: Basic, applied, and research and development.
Functional objectives of research: Preparation of courses; servicing the educational administration; comparative research.
Periodical publications: Small schools exchange (newsletter). Behavioural sciences and human services newsletter.
Monographs: Barnhardt, R.; Chilcott, J.; Wolcott, H. Anthropology and educational administration. 1979. Barnhardt, R., ed. Cross-issues in Alaskan education, vol. 2, 1982. Barnhardt, R. Culture, community and the curriculum. 1981. Curriculum resources for the Alaskan environment: small high schools project. 1981. Kleinfeld, J. Eskimo school on the Andreafsky: a study of effective bicultural education. 1979. Complete list on request.
Studies and surveys in preparation: Youth organizations as a third educational environment. Effective teachers in rural Alaska. Decentralized education in rural Alaska. Complete list on request.

Center for Educational Development

0599

Address: University of Illinois at Chicago, Health Sciences Center, 808 South Wook, 9th floor, CHICAGO, IL 60612
Parent Organization: University of Illinois
Present Head: Dr. Ronald Richards, Director
Size of staff. Total: 54 — Full time: 51 — Part time: 3
Researchers: 25 — Full time: 22 — Part time: 3
Research activities: from 25% to 50%
Educational research: more than 50%
Type of research: Basic and applied research on innovation implementation in education, cost containment in medical education, clinical education, interprofessional training, curriculum design, student and programme evaluation.
Functional objectives of research: To improve health care through innovations in health professions education; to facilitate implementation of those innovations; and to evaluate the process and results.
Periodical publications: Courier (newsletter, 4/yr). Annual report.
Monographs: Monograph currently in production on institutional self-assessment in developing countries. Competence in medical technology. 1980. Competence in clinical dietetics. 1980. Comptence in occupational therapy. 1980.
Studies and surveys in preparation: Curriculum innovation process in medical schools. Survey of problem-based medical schools in WHO innovative network. Impact of prospective reimbursement on medical education. Use of microcomputer/videodisc technology in medical education. Observations of medical clerkships.

Center for Educational Research and Evaluation

0600

Address: P.O. Box 12194, RESEARCH TRIANGLE PARK, NC 27709
Year of creation: 1971
Parent Organization: Research Triangle Institute
Present Head: Dr. J.A. Davis
Size of staff. Total: 40
Researchers: 32
Type of research: Basic and applied research.
Functional objectives of research: Evaluation of federal investment in educational activity; education statistics surveys and evaluation.

Center for Educational Research at Stanford (CERAS)

0601

Address: Stanford University, STANFORD, CA 94305
Year of creation: 1965
Parent Organization: School of Education, Stanford University
Present Head: J. Myron Atkin, Dean
Size of staff. Total: 150
Type of research: Basic and applied research.
Functional objectives of research: Carry out research projects linked to educational practice, to the improvement of American primary and secondary schools, and to educational policy and administration at local, State, and federal levels; provide a forum through conferences and workshops for educational leaders from different disciplines and backgrounds.

Monographs: Handled by individual projects — list on request.
Studies and surveys in preparation: Stanford and the schools study, investigating curriculum, educational technology, testing, personal responsibility, comprehensive high schools, teacher preparation; funded by the University and outside agencies. Several research programmes within the framework of the Institute for Research on Educational Finance and Governance, funded by the National Institute of Education. Programme for complex instruction, refining and implementing an instructional design for second to fourth-grade children using multilingual and non-lingual material called 'Finding out/Descubrimiento', funded by the Johnson Foundation. Reading research, teacher training, intercultural communication, health in youth, stress, and other projects, variously funded.

Center for Educational Technology **0602**

Address: Florida State University, TALLAHASSEE, FL 32306
Year of creation: 1974
Parent Organization: Learning Systems Institute, Florida State University
Present Head: Robert K. Branson
Size of staff. Total: 60 — Full time: 40 — Part time: 20
Researchers: 35 — Full time: 10 — Part time: 25
Research activities: more than 50%
Educational research: more than 50%
Type of research: Basic (20%), applied (50%), research and development (30%).
Functional objectives of research: Development of computer-based instruction programme in basic adult skills of reading, writing, communication, organizational effectiveness, learning strategies, stress control, etc.; many doctoral students conducting research towards the fulfilment of their degrees.
Periodical publications: The journal of instructional development (4/yr).
Monographs: Branson, R.K.; Rayner, G.T.; Kormanicki, M.J.; Erdman, A.M. Job and task analysis of Florida law enforcement officers: final report. 1981. Branson, R.K.; Rayner, G.T.; Kormanicki, M.J.; Erdman, A.M. Job and task analysis of Florida law enforcement officers: executive summary. 1981.
Studies and surveys in preparation: Project to develop basic adult skills education for the US Army, using computer-based instruction on the PLATO and TICCIT systems. Research into learning strategies, mood management, and stress reduction for students using computer-based instruction. Research into computer-based instruction-design of lessons and management of large-scale production. Research into the language used in computer-based instruction, as well as research on the writing problems of scholarly writers. Research into evaluation methods in higher education, the measurement of change due to instruction, and the employability of persons receiving certain federal welfare assistance.

Center for Innovation in Teaching the Handicapped **0603**

Address: 2805 E.10th St, Smith Research Center, Room 150, BLOOMINGTON, IN 47405
Year of creation: 1969
Parent Organization: Indiana University, Bloomington
Present Head: Dr. Herbert J. Rieth
Size of staff. Total: 60 — Full time: 40 — Part time: 20

Researchers: 50 — Full time: 40 — Part time: 10
Research activities: more than 50%
Educational research: more than 50%
Type of research: Basic, applied, research and development.
Functional objectives of research: Development of innovative instructional techniques and materials for the handicapped.
Monographs: Numerous articles in journals.
Studies and surveys in preparation: An analysis of the instructional and contextual variables that influence the efficacy of computer-based instruction for mildly handicapped secondary school students. A special project to develop and implement a microcomputer-based special teacher education and evaluation laboratory (STEEL). HCEEP: early childhood model program for serving handicapped children residing in rural environments.

Center for Instructional Research and Curriculum Evaluation

0604

Address: 1310 South Sixth Street, CHAMPAIGN, IL 61801
Year of creation: 1963
Parent Organization: University of Illinois
Present Head: Robert E. Stake
Size of staff. Total: 7 — Full time: 3 — Part time: 4
Researchers: 7 — Full time: 3 — Part time: 4
Research activities: more than 50%
Educational research: more than 50%
Type of research: Programme evaluation.
Functional objectives of research: Improve evaluation methodology.
Periodical publications: None published.
Monographs: None published.
Studies and surveys in preparation: Metaevaluation of urban programmes. School art case studies. Sex equity education demonstration (Eval). Audit of promotional gates (NYC).

Center for Needs Assessment and Planning

0605

Address: Florida State University, TALLAHASSEE, FL 32306
Year of creation: 1977
Parent Organization: Florida State University
Present Head: Roger Kaufman
Size of staff. Total: 11 — Full time: 6 — Part time: 5
Researchers: 7 — Full time: 4 — Part time: 3
Research activities: more than 50%
Educational research: more than 50%
Type of research: Needs assessment; policy analysis; formative and summative evaluation; applied history; bilingual education.
Functional objectives of research: Assist decision makers in the improvement of their organization by improving its effectiveness and efficiency.
Periodical publications: Journal of instruction and design. Educational technology. The Public historian. Florida vocational journal. Performance and instruction journal. Group and organizational studies. Educational leadership. Educational researcher. Revista Educación básica.

Monographs: A history of vocational education in Florida. Technology in education: its human potential. Evaluation without fear. Planning for organizational success: a practical guide. Needs assessment: concept and application.
Studies and surveys in preparation: Developing training manuals on needs assessment. History-based policy analysis: a history of vocational education in the State of Florida and strategic planning.

Center for Research on Learning and Teaching

0606

Address: 109 E. Madison Street, ANN ARBOR, MI 48109
Year of creation: 1962
Parent Organization: The University of Michigan
Present Head: Dr. Donald R. Brown
Size of staff. Total: 30 — Full time: 12 — Part time: 18
Researchers: 12 — Full time: 3 — Part time: 9
Type of research: Applied.
Functional objectives of research: Development of conceptual base for practice; servicing the faculty.
Periodical publications: Triennial report. CRLT Reports.
Monographs: List on request.
Studies and surveys in preparation: Student development. Personality and value change. Professionalization and socialization of professional students. Dissemination of innovations. Educational technology. Computer-assisted instruction. Research synthesis. Evaluation. Faculty development. Basic skills. Student learning.

Center for the Study of Cognitive Processes

0607

Address: Wayne State University, 71 W. Warren, DETROIT, MI 48202
Parent Organization: Merril-Palmer Institute
Present Head: Patricia Siple, PhD
Size of staff. Total: 15 — Full time: 2 — Part time: 13
Researchers: 7 — Part time: 7
Research activities: more than 50%
Educational research: from 10% to 25%
Type of research: Primarily basic.
Functional objectives of research: Basic research in cognition and language.
Periodical publications: Center report series in planning stage.
Studies and surveys in preparation: Conceptual development. Memory development. Psycholinguistics.

Center for the Study of Evaluation (CSE)

0608

Address: UCLA Graduate School of Education, 405 Hilgard Avenue, 145 Moore Hall, LOS ANGELES, CA 90024
Year of creation: 1966
Parent Organization: Graduate School of Education, University of California, Los Angeles
Present Head: Dr. Eva L. Baker
Size of staff. Total: N/A — Full time: N/A — Part time: N/A
Researchers: N/A — Full time: N/A — Part time: N/A

Type of research: Basic research.
Functional objectives of research: Produce and research findings directly applicable to meeting the increasing requirements for evaluation and social action programmers.
Periodical publications: CSE Monograph series. Evaluation comment. CSE Technical reports. CSE Resource papers.
Monographs: Complete list on request.

Center for the Study of Psychoeducational Processes (PEP Center) **0609**

Address: Ritter Annex 721, Broad & Columbia Ave, PHILADELPHIA, PA 19147
Year of creation: 1975
Parent Organization: Temple University College of Education, Department of Psychoeducational Processes
Present Head: Susan Wheelan PhD.; Marvin H. Berman M.Ed.
Size of staff. Total: 15 — Part time: 15
Researchers: 4 — Part time: 4
Research activities: from 25% to 50%
Educational research: from 25% to 50%
Type of research: Basic — group relations conference studies; applied — action research, field studies; research and development — needs analyses.
Functional objectives of research: Degree requirements; educational models evaluation; curriculum design studies.
Periodical publications: Semester reports. PEPCenter monograph series.
Monographs: The role of the teacher in the classroom. How to discipline without feeling guilty. Do you see what I see? Student-directed learning. Complete list on request.
Studies and surveys in preparation: Tavistock Group Relations Conference: an analysis of participant outcomes concerning changes in learning about self/others, groups and interpersonal relationships.

Chicago Institute for the Study of Learning Disabilities **0610**

Address: Box 4348, CHICAGO, IL 60680
Parent Organization: University of Illinois at Chicago, College of Education
Present Head: Professor Tanis Bryan, Director
Size of staff. Total: 7 — Full time: 2 — Part time: 5
Researchers: 6
Research activities: more than 50%
Educational research: more than 50%
Type of research: Applied.
Functional objectives of research: Advance knowledge of learning disabilities.
Periodical publications: Research abstract.
Monographs: Bryan, T.; Werner, M.; Pearl, R. Learning disabled children's conformity responses to prosocial and antisocial situations. Humphreys, M.; Hall, J. Do learning disabled children have a memory problem? Logical and methodological considerations. The influence of pupil behaviors and pupil status factors on teacher behaviors during oral reading lessons. Pflaum, S. The predictability of oral reading behaviors on comprehension in learning disabled and normal readers. Complete list on request.
Studies and surveys in preparation: None.

College of Education, Southern Illinois University

0611

Address: Dean's Office, Southern Illinois University-Carbondale, CARBONDALE, IL 62901
Parent Organization: Southern Illinois University
Present Head: Dr. Donald L. Beggs, Dean; Dr. Albert Somit, President; Dr. Kenneth Shaw, Chancellor
Size of staff. Total: 162 — Full time: 160 — Part time: 2
Researchers: 4 — Full time: 2 — Part time: 2
Research activities: from 10% to 25%
Educational research: from 10% to 25%
Type of research: Basic, applied, R&D.
Functional objectives of research: Create new knowledge; meet RFP requirements.
Monographs: Numerous articles in scientific and professional journals. Complete list on request.
Studies and surveys in preparation: Unavailable.

College of Education, University of Delaware

0612

Address: NEWARK, DE 19711
Year of creation: 1944
Parent Organization: University of Delaware
Present Head: Frank B. Murray, Dean, College of Education
Researchers: 42 — Full time: 38 — Part time: 4
Research activities: from 10% to 25%
Educational research: more than 50%
Type of research: Research and development.
Functional objectives of research: Partial fulfilment of degree requirements, preparation of courses, servicing the educational administration.
Periodical publications: Partnership. Research report.

College of Education, University of Georgia

0613

Address: Aderhold Hall, University of Georgia, ATHENS, GA 30607
Year of creation: 1785
Parent Organization: University of Georgia
Present Head: Dr. Alphonse Buccino, Dean
Size of staff. Total: 261 — Full time: 261
Researchers: 139 — Part time: 139
Research activities: from 10% to 25%
Educational research: more than 50%
Type of research: All: basic, applied, research and development.
Functional objectives of research: Contributing to our knowledge base about teaching, learning and schooling.
Periodical publications: Journal of research and development in education.
Studies and surveys in preparation: List on request.

College of Education, University of Missouri–Columbia

0614

Address: 109 Hill Hall, COLUMBIA, MS 65211
Parent Organization: Curators of the University of Missouri
Present Head: Dean Bob G. Woods
Size of staff. Total: 165 — Full time: 117 — Part time: 48
Researchers: 117
Research activities: from 10% to 25%
Educational research: more than 50%
Type of research: Research and development.
Functional objectives of research: Research represents one of the three major missions of the College of Education and therefore is an ongoing effort of the faculty.
Periodical publications: Journal of career education.
Monographs: Individual faculty may have had monographs published; however, the College of Education as an organization has had no such publication during the last three years.
Studies and surveys in preparation: Parental influences on emerging language. Computational estimation in mathematics. Lifelong reading. Middle school principalships. Dropouts from public schools. Career education for the handicapped. Identification of behaviour disordered children and youth. Complete list on request.

College of Education, University of South Carolina

0615

Address: Wardlaw College, COLUMBIA, SC 29208
Year of creation: 1801
Parent Organization: University of South Carolina
Present Head: Dr. John D. Mulhern, Dean
Size of staff. Total: 105 — Full time: 85 — Part time: 20
Researchers: 60
Research activities: from 25% to 50%
Type of research: Basic and applied.
Functional objectives of research: Background and preparation for courses and scholarship.

College of Human Resources and Education

0616

Address: 802 Allen Hall, P.O.Box 6122, MORGANTOWN, WV 26506-6122
Year of creation: 1967
Parent Organization: West Virginia University
Present Head: Diane L. Reinhard, Dean
Size of staff. Total: 182 — Full time: 122 — Part time: 60
Researchers: 122 — Full time: 122
Research activities: from 10% to 25%
Educational research: from 10% to 25%
Type of research: Applied, development.
Functional objectives of research: Improvement of schools and colleges; partial fulfilment of degree requirements.

Computer-Based Education Research Laboratory **0617**

Address: 103 S. Mathew, URBANA, IL 61801
Year of creation: 1960
Parent Organization: University of Illinois
Present Head: Dr. Donald L. Bitzer
Size of staff. Total: 140 — Full time: 100 — Part time: 40
Researchers: 62
Research activities: more than 50%
Educational research: from 25% to 50%
Type of research: Computer hardware, software and courseware development.
Functional objectives of research: Production of high quality compter-based education.
Studies and surveys in preparation: Continuance of studies and further development of PLATO (Programmed Logic for Automatic Teaching Operation) system, initiated by coordinated Science Laboratory at the University.

Cooperative Education Research Center, Northeastern University **0618**

Address: 360 Huntington Ave, BOSTON, MA 02115
Year of creation: 1968
Parent Organization: Northeastern University
Present Head: Dr. James W. Wilson
Size of staff. Total: 7 — Full time: 5 — Part time: 2
Researchers: 3 — Full time: 2 — Part time: 1
Research activities: more than 50%
Educational research: more than 50%
Type of research: Basic and applied.
Functional objectives of research: Extend knowledge of work-related education.
Periodical publications: Undergraduate programs of cooperative education in the United States and Canada.
Monographs: Weinstein, D. Cooperative education strategies and student career development. Weinstein, D. Cooperative education program strategies and career decision making.
Studies and surveys in preparation: Benefits/costs of employer participation in cooperative education. Impact of cooperative education on graduate's sense of power on first full time job after graduation.

Curriculum Research and Development Group **0619**

Address: 1776 University Avenue, HONOLULU, HA 96822
Year of creation: 1966
Parent Organization: College of Education, University of Hawaii
Present Head: Arthur R. King, Jr.
Size of staff. Total: 87 — Full time: 66 — Part time: 21
Researchers: 57 — Full time: 50 — Part time: 7
Research activities: more than 50%
Educational research: more than 50%
Type of research: Curriculum research and development.
Functional objectives of research: Conduct research and development in the subject areas and concerns of the school curriculum, publishes related materials, and

provides training services to schools.
Periodical publications: None published.
Monographs: Kent, G. Common heritage. Conceptual barriers to use of the oceans. Freedom of the seas: past, present and future. Marine cultural interaction. Complete list on request.
Studies and surveys in preparation: English language arts for secondary schools. Science for middle schools. Music for elementary schools. History of modern Hawaii. Nature studies for elementary schools. Marine science studies. Consumer education. Computers and other technology in mathematics education. High school physics and physiology. Computer applications in early childhood education, composition, science and nutrition. Language and telecommunications study. Complete list on request.

Department of Education, Cornell University

0620

Address: 100 Stone Hall, ITHACA, NY 14853
Year of creation: 1865
Parent Organization: State University of New York (S.U.N.Y.)
Present Head: Professor Joe P. Bail
Size of staff. Total: 100 — Full time: 40 — Part time: 60
Researchers: 30 — Part time: 30
Research activities: 50%
Educational research: more than 50%
Type of research: Basic, applied and development.
Functional objectives of research: Degree requiments; school and society problems; school organization, management and curriculum; reading.
Periodical publications: Edalus II.
Monographs: List on request.
Studies and surveys in preparation: 26 projects dealing with concept learning, aptitude, teacher education, rural education, educational economics and policy. Complete list on request.

Department of Education, University of Chicago

0621

Address: 5835 Kimbark Avenue, CHICAGO, IL 60637
Year of creation: 1897
Parent Organization: University of Chicago
Present Head: Charles E. Bidwell
Size of staff. Total: 47 — Full time: 42 — Part time: 5
Researchers: 36 — Full time: 36
Research activities: 50%
Educational research: more than 50%
Type of research: Basic.
Functional objectives of research: Scholarly publication.
Periodical publications: American journal of education.
Monographs: List on request.
Studies and surveys in preparation: Cognitive bases of instruction. Institutional frame of educational systems (intra- and cross-national). Analysis of curriculum. Theory of educational measurement and programme evaluation.

Department of General Education, Atlanta Public Schools 0622

Address: 2930 Forest Hill Drive, S.W., Suite 205, ATLANTA, GA 30315
Year of creation: 1872
Parent Organization: Board of Education of the City of Atlanta is fiscal and political bureau responsible
Present Head: Dr. Alonzo Crim; Dr. Sidney H. Estes; Dr. Mae A. Christian
Size of staff. Total: 4820 — Full time: 4820
Researchers: 20 — Full time: 20
Research activities: from 10% to 25%
Educational research: from 10% to 25%
Type of research: Applied research, R&D.
Functional objectives of research: To provide a quality education for the 69,000 children in the Atlanta Public Schools; to develop, plan, implement, assess, and build excellence in curriculum.
Periodical publications: Research and evaluation reports. Update. Connection (newsletter). "Bits, bytes, basics" (newsletter — research and evaluation, and data processing).
Monographs: Christian, M., et al. Implementation guide: semester conversion. Christian, M., et al. The humane management of the educational behavior of adults and students: a guide. Christian, M., et al. Oral skills development: an instructional approach. Christian, M., et al. Applying practical test-taking skills. Christian, M., et al. A guide for teaching reading in the content area.
Studies and surveys in preparation: High school (ninth grade) Language arts standardization model. New report cards: kindergarten, elementary and middle schools.

Department of Higher and Adult Education 0623

Address: Arizona State University, TEMPE, AZ 85287
Year of creation: 1964
Parent Organization: College of Education, Arizona State University
Present Head: Dr. Richard C. Richardson, Jr., Professor and Chair
Size of staff. Total: 14 — Full time: 10 — Part time: 4
Researchers: 9 — Full time: 5 — Part time: 4
Research activities: from 25% to 50%
Educational research: from 25% to 50%
Type of research: Comparative case studies, surveys, policy analysis.
Functional objectives of research: Colleges and universities as organizations; education as older adults; student characteristics and persistence.
Periodical publications: None published.
Monographs: List on request.
Studies and surveys in preparation: University goals and priorities. Organizational effectiveness. Subjective studies of satisfaction in adulthood.

Division of Counseling and Educational Psychology, College of Education 0624

Address: 327 CEDAR Building, The Pennsylvania State University, UNIVERSITY PARK, PA 16802
Year of creation: 1976

Parent Organization: College of Education, The Pennsylvania State University
Present Head: Dr. Eowin L. Herr
Size of staff. Total: 43 — Full time: 35 — Part time: 8
Researchers: 19 — Full time: 15 — Part time: 4
Research activities: from 25% to 50%
Educational research: from 10% to 25%
Type of research: Basic, applied, research and development.
Functional objectives of research: Partial fulfilment of degree requirements; completing contracted research studies; expanding knowledge base in education and related areas.
Periodical publications: Researchers publish in independent periodicals.
Monographs: Researchers write monographs for other publishers.
Studies and surveys in preparation: Longitudinal studies of career behaviour. Cognitive (behaviour) interventions in obesity control, anger management, rapid smoking and other social problems. Methods of drug abuse prevention. Cognitive restructuring in primary prevention. Early language development in children. Flex level testing models. Cross-cultural counselling. Intellectual assessment of children.

Drexel Early Childhood Center

0625

Address: 227 North 34th Street, PHILADELPHIA, PA 19104
Year of creation: 1924
Parent Organization: Drexel University
Present Head: Mrs. Lois Baker, Director
Size of staff. Total: 12 — Full time: 1 — Part time: 11
Researchers: 3 — Part time: 3
Research activities: less than 10%
Educational research: more than 50%
Type of research: Research and development.
Functional objectives of research: Development of new knowledge and pedagogical systems.
Monographs: Lazur, I.; Swinton, S. Education and technology (in preparation).
Studies and surveys in preparation: Use of technology with pre-school children. Use of LOGO and personal computers with pre-school children. Use of children's learning styles (auditory, visual, tactile) to develop reading skills.

Education Development Center Inc.

0626

Address: 66 Chapel Street, NEWTON, MA 02160
Year of creation: 1958
Present Head: Janet Whitla, President
Size of staff. Total: 65 — Full time: 60 — Part time: 5
Researchers: 20 — Full time: 18 — Part time: 2
Research activities: 50%
Educational research: 50%
Periodical publications: Annual report.

Education Research & Projects

0627

Address: 408 Classroom Building, STILLWATER, OK 74078
Year of creation: 1974
Parent Organization: Oklahoma State University
Present Head: Kenneth H. McKinley
Size of staff. Total: 16 — Full time: 15 — Part time: 1
Researchers: 9 — Full time: 9
Research activities: less than 10%
Educational research: more than 50%
Type of research: Developmental and applied research.
Functional objectives of research: Partial fulfilment of degree requirements; programme analysis; programme review analysis; curriculum development; policy research and applied organizational developmental research that serves the college, university, and state educational system.
Periodical publications: College of Education annual research report. Oklahoma State University annual research report.
Monographs: Diagnostic and prescriptive mathematics: issues, ideas and insights.
Studies and surveys in preparation: Oklahoma Teacher Mobility Study.

Educational Research Center, College of Education

0628

Address: New Mexico State University, Box 3R, LAS CRUCES, NM 88003
Year of creation: 1969
Parent Organization: College of Education, New Mexico State University
Present Head: Luiza B. Amodeo
Size of staff. Total: 10 — Full time: 3 — Part time: 7
Researchers: 2 — Part time: 2
Research activities: more than 50%
Educational research: more than 50%
Type of research: Educational research related to early childhood education; special education; reading; bilingual education; curriculum and instruction; educational management and development; and counselling and educational psychology.
Monographs: None published.
Studies and surveys in preparation: County Head Start Program. EQUALS-NMSU. Expanding educational opportunities in the rural Southwest. Achieving equity through development of non-biased materials for career education of young handicapped and minority girls and boys. Rural education baseline data survey. Rural schools and NCA accreditations.

Empire State College of State University of New York

0629

Address: 2 Union Avenue, SARATOGA SPRINGS, NY 12019
Year of creation: 1971
Parent Organization: State University of New York
Present Head: Dr. James W. Hall
Size of staff. Total: 505 — Full time: 283 — Part time: 222
Researchers: 4 — Full time: 3 — Part time: 1
Research activities: less than 10%
Type of research: Academic evaluation and institutional research.

Functional objectives of research: Servicing the educational administration.
Monographs: Adult learning in the context of adult development. 1978. Student leisure time activities. 1980. Students' assessment of their intellectual and personal abilities. 1979. Final report and recommendations, field test of British Open University course at WNET NYC. 1979. Colleges in partnership: four ventures in successful program collaboration. 1980. Complete list on request.

ERIC Clearinghouse on Higher Education

0630

Address: George Washington University, 1 Dupont Circle, Suite 630, WASHINGTON, D.C. 20036
Year of creation: 1968
Parent Organization: George Washington University — sponsor; National Institute of Education — funding
Present Head: Dr. Jonathan D. Fife
Size of staff. Total: 10 — Full time: 7 — Part time: 3
Research activities: from 10% to 25%
Functional objectives of research: Servicing those in educational administration and teaching.
Periodical publications: ASHE-ERIC Higher education research report series (10/yr).
Monographs: Benton, S.E. Rating college teaching: criterion validity studies of student evaluation-of-instruction instrument. Whiman, N.; Weiss, E. Faculty evaluation: the use of explicit criteria for promotion: retention and tenure. Baldridge, J.V.; Kemerer, F.R.; Green, K.C. Enrollments in the eighties: factors, actors, and impacts. Cole, Ch.C. Improving instruction: issues and alternatives for higher education. Melchiori, G.S. Planning for program discontinuance: from default to design.
Studies and surveys in preparation: The path to excellence: quality assurance in higher education. Faculty recruitment, retention, and fair employment: obligations and opportunities. The crisis in faculty careers: changes and challenges. Raising academic standards: a guide for learning improvement. Distance learning. Public service and institutions.

ERIC Clearinghouse on Urban Education

0631

Address: Box 40, Teachers College, Columbia University, NEW YORK, NY 10027
Year of creation: 1966
Parent Organization: Institute for Urban and Minority Education
Present Head: Erwin Flaxman
Size of staff. Total: 8 — Full time: 4 — Part time: 4
Researchers: 1
Research activities: from 10% to 25%
Educational research: from 10% to 25%
Type of research: Educational.
Functional objectives of research: Primarily information analysis.
Periodical publications: IRCD Bulletin. Information bulletin (newsletter, 2/yr). Equal opportunity review. Compact guides (irregular short reports–2pp.). Urban schools bibliographies.
Monographs: Ianni, F. Home, school, and community in adolescent education. 1983. Codianni, A.; Wilbur, G. More effective schooling: from research to practice. 1983. Jones, F.; Montenegro, X. Women and minorities in school administration: strategies

for making a difference. 1983. Webb, M.; Chapin, G. The urban schools bibliography 1982. 1983. Meier, E.; Lo Bosco, M. Guidebook to Hispanic organizations and information. 1983. Complete list on request.

Studies and surveys in preparation: Current studies in preparation: computers in urban education. Reform in the urban high school, with reference to several major studies that have been published or are in progress. School discipline. Asian American curriculum. Policies (strategies) for increasing number of Hispanics in higher education. Update of the urban schools bibliography and guidebook to Hispanic organizations.

Evaluation Research Center

0632

Address: School of Education, Ruffner Hall, University of Virginia, 405 Emmet Street, CHARLOTTESVILLE, VA 22903
Year of creation: 1970
Parent Organization: University of Virginia
Present Head: Michael S. Caldwell
Size of staff. Total: 16 — Full time: 3 — Part time: 13
Researchers: 15 — Full time: 2 — Part time: 13
Research activities: 50%
Educational research: more than 50%
Type of research: Applied.
Functional objectives of research: Evaluation of programme effectiveness.
Studies and surveys in preparation: Evaluation of Teaching Individuals Protective Strategies (TIPS) Programme, for Charlottesville/Albemarle public schools. Evaluation of Piedmont Regional Education Program (PREP), autism and hearing conservation project. Evaluation of Interagency Home Care Project for Central Virginia chapter of American Red Cross, Association for Retarded Citizens, and Hospice of the Piedmont. Evaluation of innovative programme for severely handicapped children. Complete list on request.

Far West Laboratory for Educational Research and Development

0633

Address: 1855 Folsom Street, SAN FRANCISCO, CA 94025
Year of creation: 1966
Present Head: William G. Spady, Ph.D.
Size of staff. Total: 85 — Full time: 70 — Part time: 15
Researchers: 41 — Full time: 35 — Part time: 6
Research activities: from 25% to 50%
Educational research: more than 50%
Type of research: Research and development.
Functional objectives of research: School improvement.
Periodical publications: RAP. Research brief. ETC: Educational technology & communications (4/yr).
Monographs: Educational Dissemination Studies Program. Collaborative arrangements that support school improvement: a synthesis of recent studies. 1983. Educational Dissemination Studies Program. The role of linking agents in school improvement: a review, analysis, and synthesis of recent major studies. 1982. New perspectives on planning in educational organizations. 1980. Alternative perspectives for viewing educational organizations. 1981. Complete list on request.

Studies and surveys in preparation: Instructional management illustrated by 12 principals. Math and science education. Microcomputers and learning. Applying research to teacher education.

Graduate School of Education and Psychology

0634

Address: 3415 Sepulveda Blvd., LOS ANGELES, CA 90034
Year of creation: 1937
Parent Organization: Pepperdine University
Present Head: Dr. William Adrian
Size of staff. Total: 81 — Full time: 47 — Part time: 34
Researchers: 29 — Full time: 12 — Part time: 17
Research activities: less than 10%
Educational research: more than 50%
Type of research: Applied research.
Functional objectives of research: Partial fulfilment of degree requirements, preparation of courses, servicing the educational administration.
Monographs: Elkins, D.; Everett, S. Parents-child relationships inventory. 1979. Elkins, D. The development of parents-child relationships inventory. The Relationships, vol. 7, no. 4, June 1980. Garcia, C.; Smith-Lawrence, P.; Simmons, B. The awareness continuum: researching the reading process naturally. Proceedings of the International Reading Association 27th Annual Convention, April 1981. Garcia, C. Guilt, shame, and embarrassment of the proficient adult reader. Proceedings of the International Reading Association 10th Southwest Regional Conference, October 1981. Garcia, C. Reading personnel and competency based education. Reading improvement, Spring 1981. McCall, C. Sampling and statistics handbook. Research in education. 1981. Stimac, M. From empathy to kenepathy. 1980. Stimac, M. Humanism begins at home. 1980. Complete list on request.

Graduate School of Education, Kent State University

0635

Address: 409 White Hall, KENT, OH 44242
Parent Organization: Kent State University
Present Head: Dean Richard Hawthorne, PhD
Size of staff. Total: 123 — Full time: 123
Researchers: 123 — Full time: 123
Research activities: from 10% to 25%
Educational research: more than 50%
Type of research: Basic and applied.
Functional objectives of research: Scholarly production for publication; doctoral dissertations.
Periodical publications: None published.
Monographs: List on request.
Studies and surveys in preparation: Complete list on request.

Graduate School of Education, University of New Jersey

0636

Address: 10 Seminary Place, NEW BRUNSWICK, NJ 08903
Year of creation: 1960
Parent Organization: Rutgers, The State University of New Jersey

Present Head: Dean Irene Athey
Size of staff. Total: 111 — Full time: 76 — Part time: 35
Researchers: 76 — Full time: 76
Research activities: 50%
Educational research: 50%
Type of research: Empirical, ethnographic, historical, sociological. Both basic and applied, and R&D.
Functional objectives of research: All full time faculty hold the doctoral degree. Research is conducted to obtain promotion, to assist doctoral students, etc.
Periodical publications: Theory and research in social education. Adult education quarterly. Inquiry/Action.
Monographs: Athey, I. Reading: the affective domain reconceptualized. In: Hutson, B.A., ed. Advances in reading/language research, vol. 1. 1981. Harold, W.; Beder, H.W.; Darkenwald, G.G. Cooperation between educational institutions and business and industry in adult education and training. 1981. Darkenwald, G.G.; Merriam, S. Adult education: foundations of practice. 1982. Hillson, M.; Cordasco, F.; Bullock, H.A. The school in the social order. Morrow, L.M. Super tips for storytelling. 1981. Complete list on request.

Institute for Research and Development in Occupational Education

0637

Address: Graduate School and University Center, City University of New York, 33 West 42nd Street, NEW YORK, NY 10036
Year of creation: 1971
Parent Organization: Center for Advanced Study in Education, Cuny
Present Head: Dr. Lee Cohen
— Full time: 8 — Part time: 100+
Researchers: 4 — Full time: 3 — Part time: 1
Research activities: from 10% to 25%
Educational research: from 10% to 25%
Type of research: New and emerging occupations; curriculum; delivery methods; special needs populations (handicapped, women, displaced workers, etc.).
Functional objectives of research: Create new information, update others, this primarily for State Education Department.
Monographs: Tobias, S. The use of computers in instruction. 1982. Abramson, T. Evaluation of new directions: vocational training for emotionally handicapped children. 1981. Flugman, B.; Goldman, L.; Katz, D. Expanding career opportunities for high school special education students: an inservice education project. 1981. Heller, B.R. Impact of experience and maturity on the responsibilities, attitudes, and capabilities of cooperative education students. 1981. Brown, J. Socioeconomic status and occupational education aspiration. 1980. Heller, B.R.; Gross, L.; Senf, R. Sex differences in cooperative education: a study of first-time cooperative education students in traditional and non-traditional occupations. 1980. West, L.J. Instructional concepts for occupational education. 1980. Complete list on request.
Studies and surveys in preparation: Futuring occupational education curriculum. Training counselors to serve handicapped persons. Training parents to serve as career educators. Interpersonal skills training.

Institute for Research on Teaching

0638

Address: College of Education, Michigan State University, EAST LANSING, MI 48824–1034
Year of creation: 1976
Parent Organization: National Institute of Education
Present Head: Jere Brophy and Andrew Porter, Co–Directors
Size of staff. Total: 78 — Full time: 1 — Part time: 77
Researchers: 34 — Part time: 34
Research activities: more than 50%
Educational research: more than 50%
Type of research: Basic and applied.
Functional objectives of research: Increased understanding and improvement of classroom teaching in elementary and secondary schools.
Periodical publications: Communication quarterly. Notes and news.
Monographs: Occasional paper series. Research series. Complete list on request.
Studies and surveys in preparation: Currently there are 15 separate research projects underway, grouped into 4 focus areas: The milieu of the classroom. The subject matter (curriculum). The students to be taught. The teachers.

International and Development Education Program

0639

Address: 5A01 Forbes Quadrangle, University of Pittsburgh, PITTSBURGH, PA 15260
Year of creation: 1964
Parent Organization: School of Education, University of Pittsburgh, PA
Present Head: Dr. Paul Watson, Director
Size of staff. Total: 11 — Full time: 6 — Part time: 5
Researchers: 5 — Part time: 5
Research activities: from 10% to 25%
Educational research: from 10% to 25%
Type of research: Educational planning.
Functional objectives of research: Course preparation for administrative work.
Periodical publications: Network news, includes clearinghouse acquisitions.
Monographs: Alemneh Dejene. Education in basic needs fulfillment: case study from Ethiopia, Bangladesh and Botswana.
Studies and surveys in preparation: Faculty consultation services.

John F. Kennedy Center for Research on Education and Human Development

0640

Address: Box 40, Peabody College, Vanderbilt University, NASHVILLE, TN 37203
Year of creation: 1965
Parent Organization: George Peabody College for Teachers of Vanderbilt University
Present Head: Alfred A. Baumeister, PhD
Size of staff. Total: 112 — Full time: 112
Researchers: 50 — Full time: 50
Type of research: Basic and applied research on mental retardation and related aspects of human development.
Functional objectives of research: To increase knowledge of the causes, social correlates and treatment of mental retardation.
Periodical publications: List on request.

Monographs: List on request.
Studies and surveys in preparation: Research is being conducted in four major areas: cognitive development, neuroscience, socioecological studies of the family, and behavioral medicine; research is also being conducted on aberrant responding.

Learning Research and Development Center (LRDC)

0641

Address: 3939 O'Hara Street, PITTSBURGH, PA 15260
Year of creation: 1963
Parent Organization: University of Pittsburgh
Present Head: Dr. Robert Glaser; Dr. Lauren Resnick, Co–Directors
Size of staff. Total: 142
Researchers: 100
Type of research: Basic and applied research on learning and schooling processes.
Functional objectives of research: To help formulate scientific grounds for the development of sound instruction and sound schooling practices through cognitive and social psychological studies, and through policy research.
Periodical publications: Complete list on request.
Studies and surveys in preparation: Research on: cognition in reading, math, science and learning skills; on computer assisted instruction; on teaching; on social processes; and on school evaluation.

Learning Systems Institute

0642

Address: 206 Dodd Hall, Florida State University, TALLAHASSEE, FA 32306
Year of creation: 1968
Parent Organization: Florida State University
Present Head: Robert M. Morgan
Size of staff. Total: 120 — Full time: 100 — Part time: 20
Researchers: 60 — Full time: 50 — Part time: 10
Research activities: more than 50%
Educational research: more than 50%
Type of research: Instructional systems; computer applications; needs assessment; instructional media; policy formation; educational planning; management; international education.
Functional objectives of research: To improve the efficiency and effectiveness of human resources development.
Periodical publications: Journal of instructional development. International educational development.
Monographs: List on request.
Studies and surveys in preparation: List on request.

Minnesota Research and Development Center for Vocational Education

0643

Address: R460 Vocational and Technical Education Building, 1954 Buford Avenue, ST. PAUL, MN 55108
Year of creation: 1968
Parent Organization: Division of Vocational Education, State Department of Education, St. Paul, MN
Present Head: Brandon B. Smith

Size of staff. Total: 8 — Full time: 4.5 — Part time: 8
Researchers: 8 — Part time: 8
Research activities: 50%
Educational research: more than 50%
Type of research: Programmatic long range applied research and development.
Functional objectives of research: Improve quality and quantity of vocational education in the State and the nation.
Monographs: Copa, G.H. Towards a strategy for planning vocational education. 1981. Smith, B.B.; Grenan, J.P. Assessing the generalizable skills of post-secondary vocational students: a validation study. 1981. Leske, G.; Frederickson, S. Needs assessment for vocational education administrators: an evolving system for staff development decision making. User's manual. 1981. Salem, M.N.; Copa, G.H. Stability in job selection patterns of post-secondary vocational education graduates in Minnesota. 1981. Complete list on request.
Studies and surveys in preparation: Review and synthesis of learning and instruction. Review and synthesis of work experience programmes. Educational adjustment for special needs learners. Instructional equity. Whole to part learning.

National Assessment of Educational Progress

0644

Address: CN 6710, PRINCETON, NJ 08541 — 6710
Parent Organization: Educational Testing Service
Educational research: more than 50%
Functional objectives of research: Collection of information on the status and trends in United States education (under a grant from the National Institute of Education).
Periodical publications: Newsletter. Extensive publications list.
Monographs: Art and young Americans, 1974–79: results from Second National Art Assessment. 1981. Mathematics technical report: summary volume. 1980. Reading comprehension of American youth: do they understand what they read? 1982. Reading, thinking and writing: results from the 1979–80 National Assessment of Reading and Literature. 1981. Changes in student performance by achievement class and modal grade: a different look at assessment data in reading, science and mathematics. 1982. Complete list on request.
Studies and surveys in preparation: 1983–84: Assessment in reading and writing. 1985–86: Assessment in reading, math, science and computer competence.

National Center for Education Statistics

0645

Address: Brown Bldg., 400 Maryland Ave. S.W., WASHINGTON, D.C. 20202
Parent Organization: U.S. Department of Education
Present Head: Marie D. Eldridge
Size of staff. Total: 130 — Full time: 130
Researchers: 20 — Full time: 20
Research activities: from 10% to 25%
Educational research: from 10% to 25%
Type of research: Data collection and analysis.
Functional objectives of research: Report the condition of education in the United States.
Periodical publications: Major publications: Digest of education statistics. Condition of education. Research reports from National Longitudinal Study and High School and

Beyond surveys of high school.
Monographs: Projections of education statistics to 1990–91. Vol. I: Analytical report. Projections of education statistics to 1990–91. Vol. II: Methodological report.
Studies and surveys in preparation: Statistical data collection surveys in elementary and secondary education, post secondary education, and vocational education on number of students, teachers and number of schools. Longitudinal follow-up surveys of high school seniors and sophomores detail reasons for continuing with education and entering the labour force. Also surveys of policy concerns such as curriculum changes. Participate in IEA Second International Mathematics Survey.

National Center for Research in Vocational Education

0646

Address: 1960 Kenny Road, COLUMBUS, OH 43210
Year of creation: 1965
Present Head: Robert E. Taylor
Size of staff. Total: 240 — Full time: 200 — Part time: 40
Research activities: more than 50%
Educational research: more than 50%
Type of research: Research and development, applied.
Functional objectives of research: Servicing career, adult and vocational education.
Periodical publications: Centergram. Vocational educator.
Monographs: Complete list on request.
Studies and surveys in preparation: Field study of newly employed youth. Preparing youth for work: a synthesis of research on schooling and employment. Schooling effectiveness for employability. Feasibility study to improve vocational education through strengthened linkages with organized labour. Assessing cooperative vocational education students' engaged time at work sites. Feasibility of satellite applications in vocational education. Complete list on request.

National Clearinghouse for Bilingual Education

0647

Address: 1555 Wilson Boulevard, Suite 605, ROSSLYN, VA 22209
Year of creation: 1978
Parent Organization: Interamerica
Present Head: Joel Gomez
Size of staff. Total: 25 — Full time: 25
Researchers: 5 — Full time: 5
Research activities: more than 50%
Educational research: more than 50%
Type of research: Applied; bilingual; education.
Functional objectives of research: Servicing bilingual education programmes.
Periodical publications: Forum (newsletter, 6/yr).
Monographs: Tucker, G.R., ed. Exploring strategies for developing a cohesive national direction toward language education in the United States. St. Clair, R.N.; Leap, W.L., eds. Language renewal among American Indian tribes: issues, problems, and prospects. Padilla, R.V., ed. Theory, technology, and public policy on bilingual education: the condition of bilingual education in the Nation, 1982. Leibowitz, A.H. Federal recognition of the rights of minority language groups. Complete list on request.
Studies and surveys in preparation: Bilingual research. On-line computerized database of

research in progress related to bilingual education.

National Institute of Education (NIE)

0648

Address: 1200 19th Street, N.W., WASHINGTON, D.C. 20208
Year of creation: 1972
Parent Organization: U.S. Department of Education
Present Head: Dr. Manuel J. Justiz
Size of staff. Total: 235 — Full time: 228 — Part time: 7
Researchers: 109 — Full time: 106 — Part time: 3
Research activities: more than 50%
Educational research: more than 50%
Type of research: Applied and basic educational research and development.
Functional objectives of research: The National Institute of Education, established by Congress in 1972 as the primary federal agency for educational research and development, supports research on critical problems faced by teachers, parents, students, and educational institutions.
Periodical publications: Resources in education (monthly journal of abstracts: recent report literature related to education), produced by Educational Resources Information Center (ERIC) of the National Institute of Education.
Monographs: Publications and papers is a catalogue listing reports published by the National Institute of Education since 1977. Available from Institute at Room 638, 1200 19th Street, N.W., Washington, D.C. 20208.
Studies and surveys in preparation: The Institute is a source of funding for institutions and organizations conducting research, development and dissemination activities. NIE's supported activities include projects on improving quality of education, effectiveness of schools and teaching, and providing assistance to States and localities. Institute's programme includes: activities to discover, examine and provide information to educators, policymakers, etc. on educational issues. Institute supports ERIC. Provides access to descriptions of programmes, research and development.

New York City Technical College

0649

Address: 300 Jay Street, Brooklyn, NEW YORK, NY 11201
Year of creation: 1946
Parent Organization: City University of New York
Present Head: Joseph S. Murphy, Chancellor, City University of New York. Ursula C. Schwerin, President, New York City Technical College
— Full time: 424 — Part time: 560
Researchers: 2 — Full time: 2
Research activities: less than 10%
Educational research: more than 50%
Type of research: Applied; research and development.
Functional objectives of research: Generating institutional statistics; servicing the educational administration and faculty.
Periodical publications: DATACORE. Student attrition study. Alumni survey. Profile of graduates study. Freshman biographical survey.
Studies and surveys in preparation: Student attrition study. DATACORE. Freshman biographical survey. Educational opportunity center survey. Alumni survey.

Non-Formal Education Information Center

0650

Address: College of Education, 237 Erickson Hall, Michigan State University, EAST LANSING, MI 48824
Year of creation: 1974
Parent Organization: Michigan State University
Present Head: Mary Joy Pigozzi
Size of staff. Total: 8 — Full time: 3 — Part time: 5
Researchers: 4 — Full time: 2 — Part time: 2
Research activities: more than 50%
Educational research: more than 50%
Type of research: Applied.
Functional objectives of research: Provide service to planners and practitioners in the field of non-formal education.
Periodical publications: The NFE Exchange (newsletter). Annotated bibliography series. Occasional papers series. Manual series.
Monographs: Brembeck, C.S. Formal education, non-formal education, and expanded conceptions of development. Hobbs, M.K. New patterns in teaching and learning: a look at the People's Republic of China. O'Gorman, F. Roles of change agents in development. Gerace, F.A.; Carkin, G. Drama in development: its integration in non-formal education. Schlueter, L.C.; Fritz, J. Journals and newsletters on non-formal education and development: a select annotated bibliography. Corvalan-Vasquez, O.E. Apprenticeship in Latin America: the INACAP Program in Chile, a case study. Complete list on request.

Northwest Regional Educational Laboratory (NWREL)

0651

Address: 300 S.W. Sixth Avenue, PORTLAND, OR 97204
Year of creation: 1966
Present Head: Dr. Robert R. Rath, Executive Director
Size of staff. Total: 129 — Full time: 112 — Part time: 17
Researchers: 78 — Full time: 66 — Part time: 12
Research activities: from 25% to 50%
Educational research: from 25% to 50%
Type of research: Research and development.
Functional objectives of research: Assistance to other agencies in improving their education programmes and processes.
Periodical publications: Northwest report newsletter.
Monographs: List on request.
Studies and surveys in preparation: Evaluation and assessment. Instructional improvement. Multicultural education. Computer technology. Complete list on request.

Office for Research and Development Services, College of Education, The Ohio State University

0652

Address: 1945 North High Street, COLUMBUS, OH 43210
Year of creation: 1980
Parent Organization: The Ohio State University, College of Education
Present Head: Dr. James J. Buffer, Jr.

Size of staff. Total: 4 — Full time: 4
Researchers: 160 — Full time: 160
Research activities: 50%
Educational research: more than 50%
Type of research: Basic and applied research.
Functional objectives of research: Knowledge generation and improved educational practice.
Periodical publications: Theory into practice (TIP). Directive teacher. Journal of teacher education.
Monographs: Occasional publications on various topics of scholarly interest. Complete list on request.
Studies and surveys in preparation: Funded and non-funded research projects are underway by faculty, staff, and graduate students representing a broad spectrum of scholarly topics in the field of learning, curriculum, pedagogy, educational policy, etc.

Office of Research, College of Education

0653

Address: NORMAL, IL 61761
Year of creation: 1857
Parent Organization: Illinois State University
Present Head: Dean William Dunifon
Size of staff. Total: 200 — Full time: 175 — Part time: 25
Researchers: 25 — Full time: 25
Research activities: from 10% to 25%
Educational research: more than 50%
Type of research: Applied and basic research.
Functional objectives of research: Applied research for policy analysis decisions; basic research for fulfillment of degree requirements.
Periodical publications: Planning and changing. Illinois school law quarterly. Illinois school research and development. College of Education (newsletter).
Monographs: Variety of papers published by the Illinois State University Centre for the Study of Finance in Education and the Center for Higher Education. Complete list on request.

Personality Research Center

0654

Address: EDA 1.218, The University of Texas at Austin, AUSTIN, TX 78712
Year of creation: 1958
Parent Organization: University of Texas
Present Head: Dr. Robert F. Peck
Size of staff. Total: 6 — Full time: 4 — Part time: 2
Researchers: 4 — Full time: 2 — Part time: 2
Research activities: more than 50%
Educational research: from 25% to 50%
Type of research: Development psychology of coping and competence; treatment effects (drug and alcohol addicts).
Functional objectives of research: Explain and assess effective coping behaviour; reduce substance abuse.
Monographs: Peck, R. et al. Coping styles and achievement.

Studies and surveys in preparation: Roots of competence; cross-cultural and longitudinal evidence. Coping and addiction: basic and applied research studies.

Queens College School of Education

0655

Address: FLUSHING, NY 11367
Year of creation: 1983
Parent Organization: City University of New York
Present Head: Dean John Lidstone
Researchers: 123 — Full time: 82 — Part time: 41
Research activities: from 10% to 25%
Educational research: more than 50%
Functional objectives of research: More effective schools.
Periodical publications: Connections. Looking at learning.
Studies and surveys in preparation: Middle school. Multicultural education. Early childhood art education. Special education. Gifted education. Computer education.

Research and Development Center for Teacher Education

0656

Address: Education Annex, University of Texas at Austin, AUSTIN, TX 78712
Year of creation: 1965
Parent Organization: University of Texas at Austin
Present Head: Dr. Oliver H. Bown, Director
Size of staff. Total: 62 — Full time: 34 — Part time: 28
Researchers: 35 — Full time: 17 — Part time: 18
Research activities: more than 50%
Educational research: more than 50%
Type of research: Basic and applied research, development and dissemination.
Functional objectives of research: To conduct long-term, programmatic research and development in the field of teacher education and the knowledge bases required to effect improvements in practice in both preservice and inservice teacher education and school improvement efforts.
Periodical publications: Catalogue of publications (1/yr). Newsletter (4/yr).
Monographs: Our catalogue of publications (100 pages) for 1983 provides an annotated listing of all recent publications. The catalogue is available upon request.
Studies and surveys in preparation: Current research and development activity of the Center is organized under four major programmes: Research on classroom learning and teaching. Research in teacher education. Research on the improvement process in schools and colleges. Research on the social context of teaching and learning.

Research Division, Bank Street College of Education

0657

Address: 610 West 112th Street, NEW YORK, NY 10025
Year of creation: 1916
Parent Organization: Bank Street College of Education
Present Head: Richard R. Ruopp, President of College
Size of staff. Total: 320 — Full time: 250 — Part time: 70
Researchers: 25 — Full time: 20 — Part time: 5
Research activities: from 10% to 25%
Educational research: more than 50%

Type of research: Basic, applied and some institutional.
Functional objectives of research: Generally furthering knowledge.
Monographs: Findings: Papers published in educational and psychological journals, books, and chapters in books.
Studies and surveys in preparation: Correlates of learning to care for others in adolescents. Sibling relationships and family structures. Stress of work and family life. Coping and resilience in children. Cognitive and social consequences of learning to use microcomputers. Cognitive demands of computer programming. Planning and decision making in adolescents. Development of identification.

School of Education, Andrews University

0658

Address: BERRIEN SPRINGS, MI 49104
Year of creation: 1960
Parent Organization: Andrews University
Present Head: George H. Akers, Ph.D., Dean
Size of staff. Total: 27 — Full time: 20 — Part time: 7
Researchers: 20 — Part time: 20
Research activities: from 10% to 25%
Educational research: more than 50%
Type of research: Applied, research and development, basic, philosophical and documentary.
Functional objectives of research: Preparation of courses, servicing the educational administration, development of tests and instruments, general advancement of knowledge.
Monographs: Habenicht, D.; Bell, A. How to teach children in Sabbath School. 1983. Knight, G.R., ed. Early Adventist educators. 1983. Lall, G.R.; Lall, B.M. Understanding the hyperactive child. 1982. Lall, G.R.; Lall, B.M. A child is not for hurting. 1982. Lall, G.R.; Lall, B.M. Comparative early childhood education. 1983. Lall, G.R.; Lall, B.M. Ways children learn. 1983. Complete list on request.
Studies and surveys in preparation: Early childhood. Design theme in selected British universities. A needs assessment manual for SDA schools. The use of psalms in elementary and secondary curriculum. An investigation into the status and problems of Christian education. Complete list on request.

School of Education, Boston University

0659

Address: 605 Commonwealth Avenue, BOSTON, MA 02215
Year of creation: 1918
Parent Organization: Boston University
Present Head: Paul B. Warren; Mary H. Shann
Size of staff. Total: 69 — Full time: 59 — Part time: 10
Researchers: 20 — Full time: 2 — Part time: 18
Research activities: from 10% to 25%
Educational research: more than 50%
Type of research: Applied research and programme development; comprehensive educational and psychological assessment.
Functional objectives of research: Degree requirements; research based teaching and learning; service to practitioners.
Periodical publications: Journal of education (4/yr).

Monographs: Giroux, H. Theory and resistance in education. 1982. Nash, P. The quiet revolution in American education: viewpoints in teaching and learning. 1982. Weaver, W.T. Contest for educational resources, equity and reform in a meritocratic society. 1982. Giroux, H. Ideology, culture and the process of schooling. 1981. Greenes, C. Beginning problem solving: problem card deck. 1983. Grabowski, S., ed. Strengthening connections between education and performance. 1983. Complete list on request.

Studies and surveys in preparation: Joint NSTA/ASE Conference on Science Education in a High Technology Society. Project TIS (Teacher Incentive Structures). Handicapped Personal Preparation Therapeutic Recreation Training Program. Complete list on request.

School of Education, Indiana State University

0660

Address: TERRE HAUTE, IN 47809
Year of creation: 1870
Parent Organization: Indiana State University
Present Head: Dr. J. Stephen Hazlett, Dean
Size of staff. Total: 86 — Full time: 86
Researchers: 86 — Part time: 86
Research activities: from 10% to 25%
Educational research: more than 50%
Type of research: Basic, applied, research and development.
Functional objectives of research: Curriculum, learning theory, administration and psychology.
Periodical publications: Contemporary education (4/year).
Monographs: Curriculum development in Indiana: analysis of the C-1 Rule and CAPPS. Twelve-year follow-up study, role and status of curriculum workers in Indiana. Using measurement and evaluation to promote learning. Socially mainstreaming handicapped students. Measurement and evaluation in Indiana public schools. Improving test taking skills. Legal aspects of pupil evaluation. Complete list on request.

School of Education, Syracuse University

0661

Address: Syracuse University, SYRACUSE, NY 13210
Year of creation: 1933
Parent Organization: Syracuse University
Present Head: Dr. Burton Blatt, Dean, School of Education
Size of staff. Total: 130 — Full time: 129 — Part time: 1
Researchers: 99 — Full time: 10 — Part time: 89
Research activities: 50%
Educational research: 50%
Type of research: Extra-mural research on education and learning; grants, contracts with numerous State, national and local agencies including private foundations; varies from basic scientific to applied research activities; development activities also included.
Functional objectives of research: Multi-functional objectives including curricular development, supports for graduate students; individual research grants in education, including reading, language, adult education, etc.

Periodical publications: The Educator (12/yr). Educational exchange (2/yr).
Studies and surveys in preparation: Approximately 75 of the faculty are currently engaged in studies and surveys funded by internal, external support, and by the university allotment of quarter-time research to each faculty member. Complete list on request.

School of Education, University of California

0662

Address: Tolman Hall, University of California, BERKELEY, CA 94720
Year of creation: 1876
Parent Organization: University of California
Present Head: Professor Bernard R. Gifford, Dean
Size of staff. Total: 130 — Full time: 115 — Part time: 15
Researchers: 50 — Full time: 40 — Part time: 10
Research activities: more than 50%
Educational research: more than 50%
Type of research: Basic and applied.
Functional objectives of research: Scholarship; improving practice.
Monographs: List on request.
Studies and surveys in preparation: Hyperactivity-Learning-Behavior Disorders Project. Learning English through bilingual instruction. Social contexts of second language learning. Sources of individual differences in second language acquisition. Complete list on request.

School of Education, University of North Carolina

0663

Address: 101 Peabody Hall, CHAPEL HILL, NC 27514
Year of creation: 1913
Parent Organization: University of North Carolina at Chapel Hill
Present Head: Dean Frank Brown
Size of staff. Total: 89 — Full time: 45 — Part time: 44
Researchers: 67 — Full time: 42 — Part time: 25
Research activities: from 25% to 50%
Educational research: more than 50%
Type of research: Applied research and research and development.
Functional objectives of research: Degree requirements; preparation of courses; contributions to the field; institutional research.
Periodical publications: The faculty of the School of Education publishes in most of the major American journals related to education.
Monographs: Within the last three years, the faculty of the School of Education has published more than 150 articles, books and monographs. All publications are in English. List on request.
Studies and surveys in preparation: Examples of some of the researches being conducted are: Research on teaching effectiveness. Development of a longitudinal database to facilitate the study of teacher education. Research in special education.

Stanford International Development Education Committee (SIDEC)

0664

Address: School of Education, Stanford University, STANFORD, CA 94305
Year of creation: 1965
Parent Organization: School of Education, Stanford University
Present Head: Dr. Hans N. Weiler
Size of staff. Total: 20 — Full time: 8 — Part time: 12
Researchers: 15 — Full time: 8 — Part time: 7
Research activities: from 25% to 50%
Educational research: from 25% to 50%
Type of research: Comparative research into social, political and economic aspects of the role of education in development.
Monographs: List on request.
Studies and surveys in preparation: List of faculty publications and Ph.D. dissertations available on request.

SWRL Educational Research and Development

0665

Address: 4665 Lampson Avenue, LOS ALAMITOS, CA 90720
Year of creation: 1966
Parent Organization: Joint-powers agency (Arizona, California, Nevada)
Present Head: Richard E. Schutz
Size of staff. Total: 100 — Full time: 95 — Part time: 5
Researchers: 60 — Full time: 55 — Part time: 5
Research activities: more than 50%
Educational research: more than 50%
Type of research: Research and development.
Functional objectives of research: Large-scale, long-term, programmatic R&D.
Periodical publications: Technical and professional papers. Working papers. General information reports.
Monographs: List on request.
Studies and surveys in preparation: National Center for Bilingual Research. Computer applications. Instructional and training system design, development and implementation. Vocational education. Complete list on request.

Teachers College, Ball State University

0666

Address: Ball State University, MUNCIE, IN 47306
Parent Organization: Deans Office, Teachers College, Ball State University
Present Head: Theodore Kowalski, Acting Dean
Size of staff. Total: 179 — Full time: 143 — Part time: 36
Research activities: from 10% to 25%
Educational research: more than 50%
Type of research: A combination of applied research and research and development.
Functional objectives of research: Most research is done in fields of education by Teachers College faculty; such research is related to the professional interest of faculty; some research is done by graduate students in partial fulfilment of degree requirements.
Periodical publications: The Teacher educator (4/yr, devoted to issues in teacher education). Changing schools (international quarterly newspaper, devoted to

alternative and innovative forms of education).
Monographs: List on request.

Teachers College–Columbia University

0667

Address: 525 W. 120 St, NEW YORK, NY 10027
Year of creation: 1887
Parent Organization: Columbia University
Present Head: Dr. Lawrence A. Cremin, President
Size of staff. Total: 250 — Full time: 150 — Part time: 100
Research activities: from 25% to 50%
Educational research: more than 50%
Type of research: Basic, applied, R&D.
Functional objectives of research: Improve the quality of programmes; improve educational practice; increase classroom effectiveness.
Periodical publications: Teachers College record.
Studies and surveys in preparation: Comprehension and mental retardation. Empathy and nursing care. Comparative juvenile law research. Complete list on request.

Vocational Studies Center, University of Wisconsin–Madison

0668

Address: 964 Educational Sciences Building, 1025 West Johnson Street, MADISON, WI 53706
Year of creation: 1971
Parent Organization: University of Wisconsin–Madison
Present Head: Dr. Merle E. Strong
Size of staff. Total: 44 — Full time: 25 — Part time: 19
Researchers: 20 — Full time: 16 — Part time: 4
Research activities: more than 50%
Educational research: more than 50%
Periodical publications: Vocational materials (catalogue). News and notes. INFORM. Vocational educator. Career currents.
Studies and surveys in preparation: Curriculum project for apprenticeship training (heating, ventilating, and air conditioning; ironwork, pipefitting, sheet metal). Development and dissemination of an inservice training package to help special educators enroll handicapped students in Job Training and Parternship Act programs. Interagency cooperation to improve services to handicapped youth. Maintenance of a central clearinghouse and dissemination process of job training-related information to facilitate the implementation of JTPA in Wisconsin. Preparation and analysis of the designated vocational instructor approach as it applies to special needs students. Preparing evaluation reports on 46 designated vocational instruction programmes. Complete list on request.

Wisconsin Center for Education Research

0669

Address: 1025 West Johnson Street, MADISON, WI 53706
Year of creation: 1964
Parent Organization: School of Education, University of Wisconsin–Madison
Present Head: Dr. Marshall S. Smith
Size of staff. Total: 115 — Full time: 25 — Part time: 90

Researchers: 75 — Part time: 75
Research activities: more than 50%
Educational research: more than 50%
Type of research: Human learning; teaching; school organization; policy.
Functional objectives of research: School improvement.
Periodical publications: NEWS. Bibliography.
Monographs: Johnson, D.D.; Chu-Chang, M., et al. Studies of vocabulary development techniques in the United States of America and the Republic of China. Bagley Marret, C. Minority females in high school mathematics and science. Newmann, M.; Sleeter, C.E. Adolescent development and secondary schooling. Wehlage, G. Effective programs for the marginal high school student.
Studies and surveys in preparation: Math education. Verb learning in children with communication disorders. National education policy. Oral communication and computer science. Understanding and the illusion of knowing. Measuring children's social skills. Complete list on request.

USSR

Eesti NSV pedagoogika teadusliku uurimise instituut/Naučno-issledovatel'skij institut pedagogiki estonskoj SSR

0670

Translation: Research Institute of Pedagogics of the Estonian SSR
Address: Ul. Tõnismägi 9, TALLINN 200105
Year of creation: 1959
Parent Organization: Ministry of Education of the Estonian SSR
Present Head: Prof. O.A. Nilson
Size of staff. Total: 65 — Full time: 65
Researchers: 50 — Full time: 50
Research activities: more than 50%
Educational research: more than 50%
Type of research: Basic and applied research.
Functional objectives of research: Methods of teaching school subjects; problems of educational psychology; servicing the educational administration.
Periodical publications: None published.
Monographs: Andresen, L. Estonskije narodnyje školy v XVII–XIX vekah. 1980. Kõverjalg, A. Metody issledovanija v professional'noj pedagogike. 1980.
Studies and surveys in preparation: School teaching of children at the age of 6. Psychodiagnostics. Methods of teaching school subjects.

Naučno-issledovatel'skij institut defektologii Akademii pedagogiceskih nauk SSSR

0671

Translation: Scientific Research Institute of Defectology of the Academy of Pedagogical Sciences of the USSR
Address: Ul. Pogodinskaja 8, MOSCOW 119121
Year of creation: 1929
Parent Organization: Academy of Pedagogical Sciences of the USSR
Present Head: Prof. T.A. Vlasova
Size of staff. Total: 390 — Full time: 390

Researchers: 309 — Full time: 309
Research activities: more than 50%
Type of research: Basic and applied research in the field of special psychology, special pedagogics, clinical and neurophysiological studying of handicapped children of preschool and school age.
Functional objectives of research: Studying, education, upbringing, vocational training and special rehabilitation of children with deficiencies in mental and physical development (deaf, hard of hearing, blind, partially sighted, speech, motor defects (cerebral palsy), developmentally backward, mental retardation).
Periodical publications: Defektologija.
Monographs: Psihologičeskie problemy korrekcionoj raboty vo vspomogatel'noj školy. 1980. Osobennosti rečevogo razvitija učaščihsja s tjaželymi narušenijami reči. 1980. Vospotanije detej s cerebral'nymi paraličom b sem'je. 1981. Metodika professional'no-trudovogo obučenija vo vspomogatel'noj škole. 1981. Formirovanije ustnoj reči u gluhih detej. 1982. Obučenije detej s zaderžkoj psihičeskogo razvitija. 1983. Čitaju sam. 1983.

Naučno-issledovatel'skij institut doškol'nogo vospitanija

0672

Translation: Scientific Research Institute of Pre-School Education
Address: Klimentovsky pereulok 1, MOSCOW 113184
Year of creation: 1960
Parent Organization: Academy of Pedagogical Sciences of the USSR
Present Head: Prof. N.N. Poddyakov
Size of staff. Total: 147
Researchers: 103
Type of research: Basic and applied research.
Functional objectives of research: Improvement of the pre-school education system.
Periodical publications: None published.
Monographs: List on request.
Studies and surveys in preparation: Pre-school education system. Combined research on forms of interconnection and combination of different aspects of pre-school education.

Naučno-issledovatel'skij institut fisiologii detej i podrostkov

0673

Translation: Scientific Research Institute of Child and Pre-Adult Physiology
Address: Ul. Pogodinskaja 8, MOSCOW 119869
Year of creation: 1944
Parent Organization: Academy of Pedagogical Sciences of the USSR
Present Head: D.V. Kolessov
Size of staff. Total: 201
Researchers: 114
Type of research: Basic and applied research.
Functional objectives of research: Age physiology; school hygiene; physical education.
Periodical publications: None published.
Monographs: List on request.

Naučno-issledovatel'skij institut hudožestvennogo vospitanija

0674

Translation: Scientific Research Institute of Art Education
Address: Kropotkinskaya nab. 15, MOSCOW 119034
Year of creation: 1947
Parent Organization: Academy of Pedagogical Sciences of the USSR
Present Head: Prof. B.T. Lihachev
Size of staff. Total: 94
Researchers: 65
Research activities: more than 50%
Educational research: more than 50%
Type of research: Basic and applied research.
Functional objectives of research: Improvement of the system of aesthetic education of pupils through literature, painting and music.
Periodical publications: None published.
Monographs: Burov, A.I. Estetika: problemy i spory. 1975. Teatr i škola. 1976. Aliev, Ju.B. Penije na urokah muzyki. 1978. Lihachev, B.T. Obščie problemy vospitanija školnikov. 1979. Rigina, G.S. Uroki muzyki v načalnyh klassah. 1979.
Studies and surveys in preparation: Improvement of the system of aesthetic education and the development of pupils' personality. Artistic education as a factor of the global development of school children's personality.

Naučno-issledovatel'skij institut nacional'nyh škol Ministerstva prosveščenija RSFSR

0675

Translation: Research Institute of National Schools of the Ministry of Education of the RSFSR
Address: Ul. Kuusinena 13, MOSCOW 125252
Year of creation: 1949
Parent Organization: Ministry of Education of the RSFSR
Present Head: Prof. P.K. Černikov
Size of staff. Total: 228
Researchers: 162
Type of research: Basic and applied research.
Functional objectives of research: Content, forms and methods of teaching native and Russian languages and literatures at schools in the RSFSR. Problems of upbringing.
Periodical publications: Problems of teaching and upbringing of children at national schools in the RSFSR.
Monographs: List on request.
Studies and surveys in preparation: Content and methods of teaching native and Russian languages in kindergartens and preparatory classes. Methods of teaching native languages and literatures at national schools. Education of students from national republics and regions in the RSFSR at teacher training colleges.

Naučno-issledovatel'skij institut obrazovanija vzroslyh

0676

Translation: Scientific Research Institute of Adult Education
Address: Naberezhnaya Kutozova 8, LENINGRAD 191187
Year of creation: 1944
Parent Organization: Academy of Pedagogical Sciences of the USSR
Present Head: Prof. V.G. Onushkin

Size of staff. Total: 162
Researchers: 102
Type of research: Basic and applied research.
Functional objectives of research: Theoretical bases for the improvement of content, form and methods in general education for adults; problems of preparation and improvement of qualifications for pedagogical staff.
Periodical publications: None published.
Monographs: List on request.

Naučno-issledovatel'skij institut obščej i pedagogičeskoj psihologii

0677

Translation: Scientific Research Institute of General and Educational Psychology
Address: Prospekt Marxa 20, MOSCOW 103009
Year of creation: 1913
Parent Organization: Academy of Pedagogical Sciences of the USSR
Present Head: Prof. A.M. Matjuschkin
Size of staff. Total: 372 — Full time: 372
Researchers: 257 — Full time: 257
Research activities: more than 50%
Educational research: from 25% to 50%
Type of research: Methodological, theoretical, experimental and applied research.
Functional objectives of research: Problems of general, differential, child and educational psychology.
Periodical publications: Voprosi psihologii. Novije issledovanija v psihologii.
Monographs: Zaporožec, A.V., et al. Cognitive processes, sensations, perceptions. 1982. Vygotskij, L.S. Works, v. 1, v. 2, v. 3, v. 5. 1982, 1983. Žinkin, N.I. Speech as an information channel. 1982.
Studies and surveys in preparation: Theoretical and methodological foundations of modern psychology. Psychological foundations of labour and professional education. Psychological problems of communication and social perception.

Naučno-issledovatel'skij institut obščej pedagogiki

0678

Translation: Research Institute of General Pedagogics
Address: Ul. Pavla Korchagina 7, MOSCOW 129278
Year of creation: 1970
Parent Organization: Academy of Pedagogical Sciences of the USSR
Present Head: Prof. Z.A. Malkova
Size of staff. Total: 245 — Full time: 245
Researchers: 202 — Full time: 202
Research activities: more than 50%
Educational research: more than 50%
Type of research: Basic and applied research.
Functional objectives of research: Methodological and theoretical problems of pedagogics; elaboration of pedagogical principles for the improvement of the effectiveness of school practice.
Monographs: List on request.
Studies and surveys in preparation: Methodological and theoretical problems of pedagogics. History of pedagogics. Modern problems of education abroad.

Naučno-issledovatelskij institut obščih problem vospitanija

0679

Translation: Scientific Research Institute of General Educational Problems
Address: Ul. Pogodinskaja 9, MOSCOW 119906
Year of creation: 1970
Parent Organization: Academy of Pedagogical Sciences of the USSR
Present Head: Prof. G.N. Filonov
Size of staff. Total: 175
Researchers: 140
Type of research: Basic and applied research.
Functional objectives of research: Combined approach to the process of forming and developing pupils' personality; influence of collectivity on pupils' personality; activities of children's organizations in pupils' upbringing.
Monographs: List on request.
Studies and surveys in preparation: Improvement of content and methods of pupils' upbringing. Theoretical bases for content and methods of educational work in comprehensive upbringing of school children.

Naučno-issledovatel'skij institut pedagogičeskih nauk Minprosa Tadžikskoj SSR

0680

Translation: Research Institute of Pedagogical Sciences of the Ministry of Education of the Tadzhik SSR
Address: Ul. Ajni 45, DUŠANBE, 734024
Year of creation: 1930
Parent Organization: Ministry of Education of the Tadzhik SSR
Present Head: Prof. O.B. Karimova
Size of staff. Total: 80
Researchers: 59
Research activities: more than 50%
Educational research: more than 50%
Type of research: Basic, applied.
Functional objectives of research: Children under school age, school children.
Periodical publications: None published.
Studies and surveys in preparation: Mechanisms of training, memory, attention, emotions and conceptions. Preparation of children for school. Professional orientation and preparation for work. Content, forms and methods of teaching native and Russian languages and literature. Teaching of history and geography in the Republic.

Naučno-issledovatel'skij institut pedagogiki im. Gogebašvili Minprosa Gruzinskoj SSR.

0681

Translation: Gogebašvili Scientific Research Institute of Pedagogics of the Ministry of Education of the Georgian SSR
Address: Ul. Džavahišvili 1, 380008 TBILISI
Year of creation: 1930
Parent Organization: Ministry of Education of the Georgian Soviet Socialist Republic
Present Head: Prof. Š.A. Amonšvili
— Full time: 119 — Part time: 15
Researchers: 129 — Full time: 115 — Part time: 14
Type of research: Applied research.

Functional objectives of research: Problems of upbringing; content, form and educational methods for compulsory secondary education; psycho-pedagogical upbringing problems of pre-school children.
Periodical publications: Šromebi (1/yr).
Monographs: Zdravstvuite deti! Problema razvitja russkoj ustnoj reči. Leksikologiisa da stilistikis scavlebis sakithebi rvaclian skolaši. Obrazovatel'naja i vospitatel'naja funkcii ocenki učenja škol'nikov. STS gamokeneba mšobliuri enisa da literaturis gakvetilebze. Estetikuri agzrdis problemebi literaturis stavlebisas.
Studies and surveys in preparation: Umcrosklaselta sastavlo-Šemecnebiti mokmedianobis motivebis formirebis pirobebi stavlebis procesši. Skolamdeli asakis bavšvis pirovnebis zneobrivi kcevis formirebis metodebi. Profesiebši mostavleta orientaciis procesis pedagogiuri martva šromisadmi mati šemokmedebiti damokidebulebis formireba. Komunisturi agzrdis problemebi. Mšobliuri enisa da literaturis šestavlis šemecnebiti mnišvneloba. Helovnebisadmi emociuri damocidebulebis formireba sašualo da ufros saskolo asakši.

Naučno-issledovatel'skij institut pedagogiki Ministerstva prosveščenija Belorusskoj
0682
Translation: Scientific Research Institute of Pedagogics of the Ministry of Education of the Byelorussian SSR
Address: ul. V. Korolja 16, 220004 MINSK 48
Year of creation: 1929
Parent Organization: Ministry of Education of the Byelorussian SSR
Present Head: Prof. M.A. Lazaruk
Size of staff. Total: 109 — Full time: 109
Researchers: 82 — Full time: 82
Research activities: more than 50%
Educational research: more than 50%
Type of research: Applied research.
Functional objectives of research: Preparation of textbooks, of teaching and audio-visual aids; modern problems of education; preschool children; problems of economics and of administration of public education.
Periodical publications: None published.
Monographs: Suprun, A.E. The content of teaching of the Russian language in primary classes of the schools with the Byelorussian language as the medium of instruction. Savel'eva, T.M. Psychological problems of mastering of the Russian language. Ogurčov, N.G. Didactical foundations of the development of the world-outlook of upper grades pupils.
Studies and surveys in preparation: Methods of teaching of Russian and Byelorussian languages and literature based on cognate bilingualism. Improvement of content, forms and methods of teaching and upbringing of schoolchildren. Improvement of content and methods of upbringing and education of preschool children in the process of preparing them for school. Work education and vocational orientation of school children. Raising the efficiency of the communist education of schoolchildren. Complete list on request.

Naučno-issledovatel'skij institut pedagogiki proftehobrazovanija

0683

Translation: Scientific Research Institute of Pedagogics of Vocational and Technical Education
Address: Ul. Lenina 10, KAZAN 420111
Year of creation: 1975
Parent Organization: Academy of Pedagogical Sciences of the USSR
Present Head: Prof. M.I. Makhmutov
Size of staff. Total: 126
Researchers: 66
Type of research: Basic and applied research.
Functional objectives of research: Content, forms and methods of general school preparation; vocational guidance and adaptation of vocational-technical school pupils.
Periodical publications: None published.
Monographs: List on request.

Naučno-issledovatel'skij institut prepodavanija russkogo jazyk v nacional'noj škole

0684

Translation: Scientific Research Institute of Russian Language Instruction in National Schools
Address: Ul. Pogodinskaja, 8, MOSCOW 119903
Year of creation: 1970
Parent Organization: Academy of Pedagogical Sciences of the USSR
Present Head: Prof. N.M. Shansky
Size of staff. Total: 72
Researchers: 61
Type of research: Basic and applied research.
Functional objectives of research: Socio-pedagogical research for the teaching of Russian in schools where the instruction language is not Russian; linguistic bases for instruction.
Periodical publications: None published.
Monographs: List on request.
Studies and surveys in preparation: Content and methods for teaching Russian in schools with other instruction languages. Preparation of Russian language teachers.

Naučno-issledovatel'skij institut problem vyssej školi

0685

Translation: Research Institute for Higher Education
Address: Podsosenskij by-street 20, 103062 MOSCOW, K-62
Year of creation: 1973
Parent Organization: Ministry of Higher and Secondary Specialized Education of the USSR
Present Head: Prof. A.Y. Savelyev
Size of staff. Total: 464 — Full time: 444 — Part time: 20
Researchers: 213 — Full time: 213
Research activities: more than 50%
Educational research: more than 50%
Type of research: Theoretical and experimental research.
Functional objectives of research: Optimization of the training of specialists at

institutions of higher education.
Periodical publications: Reviews and express information for higher and secondary specialized education.
Monographs: None published.

Naučno-issledovatel'skij institut škol'nogo oborudovanija i tehničeskih sredstv obučenija **0686**
Translation: Scientific Research Institute of School Equipment and Technical Aids in Education
Address: ul. Pogodinskaja 8, MOSCOW 119908
Year of creation: 1965
Parent Organization: Academy of Pedagogical Sciences of the USSR
Present Head: Prof. S.G. Chapovalenko
Size of staff. Total: 122
Researchers: 71
Type of research: Basic and applied research.
Functional objectives of research: Elaboration of rules for school equipment including standardization and patents.
Periodical publications: None published.
Monographs: List on request.
Studies and surveys in preparation: Theory for the creation of instructional aids. Methods for their application in the teaching and educational process. Standardization of school equipment.

Naučno-issledovatel'skij institut soderžanija i metodov obučenija **0687**
Translation: Scientific Research Institute of Educational Contents and Methodology
Address: Ul. Makarenko 5/16, MOSCOW 103062
Year of creation: 1943
Parent Organization: Academy of Pedagogical Sciences of the USSR
Present Head: Prof. V.M. Monahov
Size of staff. Total: 359
Researchers: 271
Type of research: Applied research.
Functional objectives of research: Study of the content of secondary education; development of teaching and methods for secondary education; elaboration of programmes and instructional materials.
Periodical publications: None published.
Monographs: List on request.
Studies and surveys in preparation: Educational content, methods and materials for general secondary education.

Naučno-issledovatel'skij institut trudovogo obučenija i professional'noj orientacii **0688**
Translation: Scientific Research Institute of Work Education and Vocational Guidance
Address: Ul. Pogodinskaja 8, MOSCOW 119909
Year of creation: 1960
Parent Organization: Academy of Pedagogical Sciences of the USSR
Present Head: Prof. P.R. Atutov
Size of staff. Total: 117

Researchers: 76
Research activities: more than 50%
Educational research: more than 50%
Type of research: Applied research.
Functional objectives of research: Content, forms and methods of work education; vocational guidance system.
Periodical publications: List on request.
Monographs: List on request.
Studies and surveys in preparation: Work education. Organization of work activities. Vocational guidance of school children.

VENEZUELA

Centro de Documentación e Investigación Pedagógicas

0689

Address: Facultad de Humanidades y Educación, Universidad del Zulia, Apartado aéreo 526, MARACAIBO
Year of creation: 1964
Parent Organization: Facultad de Humanidades y Educación de la Universidad del Zulia
Present Head: Yolanda Avila de Pirela, licenciada en educación, Master en administración y supervisión escolar, Presidente del Consejo de Apelaciones de la Un
Size of staff. Total: 13 — Full time: 11 — Part time: 2
Researchers: 6 — Full time: 4 — Part time: 2
Research activities: 50%
Educational research: from 25% to 50%
Type of research: Investigación aplicada.
Functional objectives of research: Conocimiento de la realidad educativa regional y de la propia institución. Apoyo a la resolución de problemas y toma de decisiones.
Periodical publications: Boletín del Centro (1/año). Boletín documental (2/año). Boletín de legislación educativa (2/año). Bibliografía educativa venezolana (2/año). Indice educacional (4/año).
Studies and surveys in preparation: Perfil academico-profesional del egresado de la Facultad de Humanidades y Educación. Estudios sobre las expectativas de formación docente generadas de la implementación de la Escuela Básica. La recreación como factor vivencial en la creatividad del niño y el joven en el Distrito Maracaibo.

Centro de Investigaciones Educativas (CIE)

0690

Address: Instituto Universitario Pedagógico Experimental de Barquisimeto, Edificio este, Final av. Varagas, BARQUISIMETO
Year of creation: 1980
Parent Organization: Instituto Universitario Pedagógico Experimental de Barquisimeto
Present Head: Licenciado Alexis Carrasco
Size of staff. Total: 5 — Full time: 4 — Part time: 1
Researchers: 3 — Full time: 3 — Part time: 1
Research activities: from 10% to 25%

Educational research: more than 50%
Type of research: Aplicada.
Functional objectives of research: Programar y desarrollar las investigaciones según las necesidades y prioridades institucionales, tanto en su ámbito interno como externo.
Periodical publications: Centro de Investigaciones Educativas: boletín informativo.
Monographs: Morles, V. La situación de postgrado en el mundo. Romero Garcia, O.; Bustamante, C. de; Romero, M. Morales de. Variables motivacionales que afectan el rendimiento académico. Equipo telemática. Elementos de aplicación de tecnologías de comunicación a la educación: proyecto telemática.
Studies and surveys in preparation: Impacto potencial de las nuevas tecnologías de la información-computación aplicada a la educación. Internalidad del estudiante, internalidad del profesor y rendimiento del estudiante. Locus de control, rendimiento académico y eficiencia docente.

Instituto Investigaciones Educativas

0691

Address: Apartado 80659, Baruta, SARTENEJAS
Year of creation: 1970
Parent Organization: Universidad Simón Bolívar
Present Head: Mercedes J. de Arnal, sociólogo, Master en educación superior
Size of staff. Total: 1
Research activities: more than 50%
Educational research: more than 50%
Type of research: Investigación interdisciplinaria sobre problemas educativos del país, investigación aplicada, seminarios, preparación de investigadores.
Functional objectives of research: Apoyo institucional a la Universidad Simón Bolívar y servicio a la institución educativa del país.
Periodical publications: No publica.
Monographs: Lista completa a disposición.
Studies and surveys in preparation: Prueba piloto de un cuestionario para obtener la opinión de los estudiantes sobre la actuación en aula del profesor. Actuación académica de los estudiantes de la cohorte 1975-76 en la Universidad Simón Bolívar. Diagnóstico precoz de la deserción y la persistencia en la Universidad Simón Bolívar con la cohorte 1982.

YEMEN

Markaz al-buḥūt wa-ăt-taṭwīr at-tarbawī

0692

Translation: Educational Research and Development Centre
Address: P.O. Box 10999, SANA'A
Year of creation: 1982
Parent Organization: Autonomous
Present Head: Mohammed Hashim El-Shahari
Size of staff. Total: 59 — Full time: 33 — Part time: 26
Researchers: 19 — Full time: 19
Research activities: more than 50%
Educational research: more than 50%

Type of research: Research and development.
Functional objectives of research: Preparation of courses.
Studies and surveys in preparation: Teacher supply and retention. Rationalization of educational expenditure. Enrolment dynamics. School facilities inventory.

Markaz al-buḥūt wa-taṭwīr at-tarbawī

0693

Translation: Educational Research and Development Centre
Address: P.O. Box 10999, SANA'A
Year of creation: 1982
Parent Organization: Ministry of Education
Present Head: Mr. Mohammed Hashim Al-Shahary
Size of staff. Total: 15 — Full time: 15
Researchers: 25 — Full time: 25
Research activities: more than 50%
Educational research: more than 50%
Type of research: Basic research.
Functional objectives of research: Servicing the educational administration.
Periodical publications: None published.
Monographs: Teacher supply and retention in Yemen Arab Republic (field survey). Enrolment dynamics at the primary level (field survey).
Studies and surveys in preparation: School facilities inventory (a field survey in data collection phase). School location planning (in preparation).

YUGOSLAVIA

Institut za pedagogijska istraživanja, OOUR Pedagogijske znanosti, Filozofski fakultet, Sveučilište u Zagrebu

0694

Translation: Institute for Educational Research, Department of Educational Sciences, Faculty of Philosophy, University of Zagreb
Address: Savska cesta 77, 41000 ZAGREB
Year of creation: 1946
Parent Organization: Department of Educational Sciences, Faculty of Philosophy, University of Zagreb
Present Head: Collective body
Researchers: 70 — Full time: 60 — Part time: 10
Research activities: more than 50%
Educational research: more than 50%
Type of research: Basic and applied research.
Functional objectives of research: R&D in the area of education.
Periodical publications: Radovi Instituta za pedagogijska istraživanja filozofskog fakulteta Sveučilišta u Zagrebu (Works of the Institute for Educational Research of the Faculty of Philosophy, University of Zagreb). Odgoj i samoupravljanje: zbornik radova. (Education and self-management: a book of readings).
Monographs: Povratno obrazovanje i promjene u politici i sistemu obrazovanja. 1981. Obrazovanje nastavnika za rad u području humanizacije odnosa medju spolovima. 1982. Training teachers for educational work in the area of humanization of

relations between the sexes. 1982. Recurrent education in Yugoslavia. 1983. Complete list on request.

Studies and surveys in preparation: Educational theory and research methodology: status and projection. Preschool education. Organization of the educational process in the contemporary school. Teaching methods in the educational process.

Institut za pedagoška istraživanja

0695

Translation: Institute of Pedagogical Research
Address: Dobrinjska 11/III, 11000 BEOGRAD
Year of creation: 1960
Parent Organization: The Assembly of the Socialist Republic of Serbia
Present Head: Dr. Vera Lukić
Size of staff. Total: 62 — Full time: 37 — Part time: 25
Researchers: 42 — Full time: 17 — Part time: 25
Research activities: more than 50%
Educational research: more than 50%
Type of research: Basic and applied research.
Functional objectives of research: Advancement of education and teaching process; development of pedagogical science.
Periodical publications: The Yearbook. Research works. Educational theory and practice. Round table.
Monographs: Knežević, V. Modeli učenja i nastave (Kibernetičko-informacioni pristup). Milanović-Nahod, S. Usvajanje pojmova zavisno od nastavnih metoda. Popović, B.V., Miočinović, L.J., Ristić, Ž. Razvoj moralnog saznanja (Rasudjivanje o osobi). Kocić, L. Pedagoški eksperiment (Karakteristike i mogućnosti). Complete list on request.
Studies and surveys in preparation: Methodological problems in comparative research in the field of education. Acquisition and widening of word meaning. Causes of school failure and models of its prevention. Development of moral values: evaluation of other people's motives and acts. Educational role of the family. Analysis of the process of acquisition of concepts.

OOUR znanstveno-nastavne djelatnosti, Pedagoski fakultet Rijeka

0696

Translation: Department of Educational Science, Faculty of Education Rijeka
Address: Narodne omladine 14, 51 000 RIJEKA
Year of creation: 1978
Parent Organization: Faculty of Education, University of Rijeka
Present Head: Prof. dr Krešimi Bezić
Size of staff. Total: 177 — Full time: 129 — Part time: 48
Researchers: 62 — Full time: 62
Research activities: more than 50%
Educational research: more than 50%
Type of research: Basic, applied, research and development.
Functional objectives of research: Conduct R&D in the area of education and teaching.
Periodical publications: Works of the Faculty of Education (1/yr).
Monographs: Permanent education of teachers.
Studies and surveys in preparation: Organization and evaluation of education. Forms and models of communication in education. Self-managing position of pupils in

education. Permanent education of teachers and innovation in education. Humanistic and esthetic education. Mathematical education. Complete list on request.

Pedagoški Inštitut pri Univerzi Edvarda Kardelja v Ljubljani

0697

Translation: Institute for Educational Research at Edvard Kardelj University in Ljubljana
Address: Gerbičeva 62, p.p. 16, 61 111 LJUBLJANA
Year of creation: 1965
Parent Organization: Univerza Edvarda Kardelja v Ljubljani
Present Head: Dr. Renata Mejak
Size of staff. Total: 33 — Full time: 31 — Part time: 2
Researchers: 19 — Full time: 17 — Part time: 2
Research activities: more than 50%
Educational research: more than 50%
Type of research: Basic, applied, R&D.
Functional objectives of research: Contribution to educational theory, educational practice and teaching.
Monographs: Gliha M. Identifikacija problemov ob uvajanju politehnične in delovne vzgoje v usmerjenem izobraževanju. 1981. Golli, D. Vplivi na izbiro smeri v izobraževanju učiteljev. 1982. Jurman, B. Elementi za oblikovanje meril vrednotenja vzgojnoizobraževalnega in drugega dela v osnovni šoli. 1981. Jurman, B. Vrednotenje vzgojnovarstvenega in drugega dela na predšolski stopnji. 1981. Jurman, B. Uresničevanje svobodne menjave dela med občinskimi izobraževalnimi skupnostmi in osnovnimi šolami na osnovi letnega delovnega načrta. 1982. Jurman, B. Uresničevanje svobodne menjave dela na področju vzgoje in izobraževanja. IV. Sistem ocenjevanja kvalitete dela v bazičnem in usmerjenem izobraževanju. 1982. Complete list on request.
Studies and surveys in preparation: Programme basis of institutional pre-school education. Language instruction in elementary school. The concept of all-day elementary school. Evaluation of secondary vocationally guided education. Development and the system of Slovene educational terminology. Personality development in self-management.

Pedagoški zavod Vojvodine

0698

Translation: Institut pour le progrès de l'enseignement général et professionnel de la province de Vojvodina
Address: Bulevar Maršala Tita 6/IV, 21000 NOVI SAD
Year of creation: 1965
Present Head: Dr. Vasilije Damjanović
Size of staff. Total: 49 — Full time: 49
Researchers: 10 — Full time: 10
Research activities: 50%
Educational research: 50%
Type of research: Recherches appliquées, recherche et développement.
Functional objectives of research: Formation et perfectionnement des enseignants.
Periodical publications: Bilteni. Monografije. Studije. Zbornici.
Monographs: Stručno-pedagoški i naučnoistraživački rad u vaspitanju i obrazovanju: zbornik. Ocenjivanje uspeha i praćenje razvoja učenika u opštem vaspitanju i

obrazovanju: monografija. Complete list on request.
Studies and surveys in preparation: Analiza vaspitnog rada u osnovnom vaspitanju i obrazovanju. Razvijenosti radnih navika, odnos prema radu i nekih osobina ličnosti značajnih u radu učenika osnovne škole. Complete list on request.

Republički zavod za unapredjivanje vaspitanja i obrazovanja SR Srbije **0699**

Translation: Institute for Development of Education in the SR of Serbia
Address: Kneza Miloša 101/III, 11000 BEOGRAD
Year of creation: 1976
Parent Organization: Founder — Republican Parliament of the SRS; Financier — Self-managing communities interested in elementary and secondary education
Present Head: Gradislav Milenović
Size of staff. Total: 88 — Full time: 88
Researchers: 60 — Full time: 60
Research activities: from 25% to 50%
Educational research: more than 50%
Type of research: Applied.
Functional objectives of research: Preparation and improvement of curricula and syllabi; improvement of educational process; inservice training of teaching staff; servicing the educational administration.
Periodical publications: Revija obrazovanja. Bibliographies (up-to-date questions in education and training). Survey of articles (in domestic and foreign pedagogical literature).
Monographs: Inostrani školski sistemi. Pregled nastavnih planova za srednje škole (opšteobrazovne i stručne) u nekim zemljama Evrope. Samoupravni preobražaj usmerenog (srednjeg) obrazovanja u SR Srbiji 1977–1981. Osnovno obrazovanje i vaspitanje u SFRJ i obavezno obrazovanje u nekim zemljama sveta. Reforma osnovnog obrazovanja u SR Srbiji 1977–1981. Usmereno obrazovanje u Jugoslaviji — informaciono-dokumentacioni pregled organizacije obrazovanja od I do V stepena stručne spreme.
Studies and surveys in preparation: Influence of pupils' prolonged staying at school on forming working habits and attaining better results in school. Inducing of students' activities in the instruction of mathematics and physics by solving of problem assignment. Way of acquiring cartographical literacy of pupils at elementary school. Methods and forms of educational and instructional work in the preparatory course with Gipsy children.

Republički zavod za unapredjivanje vaspitno-obrazovnog rada — Sarajevo **0700**

Translation: Republic Institute for Education
Address: Otokara Keršovanija 3, SARAJEVO
Year of creation: 1960
Parent Organization: Republički zavod za unapredjivanje vaspitno-obrazovnog rada
Present Head: Milan Pucar
Size of staff. Total: 38 — Full time: 36 — Part time: 2
Researchers: 8
Functional objectives of research: Improvement of education in primary and secondary schools.

Republički zavod za unapreduvanje na obrazovanieto i vospituvanjeto — Skopje

0701

Translation: Institut pédagogique pour la promotion de l'enseignement en R.S. de Macédoine
Address: Rudjer Bošković, b.b., 9100 SKOPJE, Fah 172
Year of creation: 1956
Present Head: Cvetko Smilevski, docteur ès sciences pédagogiques
Size of staff. Total: 27 — Full time: 27
Researchers: 7 — Full time: 7
Research activities: from 10% to 25%
Educational research: from 10% to 25%
Type of research: Appliquée, recherche et développement.
Functional objectives of research: Toutes sortes de perfectionnement dans le domaine de l'éducation.
Periodical publications: Bulletins (irrégulièrement).
Studies and surveys in preparation: Les effets de la réalisation des programmes des écoles primaires et secondaires. La nomenclature des professions.

Ro Republički zavod za unapredjivanje vaspitanja i obrazovanja

0702

Translation: Institution for Improvement of Pedagogy and Education
Address: Novaka Miloševa 36, P.O.Box 223, 81000 TITOGRAD
Year of creation: 1958
Parent Organization: Republic Secretariat for Education, Science and Culture in Montenegro
Present Head: Miloš Starovlah; Marko Gvozdenović; Radivoje Šuković
Size of staff. Total: 46 — Full time: 43 — Part time: 3
Researchers: 28 — Full time: 25 — Part time: 3
Research activities: from 10% to 25%
Educational research: from 10% to 25%
Type of research: Basic and applied.
Functional objectives of research: Partial fulfilment of degree requirements, servicing the educational administration.
Periodical publications: Pedagogy and education (Bulletin of Republic institute for Improvement of Pedagogy and Education).
Monographs: Hundred years of Cetinje Grammar School. Man and lifelong education. Organizations of associated work and permanent education.
Studies and surveys in preparation: Quality of pedagogy and education (internal publication). Teacher and teaching technology.

Zavod SR Slovenije za Šolstvo

0703

Translation: The Board of Education of the Socialist Republic of Slovenia
Address: Poljanska Cesta 28, 61000 LJUBLJANA
Year of creation: 1962
Present Head: Mag. Janez Sušnik
Size of staff. Total: 207
Researchers: 130
Research activities: from 25% to 50%
Educational research: from 25% to 50%

Type of research: Curricula, syllabus, text-books.
Periodical publications: Review Education (6/yr).

Zavod za prosvjetno pedagošku službu SRH 0704

Translation: Republic Institute for Education of Croatia
Address: Trg Jože Vlahovića 6, 41000 ZAGREB
Year of creation: 1977
Parent Organization: Sabor SRH (Assembly of SR of Croatia)
Present Head: Dr. Mato Jergović
Size of staff. Total: 86 — Full time: 86
Researchers: 23 — Full time: 10 — Part time: 13
Research activities: from 10% to 25%
Educational research: more than 50%
Type of research: Applied, research and development.
Functional objectives of research: Partial fulfilment of degree requirements.
Periodical publications: Obrazovanje i rad (Education and work).
Monographs: Jergović, M. Unity of education and work. Bulović, I. Bases of organization of a centre for further education.
Studies and surveys in preparation: Major research projects: Coordination of educational development with the needs of society and associated labour (13 themes). The system of education in socialist self-management society (12 themes). Socialization in the educational process and life of children and youth (5 themes).

ZAIRE

Direction des programmes scolaires et matériels didactiques 0705

Address: Avenue des Ambassadeurs, B.P. 32, KINSHASA/GOMBE
Year of creation: 1982
Parent Organization: Département de l'enseignement primaire et secondaire
Present Head: Citoyen Lwamba Lwa Nemba
Size of staff. Total: 200
Researchers: 100
Research activities: 50%
Educational research: more than 50%
Type of research: Appliquée.
Functional objectives of research: Conception et collaboration des manuels (langues-mathématique-sciences).
Periodical publications: Revue Educateur. Fiches pédagogiques.
Monographs: Manuels scolaires pour le primaire en langues vernaculaires et en français. Manuels pour le secondaire en mathématique et en sciences.
Studies and surveys in preparation: Conception des maquettes suivantes: français — 4èmc primaire; mathématique — 6ème secondaire; sciences — 3ème secondaire.

ZAMBIA

Curriculum Development Centre

0706

Address: Haile Selassie Avenue, P.O. Box 50092, Longaeres, LUSAKA
Year of creation: 1970
Parent Organization: Ministry of Higher Education
Present Head: K.A. Chali
Size of staff. Total: 39 — Full time: 31 — Part time: 1
Research activities: from 25% to 50%
Educational research: 50%
Type of research: Basic research; formative and summative evaluation.
Functional objectives of research: Preparation of courses and syllabuses.
Periodical publications: Orbit: a magazine for young Zambians.
Monographs: First steps in reading: in English or in Zambian language? Basic evaluation instruments at C.D.C.

Nkrumah Teachers College

0707

Address: P.O. Box 80404, KABWE
Year of creation: 1967
Parent Organization: University of Zambia, Ministry of Higher Education
Present Head: Mr. J.P. Kazilimani
Size of staff. Total: 40 — Full time: 40
Researchers: vari
Research activities: from 10% to 25%
Educational research: from 10% to 25%
Type of research: For higher degrees.
Functional objectives of research: For higher degrees.
Periodical publications: Nkrumah educational reviews (1/yr).

Regional institutions
Institutions régionales
Instituciones regionales

AFRICA

Bureau africain des sciences de l'éducation (BASE)

0708

Translation: African Bureau of Educational Sciences
Address: B.P. 14, KISANGANI
Country: Zaire
Year of creation: 1973
Present Head: Prof. Dr. Assindié S. Mungala, directeur général de BASE, professeur ordinaire à l'Université de Kisangani
Size of staff. Total: 148 — Full time: 145 — Part time: 3
Researchers: 41 — Full time: 38 — Part time: 15
Research activities: more than 50%
Educational research: more than 50%
Type of research: Recherches fondamentales et appliquées.
Functional objectives of research: Améliorer le processus éducatif en Afrique; inventorier et conserver le patrimoine culturel africain.
Periodical publications: Revue africaine des sciences de l'éducation (RASE). Dossier scientifique. Collection Point de vue. Collection Etudes. Répertoire et annuaire.
Monographs: Répertoire africain des institutions de recherche en éducation. Actes de la Conférence internationale sur l'éducation en Afrique. 1ère session 1975; 2ème session 1978.

GULF STATES

al-Markaz al-'arabī li-ăl-buḫūt at-tarbawiyya li-duwal al-haliğ

0709

Translation: The Gulf Arab States Educational Research Centre
Address: Shamiyah Street, P.O. Box 25566, SAFAT
Country: Kuwait
Year of creation: 1978
Parent Organization: Arab Bureau of Education for the Gulf States
Size of staff. Total: 17
Researchers: 12

Functional objectives of research: Centre in process of creation.

LATIN AMERICA

Centro Interamericano de Investigación y Documentación sobre Formación Profesional (CINTERFOR)

0710

Address: Av. Uruguay 1238, Casilla de correo 1761, MONTEVIDEO
Country: Uruguay
Year of creation: 1964
Parent Organization: Organización Internacional del Trabajo (OIT)
Present Head: Dr. João Carlos Alexim
Size of staff. Total: 29 — Full time: 25 — Part time: 4
Researchers: 5
Research activities: more than 50%
Educational research: more than 50%
Type of research: Investigación básica y aplicada.
Functional objectives of research: Impulsar y coordinar las actividades que realizan las instituciones o personas relacionadas con la formación profesional y la educación técnica en América Latina y el Caribe; preparación de cursos, seminarios, etc.
Periodical publications: Boletín Cinterfor. Cinterfor-documentación. Resúmenes de formación profesional. Serie bibliográfica-Cinterfor. Catálogos de publicaciones didácticas latinoamericanas sobre formación profesional. Catálogo de publicaciones Cinterfor. Anuario estadístico de la formación profesional en América Latina.
Monographs: Se editan sobre diferentes temas relacionados con la formación profesional, así como los informes de los seminarios, reuniones, etc. que organiza Cinterfor.
Studies and surveys in preparation: Documentación e información sobre formación profesional. Desarrollo rural y formación profesional. Tripartismo y formación profesional. Formación profesional y condiciones de trabajo. Legislación sobre formación profesional. Grupos especiales de población. Planificación de la formación profesional. Recursos técnico-pedagógicos. Certificación ocupacional. Recursos humanos para la formación profesional. Formación profesional y desarrollo empresarial.

Centro Interamericano de Investigaciones y Estudios para el Planeamiento Educativo (CINTERPLAN)

0711

Address: Apartado postal 70060, CARACAS 1071-A
Country: Venezuela
Year of creation: 1978
Parent Organization: Organización de Estados Americanos (OEA) y Gobierno de Venezuela
Present Head: Jorge Riquelme Pérez, ingeniero de negocios, economista

Size of staff. Total: 14 — Full time: 14
Researchers: 2 — Full time: 2
Research activities: 50%
Educational research: more than 50%
Type of research: Fundamentalmente documental y básica.
Functional objectives of research: Su objetivo consiste en prestar servicios a la administración educacional de los países Latinoamericanos y del Caribe.
Periodical publications: El Boletín de actividades.
Monographs: Morles, A. Un modelo para la evaluación de libros de texto. 1983. Ovalles, O. Las limitaciones ecológicas al desarrollo de la educación en Venezuela: una perspectiva a largo plazo. 1983. Lista completa a disposición.
Studies and surveys in preparation: Educación preescolar en los países Iberoamericanos. Educación superior en Venezuela.

Centro Internacional de Educación y Desarrollo Humano (CINDE)

0712

Address: Apartado aéreo 50262, MEDELLIN, Antioquia
Country: Colombia
Year of creation: 1976
Parent Organization: Ninguna
Present Head: Dra. Martha Arango de Nimnicht, M.A. en curriculum y preparación de maestros, Ph.D. en curriculum y psicolinguística
Size of staff. Total: 40 — Full time: 22 — Part time: 18
Researchers: 16 — Full time: 8 — Part time: 8
Research activities: 50%
Educational research: more than 50%
Type of research: Investigación aplicada, participativa, básica, y desarrollo.
Functional objectives of research: Desarrollar nuevas modalidades de educación con énfasis en modalidad de atención a la niñez con participación de la familia y la comunidad; formar profesionales en esta nueva linea de investigación a través de programas de postgrado y otras formas de capacitación.
Monographs: PROMESA: un desafío al cambio. Educación en el hogar. Programa para estimulación temprana. Expectativas y frustraciones en investigación. Hacía una evaluación que responda a los educandos. Lista a disposición.
Studies and surveys in preparation: Instrumento para evaluar autoconcepto en niños. Módulos de entrenamiento para promotoras rurales. Lista a disposición.

Centro Multinacional de Investigación Educativa (CEMIE)

0713

Address: Barrio Los Yoses, Calle 37, No. 40 S, SAN JOSE
Country: Costa Rica
Year of creation: 1971
Parent Organization: PREDE/OEA y Ministerio de Educación Pública de Costa Rica
Present Head: Dr. Pedro Lafourcade V.; Lic. Benedicto Orozco V.
Size of staff. Total: 12 — Full time: 9 — Part time: 3

Researchers: 6 — Full time: 5 — Part time: 1
Research activities: more than 50%
Educational research: more than 50%
Type of research: Investigación aplicada; investigación y desarrollo; investigación acción; investigación experimental.
Functional objectives of research: Prestación de servicios a la administración educacional; estudios curriculares; asesoramiento técnico en investigación a organismos ministeriales de los países latinoamericanos.
Periodical publications: Boletín. Centro Multinacional de Investigación Educativa CEMIE (4/año).
Monographs: Propuesta sobre planes de formación docente e investigaciones sobre habilidades, disposiciones de los maestros observados en el aula. 1983. Investigación evaluativa de logros del sistema educativo. 1983. Diagnóstico del colegio universitario de Cartago. 1983. Atención y desarrollo del talento y de la creatividad en niños y jóvenes del sistema educativo costarricense. 1983. Lista completa a disposición.
Studies and surveys in preparation: Evaluación de logros del sistema educativo (2a. etapa. Aplicación de una metodología de la acción institucional y extrainstitucional más garantizante de logros — I y II ciclos de la enseñanza general básica). Investigación multinacional que abarca 6 países. Diagnóstico y ensayo, alternativas, niños marginados. Atención y desarrollo del talento y de la creatividad en niños y jóvenes del sistema educativo costarricense. Creación y prueba de un modelo de administración del currículo para la región educativa central de Costa Rica. Las incidencias de la crisis socioeconómica en la deserción escolar en Costa Rica.

Centro Regional de Educación de Adultos y Alfabetización Funcional para América Latina (CREFAL)

0714

Translation: Adult Education and Functional Literacy Regional Center for Latin America
Address: CREFAL, Quinta Eréndira, 61600 PATZCUARO, Michoacán
Country: Mexico
Year of creation: 1951
Parent Organization: Secretaría de Educación Pública (SEP), Gobierno de México
Present Head: Ing. Gilberto Garza Falcón, M.S.
Size of staff. Total: 38 — Full time: 21 — Part time: 17
Researchers: 19 — Full time: 2 — Part time: 17
Research activities: from 25% to 50%
Educational research: more than 50%
Type of research: Básica, aplicada, investigación y desarrollo.
Functional objectives of research: Prestación de servicios a la administración educacional, y además preparación de cursos.
Periodical publications: Revista interamericana de educación de adultos. Boletín informativo del CREFAL. NOTICREFAL (Edición internacional). Cuadernos del CREFAL. GACIRE: Gaceta de cooperación informativa regional. Serie de resúmenes analíticos.
Monographs: Administración de la educación de adultos: cuatro experiencias. Alfabetización y educación de adultos en la Región Andina. Alfabetización y

educación de adultos: una bibliografía anotada. Alfabetización y post-alfabetización. Cultura popular y educación. Educación informal y procesos educativos informales. Lista completa a disposición.

Studies and surveys in preparation: Actualización del estudio sobre movimientos nacionales de educación de adultos en América Latina. Estudio sobre la educación de adultos y su vinculación con el mundo del trabajo. Estudio sobre la participación como elemento permanente en todos los procesos de la educación integrada de adultos para el desarrollo global de las áreas rurales. Estudios sobre la educación de adultos: análisis comparativo de la alfabetización y post-alfabetización en una perspectiva internacional; estudio sobre el aprendizaje de los adultos y estudio sobre la calidad de la educación de adultos. Thesaurus sobre educación de adultos y alfabetización. Lista completa a disposición.

WEST AFRICA

International Centre for Educational Evaluation (ICEE)

0715

Address: Institute of Education, University of Ibadan, IBADAN
Country: Nigeria
Year of creation: 1957
Parent Organization: University of Ibadan
Present Head: Prof. E.A. Yoloye
Size of staff. Total: 44
Researchers: 14
Type of research: Applied and basic research.
Functional objectives of research: Carry out R&D in the field of education; evaluate projects and programmes.
Periodical publications: West African journal of education. Careers. Evaluation in Africa (ICEE Newsletter). Annual reports.
Monographs: Occasional publications, nos 1–17. ICEE Evaluation reports, nos 1–3.
Studies and surveys in preparation: IEA 2nd Mathematics Survey. IEA Classroom Environment Study. Evaluation of West African Examinations Council examinations.

International institutions
Institutions internationales
Instituciones internacionales

INTERNATIONAL

International Institute for Educational Planning

0714

Translation: Institut international de planification de l'éducation
Address: 7–9, rue Eugène-Delacroix, 75116 PARIS
Country: France
Year of creation: 1963
Parent Organization: Unesco
Present Head: Sylvain Lourié, Director
Size of staff. Total: 37 — Full time: 35 — Part time: 2
Researchers: 9 — Full time: 9
Research activities: from 25% to 50%
Educational research: more than 50%
Type of research: Applied.
Functional objectives of research: Formulating the concepts, resources and techniques required to achieve closer integration between educational policies and development policies.
Periodical publications: IIEP Newsletter (4/yr). Bulletin of educational documentation (2/yr).
Monographs: Research reports. Case studies. Seminar documents. Training materials. Occasional papers and reference booklets. Complete catalogue available on request.
Studies and surveys in preparation: The implications for educational planning of scientific and technological development policies. The diversification of educational activities and the problems facing educational planning in relation to their articulation in a development perspective.

Unesco Institute for Education

0715

Translation: Institut de l'Unesco pour l'éducation/Unesco-Institut für Pädagogik.
Address: Feldbrunnenstrasse 58, 2000 HAMBURG 13
Country: Germany FR
Year of creation: 1951
Parent Organization: Unesco
Present Head: Dr. Ravindra H. Dave, Director
Size of staff. Total: 20 — Full time: 14 — Part time: 6

Researchers: 6 — Full time: 6

Research activities: more than 50%

Educational research: more than 50%

Type of research: Basic and applied research on the concept of lifelong education and the implications of the concept in the fields of content of education, learning strategies, evaluation and teacher education.

Functional objectives of research: To understand and analyse the significance and characteristics of the concept of lifelong education encompassing the formal, non-formal and in-formal systems of learning for the different stages of the life cycle; to study the application of the principles of lifelong education in reforming curriculum development, evaluation and other substantive aspects of formal and non-formal education; to disseminate research findings and information relevant to these fields.

Periodical publications: International review of education (4/yr). Bibliography on lifelong education (3/yr). Awareness list on lifelong education (irregular).

Monographs: Advances in lifelong education series. UIE Monographs series. UIE Case studies. UIE Studies on post-literacy and continuing education. Complete list on request.

Studies and surveys in preparation: Analysis of curricula for in-school and out-of-school education for vocational development in the framework of lifelong education. A study on the development of a common core of curriculum at the primary level of education to make it more relevant to the communities in rural environments. A study of selected innovations and experiments in the European Region aimed at integrating in the primary education curriculum basic knowledge, concepts and values necessary for all menbers of the national community. A comparative survey of curricula at school level for environmental education in the perspective of lifelong education. Identification and analysis of the content of lifelong education in selected aspects of learning and development. Development of learning strategies for post-literacy and continuing education in the perspective of lifelong education. Evaluation and monitoring of learning outcomes and larger impact of literacy, post-literacy and continuing education programmes in developing countries. The continuing education of teachers in the perspective of lifelong education.

Keywords index

ABSTRACT REASONING
0001 0002 0070 0274 0299 0534 1002 1236 1402 2035 2307 2359 2616 2644 2770 2872

ACCESS TO EDUCATION
0003 0137 1189 2919

ACHIEVEMENT RATING
0004 2137

ACTION RESEARCH
0005 1993 2689

ADMINISTRATIVE ORGANIZATION
0006 0309 0816 1792 2080 2578

ADULT EDUCATION
0007 0008 0009 0010 0011 0012 0013 0014 0015 0016 0017 0018 0019 0020 0021 0022 0023 0024 0025 0026 0027 0028 0029 0030 0031 0032 0033 0034 0035 0036 0037 0038 0039 0040 0041 0042 0043 0044 0045 0046 0047 0048 0049 0050 0051 0086 0102 0106 0108 0113 0124 0125 0127 0145 0196 0210 0244 0266 0286 0288 0326 0372 0388 0431 0446 0493 0564 0651 0653 0726 0768 0791 0805 0830 0834 0850 0855 0861 0882 0908 0953 0974 1019 1061 1094 1096 1116 1118 1131 1143 1160 1175 1178 1184 1190 1198 1207 1213 1218 1230 1233 1237 1239 1302 1320 1322 1339 1376 1400 1401 1444 1450 1488 1492 1583 1590 1594 1600 1602 1618 1630 1654 1661 1714 1730 1736 1751 1768 1779 1797 1817 1860 1897 1944 1951 1953 1956 1962 1964 2032 2033 2074 2093 2106 2107 2118 2120 2121 2122 2192 2199 2202 2217 2229 2241 2267 2311 2316 2317 2366 2370 2413 2424 2491 2496 2518 2521 2533 2557 2629 2643 2650 2652 2674 2693 2698 2721 2732 2746 2756 2788 2796 2816 2833 2844 2860 2880 2883 2889 2906 2912 2914 2916 2917 2923 2924 2929

ADULT LEARNING
0052 0833 1992 2532 2634

AFFECTIVE OBJECTIVES
0053 0295 1004 1643 2042 2432 2448 2473

AFFECTIVITY
0054 0235 0312 0993 1901 1908

AFRICA
0055 0056 0269 0374 0789 1387 1581 1900 2259 2688

AFRICAN LANGUAGES
0057 0058 0059 0060 0683 0685 1203 1258 1920 1958 2069 2104 2105 2345 2429 2430 2467 2675

AGRICULTURAL EDUCATION
0061 0062 0063 0064 0960 0961 1014 1297 1477 1478 1481 1505 1589 2109 2146 2182 2869 2870 2873 2901 2908

ALBANIA
0065 2194

ALGERIA
0066 0067 1076 1134 1497 1742 1986

ANGOLA
0068 1049

APPRENTICESHIP
0069 0104 1011 2144 2172 2329 2474 2594 2619

APTITUDE TESTS
0001 0070 0274 0299 0534 1002 2307 2359 2644 2770 2872

ARABIC

0071 0895 1950

ARGENTINA
0072 0073 0074 0075 0076 0077 0078 0079 0080 0087 0383 0694 1148 1165 1192 1225 1226 1796 1802 1810 1836 1932 2238 2323 2342 2372 2562 2567 2610 2617

ART EDUCATION
0040 0080 0081 0082 0083 0084 0085 0086 0087 0315 0558 0570 0860 0963 1042 1115 1207 1226 1424 1996 2093 2162 2184 2388 2475 2496 2640 2699 2710 2771 2832

ATHLETIC ACTIVITIES
0088 0089 1120 1232 1573 1606 1721 1725 2167 2169

AUDIOVISUAL AIDS
0090 0091 0092 0337 0355 0443 0751 0752 1018 1499 1887 1888 2426 2646

AUDIOVISUAL COMMUNICATION
0093 0678 1413 1451 1874 1978

AUDITION (PHYSIOLOGY)
0094 1007 2128 2285 2558

AUSTRALIA
0023 0046 0069 0095 0096 0097 0098 0099 0100 0101 0102 0103 0104 0105 0106 0107 0391 0392 0411 0447 0879 0880 0970 0972 0974 0975 1011 1021 1239 1375 1479 1526 1544 1617 1618 1758 1956 2057 2070 2122 2144 2145 2149 2172 2329 2336 2343 2474 2503 2594 2619 2637 2643 2654 2896 2906

AUSTRIA
0008 0022 0108 0109 0110 0111 0112 0113 0114 0115 0116 0117 0118 0119 0120 0121 0122 0222 0375 0400 0424 0531 0639 0768 0769 0951 0952 0953 0954 0956 1010 1038 1078 1079 1080 1082 1392 1426 1469 1484 1620 1716 1736 1760 1907 2068 2252 2283 2330 2444 2596 2857 2877 2904 2905 2909 2937

BAHRAIN
0123 1326 2920

BANGLADESH
0020 0124 2229 2413

BASIC EDUCATION
0014 0033 0125 0126 0127 0203 0446 0850 1143 1523 1860 2245 2693

BASIC SKILLS
0128 1223 1955 2795

BEHAVIOUR PROBLEMS
0129 0623 0754 1890

BELGIUM
0003 0130 0131 0132 0133 0134 0135 0136 0137 0138 0139 0306 0325 0333 0365 0468 0526 0587 0771 0772 0997 1008 1035 1041 1177 1189 1193 1306 1408 1441 1528 1557 1577 1790 1803 1829 1999 2039 2053 2072 2142 2154 2161 2223 2233 2244 2250 2279 2425 2438 2443 2512 2561 2656 2919

BENIN
0140 0669 1500 2073

BICULTURALISM
0141 0142 0143 0158 0290 0293 1211 1264 1324 1666 1828 1837 1840 1921 1922 1924 2045 2313 2727 2819

BILINGUAL EDUCATION
0018 0144 0145 0146 0147 0148 0149 0150 0151 0152 0159 0347 0585 0723 0981 1240 1259 1323 1334 1912 1923 2074 2160 2291 2317 2408 2531 2629 2733 2746 2753 2797 2807 2844 2887 2918

BILINGUALISM
0141 0144 0150 0152 0153 0154 0155 0156 0157 0158 0159 0160 0332 0390 0467 0528 0723 0737 0914 1029 1211 1323 1378 1454 1666 1824 1846 1910 1912 1916 1921 1923 2045 2050 2058 2205 2253 2454 2531 2691 2753 2767 2845 2849 2856

BLIND EDUCATION
0161 0167 1040 1740 2216

BOLIVIA
0162 0163 1229 1963 2240

BRAZIL
0161 0164 0165 0166 0167 0168 0169 0170 0171 0172 0173 0174 0175 0242 0373 0402 0420 0464 0697 1040 1122 1127 1205 1208 1231 1255 1256 1308 1468 1740 1943 1948 1965 2216 2218 2222 2239 2312 2504 2855 2903

BUILDING DESIGN
0176 0177 0178 0179 0182 0711 1027 1409 1645

BUILDING ENGINEERING
0177 0178 0179 0182 1027 1409 1645

BUILDING EVALUATION
0177 0178 0179 0182 1027 1409 1645

BUILDINGS
0177 0178 0179 0180 0181 0182 0541 0542 0990 1027 1409 1627 1645 1823 2840

BULGARIA
0183 0184 0185 0186 0187 0188 0189 0190 0191 0773 1055 1056 1057 1058 1204 1331 1332 1333 1418 1483 1713 1724 1754 1917 1926 1957 2059 2065 2168 2235 2416 2499 2876

BURKINA FASO
0192 0690 1981

BURMA
0193 0405

BURUNDI
0051 0194 0195 0196 0378 0670 1376 2642

CAMEROON UR
0197 0198 0199 0586 0671 0672 1504 1809 1985 2220 2232 2306 2344 2565 2591

CANADA
0034 0126 0200 0201 0202 0203 0204 0205 0206 0207 0208 0209 0210 0211 0212 0213 0214 0215 0216 0220 0324 0327 0331 0359 0394 0410 0429 0480 0512 0722 0994 1017 1071 1123 1124 1125 1160 1172 1206 1245 1279 1312 1373 1398 1506 1508 1523 1752 1816 1929 1949 2023 2052 2164 2245 2270 2282 2479 2507 2559 2585 2609 2653 2659 2916 2923 2931

CAREER COUNSELLING
0217 0218 0219 0280 0363 0422 0627 0785 1247 1260 1565 1698 2338 2574 2803 2808 2888 2892

CAREER EDUCATION
0202 0220 0221 1242 2268 2653 2799

CAREERS
0114 0222 0954 2937

CENTRAL AFRICAN REPUBLIC
0223 0379 0674

CHAD
0224

CHEMISTRY
0225 1130 1597 2004 2174 2365 2393

CHILD LANGUAGE
0226 0227 1093 1109 1596 1896

CHILD PSYCHOLOGY
0228 0229 1263 1464 2449 2726

CHILE
0054 0230 0231 0232 0233 0234 0235 0237 0238 0239 0273 0296 0312 0700 0702 0993 1104 1343 1345 1513 1560 1561 1727 1755 1901 1908 1933 2037 2112 2568 2621 2625 2636

CHINA
0240 0241 0291 1266 1671 1801 1838 2141 2611

CITIZEN PARTICIPATION
0166 0242 1468 2855 2903

CLASSROOM COMMUNICATION
0011 0243 0244 0245 0419 0682 0830 1363 1612 1714 2022 2508 2509 2518

CLASSROOM RESEARCH
0246 0247 0248 0256 0415 0427 0626 0782 1105 1185 1663 2150 2266 2276 2421 2500 2600 2786

CLINICAL DIAGNOSIS
0249 0901 2630 2846

COGNITIVE DEVELOPMENT
0250 0251 0621 0713 0729 1551 1876 2495 2685 2759

COGNITIVE PROCESSES
0248 0252 0253 0255 0256 0257 0302 0415 0425 0574 1046 1185 1241 1285 1460 1520 1663 1940 2085 2150 2421 2530 2760 2772 2798 2940

COLOMBIA
0030 0259 0260 0261 0262 0263 0264 0265 0266 0267 0272 0475 0476 0555 0556 0638 0945 0946 0950 1116 1156 1292 1391 1414 1476 1543 1553 2120 2147 2214 2231 2305 2357 2423 2588 2674 2868

COMMUNICATION
0056 0269 0789 1387 1581 1900 2259 2688

COMMUNICATION SKILLS
0270 0449 1023 1902 1909 2067 2703

COMMUNITY DEVELOPMENT
0263 0271 0272 0476 0898 1553 1966 2115 2140 2147 2304 2423

COMMUNITY EDUCATION
0001 0070 0233 0273 0274 0275 0299 0534 0702 1002 1031 1942 2112 2215 2307 2359 2644 2706 2770 2872

COMMUNITY PROBLEMS
0276 0553 0807

COMMUNITY SCHOOLS
1394 2187

COMPARATIVE EDUCATION
0031 0036 0076 0142 0143 0217 0241 0278 0279 0280 0281 0282 0283 0284 0286 0288 0289 0290 0291 0292 0293 0294 0422 0455 0457 0460 0462 0504 0527 0627 0651 0706 0749 0785 0798 0839 1052 1084 1110 1118 1148 1178 1194 1264 1266 1273 1324 1372 1389 1401 1404 1565 1619 1630 1632 1635 1653 1654 1661 1671 1746 1801 1828 1830 1831 1832 1833 1834 1836 1837 1838 1839 1840 1841 1882 1922 1924 1927 2099 2141 2189 2313 2315 2323 2338 2526 2574 2611 2709 2727 2776 2783 2819 2879 2892

COMPENSATORY EDUCATION
0053 0295 1004 1643 2042 2432 2448 2473

COMPOSITION (LITERARY)
0234 0296 0297 0482 1283 1513 1727 1806 1865 2373

COMPREHENSION
0001 0070 0274 0298 0299 0307 0534 0797 1002 1420 1634 2265 2307 2359 2644 2770 2872

COMPUTER ASSISTED INSTRUCTION
0006 0037 0054 0084 0130 0136 0211 0212 0235 0252 0298 0300 0302 0303 0304 0305 0306 0307 0309 0310 0311 0312 0313 0314 0315 0316 0317 0318 0319 0320 0321 0322 0323 0324 0325 0326 0327 0328 0329 0330 0338 0341 0384 0385 0408 0428 0480 0526 0572 0575 0587 0647 0724 0728 0732 0745 0763 0771 0797 0816 0917 0993 1012 1016 1042 1050 1066 1067 1117 1119 1149 1168 1170 1172 1177 1184 1206 1228 1287 1291 1415 1420 1430 1437 1440 1441 1448 1449 1455 1488 1501 1519 1520 1521 1568 1577 1591 1592 1599 1602 1634 1641 1712 1719 1738 1792 1795 1797 1798 1807 1815 1816 1821 1826 1878 1901 1908 1929 1940 1960 2001 2026 2038 2056 2080 2087 2095 2134 2247 2256 2265 2282 2292 2360 2415 2437 2438 2439 2457 2475 2510 2515 2545 2578 2609 2701 2711 2716 2730 2754 2758 2760 2762 2771 2773 2791 2812 2867 2883 2912

COMPUTERS

0092 0131 0133 0151 0153 0200 0317
0319 0331 0332 0333 0334 0337 0338
0339 0340 0341 0342 0344 0345 0346
0347 0348 0365 0425 0430 0443 0450
0551 0574 0607 0610 0647 0722 0737
0772 0922 1008 1018 1066 1070 1092
1117 1150 1176 1191 1200 1234 1334
1368 1433 1438 1499 1503 1535 1558
1591 1601 1614 1743 1788 1790 1803
1824 1825 1835 1977 1999 2008 2021
2034 2052 2053 2072 2085 2154 2161
2223 2233 2249 2253 2291 2396 2398
2405 2426 2462 2545 2552 2607 2646
2656 2720 2733 2767 2781 2784 2851
2856

CONGO
1383

COOPERATIVES
0350 1358 2823

COST EFFECTIVENESS
0351 0477 0579 1141 1436 1657

COSTA RICA
0352 0353 0354 0448 0619 1140 1370
1540 2143 2377 2648 2882 2935

COUNSELLING
0091 0208 0218 0355 0356 0357 0358
0359 0360 0361 0362 0363 0364 0429
0441 0512 0625 0752 0780 0869 1039
1124 1197 1201 1217 1247 1294 1398
1474 1604 1695 1696 1697 1698 1699
1787 1789 1862 1888 1949 2091 2479
2543 2803 2814 2841 2854 2865 2893
2897 2899 2921

CREATIVITY
0133 0365 0366 0367 0368 1008 1249
1369 1537 1790 1999 2233 2656 2804

CROSS CULTURAL STUDIES
0366 0368 1249 1537 2804

CUBA
0369 0370 1321 1753

CULTURAL ACTIVITIES
0025 0172 0371 0372 0373 1019 1231
1590 1951 1965 2118 2186 2218 2650
2928 2929

CULTURE
0055 0109 0374 0375 0769 2283

CURRICULUM
0376 0377 0563 0836 1174 1786 1903
2197 2288 2382 2431 2433 2523 2718
2862

CURRICULUM DEVELOPMENT
0012 0073 0095 0096 0117 0154 0168
0194 0201 0223 0300 0304 0378 0379
0380 0381 0382 0383 0384 0385 0386
0387 0388 0389 0390 0391 0392 0393
0394 0395 0396 0397 0398 0399 0400
0401 0402 0403 0404 0409 0410 0412
0467 0528 0554 0572 0670 0674 0684
0692 0724 0745 0834 0845 0879 0880
0940 1000 1010 1048 1122 1277 1296
1415 1454 1501 1512 1529 1570 1616
1701 1719 1810 1878 1934 1948 1970
2014 2023 2026 2050 2081 2084 2135
2191 2230 2319 2400 2407 2444 2471
2521 2567 2584 2585 2617 2631 2632
2659 2660 2663 2669 2686 2690 2691
2754 2769 2811 2915 2950

CURRICULUM EVALUATION
0099 0193 0201 0248 0256 0305 0386
0394 0399 0405 0406 0407 0408 0409
0410 0411 0412 0413 0414 0415 0416
0417 0753 0763 1000 1005 1133 1185
1257 1271 1453 1526 1529 1663 1879
1886 1889 1976 2023 2149 2150 2348
2421 2439 2510 2585 2593 2659 2660
2669 2671 2700 2769

CURRICULUM PLANNING
0418 0432 1253 1899

CURRICULUM RESEARCH
0044 0116 0165 0208 0217 0243 0247
0280 0320 0359 0418 0419 0420 0421
0422 0423 0424 0425 0426 0427 0428
0429 0430 0431 0432 0433 0434 0435
0512 0535 0574 0575 0627 0639 0682
0697 0785 0956 1030 1105 1119 1124
1176 1233 1253 1276 1319 1359 1392
1397 1398 1416 1426 1444 1565 1575
1601 1620 1760 1781 1899 1907 1949
2008 2022 2085 2117 2241 2249 2267

2274 2276 2292 2338 2396 2479 2500 2504 2570 2574 2586 2600 2658 2705 2711 2766 2786 2796 2818 2824 2892 2930

CYPRUS
0436

CZECHOSLOVAKIA
0092 0337 0356 0437 0438 0439 0440 0441 0442 0443 0444 0445 0536 0625 0776 0780 0781 1018 1145 1151 1470 1499 1744 1787 2206 2224 2409 2426 2564 2603 2638 2646 2858

DATA BASE
0014 0107 0125 0446 0447 0850 1375 1758 2503 2693

DEAF
0352 0448 0619 2143 2935

DEAF EDUCATION
0270 0449 1023 1902 1909 2067 2703

DECISION MAKING
0346 0450 0610 1234 2034

DELINQUENTS
0451 0788 1580 1704 2049 2281 2450 2468

DENMARK
0246 0453 0626 0782 0783 1112 2266 2572

DEVELOPING COUNTRIES
0213 0241 0279 0284 0291 0292 0294 0455 0456 0457 0460 0461 0462 0517 0518 0577 0611 0612 0617 0749 1084 1245 1266 1273 1310 1372 1382 1404 1610 1632 1642 1671 1774 1801 1831 1834 1838 1839 1841 1882 1954 2099 2141 2315 2590 2611 2687 2741 2742 2783

DEVELOPMENT EDUCATION
0164 0283 0464 1052 1833 2222 2776

DEVELOPMENTAL PSYCHOLOGY
0134 0154 0390 0466 0467 0468 0528 0630 0648 0650 0657 1035 1074 1107 1235 1454 1572 1593 1670 2050 2443 2524 2691

DISTANCE EDUCATION
0076 0079 0211 0262 0263 0272 0297 0298 0307 0324 0351 0474 0475 0476 0477 0480 0482 0556 0579 0580 0638 0797 1141 1148 1162 1172 1225 1283 1391 1419 1420 1436 1553 1578 1634 1657 1659 1735 1793 1806 1816 1836 1865 2062 2071 2147 2265 2282 2323 2373 2386 2423 2459 2610

DOCUMENTATION
0051 0196 1186 1376 1442 1664 2009 2082 2761

DOMINICAN REPUBLIC
0487 0488 0709 1514 1988

DROPOUTS
0077 1165 1796

DROPPING OUT
0490 0491 0519 0636 0941 0976 1410 2102 2136 2340 2505 2623

EARLY CHILDHOOD
1270 1609

EARLY CHILDHOOD EDUCATION
0017 0044 0431 0493 0882 1233 1444 2241 2267 2652 2796

EASTERN EUROPE
1181 1662

ECONOMIC DEVELOPMENT
2428 2492 2498 2519 2620

ECUADOR
0416 1257

EDUCATION WORK RELATIONSHIP
0499 0915 1275 1327 1328 1574 2036 2455

EDUCATIONAL ADMINISTRATION
0044 0176 0208 0281 0346 0359 0398 0429 0431 0450 0461 0504 0508 0510 0512 0517 0518 0521 0525 0527 0533 0577 0599 0602 0603 0608 0610 0611

0612 0613 0617 0645 0711 0798 0988 1037 1098 1124 1128 1158 1233 1234 1310 1382 1389 1398 1444 1472 1507 1610 1623 1625 1635 1774 1780 1885 1949 1973 1974 1975 2034 2075 2084 2158 2200 2241 2267 2280 2471 2479 2489 2490 2632 2707 2742 2796

EDUCATIONAL COUNSELLING
0490 0519 0520 0636 0941 1341 1633 1820 2136

EDUCATIONAL DEVELOPMENT
0521 1342 1780 2075

EDUCATIONAL DOCUMENTATION
0523 0524 0810 0811 1422 1852 1853

EDUCATIONAL ECONOMICS
0001 0035 0070 0115 0116 0130 0154 0274 0281 0299 0306 0390 0424 0426 0445 0467 0504 0521 0525 0526 0527 0528 0530 0531 0533 0534 0535 0536 0537 0539 0564 0587 0603 0639 0771 0798 0956 0988 1002 1030 1151 1173 1175 1222 1389 1392 1397 1400 1426 1454 1507 1588 1600 1605 1620 1625 1635 1744 1760 1780 1817 1885 1907 1973 2031 2050 2075 2217 2307 2333 2359 2370 2644 2691 2705 2770 2872 2905 2924

EDUCATIONAL ENVIRONMENT
0540 0758 1894

EDUCATIONAL EQUIPMENT
0177 0178 0179 0180 0181 0182 0541 0542 0990 1027 1409 1627 1645 1823 2840

EDUCATIONAL FINANCE
0545 0929 1517 1969 2213 2337 2339 2755

EDUCATIONAL GAMES
0052 0833 1992 2532 2634

EDUCATIONAL GOALS
0547 1516 2103

EDUCATIONAL GUIDANCE
0161 0167 0345 0490 0519 0549 0551 0636 0941 1020 1040 1200 1351 1535 1542 1740 1870 2066 2136 2216 2540 2552 2898

EDUCATIONAL HISTORY
0025 0031 0035 0083 0208 0261 0262 0276 0286 0359 0372 0377 0395 0429 0475 0512 0553 0554 0555 0556 0558 0559 0563 0564 0567 0584 0638 0651 0807 0946 0963 1019 1118 1124 1174 1175 1224 1280 1357 1391 1393 1398 1400 1458 1550 1570 1590 1600 1654 1817 1864 1873 1903 1934 1949 1951 1996 2118 2183 2184 2197 2217 2288 2370 2388 2433 2479 2553 2588 2614 2650 2718 2848 2924 2929

EDUCATIONAL IMPROVEMENT
0082 0570 0571 0735 0748 0860 1179 1386 1731 1881 2569 2605 2765 2793 2832

EDUCATIONAL INFORMATION
0304 0385 0572 0745 1501 1878

EDUCATIONAL INNOVATIONS
0320 0425 0428 0461 0517 0574 0575 0577 0611 1119 1202 1310 1610 1842 2085 2092 2212 2292 2461 2711

EDUCATIONAL LEGISLATION
0578 0609 1136 2789

EDUCATIONAL MEDIA
0351 0477 0579 0580 0581 0661 1141 1162 1329 1436 1657 1659 1679 2062

EDUCATIONAL METHODS
0559 0584 0824 0985 1457 1458 1622 2180 2635 2848

EDUCATIONAL NEEDS
0149 0585 1259 2807 2887

EDUCATIONAL OBJECTIVES
0130 0136 0198 0306 0325 0526 0586 0587 0672 0771 0936 1177 1441 1577 1800 1814 2246 2251 2344 2438 2451 2493 2580 2628 2745 2750

EDUCATIONAL PHILOSOPHY
0031 0208 0286 0359 0429 0512 0594

0651 1104 1118 1124 1313 1398 1654
1949 2479 2817

EDUCATIONAL PLANNING
0176 0340 0346 0450 0461 0508 0517
0518 0521 0533 0577 0578 0598 0599
0602 0603 0604 0605 0606 0607 0608
0609 0610 0611 0612 0613 0617 0711
0720 0747 0988 1009 1015 1025 1092
1128 1136 1234 1310 1382 1433 1472
1548 1610 1623 1625 1774 1780 1791
1825 1835 1880 1928 1974 1975 1977
1983 2034 2075 2200 2257 2280 2490
2538 2539 2542 2595 2615 2667 2679
2742 2784 2789

EDUCATIONAL POLICIES
0001 0070 0274 0299 0518 0534 0599
0612 0613 0614 0617 1002 1033 1382
1459 1472 1647 1774 2200 2262 2280
2307 2359 2644 2742 2770 2872

EDUCATIONAL PSYCHOLOGY
0031 0032 0056 0074 0116 0129 0134
0207 0217 0245 0246 0251 0255 0262
0269 0280 0286 0317 0338 0352 0356
0364 0422 0424 0426 0441 0448 0466
0468 0475 0490 0510 0519 0535 0556
0581 0619 0621 0622 0623 0624 0625
0626 0627 0630 0631 0632 0633 0634
0636 0638 0639 0642 0645 0647 0648
0649 0650 0651 0653 0654 0655 0656
0657 0658 0661 0729 0754 0762 0780
0782 0785 0789 0827 0838 0847 0862
0871 0911 0941 0956 0989 0998 1030
1035 1037 1046 1066 1074 1083 1107
1118 1123 1131 1183 1195 1220 1235
1254 1285 1294 1329 1363 1385 1387
1390 1391 1392 1393 1397 1426 1551
1552 1556 1559 1565 1569 1572 1581
1591 1593 1612 1620 1626 1654 1669
1670 1679 1699 1760 1787 1890 1900
1907 1937 1941 1945 2131 2136 2143
2153 2155 2156 2183 2190 2204 2243
2259 2260 2266 2295 2338 2366 2378
2441 2443 2508 2509 2524 2525 2530
2537 2551 2559 2574 2665 2681 2688
2705 2707 2740 2759 2763 2772 2788
2814 2834 2843 2880 2892 2907 2935

EDUCATIONAL RADIO
0038 0663 0853 0930 1190 1417 1423
1425 1452 1777 2032 2116 2133 2311
2670 2696

EDUCATIONAL REFORM
0057 0223 0379 0674 0683 2104

EDUCATIONAL RESEARCH
0001 0002 0003 0004 0005 0006 0007
0008 0009 0010 0011 0012 0013 0014
0015 0016 0017 0018 0019 0020 0021
0022 0023 0024 0025 0026 0027 0028
0029 0030 0031 0032 0033 0034 0035
0036 0037 0038 0039 0040 0041 0042
0043 0044 0045 0046 0047 0048 0049
0050 0051 0052 0053 0054 0055 0056
0057 0058 0059 0060 0061 0062 0063
0064 0065 0066 0067 0068 0069 0070
0071 0072 0073 0074 0075 0076 0077
0078 0079 0080 0081 0082 0083 0084
0085 0086 0087 0088 0089 0090 0091
0092 0093 0094 0095 0096 0097 0098
0099 0100 0101 0102 0103 0104 0105
0106 0107 0108 0109 0110 0111 0112
0113 0114 0115 0116 0117 0118 0119
0120 0121 0122 0123 0124 0125 0126
0127 0128 0129 0130 0131 0132 0133
0134 0135 0136 0137 0138 0139 0140
0141 0142 0143 0144 0145 0146 0147
0148 0149 0150 0151 0152 0153 0154
0155 0156 0157 0158 0159 0160 0161
0162 0163 0164 0165 0166 0167 0168
0169 0170 0171 0172 0173 0174 0175
0176 0177 0178 0179 0180 0181 0182
0183 0184 0185 0186 0187 0188 0189
0190 0191 0192 0193 0194 0195 0196
0197 0198 0199 0200 0201 0202 0203
0204 0205 0206 0207 0208 0209 0210
0211 0212 0213 0214 0215 0216 0217
0218 0219 0220 0221 0222 0223 0224
0225 0226 0227 0228 0229 0230 0231
0232 0233 0234 0235 0237 0238 0239
0240 0241 0242 0243 0244 0245 0246
0247 0248 0249 0250 0251 0252 0253
0255 0256 0257 0259 0260 0261 0262
0263 0264 0265 0266 0267 0269 0270
0271 0272 0273 0274 0275 0276 0278
0279 0280 0281 0282 0283 0284 0286
0288 0289 0290 0291 0292 0293 0294
0295 0296 0297 0298 0299 0300 0302
0303 0304 0305 0306 0307 0309 0310
0311 0312 0313 0314 0315 0316 0317
0318 0319 0320 0321 0322 0323 0324

0325 0326 0327 0328 0329 0330 0331
0332 0333 0334 0337 0338 0339 0340
0341 0342 0344 0345 0346 0347 0348
0350 0351 0352 0353 0354 0355 0356
0357 0358 0359 0360 0361 0362 0363
0364 0365 0366 0367 0368 0369 0370
0371 0372 0373 0374 0375 0376 0377
0378 0379 0380 0381 0382 0383 0384
0385 0386 0387 0388 0389 0390 0391
0392 0393 0394 0396 0397 0398 0399
0400 0401 0402 0403 0404 0405 0406
0407 0408 0409 0410 0411 0412 0413
0414 0415 0416 0417 0418 0419 0420
0421 0422 0423 0424 0425 0426 0427
0428 0429 0430 0431 0432 0433 0434
0435 0436 0437 0438 0439 0440 0441
0442 0443 0444 0445 0446 0447 0448
0449 0450 0451 0453 0455 0456 0457
0460 0461 0462 0464 0466 0467 0468
0474 0475 0476 0477 0480 0482 0487
0488 0490 0491 0493 0499 0504 0508
0510 0512 0517 0518 0519 0520 0521
0523 0524 0525 0526 0527 0528 0530
0531 0533 0534 0535 0536 0537 0539
0540 0541 0542 0545 0547 0549 0551
0553 0555 0556 0558 0559 0563 0564
0567 0570 0571 0572 0574 0575 0577
0578 0579 0580 0581 0584 0585 0586
0587 0594 0598 0599 0602 0603 0604
0605 0606 0607 0608 0609 0610 0611
0612 0613 0614 0617 0619 0621 0622
0623 0624 0625 0626 0627 0630 0631
0632 0633 0634 0636 0638 0639 0642
0645 0647 0648 0649 0650 0651 0653
0654 0655 0656 0657 0658 0661 0663
0669 0670 0671 0672 0674 0678 0681
0682 0683 0684 0685 0686 0688 0690
0692 0694 0697 0700 0702 0706 0709
0711 0712 0713 0715 0718 0719 0720
0722 0723 0724 0726 0728 0729 0732
0735 0737 0741 0744 0745 0747 0748
0749 0750 0751 0752 0753 0754 0756
0758 0759 0761 0762 0763 0766 0768
0769 0771 0772 0773 0776 0780 0781
0782 0783 0785 0787 0788 0789 0790
0791 0792 0794 0795 0797 0798 0800
0801 0802 0805 0806 0807 0808 0809
0810 0811 0812 0813 0815 0816 0819
0820 0824 0826 0827 0828 0830 0832
0833 0834 0835 0836 0838 0839 0841
0845 0846 0847 0850 0853 0855 0857
0858 0860 0861 0862 0865 0869 0870

0871 0872 0873 0876 0877 0879 0880
0881 0882 0885 0887 0889 0893 0895
0897 0898 0901 0902 0907 0908 0909
0911 0912 0913 0914 0915 0916 0917
0920 0922 0923 0929 0930 0934 0935
0936 0938 0939 0940 0941 0945 0946
0950 0951 0952 0953 0954 0956 0960
0961 0963 0967 0968 0970 0972 0974
0975 0976 0977 0980 0981 0983 0985
0987 0988 0989 0990 0991 0993 0994
0997 0998 1000 1001 1002 1003 1004
1005 1006 1007 1008 1009 1010 1011
1012 1013 1014 1015 1016 1017 1018
1019 1020 1021 1022 1023 1024 1025
1026 1027 1028 1029 1030 1031 1032
1033 1034 1035 1036 1037 1038 1039
1040 1041 1042 1043 1044 1045 1046
1047 1048 1049 1050 1051 1052 1053
1054 1055 1056 1057 1058 1059 1060
1061 1062 1063 1064 1065 1066 1067
1068 1069 1070 1071 1072 1073 1074
1075 1076 1078 1079 1080 1081 1082
1083 1084 1085 1086 1087 1088 1089
1090 1091 1092 1093 1094 1095 1096
1097 1098 1099 1100 1101 1102 1103
1104 1105 1106 1107 1108 1109 1110
1111 1112 1113 1114 1115 1116 1117
1118 1119 1120 1121 1122 1123 1124
1125 1126 1127 1128 1129 1130 1131
1132 1133 1134 1136 1137 1138 1139
1140 1141 1142 1143 1144 1145 1146
1147 1148 1149 1150 1151 1152 1153
1154 1155 1156 1157 1158 1159 1160
1161 1162 1163 1164 1165 1166 1167
1168 1169 1170 1171 1172 1173 1174
1175 1176 1177 1178 1179 1180 1181
1182 1183 1184 1185 1186 1187 1188
1189 1190 1191 1192 1193 1194 1195
1196 1197 1198 1199 1200 1201 1202
1203 1204 1205 1206 1207 1208 1209
1210 1211 1212 1213 1214 1215 1216
1217 1218 1219 1220 1221 1222 1223
1224 1225 1226 1227 1228 1229 1230
1231 1232 1233 1234 1235 1236 1237
1239 1240 1241 1242 1243 1244 1245
1246 1247 1248 1249 1250 1251 1252
1253 1254 1255 1256 1257 1258 1259
1260 1261 1262 1263 1264 1265 1266
1267 1268 1269 1270 1271 1272 1273
1274 1275 1276 1277 1278 1279 1280
1281 1282 1283 1284 1285 1286 1287
1288 1289 1290 1291 1292 1293 1294

1295	1296	1297	1298	1299	1300	1301
1302	1303	1304	1305	1306	1307	1308
1309	1310	1311	1312	1313	1314	1315
1316	1317	1318	1319	1320	1321	1322
1323	1324	1325	1326	1327	1327	1328
1328	1329	1330	1331	1332	1333	1334
1335	1336	1337	1338	1339	1340	1341
1342	1343	1344	1345	1346	1347	1348
1351	1352	1353	1354	1355	1356	1357
1358	1359	1360	1361	1362	1363	1364
1365	1366	1367	1368	1369	1370	1371
1372	1373	1374	1375	1376	1377	1378
1379	1380	1381	1382	1383	1384	1385
1386	1387	1388	1389	1390	1391	1392
1393	1394	1395	1396	1397	1398	1399
1400	1401	1402	1403	1404	1405	1406
1407	1408	1409	1410	1411	1412	1413
1414	1415	1416	1417	1418	1419	1420
1421	1422	1423	1424	1425	1426	1427
1428	1429	1430	1431	1432	1433	1434
1435	1436	1437	1438	1439	1440	1441
1442	1443	1444	1445	1446	1447	1448
1449	1450	1451	1452	1453	1454	1455
1456	1457	1458	1459	1460	1461	1462
1463	1464	1465	1466	1467	1468	1469
1470	1471	1472	1473	1474	1475	1476
1477	1478	1479	1480	1481	1482	1483
1484	1485	1486	1487	1488	1489	1490
1491	1492	1493	1494	1495	1496	1497
1498	1499	1500	1501	1502	1503	1504
1505	1506	1507	1508	1509	1510	1511
1512	1513	1514	1515	1516	1517	1518
1519	1520	1521	1522	1523	1525	1526
1528	1529	1530	1531	1532	1533	1534
1535	1536	1537	1538	1539	1540	1541
1542	1543	1544	1545	1546	1547	1548
1549	1550	1551	1552	1553	1554	1555
1556	1557	1558	1559	1560	1561	1564
1565	1567	1568	1569	1571	1572	1573
1574	1575	1576	1577	1578	1579	1580
1581	1582	1583	1584	1585	1586	1587
1588	1589	1590	1591	1592	1593	1594
1595	1596	1597	1598	1599	1600	1601
1602	1603	1604	1605	1606	1607	1608
1609	1610	1611	1612	1613	1614	1615
1616	1617	1618	1619	1620	1621	1622
1623	1624	1625	1626	1627	1628	1629
1630	1631	1632	1633	1634	1635	1636
1637	1638	1639	1640	1641	1642	1643
1644	1645	1646	1647	1648	1649	1650
1651	1652	1653	1654	1655	1656	1657
1658	1659	1660	1661	1662	1663	1664
1665	1666	1667	1668	1669	1670	1671
1672	1673	1674	1675	1676	1677	1678
1679	1695	1696	1697	1698	1699	1700
1701	1702	1703	1704	1705	1706	1707
1708	1709	1710	1711	1712	1713	1714
1715	1716	1717	1718	1719	1720	1721
1722	1723	1724	1725	1726	1727	1728
1729	1730	1731	1732	1733	1735	1736
1737	1738	1739	1740	1741	1742	1743
1744	1745	1746	1747	1749	1750	1751
1752	1753	1754	1755	1757	1758	1759
1760	1761	1762	1765	1767	1768	1769
1770	1771	1772	1773	1774	1775	1776
1777	1778	1779	1780	1781	1782	1783
1784	1785	1786	1787	1788	1789	1790
1791	1792	1793	1794	1795	1796	1797
1798	1799	1800	1801	1802	1803	1804
1805	1806	1807	1809	1810	1814	1815
1816	1817	1818	1819	1820	1821	1822
1823	1824	1825	1826	1828	1829	1830
1831	1832	1833	1834	1835	1836	1837
1838	1839	1840	1841	1842	1843	1844
1845	1846	1847	1848	1849	1850	1851
1852	1853	1854	1855	1856	1857	1858
1859	1860	1861	1862	1863	1864	1865
1866	1867	1868	1869	1870	1871	1872
1873	1874	1875	1876	1877	1878	1879
1880	1881	1882	1883	1884	1885	1886
1887	1888	1889	1890	1891	1893	1894
1895	1896	1897	1898	1899	1900	1901
1902	1903	1904	1905	1906	1907	1908
1909	1910	1911	1912	1913	1914	1915
1916	1917	1918	1919	1920	1921	1922
1923	1924	1925	1926	1927	1928	1929
1930	1931	1932	1933	1935	1936	1937
1938	1939	1940	1941	1942	1943	1944
1945	1946	1947	1948	1949	1950	1951
1952	1953	1954	1955	1956	1957	1958
1959	1960	1961	1962	1963	1964	1965
1966	1967	1968	1969	1970	1971	1972
1973	1974	1975	1976	1977	1978	1979
1980	1981	1982	1983	1984	1985	1986
1988	1989	1991	1992	1993	1994	1996
1997	1998	1999	2000	2001	2002	2003
2004	2005	2006	2007	2008	2009	2010
2011	2012	2013	2014	2016	2017	2019
2020	2021	2022	2023	2024	2026	2027
2028	2029	2030	2031	2032	2033	2034
2035	2036	2036	2037	2038	2039	2040
2041	2042	2043	2044	2045	2046	2047
2048	2049	2050	2051	2052	2053	2054
2056	2057	2058	2059	2060	2061	2062

2063	2064	2065	2066	2067	2068	2069
2070	2071	2072	2073	2074	2075	2076
2077	2078	2079	2080	2081	2082	2083
2084	2085	2086	2087	2090	2091	2092
2093	2094	2095	2096	2097	2098	2099
2100	2102	2103	2104	2105	2106	2107
2108	2109	2110	2112	2113	2114	2115
2116	2117	2118	2119	2120	2121	2122
2123	2124	2125	2126	2127	2128	2129
2130	2131	2132	2133	2134	2135	2136
2137	2138	2139	2140	2141	2142	2143
2144	2145	2146	2147	2148	2149	2150
2151	2153	2154	2155	2156	2157	2158
2159	2160	2161	2162	2163	2164	2165
2166	2167	2168	2169	2170	2171	2172
2173	2174	2176	2177	2178	2179	2180
2182	2183	2184	2185	2186	2187	2188
2189	2190	2191	2192	2193	2194	2195
2196	2197	2198	2199	2200	2201	2202
2203	2204	2205	2206	2207	2208	2209
2210	2211	2212	2213	2214	2215	2216
2217	2218	2219	2220	2221	2222	2223
2224	2225	2226	2227	2228	2229	2230
2231	2232	2233	2235	2236	2237	2238
2239	2240	2241	2242	2243	2244	2245
2246	2247	2248	2249	2250	2251	2252
2253	2254	2256	2257	2259	2260	2261
2262	2263	2264	2265	2266	2267	2268
2269	2270	2271	2272	2273	2274	2275
2276	2277	2278	2279	2280	2281	2282
2283	2284	2285	2286	2287	2288	2289
2290	2291	2292	2293	2294	2295	2303
2304	2305	2306	2307	2308	2309	2310
2311	2312	2313	2314	2315	2316	2317
2319	2321	2322	2323	2329	2330	2331
2332	2333	2334	2335	2336	2337	2338
2339	2340	2341	2342	2343	2344	2345
2346	2347	2348	2350	2351	2352	2353
2354	2355	2356	2357	2358	2359	2360
2361	2362	2363	2364	2365	2366	2367
2368	2369	2370	2371	2372	2373	2374
2375	2376	2377	2378	2379	2380	2381
2382	2383	2384	2385	2386	2387	2388
2389	2390	2391	2392	2393	2394	2395
2396	2397	2398	2399	2400	2401	2402
2403	2404	2405	2406	2407	2408	2409
2410	2411	2412	2413	2414	2415	2416
2417	2418	2419	2420	2421	2422	2423
2424	2425	2426	2427	2428	2429	2430
2431	2432	2433	2434	2435	2436	2437
2438	2439	2440	2441	2442	2443	2444
2445	2446	2447	2448	2449	2450	2451
2452	2453	2454	2455	2456	2457	2458
2459	2460	2461	2462	2463	2464	2465
2467	2468	2469	2470	2471	2472	2473
2474	2475	2477	2478	2479	2480	2481
2482	2483	2484	2485	2486	2487	2488
2489	2490	2491	2492	2493	2494	2495
2496	2497	2498	2499	2500	2501	2502
2503	2504	2505	2506	2507	2508	2509
2510	2511	2512	2513	2514	2515	2516
2517	2518	2519	2520	2521	2522	2523
2524	2525	2526	2527	2528	2529	2530
2531	2532	2533	2534	2535	2536	2537
2538	2539	2540	2541	2542	2543	2544
2545	2546	2547	2548	2549	2550	2551
2552	2553	2554	2555	2556	2557	2558
2559	2560	2561	2562	2563	2564	2565
2566	2567	2568	2569	2570	2571	2572
2573	2574	2575	2576	2577	2578	2579
2580	2581	2582	2583	2584	2585	2586
2587	2588	2589	2590	2591	2592	2593
2594	2595	2596	2597	2598	2599	2600
2601	2602	2603	2604	2605	2606	2607
2608	2609	2610	2611	2612	2613	2614
2615	2616	2617	2618	2619	2620	2621
2622	2623	2624	2625	2626	2628	2629
2630	2631	2632	2633	2634	2635	2636
2637	2638	2639	2640	2641	2642	2643
2644	2645	2646	2647	2648	2649	2650
2651	2652	2653	2654	2655	2656	2657
2658	2659	2660	2661	2662	2663	2664
2665	2666	2667	2668	2669	2670	2671
2672	2673	2674	2675	2676	2677	2678
2679	2680	2681	2682	2683	2684	2685
2686	2687	2688	2689	2690	2691	2692
2693	2694	2695	2696	2697	2698	2699
2700	2701	2702	2703	2704	2705	2706
2707	2708	2709	2710	2711	2712	2713
2714	2715	2716	2717	2718	2719	2720
2721	2722	2723	2724	2725	2726	2727
2728	2729	2730	2731	2732	2733	2734
2735	2736	2737	2738	2739	2740	2741
2742	2743	2744	2745	2746	2747	2748
2749	2750	2751	2752	2753	2754	2755
2756	2757	2758	2759	2760	2761	2762
2763	2764	2765	2766	2767	2768	2769
2770	2771	2772	2773	2774	2776	2777
2778	2779	2780	2781	2782	2783	2784
2785	2786	2787	2788	2789	2790	2791
2792	2793	2794	2795	2796	2797	2798
2799	2800	2801	2802	2803	2804	2805
2806	2807	2808	2809	2810	2811	2812
2813	2814	2815	2816	2817	2818	2819

2820 2821 2822 2823 2824 2825 2826
2827 2828 2829 2830 2831 2832 2833
2834 2835 2836 2837 2838 2839 2840
2841 2842 2843 2844 2845 2846 2847
2848 2849 2850 2851 2852 2853 2854
2855 2856 2857 2858 2859 2860 2861
2862 2863 2864 2865 2866 2867 2868
2869 2870 2871 2872 2873 2874 2875
2876 2877 2878 2879 2880 2881 2882
2883 2884 2885 2886 2887 2888 2889
2890 2891 2892 2893 2894 2895 2896
2897 2898 2899 2900 2901 2902 2903
2904 2905 2906 2907 2908 2909 2910
2911 2912 2913 2914 2915 2916 2917
2918 2919 2920 2921 2922 2923 2924
2925 2926 2927 2928 2929 2930 2931
2932 2933 2934 2935 2936 2937 2938
2939 2940 2941 2942 2943 2944 2945
2946 2947 2948 2949 2950 2951

EDUCATIONAL SOCIOLOGY
0002 0035 0036 0056 0116 0139 0208
0262 0269 0281 0288 0292 0359 0424
0426 0429 0460 0475 0504 0512 0527
0535 0556 0564 0638 0639 0735 0789
0795 0798 0911 0956 1026 1030 1124
1138 1175 1178 1236 1273 1278 1286
1298 1306 1385 1386 1387 1388 1389
1390 1391 1392 1393 1394 1395 1396
1397 1398 1399 1400 1401 1402 1403
1404 1405 1406 1407 1408 1426 1447
1549 1554 1555 1557 1569 1581 1587
1600 1620 1630 1632 1635 1644 1661
1672 1674 1760 1817 1839 1900 1907
1949 2035 2086 2096 2142 2156 2183
2187 2217 2259 2334 2370 2479 2547
2569 2616 2688 2705 2749 2765 2815
2910 2924 2932 2936

EDUCATIONAL SPACES
0177 0178 0179 0182 1027 1409 1645

EDUCATIONAL STATISTICS
0491 0976 1244 1410 1411 1536 2011
2102 2340 2505 2623 2801

EDUCATIONAL STRATEGIES
1412 1994 2114 2226 2697 2927

EDUCATIONAL TECHNOLOGY
0044 0049 0081 0093 0116 0136 0183
0259 0298 0300 0307 0316 0321 0322
0325 0329 0330 0340 0342 0351 0384
0421 0424 0431 0477 0524 0579 0607
0639 0663 0678 0724 0773 0797 0811
0853 0930 0956 0983 1022 1050 1053
1090 1092 1101 1108 1141 1149 1150
1163 1168 1177 1186 1199 1233 1269
1272 1278 1287 1291 1322 1392 1405
1413 1414 1415 1416 1417 1418 1419
1420 1421 1422 1423 1424 1425 1426
1427 1428 1429 1430 1431 1432 1433
1434 1435 1436 1437 1438 1439 1440
1441 1442 1443 1444 1445 1446 1447
1448 1449 1450 1451 1452 1577 1578
1603 1620 1634 1636 1657 1664 1672
1713 1719 1723 1739 1743 1760 1769
1770 1777 1807 1825 1835 1853 1859
1863 1874 1907 1977 1978 2009 2026
2071 2083 2116 2133 2134 2162 2219
2241 2265 2267 2274 2361 2438 2478
2513 2549 2570 2601 2608 2640 2658
2670 2684 2696 2699 2702 2716 2728
2730 2732 2754 2766 2773 2777 2784
2791 2796 2812 2851 2861 2930

EDUCATIONAL TELEVISION
0093 0154 0390 0407 0467 0528 0663
0678 0753 1413 1417 1451 1452 1453
1454 1777 1874 1889 1978 2050 2691

EDUCATIONAL TESTING
0328 1228 1455 1798 2095

EDUCATIONAL TESTS
0801 1456 1638

EDUCATIONAL THEORIES
0257 0559 0584 0824 1033 1241 1457
1458 1459 1460 1647 2180 2798 2848

EGYPT
0228 0885 0887 1303 1461 1462 1463
1464 1465 1466 2354 2383 2384

EMOTIONALLY DISTURBED
1268 1467 1707 1938 2097 2482

EMPLOYMENT
0037 0048 0061 0062 0063 0098 0110
0121 0166 0185 0242 0264 0326 0357
0442 0599 0613 0781 0787 0865 0869
0873 0960 0961 0970 0991 1014 1054
1056 1080 1081 1139 1153 1184 1209

1251 1252 1320 1362 1362 1364 1468
1469 1470 1471 1472 1473 1474 1475
1476 1477 1478 1479 1480 1481 1482
1483 1484 1485 1486 1487 1488 1489
1490 1491 1492 1493 1493 1494 1494
1495 1496 1505 1546 1579 1589 1602
1608 1628 1651 1665 1709 1797 2132
2146 2182 2192 2200 2252 2280 2305
2331 2481 2485 2638 2641 2714 2752
2778 2806 2826 2826 2837 2841 2853
2855 2857 2858 2859 2864 2865 2866
2868 2869 2870 2871 2873 2875 2876
2877 2878 2881 2883 2884 2885 2886
2889 2890 2890 2891 2893 2896 2900
2901 2903 2904 2908 2909 2911 2912
2913 2914 2921 2939

EMPLOYMENT OPPORTUNITIES
0067 0787 1134 1471 1496 1497 1579
1742 2331 2859

ENGINEERING EDUCATION
0092 0337 0443 1013 1018 1498 1499
1531 2248 2426 2645 2646

ENVIRONMENTAL EDUCATION
0063 0140 0199 0304 0334 0385 0572
0669 0745 0922 1014 1481 1500 1501
1502 1503 1504 1505 1589 1878 1985
2073 2146 2232 2284 2306 2410 2462
2591 2695 2873 2901 2908

ENVIRONMENTAL INFLUENCES
0205 1017 1506 1508 2931

EQUAL EDUCATION
0205 0525 1017 1506 1507 1508 1885
1973 2931

ETHIOPIA
1509 1510 1511 1703 2419 2511

EVALUATION
0099 0126 0132 0203 0234 0252 0296
0302 0303 0345 0354 0366 0368 0380
0399 0411 0412 0488 0491 0547 0551
0684 0709 0712 0728 0732 0841 0967
0976 0997 1000 1006 1013 1043 1152
1196 1200 1244 1249 1267 1309 1370
1371 1410 1411 1498 1509 1511 1512
1513 1514 1515 1516 1517 1518 1519
1520 1521 1522 1523 1525 1526 1528
1529 1530 1531 1532 1533 1534 1535
1536 1537 1538 1539 1540 1541 1545
1712 1727 1794 1821 1844 1884 1940
1997 2011 2039 2102 2103 2149 2245
2248 2272 2279 2321 2335 2339 2340
2377 2425 2434 2465 2505 2512 2515
2528 2534 2535 2552 2623 2645 2657
2660 2662 2713 2755 2757 2758 2760
2762 2769 2801 2804 2810 2827 2915

EVALUATION METHODS
0549 1020 1542 2066 2540

EXAMINATIONS
0105 0265 0950 1021 1152 1153 1487
1533 1543 1544 1545 1546 2057 2070
2145 2335 2336 2357 2637 2713 2714
2853

EXPERIMENTAL EDUCATION
0606 0792 1025 1547 1548 1584 2542
2595

FAILURE FACTORS
1138 1280 1399 1549 1550 1555 1864
2334 2547 2910

FAMILY (SOCIOLOGICAL UNIT)
0251 0621 0729 1551 2759

FAMILY EDUCATION
0139 0263 0272 0476 0624 0654 0762
1026 1138 1183 1306 1396 1399 1408
1549 1552 1553 1554 1555 1556 1557
1559 1644 2142 2147 2204 2243 2334
2423 2547 2551 2665 2910 2932 2936

FAMILY RELATIONSHIP
0339 0654 1070 1183 1556 1558 1559
1788 2551 2781

FAMILY ROLE
0230 1560 1933 2037 2636

FAMILY SCHOOL RELATIONSHIP
0128 0217 0231 0280 0422 0627 0700
0785 1223 1561 1565 1955 2338 2574
2795 2892

FINLAND
0019 0088 0217 0280 0310 0395 0422
0433 0554 0627 0650 0785 0908 0909

0911 1086 1107 1120 1275 1276 1390 1564 1565 1567 1568 1569 1570 1571 1572 1573 1574 1575 1721 1815 1934 2041 2167 2338 2573 2574 2598 2867 2892

FORMATIVE EVALUATION
0136 0325 1177 1441 1576 1577 2438 2514 2556

FRANCE
0009 0025 0027 0035 0037 0056 0063 0089 0225 0227 0245 0269 0317 0318 0323 0326 0338 0348 0362 0372 0430 0451 0461 0517 0530 0539 0564 0577 0611 0647 0648 0787 0788 0789 0790 0791 0792 0794 0795 1014 1019 1066 1067 1074 1106 1109 1130 1166 1170 1175 1176 1184 1199 1217 1222 1232 1248 1252 1270 1310 1335 1363 1365 1368 1387 1388 1400 1419 1443 1471 1481 1488 1491 1496 1505 1547 1578 1579 1580 1581 1582 1583 1584 1585 1586 1587 1588 1589 1590 1591 1592 1593 1594 1595 1596 1597 1598 1599 1600 1601 1602 1603 1604 1605 1606 1607 1608 1609 1610 1611 1612 1613 1614 1615 1697 1704 1710 1718 1725 1789 1797 1817 1900 1913 1918 1919 1951 1953 2001 2004 2008 2013 2017 2021 2040 2043 2047 2049 2054 2060 2063 2071 2118 2132 2146 2169 2174 2217 2249 2259 2281 2293 2331 2333 2365 2370 2393 2396 2402 2405 2450 2468 2486 2508 2509 2513 2608 2650 2688 2859 2860 2873 2883 2886 2901 2908 2912 2924 2929

FRENCH
1585 1615 1913 2040 2047

FUNCTIONAL LITERACY
0397 0940 1616 2135 2230

FURNITURE DESIGN
0101 1617

FURTHER TRAINING
0023 0102 0974 1110 1618 1619 1653 2643 2709 2879 2906

GEOGRAPHY INSTRUCTION
0116 0424 0639 0956 1392 1426 1620 1760 1907

GERMAN DR
0036 0181 0288 0292 0460 0508 0520 0533 0542 0602 0603 0985 0987 0988 0989 0990 0991 1034 1178 1265 1273 1341 1401 1404 1480 1621 1622 1623 1624 1625 1626 1627 1628 1629 1630 1631 1632 1633 1661 1820 1839 1941 1974 1998 2198 2358 2389 2575 2635 2649 2871

GERMANY FR
0031 0036 0050 0053 0141 0158 0177 0178 0179 0182 0241 0248 0256 0281 0286 0288 0291 0295 0298 0307 0351 0415 0456 0477 0504 0527 0579 0580 0581 0651 0656 0657 0661 0797 0798 0800 0801 0802 1004 1026 1027 1032 1033 1059 1065 1072 1081 1087 1110 1118 1126 1132 1141 1159 1162 1167 1178 1181 1185 1186 1209 1211 1212 1216 1220 1235 1266 1278 1282 1286 1288 1289 1301 1325 1329 1339 1348 1364 1389 1396 1401 1405 1406 1409 1420 1421 1436 1442 1447 1456 1459 1485 1489 1495 1554 1619 1630 1634 1635 1636 1637 1638 1639 1640 1641 1642 1643 1644 1645 1646 1647 1648 1649 1650 1651 1652 1653 1654 1655 1656 1657 1658 1659 1660 1661 1662 1663 1664 1665 1666 1667 1668 1669 1670 1671 1672 1673 1674 1675 1676 1677 1678 1679 1709 1726 1747 1757 1801 1838 1921 1925 1954 1991 2003 2007 2009 2010 2038 2042 2045 2062 2064 2141 2150 2170 2173 2176 2236 2237 2265 2353 2364 2381 2392 2395 2399 2417 2421 2432 2437 2448 2473 2477 2485 2590 2602 2611 2673 2687 2709 2741 2861 2874 2878 2879 2884 2891 2900 2902 2913 2932 2933 2936

GHANA
1069 1342 2363 2378

GRADE REPETITION
0232 2568 2621 2625

GREECE
0010 0805 1366 1381 1819 2199

GUATEMALA
0176 0711 1728 2346 2497

GUIDANCE
0218 0356 0357 0358 0360 0361 0362
0363 0364 0441 0625 0780 0869 1039
1197 1201 1217 1247 1294 1474 1604
1695 1696 1697 1698 1699 1787 1789
1862 2091 2543 2803 2814 2841 2854
2865 2893 2897 2899 2921

GULF STATES
0889 1700

GUYANA
0393 0897 1701 1702 2584

HANDICAPPED
0451 0788 0857 1003 1268 1353 1364
1365 1467 1495 1510 1580 1613 1703
1704 1705 1706 1707 1708 1709 1710
1718 1938 2049 2097 2127 2281 2293
2419 2450 2468 2470 2472 2482 2484
2485 2486 2511 2592 2633 2820 2829
2891 2900

HANDICAPPED EDUCATION
1711 2387 2464

HANDICAPPED STUDENTS
0011 0118 0183 0244 0728 0773 0830
0923 1038 1246 1365 1418 1519 1613
1710 1712 1713 1714 1715 1716 1717
1718 2012 2068 2293 2330 2463 2480
2486 2515 2518 2758 2802 2894

HEALTH EDUCATION
0088 0089 0188 0300 0384 0724 1120
1146 1163 1204 1232 1289 1415 1439
1573 1606 1676 1719 1720 1721 1722
1723 1724 1725 1726 1773 2026 2051
2163 2167 2168 2169 2170 2367 2549
2712 2754 2831

HIGHER EDUCATION
0007 0022 0047 0067 0107 0113 0161
0167 0190 0215 0234 0237 0238 0289
0296 0313 0342 0370 0445 0447 0474
0536 0539 0715 0726 0748 0902 0953
1012 1022 1040 1064 1134 1150 1151
1154 1194 1212 1222 1261 1293 1302
1312 1321 1332 1343 1345 1348 1375
1429 1438 1497 1513 1605 1667 1727
1728 1729 1730 1731 1732 1733 1735
1736 1737 1738 1739 1740 1741 1742
1743 1744 1745 1746 1747 1749 1750
1751 1752 1753 1754 1755 1757 1758
1759 1793 1845 1881 2029 2078 2087
2189 2216 2247 2271 2346 2356 2360
2361 2386 2458 2459 2494 2497 2501
2503 2560 2589 2702 2756 2809 2813
2816 2847 2851 2852 2951

HISTORY INSTRUCTION
0116 0424 0639 0956 1157 1392 1426
1620 1759 1760 1761 1907 1935 2271
2356 2368 2458 2715

HOLY SEE
1161 1762 1861 2286

HONDURAS
0712 1515 2321

HUMAN RELATIONS
1187 2273 2794

HUNGARY
0024 0276 0553 0806 0807 0808 0983
1108 1311 1318 1428 1435 1765 1767
1768 1769 1770 1771 1772 2424 2576
2601

HYGIENE
1720 1773 2163 2831

IIEP
0518 0612 0617 1382 1774 2742

INDIA
0021 0423 0521 0663 0741 0934 1367
1417 1452 1775 1776 1777 1778 1779
1780 1781 1782 1783 1804 2075 2117
2303 2314 2347 2571 2586 2917

INDIVIDUAL CHARACTERISTICS
1784 1785 2179

INDIVIDUAL DEVELOPMENT
1784 1785 2179

INDIVIDUAL DIFFERENCES
0376 0836 1786 2382 2431 2523 2862

INDIVIDUAL PSYCHOLOGY
0339 0356 0362 0441 0625 0780 1070 1217 1558 1604 1697 1787 1788 1789 2781

INDIVIDUALIZED CURRICULUM
0133 0365 1008 1790 1999 2233 2656

INDIVIDUALIZED INSTRUCTION
0006 0037 0077 0309 0314 0326 0328 0474 0747 0816 0967 1016 1165 1184 1228 1455 1488 1525 1602 1735 1791 1792 1793 1794 1795 1796 1797 1798 1826 1880 1960 1983 1997 2056 2080 2095 2272 2386 2415 2459 2535 2578 2701 2883 2912

INDONESIA
0241 0291 0935 0936 1266 1671 1799 1800 1801 1838 2141 2246 2251 2493 2611 2745 2750

INFANTS
0072 0694 1802 1932 2562

INFORMAL EDUCATION
0131 0333 0772 1803 2053 2072 2154 2161 2223

INFORMATION DISSEMINATION
1775 1804 1805 2571 2692

INFORMATION SCIENCE
0297 0482 1283 1806 1865 2373

INFORMATION SYSTEMS
0322 1168 1440 1807 2134 2716

INSERVICE EDUCATION
0005 1993 2689

INSERVICE TEACHER EDUCATION
0035 0073 0197 0211 0310 0324 0383 0440 0480 0564 0671 0750 1172 1175 1284 1381 1400 1568 1600 1775 1804 1809 1810 1814 1815 1816 1817 1818 1819 1866 1883 2046 2217 2220 2282 2370 2451 2565 2567 2571 2580 2617 2628 2867 2924

INSTRUCTION
0520 1341 1633 1820

INSTRUCTIONAL IMPROVEMENT
0303 0732 1521 1821 2762

INSTRUCTIONAL MATERIALS
0180 0541 1822 1823 1893 2840

INSTRUCTIONAL PROGRAMMES
0153 0332 0340 0607 0737 1092 1433 1824 1825 1835 1977 2253 2767 2784 2856

INTEGRATED ACTIVITIES
0314 1016 1795 1826 1960 2056 2415 2701

INTEGRATED CURRICULUM
1304 2435

INTERCULTURAL PROGRAMMES
0142 0290 1264 1828 1837 1922 2727

INTERDISCIPLINARY APPROACH
0135 1041 1829

INTERNATIONAL EDUCATION
0076 0142 0143 0241 0278 0279 0282 0283 0284 0290 0291 0292 0293 0294 0340 0455 0457 0460 0462 0607 0706 0749 0839 1052 1084 1092 1148 1264 1266 1273 1324 1372 1404 1433 1632 1671 1801 1825 1828 1830 1831 1832 1833 1834 1835 1836 1837 1838 1839 1840 1841 1882 1922 1924 1927 1977 2099 2141 2313 2315 2323 2526 2611 2727 2776 2783 2784 2819

INTERNATIONAL SCHOOLS
1202 1842 2092

INTERPERSONAL RELATIONSHIP
1355 1843 1946 2821

IRAN (ISLAMIC REPUBLIC)
1043 1532 1844 2662

IRAQ
1737 1845 2589

IRELAND
0157 1029 1068 1846 1847 1916 2058

ISRAEL

0744 1330 1347 1361 1848 1849 1850 1851 2016 2019 2275 2277 2375 2401 2404

ITALY
0033 0127 0297 0360 0482 0523 0524 0567 0810 0811 0812 1060 1085 1088 1089 1090 1143 1161 1197 1269 1280 1283 1284 1305 1307 1338 1351 1352 1354 1357 1422 1432 1445 1550 1695 1762 1806 1818 1852 1853 1854 1855 1856 1857 1858 1859 1860 1861 1862 1863 1864 1865 1866 1867 1868 1869 1870 1871 1872 1873 2046 2195 2286 2373 2418 2597 2599 2614 2747 2897 2898 2934

IVORY COAST
0093 0678 1413 1451 1874 1875 1978 2221

JAMAICA
0250 0713 1113 1876 1877 1961 2495 2685

JAPAN
0279 0304 0385 0406 0455 0572 0745 0747 0748 0749 0750 1501 1731 1791 1831 1878 1879 1880 1881 1882 1883 1983 2348

JORDAN
1309 1539 1884

KENYA
0417 0525 1271 1507 1885 1886 1973

KOREA R
0028 0090 0091 0129 0226 0355 0407 0540 0623 0751 0752 0753 0754 0756 0758 0759 1093 1094 1453 1822 1887 1888 1889 1890 1891 1893 1894 1895 1896 1897 2350 2622

KUWAIT
0418 0432 1253 1898 1899

LANGUAGE DEVELOPMENT
0054 0056 0235 0269 0270 0312 0377 0449 0563 0789 0993 1023 1174 1387 1581 1900 1901 1902 1903 1908 1909 2067 2197 2259 2288 2433 2688 2703 2718

LANGUAGE INSTRUCTION
0054 0116 0160 0235 0270 0312 0424 0449 0639 0912 0916 0956 0993 1023 1378 1392 1426 1620 1760 1901 1902 1904 1905 1906 1907 1908 1909 1910 1915 1947 2067 2355 2385 2452 2456 2703 2838 2849

LANGUAGE RESEARCH
0828 1911 1914

LANGUAGES
0059 0141 0142 0143 0144 0150 0152 0157 0158 0159 0187 0189 0290 0293 0723 0828 1029 1058 1106 1166 1203 1211 1264 1323 1324 1325 1331 1585 1595 1598 1615 1666 1678 1828 1837 1840 1846 1904 1911 1912 1913 1914 1915 1916 1917 1918 1919 1920 1921 1922 1923 1924 1925 1926 1957 1958 2040 2043 2045 2047 2058 2059 2060 2063 2064 2065 2069 2313 2429 2531 2727 2753 2819 2838

LATIN AMERICA
0278 0706 0720 1830 1927 1928

LEARNING
0212 0327 1206 1314 1929 1930 2609 2946

LEARNING ACTIVITIES
1931 2768

LEARNING DIFFICULTIES
0072 0230 0395 0554 0694 1157 1262 1560 1570 1761 1802 1932 1933 1934 1935 1936 2037 2368 2562 2636 2715 2725

LEARNING DISABILITIES
0658 1254 1268 1360 1467 1707 1937 1938 1939 1945 2097 2131 2482 2825

LEARNING PROCESSES
0045 0169 0252 0275 0302 0658 0989 1031 1127 1237 1254 1355 1520 1626 1843 1937 1940 1941 1942 1943 1944 1945 1946 2131 2215 2491 2706 2760 2821

LEARNING THEORIES
0168 0208 0359 0402 0429 0512 0916 1122 1124 1398 1906 1947 1948 1949 2385 2456 2479

LEBANON
0071 0895 1950

LEISURE
0025 0372 1019 1590 1951 2118 2650 2929

LIBERIA
0907 1952

LIFELONG EDUCATION
0009 0046 0106 0128 0456 0791 1223 1239 1583 1642 1953 1954 1955 1956 2122 2590 2687 2741 2795 2860

LINGUISTICS
0059 0187 1058 1203 1917 1920 1957 1958 2059 2069 2429

LITERACY
0039 0043 0163 0172 0314 0373 1001 1016 1113 1198 1229 1230 1231 1795 1826 1877 1959 1960 1961 1962 1963 1964 1965 2033 2048 2056 2106 2121 2166 2218 2240 2415 2442 2527 2655 2701

LITERACY CAMPAIGNS
0271 0898 1966 2115 2140 2304

LUXEMBOURG
0813 1182 1967 1968 2044 2207 2225

MALAYSIA
0396 0545 0929 1969 1970 2213 2337 2407 2631

MALI
0681 1971 1979

MALTA
0809 1972 2577

MANAGEMENT
0508 0525 0602 0608 1128 1507 1623 1885 1973 1974 1975 2490

MANAGEMENT EDUCATION
0413 1005 1976 2593 2700

MANAGEMENT SYSTEMS
0340 0607 1092 1433 1825 1835 1977 2784

MASS MEDIA
0093 0678 1413 1451 1874 1978

MATERIALS PREPARATION
0066 0192 0199 0434 0681 0686 0690 0719 0747 0761 1076 1319 1504 1791 1880 1971 1979 1980 1981 1982 1983 1984 1985 1986 2232 2264 2306 2427 2487 2591 2751 2818

MATHEMATICS INSTRUCTION
0005 0052 0083 0116 0131 0133 0225 0318 0333 0348 0365 0403 0424 0430 0487 0558 0639 0766 0772 0800 0833 0956 0963 0967 0987 1008 1028 1067 1095 1126 1130 1155 1164 1167 1176 1186 1216 1244 1246 1248 1277 1290 1330 1335 1346 1347 1356 1368 1392 1411 1412 1426 1442 1525 1536 1592 1597 1601 1607 1611 1614 1620 1624 1637 1655 1660 1664 1668 1717 1760 1790 1794 1803 1849 1850 1907 1988 1989 1991 1992 1993 1994 1996 1997 1998 1999 2000 2001 2002 2003 2004 2005 2006 2007 2008 2009 2010 2011 2012 2013 2014 2016 2017 2019 2020 2021 2053 2072 2114 2154 2161 2173 2174 2184 2201 2223 2226 2233 2249 2272 2352 2353 2358 2362 2364 2365 2369 2374 2375 2376 2380 2381 2388 2389 2390 2391 2392 2393 2394 2395 2396 2399 2400 2401 2402 2403 2404 2405 2480 2532 2535 2548 2550 2624 2634 2656 2668 2689 2697 2704 2729 2737 2801 2802 2811 2822 2927

MAURITIUS
0243 0419 0682 2022

MEASUREMENT
0201 0394 0410 1036 2023 2024 2585 2659

MEASUREMENT TECHNIQUES
1121 2030 2647

MEDICAL EDUCATION
0300 0384 0724 1227 1415 1719 2026 2027 2554 2754

MEXICO
0002 0038 0043 0346 0450 0537 0610 0715 1121 1173 1190 1230 1234 1236 1327 1328 1402 1729 1964 2028 2029 2030 2031 2032 2033 2034 2035 2036 2113 2121 2311 2616 2647

MICROTEACHING
0132 0230 0997 1528 1560 1641 1933 2037 2038 2039 2279 2425 2437 2512 2636

MIGRANT EDUCATION
0053 0141 0158 0295 0909 1004 1106 1182 1211 1284 1567 1585 1595 1615 1643 1666 1818 1866 1913 1918 1921 1968 2040 2041 2042 2043 2044 2045 2046 2047 2060 2432 2448 2473

MIGRANT PROBLEMS
1001 1585 1615 1913 1959 2040 2047 2048 2166 2442 2527 2655

MINORITY GROUP CHILDREN
0154 0390 0451 0467 0528 0788 1454 1580 1704 2049 2050 2281 2450 2468 2691

MINORITY GROUPS
1146 1722 2051 2367 2712

MODERN LANGUAGE INSTRUCTION
0105 0131 0157 0187 0189 0200 0314 0331 0333 0580 0722 0772 0790 1016 1021 1029 1058 1106 1142 1162 1166 1325 1331 1544 1582 1585 1595 1598 1615 1659 1678 1795 1803 1826 1846 1913 1916 1917 1918 1919 1925 1926 1957 1960 2040 2043 2047 2052 2053 2054 2056 2057 2058 2059 2060 2061 2062 2063 2064 2065 2070 2072 2145 2154 2161 2188 2196 2223 2336 2415 2637 2701

MOTHER TONGUE INSTRUCTION
0059 0118 0270 0449 0549 1020 1023 1038 1203 1542 1716 1902 1909 1920 1958 2066 2067 2068 2069 2330 2429 2540 2703

MOTHERS
0105 1021 1544 2057 2070 2145 2336 2637

MULTIMEDIA INSTRUCTION
1419 1578 2071

MUSIC EDUCATION
0131 0333 0772 1803 2053 2072 2154 2161 2223

NATIONAL LANGUAGE
0018 0140 0145 0669 1500 2073 2074 2317 2629 2746 2844

NATIONAL REGIONAL DISPARITIES
0521 1780 2075

NEPAL
0938 0939 2076 2077 2516 2563 2587 2661

NETHERLANDS
0006 0040 0086 0294 0309 0313 0328 0361 0387 0398 0425 0462 0574 0815 0816 1012 1013 1036 1147 1201 1202 1207 1210 1228 1268 1274 1372 1395 1403 1427 1455 1467 1498 1531 1696 1707 1732 1738 1792 1798 1841 1842 1938 2024 2078 2079 2080 2081 2082 2083 2084 2085 2086 2087 2090 2091 2092 2093 2094 2095 2096 2097 2098 2099 2247 2248 2315 2360 2422 2471 2482 2496 2578 2632 2645

NEW ZEALAND
0017 0491 0493 0881 0882 0976 1410 2100 2102 2340 2505 2623 2652

NICARAGUA
0547 1516 2103

NIGER
0057 0683 2104

NIGERIA
0039 0042 0058 0064 0685 1198 1218 1295 1297 1299 1962 2105 2106 2107 2108 2109 2110 2171 2345 2406 2467

2612

NONFORMAL EDUCATION
0025 0030 0043 0046 0106 0140 0233 0266 0271 0273 0372 0423 0669 0702 0898 0930 1019 1114 1116 1230 1239 1250 1412 1425 1500 1590 1781 1951 1956 1964 1966 1994 2028 2033 2073 2112 2113 2114 2115 2116 2117 2118 2119 2120 2121 2122 2123 2140 2157 2226 2304 2310 2586 2650 2670 2674 2697 2805 2927 2929

NORWAY
0094 0658 0819 0820 0968 1003 1007 1075 1111 1254 1706 1937 1945 2124 2125 2126 2127 2128 2129 2130 2131 2285 2322 2472 2558 2592 2633 2895

OCCUPATIONAL SURVEYS
1252 1491 1608 2132 2886

OPEN LEARNING SYSTEMS
0322 0853 1168 1423 1440 1807 2133 2134 2696 2716

PAKISTAN
0004 0397 0490 0519 0636 0940 0941 0980 1091 1616 2135 2136 2137 2138 2139 2230 2414 2420

PAPUA NEW GUINEA
0271 0898 1966 2115 2140 2304

PARAGUAY
0241 0291 1266 1671 1801 1838 2141 2611

PARENT CHILD RELATIONSHIP
0139 1306 1408 1557 2142

PARENT EDUCATION PROGRAMMES
0352 0448 0619 2143 2935

PARENT PARTICIPATION
0069 0104 1011 2144 2172 2329 2474 2594 2619

PARENTS
0105 1021 1544 2057 2070 2145 2336 2637

PART TIME TRAINING
0063 1014 1481 1505 1589 2146 2873 2901 2908

PEER TEACHING
0263 0272 0476 1553 2147 2423

PERFORMANCE FACTORS
1024 2148 2506 2541 2618

PERFORMANCE TESTS
0099 0248 0256 0411 0415 1185 1526 1663 2149 2150 2421

PERSONALITY DEVELOPMENT
2151 2835

PERSONALITY PROBLEMS
0276 0553 0807

PERSONALITY STUDIES
0131 0333 0622 0642 0772 0998 1803 2053 2072 2153 2154 2155 2161 2223 2537 2763 2907

PERU
1114 1158 1385 2119 2156 2157 2158 2310

PHILIPPINES
0147 0981 2159 2160 2351 2379 2918

PHYSICAL EDUCATION
0081 0088 0089 0131 0188 0204 0333 0772 0994 1001 1120 1204 1232 1289 1299 1424 1573 1606 1676 1720 1721 1724 1725 1726 1773 1803 1959 2048 2053 2072 2110 2154 2161 2162 2163 2164 2165 2166 2167 2168 2169 2170 2171 2223 2406 2442 2527 2536 2640 2655 2699 2831

PHYSICAL HANDICAPS
0069 0104 1011 2144 2172 2329 2474 2594 2619

PHYSICS
0225 1126 1130 1335 1597 1611 1655 2003 2004 2017 2173 2174 2364 2365 2392 2393 2402

PLAY

1159 1658 2176 2237 2417 2673

POLAND
0048 0061 0062 0083 0289 0371 0404 0558 0655 0824 0960 0961 0963 1142 1194 1195 1296 1320 1374 1393 1394 1457 1477 1478 1492 1746 1784 1785 1996 2061 2177 2178 2179 2180 2182 2183 2184 2185 2186 2187 2188 2189 2190 2191 2192 2193 2196 2388 2517 2579 2663 2869 2870 2889 2914 2928

POLITICAL EDUCATION
0065 0377 0563 0812 1142 1174 1854 1903 2061 2188 2194 2195 2196 2197 2288 2433 2718

POLYTECHNICAL EDUCATION
1265 1631 2198 2649

POPULATION EDUCATION
0010 0805 2199

PORTUGAL
0029 0599 0613 1095 1096 1344 1472 2002 2200 2201 2202 2203 2280 2316 2391

PREPRIMARY CHILDREN
0155 0624 0762 1552 2204 2205 2243 2665 2845

PREPRIMARY EDUCATION
0035 0161 0167 0172 0260 0275 0373 0438 0545 0564 0813 0858 0870 0872 0929 0945 1031 1040 1175 1231 1400 1600 1740 1817 1942 1965 1967 1969 2206 2207 2208 2209 2210 2211 2212 2213 2214 2215 2216 2217 2218 2224 2225 2227 2228 2231 2337 2370 2409 2411 2412 2461 2706 2739 2830 2836 2842 2922 2924 2938

PRESCHOOL LEARNING
1053 1431 2219 2777

PRIMARY EDUCATION
0020 0044 0078 0124 0131 0133 0163 0164 0171 0186 0197 0199 0260 0333 0365 0397 0431 0438 0464 0605 0671 0772 0813 0870 0872 0940 0945 1008 1015 1057 1072 1159 1192 1208 1229 1233 1340 1412 1444 1504 1616 1650 1658 1790 1803 1809 1875 1963 1967 1985 1994 1999 2053 2072 2114 2135 2154 2161 2176 2206 2207 2210 2211 2214 2220 2221 2222 2223 2224 2225 2226 2227 2228 2229 2230 2231 2232 2233 2235 2236 2237 2238 2239 2240 2241 2242 2257 2267 2306 2312 2372 2409 2412 2413 2416 2417 2539 2565 2591 2656 2673 2697 2736 2739 2796 2842 2922 2927 2938

PRIMARY SCHOOL STUDENTS
0624 0762 1552 2204 2243 2665

PRINCIPALS
0138 1193 2244 2250 2561

PRIVATE EDUCATION
0126 0203 0936 1523 1800 2245 2246 2251 2493 2745 2750

PROBLEM SOLVING
0138 0313 0430 1012 1013 1176 1193 1498 1531 1601 1738 2008 2087 2244 2247 2248 2249 2250 2360 2396 2561 2645

PRODUCTIVITY
0936 1800 2246 2251 2493 2745 2750

PROFESSIONAL EDUCATION
0121 1080 1484 2252 2877 2909

PROGRAMME DESIGN
0153 0332 0737 1824 2253 2254 2767 2856 2944

PROGRAMME EVALUATION
0311 0598 0605 0917 1015 1182 1968 2044 2256 2257 2457 2539 2667

PSYCHOLOGICAL TESTING
0056 0269 0789 1387 1581 1900 2259 2688

PSYCHOLOGY
0633 0862 2260 2441 2834

PUBLIC SCHOOLS
2261 2764

QATAR
0614 2262 2263 2269 2583

READABILITY
0298 0307 0761 0797 1420 1634 1984 2264 2265 2487

READING
0044 0221 0246 0431 0626 0782 1233 1242 1444 2241 2266 2267 2268 2796 2799

READING DIFFICULTY
0209 1125 2263 2269 2270 2507 2583

READING INSTRUCTION
0967 1525 1759 1794 1997 2271 2272 2356 2458 2535

READING PROCESSES
1187 2273 2794

READING RESEARCH
0247 0421 0427 0744 1105 1361 1416 1848 1851 2274 2275 2276 2277 2500 2570 2600 2658 2766 2786 2930

RECREATION
2278 2332 2850

REFERENCE MATERIALS
0132 0997 1528 2039 2279 2425 2512

REGIONAL PLANNING
0599 0613 1472 2200 2280

REHABILITATION
0451 0788 1580 1704 2049 2281 2450 2468

REHABILITATION PROGRAMMES
0211 0324 0480 1172 1816 2282

RELIGIOUS EDUCATION
0094 0109 0151 0347 0375 0377 0563 0769 1007 1161 1169 1174 1188 1243 1334 1502 1762 1861 1903 2128 2197 2283 2284 2285 2286 2287 2288 2289 2290 2291 2410 2433 2529 2558 2604 2695 2717 2718 2733 2800

RESEARCH METHODOLOGY
0320 0428 0575 1119 2292 2711

RETARDED CHILDREN
1365 1613 1710 1718 2293 2486

ROMANIA
0367 0649 0826 0827 0828 1083 1369 1911 1914 2294 2295

RURAL DEVELOPMENT
0147 0231 0264 0700 0981 1139 1367 1476 1486 1561 1783 2160 2303 2305 2314 2752 2868 2881 2911 2918

RURAL EDUCATION
0001 0038 0070 0143 0171 0199 0264 0271 0274 0293 0294 0299 0462 0534 0898 1002 1047 1103 1114 1190 1208 1324 1367 1372 1476 1504 1783 1840 1841 1924 1966 1985 2032 2099 2115 2119 2140 2157 2232 2239 2303 2304 2305 2306 2307 2308 2309 2310 2311 2312 2313 2314 2315 2359 2591 2644 2770 2785 2819 2868 2872

RURAL POPULATION
0029 1096 2202 2316

RUSSIAN
0018 0145 2074 2317 2629 2746 2844

RWANDA
0401 1047 1048 2308 2319

SAUDI ARABIA

SCHOOL COMMUNITY RELATIONSHIP
0076 0712 0968 1148 1515 1836 2126 2321 2322 2323 2895

SCHOOL INDUSTRY RELATIONSHIP
0369 0571 0827 0877 1179 1209 1489 1665 2295 2447 2605 2793 2884 2913 2943

SCHOOL INTEGRATION
0069 0104 0118 1011 1038 1716 2068 2144 2172 2329 2330 2474 2594 2619

SCHOOL LEAVERS

0787 1471 1496 1579 2331 2859

SCHOOL LEAVING
0530 1138 1152 1399 1533 1545 1549 1555 1588 2278 2332 2333 2334 2335 2547 2713 2850 2910

SCHOOL LIBRARIES
0105 1021 1544 2057 2070 2145 2336 2637

SCHOOL MAPPING
0545 0929 1969 2213 2337

SCHOOL ORGANIZATION
0217 0280 0422 0627 0785 1565 2338 2574 2892

SCHOOL STATISTICS
0491 0976 1336 1410 1517 2102 2339 2340 2341 2505 2623 2734 2755

SCHOOL SYSTEMS
0075 0103 0975 2342 2343

SCIENCE EDUCATION
0001 0032 0035 0058 0070 0078 0198 0225 0265 0274 0297 0299 0313 0354 0406 0482 0534 0564 0586 0653 0672 0685 0756 0759 0766 0800 0885 0912 0950 0987 1002 1012 1022 1028 1069 1126 1130 1131 1146 1157 1164 1175 1180 1192 1283 1290 1330 1346 1370 1400 1429 1463 1540 1543 1597 1600 1624 1637 1655 1722 1728 1738 1739 1759 1761 1778 1806 1817 1849 1865 1879 1895 1905 1935 1989 1991 1998 2000 2003 2004 2006 2016 2051 2087 2105 2159 2173 2174 2217 2238 2247 2271 2307 2344 2345 2346 2347 2348 2350 2351 2352 2353 2354 2355 2356 2357 2358 2359 2360 2361 2362 2363 2364 2365 2366 2367 2368 2369 2370 2371 2372 2373 2374 2375 2376 2377 2379 2380 2381 2383 2389 2390 2392 2393 2394 2397 2401 2403 2452 2458 2467 2497 2550 2606 2622 2644 2668 2702 2704 2712 2715 2719 2729 2737 2770 2788 2872 2880 2924

SCIENCE INSTRUCTION
0083 0225 0344 0348 0376 0403 0430 0474 0558 0766 0800 0836 0885 0887 0916 0963 0987 1028 1095 1126 1130 1164 1167 1176 1180 1191 1216 1277 1330 1335 1346 1347 1368 1463 1465 1597 1601 1611 1614 1624 1637 1655 1660 1668 1711 1735 1786 1793 1849 1850 1906 1947 1989 1991 1996 1998 2000 2002 2003 2004 2006 2007 2008 2010 2014 2016 2017 2019 2021 2159 2173 2174 2184 2201 2249 2351 2352 2353 2354 2358 2362 2364 2365 2369 2371 2375 2376 2378 2379 2380 2381 2382 2383 2384 2385 2386 2387 2388 2389 2390 2391 2392 2393 2394 2395 2396 2397 2398 2399 2400 2401 2402 2403 2404 2405 2431 2456 2459 2464 2523 2550 2606 2607 2668 2704 2719 2720 2737 2811 2862

SCIENCE TEACHERS
1299 2110 2171 2406

SCIENTIFIC RESEARCH
0396 1970 2407 2631

SECOND LANGUAGES
0148 1240 2408 2797

SECONDARY EDUCATION
0020 0124 0186 0314 0438 0872 0980 1016 1057 1159 1338 1502 1658 1795 1826 1869 1960 2056 2138 2176 2206 2209 2211 2224 2228 2229 2235 2237 2284 2409 2410 2411 2412 2413 2414 2415 2416 2417 2418 2420 2673 2695 2701 2836 2938

SECONDARY SCHOOL STUDENTS
0248 0256 0415 0980 1185 1510 1663 1703 2138 2150 2414 2419 2420 2421 2511

SECONDARY SCHOOLS
1210 2094 2422

SELF CONCEPT
0263 0272 0476 1553 2147 2423

SELF INSTRUCTIONAL METHODS
0024 0092 0132 0337 0443 0997 1018 1499 1528 1768 2039 2279 2424 2425 2426 2512 2646

SENEGAL
0059 0060 0686 1203 1258 1920 1958 1980 2069 2427 2428 2429 2430 2492 2675

SEX DIFFERENCES
0053 0295 0376 0377 0563 0836 1004 1174 1643 1786 1903 2042 2197 2288 2382 2431 2432 2433 2448 2473 2523 2718 2862

SIERRA LEONE
1196 1304 1377 1534 2434 2435 2436 2657

SIMULATION
0136 0325 1177 1441 1577 1641 2038 2437 2438

SINGAPORE
0305 0408 0763 1102 2439 2440 2510

SOCIAL PSYCHOLOGY
0134 0468 0633 0862 1001 1035 1959 2048 2166 2260 2441 2442 2443 2527 2655 2834

SOCIAL SCIENCES
0117 0400 1010 2444

SOCIAL STUDIES
0718 2445 2676

SOCIALIZATION
0053 0229 0295 0832 0877 1004 1263 1643 2042 2432 2446 2447 2448 2449 2469 2473 2520 2581 2726 2943

SOCIALLY MALADJUSTED
0451 0788 1580 1704 2049 2281 2450 2468

SPAIN
0146 0156 0311 0334 0474 0499 0912 0913 0914 0915 0916 0917 0920 0922 0923 1503 1711 1715 1735 1759 1793 1814 1905 1906 1947 2212 2256 2271 2355 2356 2385 2386 2387 2451 2452 2453 2454 2455 2456 2457 2458 2459 2460 2461 2462 2463 2464 2465 2580 2628 2894

SPECIAL EDUCATION
0053 0058 0069 0084 0104 0208 0295 0315 0359 0398 0429 0451 0512 0685 0788 0832 0857 1003 1004 1011 1042 1059 1101 1124 1246 1251 1268 1353 1364 1365 1398 1434 1467 1490 1495 1580 1613 1643 1648 1704 1705 1706 1707 1708 1709 1710 1717 1718 1938 1949 2012 2042 2049 2084 2097 2105 2127 2144 2172 2281 2293 2329 2345 2432 2446 2448 2450 2467 2468 2469 2470 2471 2472 2473 2474 2475 2476 2477 2478 2479 2480 2481 2482 2483 2484 2485 2486 2520 2581 2592 2594 2613 2619 2627 2632 2633 2684 2738 2771 2775 2802 2806 2820 2829 2885 2891 2900

SRI LANKA
0045 0608 0761 1097 1098 1128 1237 1944 1975 1984 2264 2487 2488 2489 2490 2491

STUDENT ATTITUDES
2428 2492

STUDENT CHARACTERISTICS
0936 1154 1745 1800 2246 2251 2493 2494 2560 2745 2750 2852

STUDENT EVALUATION
0250 0713 1876 2495 2685

STUDENT MOTIVATION
0040 0086 1207 2093 2496

STUDENT RESEARCH
0107 0184 0247 0427 0447 1055 1105 1261 1317 1375 1728 1749 1758 2276 2346 2497 2498 2499 2500 2501 2502 2503 2519 2600 2620 2731 2786 2809

STUDENT TEACHER RELATIONSHIP
0165 0209 0245 0245 0420 0491 0697 0976 1024 1125 1363 1363 1410 1612 1612 2102 2148 2270 2340 2504 2505 2506 2507 2508 2508 2509 2509 2541 2618 2623

STUDENT TEACHERS
0305 0408 0763 2439 2510

STUDY HABITS
1510 1703 2419 2511

STUDY SKILLS
0132 0997 1528 2039 2279 2425 2512

SUCCESS FACTORS
1199 1443 1603 2513 2608

SUMMATIVE EVALUATION
0728 1519 1576 1712 2514 2515 2556 2758

SUPERVISION
0938 2076 2516 2661

SUPERVISORS
2177 2517 2579

SWEDEN
0011 0012 0150 0159 0244 0282 0376 0388 0466 0630 0631 0830 0832 0834 0835 0836 0838 0839 1001 1006 1188 1285 1323 1530 1714 1786 1832 1923 1959 2048 2166 2289 2382 2431 2442 2446 2469 2498 2518 2519 2520 2521 2522 2523 2524 2525 2526 2527 2528 2529 2530 2531 2581 2620 2655 2862

SWITZERLAND
0013 0052 0319 0341 0345 0358 0549 0551 0604 0605 0606 0642 0654 0833 0841 0967 0998 1009 1015 1020 1024 1025 1039 1044 1117 1137 1138 1155 1163 1164 1183 1200 1224 1227 1399 1439 1522 1525 1535 1542 1548 1549 1555 1556 1559 1723 1794 1992 1997 2005 2006 2027 2066 2148 2155 2165 2257 2272 2334 2369 2394 2506 2532 2533 2534 2535 2536 2537 2538 2539 2540 2541 2542 2543 2544 2545 2546 2547 2548 2549 2550 2551 2552 2553 2554 2595 2615 2618 2634 2854 2899 2907 2910

SYRIAN AR
0893 2555

TANZANIA UR
0026 1061 1576 2514 2556 2557

TEACHER BEHAVIOUR
0094 0138 0207 1007 1123 1154 1193 1745 2128 2244 2250 2285 2494 2558 2559 2560 2561 2852

TEACHER CHARACTERISTICS
0072 0444 0694 0939 1145 1802 1932 2077 2562 2563 2564 2587 2603

TEACHER EDUCATION
0006 0069 0073 0079 0104 0122 0197 0199 0201 0212 0217 0232 0241 0247 0261 0280 0291 0309 0327 0344 0383 0393 0394 0410 0413 0421 0422 0423 0427 0444 0453 0456 0555 0567 0571 0606 0627 0671 0688 0735 0783 0785 0806 0809 0816 0832 0939 0946 1003 1005 1011 1025 1082 1085 1086 1088 1105 1108 1132 1145 1169 1179 1180 1191 1199 1206 1225 1266 1295 1357 1386 1416 1435 1443 1504 1548 1564 1565 1571 1603 1621 1642 1656 1671 1701 1706 1737 1765 1770 1775 1781 1792 1801 1804 1809 1810 1814 1838 1845 1856 1857 1873 1929 1954 1972 1976 1985 2023 2077 2080 2108 2117 2127 2141 2144 2172 2177 2220 2232 2263 2269 2274 2276 2287 2306 2329 2338 2371 2397 2398 2446 2451 2469 2472 2474 2483 2500 2513 2517 2520 2542 2563 2564 2565 2566 2567 2568 2569 2570 2571 2572 2573 2574 2575 2576 2577 2578 2579 2580 2581 2582 2583 2584 2585 2586 2587 2588 2589 2590 2591 2592 2593 2594 2595 2596 2597 2598 2599 2600 2601 2602 2603 2604 2605 2606 2607 2608 2609 2610 2611 2612 2613 2614 2617 2619 2621 2625 2628 2633 2639 2658 2659 2672 2678 2687 2700 2717 2719 2720 2738 2741 2765 2766 2786 2793 2863 2892 2930

TEACHER EDUCATOR EDUCATION
0604 1009 2538 2615

TEACHER EVALUATION
0002 1236 1402 2035 2616

TEACHER IMPROVEMENT
0073 0383 1810 2567 2617

TEACHER INFLUENCE

1024 2148 2506 2541 2618

TEACHER MOBILITY
0069 0104 1011 2144 2172 2329 2474 2594 2619

TEACHER ROLE
2498 2519 2620

TEACHER STATUS
0232 0491 0759 0976 1356 1410 1895 2020 2102 2340 2350 2505 2568 2621 2622 2623 2624 2625 2822

TEACHER SUPPLY AND DEMAND
0232 1221 2568 2621 2625 2626 2925

TEACHING
2476 2627 2775

TEACHING METHODS
0018 0145 0249 0396 0398 0901 1003 1706 1814 1970 2074 2084 2127 2317 2407 2451 2471 2472 2580 2592 2628 2629 2630 2631 2632 2633 2746 2844 2846

TEACHING PROCEDURES
0052 0833 0985 1622 1992 2532 2634 2635

TEAMWORK
0105 0230 1021 1544 1560 1933 2037 2057 2070 2145 2336 2636 2637

TECHNICAL EDUCATION
0001 0023 0070 0081 0092 0102 0195 0274 0299 0337 0353 0442 0443 0534 0781 0865 0974 1002 1013 1018 1121 1140 1265 1424 1470 1473 1498 1499 1531 1618 1631 2030 2162 2198 2248 2307 2359 2426 2582 2638 2639 2640 2641 2642 2643 2644 2645 2646 2647 2648 2649 2678 2699 2770 2837 2858 2863 2864 2872 2882 2906

TELEVISION
0025 0372 1019 1214 1590 1951 2118 2650 2651 2722 2929

TEST CONSTRUCTION
0017 0097 0133 0202 0220 0365 0493 0882 1001 1008 1196 1534 1790 1959 1999 2048 2166 2233 2434 2442 2527 2652 2653 2654 2655 2656 2657

TESTING
0201 0394 0399 0410 0412 0421 1000 1416 1529 2023 2274 2570 2585 2658 2659 2660 2766 2769 2930

TEXTBOOK
0404 0938 1043 1296 1379 1532 1844 2076 2191 2516 2661 2662 2663 2664 2949

THAILAND
0386 0409 0414 0598 0624 0762 0766 0930 1133 1425 1552 1989 2116 2204 2243 2352 2380 2665 2666 2667 2668 2669 2670 2671

TOGO
0688 2566 2672

TOYS
1159 1658 2176 2237 2417 2673

TRADE UNIONS
0030 0266 1116 2120 2674

TRADITIONAL EDUCATION
0060 1258 2430 2675

TRINIDAD AND TOBAGO
0718 2445 2676

TUNISIA
0977 2677

TURKEY
0632 0846 0847 1099 1100 1101 1434 2478 2582 2639 2678 2679 2680 2681 2682 2683 2684 2863

TUTORING
0250 0713 1876 2495 2685

UGANDA
0381 2686

UIEH
0456 1642 1954 2590 2687 2741

UK
0005 0014 0015 0041 0049 0056 0081
0085 0125 0142 0151 0154 0229 0269
0270 0275 0290 0314 0320 0322 0330
0344 0347 0377 0389 0390 0413 0426
0428 0446 0449 0467 0510 0528 0535
0563 0575 0645 0789 0845 0850 0853
0855 1005 1016 1022 1023 1028 1030
1031 1037 1045 1110 1115 1119 1146
1152 1153 1157 1168 1169 1174 1180
1191 1213 1214 1215 1219 1262 1263
1264 1272 1290 1291 1317 1322 1334
1336 1337 1340 1346 1387 1397 1412
1423 1424 1429 1440 1446 1449 1450
1454 1487 1502 1533 1545 1546 1581
1619 1653 1722 1739 1761 1795 1805
1807 1826 1828 1837 1900 1902 1903
1909 1922 1935 1936 1942 1960 1976
1993 1994 2000 2050 2051 2056 2067
2114 2133 2134 2162 2197 2215 2226
2242 2259 2284 2287 2288 2291 2292
2335 2341 2361 2362 2367 2368 2371
2374 2376 2390 2397 2398 2403 2410
2415 2433 2449 2483 2502 2593 2604
2606 2607 2613 2640 2651 2688 2689
2690 2691 2692 2693 2694 2695 2696
2697 2698 2699 2700 2701 2702 2703
2704 2705 2706 2707 2708 2709 2710
2711 2712 2713 2714 2715 2716 2717
2718 2719 2720 2721 2722 2723 2724
2725 2726 2727 2728 2729 2730 2731
2732 2733 2734 2735 2736 2737 2738
2748 2853 2879 2927

UKRAINIAN SSR
0634 0870 0871 2210 2227 2739 2740
2842 2843 2922

UNESCO
0456 0518 0612 0617 1382 1642 1774
1954 2590 2687 2741 2742

UNITED ARAB EMIRATES
1300 2743 2744

UNIVERSITIES
0936 1800 2246 2251 2493 2745 2750

UPBRINGING
0018 0145 2074 2317 2629 2746 2844

UPPER SECONDARY EDUCATION
1307 1868 2747

URBAN EDUCATION
1045 1298 1407 2708 2748 2749 2815

URBAN YOUTH
0936 1800 2246 2251 2493 2745 2750

URUGUAY
0719 1139 1486 1982 2751 2752 2881
2911

USA
0001 0007 0032 0044 0047 0070 0084
0128 0143 0144 0148 0149 0152 0153
0218 0219 0221 0247 0251 0252 0255
0257 0274 0283 0284 0293 0299 0300
0302 0303 0315 0316 0321 0329 0332
0339 0340 0350 0363 0364 0366 0368
0384 0399 0403 0412 0421 0427 0431
0434 0435 0457 0534 0571 0578 0585
0594 0607 0609 0621 0622 0653 0723
0724 0726 0728 0729 0732 0735 0737
1000 1002 1042 1046 1050 1051 1052
1053 1054 1062 1063 1070 1073 1084
1092 1103 1105 1129 1131 1136 1144
1149 1171 1179 1187 1223 1233 1240
1241 1242 1243 1244 1246 1247 1249
1250 1251 1259 1260 1261 1267 1277
1287 1293 1294 1298 1302 1313 1319
1324 1353 1355 1356 1358 1359 1360
1362 1371 1380 1386 1407 1411 1415
1416 1430 1431 1433 1437 1444 1448
1460 1482 1490 1493 1494 1517 1518
1519 1520 1521 1529 1536 1537 1538
1541 1551 1558 1698 1699 1708 1712
1717 1719 1730 1749 1750 1751 1788
1821 1824 1825 1833 1834 1835 1840
1843 1912 1924 1931 1939 1940 1946
1955 1977 2011 2012 2014 2020 2026
2123 2153 2219 2241 2253 2261 2267
2268 2273 2274 2276 2290 2307 2309
2313 2339 2359 2366 2400 2408 2475
2476 2480 2481 2484 2500 2501 2515
2569 2570 2600 2605 2624 2627 2644
2658 2660 2749 2753 2754 2755 2756
2757 2758 2759 2760 2761 2762 2763
2764 2765 2766 2767 2768 2769 2770
2771 2772 2773 2774 2775 2776 2777
2778 2779 2780 2781 2782 2783 2784
2785 2786 2787 2788 2789 2790 2791
2792 2793 2794 2795 2796 2797 2798

2799 2800 2801 2802 2803 2804 2805
2806 2807 2808 2809 2810 2811 2812
2813 2814 2815 2816 2817 2818 2819
2820 2821 2822 2823 2824 2825 2826
2827 2828 2856 2872 2875 2880 2885
2887 2888 2890 2930

USSR
0016 0018 0082 0145 0155 0160 0180
0249 0357 0541 0559 0570 0584 0633
0634 0857 0858 0860 0861 0862 0865
0869 0870 0871 0901 0902 1378 1458
1473 1474 1705 1720 1733 1773 1823
1904 1910 1915 2074 2151 2163 2205
2208 2209 2210 2227 2260 2317 2411
2441 2470 2629 2630 2641 2739 2740
2746 2829 2830 2831 2832 2833 2834
2835 2836 2837 2838 2839 2840 2841
2842 2843 2844 2845 2846 2847 2848
2849 2864 2865 2893 2921 2922

VENEZUELA
0342 1150 1154 1438 1743 1745 2278
2332 2494 2560 2850 2851 2852

VISUAL HANDICAPS
1153 1487 1546 2714 2853

VOCATIONAL ADJUSTMENT
0358 1039 2543 2854 2899

VOCATIONAL EDUCATION
0001 0009 0032 0037 0048 0061 0062
0063 0070 0110 0121 0149 0153 0166
0185 0219 0242 0264 0274 0299 0310
0326 0332 0353 0357 0376 0442 0534
0585 0653 0737 0781 0787 0791 0836
0865 0869 0873 0960 0961 0991 1002
1014 1032 1054 1056 1080 1081 1110
1131 1139 1140 1184 1209 1251 1252
1259 1260 1320 1362 1364 1421 1468
1469 1470 1471 1473 1474 1475 1476
1477 1478 1480 1481 1482 1483 1484
1485 1486 1488 1489 1490 1491 1492
1493 1494 1495 1496 1505 1568 1579
1583 1589 1602 1608 1619 1628 1636
1646 1651 1653 1665 1709 1786 1797
1815 1824 1953 2132 2146 2182 2192
2252 2253 2305 2307 2331 2359 2366
2382 2431 2481 2485 2523 2582 2638
2639 2641 2644 2648 2678 2709 2752
2767 2770 2778 2788 2806 2807 2808
2826 2837 2841 2855 2856 2857 2858
2859 2860 2861 2862 2863 2864 2865
2866 2867 2868 2869 2870 2871 2872
2873 2874 2875 2876 2877 2878 2879
2880 2881 2882 2883 2884 2885 2886
2887 2888 2889 2890 2891 2893 2900
2901 2902 2903 2904 2908 2909 2911
2912 2913 2914 2921 2939

VOCATIONAL GUIDANCE
0098 0217 0280 0357 0360 0422 0627
0785 0869 0923 0968 0970 1197 1351
1474 1479 1565 1695 1715 1862 1870
2126 2322 2338 2463 2574 2841 2865
2892 2893 2894 2895 2896 2897 2898
2921

VOCATIONAL INTERESTS
0358 1039 2543 2854 2899

VOCATIONAL REHABILITATION
1364 1495 1709 2485 2891 2900

VOCATIONAL SCHOOL CURRICULUM
0063 1014 1481 1505 1589 2146 2873
2901 2908

VOCATIONAL SCHOOLS
1032 1646 2874 2902

VOCATIONAL TRAINING
0023 0037 0048 0063 0102 0110 0115
0121 0166 0242 0326 0531 0642 0974
0998 1014 1080 1138 1139 1184 1209
1320 1399 1468 1469 1481 1484 1486
1488 1489 1492 1505 1549 1555 1589
1602 1618 1665 1797 2146 2155 2192
2252 2334 2537 2547 2643 2752 2855
2857 2873 2877 2881 2883 2884 2889
2901 2903 2904 2905 2906 2907 2908
2909 2910 2911 2912 2913 2914

WEST AFRICA
0380 0684 1512 2915

WOMEN
0034 0210 1160 2916 2923

WOMENS EDUCATION
0003 0021 0123 0137 0147 0981 1189
1326 1779 2160 2917 2918 2919 2920

WORK EDUCATION
0357 0869 0870 1474 2210 2227 2739
2841 2842 2865 2893 2921 2922

WORKERS EDUCATION
0034 0035 0210 0564 1160 1175 1400
1600 1817 2217 2370 2916 2923 2924

YEMEN
1221 1384 2626 2925 2926

YOUNG ADULTS
1412 1994 2114 2226 2697 2927

YOUTH
0371 2186 2928

YOUTH OPPORTUNITIES
0025 0372 1019 1590 1951 2118 2650
2929

YOUTH PROBLEMS
0205 0421 1017 1026 1301 1352 1396
1416 1506 1508 1554 1644 1677 1871
2274 2570 2658 2766 2930 2931 2932
2933 2934 2936

YOUTH PROGRAMMES
0352 0448 0619 1026 1396 1554 1644
2143 2932 2935 2936

YOUTH UNEMPLOYMENT
0114 0222 0954 2937

YUGOSLAVIA
0253 0872 0873 0876 0877 1281 1314
1315 1316 1475 1930 2211 2228 2254
2412 2447 2866 2938 2939 2940 2941
2942 2943 2944 2945 2946 2947 2948

ZAIRE
1379 2664 2949

ZAMBIA
0382 0692 1064 1741 2950 2951

Index des mots clés

ABANDON EN COURS D'ETUDES
0490 0491 0519 0636 0941 0976 1410 2102 2136 2340 2505 2623

ACCES A L'EDUCATION
0003 0137 1189 2919

ACTIVITE CULTURELLE
0025 0172 0371 0372 0373 1019 1231 1590 1951 1965 2118 2186 2218 2650 2928 2929

ACTIVITE D'APPRENTISSAGE
1931 2768

ACTIVITE INTEGREE
0314 1016 1795 1826 1960 2056 2415 2701

ACTIVITE SPORTIVE
0088 0089 1120 1232 1573 1606 1721 1725 2167 2169

ADAPTATION PROFESSIONNELLE
0358 1039 2543 2854 2899

ADMINISTRATION DE L'EDUCATION
0044 0176 0208 0281 0346 0359 0398 0429 0431 0450 0461 0504 0508 0510 0512 0517 0518 0521 0525 0527 0533 0577 0599 0602 0603 0608 0610 0611 0612 0613 0617 0645 0711 0798 0988 1037 1098 1124 1128 1158 1233 1234 1310 1382 1389 1398 1444 1472 1507 1610 1623 1625 1635 1774 1780 1885 1949 1973 1974 1975 2034 2075 2084 2158 2200 2241 2267 2280 2471 2479 2489 2490 2632 2707 2742 2796

ADMINISTRATION DE TEST SCOLAIRE
0328 1228 1455 1798 2095

ADMINISTRATION DE TESTS
0201 0394 0399 0410 0412 0421 1000 1416 1529 2023 2274 2570 2585 2658 2659 2660 2766 2769 2930

ADMINISTRATION DE TESTS PSYCHOLOGIQUES
0056 0269 0789 1387 1581 1900 2259 2688

AFFECTIVITE
0054 0235 0312 0993 1901 1908

AFRIQUE
0055 0056 0269 0374 0789 1387 1581 1900 2259 2688

AFRIQUE OCCIDENTALE
0380 0684 1512 2915

ALBANIE
0065 2194

ALGERIE
0066 0067 1076 1134 1497 1742 1986

ALLEMAGNE (REPUBLIQUE FEDERALE)
0031 0036 0050 0053 0141 0158 0177 0178 0179 0182 0241 0248 0256 0281 0286 0288 0291 0295 0298 0307 0351 0415 0456 0477 0504 0527 0579 0580 0581 0651 0656 0657 0661 0797 0798 0800 0801 0802 1004 1026 1027 1032 1033 1059 1065 1072 1081 1087 1110 1118 1126 1132 1141 1159 1162 1167 1178 1181 1185 1186 1209 1211 1212 1216 1220 1235 1266 1278 1282 1286 1288 1289 1301 1325 1329 1339 1348 1364 1389 1396 1401 1405 1406 1409 1420 1421 1436 1442 1447 1456 1459 1485 1489 1495 1553 1619 1630 1634 1635 1636 1637 1638 1639 1640 1641 1642 1643 1644 1645 1646 1647 1648

1649 1650 1651 1652 1653 1654 1655 1656 1657 1658 1659 1660 1661 1662 1663 1664 1665 1666 1667 1668 1669 1670 1671 1672 1673 1674 1675 1676 1677 1678 1679 1709 1726 1747 1757 1801 1838 1921 1925 1954 1991 2003 2007 2009 2010 2038 2042 2045 2062 2064 2141 2150 2170 2173 2176 2236 2237 2265 2353 2364 2381 2392 2395 2399 2417 2421 2432 2437 2448 2473 2477 2485 2590 2602 2611 2673 2687 2709 2741 2861 2874 2878 2879 2884 2891 2900 2902 2913 2932 2933 2936

ALPHABETISATION
0039 0043 0163 0172 0314 0373 1001 1016 1113 1198 1229 1230 1231 1795 1826 1877 1959 1960 1961 1962 1963 1964 1965 2033 2048 2056 2106 2121 2166 2218 2240 2415 2442 2527 2655 2701

ALPHABETISATION FONCTIONNELLE
0397 0940 1616 2135 2230

AMELIORATION DE L'EDUCATION
0082 0570 0571 0735 0748 0860 1179 1386 1731 1881 2569 2605 2765 2793 2832

AMERIQUE LATINE
0278 0706 0720 1830 1927 1928

ANGOLA
0068 1049

APPRENTISSAGE
0212 0327 1206 1314 1929 1930 2609 2946

APPRENTISSAGE A L'AGE ADULTE
0052 0833 1992 2532 2634

APPRENTISSAGE (METIERS)
0069 0104 1011 2144 2172 2329 2474 2594 2619

APPRENTISSAGE PRESCOLAIRE
1053 1431 2219 2777

APPROCHE INTERDISCIPLINAIRE
0135 1041 1829

APTITUDE A COMMUNIQUER
0270 0449 1023 1902 1909 2067 2703

APTITUDE AUX ETUDES
0132 0997 1528 2039 2279 2425 2512

ARABIE SAOUDITE

ARGENTINE
0072 0073 0074 0075 0076 0077 0078 0079 0080 0087 0383 0694 1148 1165 1192 1225 1226 1796 1802 1810 1836 1932 2238 2323 2342 2372 2562 2567 2610 2617

ATTITUDE DE L'ELEVE
2428 2492

AUDITION (PHYSIOLOGIE)
0094 1007 2128 2285 2558

AUSTRALIE
0023 0046 0069 0095 0096 0097 0098 0099 0100 0101 0102 0103 0104 0105 0106 0107 0391 0392 0411 0447 0879 0880 0970 0972 0974 0975 1011 1021 1239 1375 1479 1526 1544 1617 1618 1758 1956 2057 2070 2122 2144 2145 2149 2172 2329 2336 2343 2474 2503 2594 2619 2637 2643 2654 2896 2906

AUTRICHE
0008 0022 0108 0109 0110 0111 0112 0113 0114 0115 0116 0117 0118 0119 0120 0121 0122 0222 0375 0400 0424 0531 0639 0768 0769 0951 0952 0953 0954 0956 1010 1038 1078 1079 1080 1082 1392 1426 1469 1484 1620 1716 1736 1760 1907 2068 2252 2283 2330 2444 2596 2857 2877 2904 2905 2909 2937

AUXILIAIRE AUDIOVISUEL
0090 0091 0092 0337 0355 0443 0751 0752 1018 1499 1887 1888 2426 2646

BAHREIN
0123 1326 2920

BANGLADESH
0020 0124 2229 2413

BASE DE DONNEES
0014 0107 0125 0446 0447 0850 1375 1758 2503 2693

BATIMENT
0177 0178 0179 0180 0181 0182 0541 0542 0990 1027 1409 1627 1645 1823 2840

BELGIQUE
0003 0130 0131 0132 0133 0134 0135 0136 0137 0138 0139 0306 0325 0333 0365 0468 0526 0587 0771 0772 0997 1008 1035 1041 1177 1189 1193 1306 1408 1441 1528 1556 1577 1790 1803 1829 1999 2039 2053 2072 2142 2154 2161 2223 2233 2244 2250 2279 2425 2438 2443 2512 2561 2656 2919

BENIN
0140 0669 1500 2073

BESOIN EDUCATIONNEL
0149 0585 1259 2807 2887

BIBLIOTHEQUE SCOLAIRE
0105 1021 1544 2057 2070 2145 2336 2637

BICULTURALISME
0141 0142 0143 0158 0290 0293 1211 1264 1324 1666 1828 1837 1840 1921 1922 1924 2045 2313 2727 2819

BILINGUISME
0141 0144 0150 0152 0153 0154 0155 0156 0157 0158 0159 0160 0332 0390 0467 0528 0723 0737 0914 1029 1211 1323 1378 1454 1666 1824 1846 1910 1912 1916 1921 1923 2045 2050 2058 2205 2253 2454 2531 2691 2753 2767 2845 2849 2856

BIRMANIE
0193 0405

BOLIVIE
0162 0163 1229 1963 2240

BRESIL
0161 0164 0165 0166 0167 0168 0169 0170 0171 0172 0173 0174 0175 0242 0373 0402 0420 0464 0697 1040 1122 1127 1205 1208 1231 1255 1256 1308 1468 1740 1943 1948 1965 2216 2218 2222 2239 2312 2504 2855 2903

BULGARIE
0183 0184 0185 0186 0187 0188 0189 0190 0191 0773 1055 1056 1057 1058 1204 1331 1332 1333 1418 1483 1713 1724 1754 1917 1926 1957 2059 2065 2168 2235 2416 2499 2876

BURKINA FASO
0192 0690 1981

BURUNDI
0051 0194 0195 0196 0378 0670 1376 2642

CAMEROUN (REPUBLIQUE UNIE)
0197 0198 0199 0586 0671 0672 1504 1809 1985 2220 2232 2306 2344 2565 2591

CAMPAGNE D'ALPHABETISATION
0271 0898 1966 2115 2140 2304

CANADA
0034 0126 0200 0201 0202 0203 0204 0205 0206 0207 0208 0209 0210 0211 0212 0213 0214 0215 0216 0220 0324 0327 0331 0359 0394 0410 0429 0480 0512 0722 0994 1017 1071 1123 1124 1125 1160 1172 1206 1245 1279 1312 1373 1398 1506 1508 1523 1752 1816 1929 1949 2023 2052 2164 2245 2270 2282 2479 2507 2559 2585 2609 2653 2659 2916 2923 2931

CARACTERIEL
1268 1467 1707 1938 2097 2482

CARACTERISTIQUE DE L'ELEVE
0936 1154 1745 1800 2246 2251 2493 2494 2560 2745 2750 2852

CARACTERISTIQUE DE L'ENSEIGNANT

0072 0444 0694 0939 1145 1802 1932 2077 2562 2563 2564 2587 2603

CARACTERISTIQUE INDIVIDUELLE
1784 1785 2179

CARRIERE
0114 0222 0954 2937

CARTE SCOLAIRE
0545 0929 1969 2213 2337

CHILI
0054 0230 0231 0232 0233 0234 0235 0237 0238 0239 0273 0296 0312 0700 0702 0993 1104 1343 1345 1513 1559 1560 1727 1755 1901 1908 1933 2037 2112 2568 2621 2625 2636

CHIMIE
0225 1130 1597 2004 2174 2365 2393

CHINE
0240 0241 0291 1266 1671 1801 1838 2141 2611

CHOMAGE DES JEUNES
0114 0222 0954 2937

CHYPRE
0436

CLASSIFICATION DES PERFORMANCES
0004 2137

COLOMBIE
0030 0259 0260 0261 0262 0263 0264 0265 0266 0267 0272 0475 0476 0555 0556 0638 0945 0946 0950 1116 1156 1292 1391 1414 1476 1543 1552 2120 2147 2214 2231 2305 2357 2423 2588 2674 2868

COMMUNICATION
0056 0269 0789 1387 1581 1900 2259 2688

COMMUNICATION AUDIOVISUELLE
0093 0678 1413 1451 1874 1978

COMMUNICATION EN CLASSE
0011 0243 0244 0245 0419 0682 0830 1363 1612 1714 2022 2508 2509 2518

COMPETENCE FONDAMENTALE
0128 1223 1955 2795

COMPORTEMENT DE L'ENSEIGNANT
0094 0138 0207 1007 1123 1154 1193 1745 2128 2244 2250 2285 2494 2558 2559 2560 2561 2852

COMPREHENSION
0001 0070 0274 0298 0299 0307 0534 0797 1002 1420 1634 2265 2307 2359 2644 2770 2872

CONCEPTION DE MOBILIER
0101 1617

CONCEPTION DE PROGRAMME
0153 0332 0737 1824 2253 2254 2767 2856 2944

CONCEPTION DES BATIMENTS
0176 0177 0178 0179 0182 0711 1027 1409 1645

CONGO
1383

CONSEILLER PEDAGOGIQUE
2177 2517 2579

CONSULTATION D'ORIENTATION
0091 0208 0218 0355 0356 0357 0358 0359 0360 0361 0362 0363 0364 0429 0441 0512 0625 0752 0780 0869 1039 1124 1197 1201 1217 1247 1294 1398 1474 1604 1695 1696 1697 1698 1699 1787 1789 1862 1888 1949 2091 2479 2543 2803 2814 2841 2854 2865 2893 2897 2899 2921

CONSULTATION EDUCATIVE
0490 0519 0520 0636 0941 1341 1633 1820 2136

CONSULTATION SUR LA CARRIERE
0217 0218 0219 0280 0363 0422 0627

0785 1247 1260 1561 1565 1698 2338 2574 2803 2808 2888 2892

COOPERATIVE
0350 1358 2823

COREE (REPUBLIQUE)
0028 0090 0091 0129 0226 0355 0407 0540 0623 0751 0752 0753 0754 0756 0758 0759 1093 1094 1453 1822 1887 1888 1889 1890 1891 1893 1894 1895 1896 1897 2350 2622

COSTA RICA
0352 0353 0354 0448 0619 1140 1370 1540 2143 2377 2648 2882 2935

COTE D'IVOIRE
0093 0678 1413 1451 1874 1875 1978 2221

CREATIVITE
0133 0365 0366 0367 0368 1008 1249 1369 1537 1790 1999 2233 2656 2804

CUBA
0369 0370 1321 1753

CULTURE
0055 0109 0374 0375 0769 2283

CURRICULUM
0376 0377 0563 0836 1174 1786 1903 2197 2288 2382 2431 2433 2523 2718 2862

DANEMARK
0246 0453 0626 0782 0783 1112 2266 2572

DEFICIENCE VISUELLE
1153 1487 1546 2714 2853

DELINQUANT
0451 0788 1580 1704 2049 2281 2450 2468

DEVELOPPEMENT COGNITIF
0250 0251 0621 0713 0729 1876 2495 2685 2759

DEVELOPPEMENT COMMUNAUTAIRE
0263 0271 0272 0476 0898 1552 1966 2115 2140 2147 2304 2423

DÉVELOPPEMENT DE CURRICULUM
0012 0073 0095 0096 0117 0154 0168 0194 0201 0223 0300 0304 0378 0379 0380 0381 0382 0383 0384 0385 0386 0387 0388 0389 0390 0391 0392 0393 0394 0395 0396 0397 0398 0399 0400 0401 0402 0403 0404 0409 0410 0412 0467 0528 0554 0572 0670 0674 0684 0692 0724 0745 0834 0845 0879 0880 0940 1000 1010 1048 1122 1277 1296 1415 1454 1501 1512 1529 1570 1616 1701 1719 1810 1878 1934 1948 1970 2014 2023 2026 2050 2081 2084 2135 2191 2230 2319 2400 2407 2444 2471 2521 2567 2584 2585 2617 2631 2632 2659 2660 2663 2669 2686 2690 2691 2754 2769 2811 2915 2950

DEVELOPPEMENT DE LA PERSONNALITE
2151 2835

DEVELOPPEMENT DE L'EDUCATION
0521 1342 1780 2075

DEVELOPPEMENT DU LANGAGE
0054 0056 0235 0269 0270 0312 0377 0449 0563 0789 0993 1023 1174 1387 1581 1900 1901 1902 1903 1908 1909 2067 2197 2259 2288 2433 2688 2703 2718

DEVELOPPEMENT ECONOMIQUE
2428 2492 2498 2519 2620

DEVELOPPEMENT INDIVIDUEL
1784 1785 2179

DEVELOPPEMENT RURAL
0147 0231 0264 0700 0981 1139 1367 1476 1486 1560 1783 2160 2303 2305 2314 2752 2868 2881 2911 2918

DIAGNOSTIC CLINIQUE

0249 0901 2630 2846

DIFFERENCE ENTRE SEXES
0053 0295 0376 0377 0563 0836 1004 1174 1643 1786 1903 2042 2197 2288 2382 2431 2432 2433 2448 2473 2523 2718 2862

DIFFERENCE INDIVIDUELLE
0376 0836 1786 2382 2431 2523 2862

DIFFICULTE DE L'APPRENTISSAGE
0658 1254 1268 1360 1467 1707 1937 1938 1939 1945 2097 2131 2482 2825

DIFFICULTE EN LECTURE
0209 1125 2263 2269 2270 2507 2583

DIFFUSION DE L'INFORMATION
1775 1804 1805 2571 2692

DIRECTEUR D'ETABLISSEMENT
0138 1193 2244 2250 2561

DIRECTION D'ETUDES
0250 0713 1876 2495 2685

DISPARITE NATIONALE INTERREGIONALE
0521 1780 2075

DOCIMOLOGIE
0201 0394 0410 1036 2023 2024 2585 2659

DOCUMENTATION
0051 0196 1186 1376 1442 1664 2009 2082 2761

DOCUMENTATION SUR L'EDUCATION
0523 0524 0810 0811 1422 1852 1853

ECOLE COMMUNAUTAIRE
1394 2187

ECOLE INTERNATIONALE
1202 1842 2092

ECOLE PROFESSIONNELLE
1032 1646 2874 2902

ECOLE PUBLIQUE
2261 2764

ECOLE SECONDAIRE
1210 2094 2422

ECONOMIE DE L'EDUCATION
0001 0035 0070 0115 0116 0130 0154 0274 0281 0299 0306 0390 0424 0426 0445 0467 0504 0521 0525 0526 0527 0528 0530 0531 0533 0534 0535 0536 0537 0539 0564 0587 0603 0639 0771 0798 0956 0988 1002 1030 1151 1173 1175 1222 1389 1392 1397 1400 1426 1454 1507 1588 1600 1605 1620 1625 1635 1744 1760 1780 1817 1885 1907 1973 2031 2050 2075 2217 2307 2333 2359 2370 2644 2691 2705 2770 2872 2905 2924

EDUCATION ARTISTIQUE
0040 0080 0081 0082 0083 0084 0085 0086 0087 0315 0558 0570 0860 0963 1042 1115 1207 1226 1424 1996 2093 2162 2184 2388 2475 2496 2640 2699 2710 2771 2832

EDUCATION COMMUNAUTAIRE
0001 0070 0233 0273 0274 0275 0299 0534 0702 1002 1031 1942 2112 2215 2307 2359 2644 2706 2770 2872

EDUCATION COMPAREE
0031 0036 0076 0142 0143 0217 0241 0278 0279 0280 0281 0282 0283 0284 0286 0288 0289 0290 0291 0292 0293 0294 0422 0455 0457 0460 0462 0504 0527 0627 0651 0706 0749 0785 0798 0839 1052 1084 1110 1118 1148 1178 1194 1264 1266 1273 1324 1372 1389 1401 1404 1561 1565 1619 1630 1632 1635 1653 1654 1661 1671 1746 1801 1828 1830 1831 1832 1833 1834 1836 1837 1838 1839 1840 1841 1882 1922 1924 1927 2099 2141 2189 2313 2315 2323 2338 2526 2574 2611 2709 2727 2776 2783 2819 2879 2892

EDUCATION COMPENSATOIRE
0053 0295 1004 1643 2042 2432 2448 2473

EDUCATION DE BASE
0014 0033 0125 0126 0127 0203 0446 0850 1143 1523 1860 2245 2693

EDUCATION DE LA PREMIERE ENFANCE
0017 0044 0431 0493 0882 1233 1444 2241 2267 2652 2796

EDUCATION DE L'ENFANT
0018 0145 2074 2317 2629 2746 2844

EDUCATION DES ADULTES
0007 0008 0009 0010 0011 0012 0013 0014 0015 0016 0017 0018 0019 0020 0021 0022 0023 0024 0025 0026 0027 0028 0029 0030 0031 0032 0033 0034 0035 0036 0037 0038 0039 0040 0041 0042 0043 0044 0045 0046 0047 0048 0049 0050 0051 0086 0102 0106 0108 0113 0124 0125 0127 0145 0196 0210 0244 0266 0286 0288 0326 0372 0388 0431 0446 0493 0564 0651 0653 0726 0768 0791 0805 0830 0834 0850 0855 0861 0882 0908 0953 0974 1019 1061 1094 1096 1116 1118 1131 1143 1160 1175 1178 1184 1190 1198 1207 1213 1218 1230 1233 1237 1239 1302 1320 1322 1339 1376 1400 1401 1444 1450 1488 1492 1583 1590 1594 1600 1602 1618 1630 1654 1661 1714 1730 1736 1751 1768 1779 1797 1817 1860 1897 1944 1951 1953 1956 1962 1964 2032 2033 2074 2093 2106 2107 2118 2120 2121 2122 2192 2199 2202 2217 2229 2241 2267 2311 2316 2317 2366 2370 2413 2424 2491 2496 2518 2521 2533 2557 2629 2643 2650 2652 2674 2693 2698 2721 2732 2746 2756 2788 2796 2816 2833 2844 2860 2880 2883 2889 2906 2912 2914 2916 2917 2923 2924 2929

EDUCATION DES AVEUGLES
0161 0167 1040 1740 2216

EDUCATION DES FEMMES
0003 0021 0123 0137 0147 0981 1189 1326 1779 2160 2917 2918 2919 2920

EDUCATION DES HANDICAPES
1711 2387 2464

EDUCATION DES MIGRANTS
0053 0141 0158 0295 0909 1004 1106 1182 1211 1284 1567 1585 1595 1615 1643 1666 1818 1866 1913 1918 1921 1968 2040 2041 2042 2043 2044 2045 2046 2047 2060 2432 2448 2473

EDUCATION DES SOURDS
0270 0449 1023 1902 1909 2067 2703

EDUCATION DIFFUSE
0131 0333 0772 1803 2053 2072 2154 2161 2223

EDUCATION EN MATIERE DE POPULATION
0010 0805 2199

ÉDUCATION EN MATIÈRE DE SANTÉ
0088 0089 0188 0300 0384 0724 1120 1146 1163 1204 1232 1289 1415 1439 1573 1606 1676 1719 1720 1721 1722 1723 1724 1725 1726 1773 2026 2051 2163 2167 2168 2169 2170 2367 2549 2712 2754 2831

EDUCATION FAMILIALE
0139 0263 0272 0476 0624 0654 0762 1026 1138 1183 1306 1396 1399 1408 1549 1551 1552 1553 1554 1555 1556 1558 1644 2142 2147 2204 2243 2334 2423 2547 2551 2665 2910 2932 2936

EDUCATION INTERNATIONALE
0076 0142 0143 0241 0278 0279 0282 0283 0284 0290 0291 0292 0293 0294 0340 0455 0457 0460 0462 0607 0706 0749 0839 1052 1084 1092 1148 1264 1266 1273 1324 1372 1404 1433 1632 1671 1801 1825 1828 1830 1831 1832 1833 1834 1835 1836 1837 1838 1839 1840 1841 1882 1922 1924 1927 1977 2099 2141 2313 2315 2323 2526 2611 2727 2776 2783 2784 2819

EDUCATION MUSICALE
0131 0333 0772 1803 2053 2072 2154 2161 2223

EDUCATION NON FORMELLE
0025 0030 0043 0046 0106 0140 0233
0266 0271 0273 0372 0423 0669 0702
0898 0930 1019 1114 1116 1230 1239
1250 1412 1425 1500 1590 1781 1951
1956 1964 1966 1994 2028 2033 2073
2112 2113 2114 2115 2116 2117 2118
2119 2120 2121 2122 2123 2140 2157
2226 2304 2310 2586 2650 2670 2674
2697 2805 2927 2929

EDUCATION OUVRIERE
0034 0035 0210 0564 1160 1175 1400
1600 1817 2217 2370 2916 2923 2924

EDUCATION PERMANENTE
0009 0046 0106 0128 0456 0791 1223
1239 1583 1642 1953 1954 1955 1956
2122 2590 2687 2741 2795 2860

EDUCATION PHYSIQUE
0081 0088 0089 0131 0188 0204 0333
0772 0994 1001 1120 1204 1232 1289
1299 1424 1573 1606 1676 1720 1721
1724 1725 1726 1773 1803 1959 2048
2053 2072 2110 2154 2161 2162 2163
2164 2165 2166 2167 2168 2169 2170
2171 2223 2406 2442 2527 2536 2640
2655 2699 2831

EDUCATION POLITIQUE
0065 0377 0563 0812 1142 1174 1854
1903 2061 2188 2194 2195 2196 2197
2288 2433 2718

EDUCATION POUR LE DEVELOPPEMENT
0164 0283 0464 1052 1833 2222 2776

EDUCATION POUR LE TRAVAIL
0357 0869 0870 1474 2210 2227 2739
2841 2842 2865 2893 2921 2922

EDUCATION PREPRIMAIRE
0035 0161 0167 0172 0260 0275 0373
0438 0545 0564 0813 0858 0870 0872
0929 0945 1031 1040 1175 1231 1400
1600 1740 1817 1942 1965 1967 1969
2206 2207 2208 2209 2210 2211 2212
2213 2214 2215 2216 2217 2218 2224
2225 2227 2228 2231 2337 2370 2409
2411 2412 2461 2706 2739 2830 2836
2842 2922 2924 2938

EDUCATION RELATIVE A L'ENVIRONNEMENT
0063 0140 0199 0304 0334 0385 0572
0669 0745 0922 1014 1481 1500 1501
1502 1503 1504 1505 1589 1878 1985
2073 2146 2232 2284 2306 2410 2462
2591 2695 2873 2901 2908

EDUCATION RELIGIEUSE
0094 0109 0151 0347 0375 0377 0563
0769 1007 1161 1169 1174 1188 1243
1334 1502 1762 1861 1903 2128 2197
2283 2284 2285 2286 2287 2288 2289
2290 2291 2410 2433 2529 2558 2604
2695 2717 2718 2733 2800

EDUCATION RURALE
0001 0038 0070 0143 0171 0199 0264
0271 0274 0293 0294 0299 0462 0534
0898 1002 1047 1103 1114 1190 1208
1324 1367 1372 1476 1504 1783 1840
1841 1924 1966 1985 2032 2099 2115
2119 2140 2157 2232 2239 2303 2304
2305 2306 2307 2308 2309 2310 2311
2312 2313 2314 2315 2359 2591 2644
2770 2785 2819 2868 2872

ÉDUCATION SCIENTIFIQUE
0001 0032 0035 0058 0070 0078 0198
0225 0265 0274 0297 0299 0313 0354
0406 0482 0534 0564 0586 0653 0672
0685 0756 0759 0766 0800 0885 0912
0950 0987 1002 1012 1022 1028 1069
1126 1130 1131 1146 1157 1164 1175
1180 1192 1283 1290 1330 1346 1370
1400 1429 1463 1540 1543 1597 1600
1624 1637 1655 1722 1728 1738 1739
1759 1761 1778 1806 1817 1849 1865
1879 1895 1905 1935 1989 1991 1998
2000 2003 2004 2006 2016 2051 2087
2105 2159 2173 2174 2217 2238 2247
2271 2307 2344 2345 2346 2347 2348
2350 2351 2352 2353 2354 2355 2356
2357 2358 2359 2360 2361 2362 2363
2364 2365 2366 2367 2368 2369 2370
2371 2372 2373 2374 2375 2376 2377
2379 2380 2381 2383 2389 2390 2392
2393 2394 2397 2401 2403 2452 2458

2467 2497 2550 2606 2622 2644 2668 2702 2704 2712 2715 2719 2729 2737 2770 2788 2872 2880 2924

EDUCATION SPECIALE
0053 0058 0069 0084 0104 0208 0295 0315 0359 0398 0429 0451 0512 0685 0788 0832 0857 1003 1004 1011 1042 1059 1101 1124 1246 1251 1268 1353 1364 1365 1398 1434 1467 1490 1495 1580 1613 1643 1648 1704 1705 1706 1707 1708 1709 1710 1717 1718 1938 1949 2012 2042 2049 2084 2097 2105 2127 2144 2172 2281 2293 2329 2345 2432 2446 2448 2450 2467 2468 2469 2470 2471 2472 2473 2474 2475 2476 2477 2478 2479 2480 2481 2482 2483 2484 2485 2486 2520 2581 2592 2594 2613 2619 2627 2632 2633 2684 2738 2771 2775 2802 2806 2820 2829 2885 2891 2900

EDUCATION TRADITIONNELLE
0060 1258 2430 2675

EDUCATION URBAINE
1045 1298 1407 2708 2748 2749 2815

EGALITE DEVANT L'EDUCATION
0205 0525 1017 1506 1507 1508 1885 1973 2931

EGYPTE
0228 0885 0887 1303 1461 1462 1463 1464 1465 1466 2354 2383 2384

ELABORATION DE TESTS
0017 0097 0133 0202 0220 0365 0493 0882 1001 1008 1196 1534 1790 1959 1999 2048 2166 2233 2434 2442 2527 2652 2653 2654 2655 2656 2657

ELEVE ABANDONNANT LA SCOLARITE
0077 1165 1796

ELEVE DU PREPRIMAIRE
0155 0624 0762 1551 2204 2205 2243 2665 2845

ELEVE DU PRIMAIRE
0624 0762 1551 2204 2243 2665

ELEVE DU SECONDAIRE
0248 0256 0415 0980 1185 1510 1663 1703 2138 2150 2414 2419 2420 2421 2511

ELEVE HANDICAPE
0011 0118 0183 0244 0728 0773 0830 0923 1038 1246 1365 1418 1519 1613 1710 1712 1713 1714 1715 1716 1717 1718 2012 2068 2293 2330 2463 2480 2486 2515 2518 2758 2802 2894

ELEVE SORTANT
0787 1471 1496 1579 2331 2859

ELEVE-MAITRE
0305 0408 0763 2439 2510

EMIRATS ARABES UNIS
1300 2743 2744

EMPLOI
0037 0048 0061 0062 0063 0098 0110 0121 0166 0185 0242 0264 0326 0357 0442 0599 0613 0781 0787 0865 0869 0873 0960 0961 0970 0991 1014 1054 1056 1080 1081 1139 1153 1184 1209 1251 1252 1320 1362 1362 1364 1468 1469 1470 1471 1472 1473 1474 1475 1476 1477 1478 1479 1480 1481 1482 1483 1484 1485 1486 1487 1488 1489 1490 1491 1492 1493 1493 1494 1494 1495 1496 1505 1546 1579 1589 1602 1608 1628 1651 1665 1709 1797 2132 2146 2182 2192 2200 2252 2280 2305 2331 2481 2485 2638 2641 2714 2752 2778 2806 2826 2826 2837 2841 2853 2855 2857 2858 2859 2864 2865 2866 2868 2869 2870 2871 2873 2875 2876 2877 2878 2881 2883 2884 2885 2886 2889 2890 2890 2891 2893 2896 2900 2901 2903 2904 2908 2909 2911 2912 2913 2914 2921 2939

ENFANT DE GROUPE MINORITAIRE
0154 0390 0451 0467 0528 0788 1454 1580 1704 2049 2050 2281 2450 2468 2691

ENFANT DU PREMIER AGE
0072 0694 1802 1932 2562

ENFANT RETARDE
1365 1613 1710 1718 2293 2486

ENQUETE SUR L'EMPLOI
1252 1491 1608 2132 2886

ENSEIGNEMENT
2476 2627 2775

ENSEIGNEMENT AGRICOLE
0061 0062 0063 0064 0960 0961 1014 1297 1477 1478 1481 1505 1589 2109 2146 2182 2869 2870 2873 2901 2908

ENSEIGNEMENT ASSISTE PAR ORDINATEUR
0006 0037 0054 0084 0130 0136 0211 0212 0235 0252 0298 0300 0302 0303 0304 0305 0306 0307 0309 0310 0311 0312 0313 0314 0315 0316 0317 0318 0319 0320 0321 0322 0323 0324 0325 0326 0327 0328 0329 0330 0338 0341 0384 0385 0408 0428 0480 0526 0572 0575 0587 0647 0724 0728 0732 0745 0763 0771 0797 0816 0917 0993 1012 1016 1042 1050 1066 1067 1117 1119 1149 1168 1170 1172 1177 1184 1206 1228 1287 1291 1415 1420 1430 1437 1440 1441 1448 1449 1455 1488 1501 1519 1520 1521 1568 1577 1591 1592 1599 1602 1634 1641 1712 1719 1738 1792 1795 1797 1798 1807 1815 1816 1821 1826 1878 1901 1908 1929 1940 1960 2001 2026 2038 2056 2080 2087 2095 2134 2247 2256 2265 2282 2292 2360 2415 2437 2438 2439 2457 2475 2510 2515 2545 2578 2609 2701 2711 2716 2730 2754 2758 2760 2762 2771 2773 2791 2812 2867 2883 2912

ENSEIGNEMENT BILINGUE
0018 0144 0145 0146 0147 0148 0149 0150 0151 0152 0159 0347 0585 0723 0981 1240 1259 1323 1334 1912 1923 2074 2160 2291 2317 2408 2531 2629 2733 2746 2753 2797 2807 2844 2887 2918

ENSEIGNEMENT DE LA GEOGRAPHIE
0116 0424 0639 0956 1392 1426 1620 1760 1907

ENSEIGNEMENT DE LA LANGUE MATERNELLE
0059 0118 0270 0449 0549 1020 1023 1038 1203 1542 1716 1902 1909 1920 1958 2066 2067 2068 2069 2330 2429 2540 2703

ENSEIGNEMENT DE LA LECTURE
0967 1525 1759 1794 1997 2271 2272 2356 2458 2535

ENSEIGNEMENT DE L'HISTOIRE
0116 0424 0639 0956 1157 1392 1426 1620 1759 1760 1761 1907 1935 2271 2356 2368 2458 2715

ENSEIGNEMENT DES LANGUES
0054 0116 0160 0235 0270 0312 0424 0449 0639 0912 0916 0956 0993 1023 1378 1392 1426 1620 1760 1901 1902 1904 1905 1906 1907 1908 1909 1910 1915 1947 2067 2355 2385 2452 2456 2703 2838 2849

ENSEIGNEMENT DES MATHEMATIQUES
0005 0052 0083 0116 0131 0133 0225 0318 0333 0348 0365 0403 0424 0430 0487 0558 0639 0766 0772 0800 0833 0956 0963 0967 0987 1008 1028 1067 1095 1126 1130 1155 1164 1167 1176 1186 1216 1244 1246 1248 1277 1290 1330 1335 1346 1347 1356 1368 1392 1411 1412 1426 1442 1525 1536 1592 1597 1601 1607 1611 1614 1620 1624 1637 1655 1660 1664 1668 1717 1760 1790 1794 1803 1849 1850 1907 1988 1989 1991 1992 1993 1994 1996 1997 1998 1999 2000 2001 2002 2003 2004 2005 2006 2007 2008 2009 2010 2011 2012 2013 2014 2016 2017 2019 2020 2021 2053 2072 2114 2154 2161 2173 2174 2184 2201 2223 2226 2233 2249 2272 2352 2353 2358 2362 2364 2365 2369 2374 2375 2376 2380 2381 2388 2389 2390 2391 2392 2393 2394 2395

2396 2399 2400 2401 2402 2403 2404 2405 2480 2532 2535 2548 2550 2624 2634 2656 2668 2689 2697 2704 2729 2737 2801 2802 2811 2822 2927

ENSEIGNEMENT DES SCIENCES
0083 0225 0344 0348 0376 0403 0430 0474 0558 0766 0800 0836 0885 0887 0916 0963 0987 1028 1095 1126 1130 1164 1167 1176 1180 1191 1216 1277 1330 1335 1346 1347 1368 1463 1465 1597 1601 1611 1614 1624 1637 1655 1660 1668 1711 1735 1786 1793 1849 1850 1906 1947 1989 1991 1996 1998 2000 2002 2003 2004 2006 2007 2008 2010 2014 2016 2017 2019 2021 2159 2173 2174 2184 2201 2249 2351 2352 2353 2354 2358 2362 2364 2365 2369 2371 2375 2376 2378 2379 2380 2381 2382 2383 2384 2385 2386 2387 2388 2389 2390 2391 2392 2393 2394 2395 2396 2397 2398 2399 2400 2401 2402 2403 2404 2405 2431 2456 2459 2464 2523 2550 2606 2607 2668 2704 2719 2720 2737 2811 2862

ENSEIGNEMENT D'UNE LANGUE VIVANTE
0105 0131 0157 0187 0189 0200 0314 0331 0333 0580 0722 0772 0790 1016 1021 1029 1058 1106 1142 1162 1166 1325 1331 1544 1582 1585 1595 1598 1615 1659 1678 1795 1803 1826 1846 1913 1916 1917 1918 1919 1925 1926 1957 1960 2040 2043 2047 2052 2053 2054 2056 2057 2058 2059 2060 2061 2062 2063 2064 2065 2070 2072 2145 2154 2161 2188 2196 2223 2336 2415 2637 2701

ENSEIGNEMENT INDIVIDUALISE
0006 0037 0077 0309 0314 0326 0328 0474 0747 0816 0967 1016 1165 1184 1228 1455 1488 1525 1602 1735 1791 1792 1793 1794 1795 1796 1797 1798 1826 1880 1960 1983 1997 2056 2080 2095 2272 2386 2415 2459 2535 2578 2701 2883 2912

ENSEIGNEMENT MUTUEL
0263 0272 0476 1552 2147 2423

ENSEIGNEMENT PAR MULTIMEDIA
1419 1578 2071

ENSEIGNEMENT POLYTECHNIQUE
1265 1631 2198 2649

ENSEIGNEMENT PRIMAIRE
0020 0044 0078 0124 0131 0133 0163 0164 0171 0186 0197 0199 0260 0333 0365 0397 0431 0438 0464 0605 0671 0772 0813 0870 0872 0940 0945 1008 1015 1057 1072 1159 1192 1208 1229 1233 1340 1412 1444 1504 1616 1650 1658 1790 1803 1809 1875 1963 1967 1985 1994 1999 2053 2072 2114 2135 2154 2161 2176 2206 2207 2210 2211 2214 2220 2221 2222 2223 2224 2225 2226 2227 2228 2229 2230 2231 2232 2233 2235 2236 2237 2238 2239 2240 2241 2242 2257 2267 2306 2312 2372 2409 2412 2413 2416 2417 2539 2565 2591 2656 2673 2697 2736 2739 2796 2842 2922 2927 2938

ENSEIGNEMENT PRIVE
0126 0203 0936 1523 1800 2245 2246 2251 2493 2745 2750

ENSEIGNEMENT PROFESSIONNEL
0001 0009 0032 0037 0048 0061 0062 0063 0070 0110 0121 0149 0153 0166 0185 0219 0242 0264 0274 0299 0310 0326 0332 0353 0357 0376 0442 0534 0585 0653 0737 0781 0787 0791 0836 0865 0869 0873 0960 0961 0991 1002 1014 1032 1054 1056 1080 1081 1110 1131 1139 1140 1184 1209 1251 1252 1259 1260 1320 1362 1364 1421 1468 1469 1470 1471 1473 1474 1475 1476 1477 1478 1480 1481 1482 1483 1484 1485 1486 1488 1489 1490 1491 1492 1493 1494 1495 1496 1505 1568 1579 1583 1589 1602 1608 1619 1628 1636 1646 1651 1653 1665 1709 1786 1797 1815 1824 1953 2132 2146 2182 2192 2252 2253 2305 2307 2331 2359 2366 2382 2431 2481 2485 2523 2582 2638 2639 2641 2644 2648 2678 2709 2752 2767 2770 2778 2788 2806 2807 2808 2826 2837 2841 2855 2856 2857 2858 2859 2860 2861 2862 2863 2864 2865

2866 2867 2868 2869 2870 2871 2872 2873 2874 2875 2876 2877 2878 2879 2880 2881 2882 2883 2884 2885 2886 2887 2888 2889 2890 2891 2893 2900 2901 2902 2903 2904 2908 2909 2911 2912 2913 2914 2921 2939

ENSEIGNEMENT SECONDAIRE (2E CYCLE)
1307 1868 2747

ENSEIGNEMENT SECONDAIRE
0020 0124 0186 0314 0438 0872 0980 1016 1057 1159 1338 1502 1658 1795 1826 1869 1960 2056 2138 2176 2206 2209 2211 2224 2228 2229 2235 2237 2284 2409 2410 2411 2412 2413 2414 2415 2416 2417 2418 2420 2673 2695 2701 2836 2938

ENSEIGNEMENT SUPERIEUR
0007 0022 0047 0067 0107 0113 0161 0167 0190 0215 0234 0237 0238 0289 0296 0313 0342 0370 0445 0447 0474 0536 0539 0715 0726 0748 0902 0953 1012 1022 1040 1064 1134 1150 1151 1154 1194 1212 1222 1261 1293 1302 1312 1321 1332 1343 1345 1348 1375 1429 1438 1497 1513 1605 1667 1727 1728 1729 1730 1731 1732 1733 1735 1736 1737 1738 1739 1740 1741 1742 1743 1744 1745 1746 1747 1749 1750 1751 1752 1753 1754 1755 1757 1758 1759 1793 1845 1881 2029 2078 2087 2189 2216 2247 2271 2346 2356 2360 2361 2386 2458 2459 2494 2497 2501 2503 2560 2589 2702 2756 2809 2813 2816 2847 2851 2852 2951

ENSEIGNEMENT SUPERIEUR PROFESSIONNEL
0121 1080 1484 2252 2877 2909

ENSEIGNEMENT TECHNIQUE
0001 0023 0070 0081 0092 0102 0195 0274 0299 0337 0353 0442 0443 0534 0781 0865 0974 1002 1013 1018 1121 1140 1265 1424 1470 1473 1498 1499 1531 1618 1631 2030 2162 2198 2248 2307 2359 2426 2582 2638 2639 2640 2641 2642 2643 2644 2645 2646 2647 2648 2649 2678 2699 2770 2837 2858 2863 2864 2872 2882 2906

EQUATEUR
0416 1257

EQUIPEMENT EDUCATIF
0177 0178 0179 0180 0181 0182 0541 0542 0990 1027 1409 1627 1645 1823 2840

ESPACE EDUCATIF
0177 0178 0179 0182 1027 1409 1645

ESPAGNE
0146 0156 0311 0334 0474 0499 0912 0913 0914 0915 0916 0917 0920 0922 0923 1503 1711 1715 1735 1759 1793 1814 1905 1906 1947 2212 2256 2271 2355 2356 2385 2386 2387 2451 2452 2453 2454 2455 2456 2457 2458 2459 2460 2461 2462 2463 2464 2465 2580 2628 2894

ETATS DU GOLFE
0889 1700

ETATS-UNIS D'AMERIQUE
0001 0007 0032 0044 0047 0070 0084 0128 0143 0144 0148 0149 0152 0153 0218 0219 0221 0247 0251 0252 0255 0257 0274 0283 0284 0293 0299 0300 0302 0303 0315 0316 0321 0329 0332 0339 0340 0350 0363 0364 0366 0368 0384 0399 0403 0412 0421 0427 0431 0434 0435 0457 0534 0571 0578 0585 0594 0607 0609 0621 0622 0653 0723 0724 0726 0728 0729 0732 0735 0737 1000 1002 1042 1046 1050 1051 1052 1053 1054 1062 1063 1070 1073 1084 1092 1103 1105 1129 1131 1136 1144 1149 1171 1179 1187 1223 1233 1240 1241 1242 1243 1244 1246 1247 1249 1250 1251 1259 1260 1261 1267 1277 1287 1293 1294 1298 1302 1313 1319 1324 1353 1355 1356 1358 1359 1360 1362 1371 1380 1386 1407 1411 1415 1416 1430 1431 1433 1437 1444 1448 1460 1482 1490 1493 1494 1517 1518 1519 1520 1521 1529 1536 1537 1538 1541 1557 1698 1699 1708 1712 1717

1719 1730 1749 1750 1751 1788 1821
1824 1825 1833 1834 1835 1840 1843
1912 1924 1931 1939 1940 1946 1955
1977 2011 2012 2014 2020 2026 2123
2153 2219 2241 2253 2261 2267 2268
2273 2274 2276 2290 2307 2309 2313
2339 2359 2366 2400 2408 2475 2476
2480 2481 2484 2500 2501 2515 2569
2570 2600 2605 2624 2627 2644 2658
2660 2749 2753 2754 2755 2756 2757
2758 2759 2760 2761 2762 2763 2764
2765 2766 2767 2768 2769 2770 2771
2772 2773 2774 2775 2776 2777 2778
2779 2780 2781 2782 2783 2784 2785
2786 2787 2788 2789 2790 2791 2792
2793 2794 2795 2796 2797 2798 2799
2800 2801 2802 2803 2804 2805 2806
2807 2808 2809 2810 2811 2812 2813
2814 2815 2816 2817 2818 2819 2820
2821 2822 2823 2824 2825 2826 2827
2828 2856 2872 2875 2880 2885 2887
2888 2890 2930

ETHIOPIE
1509 1510 1511 1703 2419 2511

ETUDE DE LA PERSONNALITE
0131 0333 0622 0642 0772 0998 1803
2053 2072 2153 2154 2155 2161 2223
2537 2763 2907

ETUDE TRANSCULTURELLE
0366 0368 1249 1537 2804

ETUDES SOCIALES
0718 2445 2676

EUROPE ORIENTALE
1181 1662

EVALUATION
0099 0126 0132 0203 0234 0252 0296
0302 0303 0345 0354 0366 0368 0380
0399 0411 0412 0488 0491 0547 0551
0684 0709 0712 0728 0732 0841 0967
0976 0997 1000 1006 1013 1043 1152
1196 1200 1244 1249 1267 1309 1370
1371 1410 1411 1498 1509 1511 1512
1513 1514 1515 1516 1517 1518 1519
1520 1521 1522 1523 1525 1526 1528
1529 1530 1531 1532 1533 1534 1535
1536 1537 1538 1539 1540 1541 1545
1712 1727 1794 1821 1844 1884 1940
1997 2011 2039 2102 2103 2149 2245
2248 2272 2279 2321 2335 2339 2340
2377 2425 2434 2465 2505 2512 2515
2528 2534 2535 2552 2623 2645 2657
2660 2662 2713 2755 2757 2758 2760
2762 2769 2801 2804 2810 2827 2915

EVALUATION DES BATIMENTS
0177 0178 0179 0182 1027 1409 1645

EVALUATION DES ENSEIGNANTS
0002 1236 1402 2035 2616

EVALUATION DES ETUDIANTS
0250 0713 1876 2495 2685

EVALUATION DU CURRICULUM
0099 0193 0201 0248 0256 0305 0386
0394 0399 0405 0406 0407 0408 0409
0410 0411 0412 0413 0414 0415 0416
0417 0753 0763 1000 1005 1133 1185
1257 1271 1453 1526 1529 1663 1879
1886 1889 1976 2023 2149 2150 2348
2421 2439 2510 2585 2593 2659 2660
2669 2671 2700 2769

EVALUATION DU PROGRAMME
0311 0598 0605 0917 1015 1182 1968
2044 2256 2257 2457 2539 2667

EVALUATION OPERATIONNELLE
0136 0325 1177 1441 1576 1577 2438
2514 2556

EVALUATION SOMMATIVE
0728 1519 1576 1712 2514 2515 2556
2758

EXAMEN
0105 0265 0950 1021 1152 1153 1487
1533 1543 1544 1545 1546 2057 2070
2145 2335 2336 2357 2637 2713 2714
2853

EXEAT SCOLAIRE
0530 1138 1152 1399 1533 1545 1549
1554 1588 2278 2332 2333 2334 2335
2547 2713 2850 2910

FACTEUR DE PERFORMANCE
1024 2148 2506 2541 2618

FACTEUR DE SUCCES
1199 1443 1603 2513 2608

FACTEUR D'ECHEC
1138 1280 1399 1549 1550 1554 1864
2334 2547 2910

FAMILLE (UNITE SOCIOLOGIQUE)
0251 0621 0729 2759

FEMME
0034 0210 1160 2916 2923

FINALITE DE L'EDUCATION
0547 1516 2103

FINANCEMENT DE L'EDUCATION
0545 0929 1517 1969 2213 2337 2339
2755

FINLANDE
0019 0088 0217 0280 0310 0395 0422
0433 0554 0627 0650 0785 0908 0909
0911 1086 1107 1120 1275 1276 1390
1561 1564 1565 1567 1568 1569 1570
1571 1572 1573 1574 1575 1721 1815
1934 2041 2167 2338 2573 2574 2598
2867 2892

FORMATION A TEMPS PARTIEL
0063 1014 1481 1505 1589 2146 2873
2901 2908

FORMATION DES ENSEIGNANTS
0006 0069 0073 0079 0104 0122 0197
0199 0201 0212 0217 0232 0241 0247
0261 0280 0291 0309 0327 0344 0383
0393 0394 0410 0413 0421 0422 0423
0427 0444 0453 0456 0555 0567 0571
0606 0627 0671 0688 0735 0783 0785
0806 0809 0816 0832 0939 0946 1003
1005 1011 1025 1082 1085 1086 1088
1105 1108 1132 1145 1169 1179 1180
1191 1199 1206 1225 1266 1295 1357
1386 1416 1435 1443 1504 1548 1561
1564 1565 1571 1603 1621 1642 1656
1671 1701 1706 1737 1765 1770 1775
1781 1792 1801 1804 1809 1810 1814
1838 1845 1856 1857 1873 1929 1954
1972 1976 1985 2023 2077 2080 2108
2117 2127 2141 2144 2172 2177 2220
2232 2263 2269 2274 2276 2287 2306
2329 2338 2371 2397 2398 2446 2451
2469 2472 2474 2483 2500 2513 2517
2520 2542 2563 2564 2565 2566 2567
2568 2569 2570 2571 2572 2573 2574
2575 2576 2577 2578 2579 2580 2581
2582 2583 2584 2585 2586 2587 2588
2589 2590 2591 2592 2593 2594 2595
2596 2597 2598 2599 2600 2601 2602
2603 2604 2605 2606 2607 2608 2609
2610 2611 2612 2613 2614 2617 2619
2621 2625 2628 2633 2639 2658 2659
2672 2678 2687 2700 2717 2719 2720
2738 2741 2765 2766 2786 2793 2863
2892 2930

FORMATION DES FORMATEURS
0604 1009 2538 2615

FORMATION DES GESTIONNAIRES
0413 1005 1976 2593 2700

FORMATION DES INGENIEURS
0092 0337 0443 1013 1018 1498 1499
1531 2248 2426 2645 2646

FORMATION DES MAITRES EN EXERCICE
0035 0073 0197 0211 0310 0324 0383
0440 0480 0564 0671 0750 1172 1175
1284 1381 1400 1568 1600 1775 1804
1809 1810 1814 1815 1816 1817 1818
1819 1866 1883 2046 2217 2220 2282
2370 2451 2565 2567 2571 2580 2617
2628 2867 2924

FORMATION EN COURS D'EMPLOI
0005 1993 2689

FORMATION MEDICALE
0300 0384 0724 1227 1415 1719 2026
2027 2554 2754

FORMATION PROFESSIONNELLE
0023 0037 0048 0063 0102 0110 0115
0121 0166 0242 0326 0531 0642 0974
0998 1014 1080 1138 1139 1184 1209
1320 1399 1468 1469 1481 1484 1486

1488 1489 1492 1505 1549 1554 1589 1602 1618 1665 1797 2146 2155 2192 2252 2334 2537 2547 2643 2752 2855 2857 2873 2877 2881 2883 2884 2889 2901 2903 2904 2905 2906 2907 2908 2909 2910 2911 2912 2913 2914

FRANCE
0009 0025 0027 0035 0037 0056 0063 0089 0225 0227 0245 0269 0317 0318 0323 0326 0338 0348 0362 0372 0430 0451 0461 0517 0530 0539 0564 0577 0611 0647 0648 0787 0788 0789 0790 0791 0792 0794 0795 1014 1019 1066 1067 1074 1106 1109 1130 1166 1170 1175 1176 1184 1199 1217 1222 1232 1248 1252 1270 1310 1335 1363 1365 1368 1387 1388 1400 1419 1443 1471 1481 1488 1491 1496 1505 1547 1578 1579 1580 1581 1582 1583 1584 1585 1586 1587 1588 1589 1590 1591 1592 1593 1594 1595 1596 1597 1598 1599 1600 1601 1602 1603 1604 1605 1606 1607 1608 1609 1610 1611 1612 1613 1614 1615 1697 1704 1710 1718 1725 1789 1797 1817 1900 1913 1918 1919 1951 1953 2001 2004 2008 2013 2017 2021 2040 2043 2047 2049 2054 2060 2063 2071 2118 2132 2146 2169 2174 2217 2249 2259 2281 2293 2331 2333 2365 2370 2393 2396 2402 2405 2450 2468 2486 2508 2509 2513 2608 2650 2688 2859 2860 2873 2883 2886 2901 2908 2912 2924 2929

GESTION
0508 0525 0602 0608 1128 1507 1623 1885 1973 1974 1975 2490

GHANA
1069 1342 2363 2378

GRECE
0010 0805 1366 1381 1819 2199

GROUPE MINORITAIRE
1146 1722 2051 2367 2712

GUATEMALA
0176 0711 1728 2346 2497

GUYANE
0393 0897 1701 1702 2584

HANDICAP PHYSIQUE
0069 0104 1011 2144 2172 2329 2474 2594 2619

HANDICAPE
0451 0788 0857 1003 1268 1353 1364 1365 1467 1495 1510 1580 1613 1703 1704 1705 1706 1707 1708 1709 1710 1718 1938 2049 2097 2127 2281 2293 2419 2450 2468 2470 2472 2482 2484 2485 2486 2511 2592 2633 2820 2829 2891 2900

HISTOIRE DE L'EDUCATION
0025 0031 0035 0083 0208 0261 0262 0276 0286 0359 0372 0377 0395 0429 0475 0512 0553 0554 0555 0556 0558 0559 0563 0564 0567 0584 0638 0651 0807 0946 0963 1019 1118 1124 1174 1175 1224 1280 1357 1391 1393 1398 1400 1458 1550 1570 1590 1600 1654 1817 1864 1873 1903 1934 1949 1951 1996 2118 2183 2184 2197 2217 2288 2370 2388 2433 2479 2553 2588 2614 2650 2718 2848 2924 2929

HONDURAS
0712 1515 2321

HONGRIE
0024 0276 0553 0806 0807 0808 0983 1108 1311 1318 1428 1435 1765 1767 1768 1769 1770 1771 1772 2424 2576 2601

HYGIENE
1720 1773 2163 2831

IIPE
0518 0612 0617 1382 1774 2742

IMAGE DE SOI
0263 0272 0476 1552 2147 2423

INADAPTE SOCIAL
0451 0788 1580 1704 2049 2281 2450 2468

INDE
0021 0423 0521 0663 0741 0934 1367 1417 1452 1775 1776 1777 1778 1779 1780 1781 1782 1783 1804 2075 2117 2303 2314 2347 2571 2586 2917

INDONESIE
0241 0291 0935 0936 1266 1671 1799 1800 1801 1838 2141 2246 2251 2493 2611 2745 2750

INFLUENCE DE L'ENSEIGNANT
1024 2148 2506 2541 2618

INFLUENCE DE L'ENVIRONNEMENT
0205 1017 1506 1508 2931

INFORMATION SUR L'EDUCATION
0304 0385 0572 0745 1501 1878

INGENIERIE DU BATIMENT
0177 0178 0179 0182 1027 1409 1645

INNOVATION EDUCATIVE
0320 0425 0428 0461 0517 0574 0575 0577 0611 1119 1202 1310 1610 1842 2085 2092 2212 2292 2461 2711

INSPECTION
0938 2076 2516 2661

INSTRUCTION
0520 1341 1633 1820

INTEGRATION SCOLAIRE
0069 0104 0118 1011 1038 1716 2068 2144 2172 2329 2330 2474 2594 2619

INTERET PROFESSIONNEL
0358 1039 2543 2854 2899

IRAK
1737 1845 2589

IRAN (REPUBLIQUE ISLAMIQUE)
1043 1532 1844 2662

IRLANDE
0157 1029 1068 1846 1847 1916 2058

ISRAEL
0744 1330 1347 1361 1848 1849 1850 1851 2016 2019 2275 2277 2375 2401 2404

ITALIE
0033 0127 0297 0360 0482 0523 0524 0567 0810 0811 0812 1060 1085 1088 1089 1090 1143 1161 1197 1269 1280 1283 1284 1305 1307 1338 1351 1352 1354 1357 1422 1432 1445 1550 1695 1762 1806 1818 1852 1853 1854 1855 1856 1857 1858 1859 1860 1861 1862 1863 1864 1865 1866 1867 1868 1869 1870 1871 1872 1873 2046 2195 2286 2373 2418 2597 2599 2614 2747 2897 2898 2934

IUEH
0456 1642 1954 2590 2687 2741

JAMAIQUE
0250 0713 1113 1876 1877 1961 2495 2685

JAPON
0279 0304 0385 0406 0455 0572 0745 0747 0748 0749 0750 1501 1731 1791 1831 1878 1879 1880 1881 1882 1883 1983 2348

JEU
1159 1658 2176 2237 2417 2673

JEU EDUCATIF
0052 0833 1992 2532 2634

JEUNE ADULTE
1412 1994 2114 2226 2697 2927

JEUNESSE
0371 2186 2928

JEUNESSE URBAINE
0936 1800 2246 2251 2493 2745 2750

JORDANIE
1309 1539 1884

JOUET
1159 1658 2176 2237 2417 2673

KENYA
0417 0525 1271 1507 1885 1886 1973

KOWEIT
0418 0432 1253 1898 1899

LANGAGE DE L'ENFANT
0226 0227 1093 1109 1596 1896

LANGUE ARABE
0071 0895 1950

LANGUE FRANCAISE
1585 1615 1913 2040 2047

LANGUE NATIONALE
0018 0140 0145 0669 1500 2073 2074 2317 2629 2746 2844

LANGUE RUSSE
0018 0145 2074 2317 2629 2746 2844

LANGUE SECONDE
0148 1240 2408 2797

LANGUES
0059 0141 0142 0143 0144 0150 0152 0157 0158 0159 0187 0189 0290 0293 0723 0828 1029 1058 1106 1166 1203 1211 1264 1323 1324 1325 1331 1585 1595 1598 1615 1666 1678 1828 1837 1840 1846 1904 1911 1912 1913 1914 1915 1916 1917 1918 1919 1920 1921 1922 1923 1924 1925 1926 1957 1958 2040 2043 2045 2047 2058 2059 2060 2063 2064 2065 2069 2313 2429 2531 2727 2753 2819 2838

LANGUES AFRICAINES
0057 0058 0059 0060 0683 0685 1203 1258 1920 1958 2069 2104 2105 2345 2429 2430 2467 2675

LECTURE
0044 0221 0246 0431 0626 0782 1233 1242 1444 2241 2266 2267 2268 2796 2799

LEGISLATION DE L'EDUCATION
0578 0609 1136 2789

LIBAN
0071 0895 1950

LIBERIA
0907 1952

LINGUISTIQUE
0059 0187 1058 1203 1917 1920 1957 1958 2059 2069 2429

LISIBILITE
0298 0307 0761 0797 1420 1634 1984 2264 2265 2487

LIVRE DE TEXTES
0404 0938 1043 1296 1379 1532 1844 2076 2191 2516 2661 2662 2663 2664 2949

LOISIR
0025 0372 1019 1590 1951 2118 2650 2929

LUXEMBOURG
0813 1182 1967 1968 2044 2207 2225

MALAISIE
0396 0545 0929 1969 1970 2213 2337 2407 2631

MALI
0681 1971 1979

MALTE
0809 1972 2577

MATERIEL DIDACTIQUE
0180 0541 1822 1823 1893 2840

MAURICE
0243 0419 0682 2022

MERE
0105 1021 1544 2057 2070 2145 2336 2637

METHODE AUTODIDACTIQUE
0024 0092 0132 0337 0443 0997 1018 1499 1528 1768 2039 2279 2424 2425 2426 2512 2646

METHODE D'EVALUATION
0549 1020 1542 2066 2540

METHODE EDUCATIVE
0559 0584 0824 0985 1457 1458 1622 2180 2635 2848

METHODE PEDAGOGIQUE
0018 0145 0249 0396 0398 0901 1003 1706 1814 1970 2074 2084 2127 2317 2407 2451 2471 2472 2580 2592 2628 2629 2630 2631 2632 2633 2746 2844 2846

METHODOLOGIE DE LA RECHERCHE
0320 0428 0575 1119 2292 2711

MEXIQUE
0002 0038 0043 0346 0450 0537 0610 0715 1121 1173 1190 1230 1234 1236 1327 1328 1402 1729 1964 2028 2029 2030 2031 2032 2033 2034 2035 2036 2113 2121 2311 2616 2647

MICRO-ENSEIGNEMENT
0132 0230 0997 1528 1559 1641 1933 2037 2038 2039 2279 2425 2437 2512 2636

MILIEU EDUCATIF
0540 0758 1894

MOBILITE DES ENSEIGNANTS
0069 0104 1011 2144 2172 2329 2474 2594 2619

MODE D'ETUDE
1510 1703 2419 2511

MOTIVATION DE L'ELEVE
0040 0086 1207 2093 2496

MOYEN D'ENSEIGNEMENT
0351 0477 0579 0580 0581 0661 1141 1162 1329 1436 1657 1659 1679 2062

MOYEN D'INFORMATION DE MASSE
0093 0678 1413 1451 1874 1978

NEPAL
0938 0939 2076 2077 2516 2563 2587 2661

NICARAGUA
0547 1516 2103

NIGER
0057 0683 2104

NIGERIA
0039 0042 0058 0064 0685 1198 1218 1295 1297 1299 1962 2105 2106 2107 2108 2109 2110 2171 2345 2406 2467 2612

NORVEGE
0094 0658 0819 0820 0968 1003 1007 1075 1111 1254 1706 1937 1945 2124 2125 2126 2127 2128 2129 2130 2131 2285 2322 2472 2558 2592 2633 2895

NOUVELLE ZELANDE
0017 0491 0493 0881 0882 0976 1410 2100 2102 2340 2505 2623 2652

OBJECTIF AFFECTIF
0053 0295 1004 1643 2042 2432 2448 2473

OBJECTIF EDUCATIF
0130 0136 0198 0306 0325 0526 0586 0587 0672 0771 0936 1177 1441 1577 1800 1814 2246 2251 2344 2438 2451 2493 2580 2628 2745 2750

OFFRE ET DEMANDE D'ENSEIGNANTS
0232 1221 2568 2621 2625 2626 2925

ORDINATEUR
0092 0131 0133 0151 0153 0200 0317 0319 0331 0332 0333 0334 0337 0338 0339 0340 0341 0342 0344 0345 0346 0347 0348 0365 0425 0430 0443 0450 0551 0574 0607 0610 0647 0722 0737 0772 0922 1008 1018 1066 1070 1092 1117 1150 1176 1191 1200 1234 1334 1368 1433 1438 1499 1503 1535 1557 1591 1601 1614 1743 1788 1790 1803 1824 1825 1835 1977 1999 2008 2021

2034 2052 2053 2072 2085 2154 2161 2223 2233 2249 2253 2291 2396 2398 2405 2426 2462 2545 2552 2607 2646 2656 2720 2733 2767 2781 2784 2851 2856

ORGANISATION ADMINISTRATIVE
0006 0309 0816 1792 2080 2578

ORGANISATION SCOLAIRE
0217 0280 0422 0627 0785 1561 1565 2338 2574 2892

ORIENTATION
0218 0356 0357 0358 0360 0361 0362 0363 0364 0441 0625 0780 0869 1039 1197 1201 1217 1247 1294 1474 1604 1695 1696 1697 1698 1699 1787 1789 1862 2091 2543 2803 2814 2841 2854 2865 2893 2897 2899 2921

ORIENTATION PROFESSIONNELLE
0098 0217 0280 0357 0360 0422 0627 0785 0869 0923 0968 0970 1197 1351 1474 1479 1561 1565 1695 1715 1862 1870 2126 2322 2338 2463 2574 2841 2865 2892 2893 2894 2895 2896 2897 2898 2921

ORIENTATION SCOLAIRE
0161 0167 0345 0490 0519 0549 0551 0636 0941 1020 1040 1200 1351 1535 1542 1740 1870 2066 2136 2216 2540 2552 2898

OUGANDA
0381 2686

OUVRAGE DE REFERENCE
0132 0997 1528 2039 2279 2425 2512

PAKISTAN
0004 0397 0490 0519 0636 0940 0941 0980 1091 1616 2135 2136 2137 2138 2139 2230 2414 2420

PAPOUASIE-NOUVELLE-GUINEE
0271 0898 1966 2115 2140 2304

PARAGUAY
0241 0291 1266 1671 1801 1838 2141 2611

PARENTS
0105 1021 1544 2057 2070 2145 2336 2637

PARTICIPATION DES PARENTS
0069 0104 1011 2144 2172 2329 2474 2594 2619

PARTICIPATION DU CITOYEN
0166 0242 1468 2855 2903

PAYS EN DEVELOPPEMENT
0213 0241 0279 0284 0291 0292 0294 0455 0456 0457 0460 0461 0462 0517 0518 0577 0611 0612 0617 0749 1084 1245 1266 1273 1310 1372 1382 1404 1610 1632 1642 1671 1774 1801 1831 1834 1838 1839 1841 1882 1954 2099 2141 2315 2590 2611 2687 2741 2742 2783

PAYS-BAS
0006 0040 0086 0294 0309 0313 0328 0361 0387 0398 0425 0462 0574 0815 0816 1012 1013 1036 1147 1201 1202 1207 1210 1228 1268 1274 1372 1395 1403 1427 1455 1467 1498 1531 1696 1707 1732 1738 1792 1798 1841 1842 1938 2024 2078 2079 2080 2081 2082 2083 2084 2085 2086 2087 2090 2091 2092 2093 2094 2095 2096 2097 2098 2099 2247 2248 2315 2360 2422 2471 2482 2496 2578 2632 2645

PEDAGOGIE EXPERIMENTALE
0606 0792 1025 1547 1548 1584 2542 2595

PERFECTIONNEMENT
0023 0102 0974 1110 1618 1619 1653 2643 2709 2879 2906

PERFECTIONNEMENT DES ENSEIGNANTS
0073 0383 1810 2567 2617

PEROU
1114 1158 1385 2119 2156 2157 2158 2310

PHILIPPINES
0147 0981 2159 2160 2351 2379 2918

PHILOSOPHIE DE L'EDUCATION
0031 0208 0286 0359 0429 0512 0594
0651 1104 1118 1124 1313 1398 1654
1949 2479 2817

PHYSIQUE
0225 1126 1130 1335 1597 1611 1655
2003 2004 2017 2173 2174 2364 2365
2392 2393 2402

PLANIFICATION DE L'EDUCATION
0176 0340 0346 0450 0461 0508 0517
0518 0521 0533 0577 0578 0598 0599
0602 0603 0604 0605 0606 0607 0608
0609 0610 0611 0612 0613 0617 0711
0720 0747 0988 1009 1015 1025 1092
1128 1136 1234 1310 1382 1433 1472
1548 1610 1623 1625 1774 1780 1791
1825 1835 1880 1928 1974 1975 1977
1983 2034 2075 2200 2257 2280 2490
2538 2539 2542 2595 2615 2667 2679
2742 2784 2789

PLANIFICATION DU CURRICULUM
0418 0432 1253 1899

PLANIFICATION REGIONALE
0599 0613 1472 2200 2280

POLITIQUE D'EDUCATION
0001 0070 0274 0299 0518 0534 0599
0612 0613 0614 0617 1002 1033 1382
1459 1472 1647 1774 2200 2262 2280
2307 2359 2644 2742 2770 2872

POLOGNE
0048 0061 0062 0083 0289 0371 0404
0558 0655 0824 0960 0961 0963 1142
1194 1195 1296 1320 1374 1393 1394
1457 1477 1478 1492 1746 1784 1785
1996 2061 2177 2178 2179 2180 2182
2183 2184 2185 2186 2187 2188 2189
2190 2191 2192 2193 2196 2388 2517
2579 2663 2869 2870 2889 2914 2928

POPULATION RURALE
0029 1096 2202 2316

PORTUGAL
0029 0599 0613 1095 1096 1344 1472
2002 2200 2201 2202 2203 2280 2316
2391

POSSIBILITE D'EMPLOI
0067 0787 1134 1471 1496 1497 1579
1742 2331 2859

POSSIBILITE OFFERTE AUX JEUNES
0025 0372 1019 1590 1951 2118 2650
2929

PREMIERE ENFANCE
1270 1609

PREPARATION A LA VIE ACTIVE
0202 0220 0221 1242 2268 2653 2799

PREPARATION DU MATERIEL DIDACTIQUE
0066 0192 0199 0434 0681 0686 0690
0719 0747 0761 1076 1319 1504 1791
1880 1971 1979 1980 1981 1982 1983
1984 1985 1986 2232 2264 2306 2427
2487 2591 2751 2818

PRISE DE DECISION
0346 0450 0610 1234 2034

PROBLEME COMMUNAUTAIRE
0276 0553 0807

PROBLEME DE COMPORTEMENT
0129 0623 0754 1890

PROBLEME DE MIGRATION
1001 1585 1615 1913 1959 2040 2047
2048 2166 2442 2527 2655

PROBLEME DE PERSONNALITE
0276 0553 0807

PROBLEME DES JEUNES
0205 0421 1017 1026 1301 1352 1396
1416 1506 1508 1553 1644 1677 1871
2274 2570 2658 2766 2930 2931 2932
2933 2934 2936

PROCEDE PEDAGOGIQUE

0052 0833 0985 1622 1992 2532 2634 2635

PROCESSUS COGNITIF
0248 0252 0253 0255 0256 0257 0302 0415 0425 0574 1046 1185 1241 1285 1460 1520 1663 1940 2085 2150 2421 2530 2760 2772 2798 2940

PROCESSUS D'APPRENTISSAGE
0045 0169 0252 0275 0302 0658 0989 1031 1127 1237 1254 1355 1520 1626 1843 1937 1940 1941 1942 1943 1944 1945 1946 2131 2215 2491 2706 2760 2821

PROCESSUS DE LECTURE
1187 2273 2794

PRODUCTIVITE
0936 1800 2246 2251 2493 2745 2750

PROFESSEUR DE SCIENCES
1299 2110 2171 2406

PROGRAMME DE READAPTATION
0211 0324 0480 1172 1816 2282

PROGRAMME D'EDUCATION DES PARENTS
0352 0448 0619 2143 2935

PROGRAMME D'ENSEIGNEMENT
0153 0332 0340 0607 0737 1092 1433 1824 1825 1835 1977 2253 2767 2784 2856

PROGRAMME INTERCULTUREL
0142 0290 1264 1828 1837 1922 2727

PROGRAMME POUR LA JEUNESSE
0352 0448 0619 1026 1396 1553 1644 2143 2932 2935 2936

PROGRAMMES D'ENSEIGNEMENT PROFESSIONNEL
0063 1014 1481 1505 1589 2146 2873 2901 2908

PROGRAMMES INDIVIDUALISES
0133 0365 1008 1790 1999 2233 2656

PROGRAMMES INTEGRES
1304 2435

PROGRES PEDAGOGIQUE
0303 0732 1521 1821 2762

PSYCHOLOGIE
0633 0862 2260 2441 2834

PSYCHOLOGIE DE L'EDUCATION
0031 0032 0056 0074 0116 0129 0134 0207 0217 0245 0246 0251 0255 0262 0269 0280 0286 0317 0338 0352 0356 0364 0422 0424 0426 0441 0448 0466 0468 0475 0490 0510 0519 0535 0556 0581 0619 0621 0622 0623 0624 0625 0626 0627 0630 0631 0632 0633 0634 0636 0638 0639 0642 0645 0647 0648 0649 0650 0651 0653 0654 0655 0656 0657 0658 0661 0729 0754 0762 0780 0782 0785 0789 0827 0838 0847 0862 0871 0911 0941 0956 0989 0998 1030 1035 1037 1046 1066 1074 1083 1107 1118 1123 1131 1183 1195 1220 1235 1254 1285 1294 1329 1363 1385 1387 1390 1391 1392 1393 1397 1426 1551 1555 1558 1561 1565 1569 1572 1581 1591 1593 1612 1620 1626 1654 1669 1670 1679 1699 1760 1787 1890 1900 1907 1937 1941 1945 2131 2136 2143 2153 2155 2156 2183 2190 2204 2243 2259 2260 2266 2295 2338 2366 2378 2441 2443 2508 2509 2524 2525 2530 2537 2551 2559 2574 2665 2681 2688 2705 2707 2740 2759 2763 2772 2788 2814 2834 2843 2880 2892 2907 2935

PSYCHOLOGIE DE L'ENFANT
0228 0229 1263 1464 2449 2726

PSYCHOLOGIE GENERALE
0339 0356 0362 0441 0625 0780 1070 1217 1557 1604 1697 1787 1788 1789 2781

PSYCHOLOGIE GENETIQUE
0134 0154 0390 0466 0467 0468 0528 0630 0648 0650 0657 1035 1074 1107 1235 1454 1572 1593 1670 2050 2443 2524 2691

0578	0579	0580	0581	0584	0585	0586
0587	0594	0598	0599	0602	0603	0604
0605	0606	0607	0608	0609	0610	0611
0612	0613	0614	0617	0619	0621	0622
0623	0624	0625	0626	0627	0630	0631
0632	0633	0634	0636	0638	0639	0642
0645	0647	0648	0649	0650	0651	0653
0654	0655	0656	0657	0658	0661	0663
0669	0670	0671	0672	0674	0678	0681
0682	0683	0684	0685	0686	0688	0690
0692	0694	0697	0700	0702	0706	0709
0711	0712	0713	0715	0718	0719	0720
0722	0723	0724	0726	0728	0729	0732
0735	0737	0741	0744	0745	0747	0748
0749	0750	0751	0752	0753	0754	0756
0758	0759	0761	0762	0763	0766	0768
0769	0771	0772	0773	0776	0780	0781
0782	0783	0785	0787	0788	0789	0790
0791	0792	0794	0795	0797	0798	0800
0801	0802	0805	0806	0807	0808	0809
0810	0811	0812	0813	0815	0816	0819
0820	0824	0826	0827	0828	0830	0832
0833	0834	0835	0836	0838	0839	0841
0845	0846	0847	0850	0853	0855	0857
0858	0860	0861	0862	0865	0869	0870
0871	0872	0873	0876	0877	0879	0880
0881	0882	0885	0887	0889	0893	0895
0897	0898	0901	0902	0907	0908	0909
0911	0912	0913	0914	0915	0916	0917
0920	0922	0923	0929	0930	0934	0935
0936	0938	0939	0940	0941	0945	0946
0950	0951	0952	0953	0954	0956	0960
0961	0963	0967	0968	0970	0972	0974
0975	0976	0977	0980	0981	0983	0985
0987	0988	0989	0990	0991	0993	0994
0997	0998	1000	1001	1002	1003	1004
1005	1006	1007	1008	1009	1010	1011
1012	1013	1014	1015	1016	1017	1018
1019	1020	1021	1022	1023	1024	1025
1026	1027	1028	1029	1030	1031	1032
1033	1034	1035	1036	1037	1038	1039
1040	1041	1042	1043	1044	1045	1046
1047	1048	1049	1050	1051	1052	1053
1054	1055	1056	1057	1058	1059	1060
1061	1062	1063	1064	1065	1066	1067
1068	1069	1070	1071	1072	1073	1074
1075	1076	1078	1079	1080	1081	1082
1083	1084	1085	1086	1087	1088	1089
1090	1091	1092	1093	1094	1095	1096
1097	1098	1099	1100	1101	1102	1103
1104	1105	1106	1107	1108	1109	1110
1111	1112	1113	1114	1115	1116	1117
1118	1119	1120	1121	1122	1123	1124
1125	1126	1127	1128	1129	1130	1131
1132	1133	1134	1136	1137	1138	1139
1140	1141	1142	1143	1144	1145	1146
1147	1148	1149	1150	1151	1152	1153
1154	1155	1156	1157	1158	1159	1160
1161	1162	1163	1164	1165	1166	1167
1168	1169	1170	1171	1172	1173	1174
1175	1176	1177	1178	1179	1180	1181
1182	1183	1184	1185	1186	1187	1188
1189	1190	1191	1192	1193	1194	1195
1196	1197	1198	1199	1200	1201	1202
1203	1204	1205	1206	1207	1208	1209
1210	1211	1212	1213	1214	1215	1216
1217	1218	1219	1220	1221	1222	1223
1224	1225	1226	1227	1228	1229	1230
1231	1232	1233	1234	1235	1236	1237
1239	1240	1241	1242	1243	1244	1245
1246	1247	1248	1249	1250	1251	1252
1253	1254	1255	1256	1257	1258	1259
1260	1261	1262	1263	1264	1265	1266
1267	1268	1269	1270	1271	1272	1273
1274	1275	1276	1277	1278	1279	1280
1281	1282	1283	1284	1285	1286	1287
1288	1289	1290	1291	1292	1293	1294
1295	1296	1297	1298	1299	1300	1301
1302	1303	1304	1305	1306	1307	1308
1309	1310	1311	1312	1313	1314	1315
1316	1317	1318	1319	1320	1321	1322
1323	1324	1325	1326	1327	1327	1328
1328	1329	1330	1331	1332	1333	1334
1335	1336	1337	1338	1339	1340	1341
1342	1343	1344	1345	1346	1347	1348
1351	1352	1353	1354	1355	1356	1357
1358	1359	1360	1361	1362	1363	1364
1365	1366	1367	1368	1369	1370	1371
1372	1373	1374	1375	1376	1377	1378
1379	1380	1381	1382	1383	1384	1385
1386	1387	1388	1389	1390	1391	1392
1393	1394	1395	1396	1397	1398	1399
1400	1401	1402	1403	1404	1405	1406
1407	1408	1409	1410	1411	1412	1413
1414	1415	1416	1417	1418	1419	1420
1421	1422	1423	1424	1425	1426	1427
1428	1429	1430	1431	1432	1433	1434
1435	1436	1437	1438	1439	1440	1441
1442	1443	1444	1445	1446	1447	1448
1449	1450	1451	1452	1453	1454	1455
1456	1457	1458	1459	1460	1461	1462
1463	1464	1465	1466	1467	1468	1469

1470	1471	1472	1473	1474	1475	1476
1477	1478	1479	1480	1481	1482	1483
1484	1485	1486	1487	1488	1489	1490
1491	1492	1493	1494	1495	1496	1497
1498	1499	1500	1501	1502	1503	1504
1505	1506	1507	1508	1509	1510	1511
1512	1513	1514	1515	1516	1517	1518
1519	1520	1521	1522	1523	1525	1526
1528	1529	1530	1531	1532	1533	1534
1535	1536	1537	1538	1539	1540	1541
1542	1543	1544	1545	1546	1547	1548
1549	1550	1551	1552	1553	1554	1555
1556	1557	1558	1559	1560	1561	1564
1565	1567	1568	1569	1571	1572	1573
1574	1575	1576	1577	1578	1579	1580
1581	1582	1583	1584	1585	1586	1587
1588	1589	1590	1591	1592	1593	1594
1595	1596	1597	1598	1599	1600	1601
1602	1603	1604	1605	1606	1607	1608
1609	1610	1611	1612	1613	1614	1615
1616	1617	1618	1619	1620	1621	1622
1623	1624	1625	1626	1627	1628	1629
1630	1631	1632	1633	1634	1635	1636
1637	1638	1639	1640	1641	1642	1643
1644	1645	1646	1647	1648	1649	1650
1651	1652	1653	1654	1655	1656	1657
1658	1659	1660	1661	1662	1663	1664
1665	1666	1667	1668	1669	1670	1671
1672	1673	1674	1675	1676	1677	1678
1679	1695	1696	1697	1698	1699	1700
1701	1702	1703	1704	1705	1706	1707
1708	1709	1710	1711	1712	1713	1714
1715	1716	1717	1718	1719	1720	1721
1722	1723	1724	1725	1726	1727	1728
1729	1730	1731	1732	1733	1735	1736
1737	1738	1739	1740	1741	1742	1743
1744	1745	1746	1747	1749	1750	1751
1752	1753	1754	1755	1757	1758	1759
1760	1761	1762	1765	1767	1768	1769
1770	1771	1772	1773	1774	1775	1776
1777	1778	1779	1780	1781	1782	1783
1784	1785	1786	1787	1788	1789	1790
1791	1792	1793	1794	1795	1796	1797
1798	1799	1800	1801	1802	1803	1804
1805	1806	1807	1809	1810	1814	1815
1816	1817	1818	1819	1820	1821	1822
1823	1824	1825	1826	1828	1829	1830
1831	1832	1833	1834	1835	1836	1837
1838	1839	1840	1841	1842	1843	1844
1845	1846	1847	1848	1849	1850	1851
1852	1853	1854	1855	1856	1857	1858

1859	1860	1861	1862	1863	1864	1865
1866	1867	1868	1869	1870	1871	1872
1873	1874	1875	1876	1877	1878	1879
1880	1881	1882	1883	1884	1885	1886
1887	1888	1889	1890	1891	1893	1894
1895	1896	1897	1898	1899	1900	1901
1902	1903	1904	1905	1906	1907	1908
1909	1910	1911	1912	1913	1914	1915
1916	1917	1918	1919	1920	1921	1922
1923	1924	1925	1926	1927	1928	1929
1930	1931	1932	1933	1935	1936	1937
1938	1939	1940	1941	1942	1943	1944
1945	1946	1947	1948	1949	1950	1951
1952	1953	1954	1955	1956	1957	1958
1959	1960	1961	1962	1963	1964	1965
1966	1967	1968	1969	1970	1971	1972
1973	1974	1975	1976	1977	1978	1979
1980	1981	1982	1983	1984	1985	1986
1988	1989	1991	1992	1993	1994	1996
1997	1998	1999	2000	2001	2002	2003
2004	2005	2006	2007	2008	2009	2010
2011	2012	2013	2014	2016	2017	2019
2020	2021	2022	2023	2024	2026	2027
2028	2029	2030	2031	2032	2033	2034
2035	2036	2036	2037	2038	2039	2040
2041	2042	2043	2044	2045	2046	2047
2048	2049	2050	2051	2052	2053	2054
2056	2057	2058	2059	2060	2061	2062
2063	2064	2065	2066	2067	2068	2069
2070	2071	2072	2073	2074	2075	2076
2077	2078	2079	2080	2081	2082	2083
2084	2085	2086	2087	2090	2091	2092
2093	2094	2095	2096	2097	2098	2099
2100	2102	2103	2104	2105	2106	2107
2108	2109	2110	2112	2113	2114	2115
2116	2117	2118	2119	2120	2121	2122
2123	2124	2125	2126	2127	2128	2129
2130	2131	2132	2133	2134	2135	2136
2137	2138	2139	2140	2141	2142	2143
2144	2145	2146	2147	2148	2149	2150
2151	2153	2154	2155	2156	2157	2158
2159	2160	2161	2162	2163	2164	2165
2166	2167	2168	2169	2170	2171	2172
2173	2174	2176	2177	2178	2179	2180
2182	2183	2184	2185	2186	2187	2188
2189	2190	2191	2192	2193	2194	2195
2196	2197	2198	2199	2200	2201	2202
2203	2204	2205	2206	2207	2208	2209
2210	2211	2212	2213	2214	2215	2216
2217	2218	2219	2220	2221	2222	2223
2224	2225	2226	2227	2228	2229	2230

2231 2232 2233 2235 2236 2237 2238
2239 2240 2241 2242 2243 2244 2245
2246 2247 2248 2249 2250 2251 2252
2253 2254 2256 2257 2259 2260 2261
2262 2263 2264 2265 2266 2267 2268
2269 2270 2271 2272 2273 2274 2275
2276 2277 2278 2279 2280 2281 2282
2283 2284 2285 2286 2287 2288 2289
2290 2291 2292 2293 2294 2295 2303
2304 2305 2306 2307 2308 2309 2310
2311 2312 2313 2314 2315 2316 2317
2319 2321 2322 2323 2329 2330 2331
2332 2333 2334 2335 2336 2337 2338
2339 2340 2341 2342 2343 2344 2345
2346 2347 2348 2350 2351 2352 2353
2354 2355 2356 2357 2358 2359 2360
2361 2362 2363 2364 2365 2366 2367
2368 2369 2370 2371 2372 2373 2374
2375 2376 2377 2378 2379 2380 2381
2382 2383 2384 2385 2386 2387 2388
2389 2390 2391 2392 2393 2394 2395
2396 2397 2398 2399 2400 2401 2402
2403 2404 2405 2406 2407 2408 2409
2410 2411 2412 2413 2414 2415 2416
2417 2418 2419 2420 2421 2422 2423
2424 2425 2426 2427 2428 2429 2430
2431 2432 2433 2434 2435 2436 2437
2438 2439 2440 2441 2442 2443 2444
2445 2446 2447 2448 2449 2450 2451
2452 2453 2454 2455 2456 2457 2458
2459 2460 2461 2462 2463 2464 2465
2467 2468 2469 2470 2471 2472 2473
2474 2475 2477 2478 2479 2480 2481
2482 2483 2484 2485 2486 2487 2488
2489 2490 2491 2492 2493 2494 2495
2496 2497 2498 2499 2500 2501 2502
2503 2504 2505 2506 2507 2508 2509
2510 2511 2512 2513 2514 2515 2516
2517 2518 2519 2520 2521 2522 2523
2524 2525 2526 2527 2528 2529 2530
2531 2532 2533 2534 2535 2536 2537
2538 2539 2540 2541 2542 2543 2544
2545 2546 2547 2548 2549 2550 2551
2552 2553 2554 2555 2556 2557 2558
2559 2560 2561 2562 2563 2564 2565
2566 2567 2568 2569 2570 2571 2572
2573 2574 2575 2576 2577 2578 2579
2580 2581 2582 2583 2584 2585 2586
2587 2588 2589 2590 2591 2592 2593
2594 2595 2596 2597 2598 2599 2600
2601 2602 2603 2604 2605 2606 2607
2608 2609 2610 2611 2612 2613 2614
2615 2616 2617 2618 2619 2620 2621
2622 2623 2624 2625 2626 2628 2629
2630 2631 2632 2633 2634 2635 2636
2637 2638 2639 2640 2641 2642 2643
2644 2645 2646 2647 2648 2649 2650
2651 2652 2653 2654 2655 2656 2657
2658 2659 2660 2661 2662 2663 2664
2665 2666 2667 2668 2669 2670 2671
2672 2673 2674 2675 2676 2677 2678
2679 2680 2681 2682 2683 2684 2685
2686 2687 2688 2689 2690 2691 2692
2693 2694 2695 2696 2697 2698 2699
2700 2701 2702 2703 2704 2705 2706
2707 2708 2709 2710 2711 2712 2713
2714 2715 2716 2717 2718 2719 2720
2721 2722 2723 2724 2725 2726 2727
2728 2729 2730 2731 2732 2733 2734
2735 2736 2737 2738 2739 2740 2741
2742 2743 2744 2745 2746 2747 2748
2749 2750 2751 2752 2753 2754 2755
2756 2757 2758 2759 2760 2761 2762
2763 2764 2765 2766 2767 2768 2769
2770 2771 2772 2773 2774 2776 2777
2778 2779 2780 2781 2782 2783 2784
2785 2786 2787 2788 2789 2790 2791
2792 2793 2794 2795 2796 2797 2798
2799 2800 2801 2802 2803 2804 2805
2806 2807 2808 2809 2810 2811 2812
2813 2814 2815 2816 2817 2818 2819
2820 2821 2822 2823 2824 2825 2826
2827 2828 2829 2830 2831 2832 2833
2834 2835 2836 2837 2838 2839 2840
2841 2842 2843 2844 2845 2846 2847
2848 2849 2850 2851 2852 2853 2854
2855 2856 2857 2858 2859 2860 2861
2862 2863 2864 2865 2866 2867 2868
2869 2870 2871 2872 2873 2874 2875
2876 2877 2878 2879 2880 2881 2882
2883 2884 2885 2886 2887 2888 2889
2890 2891 2892 2893 2894 2895 2896
2897 2898 2899 2900 2901 2902 2903
2904 2905 2906 2907 2908 2909 2910
2911 2912 2913 2914 2915 2916 2917
2918 2919 2920 2921 2922 2923 2924
2925 2926 2927 2928 2929 2930 2931
2932 2933 2934 2935 2936 2937 2938
2939 2940 2941 2942 2943 2944 2945
2946 2947 2948 2949 2950 2951

RECHERCHE FAITE PAR LES

ELEVES
0107 0184 0247 0427 0447 1055 1105 1261 1317 1375 1728 1749 1758 2276 2346 2497 2498 2499 2500 2501 2502 2503 2519 2600 2620 2731 2786 2809

RECHERCHE LINGUISTIQUE
0828 1911 1914

RECHERCHE PEDAGOGIQUE APPLIQUEE
0246 0247 0248 0256 0415 0427 0626 0782 1105 1185 1663 2150 2266 2276 2421 2500 2600 2786

RECHERCHE SCIENTIFIQUE
0396 1970 2407 2631

RECHERCHE SUR LA LECTURE
0247 0421 0427 0744 1105 1361 1416 1848 1851 2274 2275 2276 2277 2500 2570 2600 2658 2766 2786 2930

RECHERCHE SUR LE CURRICULUM
0044 0116 0165 0208 0217 0243 0247 0280 0320 0359 0418 0419 0420 0421 0422 0423 0424 0425 0426 0427 0428 0429 0430 0431 0432 0433 0434 0435 0512 0535 0574 0575 0627 0639 0682 0697 0785 0956 1030 1105 1119 1124 1176 1233 1253 1276 1319 1359 1392 1397 1398 1416 1426 1444 1561 1565 1575 1601 1620 1760 1781 1899 1907 1949 2008 2022 2085 2117 2241 2249 2267 2274 2276 2292 2338 2396 2479 2500 2504 2570 2574 2586 2600 2658 2705 2711 2766 2786 2796 2818 2824 2892 2930

RECHERCHE-ACTION
0005 1993 2689

RECREATION
2278 2332 2850

REDACTION
0234 0296 0297 0482 1283 1513 1727 1806 1865 2373

REDOUBLEMENT
0232 2568 2621 2625

REFORME DE L'EDUCATION
0057 0223 0379 0674 0683 2104

RELATION TRAVAIL-EDUCATION
0499 0915 1275 1327 1328 1574 2036 2455

RELATIONS ECOLE-COLLECTIVITE
0076 0712 0968 1148 1515 1836 2126 2321 2322 2323 2895

RELATIONS ECOLE-FAMILLE
0128 0217 0231 0280 0422 0627 0700 0785 1223 1560 1561 1565 1955 2338 2574 2795 2892

RELATIONS ECOLE-INDUSTRIE
0369 0571 0827 0877 1179 1209 1489 1665 2295 2447 2605 2793 2884 2913 2943

RELATIONS FAMILIALES
0339 0654 1070 1183 1555 1557 1558 1788 2551 2781

RELATIONS HUMAINES
1187 2273 2794

RELATIONS INTERPERSONNELLES
1355 1843 1946 2821

RELATIONS MAITRE-ELEVE
0165 0209 0245 0245 0420 0491 0697 0976 1024 1125 1363 1363 1410 1612 1612 2102 2148 2270 2340 2504 2505 2506 2507 2508 2508 2509 2509 2541 2618 2623

RELATIONS PARENTS-ENFANTS
0139 1306 1408 1556 2142

REPUBLIQUE ARABE SYRIENNE
0893 2555

REPUBLIQUE CENTRAFRICAINE
0223 0379 0674

REPUBLIQUE DEMOCRATIQUE ALLEMANDE

0036 0181 0288 0292 0460 0508 0520 0533 0542 0602 0603 0985 0987 0988 0989 0990 0991 1034 1178 1265 1273 1341 1401 1404 1480 1621 1622 1623 1624 1625 1626 1627 1628 1629 1630 1631 1632 1633 1661 1820 1839 1941 1974 1998 2198 2358 2389 2575 2635 2649 2871

REPUBLIQUE DOMINICAINE
0487 0488 0709 1514 1988

RESOLUTION DE PROBLEMES
0138 0313 0430 1012 1013 1176 1193 1498 1531 1601 1738 2008 2087 2244 2247 2248 2249 2250 2360 2396 2561 2645

ROLE DE LA FAMILLE
0230 1559 1933 2037 2636

ROLE DE L'ENSEIGNANT
2498 2519 2620

ROUMANIE
0367 0649 0826 0827 0828 1083 1369 1911 1914 2294 2295

ROYAUME-UNI
0005 0014 0015 0041 0049 0056 0081 0085 0125 0142 0151 0154 0229 0269 0270 0275 0290 0314 0320 0322 0330 0344 0347 0377 0389 0390 0413 0426 0428 0446 0449 0467 0510 0528 0535 0563 0575 0645 0789 0845 0850 0853 0855 1005 1016 1022 1023 1028 1030 1031 1037 1045 1110 1115 1119 1146 1152 1153 1157 1168 1169 1174 1180 1191 1213 1214 1215 1219 1262 1263 1264 1272 1290 1291 1317 1322 1334 1336 1337 1340 1346 1387 1397 1412 1423 1424 1429 1440 1446 1449 1450 1454 1487 1502 1533 1545 1546 1581 1619 1653 1722 1739 1761 1795 1805 1807 1826 1828 1837 1900 1902 1903 1909 1922 1935 1936 1942 1960 1976 1993 1994 2000 2050 2051 2056 2067 2114 2133 2134 2162 2197 2215 2226 2242 2259 2284 2287 2288 2291 2292 2335 2341 2361 2362 2367 2368 2371 2374 2376 2390 2397 2398 2403 2410 2415 2433 2449 2483 2502 2593 2604 2606 2607 2613 2640 2651 2688 2689 2690 2691 2692 2693 2694 2695 2696 2697 2698 2699 2700 2701 2702 2703 2704 2705 2706 2707 2708 2709 2710 2711 2712 2713 2714 2715 2716 2717 2718 2719 2720 2721 2722 2723 2724 2725 2726 2727 2728 2729 2730 2731 2732 2733 2734 2735 2736 2737 2738 2748 2853 2879 2927

RSS D'UKRAINE
0634 0870 0871 2210 2227 2739 2740 2842 2843 2922

RWANDA
0401 1047 1048 2308 2319

SAINT-SIEGE
1161 1762 1861 2286

SCIENCES DE L'INFORMATION
0297 0482 1283 1806 1865 2373

SCIENCES SOCIALES
0117 0400 1010 2444

SENEGAL
0059 0060 0686 1203 1258 1920 1958 1980 2069 2427 2428 2429 2430 2492 2675

SIERRA LEONE
1196 1304 1377 1534 2434 2435 2436 2657

SIMULATION
0136 0325 1177 1441 1577 1641 2038 2437 2438

SINGAPOUR
0305 0408 0763 1102 2439 2440 2510

SOCIALISATION
0053 0229 0295 0832 0877 1004 1263 1643 2042 2432 2446 2447 2448 2449 2469 2473 2520 2581 2726 2943

SOCIOLOGIE DE L'EDUCATION
0002 0035 0036 0056 0116 0139 0208 0262 0269 0281 0288 0292 0359 0424

0426 0429 0460 0475 0504 0512 0527 0535 0556 0564 0638 0639 0735 0789 0795 0798 0911 0956 1026 1030 1124 1138 1175 1178 1236 1273 1278 1286 1298 1306 1385 1386 1387 1388 1389 1390 1391 1392 1393 1394 1395 1396 1397 1398 1399 1400 1401 1402 1403 1404 1405 1406 1407 1408 1426 1447 1549 1553 1554 1556 1569 1581 1587 1600 1620 1630 1632 1635 1644 1661 1672 1674 1760 1817 1839 1900 1907 1949 2035 2086 2096 2142 2156 2183 2187 2217 2259 2334 2370 2479 2547 2569 2616 2688 2705 2749 2765 2815 2910 2924 2932 2936

SOURD
0352 0448 0619 2143 2935

SRI LANKA
0045 0608 0761 1097 1098 1128 1237 1944 1975 1984 2264 2487 2488 2489 2490 2491

STATISTIQUES DE L'EDUCATION
0491 0976 1244 1410 1411 1536 2011 2102 2340 2505 2623 2801

STATISTIQUES SCOLAIRES
0491 0976 1336 1410 1517 2102 2339 2340 2341 2505 2623 2734 2755

STATUT DE L'ENSEIGNANT
0232 0491 0759 0976 1356 1410 1895 2020 2102 2340 2350 2505 2568 2621 2622 2623 2624 2625 2822

STRATEGIE DE L'EDUCATION
1412 1994 2114 2226 2697 2927

SUEDE
0011 0012 0150 0159 0244 0282 0376 0388 0466 0630 0631 0830 0832 0834 0835 0836 0838 0839 1001 1006 1188 1285 1323 1530 1714 1786 1832 1923 1959 2048 2166 2289 2382 2431 2442 2446 2469 2498 2518 2519 2520 2521 2522 2523 2524 2525 2526 2527 2528 2529 2530 2531 2581 2620 2655 2862

SUISSE
0013 0052 0319 0341 0345 0358 0549 0551 0604 0605 0606 0642 0654 0833 0841 0967 0998 1009 1015 1020 1024 1025 1039 1044 1117 1137 1138 1155 1163 1164 1183 1200 1224 1227 1399 1439 1522 1525 1535 1542 1548 1549 1554 1555 1558 1723 1794 1992 1997 2005 2006 2027 2066 2148 2155 2165 2257 2272 2334 2369 2394 2506 2532 2533 2534 2535 2536 2537 2538 2539 2540 2541 2542 2543 2544 2545 2546 2547 2548 2549 2550 2551 2552 2553 2554 2595 2615 2618 2634 2854 2899 2907 2910

SYNDICAT
0030 0266 1116 2120 2674

SYSTEME DE GESTION
0340 0607 1092 1433 1825 1835 1977 2784

SYSTEME D'INFORMATION
0322 1168 1440 1807 2134 2716

SYSTEME OUVERT D'ENSEIGNEMENT
0322 0853 1168 1423 1440 1807 2133 2134 2696 2716

SYSTEME SCOLAIRE
0075 0103 0975 2342 2343

TANZANIE (REPUBLIQUE UNIE)
0026 1061 1576 2514 2556 2557

TCHAD
0224

TCHECOSLOVAQUIE
0092 0337 0356 0437 0438 0439 0440 0441 0442 0443 0444 0445 0536 0625 0776 0780 0781 1018 1145 1151 1470 1499 1744 1787 2206 2224 2409 2426 2564 2603 2638 2646 2858

TECHNIQUE DOCIMOLOGIQUE
1121 2030 2647

TECHNOLOGIE DE L'EDUCATION
0044 0049 0081 0093 0116 0136 0183

0259 0298 0300 0307 0316 0321 0322
0325 0329 0330 0340 0342 0351 0384
0421 0424 0431 0477 0524 0579 0607
0639 0663 0678 0724 0773 0797 0811
0853 0930 0956 0983 1022 1050 1053
1090 1092 1101 1108 1141 1149 1150
1163 1168 1177 1186 1199 1233 1269
1272 1278 1287 1291 1322 1392 1405
1413 1414 1415 1416 1417 1418 1419
1420 1421 1422 1423 1424 1425 1426
1427 1428 1429 1430 1431 1432 1433
1434 1435 1436 1437 1438 1439 1440
1441 1442 1443 1444 1445 1446 1447
1448 1449 1450 1451 1452 1577 1578
1603 1620 1634 1636 1657 1664 1672
1713 1719 1723 1739 1743 1760 1769
1770 1777 1807 1825 1835 1853 1859
1863 1874 1907 1977 1978 2009 2026
2071 2083 2116 2133 2134 2162 2219
2241 2265 2267 2274 2361 2438 2478
2513 2549 2570 2601 2608 2640 2658
2670 2684 2696 2699 2702 2716 2728
2730 2732 2754 2766 2773 2777 2784
2791 2796 2812 2851 2861 2930

TELE-ENSEIGNEMENT
0076 0079 0211 0262 0263 0272 0297
0298 0307 0324 0351 0474 0475 0476
0477 0480 0482 0556 0579 0580 0638
0797 1141 1148 1162 1172 1225 1283
1391 1419 1420 1436 1552 1578 1634
1657 1659 1735 1793 1806 1816 1836
1865 2062 2071 2147 2265 2282 2323
2373 2386 2423 2459 2610

TELEVISION
0025 0372 1019 1214 1590 1951 2118
2650 2651 2722 2929

TELEVISION EDUCATIVE
0093 0154 0390 0407 0467 0528 0663
0678 0753 1413 1417 1451 1452 1453
1454 1777 1874 1889 1978 2050 2691

TEST D'APTITUDES
0001 0070 0274 0299 0534 1002 2307
2359 2644 2770 2872

TEST DE PERFORMANCE
0099 0248 0256 0411 0415 1185 1526
1663 2149 2150 2421

TEST SCOLAIRE
0801 1456 1638

THAILANDE
0386 0409 0414 0598 0624 0762 0766
0930 1133 1425 1551 1989 2116 2204
2243 2352 2380 2665 2666 2667 2668
2669 2670 2671

THEORIE DE L'APPRENTISSAGE
0168 0208 0359 0402 0429 0512 0916
1122 1124 1398 1906 1947 1948 1949
2385 2456 2479

THEORIE DE L'EDUCATION
0257 0559 0584 0824 1033 1241 1457
1458 1459 1460 1647 2180 2798 2848

TOGO
0688 2566 2672

TRAVAIL D'EQUIPE
0105 0230 1021 1544 1559 1933 2037
2057 2070 2145 2336 2636 2637

TRINITE ET TOBAGO
0718 2445 2676

TROUBLE D'APPRENTISSAGE
0072 0230 0395 0554 0694 1157 1262
1559 1570 1761 1802 1932 1933 1934
1935 1936 2037 2368 2562 2636 2715
2725

TUNISIE
0977 2677

TURQUIE
0632 0846 0847 1099 1100 1101 1434
2478 2582 2639 2678 2679 2680 2681
2682 2683 2684 2863

UNESCO
0456 0518 0612 0617 1382 1642 1774
1954 2590 2687 2741 2742

UNIVERSITE
0936 1800 2246 2251 2493 2745 2750

URSS
0016 0018 0082 0145 0155 0160 0180

Indice de palabras claves

ACCESO A LA EDUCACION
0003 0137 1189 2919

ACTITUD DEL ALUMNO
2428 2492

ACTIVIDAD CULTURAL
0025 0172 0371 0372 0373 1019 1231 1590 1951 1965 2118 2186 2218 2650 2928 2929

ACTIVIDAD DE APRENDIZAJE
1931 2768

ACTIVIDAD DEPORTIVA
0088 0089 1120 1232 1573 1606 1721 1725 2167 2169

ACTIVIDAD INTEGRADA
0314 1016 1795 1826 1960 2056 2415 2701

ADAPTACION PROFESIONAL
0358 1039 2543 2854 2899

ADMINISTRACION DE LA EDUCACION
0044 0176 0208 0281 0346 0359 0398 0429 0431 0450 0461 0504 0508 0510 0512 0517 0518 0521 0525 0527 0533 0577 0599 0602 0603 0608 0610 0611 0612 0613 0617 0645 0711 0798 0988 1037 1098 1124 1128 1158 1233 1234 1310 1382 1389 1398 1444 1472 1507 1610 1623 1625 1635 1774 1780 1885 1949 1973 1974 1975 2034 2075 2084 2158 2200 2241 2267 2280 2471 2479 2489 2490 2632 2707 2742 2796

AFECTIVAMENTE INADAPTADO
1268 1467 1707 1938 2097 2482

AFECTIVIDAD
0054 0235 0312 0993 1901 1908

AFRICA
0055 0056 0269 0374 0789 1387 1581 1900 2259 2688

AFRICA OCCIDENTAL
0380 0684 1512 2915

ALBANIA
0065 2194

ALEMANIA (REPUBLICA FEDERAL)
0031 0036 0050 0053 0141 0158 0177 0178 0179 0182 0241 0248 0256 0281 0286 0288 0291 0295 0298 0307 0351 0415 0456 0477 0504 0527 0579 0580 0581 0651 0656 0657 0661 0797 0798 0800 0801 0802 1004 1026 1027 1032 1033 1059 1065 1072 1081 1087 1110 1118 1126 1132 1141 1159 1162 1167 1178 1181 1185 1186 1209 1211 1212 1216 1220 1235 1266 1278 1282 1286 1288 1289 1301 1325 1329 1339 1348 1364 1389 1396 1401 1405 1406 1409 1420 1421 1436 1442 1447 1456 1459 1485 1489 1495 1553 1619 1630 1634 1635 1636 1637 1638 1639 1640 1641 1642 1643 1644 1645 1646 1647 1648 1649 1650 1651 1652 1653 1654 1655 1656 1657 1658 1659 1660 1661 1662 1663 1664 1665 1666 1667 1668 1669 1670 1671 1672 1673 1674 1675 1676 1677 1678 1679 1709 1726 1747 1757 1801 1838 1921 1925 1954 1991 2003 2007 2009 2010 2038 2042 2045 2062 2064 2141 2150 2170 2173 2176 2236 2237 2265 2353 2364 2381 2392 2395 2399 2417 2421 2432 2437 2448 2473 2477 2485 2590 2602 2611 2673 2687 2709 2741 2861 2874 2878 2879 2884 2891 2900 2902 2913 2932 2933 2936

ALFABETIZACION
0039 0043 0163 0172 0314 0373 1001 1016 1113 1198 1229 1230 1231 1795

1826 1877 1959 1960 1961 1962 1963 1964 1965 2033 2048 2056 2106 2121 2166 2218 2240 2415 2442 2527 2655 2701

ALFABETIZACION FUNCIONAL
0397 0940 1616 2135 2230

ALUMNO DE ESCUELA PRIMARIA
0624 0762 1551 2204 2243 2665

ALUMNO DE PREPRIMARIA
0155 0624 0762 1551 2204 2205 2243 2665 2845

ALUMNO DE SECUNDARIA
0248 0256 0415 0980 1185 1510 1663 1703 2138 2150 2414 2419 2420 2421 2511

ALUMNO DEFICIENTE
0011 0118 0183 0244 0728 0773 0830 0923 1038 1246 1365 1418 1519 1613 1710 1712 1713 1714 1715 1716 1717 1718 2012 2068 2293 2330 2463 2480 2486 2515 2518 2758 2802 2894

ALUMNO DESERTOR
0077 1165 1796

ALUMNO-DOCENTE
0305 0408 0763 2439 2510

AMBIENTE EDUCACIONAL
0540 0758 1894

AMERICA LATINA
0278 0706 0720 1830 1927 1928

ANGOLA
0068 1049

APRENDIZAJE
0212 0327 1206 1314 1929 1930 2609 2946

APRENDIZAJE DE ADULTOS
0052 0833 1992 2532 2634

APRENDIZAJE (OFICIOS)
0069 0104 1011 2144 2172 2329 2474 2594 2619

APRENDIZAJE PREESCOLAR
1053 1431 2219 2777

APTITUD PARA LA COMUNICACION
0270 0449 1023 1902 1909 2067 2703

APTITUD PARA LOS ESTUDIOS
0132 0997 1528 2039 2279 2425 2512

ARABIA SAUDITA

ARGELIA
0066 0067 1076 1134 1497 1742 1986

ARGENTINA
0072 0073 0074 0075 0076 0077 0078 0079 0080 0087 0383 0694 1148 1165 1192 1225 1226 1796 1802 1810 1836 1932 2238 2323 2342 2372 2562 2567 2610 2617

ASESORAMIENTO
0091 0208 0218 0355 0356 0357 0358 0359 0360 0361 0362 0363 0364 0429 0441 0512 0625 0752 0780 0869 1039 1124 1197 1201 1217 1247 1294 1398 1474 1604 1695 1696 1697 1698 1699 1787 1789 1862 1888 1949 2091 2479 2543 2803 2814 2841 2854 2865 2893 2897 2899 2921

ASESORAMIENTO SOBRE LA CARRERA
0217 0218 0219 0280 0363 0422 0627 0785 1247 1260 1561 1565 1698 2338 2574 2803 2808 2888 2892

AUDICION (FISIOLOGIA)
0094 1007 2128 2285 2558

AUSTRALIA
0023 0046 0069 0095 0096 0097 0098 0099 0100 0101 0102 0103 0104 0105 0106 0107 0391 0392 0411 0447 0879 0880 0970 0972 0974 0975 1011 1021 1239 1375 1479 1526 1544 1617 1618 1758 1956 2057 2070 2122 2144 2145 2149 2172 2329 2336 2343 2474 2503

1929 1949 2023 2052 2164 2245 2270 2282 2479 2507 2559 2585 2609 2653 2659 2916 2923 2931

CARACTERISTICA INDIVIDUAL
1784 1785 2179

CARACTERISTICAS DEL DOCENTE
0072 0444 0694 0939 1145 1802 1932 2077 2562 2563 2564 2587 2603

CARACTERISTICAS DEL ESTUDIANTE
0936 1154 1745 1800 2246 2251 2493 2494 2560 2745 2750 2852

CARRERA
0114 0222 0954 2937

CHAD
0224

CHECOSLOVAQUIA
0092 0337 0356 0437 0438 0439 0440 0441 0442 0443 0444 0445 0536 0625 0776 0780 0781 1018 1145 1151 1470 1499 1744 1787 2206 2224 2409 2426 2564 2603 2638 2646 2858

CHILE
0054 0230 0231 0232 0233 0234 0235 0237 0238 0239 0273 0296 0312 0700 0702 0993 1104 1343 1345 1513 1559 1560 1727 1755 1901 1908 1933 2037 2112 2568 2621 2625 2636

CHINA
0240 0241 0291 1266 1671 1801 1838 2141 2611

CHIPRE
0436

CIENCIAS DE LA INFORMACION
0297 0482 1283 1806 1865 2373

CIENCIAS SOCIALES
0117 0400 1010 2444

COLOMBIA
0030 0259 0260 0261 0262 0263 0264 0265 0266 0267 0272 0475 0476 0555 0556 0638 0945 0946 0950 1116 1156 1292 1391 1414 1476 1543 1552 2120 2147 2214 2231 2305 2357 2423 2588 2674 2868

COMPORTAMIENTO DEL DOCENTE
0094 0138 0207 1007 1123 1154 1193 1745 2128 2244 2250 2285 2494 2558 2559 2560 2561 2852

COMPRENSION
0001 0070 0274 0298 0299 0307 0534 0797 1002 1420 1634 2265 2307 2359 2644 2770 2872

COMPUTADORA
0092 0131 0133 0151 0153 0200 0317 0319 0331 0332 0333 0334 0337 0338 0339 0340 0341 0342 0344 0345 0346 0347 0348 0365 0425 0430 0443 0450 0551 0574 0607 0610 0647 0722 0737 0772 0922 1008 1018 1066 1070 1092 1117 1150 1176 1191 1200 1234 1334 1368 1433 1438 1499 1503 1535 1557 1591 1601 1614 1743 1788 1790 1803 1824 1825 1835 1977 1999 2008 2021 2034 2052 2053 2072 2085 2154 2161 2223 2233 2249 2253 2291 2396 2398 2405 2426 2462 2545 2552 2607 2646 2656 2720 2733 2767 2781 2784 2851 2856

COMUNICACION
0056 0269 0789 1387 1581 1900 2259 2688

COMUNICACION AUDIOVISUAL
0093 0678 1413 1451 1874 1978

COMUNICACION EN LA CLASE
0011 0243 0244 0245 0419 0682 0830 1363 1612 1714 2022 2508 2509 2518

CONCEPCION DEL PROGRAMA
0153 0332 0737 1824 2253 2254 2767 2856 2944

CONCEPTO DE SI MISMO
0263 0272 0476 1552 2147 2423

CONDICION DEL DOCENTE
0232 0491 0759 0976 1356 1410 1895
2020 2102 2340 2350 2505 2568 2621
2622 2623 2624 2625 2822

CONGO
1383

CONSEJERIA EDUCACIONAL
0490 0519 0520 0636 0941 1341 1633
1820 2136

CONSEJERO PEDAGOGICO
2177 2517 2579

COOPERATIVA
0350 1358 2823

COREA (REPUBLICA)
0028 0090 0091 0129 0226 0355 0407
0540 0623 0751 0752 0753 0754 0756
0758 0759 1093 1094 1453 1822 1887
1888 1889 1890 1891 1893 1894 1895
1896 1897 2350 2622

COSTA DE MARFIL
0093 0678 1413 1451 1874 1875 1978
2221

COSTA RICA
0352 0353 0354 0448 0619 1140 1370
1540 2143 2377 2648 2882 2935

CREATIVIDAD
0133 0365 0366 0367 0368 1008 1249
1369 1537 1790 1999 2233 2656 2804

CUBA
0369 0370 1321 1753

CULTURA
0055 0109 0374 0375 0769 2283

CURRICULO
0376 0377 0563 0836 1174 1786 1903
2197 2288 2382 2431 2433 2523 2718
2862

CURRICULO DE ESCUELA PROFESIONAL
0063 1014 1481 1505 1589 2146 2873
2901 2908

CURRICULO INTEGRADO
1304 2435

DEFICIENCIA FISICA
0069 0104 1011 2144 2172 2329 2474
2594 2619

DEFICIENCIA VISUAL
1153 1487 1546 2714 2853

DEFICIENTE
0451 0788 0857 1003 1268 1353 1364
1365 1467 1495 1510 1580 1613 1703
1704 1705 1706 1707 1708 1709 1710
1718 1938 2049 2097 2127 2281 2293
2419 2450 2468 2470 2472 2482 2484
2485 2486 2511 2592 2633 2820 2829
2891 2900

DELINCUENTE
0451 0788 1580 1704 2049 2281 2450
2468

DESARROLLO COGNOSCITIVO
0250 0251 0621 0713 0729 1876 2495
2685 2759

DESARROLLO COMUNITARIO
0263 0271 0272 0476 0898 1552 1966
2115 2140 2147 2304 2423

DESARROLLO DE LA EDUCACION
0521 1342 1780 2075

DESARROLLO DE LA PERSONALIDAD
2151 2835

DESARROLLO DEL LENGUAJE
0054 0056 0235 0269 0270 0312 0377
0449 0563 0789 0993 1023 1174 1387
1581 1900 1901 1902 1903 1908 1909
2067 2197 2259 2288 2433 2688 2703
2718

DESARROLLO ECONOMICO
2428 2492 2498 2519 2620

DESARROLLO INDIVIDUAL

1784 1785 2179

DESARROLLO RURAL
0147 0231 0264 0700 0981 1139 1367 1476 1486 1560 1783 2160 2303 2305 2314 2752 2868 2881 2911 2918

DESERCION
0490 0491 0519 0636 0941 0976 1410 2102 2136 2340 2505 2623

DESIGUALDAD NACIONAL ENTRE REGIONES
0521 1780 2075

DESOCUPACION DE LOS JOVENES
0114 0222 0954 2937

DIAGNOSTICO CLINICO
0249 0901 2630 2846

DIFERENCIA ENTRE SEXOS
0053 0295 0376 0377 0563 0836 1004 1174 1643 1786 1903 2042 2197 2288 2382 2431 2432 2433 2448 2473 2523 2718 2862

DIFERENCIAS INDIVIDUALES
0376 0836 1786 2382 2431 2523 2862

DIFICULTAD EN LA LECTURA
0209 1125 2263 2269 2270 2507 2583

DIFICULTADES EN EL APRENDIZAJE
0072 0230 0395 0554 0694 1157 1262 1559 1570 1761 1802 1932 1933 1934 1935 1936 2037 2368 2562 2636 2715 2725

DIFUSION DE LA INFORMACION
1775 1804 1805 2571 2692

DINAMARCA
0246 0453 0626 0782 0783 1112 2266 2572

DIRECTOR DE ESTABLECIMIENTO
0138 1193 2244 2250 2561

DISEÑO DE EDIFICIOS
0176 0177 0178 0179 0182 0711 1027 1409 1645

DISEÑO DEL MOBILIARIO
0101 1617

DOCUMENTACION
0051 0196 1186 1376 1442 1664 2009 2082 2761

DOCUMENTACION SOBRE EDUCACION
0523 0524 0810 0811 1422 1852 1853

DOCUMENTO DE REFERENCIA
0132 0997 1528 2039 2279 2425 2512

ECONOMIA DE LA EDUCACION
0001 0035 0070 0115 0116 0130 0154 0274 0281 0299 0306 0390 0424 0426 0445 0467 0504 0521 0525 0526 0527 0528 0530 0531 0533 0534 0535 0536 0537 0539 0564 0587 0603 0639 0771 0798 0956 0988 1002 1030 1151 1173 1175 1222 1389 1392 1397 1400 1426 1454 1507 1588 1600 1605 1620 1625 1635 1744 1760 1780 1817 1885 1907 1973 2031 2050 2075 2217 2307 2333 2359 2370 2644 2691 2705 2770 2872 2905 2924

ECUADOR
0416 1257

EDIFICIO
0177 0178 0179 0180 0181 0182 0541 0542 0990 1027 1409 1627 1645 1823 2840

EDUCACION AMBIENTAL
0063 0140 0199 0304 0334 0385 0572 0669 0745 0922 1014 1481 1500 1501 1502 1503 1504 1505 1589 1878 1985 2073 2146 2232 2284 2306 2410 2462 2591 2695 2873 2901 2908

EDUCACION ARTISTICA
0040 0080 0081 0082 0083 0084 0085 0086 0087 0315 0558 0570 0860 0963 1042 1115 1207 1226 1424 1996 2093 2162 2184 2388 2475 2496 2640 2699

2710 2771 2832

EDUCACION BASICA
0014 0033 0125 0126 0127 0203 0446 0850 1143 1523 1860 2245 2693

EDUCACION BILINGUE
0018 0144 0145 0146 0147 0148 0149 0150 0151 0152 0159 0347 0585 0723 0981 1240 1259 1323 1334 1912 1923 2074 2160 2291 2317 2408 2531 2629 2733 2746 2753 2797 2807 2844 2887 2918

EDUCACIÓN CIENTÍFICA
0001 0032 0035 0058 0070 0078 0198 0225 0265 0274 0297 0299 0313 0354 0406 0482 0534 0564 0586 0653 0672 0685 0756 0759 0766 0800 0885 0912 0950 0987 1002 1012 1022 1028 1069 1126 1130 1131 1146 1157 1164 1175 1180 1192 1283 1290 1330 1346 1370 1400 1429 1463 1540 1543 1597 1600 1624 1637 1655 1722 1728 1738 1739 1759 1761 1778 1806 1817 1849 1865 1879 1895 1905 1935 1989 1991 1998 2000 2003 2004 2006 2016 2051 2087 2105 2159 2173 2174 2217 2238 2247 2271 2307 2344 2345 2346 2347 2348 2350 2351 2352 2353 2354 2355 2356 2357 2358 2359 2360 2361 2362 2363 2364 2365 2366 2367 2368 2369 2370 2371 2372 2373 2374 2375 2376 2377 2379 2380 2381 2383 2389 2390 2392 2393 2394 2397 2401 2403 2452 2458 2467 2497 2550 2606 2622 2644 2668 2702 2704 2712 2715 2719 2729 2737 2770 2788 2872 2880 2924

EDUCACION COMPARADA
0031 0036 0076 0142 0143 0217 0241 0278 0279 0280 0281 0282 0283 0284 0286 0288 0289 0290 0291 0292 0293 0294 0422 0455 0457 0460 0462 0504 0527 0627 0651 0706 0749 0785 0798 0839 1052 1084 1110 1118 1148 1178 1194 1264 1266 1273 1324 1372 1389 1401 1404 1561 1565 1619 1630 1632 1635 1653 1654 1661 1671 1746 1801 1828 1830 1831 1832 1833 1834 1836 1837 1838 1839 1840 1841 1882 1922 1924 1927 2099 2141 2189 2313 2315 2323 2338 2526 2574 2611 2709 2727 2776 2783 2819 2879 2892

EDUCACION COMPENSATORIA
0053 0295 1004 1643 2042 2432 2448 2473

EDUCACION COMUNITARIA
0001 0070 0233 0273 0274 0275 0299 0534 0702 1002 1031 1942 2112 2215 2307 2359 2644 2706 2770 2872

EDUCACION DE ADULTOS
0007 0008 0009 0010 0011 0012 0013 0014 0015 0016 0017 0018 0019 0020 0021 0022 0023 0024 0025 0026 0027 0028 0029 0030 0031 0032 0033 0034 0035 0036 0037 0038 0039 0040 0041 0042 0043 0044 0045 0046 0047 0048 0049 0050 0051 0086 0102 0106 0108 0113 0124 0125 0127 0145 0196 0210 0244 0266 0286 0288 0326 0372 0388 0431 0446 0493 0564 0651 0653 0726 0768 0791 0805 0830 0834 0850 0855 0861 0882 0908 0953 0974 1019 1061 1094 1096 1116 1118 1131 1143 1160 1175 1178 1184 1190 1198 1207 1213 1218 1230 1233 1237 1239 1302 1320 1322 1339 1376 1400 1401 1444 1450 1488 1492 1583 1590 1594 1600 1602 1618 1630 1654 1661 1714 1730 1736 1751 1768 1779 1797 1817 1860 1897 1944 1951 1953 1956 1962 1964 2032 2033 2074 2093 2106 2107 2118 2120 2121 2122 2192 2199 2202 2217 2229 2241 2267 2311 2316 2317 2366 2370 2413 2424 2491 2496 2518 2521 2533 2557 2629 2643 2650 2652 2674 2693 2698 2721 2732 2746 2756 2788 2796 2816 2833 2844 2860 2880 2883 2889 2906 2912 2914 2916 2917 2923 2924 2929

EDUCACION DE CIEGOS
0161 0167 1040 1740 2216

EDUCACION DE LA MUJER
0003 0021 0123 0137 0147 0981 1189 1326 1779 2160 2917 2918 2919 2920

EDUCACION DE LA PRIMERA INFANCIA
0017 0044 0431 0493 0882 1233 1444 2241 2267 2652 2796

EDUCACION DE SORDOS
0270 0449 1023 1902 1909 2067 2703

EDUCACION DEL MIGRANTE
0053 0141 0158 0295 0909 1004 1106 1182 1211 1284 1567 1585 1595 1615 1643 1666 1818 1866 1913 1918 1921 1968 2040 2041 2042 2043 2044 2045 2046 2047 2060 2432 2448 2473

EDUCACION DEL NIÑO
0018 0145 2074 2317 2629 2746 2844

EDUCACIÓN EN MATERIA DE POBLACIÓN
0010 0805 2199

EDUCACIÓN EN MATERIA DE SALUD
0088 0089 0188 0300 0384 0724 1120 1146 1163 1204 1232 1289 1415 1439 1573 1606 1676 1719 1720 1721 1722 1723 1724 1725 1726 1773 2026 2051 2163 2167 2168 2169 2170 2367 2549 2712 2754 2831

EDUCACION ESPECIAL
0053 0058 0069 0084 0104 0208 0295 0315 0359 0398 0429 0451 0512 0685 0788 0832 0857 1003 1004 1011 1042 1059 1101 1124 1246 1251 1268 1353 1364 1365 1398 1434 1467 1490 1495 1580 1613 1643 1648 1704 1705 1706 1707 1708 1709 1710 1717 1718 1938 1949 2012 2042 2049 2084 2097 2105 2127 2144 2172 2281 2293 2329 2345 2432 2446 2448 2450 2467 2468 2469 2470 2471 2472 2473 2474 2475 2476 2477 2478 2479 2480 2481 2482 2483 2484 2485 2486 2520 2581 2592 2594 2613 2619 2627 2632 2633 2684 2738 2771 2775 2802 2806 2820 2829 2885 2891 2900

EDUCACION FAMILIAR
0139 0263 0272 0476 0624 0654 0762 1026 1138 1183 1306 1396 1399 1408 1549 1551 1552 1553 1554 1555 1556 1558 1644 2142 2147 2204 2243 2334 2423 2547 2551 2665 2910 2932 2936

EDUCACION FISICA
0081 0088 0089 0131 0188 0204 0333 0772 0994 1001 1120 1204 1232 1289 1299 1424 1573 1606 1676 1720 1721 1724 1725 1726 1773 1803 1959 2048 2053 2072 2110 2154 2161 2162 2163 2164 2165 2166 2167 2168 2169 2170 2171 2223 2406 2442 2527 2536 2640 2655 2699 2831

EDUCACION INFORMAL
0131 0333 0772 1803 2053 2072 2154 2161 2223

EDUCACION INTERNACIONAL
0076 0142 0143 0241 0278 0279 0282 0283 0284 0290 0291 0292 0293 0294 0340 0455 0457 0460 0462 0607 0706 0749 0839 1052 1084 1092 1148 1264 1266 1273 1324 1372 1404 1433 1632 1671 1801 1825 1828 1830 1831 1832 1833 1834 1835 1836 1837 1838 1839 1840 1841 1882 1922 1924 1927 1977 2099 2141 2313 2315 2323 2526 2611 2727 2776 2783 2784 2819

EDUCACION MUSICAL
0131 0333 0772 1803 2053 2072 2154 2161 2223

EDUCACION NO FORMAL
0025 0030 0043 0046 0106 0140 0233 0266 0271 0273 0372 0423 0669 0702 0898 0930 1019 1114 1116 1230 1239 1250 1412 1425 1500 1590 1781 1951 1956 1964 1966 1994 2028 2033 2073 2112 2113 2114 2115 2116 2117 2118 2119 2120 2121 2122 2123 2140 2157 2226 2304 2310 2586 2650 2670 2674 2697 2805 2927 2929

EDUCACION OBRERA
0034 0035 0210 0564 1160 1175 1400 1600 1817 2217 2370 2916 2923 2924

EDUCACION PARA DEFICIENTES

1711 2387 2464

EDUCACION PARA EL DESARROLLO
0164 0283 0464 1052 1833 2222 2776

EDUCACION PARA EL TRABAJO
0357 0869 0870 1474 2210 2227 2739 2841 2842 2865 2893 2921 2922

EDUCACION PERMANENTE
0009 0046 0106 0128 0456 0791 1223 1239 1583 1642 1953 1954 1955 1956 2122 2590 2687 2741 2795 2860

EDUCACION PREESCOLAR
0035 0161 0167 0172 0260 0275 0373 0438 0545 0564 0813 0858 0870 0872 0929 0945 1031 1040 1175 1231 1400 1600 1740 1817 1942 1965 1967 1969 2206 2207 2208 2209 2210 2211 2212 2213 2214 2215 2216 2217 2218 2224 2225 2227 2228 2231 2337 2370 2409 2411 2412 2461 2706 2739 2830 2836 2842 2922 2924 2938

EDUCACION RELIGIOSA
0094 0109 0151 0347 0375 0377 0563 0769 1007 1161 1169 1174 1188 1243 1334 1502 1762 1861 1903 2128 2197 2283 2284 2285 2286 2287 2288 2289 2290 2291 2410 2433 2529 2558 2604 2695 2717 2718 2733 2800

EDUCACION RURAL
0001 0038 0070 0143 0171 0199 0264 0271 0274 0293 0294 0299 0462 0534 0898 1002 1047 1103 1114 1190 1208 1324 1367 1372 1476 1504 1783 1840 1841 1924 1966 1985 2032 2099 2115 2119 2140 2157 2232 2239 2303 2304 2305 2306 2307 2308 2309 2310 2311 2312 2313 2314 2315 2359 2591 2644 2770 2785 2819 2868 2872

EDUCACION TRADICIONAL
0060 1258 2430 2675

EDUCACION URBANA
1045 1298 1407 2708 2748 2749 2815

EGIPTO
0228 0885 0887 1303 1461 1462 1463 1464 1465 1466 2354 2383 2384

EGRESADO ESCOLAR
0787 1471 1496 1579 2331 2859

EGRESO DE LA ESCUELA
0530 1138 1152 1399 1533 1545 1549 1554 1588 2278 2332 2333 2334 2335 2547 2713 2850 2910

ELABORACION DE PRUEBAS
0017 0097 0133 0202 0220 0365 0493 0882 1001 1008 1196 1534 1790 1959 1999 2048 2166 2233 2434 2442 2527 2652 2653 2654 2655 2656 2657

ELABORACION DEL CURRICULO
0012 0073 0095 0096 0117 0154 0168 0194 0201 0223 0300 0304 0378 0379 0380 0381 0382 0383 0384 0385 0386 0387 0388 0389 0390 0391 0392 0393 0394 0395 0396 0397 0398 0399 0400 0401 0402 0403 0404 0409 0410 0412 0467 0528 0554 0572 0670 0674 0684 0692 0724 0745 0834 0845 0879 0880 0940 1000 1010 1048 1122 1277 1296 1415 1454 1501 1512 1529 1570 1616 1701 1719 1810 1878 1934 1948 1970 2014 2023 2026 2050 2081 2084 2135 2191 2230 2319 2400 2407 2444 2471 2521 2567 2584 2585 2617 2631 2632 2659 2660 2663 2669 2686 2690 2691 2754 2769 2811 2915 2950

EMIRATOS ARABES UNIDOS
1300 2743 2744

EMPLEO
0037 0048 0061 0062 0063 0098 0110 0121 0166 0185 0242 0264 0326 0357 0442 0599 0613 0781 0787 0865 0869 0873 0960 0961 0970 0991 1014 1054 1056 1080 1081 1139 1153 1184 1209 1251 1252 1320 1362 1362 1364 1468 1469 1470 1471 1472 1473 1474 1475 1476 1477 1478 1479 1480 1481 1482 1483 1484 1485 1486 1487 1488 1489 1490 1491 1492 1493 1493 1494 1494 1495 1496 1505 1546 1579 1589 1602

1608 1628 1651 1665 1709 1797 2132
2146 2182 2192 2200 2252 2280 2305
2331 2481 2485 2638 2641 2714 2752
2778 2806 2826 2826 2837 2841 2853
2855 2857 2858 2859 2864 2865 2866
2868 2869 2870 2871 2873 2875 2876
2877 2878 2881 2883 2884 2885 2886
2889 2890 2890 2891 2893 2896 2900
2901 2903 2904 2908 2909 2911 2912
2913 2914 2921 2939

ENCUESTA OCUPACIONAL
1252 1491 1608 2132 2886

ENFOQUE INTERDISCIPLINARIO
0135 1041 1829

ENSEÑANZA
2476 2627 2775

ENSEÑANZA A DISTANCIA
0076 0079 0211 0262 0263 0272 0297
0298 0307 0324 0351 0474 0475 0476
0477 0480 0482 0556 0579 0580 0638
0797 1141 1148 1162 1172 1225 1283
1391 1419 1420 1436 1552 1578 1634
1657 1659 1735 1793 1806 1816 1836
1865 2062 2071 2147 2265 2282 2323
2373 2386 2423 2459 2610

ENSEÑANZA AGRICOLA
0061 0062 0063 0064 0960 0961 1014
1297 1477 1478 1481 1505 1589 2109
2146 2182 2869 2870 2873 2901 2908

ENSEÑANZA DE IDIOMAS
0054 0116 0160 0235 0270 0312 0424
0449 0639 0912 0916 0956 0993 1023
1378 1392 1426 1620 1760 1901 1902
1904 1905 1906 1907 1908 1909 1910
1915 1947 2067 2355 2385 2452 2456
2703 2838 2849

ENSEÑANZA DE LA CIENCIA
0083 0225 0344 0348 0376 0403 0430
0474 0558 0766 0800 0836 0885 0887
0916 0963 0987 1028 1095 1126 1130
1164 1167 1176 1180 1191 1216 1277
1330 1335 1346 1347 1368 1463 1465
1597 1601 1611 1614 1624 1637 1655
1660 1668 1711 1735 1786 1793 1849
1850 1906 1947 1989 1991 1996 1998
2000 2002 2003 2004 2006 2007 2008
2010 2014 2016 2017 2019 2021 2159
2173 2174 2184 2201 2249 2351 2352
2353 2354 2358 2362 2364 2365 2369
2371 2375 2376 2378 2379 2380 2381
2382 2383 2384 2385 2386 2387 2388
2389 2390 2391 2392 2393 2394 2395
2396 2397 2398 2399 2400 2401 2402
2403 2404 2405 2431 2456 2459 2464
2523 2550 2606 2607 2668 2704 2719
2720 2737 2811 2862

ENSEÑANZA DE LA GEOGRAFIA
0116 0424 0639 0956 1392 1426 1620
1760 1907

ENSEÑANZA DE LA HISTORIA
0116 0424 0639 0956 1157 1392 1426
1620 1759 1760 1761 1907 1935 2271
2356 2368 2458 2715

ENSEÑANZA DE LA LECTURA
0967 1525 1759 1794 1997 2271 2272
2356 2458 2535

ENSEÑANZA DE LA LENGUA MATERNA
0059 0118 0270 0449 0549 1020 1023
1038 1203 1542 1716 1902 1909 1920
1958 2066 2067 2068 2069 2330 2429
2540 2703

ENSEÑANZA DE LAS MATEMATICAS
0005 0052 0083 0116 0131 0133 0225
0318 0333 0348 0365 0403 0424 0430
0487 0558 0639 0766 0772 0800 0833
0956 0963 0967 0987 1008 1028 1067
1095 1126 1130 1155 1164 1167 1176
1186 1216 1244 1246 1248 1277 1290
1330 1335 1346 1347 1356 1368 1392
1411 1412 1426 1442 1525 1536 1592
1597 1601 1607 1611 1614 1620 1624
1637 1655 1660 1664 1668 1717 1760
1790 1794 1803 1849 1850 1907 1988
1989 1991 1992 1993 1994 1996 1997
1998 1999 2000 2001 2002 2003 2004
2005 2006 2007 2008 2009 2010 2011
2012 2013 2014 2016 2017 2019 2020
2021 2053 2072 2114 2154 2161 2173

0491 0976 1336 1410 1517 2102 2339
2340 2341 2505 2623 2734 2755

ESTADISTICAS EDUCACIONALES
0491 0976 1244 1410 1411 1536 2011
2102 2340 2505 2623 2801

ESTADOS DEL GOLFO
0889 1700

ESTADOS UNIDOS DE AMERICA
0001 0007 0032 0044 0047 0070 0084
0128 0143 0144 0148 0149 0152 0153
0218 0219 0221 0247 0251 0252 0255
0257 0274 0283 0284 0293 0299 0300
0302 0303 0315 0316 0321 0329 0332
0339 0340 0350 0363 0364 0366 0368
0384 0399 0403 0412 0421 0427 0431
0434 0435 0457 0534 0571 0578 0585
0594 0607 0609 0621 0622 0653 0723
0724 0726 0728 0729 0732 0735 0737
1000 1002 1042 1046 1050 1051 1052
1053 1054 1062 1063 1070 1073 1084
1092 1103 1105 1129 1131 1136 1144
1149 1171 1179 1187 1223 1233 1240
1241 1242 1243 1244 1246 1247 1249
1250 1251 1259 1260 1261 1267 1277
1287 1293 1294 1298 1302 1313 1319
1324 1353 1355 1356 1358 1359 1360
1362 1371 1380 1386 1407 1411 1415
1416 1430 1431 1433 1437 1444 1448
1460 1482 1490 1493 1494 1517 1518
1519 1520 1521 1529 1536 1537 1538
1541 1557 1698 1699 1708 1712 1717
1719 1730 1749 1750 1751 1788 1821
1824 1825 1833 1834 1835 1840 1843
1912 1924 1931 1939 1940 1946 1955
1977 2011 2012 2014 2020 2026 2123
2153 2219 2241 2253 2261 2267 2268
2273 2274 2276 2290 2307 2309 2313
2339 2359 2366 2400 2408 2475 2476
2480 2481 2484 2500 2501 2515 2569
2570 2600 2605 2624 2627 2644 2658
2660 2749 2753 2754 2755 2756 2757
2758 2759 2760 2761 2762 2763 2764
2765 2766 2767 2768 2769 2770 2771
2772 2773 2774 2775 2776 2777 2778
2779 2780 2781 2782 2783 2784 2785
2786 2787 2788 2789 2790 2791 2792
2793 2794 2795 2796 2797 2798 2799
2800 2801 2802 2803 2804 2805 2806
2807 2808 2809 2810 2811 2812 2813
2814 2815 2816 2817 2818 2819 2820
2821 2822 2823 2824 2825 2826 2827
2828 2856 2872 2875 2880 2885 2887
2888 2890 2930

ESTRATEGIAS DE LA EDUCACION
1412 1994 2114 2226 2697 2927

ESTUDIO DE LA PERSONALIDAD
0131 0333 0622 0642 0772 0998 1803
2053 2072 2153 2154 2155 2161 2223
2537 2763 2907

ESTUDIO INTERCULTURAL
0366 0368 1249 1537 2804

ESTUDIOS SOCIALES
0718 2445 2676

ETIOPIA
1509 1510 1511 1703 2419 2511

EUROPA ORIENTAL
1181 1662

EVALUACION
0099 0126 0132 0203 0234 0252 0296
0302 0303 0345 0354 0366 0368 0380
0399 0411 0412 0488 0491 0547 0551
0684 0709 0712 0728 0732 0841 0967
0976 0997 1000 1006 1013 1043 1152
1196 1200 1244 1249 1267 1309 1370
1371 1410 1411 1498 1509 1511 1512
1513 1514 1515 1516 1517 1518 1519
1520 1521 1522 1523 1525 1526 1528
1529 1530 1531 1532 1533 1534 1535
1536 1537 1538 1539 1540 1541 1545
1712 1727 1794 1821 1844 1884 1940
1997 2011 2039 2102 2103 2149 2245
2248 2272 2279 2321 2335 2339 2340
2377 2425 2434 2465 2505 2512 2515
2528 2534 2535 2552 2623 2645 2657
2660 2662 2713 2755 2757 2758 2760
2762 2769 2801 2804 2810 2827 2915

EVALUACION ACUMULATIVA
0728 1519 1576 1712 2514 2515 2556
2758

EVALUACION DE LOS EDIFICIOS

0177 0178 0179 0182 1027 1409 1645

EVALUACION DEL ALUMNO
0250 0713 1876 2495 2685

EVALUACION DEL CURRICULO
0099 0193 0201 0248 0256 0305 0386 0394 0399 0405 0406 0407 0408 0409 0410 0411 0412 0413 0414 0415 0416 0417 0753 0763 1000 1005 1133 1185 1257 1271 1453 1526 1529 1663 1879 1886 1889 1976 2023 2149 2150 2348 2421 2439 2510 2585 2593 2659 2660 2669 2671 2700 2769

EVALUACION DEL DOCENTE
0002 1236 1402 2035 2616

EVALUACION DEL PROGRAMA
0311 0598 0605 0917 1015 1182 1968 2044 2256 2257 2457 2539 2667

EVALUACION OPERACIONAL
0136 0325 1177 1441 1576 1577 2438 2514 2556

EXAMEN
0105 0265 0950 1021 1152 1153 1487 1533 1543 1544 1545 1546 2057 2070 2145 2335 2336 2357 2637 2713 2714 2853

EXAMEN PSICOLOGICO
0056 0269 0789 1387 1581 1900 2259 2688

FACTOR DE EXITO
1199 1443 1603 2513 2608

FACTOR DE FRACASO
1138 1280 1399 1549 1550 1554 1864 2334 2547 2910

FACTOR DE RENDIMIENTO
1024 2148 2506 2541 2618

FAMILIA (UNIDAD SOCIOLOGICA)
0251 0621 0729 2759

FILIPINAS
0147 0981 2159 2160 2351 2379 2918

FILOSOFIA DE LA EDUCACION
0031 0208 0286 0359 0429 0512 0594 0651 1104 1118 1124 1313 1398 1654 1949 2479 2817

FINALIDADES DE LA EDUCACION
0547 1516 2103

FINANCIAMIENTO DE LA EDUCACION
0545 0929 1517 1969 2213 2337 2339 2755

FINLANDIA
0019 0088 0217 0280 0310 0395 0422 0433 0554 0627 0650 0785 0908 0909 0911 1086 1107 1120 1275 1276 1390 1561 1564 1565 1567 1568 1569 1570 1571 1572 1573 1574 1575 1721 1815 1934 2041 2167 2338 2573 2574 2598 2867 2892

FISICA
0225 1126 1130 1335 1597 1611 1655 2003 2004 2017 2173 2174 2364 2365 2392 2393 2402

FORMACION A TIEMPO PARCIAL
0063 1014 1481 1505 1589 2146 2873 2901 2908

FORMACION DE ADMINISTRADORES
0413 1005 1976 2593 2700

FORMACION DE DOCENTES
0006 0069 0073 0079 0104 0122 0197 0199 0201 0212 0217 0232 0241 0247 0261 0280 0291 0309 0327 0344 0383 0393 0394 0410 0413 0421 0422 0423 0427 0444 0453 0456 0555 0567 0571 0606 0627 0671 0688 0735 0783 0785 0806 0809 0816 0832 0939 0946 1003 1005 1011 1025 1082 1085 1086 1088 1105 1108 1132 1145 1169 1179 1180 1191 1199 1206 1225 1266 1295 1357 1386 1416 1435 1443 1504 1548 1561 1564 1565 1571 1603 1621 1642 1656 1671 1701 1706 1737 1765 1770 1775 1781 1792 1801 1804 1809 1810 1814 1838 1845 1856 1857 1873 1929 1954

1972 1976 1985 2023 2077 2080 2108 2117 2127 2141 2144 2172 2177 2220 2232 2263 2269 2274 2276 2287 2306 2329 2338 2371 2397 2398 2446 2451 2469 2472 2474 2483 2500 2513 2517 2520 2542 2563 2564 2565 2566 2567 2568 2569 2570 2571 2572 2573 2574 2575 2576 2577 2578 2579 2580 2581 2582 2583 2584 2585 2586 2587 2588 2589 2590 2591 2592 2593 2594 2595 2596 2597 2598 2599 2600 2601 2602 2603 2604 2605 2606 2607 2608 2609 2610 2611 2612 2613 2614 2617 2619 2621 2625 2628 2633 2639 2658 2659 2672 2678 2687 2700 2717 2719 2720 2738 2741 2765 2766 2786 2793 2863 2892 2930

FORMACION DE DOCENTES EN EJERCICIO
0035 0073 0197 0211 0310 0324 0383 0440 0480 0564 0671 0750 1172 1175 1284 1381 1400 1568 1600 1775 1804 1809 1810 1814 1815 1816 1817 1818 1819 1866 1883 2046 2217 2220 2282 2370 2451 2565 2567 2571 2580 2617 2628 2867 2924

FORMACION DE FORMADORES DE DOCENTES
0604 1009 2538 2615

FORMACION DE INGENIEROS
0092 0337 0443 1013 1018 1498 1499 1531 2248 2426 2645 2646

FORMACION EN EJERCICIO
0005 1993 2689

FORMACION MEDICA
0300 0384 0724 1227 1415 1719 2026 2027 2554 2754

FORMACION POLITICA
0065 0377 0563 0812 1142 1174 1854 1903 2061 2188 2194 2195 2196 2197 2288 2433 2718

FORMACION PROFESIONAL
0023 0037 0048 0063 0102 0110 0115 0121 0166 0242 0326 0531 0642 0974 0998 1014 1080 1138 1139 1184 1209 1320 1399 1468 1469 1481 1484 1486 1488 1489 1492 1505 1549 1554 1589 1602 1618 1665 1797 2146 2155 2192 2252 2334 2537 2547 2643 2752 2855 2857 2873 2877 2881 2883 2884 2889 2901 2903 2904 2905 2906 2907 2908 2909 2910 2911 2912 2913 2914

FRANCIA
0009 0025 0027 0035 0037 0056 0063 0089 0225 0227 0245 0269 0317 0318 0323 0326 0338 0348 0362 0372 0430 0451 0461 0517 0530 0539 0564 0577 0611 0647 0648 0787 0788 0789 0790 0791 0792 0794 0795 1014 1019 1066 1067 1074 1106 1109 1130 1166 1170 1175 1176 1184 1199 1217 1222 1232 1248 1252 1270 1310 1335 1363 1365 1368 1387 1388 1400 1419 1443 1471 1481 1488 1491 1496 1505 1547 1578 1579 1580 1581 1582 1583 1584 1585 1586 1587 1588 1589 1590 1591 1592 1593 1594 1595 1596 1597 1598 1599 1600 1601 1602 1603 1604 1605 1606 1607 1608 1609 1610 1611 1612 1613 1614 1615 1697 1704 1710 1718 1725 1789 1797 1817 1900 1913 1918 1919 1951 1953 2001 2004 2008 2013 2017 2021 2040 2043 2047 2049 2054 2060 2063 2071 2118 2132 2146 2169 2174 2217 2249 2259 2281 2293 2331 2333 2365 2370 2393 2396 2402 2405 2450 2468 2486 2508 2509 2513 2608 2650 2688 2859 2860 2873 2883 2886 2901 2908 2912 2924 2929

GESTION
0508 0525 0602 0608 1128 1507 1623 1885 1973 1974 1975 2490

GHANA
1069 1342 2363 2378

GRECIA
0010 0805 1366 1381 1819 2199

GRUPO MINORITARIO
1146 1722 2051 2367 2712

GUATEMALA

0176 0711 1728 2346 2497

GUAYANA
0393 0897 1701 1702 2584

HABILIDADES BASICAS
0128 1223 1955 2795

HIGIENE
1720 1773 2163 2831

HISTORIA DE LA EDUCACION
0025 0031 0035 0083 0208 0261 0262 0276 0286 0359 0372 0377 0395 0429 0475 0512 0553 0554 0555 0556 0558 0559 0563 0564 0567 0584 0638 0651 0807 0946 0963 1019 1118 1124 1174 1175 1224 1280 1357 1391 1393 1398 1400 1458 1550 1570 1590 1600 1654 1817 1864 1873 1903 1934 1949 1951 1996 2118 2183 2184 2197 2217 2288 2370 2388 2433 2479 2553 2588 2614 2650 2718 2848 2924 2929

HONDURAS
0712 1515 2321

HUNGRIA
0024 0276 0553 0806 0807 0808 0983 1108 1311 1318 1428 1435 1765 1767 1768 1769 1770 1771 1772 2424 2576 2601

IGUALDAD DE EDUCACION
0205 0525 1017 1506 1507 1508 1885 1973 2931

IIPE
0518 0612 0617 1382 1774 2742

INADAPTADO SOCIAL
0451 0788 1580 1704 2049 2281 2450 2468

INCAPACIDAD PARA EL APRENDIZAJE
0658 1254 1268 1360 1467 1707 1937 1938 1939 1945 2097 2131 2482 2825

INDIA
0021 0423 0521 0663 0741 0934 1367 1417 1452 1775 1776 1777 1778 1779 1780 1781 1782 1783 1804 2075 2117 2303 2314 2347 2571 2586 2917

INDONESIA
0241 0291 0935 0936 1266 1671 1799 1800 1801 1838 2141 2246 2251 2493 2611 2745 2750

INFLUENCIA DEL AMBIENTE
0205 1017 1506 1508 2931

INFLUENCIA DEL DOCENTE
1024 2148 2506 2541 2618

INFORMACION SOBRE EDUCACION
0304 0385 0572 0745 1501 1878

INGENIERIA DE CONSTRUCCION
0177 0178 0179 0182 1027 1409 1645

INNOVACION EDUCACIONAL
0320 0425 0428 0461 0517 0574 0575 0577 0611 1119 1202 1310 1610 1842 2085 2092 2212 2292 2461 2711

INSPECCION
0938 2076 2516 2661

INSTRUCCION
0520 1341 1633 1820

INTEGRACION ESCOLAR
0069 0104 0118 1011 1038 1716 2068 2144 2172 2329 2330 2474 2594 2619

INTERES PROFESIONAL
0358 1039 2543 2854 2899

INVESTIGACION CIENTIFICA
0396 1970 2407 2631

INVESTIGACION CURRICULAR
0044 0116 0165 0208 0217 0243 0247 0280 0320 0359 0418 0419 0420 0421 0422 0423 0424 0425 0426 0427 0428 0429 0430 0431 0432 0433 0434 0435 0512 0535 0574 0575 0627 0639 0682 0697 0785 0956 1030 1105 1119 1124 1176 1233 1253 1276 1319 1359 1392

1397 1398 1416 1426 1444 1561 1565
1575 1601 1620 1760 1781 1899 1907
1949 2008 2022 2085 2117 2241 2249
2267 2274 2276 2292 2338 2396 2479
2500 2504 2570 2574 2586 2600 2658
2705 2711 2766 2786 2796 2818 2824
2892 2930

INVESTIGACION EDUCACIONAL

0001 0002 0003 0004 0005 0006 0007
0008 0009 0010 0011 0012 0013 0014
0015 0016 0017 0018 0019 0020 0021
0022 0023 0024 0025 0026 0027 0028
0029 0030 0031 0032 0033 0034 0035
0036 0037 0038 0039 0040 0041 0042
0043 0044 0045 0046 0047 0048 0049
0050 0051 0052 0053 0054 0055 0056
0057 0058 0059 0060 0061 0062 0063
0064 0065 0066 0067 0068 0069 0070
0071 0072 0073 0074 0075 0076 0077
0078 0079 0080 0081 0082 0083 0084
0085 0086 0087 0088 0089 0090 0091
0092 0093 0094 0095 0096 0097 0098
0099 0100 0101 0102 0103 0104 0105
0106 0107 0108 0109 0110 0111 0112
0113 0114 0115 0116 0117 0118 0119
0120 0121 0122 0123 0124 0125 0126
0127 0128 0129 0130 0131 0132 0133
0134 0135 0136 0137 0138 0139 0140
0141 0142 0143 0144 0145 0146 0147
0148 0149 0150 0151 0152 0153 0154
0155 0156 0157 0158 0159 0160 0161
0162 0163 0164 0165 0166 0167 0168
0169 0170 0171 0172 0173 0174 0175
0176 0177 0178 0179 0180 0181 0182
0183 0184 0185 0186 0187 0188 0189
0190 0191 0192 0193 0194 0195 0196
0197 0198 0199 0200 0201 0202 0203
0204 0205 0206 0207 0208 0209 0210
0211 0212 0213 0214 0215 0216 0217
0218 0219 0220 0221 0222 0223 0224
0225 0226 0227 0228 0229 0230 0231
0232 0233 0234 0235 0237 0238 0239
0240 0241 0242 0243 0244 0245 0246
0247 0248 0249 0250 0251 0252 0253
0255 0256 0257 0259 0260 0261 0262
0263 0264 0265 0266 0267 0269 0270
0271 0272 0273 0274 0275 0276 0278
0279 0280 0281 0282 0283 0284 0286
0288 0289 0290 0291 0292 0293 0294
0295 0296 0297 0298 0299 0300 0302
0303 0304 0305 0306 0307 0309 0310
0311 0312 0313 0314 0315 0316 0317
0318 0319 0320 0321 0322 0323 0324
0325 0326 0327 0328 0329 0330 0331
0332 0333 0334 0337 0338 0339 0340
0341 0342 0344 0345 0346 0347 0348
0350 0351 0352 0353 0354 0355 0356
0357 0358 0359 0360 0361 0362 0363
0364 0365 0366 0367 0368 0369 0370
0371 0372 0373 0374 0375 0376 0377
0378 0379 0380 0381 0382 0383 0384
0385 0386 0387 0388 0389 0390 0391
0392 0393 0394 0396 0397 0398 0399
0400 0401 0402 0403 0404 0405 0406
0407 0408 0409 0410 0411 0412 0413
0414 0415 0416 0417 0418 0419 0420
0421 0422 0423 0424 0425 0426 0427
0428 0429 0430 0431 0432 0433 0434
0435 0436 0437 0438 0439 0440 0441
0442 0443 0444 0445 0446 0447 0448
0449 0450 0451 0453 0455 0456 0457
0460 0461 0462 0464 0466 0467 0468
0474 0475 0476 0477 0480 0482 0487
0488 0490 0491 0493 0499 0504 0508
0510 0512 0517 0518 0519 0520 0521
0523 0524 0525 0526 0527 0528 0530
0531 0533 0534 0535 0536 0537 0539
0540 0541 0542 0545 0547 0549 0551
0553 0555 0556 0558 0559 0563 0564
0567 0570 0571 0572 0574 0575 0577
0578 0579 0580 0581 0584 0585 0586
0587 0594 0598 0599 0602 0603 0604
0605 0606 0607 0608 0609 0610 0611
0612 0613 0614 0617 0619 0621 0622
0623 0624 0625 0626 0627 0630 0631
0632 0633 0634 0636 0638 0639 0642
0645 0647 0648 0649 0650 0651 0653
0654 0655 0656 0657 0658 0661 0663
0669 0670 0671 0672 0674 0678 0681
0682 0683 0684 0685 0686 0688 0690
0692 0694 0697 0700 0702 0706 0709
0711 0712 0713 0715 0718 0719 0720
0722 0723 0724 0726 0728 0729 0732
0735 0737 0741 0744 0745 0747 0748
0749 0750 0751 0752 0753 0754 0756
0758 0759 0761 0762 0763 0766 0768
0769 0771 0772 0773 0776 0780 0781
0782 0783 0785 0787 0788 0789 0790
0791 0792 0794 0795 0797 0798 0800
0801 0802 0805 0806 0807 0808 0809
0810 0811 0812 0813 0815 0816 0819

0820 0824 0826 0827 0828 0830 0832
0833 0834 0835 0836 0838 0839 0841
0845 0846 0847 0850 0853 0855 0857
0858 0860 0861 0862 0865 0869 0870
0871 0872 0873 0876 0877 0879 0880
0881 0882 0885 0887 0889 0893 0895
0897 0898 0901 0902 0907 0908 0909
0911 0912 0913 0914 0915 0916 0917
0920 0922 0923 0929 0930 0934 0935
0936 0938 0939 0940 0941 0945 0946
0950 0951 0952 0953 0954 0956 0960
0961 0963 0967 0968 0970 0972 0974
0975 0976 0977 0980 0981 0983 0985
0987 0988 0989 0990 0991 0993 0994
0997 0998 1000 1001 1002 1003 1004
1005 1006 1007 1008 1009 1010 1011
1012 1013 1014 1015 1016 1017 1018
1019 1020 1021 1022 1023 1024 1025
1026 1027 1028 1029 1030 1031 1032
1033 1034 1035 1036 1037 1038 1039
1040 1041 1042 1043 1044 1045 1046
1047 1048 1049 1050 1051 1052 1053
1054 1055 1056 1057 1058 1059 1060
1061 1062 1063 1064 1065 1066 1067
1068 1069 1070 1071 1072 1073 1074
1075 1076 1078 1079 1080 1081 1082
1083 1084 1085 1086 1087 1088 1089
1090 1091 1092 1093 1094 1095 1096
1097 1098 1099 1100 1101 1102 1103
1104 1105 1106 1107 1108 1109 1110
1111 1112 1113 1114 1115 1116 1117
1118 1119 1120 1121 1122 1123 1124
1125 1126 1127 1128 1129 1130 1131
1132 1133 1134 1136 1137 1138 1139
1140 1141 1142 1143 1144 1145 1146
1147 1148 1149 1150 1151 1152 1153
1154 1155 1156 1157 1158 1159 1160
1161 1162 1163 1164 1165 1166 1167
1168 1169 1170 1171 1172 1173 1174
1175 1176 1177 1178 1179 1180 1181
1182 1183 1184 1185 1186 1187 1188
1189 1190 1191 1192 1193 1194 1195
1196 1197 1198 1199 1200 1201 1202
1203 1204 1205 1206 1207 1208 1209
1210 1211 1212 1213 1214 1215 1216
1217 1218 1219 1220 1221 1222 1223
1224 1225 1226 1227 1228 1229 1230
1231 1232 1233 1234 1235 1236 1237
1239 1240 1241 1242 1243 1244 1245
1246 1247 1248 1249 1250 1251 1252
1253 1254 1255 1256 1257 1258 1259

1260 1261 1262 1263 1264 1265 1266
1267 1268 1269 1270 1271 1272 1273
1274 1275 1276 1277 1278 1279 1280
1281 1282 1283 1284 1285 1286 1287
1288 1289 1290 1291 1292 1293 1294
1295 1296 1297 1298 1299 1300 1301
1302 1303 1304 1305 1306 1307 1308
1309 1310 1311 1312 1313 1314 1315
1316 1317 1318 1319 1320 1321 1322
1323 1324 1325 1326 1327 1327 1328
1328 1329 1330 1331 1332 1333 1334
1335 1336 1337 1338 1339 1340 1341
1342 1343 1344 1345 1346 1347 1348
1351 1352 1353 1354 1355 1356 1357
1358 1359 1360 1361 1362 1363 1364
1365 1366 1367 1368 1369 1370 1371
1372 1373 1374 1375 1376 1377 1378
1379 1380 1381 1382 1383 1384 1385
1386 1387 1388 1389 1390 1391 1392
1393 1394 1395 1396 1397 1398 1399
1400 1401 1402 1403 1404 1405 1406
1407 1408 1409 1410 1411 1412 1413
1414 1415 1416 1417 1418 1419 1420
1421 1422 1423 1424 1425 1426 1427
1428 1429 1430 1431 1432 1433 1434
1435 1436 1437 1438 1439 1440 1441
1442 1443 1444 1445 1446 1447 1448
1449 1450 1451 1452 1453 1454 1455
1456 1457 1458 1459 1460 1461 1462
1463 1464 1465 1466 1467 1468 1469
1470 1471 1472 1473 1474 1475 1476
1477 1478 1479 1480 1481 1482 1483
1484 1485 1486 1487 1488 1489 1490
1491 1492 1493 1494 1495 1496 1497
1498 1499 1500 1501 1502 1503 1504
1505 1506 1507 1508 1509 1510 1511
1512 1513 1514 1515 1516 1517 1518
1519 1520 1521 1522 1523 1525 1526
1528 1529 1530 1531 1532 1533 1534
1535 1536 1537 1538 1539 1540 1541
1542 1543 1544 1545 1546 1547 1548
1549 1550 1551 1552 1553 1554 1555
1556 1557 1558 1559 1560 1561 1564
1565 1567 1568 1569 1571 1572 1573
1574 1575 1576 1577 1578 1579 1580
1581 1582 1583 1584 1585 1586 1587
1588 1589 1590 1591 1592 1593 1594
1595 1596 1597 1598 1599 1600 1601
1602 1603 1604 1605 1606 1607 1608
1609 1610 1611 1612 1613 1614 1615
1616 1617 1618 1619 1620 1621 1622

1623 1624 1625 1626 1627 1628 1629
1630 1631 1632 1633 1634 1635 1636
1637 1638 1639 1640 1641 1642 1643
1644 1645 1646 1647 1648 1649 1650
1651 1652 1653 1654 1655 1656 1657
1658 1659 1660 1661 1662 1663 1664
1665 1666 1667 1668 1669 1670 1671
1672 1673 1674 1675 1676 1677 1678
1679 1695 1696 1697 1698 1699 1700
1701 1702 1703 1704 1705 1706 1707
1708 1709 1710 1711 1712 1713 1714
1715 1716 1717 1718 1719 1720 1721
1722 1723 1724 1725 1726 1727 1728
1729 1730 1731 1732 1733 1735 1736
1737 1738 1739 1740 1741 1742 1743
1744 1745 1746 1747 1749 1750 1751
1752 1753 1754 1755 1757 1758 1759
1760 1761 1762 1765 1767 1768 1769
1770 1771 1772 1773 1774 1775 1776
1777 1778 1779 1780 1781 1782 1783
1784 1785 1786 1787 1788 1789 1790
1791 1792 1793 1794 1795 1796 1797
1798 1799 1800 1801 1802 1803 1804
1805 1806 1807 1809 1810 1814 1815
1816 1817 1818 1819 1820 1821 1822
1823 1824 1825 1826 1828 1829 1830
1831 1832 1833 1834 1835 1836 1837
1838 1839 1840 1841 1842 1843 1844
1845 1846 1847 1848 1849 1850 1851
1852 1853 1854 1855 1856 1857 1858
1859 1860 1861 1862 1863 1864 1865
1866 1867 1868 1869 1870 1871 1872
1873 1874 1875 1876 1877 1878 1879
1880 1881 1882 1883 1884 1885 1886
1887 1888 1889 1890 1891 1893 1894
1895 1896 1897 1898 1899 1900 1901
1902 1903 1904 1905 1906 1907 1908
1909 1910 1911 1912 1913 1914 1915
1916 1917 1918 1919 1920 1921 1922
1923 1924 1925 1926 1927 1928 1929
1930 1931 1932 1933 1935 1936 1937
1938 1939 1940 1941 1942 1943 1944
1945 1946 1947 1948 1949 1950 1951
1952 1953 1954 1955 1956 1957 1958
1959 1960 1961 1962 1963 1964 1965
1966 1967 1968 1969 1970 1971 1972
1973 1974 1975 1976 1977 1978 1979
1980 1981 1982 1983 1984 1985 1986
1988 1989 1991 1992 1993 1994 1996
1997 1998 1999 2000 2001 2002 2003
2004 2005 2006 2007 2008 2009 2010

2011 2012 2013 2014 2016 2017 2019
2020 2021 2022 2023 2024 2026 2027
2028 2029 2030 2031 2032 2033 2034
2035 2036 2036 2037 2038 2039 2040
2041 2042 2043 2044 2045 2046 2047
2048 2049 2050 2051 2052 2053 2054
2056 2057 2058 2059 2060 2061 2062
2063 2064 2065 2066 2067 2068 2069
2070 2071 2072 2073 2074 2075 2076
2077 2078 2079 2080 2081 2082 2083
2084 2085 2086 2087 2090 2091 2092
2093 2094 2095 2096 2097 2098 2099
2100 2102 2103 2104 2105 2106 2107
2108 2109 2110 2112 2113 2114 2115
2116 2117 2118 2119 2120 2121 2122
2123 2124 2125 2126 2127 2128 2129
2130 2131 2132 2133 2134 2135 2136
2137 2138 2139 2140 2141 2142 2143
2144 2145 2146 2147 2148 2149 2150
2151 2153 2154 2155 2156 2157 2158
2159 2160 2161 2162 2163 2164 2165
2166 2167 2168 2169 2170 2171 2172
2173 2174 2176 2177 2178 2179 2180
2182 2183 2184 2185 2186 2187 2188
2189 2190 2191 2192 2193 2194 2195
2196 2197 2198 2199 2200 2201 2202
2203 2204 2205 2206 2207 2208 2209
2210 2211 2212 2213 2214 2215 2216
2217 2218 2219 2220 2221 2222 2223
2224 2225 2226 2227 2228 2229 2230
2231 2232 2233 2235 2236 2237 2238
2239 2240 2241 2242 2243 2244 2245
2246 2247 2248 2249 2250 2251 2252
2253 2254 2256 2257 2259 2260 2261
2262 2263 2264 2265 2266 2267 2268
2269 2270 2271 2272 2273 2274 2275
2276 2277 2278 2279 2280 2281 2282
2283 2284 2285 2286 2287 2288 2289
2290 2291 2292 2293 2294 2295 2303
2304 2305 2306 2307 2308 2309 2310
2311 2312 2313 2314 2315 2316 2317
2319 2321 2322 2323 2329 2330 2331
2332 2333 2334 2335 2336 2337 2338
2339 2340 2341 2342 2343 2344 2345
2346 2347 2348 2350 2351 2352 2353
2354 2355 2356 2357 2358 2359 2360
2361 2362 2363 2364 2365 2366 2367
2368 2369 2370 2371 2372 2373 2374
2375 2376 2377 2378 2379 2380 2381
2382 2383 2384 2385 2386 2387 2388
2389 2390 2391 2392 2393 2394 2395

2570 2600 2658 2766 2786 2930

IRAN (REPUBLICA ISLAMICA)
1043 1532 1844 2662

IRAQ
1737 1845 2589

IRLANDA
0157 1029 1068 1846 1847 1916 2058

ISRAEL
0744 1330 1347 1361 1848 1849 1850 1851 2016 2019 2275 2277 2375 2401 2404

ITALIA
0033 0127 0297 0360 0482 0523 0524 0567 0810 0811 0812 1060 1085 1088 1089 1090 1143 1161 1197 1269 1280 1283 1284 1305 1307 1338 1351 1352 1354 1357 1422 1432 1445 1550 1695 1762 1806 1818 1852 1853 1854 1855 1856 1857 1858 1859 1860 1861 1862 1863 1864 1865 1866 1867 1868 1869 1870 1871 1872 1873 2046 2195 2286 2373 2418 2597 2599 2614 2747 2897 2898 2934

IUEH
0456 1642 1954 2590 2687 2741

JAMAICA
0250 0713 1113 1876 1877 1961 2495 2685

JAPON
0279 0304 0385 0406 0455 0572 0745 0747 0748 0749 0750 1501 1731 1791 1831 1878 1879 1880 1881 1882 1883 1983 2348

JORDANIA
1309 1539 1884

JOVENES
1412 1994 2114 2226 2697 2927

JUEGO
1159 1658 2176 2237 2417 2673

JUEGO EDUCATIVO
0052 0833 1992 2532 2634

JUGUETE
1159 1658 2176 2237 2417 2673

JUVENTUD
0371 2186 2928

JUVENTUD URBANA
0936 1800 2246 2251 2493 2745 2750

KENYA
0417 0525 1271 1507 1885 1886 1973

KUWAIT
0418 0432 1253 1898 1899

LECTURA
0044 0221 0246 0431 0626 0782 1233 1242 1444 2241 2266 2267 2268 2796 2799

LEGIBILIDAD
0298 0307 0761 0797 1420 1634 1984 2264 2265 2487

LEGISLACION DE LA EDUCACION
0578 0609 1136 2789

LENGUA ARABE
0071 0895 1950

LENGUA FRANCESA
1585 1615 1913 2040 2047

LENGUA NACIONAL
0018 0140 0145 0669 1500 2073 2074 2317 2629 2746 2844

LENGUA RUSA
0018 0145 2074 2317 2629 2746 2844

LENGUAJE INFANTIL
0226 0227 1093 1109 1596 1896

LENGUAS
0059 0141 0142 0143 0144 0150 0152 0157 0158 0159 0187 0189 0290 0293 0723 0828 1029 1058 1106 1166 1203 1211 1264 1323 1324 1325 1331 1585

1595 1598 1615 1666 1678 1828 1837 1840 1846 1904 1911 1912 1913 1914 1915 1916 1917 1918 1919 1920 1921 1922 1923 1924 1925 1926 1957 1958 2040 2043 2045 2047 2058 2059 2060 2063 2064 2065 2069 2313 2429 2531 2727 2753 2819 2838

LENGUAS AFRICANAS
0057 0058 0059 0060 0683 0685 1203 1258 1920 1958 2069 2104 2105 2345 2429 2430 2467 2675

LIBANO
0071 0895 1950

LIBERIA
0907 1952

LIBRO DE TEXTO
0404 0938 1043 1296 1379 1532 1844 2076 2191 2516 2661 2662 2663 2664 2949

LINGUISTICA
0059 0187 1058 1203 1917 1920 1957 1958 2059 2069 2429

LUXEMBURGO
0813 1182 1967 1968 2044 2207 2225

MADRE
0105 1021 1544 2057 2070 2145 2336 2637

MALASIA
0396 0545 0929 1969 1970 2213 2337 2407 2631

MALI
0681 1971 1979

MALTA
0809 1972 2577

MANERA DE ESTUDIAR
1510 1703 2419 2511

MAPA ESCOLAR
0545 0929 1969 2213 2337

MATERIAL DIDACTICO
0180 0541 1822 1823 1893 2840

MAURICIO
0243 0419 0682 2022

MEDICION
0201 0394 0410 1036 2023 2024 2585 2659

MEDIOS DE COMUNICACION MASIVA
0093 0678 1413 1451 1874 1978

MEDIOS DE ENSEÑANZA
0351 0477 0579 0580 0581 0661 1141 1162 1329 1436 1657 1659 1679 2062

MEJORA PEDAGOGICA
0303 0732 1521 1821 2762

MEJORAMIENTO DE LA EDUCACION
0082 0570 0571 0735 0748 0860 1179 1386 1731 1881 2569 2605 2765 2793 2832

METODO AUTODIDACTICO
0024 0092 0132 0337 0443 0997 1018 1499 1528 1768 2039 2279 2424 2425 2426 2512 2646

METODO DE ENSEÑANZA
0018 0145 0249 0396 0398 0901 1003 1706 1814 1970 2074 2084 2127 2317 2407 2451 2471 2472 2580 2592 2628 2629 2630 2631 2632 2633 2746 2844 2846

METODO DE EVALUACION
0549 1020 1542 2066 2540

METODO EDUCACIONAL
0559 0584 0824 0985 1457 1458 1622 2180 2635 2848

METODOLOGIA DE LA INVESTIGACION
0320 0428 0575 1119 2292 2711

MEXICO

0002 0038 0043 0346 0450 0537 0610
0715 1121 1173 1190 1230 1234 1236
1327 1328 1402 1729 1964 2028 2029
2030 2031 2032 2033 2034 2035 2036
2113 2121 2311 2616 2647

MICROENSEÑANZA
0132 0230 0997 1528 1559 1641 1933
2037 2038 2039 2279 2425 2437 2512
2636

MOTIVACION DEL ALUMNO
0040 0086 1207 2093 2496

MOVILIDAD DE LOS DOCENTES
0069 0104 1011 2144 2172 2329 2474
2594 2619

MUJER
0034 0210 1160 2916 2923

NECESIDADES EDUCACIONALES
0149 0585 1259 2807 2887

NEPAL
0938 0939 2076 2077 2516 2563 2587
2661

NICARAGUA
0547 1516 2103

NIGER
0057 0683 2104

NIGERIA
0039 0042 0058 0064 0685 1198 1218
1295 1297 1299 1962 2105 2106 2107
2108 2109 2110 2171 2345 2406 2467
2612

NIÑO DE GRUPO MINORITARIO
0154 0390 0451 0467 0528 0788 1454
1580 1704 2049 2050 2281 2450 2468
2691

NIÑO RETARDADO
1365 1613 1710 1718 2293 2486

NORUEGA
0094 0658 0819 0820 0968 1003 1007
1075 1111 1254 1706 1937 1945 2124
2125 2126 2127 2128 2129 2130 2131
2285 2322 2472 2558 2592 2633 2895

NUEVA ZELANDIA
0017 0491 0493 0881 0882 0976 1410
2100 2102 2340 2505 2623 2652

OBJETIVO AFECTIVO
0053 0295 1004 1643 2042 2432 2448
2473

OBJETIVO EDUCACIONAL
0130 0136 0198 0306 0325 0526 0586
0587 0672 0771 0936 1177 1441 1577
1800 1814 2246 2251 2344 2438 2451
2493 2580 2628 2745 2750

OFERTA Y DEMANDA DE DOCENTES
0232 1221 2568 2621 2625 2626 2925

OPORTUNIDAD DE EMPLEO
0067 0787 1134 1471 1496 1497 1579
1742 2331 2859

OPORTUNIDAD PARA LA JUVENTUD
0025 0372 1019 1590 1951 2118 2650
2929

ORGANIZACION ADMINISTRATIVA
0006 0309 0816 1792 2080 2578

ORGANIZACION ESCOLAR
0217 0280 0422 0627 0785 1561 1565
2338 2574 2892

ORIENTACION
0218 0356 0357 0358 0360 0361 0362
0363 0364 0441 0625 0780 0869 1039
1197 1201 1217 1247 1294 1474 1604
1695 1696 1697 1698 1699 1787 1789
1862 2091 2543 2803 2814 2841 2854
2865 2893 2897 2899 2921

ORIENTACION EDUCACIONAL
0161 0167 0345 0490 0519 0549 0551
0636 0941 1020 1040 1200 1351 1535
1542 1740 1870 2066 2136 2216 2540
2552 2898

ORIENTACION PROFESIONAL
0098 0217 0280 0357 0360 0422 0627 0785 0869 0923 0968 0970 1197 1351 1474 1479 1561 1565 1695 1715 1862 1870 2126 2322 2338 2463 2574 2841 2865 2892 2893 2894 2895 2896 2897 2898 2921

PADRES
0105 1021 1544 2057 2070 2145 2336 2637

PAISES BAJOS
0006 0040 0086 0294 0309 0313 0328 0361 0387 0398 0425 0462 0574 0815 0816 1012 1013 1036 1147 1201 1202 1207 1210 1228 1268 1274 1372 1395 1403 1427 1455 1467 1498 1531 1696 1707 1732 1738 1792 1798 1841 1842 1938 2024 2078 2079 2080 2081 2082 2083 2084 2085 2086 2087 2090 2091 2092 2093 2094 2095 2096 2097 2098 2099 2247 2248 2315 2360 2422 2471 2482 2496 2578 2632 2645

PAISES EN DESARROLLO
0213 0241 0279 0284 0291 0292 0294 0455 0456 0457 0460 0461 0462 0517 0518 0577 0611 0612 0617 0749 1084 1245 1266 1273 1310 1372 1382 1404 1610 1632 1642 1671 1774 1801 1831 1834 1838 1839 1841 1882 1954 2099 2141 2315 2590 2611 2687 2741 2742 2783

PAKISTAN
0004 0397 0490 0519 0636 0940 0941 0980 1091 1616 2135 2136 2137 2138 2139 2230 2414 2420

PAPEL DE LA FAMILIA
0230 1559 1933 2037 2636

PAPEL DEL DOCENTE
2498 2519 2620

PAPUA NUEVA GUINEA
0271 0898 1966 2115 2140 2304

PARAGUAY
0241 0291 1266 1671 1801 1838 2141 2611

PARTICIPACION DE LOS PADRES
0069 0104 1011 2144 2172 2329 2474 2594 2619

PARTICIPACION DEL CIUDADANO
0166 0242 1468 2855 2903

PARVULO
0072 0694 1802 1932 2562

PEDAGOGIA EXPERIMENTAL
0606 0792 1025 1547 1548 1584 2542 2595

PERFECCIONAMIENTO
0023 0102 0974 1110 1618 1619 1653 2643 2709 2879 2906

PERFECCIONAMIENTO DEL DOCENTE
0073 0383 1810 2567 2617

PERU
1114 1158 1385 2119 2156 2157 2158 2310

PLANIFICACION DE LA EDUCACION
0176 0340 0346 0450 0461 0508 0517 0518 0521 0533 0577 0578 0598 0599 0602 0603 0604 0605 0606 0607 0608 0609 0610 0611 0612 0613 0617 0711 0720 0747 0988 1009 1015 1025 1092 1128 1136 1234 1310 1382 1433 1472 1548 1610 1623 1625 1774 1780 1791 1825 1835 1880 1928 1974 1975 1977 1983 2034 2075 2200 2257 2280 2490 2538 2539 2542 2595 2615 2667 2679 2742 2784 2789

PLANIFICACION DEL CURRICULO
0418 0432 1253 1899

PLANIFICACION REGIONAL
0599 0613 1472 2200 2280

POBLACION RURAL
0029 1096 2202 2316

POLITICA EDUCACIONAL
0001 0070 0274 0299 0518 0534 0599 0612 0613 0614 0617 1002 1033 1382 1459 1472 1647 1774 2200 2262 2280 2307 2359 2644 2742 2770 2872

POLONIA
0048 0061 0062 0083 0289 0371 0404 0558 0655 0824 0960 0961 0963 1142 1194 1195 1296 1320 1374 1393 1394 1457 1477 1478 1492 1746 1784 1785 1996 2061 2177 2178 2179 2180 2182 2183 2184 2185 2186 2187 2188 2189 2190 2191 2192 2193 2196 2388 2517 2579 2663 2869 2870 2889 2914 2928

PORTUGAL
0029 0599 0613 1095 1096 1344 1472 2002 2200 2201 2202 2203 2280 2316 2391

PREPARACION DE MATERIAL DIDACTICO
0066 0192 0199 0434 0681 0686 0690 0719 0747 0761 1076 1319 1504 1791 1880 1971 1979 1980 1981 1982 1983 1984 1985 1986 2232 2264 2306 2427 2487 2591 2751 2818

PREPARACION PARA LA VIDA ACTIVA
0202 0220 0221 1242 2268 2653 2799

PRIMERA INFANCIA
1270 1609

PROBLEMAS DE COMPORTAMIENTO
0129 0623 0754 1890

PROBLEMAS DE LA COMUNIDAD
0276 0553 0807

PROBLEMAS DE LA JUVENTUD
0205 0421 1017 1026 1301 1352 1396 1416 1506 1508 1553 1644 1677 1871 2274 2570 2658 2766 2930 2931 2932 2933 2934 2936

PROBLEMAS DE LA PERSONALIDAD
0276 0553 0807

PROBLEMAS DEL INMIGRANTE
1001 1585 1615 1913 1959 2040 2047 2048 2166 2442 2527 2655

PROCEDIMIENTO PEDAGOGICO
0052 0833 0985 1622 1992 2532 2634 2635

PROCESO COGNOSCITIVO
0248 0252 0253 0255 0256 0257 0302 0415 0425 0574 1046 1185 1241 1285 1460 1520 1663 1940 2085 2150 2421 2530 2760 2772 2798 2940

PROCESO DE APRENDIZAJE
0045 0169 0252 0275 0302 0658 0989 1031 1127 1237 1254 1355 1520 1626 1843 1937 1940 1941 1942 1943 1944 1945 1946 2131 2215 2491 2706 2760 2821

PROCESO DE LECTURA
1187 2273 2794

PRODUCTIVIDAD
0936 1800 2246 2251 2493 2745 2750

PROFESOR DE CIENCIAS
1299 2110 2171 2406

PROGRAMA DE EDUCACION DE LOS PADRES
0352 0448 0619 2143 2935

PROGRAMA DE ENSEÑANZA
0153 0332 0340 0607 0737 1092 1433 1824 1825 1835 1977 2253 2767 2784 2856

PROGRAMA DE REHABILITACION
0211 0324 0480 1172 1816 2282

PROGRAMA INDIVIDUALIZADO
0133 0365 1008 1790 1999 2233 2656

PROGRAMA INTERCULTURAL
0142 0290 1264 1828 1837 1922 2727

PROGRAMA PARA LA JUVENTUD

0352 0448 0619 1026 1396 1553 1644
2143 2932 2935 2936

PRUEBA DE APTITUD
0001 0070 0274 0299 0534 1002 2307
2359 2644 2770 2872

PRUEBA DE RENDIMIENTO
0099 0248 0256 0411 0415 1185 1526
1663 2149 2150 2421

PRUEBA ESCOLAR
0801 1456 1638

PRUEBAS
0201 0394 0399 0410 0412 0421 1000
1416 1529 2023 2274 2570 2585 2658
2659 2660 2766 2769 2930

PSICOLOGIA
0633 0862 2260 2441 2834

PSICOLOGIA DE LA EDUCACION
0031 0032 0056 0074 0116 0129 0134
0207 0217 0245 0246 0251 0255 0262
0269 0280 0286 0317 0338 0352 0356
0364 0422 0424 0426 0441 0448 0466
0468 0475 0490 0510 0519 0535 0556
0581 0619 0621 0622 0623 0624 0625
0626 0627 0630 0631 0632 0633 0634
0636 0638 0639 0642 0645 0647 0648
0649 0650 0651 0653 0654 0655 0656
0657 0658 0661 0729 0754 0762 0780
0782 0785 0789 0827 0838 0847 0862
0871 0911 0941 0956 0989 0998 1030
1035 1037 1046 1066 1074 1083 1107
1118 1123 1131 1183 1195 1220 1235
1254 1285 1294 1329 1363 1385 1387
1390 1391 1392 1393 1397 1426 1551
1555 1558 1561 1565 1569 1572 1581
1591 1593 1612 1620 1626 1654 1669
1670 1679 1699 1760 1787 1890 1900
1907 1937 1941 1945 2131 2136 2143
2153 2155 2156 2183 2190 2204 2243
2259 2260 2266 2295 2338 2366 2378
2441 2443 2508 2509 2524 2525 2530
2537 2551 2559 2574 2665 2681 2688
2705 2707 2740 2759 2763 2772 2788
2814 2834 2843 2880 2892 2907 2935

PSICOLOGIA DEL NIÑO
0228 0229 1263 1464 2449 2726

PSICOLOGIA EVOLUTIVA
0134 0154 0390 0466 0467 0468 0528
0630 0648 0650 0657 1035 1074 1107
1235 1454 1572 1593 1670 2050 2443
2524 2691

PSICOLOGIA GENERAL
0339 0356 0362 0441 0625 0780 1070
1217 1557 1604 1697 1787 1788 1789
2781

PSICOLOGIA SOCIAL
0134 0468 0633 0862 1001 1035 1959
2048 2166 2260 2441 2442 2443 2527
2655 2834

QATAR
0614 2262 2263 2269 2583

QUIMICA
0225 1130 1597 2004 2174 2365 2393

RADIO EDUCATIVA
0038 0663 0853 0930 1190 1417 1423
1425 1452 1777 2032 2116 2133 2311
2670 2696

RAZONAMIENTO ABSTRACTO
0001 0002 0070 0274 0299 0534 1002
1236 1402 2035 2307 2359 2616 2644
2770 2872

READAPTACION PROFESIONAL
1364 1495 1709 2485 2891 2900

RECREACION
2278 2332 2850

REDACCION
0234 0296 0297 0482 1283 1513 1727
1806 1865 2373

REFORMA DE LA EDUCACION
0057 0223 0379 0674 0683 2104

REHABILITACION
0451 0788 1580 1704 2049 2281 2450
2468

RSS DE UCRANIA
0634 0870 0871 2210 2227 2739 2740 2842 2843 2922

RUMANIA
0367 0649 0826 0827 0828 1083 1369 1911 1914 2294 2295

RWANDA
0401 1047 1048 2308 2319

SANTA SEDE
1161 1762 1861 2286

SEGUNDA LENGUA
0148 1240 2408 2797

SENEGAL
0059 0060 0686 1203 1258 1920 1958 1980 2069 2427 2428 2429 2430 2492 2675

SIERRA LEONA
1196 1304 1377 1534 2434 2435 2436 2657

SIMULACION
0136 0325 1177 1441 1577 1641 2038 2437 2438

SINDICATOS
0030 0266 1116 2120 2674

SINGAPUR
0305 0408 0763 1102 2439 2440 2510

SISTEMA DE ENSEÑANZA ABIERTO
0322 0853 1168 1423 1440 1807 2133 2134 2696 2716

SISTEMA DE GESTION
0340 0607 1092 1433 1825 1835 1977 2784

SISTEMA DE INFORMACION
0322 1168 1440 1807 2134 2716

SISTEMA ESCOLAR
0075 0103 0975 2342 2343

SOCIALIZACION
0053 0229 0295 0832 0877 1004 1263 1643 2042 2432 2446 2447 2448 2449 2469 2473 2520 2581 2726 2943

SOCIOLOGIA DE LA EDUCACION
0002 0035 0036 0056 0116 0139 0208 0262 0269 0281 0288 0292 0359 0424 0426 0429 0460 0475 0504 0512 0527 0535 0556 0564 0638 0639 0735 0789 0795 0798 0911 0956 1026 1030 1124 1138 1175 1178 1236 1273 1278 1286 1298 1306 1385 1386 1387 1388 1389 1390 1391 1392 1393 1394 1395 1396 1397 1398 1399 1400 1401 1402 1403 1404 1405 1406 1407 1408 1426 1447 1549 1553 1554 1556 1569 1581 1587 1600 1620 1630 1632 1635 1644 1661 1672 1674 1760 1817 1839 1900 1907 1949 2035 2086 2096 2142 2156 2183 2187 2217 2259 2334 2370 2479 2547 2569 2616 2688 2705 2749 2765 2815 2910 2924 2932 2936

SOMETER A PRUEBAS EDUCACIONALES
0328 1228 1455 1798 2095

SORDO
0352 0448 0619 2143 2935

SRI LANKA
0045 0608 0761 1097 1098 1128 1237 1944 1975 1984 2264 2487 2488 2489 2490 2491

SUECIA
0011 0012 0150 0159 0244 0282 0376 0388 0466 0630 0631 0830 0832 0834 0835 0836 0838 0839 1001 1006 1188 1285 1323 1530 1714 1786 1832 1923 1959 2048 2166 2289 2382 2431 2442 2446 2469 2498 2518 2519 2520 2521 2522 2523 2524 2525 2526 2527 2528 2529 2530 2531 2581 2620 2655 2862

SUIZA
0013 0052 0319 0341 0345 0358 0549 0551 0604 0605 0606 0642 0654 0833 0841 0967 0998 1009 1015 1020 1024 1025 1039 1044 1117 1137 1138 1155 1163 1164 1183 1200 1224 1227 1399

Main subject index

ADULT EDUCATION
0001 0002 0003 0004 0005 0006 0007 0008 0009 0010 0011 0012 0013 0014 0015 0016 0017 0018 0019 0020 0021 0022 0023 0024 0025 0026 0027 0028 0150 0189 0279

BUILDINGS
0029 0030 0031 0064 0065 0066

COMPARATIVE EDUCATION
0032 0033 0034 0035 0036 0037 0038 0039 0040 0041 0042 0107 0204 0205 0206 0207 0208 0209 0210 0211 0212 0213 0214 0225 0227

COUNSELLING
0043 0044 0045 0046 0047 0048 0049 0050 0081 0098 0138 0168 0169 0170 0171 0172 0173 0174 0175 0289

EDUCATIONAL ADMINISTRATION
0051 0052 0053 0054 0055 0056 0057 0058 0059 0061 0067 0068 0069 0070 0071 0072 0073 0074 0075

EDUCATIONAL ECONOMICS
0055 0060 0061 0062 0063 0071

EDUCATIONAL EQUIPMENT
0029 0030 0031 0064 0065 0066

EDUCATIONAL PLANNING
0051 0052 0053 0054 0055 0056 0057 0058 0059 0061 0067 0068 0069 0070 0071 0072 0073 0074 0075

EDUCATIONAL PSYCHOLOGY
0043 0050 0076 0077 0078 0079 0080 0081 0082 0083 0084 0085 0086 0087 0088 0089 0090 0091 0092 0093 0094 0095 0096 0097 0098 0099 0100 0101 0168 0175

EDUCATIONAL SOCIOLOGY
0040 0082 0101 0102 0103 0104 0105 0106 0107 0108 0109 0110 0111 0212

EDUCATIONAL STATISTICS
0112 0113 0161 0165

EDUCATIONAL TECHNOLOGY
0114 0115 0116 0117 0118 0119 0120 0121 0122 0123 0124 0125 0126 0127 0128 0129 0130 0131 0132

EMPLOYMENT
0021 0044 0133 0134 0135 0136 0137 0138 0139 0140 0141 0142 0143 0144 0145 0146 0147 0148 0149 0150 0151 0152 0153 0154 0155 0156 0169 0181 0274 0276 0284 0286 0288 0289 0290 0291 0292 0293 0294 0295 0296 0297 0298 0299 0300 0302 0303 0304 0305 0306 0307

EVALUATION
0112 0113 0157 0158 0159 0160 0161 0162 0163 0164 0165 0166 0167

GUIDANCE
0043 0044 0045 0046 0047 0048 0049 0050 0081 0098 0138 0168 0169 0170 0171 0172 0173 0174 0175 0289

HANDICAPPED
0156 0176 0177 0178 0179 0180 0181 0182 0269 0270 0271 0272 0273 0274 0275 0307

HEALTH EDUCATION
0183 0184 0185 0186 0187 0247 0248 0249 0250 0251

HIGHER EDUCATION
0001 0188 0189 0190 0191 0192 0193 0194 0195 0196 0197 0198 0199 0200 0201 0202 0203

INTERNATIONAL EDUCATION

0032 0033 0034 0035 0036 0037 0038
0039 0040 0041 0042 0107 0204 0205
0206 0207 0208 0209 0210 0211 0212
0213 0214 0225 0227

LANGUAGES
0038 0041 0210 0213 0215 0216 0217
0218 0219 0220 0221 0222 0223 0224
0225 0226 0227 0228 0229

MATHEMATICS INSTRUCTION
0230 0231 0232 0233 0234 0235 0237
0238 0239 0240 0241 0242 0243 0244
0245 0246 0252 0253 0255 0256 0257
0259 0260 0261 0262 0263 0264 0265
0266 0267

PHYSICAL EDUCATION
0183 0184 0185 0186 0187 0247 0248
0249 0250 0251

SCIENCE INSTRUCTION
0230 0231 0232 0233 0234 0235 0237
0238 0239 0240 0241 0242 0243 0244
0245 0246 0252 0253 0255 0256 0257
0259 0260 0261 0262 0263 0264 0265
0266 0267

SPECIAL EDUCATION
0156 0176 0177 0178 0179 0180 0181
0182 0269 0270 0271 0272 0273 0274
0275 0307

TECHNICAL EDUCATION
0012 0135 0137 0276 0278 0279 0280
0281 0282 0283 0286 0288

VOCATIONAL EDUCATION
0021 0044 0133 0134 0135 0136 0137
0138 0139 0140 0141 0142 0143 0144
0145 0146 0147 0148 0149 0150 0151
0152 0153 0154 0155 0156 0169 0181
0274 0276 0284 0286 0288 0289 0290
0291 0292 0293 0294 0295 0296 0297
0298 0299 0300 0302 0303 0304 0305
0306 0307

Index des matières principales

ENSEIGNEMENT TECHNIQUE
0012 0135 0137 0276 0278 0279 0280
0281 0282 0283 0286 0288

EQUIPEMENT EDUCATIF
0029 0030 0031 0064 0065 0066

EVALUATION
0112 0113 0157 0158 0159 0160 0161
0162 0163 0164 0165 0166 0167

HANDICAPE
0156 0176 0177 0178 0179 0180 0181
0182 0269 0270 0271 0272 0273 0274
0275 0307

LANGUES
0038 0041 0210 0213 0215 0216 0217
0218 0219 0220 0221 0222 0223 0224
0225 0226 0227 0228 0229

ORIENTATION
0043 0044 0045 0046 0047 0048 0049
0050 0081 0098 0138 0168 0169 0170
0171 0172 0173 0174 0175 0289

PLANIFICATION DE L'EDUCATION
0051 0052 0053 0054 0055 0056 0057
0058 0059 0061 0067 0068 0069 0070
0071 0072 0073 0074 0075

PSYCHOLOGIE DE L'EDUCATION
0043 0050 0076 0077 0078 0079 0080
0081 0082 0083 0084 0085 0086 0087
0088 0089 0090 0091 0092 0093 0094
0095 0096 0097 0098 0099 0100 0101
0168 0175

SOCIOLOGIE DE L'EDUCATION
0040 0082 0101 0102 0103 0104 0105
0106 0107 0108 0109 0110 0111 0212

STATISTIQUES DE L'EDUCATION
0112 0113 0161 0165

TECHNOLOGIE DE L'EDUCATION
0114 0115 0116 0117 0118 0119 0120
0121 0122 0123 0124 0125 0126 0127
0128 0129 0130 0131 0132

Indice de materias principales

ADMINISTRACION DE LA EDUCACION
0051 0052 0053 0054 0055 0056 0057 0058 0059 0061 0067 0068 0069 0070 0071 0072 0073 0074 0075

ASESORAMIENTO
0043 0044 0045 0046 0047 0048 0049 0050 0081 0098 0138 0168 0169 0170 0171 0172 0173 0174 0175 0289

DEFICIENTE
0156 0176 0177 0178 0179 0180 0181 0182 0269 0270 0271 0272 0273 0274 0275 0307

ECONOMIA DE LA EDUCACION
0055 0060 0061 0062 0063 0071

EDIFICIO
0029 0030 0031 0064 0065 0066

EDUCACION COMPARADA
0032 0033 0034 0035 0036 0037 0038 0039 0040 0041 0042 0107 0204 0205 0206 0207 0208 0209 0210 0211 0212 0213 0214 0225 0227

EDUCACION DE ADULTOS
0001 0002 0003 0004 0005 0006 0007 0008 0009 0010 0011 0012 0013 0014 0015 0016 0017 0018 0019 0020 0021 0022 0023 0024 0025 0026 0027 0028 0150 0189 0279

EDUCACIÓN EN MATERIA DE SALUD
0183 0184 0185 0186 0187 0247 0248 0249 0250 0251

EDUCACION ESPECIAL
0156 0176 0177 0178 0179 0180 0181 0182 0269 0270 0271 0272 0273 0274 0275 0307

EDUCACION FISICA
0183 0184 0185 0186 0187 0247 0248 0249 0250 0251

EDUCACION INTERNACIONAL
0032 0033 0034 0035 0036 0037 0038 0039 0040 0041 0042 0107 0204 0205 0206 0207 0208 0209 0210 0211 0212 0213 0214 0225 0227

EMPLEO
0021 0044 0133 0134 0135 0136 0137 0138 0139 0140 0141 0142 0143 0144 0145 0146 0147 0148 0149 0150 0151 0152 0153 0154 0155 0156 0169 0181 0274 0276 0284 0286 0288 0289 0290 0291 0292 0293 0294 0295 0296 0297 0298 0299 0300 0302 0303 0304 0305 0306 0307

ENSEÑANZA DE LA CIENCIA
0230 0231 0232 0233 0234 0235 0237 0238 0239 0240 0241 0242 0243 0244 0245 0246 0252 0253 0255 0256 0257 0259 0260 0261 0262 0263 0264 0265 0266 0267

ENSEÑANZA DE LAS MATEMATICAS
0230 0231 0232 0233 0234 0235 0237 0238 0239 0240 0241 0242 0243 0244 0245 0246 0252 0253 0255 0256 0257 0259 0260 0261 0262 0263 0264 0265 0266 0267

ENSEÑANZA PROFESIONAL
0021 0044 0133 0134 0135 0136 0137 0138 0139 0140 0141 0142 0143 0144 0145 0146 0147 0148 0149 0150 0151 0152 0153 0154 0155 0156 0169 0181 0274 0276 0284 0286 0288 0289 0290 0291 0292 0293 0294 0295 0296 0297 0298 0299 0300 0302 0303 0304 0305 0306 0307

WORKSHEET

If you have any additions or changes which you wish to be included in the next edition of this directory, please complete the worksheet on the adjacent page and send it to: Documentation Office, Unesco: International Bureau of Education, C.P. 199, 1211 Geneva 20, Switzerland.

The following information is an explanation of some of the coding instructions and is intended to assist you in filling in the worksheet. Your answers may be given in English, French or Spanish.

EXPLANATION OF HEADINGS

1. Name of the institution in the official language. If the alphabet is other than Roman, please transliterate.
2. Translation of the title into English, French or Spanish.
3. Street address and city. Add post-office box number and postal zone, if they exist.
4. Name of country.
6. Organization on which the institution depends administratively.
8. Give figures only.
9. Give figures only.
10. If the institution has other activities than research (instruction/training, administration, documentation, etc.), estimate roughly as a percentage the position occupied by research among the activities as a whole.
11. If the research is not conducted entirely in the field of education, estimate the percentage relating directly to education.
12. E.g., 'basic', 'applied', 'research and development'.
13. Objectives of the research, for instance: partial fulfilment of degree requirements, preparation of courses, servicing the educational administration.
14. Give titles of your periodical publications: journals, bulletins, etc. If necessary, use a separate sheet.
15. Give, in the language of publication, titles of monographs published in the last three years. If the alphabet is other than Roman, please transliterate.
16. Give major themes of research work and studies now in progress, together with author and his title. If necessary, use a separate sheet.
17. Leave blank.

FORMULAIRE

Si vous avez une addition ou une modification à suggérer pour la prochaine édition de ce répertoire, veuillez remplir le présent formulaire et le renvoyer au Centre de documentation, Unesco : Bureau international d'éducation, C.P. 199, 1211 Genève 20, Suisse.

Les informations qui suivent donnent quelques éclaircissements sur certaines instructions de programmation et ont pour objet de vous aider à compléter le formulaire. Celui-ci peut être rempli en français, en anglais ou en espagnol.

EXPLICATION DES RUBRIQUES

1. Nom de l'institution dans la langue officielle. Si l'alphabet n'est pas latin, prière de procéder à une translittération.
2. Traduction en anglais, en français ou en espagnol.
3. Adresse et nom de la ville. Case et code postaux s'ils existent. Téléphone. Télex.
4. Nom du pays.
6. Organisation dont dépend l'institution du point de vue administratif.
7. Donnez, avec le nom, le titre universitaire et éventuellement les fonctions autres que la direction de l'institution.
8. Ne donnez que des chiffres.
9. Ne donnez que des chiffres.
10. Dans le cas où l'institution a d'autres activités que la recherche (enseignement/formation, administration, documentation, etc.), estimez approximativement en pourcentage la place tenue par la recherche dans l'ensemble de ces activités.
11. L'activité de recherche ne s'exerce peut-être pas uniquement dans le domaine de l'éducation. Estimez le pourcentage de la recherche directement en rapport avec l'éducation.
12. Par exemple : "fondamentale", "appliquée", "recherche et développement", etc.
13. Objectif de la recherche, par exemple : satisfaire partiellement aux conditions d'obtention d'un grade ; préparation de cours ; fournir des prestations à l'administration de l'éducation.
14. Donnez les titres de vos publications périodiques : revues, bulletins, etc. Si nécessaire, utilisez une feuille séparée.
15. Donnez, dans la langue de la publication, le titre des monographies parues au cours des trois dernières années. Si l'alphabet n'est pas latin, prière de procéder à une translittération.
16. Donnez les thèmes des recherches et des études actuellement en cours, ainsi que le nom de l'auteur et son titre. Si nécessaire, utilisez une feuille séparée.
17. Laissez en blanc.

FORMULARIO

Si tiene alguna sugerencia sobre ampliaciones o modificaciones que puedan ser introducidas en la próxima edición de este repertorio, tenga a bien completar el formulario adjunto y enviarlo al Centro de documentación, Unesco: Oficina Internacional de Educación, C.P. 199, 1211 Ginebra 20, Suiza.

A continuación se aclaran ciertos aspectos de las instrucciones de programación. El formulario puede escribirse en español, francés o inglés.

RUBRICA N.°

1. Nombre de la institución en el idioma oficial. Si no estuviera excrito en alfabeto latino efectuar su transcripción.
2. Nombre traducido al español, al francés o al inglés.
3. Dirección completa, número de la casilla y del código postal, si hubiere.
4. Nombre del país.
6. Organismo o entidad de la cual depende administrativamente la institución.
7. Escribir el nombre, el título universitario y eventualmente las otras funciones que desempeña, además de la dirección de la institución.
8. Dar cifras solamente.
9. Dar cifras solamente.
10. Si la institución desarrolla otras actividades, además de la investigación, (enseñanza/formación, administración, documentación, etc.) dentro del conjunto de actividades estimar aproximadamente el porcentaje que la institución dedica a la investigación.
11. Si la actividad de investigación no está orientada solamente a la educación, estimar el porcentaje de la investigación que esta en relación directa con la educación.
12. Indicar, por ejempleo, si la investigación es 'básica', 'aplicada', 'investigación y desarrollo'.
13. Objectivos de la investigación, por ejemplo: cumplimiento parcial de requisitos para obtener grados, preparación de cursos, prestación de servicios a la administración educacional.
14. Mencionar los títulos desus publicaciones periódicas: revistas, boletines, etc. En caso necesario pueden utilizarse hojas adicionales.
15. Mencionar los títulos (en el idioma de la publicación) de las monografías publicadas en los últimos tres años. Si el alfabeto no fuere latino efectuar su transcripción.
16. Mencionar los temas de las principales investigaciones y estudios en curso así como el título y el nombre del autor. En caso necesario pueden utilizarse hojas adicionales.
17. Dejar en blanco.

Worksheet IBECENT: Research Institutions
Formulaire IBECENT: Institutions de recherche
Formulario IBECENT: Instituciones de Investigación

Control number Numéro de contrôle *Número de control*	**Code number** Numéro de code *Número de código*	**Date** Date *Fecha*
1. **Official name** Nom officiel *Nombre oficial* 10		
2. **Translation** Traduction *Traducción* 11		
3. **Address** Adresse *Dirección* 12		
4. **Country** Pays *País* 13	5. **Year of creation** Année de création *Año de creación* 00/Y	
6. **Parent organization** Organisation-mère *Organismo del que depende* 15		
7. **Present Head** Directeur actuel *Director actual* 20		
8. **Size of staff: total** Effectif du personnel : total *Personal total* 30	**Full time** A temps complet *Tiempo completo* 28	**Part-time** A temps partiel *Tiempo parcial* 29
9. **Researchers** Chercheurs *Investigadores* 61	**Full time** A temps complet *Tiempo completo* 65	**Part-time** A temps partiel *Tiempo parcial* 63

10. Research activities (%)
Activités de recherche (%)
Actividades de investigación (%)

☐	☐	☐	☐	☐
Less than 10% Moins de 10% *Menos del 10%*	**From 10% to 25%** De 10% à 25% *De 10% a 25%*	**From 25% to 50%** De 25% à 50% *De 25% a 50%*	**50%**	**More than 50%** Plus de 50% *Más de 50%*
51	52	53	54	56

11. Educational research (%)
Recherche en éducation (%)
Investigación educacional (%)

☐	☐	☐	☐	☐
Less than 10% Moins de 10% *Menos del 10%*	**From 10% to 25%** De 10% à 25% *De 10% a 25%*	**From 25% to 50%** De 25% à 50% *De 25% a 50%*	**50%**	**More than 50%** Plus de 50% *Mas de 50%*
03	04	05	06	07

12. Type of research
Type de recherche
Tipo de investigaciones

22

13. Functional objectives of research
Objectifs fonctionnels de la recherche
Objetivos funcionales de la investigación

57

14. Periodical publications
Publications périodiques
Publicaciones periódicas

50

15. Monographs
Monographies
Monografías

55

16. Studies and surveys in preparation
Etudes et enquêtes en préparation
Investigaciones y estudios en curso

60

17. Index
Index
Indice

70